BRIDGE OF SIGHS

Richard Russo is the author of *Mohawk*, *The Risk Pool*, *Nobody's Fool* (filmed with Paul Newman) and *Straight Man*, as well as a collection of short stories, *The Whore's Child*. In 2002, his fifth novel, *Empire Falls*, won a Pulitzer prize and was a *New York Times* bestseller. It was also made into a TV mini-series, starring Paul Newman, Ed Harris, Philip Seymour Hoffman and Helen Hunt. He has collaborated with Robert Benton on the screenplays for *Nobody's Fool*, *Twilight* and *The Ice Harvest*. His original screenplay is the basis for Rowan Atkinson's film *Keeping Mum*, with Maggie Smith and Kristin Scott Thomas. He lives in Maine with his wife, and they have two daughters.

ALSO BY RICHARD RUSSO

For Gary Fisketjon

Bridge of Sighs

BERMAN COURT

FIRST, THE FACTS.
My name is Louis Charles Lynch. I am sixty years old, and for nearly forty of those years I've been a devoted if not terribly exciting husband to the same lovely woman, as well as a doting father to Owen, our son, who is now himself a grown, married man. He and his wife are childless and likely, alas, to so remain. Earlier in my marriage it appeared as if we'd be blessed with a daughter, but a car accident when my wife was in her fourth month caused her to miscarry. That was a long time ago, but Sarah still thinks about the child and so do I.

Perhaps what's most remarkable about my life is that I've lived all of it in the same small town in upstate New York, a thing unheard of in this day and age. My wife's parents moved here when she was a little girl, so she has few memories before Thomaston, and her situation isn't much different from my own. Some people, upon learning how we've lived our lives, are unable to conceal their chagrin on our behalf, that our lives should be so limited, as if experience so geographically circumscribed could be neither rich nor satisfying. When I assure them that it has been both, their smiles suggest we've been blessed with self-deception by way of compensation for all we've missed. I remind such people that until fairly recently the vast majority of humans have been circumscribed in precisely this manner and that lives can also be constrained by a great many other things: want, illness, ignorance, loneliness and lack of faith, to name just a few. But it's probably true my wife would have traveled more if she'd married someone else, and my unwillingness to become the vagabond is just one of the ways I've been, as I said, an unexciting if loyal and unwavering companion. She's heard all of my arguments, philosophical and other, for staying put; in her mind they all amount to little more than my natural inclination, inertia rationalized. She may be right. That said, I don't think Sarah has been unhappy in our marriage. She loves me and our son and, I think, our life. She assured me of this not long ago when it appeared she might lose her own and, sick with worry, I asked if she'd regretted the good simple life we've made together.

Though our pace, never breakneck, has slowed recently, I like to think that the real reason we've not seen more of the world is that Thomaston itself has always been both luxuriant and demanding. In addition to the corner store we inherited from my parents, we now own and operate two other convenience stores. My son wryly refers to these as "the Lynch Empire," and while the demands of running them are not overwhelming, they are relentless and time-consuming. Each is like a pet that refuses to be housebroken and resents being left alone. In addition to these demands on my time, I also serve on a great many committees, so many, in fact, that late in life I've acquired a nickname, *Mr. Mayor*—a tribute to my civic-mindedness that contains, I'm well aware, an element of gentle derision. Sarah believes that people take advantage of my good nature, my willingness to listen carefully to everyone, even after it's become clear they have nothing to say. She worries that I often return home late in the evening and then not in the best of humors, a natural result of the fact that the civic pie we divide grows smaller each year, even as our community's needs continue dutifully to grow. Every year the arguments over how we spend our diminished and diminishing assets become less civil, less respectful, and my wife believes it's high time for younger men to shoulder their fair share of the responsibility, not to mention the attendant abuse. In principle I heartily agree, though in practice I no sooner resign from one committee than I'm persuaded to join another. And Sarah's no one to talk, serving as she has, until her recent illness, on far too many boards and development committees.

Be all that as it may, the well-established rhythms of our adult lives will soon be interrupted most violently, for despite my inclination to stay put, we are soon to travel, my wife and I. I have but one month to prepare for this momentous change and mentally adjust to the loss of my precious routines—my rounds, I call them—that take me into every part of town on an almost daily basis. Too little time, I maintain, for a man so set in his ways, but I have agreed to all of it. I've had my passport photo taken, filled out my application at the post office and mailed all the necessary documents to the State Department, all under the watchful eye of my wife and son, who seem to believe that my lifelong aversion to travel might actually cause me to sabotage our plans. Owen in particular sustains this unkind view of his father, as if I'd deny his mother anything, after all she's been through. "Watch him, Ma," he advises, narrowing his eyes at me in what I hope is mock suspicion. "You know how he is."

Italy. We will go to Italy. Rome, then Florence, and finally Venice.

No sooner did I agree than we were marooned in a sea of guidebooks that my wife now studies like a madwoman. "*Aqua alta,*" she said last night after she'd finally turned off the light, her voice near and intimate in the dark. She found my hand and gave it a squeeze under the covers. "In Venice there's something called *aqua alta.* High water."

"How high?" I said.

"The *calle*s flood."

"What's a *calle*?"

"If you'd do some reading, you'd know that streets in Italy are called *calle*s."

"How many of us need to know that?" I asked her. "You're going to be there, right? I'm not going alone, am I?"

"When the *aqua alta* is bad, all of St. Mark's is underwater."

"The whole church?" I said. "How tall is it?"

She sighed loudly. "St. Mark's isn't a church. It's a plaza. The plaza of San Marco. Do you need me to explain what a plaza is?"

Actually, I'd known that *calle*s were streets and hadn't really needed an explanation of *aqua alta* either. But my militant ignorance on the subject of all things Italian has quickly become a game between us, one we both enjoy.

"We may need boots," my wife ventured.

"We have boots."

"Rubber boots. *Aqua alta* boots. They sound a siren."

"If you don't have the right boots, they sound a siren?"

She gave me a swift kick under the covers. "To warn you. That the high water's coming. So you'll wear your boots."

"Who lives like this?"

"Venetians."

"Maybe I'll just sit in the car and wait for the water to recede."

Another kick. "No cars."

"Right. No cars."

"Lou?"

"No cars," I repeated. "Got it. *Calle*s where the streets should be. No cars in the *calle*s, though, not one."

"We haven't heard back from Bobby."

Our old friend. Our third musketeer from senior year of high school. Long, long gone from us. She didn't have to tell me we hadn't heard back. "Maybe he's moved. Maybe he doesn't live in Venice anymore."

"Maybe he'd rather not see us."

"Why? Why would he not want to see us?"

I could feel my wife shrug in the dark, and feel our sense of play running aground. "How's your story coming?"

"Good," I told her. "I've been born already. A chronological approach is best, don't you think?"

"I thought you were writing a history of Thomaston," she said.

"Thomaston's in it, but so am I."

"How about me?" she said, taking my hand again.

"Not yet. I'm still just a baby. You're still downstate. Out of sight, out of mind."

"You could lie. You could say I lived next door. That way we'd always be together." Playful again, now.

"I'll think about it," I said. "But the people who actually lived next door are the problem. I'd have to evict them."

"I wouldn't want you to do that."

"It is tempting to lie, though," I admitted.

"About what?" She yawned, and I knew she'd be asleep and snoring peacefully in another minute or two.

"Everything."

"Lou?"

"What."

"Promise me you won't let it become an obsession."

It's true. I'm prone to obsession. "It won't be," I promised her.

But I'm not the only reason my wife is on guard against obsession. Her father, who taught English at the high school, spent his summers writing a novel that by the end had swollen to more than a thousand single-spaced pages and still with no end in sight. I myself am drawn to shorter narratives. Of late, obituaries. It troubles my wife that I read them with my morning coffee, going directly to that section of the newspaper, but turning sixty does that, does it not? Death isn't an obsession, just a reality. Last month I read of the death—in yet another car accident—of a man whose life had been intertwined with mine since we were boys. I slipped it into the envelope that contained my wife's letter, the one that announced our forthcoming travels, to our old friend Bobby, who will remember him well. Obituaries, I believe, are really less about death than the odd shapes life takes, the patterns that death allows us to see. At sixty, these patterns are important.

"I'm thinking fifty pages should do it. A hundred, tops. And I've already got a title: *The Dullest Story Ever Told*."

When she had no response to this, I glanced over and saw that her breathing had become regular, that her eyes were closed, lids fluttering.

It's possible, of course, that Bobby might prefer not to see us, his oldest friends. Not everyone, Sarah reminds me, values the past as I do. Dwells on it, she no doubt means. Loves it. Is troubled by it. Alludes to it in conversation without appropriate transition. Had I finished my university degree, as my mother desperately wanted me to, it would have been in history, and that might have afforded me ample justification for this inclination to gaze backward. But Bobby—having fled our town, state and nation at eighteen—may have little desire to stroll down memory lane. After living all over Europe, he might well have all but forgotten those he fled. I can joke about mine being "the dullest story ever told," but to a man like Bobby it probably isn't so very far from the truth. I could go back over my correspondence with him, though I think I know what I'd find in it—polite acknowledgment of whatever I've sent him, news that someone we'd both known as boys has married, or divorced, or been arrested, or diagnosed, or died. But little beyond acknowledgment. His responses to my newsy letters will contain no requests for further information, no Do you ever hear from so-and-so anymore? Still, I'm confident Bobby would be happy to see us, that my wife and I haven't become inconsequential to him.

Why not admit it? Of late, he has been much on my mind.

M Y FATHER WAS Louis Patrick Lynch—Big Lou, to his friends. In christening me Louis Charles—the Charles for my mother's father—they meant for me to be called Lou as well, though I've been known all my life by the nickname given to me on the first day of kindergarten at Cayoga Elementary School. Miss Vincent's roll sheet contained her students' first names, their middle initials and, of course, their surnames. If that's what she'd read that first morning—Louis C. Lynch—I suspect I'd have had a different childhood, though if she hadn't made the mistake, maybe somebody else would've later. She knew my father, and you couldn't blame her for assuming I was called Lou, and if she'd said "Lou Lynch," everything would have been fine. But for some reason she chose also to read my middle initial. Lou C. Lynch was the name she called, and when she did, I raised my hand. The other children turned to look at me, and I could tell by their puzzled looks that something had occurred, something I alone had missed. Even then all might have been fine if Miss Vincent had simply noted my raised hand and proceeded down her list to the next name. Instead she paused, her ear registering what her eye had missed, and in her hesitation, that empty beat, someone said, "His name's Lucy?"

After school, I told my mother how everyone had laughed at me, that I'd been called Lucy all day. She nodded and sighed, conceding sadly, "Children are cruel. Don't let them know it hurts your feelings and they'll forget."

"How?" I asked, meaning how could I keep them from knowing.

"Laugh along with them," she suggested.

She must have suspected that this would be impossible for me, and my father must have known it, too, because when I told him the story that evening, his eyes were instantly full. "For heaven's sake, Lou," my mother said when she saw this. I don't know whether he felt bad about the derision I'd endured my first day of school or guilty because in naming me he and my mother hadn't anticipated what might happen or whether he'd understood what my mother did not—that my schoolmates would never forget, never tire of the joke, and that I'd be known for the rest of my life as Lucy. As I have been.

Thomaston, New York, is a place you've never heard of, unless you're a history buff, an art lover or a cancer researcher. The town was named for Sir Thomas Whitcombe, of French and Indian War fame. Our other claim to fame, Robert Noonan, the painter, grew up in Thomaston, though he left when he was barely eighteen and has lived his adult life abroad.

Otherwise, as I say, you're unlikely to have heard of Thomaston, unless you work in medical research, in which case you may remember the now-famous study done years ago to explain why our cancer statistics were off any actuarial chart. The principal culprit was, as we all suspected, the old tannery, boarded up these last forty years, which dumped its dyes and chemicals into the Cayoga Stream, which meanders through most of Thomaston before finally emptying into the Barge Canal five miles to the south. Throughout my youth the Cayoga ran different colors, according to that day's dye batch. Red, of course, for those who know their history and are susceptible to metaphor, was the most unnerving. Historians will recall that the Adirondack headwaters of our modest stream were the site of the Cayoga Massacre the year before the start of the American Revolution. For reasons largely obscured by time, a garrison of soldiers from then largely Dutch Albany was en route to Montreal when a band of Mohawks, stirred up by local Tories, fell upon them. Completely surprised by the ambush, two hundred men were butchered in a matter of hours. According to local legend, so much blood was shed that the Cayoga ran red down from the Adirondacks and through the farmlands to the south all the way to Albany, though this last is likely a political statement.

Some have suggested that the owners of the old tannery, having exterminated everything in a living stream and poisoned the people along its banks, should all be behind bars, and they may be right, but it's worth remembering that this same tannery sustained our lives for more than a century, that the very dyes that had caused the Cayoga to run red every fourth or fifth day also put bread and meat on our tables. When I was a boy, people were afraid only when the stream *didn't* change color, because that meant layoffs and hard times would soon follow. Without admitting it, however, everyone was wary of the stream, and those who could afford to built homes away from its banks. When the cancer study was published, it merely reinforced the wisdom of our common practice. The nearer you lived to the Cayoga, the more likely that you'd contract cancer, even the most exotic varieties of which are represented in unnatural abundance.

Can it be that what provides for us is the very thing that poisons us? Who hasn't considered this terrible possibility?

THOUGH SOME of the very first fortunes of the New World were made right in our valley, Thomaston is today a poor town. Like Gaul it is divided into three parts, though these are by no means equal. The two largest sectors are located on opposite sides of— if you can believe it—Division Street. The East End, where I spent much of my youth, is lower middle class, whereas the West End is industrial and poor. Thomaston's few black families reside in a West End neighborhood called the Hill. None of them, according to my research, descend from the slaves who were kept at Whitcombe Hall, though it's true that Sir Thomas, like so many Tories, was a slaveholder. But the ancestors of our black families moved here from the South and Midwest just before the First World War.

The third section of Thomaston—the Borough—is located in the northeast sector, contiguous to both the East End and Whitcombe Park, and while it's smaller than the East and West Ends in terms of both geography and population, what little wealth we have is concentrated here. Needless to say, this is where you'll find Thomaston Country Club and the prettiest of our town parks, the one that houses a band shell for summer concerts, as well as the most desirable elementary school (Thomaston children have never been bused). Borough streets are wide and tree lined, our houses set back from the pavement and our lawns well tended, for the most part by ourselves; our elderly hire their neighbors' children to mow in the summer, rake in the autumn and shovel during our long upstate winters. Borough sidewalks run flat and true so our children won't be injured on their bicycles and Rollerblades. As kids growing up, we rode bikes with little regard for safety; in the summer all the boys wore shorts and rode shirtless, sometimes even shoeless, and whenever we went over the handlebars, we bled from our knees, elbows and foreheads. Now, decades later, recalling our injuries, we Borough parents spare our children similar scrapes and bruises by dressing them in high-tech helmets plus neon-colored knee and elbow pads. Nor do we mind if they're scoffed at by kids from the less affluent West or East End. We have the wherewithal to keep our children safe, so we do.

Borough residents are mostly Protestant and politically conservative, descendants of Tories like Sir Thomas Whitcombe, who settled our valley and built the great Halls. Loyal to King George, if they'd had their way, they would've preserved the Adirondacks, if not all of America, as a giant game reserve for aristocratic Englishmen. My wife's father used to argue that instead of restoring the Hall, as Sir Thomas's great residence is locally known, to its former splendor, the town fathers should have razed it and erected a discount store in its place. But he was a man of many opinions, most of them outrageous, and in any case the Hall, by then a mere shell, caught fire years ago and burned to its foundations.

Though we in the Borough are outnumbered by the ethnic Catholics and registered Democrats in both the East and West Ends, our town always has a Republican mayor and is considered a write-off by downstate liberals who don't waste much campaign money in our local television market. As an East End boy, I wondered how a majority could be outvoted by a minority, and my father could offer no explanation except that this was the way it had always been. My mother, on the other hand, knew why. The reason was fingernails. People in the Borough had clean fingernails because they never had to get them dirty, whereas West Enders got them so dirty, day after day, that they never came entirely clean, and eventually they stopped trying; East Enders like us worked hard, too, my mother claimed, but it was our nature to scrub ourselves raw with stiff brushes and coarse soap, to scrub until we bled, so our fingernails were as clean as those that never dirtied them to begin with. It was human nature, she explained. You don't identify with people worse off than you are. You make your deals, if you can, with those who have more, because you hope one day to have more yourself. Understand that, she claimed, and you understand America, not just Thomaston. When I asked if it would always be that way, she opened her mouth to answer, then closed it again. "How about I ask *you* that question in about twenty years?" she suggested. I agreed enthusiastically, enjoying the idea that in twenty years I might be smart enough to figure out what she couldn't, so we set the date and pledged not to forget, but of course we did.

Though we now live in the Borough and have done so for years, I doubt anyone in Thomaston is more democratic and egalitarian than my wife and me. I myself, in a sense, am spread all over town by virtue of owning property in both the West and

13

East Ends, and I've been a walker of Thomaston streets all my life. Even now, I walk at least an hour a day through Thomaston's different neighborhoods, where I'm recognized and, I hope and trust, respected in all of them. "One of these days you're going to meet yourself either coming or going, Pop," our son, also a lifelong resident of our town, often observes, and there's a good deal of symbolic truth to this remark. Almost nowhere in Thomaston am I not within sight of a personal memory.

The self I meet coming and going is, I confess, relentlessly unexceptional. I'm a large man, like my father, and the resemblance has always been a source of pleasure to me. I loved him more than I can say, so much that even now, many years after his death, it's hard for me to hear, much less speak, a word against him. Still, there's also something bittersweet about our resemblance. I am, I believe, an intelligent man, but I'll admit this isn't always the impression I convey to others. Over the course of a lifetime a man will overhear a fair number of remarks about himself and learn from them how very wide is the gulf between his public perception and the image he hopes to project. I've always known that there's more going on inside me than finds its way into the world, but this is probably true of everyone. Who doesn't regret that he isn't more fully understood? I tend to be both self-conscious and reticent. Where others regret speaking in haste, wishing they could recall some unkind or ill-considered opinion, I more often have occasion to regret what I've not said. Worse, these regrets accumulate and become a kind of verbal dam, preventing utterance of any sort until the dam finally breaks and I blurt something with inappropriate urgency, the time for that particular observation having long passed. As a result, until people get to know me, they often conclude that I'm slow, and in this I'm also like my father.

I don't remember how old I was the first time I overheard somebody call Big Lou Lynch a buffoon, but it so surprised me that I looked the word up in the dictionary, convinced I'd somehow mistaken its meaning. This was probably the first time I recognized how deeply unkindness burrows and how helpless we are against it. At any rate, I've noticed that people who eventually come to like me often seem embarrassed to, almost as if they need to explain. Though I've been well and truly loved, perhaps more than I've deserved, my father is the only person in my life to love me uncritically, which may be why I find it impossible to be critical of him. In one other respect, I'm also my father's son: we both are optimists. It is our nature to dwell upon our blessings. What's given is to us more important than what's withheld, or what's given for a time and then taken away. Until he had to surrender it, too young, my father was glad to have his life, as I am to have mine.

THOUGH I GREW UP in Thomaston, my earliest memories are of living with my maternal grandparents in a tiny house three miles to the south, its backyard sloping down to the Cayoga Stream. When the winter trees were bare I could see the water sparkling from the upstairs windows, but I wasn't allowed to play along the banks. My grandfather owned a car, and by the time I awoke in the bedroom I shared with my parents, he and my father had already left for work. I vaguely remember my mother being unhappy about living "in each other's laps" and that we were saving for the day we could afford a flat of our own in town. With no other children nearby, I'd become a quiet, solitary child, and my mother was determined that I attend kindergarten in town and make friends. With a year of business school under her belt, she was confident she could get part-time work as a bookkeeper once I was in school.

We couldn't have saved much money, because when the time came to enroll me in kindergarten, the place my parents rented was in Thomaston's West End on Berman Court. There were only five houses on Berman, two on each side of the street and another—a three-story building—at the dead end where the land fell sharply away to the Cayoga Stream. I remember having a hard time understanding how this was the same river I could see from my grandparents' house, which felt like a different world to me. My new bedroom window, in the back of the building, was impossibly high, and I remember being afraid of falling from it, down the steep bank and into the stream. Most of the houses in our new neighborhood were slapdash affairs that almost from the day of their construction began to slope and tilt dangerously, their chimneys sporting large fissures and some-times toppling onto the roofs of their neighbors' sloping porches. I remember, too, the dank chemical smell of the Cayoga itself, which always permeated the stairwell that led up to our rooms, an odor that was nothing like the overheated apartments, which were ripe with pungent cooking oils and unbathed pets kept too long indoors.

My father was a milkman. His dairy job had paid enough to support us when we lived with my grandparents, but not now, though I was unaware of this at the time. I was proud that everyone in Thomaston seemed to know and like my father, that no matter where we went people would toot their horns or call to him from across Division Street or want to shake his hand in the doorway of the barbershop. My mother, by contrast, lacked this great popularity, and though I loved her, I sometimes wondered why my father had married her. She was terribly thin and angular, and her eyebrows met in the middle of her forehead when she frowned, which was most of the time. Old photo-graphs suggested that she had never been pretty. I don't mean that she was homely, just the kind of girl you wouldn't notice, and now that she was a woman people always seemed to be trying to place her. Whenever anyone offered the slightest hesitation, she would supply her name, as if she understood their predicament all too well. I thought it was a shame she didn't have my father's good-natured, jovial temperament, because at least that might have made some sort of impression.

After we moved to Berman Court, when my father went out on his milk route, my mother worked at home, keeping the books for several small local businesses, the extra income allowing my father the largesse for which, in those early days, he was well known. "Acting like a big wheel" was what my mother called his willingness to loan a dollar or buy a cup of coffee. I don't think it occurred to me that we were poor, but my parents often disagreed about money. My father loved to buy things for a quarter or fifty cents at yard sales, items that he claimed were worth far more than he paid for them and that my mother regarded as worthless because we had no use for them. He'd buy a tire for a dollar if it still had tread on it, even though at the time we didn't own a car. (The milk truck he drove wasn't for personal use, but he had special permission to use it to buy groceries at the A&P when he finished his shift on Saturday morning.) "I know a guy'll give me two, three bucks for that, easy," he'd tell my mother in reference to the tire, and most of the time he was right. When he brought what she called junk home from yard sales, she'd take one look and say, "What in the world did you buy *that* for," and he'd reply, "A quarter." Nor could he resist a lottery ticket or a fifty-cent chance on a Rotary Club raffle, even though my mother insisted that these were "taxes on ignorance." Winning, which he seemed to do a lot, allowed him to feel vindicated, even when what he won wasn't something we needed or even wanted. "What if first prize had been a head cold?" my mother would ask when presented with the fishbowl of jelly beans he'd won by guessing how many it contained. "Would you have bought a ticket? You don't even like jelly beans." He just replied that he supposed he could *learn* to like them. In fact, he'd have nine hundred and seventy-three opportunities. "Besides," he continued, "our Louie here likes jelly beans, don't you?" And I said I did, though in truth I wasn't overly fond of them. "Great," my mother said. "Fifty dollars' worth of cavities, minimum." But it was true, my father was always winning things, and if I had to explain why our family was

17

so fortunate, I'd have said it was due to my father's luck. I felt lucky just standing next to him, confident that I, too, would come up a winner.

If my mother thought moving into town would guarantee me friends, she was mistaken. That first day of kindergarten, when I got my nickname, made me wary of the other children, and a year after we'd moved to Berman Court I was still nearly as solitary as I'd been in the country at my grandparents'. I say "nearly" because I did have one friend, of a sort, in Bobby Marconi, whose family lived on the second floor of our building. His father worked nights as a desk clerk at the hotel but was trying to get on at the post office, where he filled in whenever a letter carrier got sick. Ours was, alas, mostly a walk-to-and-from-school sort of friendship. Once we arrived back at Berman Court we seldom saw each other until the following morning, and we never played together on weekends. On Sundays, of course, the Marconis attended Mount Carmel with the Italians, and we Lynches worshipped with the Irish of St. Francis. It was exasperating to have my only friend right there in the building and yet have so little access to him. My mother explained that the Marconis preferred to keep to themselves, and when I asked why, she said it was just the way they were. You couldn't make people want friends, and we certainly couldn't make the Marconis want *us* for friends.

Neither of these observations made much sense to me. My father always said you couldn't have too many friends, so why would the Marconis consider them a liability, especially people as likable and interesting as us Lynches? But my mother explained that not everybody was like us. Other people went about things differently. It was our way—or my father's, she said—to keep people abreast of what we were up to, especially when fortune smiled on us. If he won twenty dollars at a church raffle, he thought people should know. Somebody else, she concluded, might keep the lucky event a secret to ward off envy or requests for a small loan. To me, such logic was both new and disconcerting. Just before we'd moved to Berman Court, my grandparents had bought a television, perhaps as an inducement for us to remain with them. My father liked watching television almost as much as I did, and recently I'd overheard my parents talking about buying a used one for our flat. My father didn't see why we couldn't afford one, and my mother, who paid the bills and balanced the checkbook, did. I happened to know that the Marconis were also debating the same purchase, and I gave Bobby to understand that if we got ours first, we'd invite them up to watch our favorite shows. I made this offer, without consulting my parents, as a hedge against the possibility that they'd get one first, in which event we could watch with them until we could afford our own. Something like a television couldn't help but draw people together had been my thinking, which I now understood to be flawed. Instead of opening their front door, it could in fact shut it tighter than before.

I got the distinct impression that, left to themselves, my mother and Mrs. Marconi might have been friends, like Bobby and me, but for some reason this was not allowed. Mrs. Marconi, a pale, nervous woman of Irish descent, seemed never to leave the apartment. When Bobby and I arrived home from school, we'd sometimes find our mothers in furtive conversation in the hall downstairs. Mrs. Marconi always had one of Bobby's little brothers on her hip, and there was usually another small, liquid eye peering out from behind the cracked door, but when she saw Bobby and me, she quickly disappeared inside, as if she'd been doing something wrong and I might be a spy ready to report her indiscretion.

Being a child, I had a child's intolerance of mystery and vagueness, so I kept after my mother relentlessly. Why couldn't she and Mrs. Marconi be friends? Why was my own friendship with Bobby restricted to walking to and from school? Why couldn't our *families* be friends? To which my mother responded, with yet more vagueness, that we had very different notions about how to go about doing things and therefore little

19

in common. Little in common? Weren't we mirror images of each other? My father was Irish, my mother Italian, the Marconis the reverse. When we first moved to Berman Court and met them I remember wondering if our families hadn't somehow gotten tangled up. Mrs. Marconi had a softness about her that made her a better match for my father than the man she married, and I couldn't help thinking she wouldn't have been so nervous all the time if she lived with a man as good-natured as Big Lou Lynch. And while I wouldn't have wished for this, my mother, a woman who knew her own mind and didn't spook easily, seemed a better match for Mr. Marconi. That way, when they went to church at Mount Carmel and we went to St. Francis, everybody would be where they belonged. I was just a boy, of course, and it didn't occur to me that had things been arranged in this fashion neither Bobby nor I would have existed. It just seemed like a more workable situation, and I was surprised nobody else had thought about it.

Gradually, I came to understand that the real reason Bobby and I couldn't be better friends was that his father had something against mine. And since everybody liked my father, Mr. Marconi's refusal to do so seemed willful and perverse. I studied him carefully every chance I got, hoping to understand what was wrong. He wasn't nearly as large a man as my father, but he was compact and muscular, and he had a way of leaning slightly forward, his hands clenching into fists and then unclenching again, as if he had to remind himself not to be angry. On his forehead, just below the hairline, he had a purple birthmark that seemed to change in size and vividness, growing larger and darker when his fists were clenched than when he relaxed them. But what could he possibly have against my father? Of all the things I wanted to understand, this was the most urgent because it seemed the most inexplicable. It seemed to have something to do with the army. Mr. Marconi had served and my father hadn't, and apparently he held it against him, though it was flat feet and not unwillingness or cowardice that kept my father out. He'd taken some pains to explain this to Mr. Marconi, who just smiled and said, "Funny how that works," then claimed to know plenty of other flat-footed guys who'd managed to serve. "Too bad, anyhow," he concluded. "We could've used a guy like you who knows the right way to do everything."

"You'd think he was part of the Normandy invasion." My mother snorted when my father told her about this conversation. From what Mrs. Marconi had said, by the time her husband had arrived in Europe the war was already over, which to my mother's way of thinking explained why he was still fighting it. "Don't you dare repeat that," she said when she remembered I was in the room and taking it all in. "Bobby's mother isn't supposed to talk about the family, so I'm not supposed to know."

Dressed in his postman's uniform, Mr. Marconi did have a military bearing, and I half expected to look up one day and see him wearing a sidearm. According to my mother he ran his family on a military model, with the emphasis on discipline. In our house it was my mother who was in charge of that, though there was little need of it. I'd never been a willful or disobedient child, and a reproachful look was enough to improve my conduct. Neither of my parents had ever raised a hand to me. Apparently at the Marconis it was different. Mr. Marconi alone handled discipline, and my mother feared it was often harsh. Could that be another reason he didn't like my father, a man who spared the rod?

If I had a hard time understanding Mr. Marconi's resentment, I wasn't alone. My father couldn't understand it either, and whenever they met in the hall, he was even friendlier than he was with other people. "Lou," my mother said, "leave the man alone. If he doesn't like you, he doesn't like you."

"What'd I ever do to him, that's all I want to know. I never done nothing to him."

"I know that, Lou," my mother said. "Leave him alone anyway."

But he couldn't. Even I knew that. He kept an eye peeled and would waylay him by the mailboxes or in the hall, determined, I could tell, to be liked or know why he wasn't. The subject he usually tried to introduce as an icebreaker was money and how much things cost anymore, that there seemed to be no end in sight and you had all you could do to keep up, never mind get ahead. These were subjects my father considered to be of universal appeal and easy enough for anybody to talk about and share as common ground. "What Tessa spent on winter clothes for our Louie this weekend?" he'd venture. "I couldn't hardly believe it. And one kid's all we got. With three, that's gotta be rough." Here he'd let his voice fall so Mr. Marconi could commiserate or, if he felt like it, compare notes about the cost of children's coats and boots. I think my father suspected that Mr. Marconi, between his two jobs, made more money than he did at the dairy, but having three kids and another on the way, he figured, put them in pretty much the same boat, moneywise. Also, there were rumors the hotel was going to close. "I told Tessa she ain't gotta pay Calloway's prices," he continued when Mr. Marconi declined to comment. "She could go down to Foreman's for cheaper, but thinks cheaper's more expensive in the long run, and I guess she's right." Actually, that wasn't how he'd reacted the night before when he found out how much my winter clothes had cost, but now he'd slept on it, and I could tell spending all that money had become a source of pride. "Besides, if you've got the money, why shortchange your kids? If you ain't *got* it, sure, that's another thing, but if you *do*, why not spend the extra buck?"

"Because you might need it tomorrow," Mr. Marconi finally said, pushing past my father and closing the door in his face, rather more forcefully, it seemed to me, than was necessary.

"Don't always be bragging to that man," my mother told him. "You know they dress those boys out of the thrift shop."

"Well, what's he spend their money on, then?" my father said.

"Lou, that's none of our business. Leave him alone. He doesn't like you."

"I just wish I knew why, is all. I never done nothing to him."

Which caused my mother to rub her temples.

About the only thing the Lynches and the Marconis *did* have in common was a determination to leave the West End as soon as we could afford to. My mother in particular saw Berman Court as temporary. She'd wanted to rent in the East End from the start, but having grown up at the end of the Depression, she was wary and said she preferred to not have something at all than to have it today and lose it tomorrow. She felt bad for Mrs. Marconi, who was always pregnant. With each new baby, my mother claimed, the poor woman was tethered to the West End that much more securely.

I remember knocking on the Marconis' door late one afternoon and waiting in the hall for a long time. There were sounds inside, so I knew someone was home, someone, I sensed, was right on the other side of the door, listening and hoping whoever it was would go away. Only when I knocked a second time did Mrs. Marconi respond, her voice very near, "Who is it?" she wanted to know, her voice tremulous. "Bobby can't come out," she said once I'd identified myself, though I was there to return something my mother had borrowed the day before.

"That woman is terrified," she said when I told her what had happened. But when I asked what Bobby's mother might be afraid of, she claimed not to know. I didn't believe her, and it frightened me to think some unnamed thing in our own building could scare a grown woman, and I wondered if my father could protect us from it.

St. Francis was Thomaston's only parochial elementary school. After kindergarten my mother had been talked into enrolling me there by Father Gluck, our parish priest, and I suspect she also hoped—in vain—that my nickname wouldn't follow me there. Bobby's parents had reluctantly enrolled him in

St. Francis in third grade because at Cayoga Elementary he'd fallen in with a group of rough boys and been suspended, more than once, for fighting, which particularly worried Mrs. Marconi. In one of their furtive hallway conversations, my mother may have suggested that St. Francis boys weren't so combative, and that having Bobby there would be good for me, too. We could be friends and walk to and from school together. Mrs. Marconi liked that idea but didn't think her husband would spend the extra money, so we were all surprised when she prevailed. My mother speculated afterward that Mr. Marconi may have been swayed by the fact that St. Francis boys wore uniforms, of which he heartily approved, believing that dress impacted behavior.

Cayoga Elementary had been a short block from Berman Court, but St. Francis was a half-dozen blocks farther, in the opposite direction. It was also on the other side of the Cayoga Stream, which we crossed, coming and going, by means of a narrow footbridge. Both schools dismissed students by grade, ten minutes apart, lower grades first. If you were a first grader with a brother or sister in second or third grade, you were allowed to wait in the office until the higher grade was let out. Otherwise, you were to go straight home. The flaw in the system was that older kids in the public school were being let out at the same time as the younger ones from the parochial. St. Francis kids were already objects of scorn because we wore uniforms and were taught by nuns, and those who left by the front door often had to run a gantlet of ridicule. For others of us, though, the most direct route home was out the back and across the small school yard, then out through a gap in the fence. From there we followed a path through the trees down the steep bank of the Cayoga Stream, crossed the footbridge and climbed up the far embankment. From there it was, for Bobby and me, three short blocks home to Berman Court.

The scary part of the journey was the bridge itself. Thanks to the depth of the ravine, it was visible from neither the school on one side nor the street on the other. The whole journey, down one bank and up the other, took only a minute, but if the public school boys arrived at the footbridge first, and no parents were around, St. Francis kids had to "pay a toll" in order to pass. The toll could be whatever you had: a penny, a marble, an old Necco Wafer. If you had nothing, or maybe just a broken pencil, you found yourself in a headlock and tossed over a hip and onto the hard ground and then laughed at as you raced toward safety back where you'd come from. Whenever Bobby Marconi stayed home from school, I made sure I had something for the toll.

That was the thing about Bobby: he never had to pay the toll, nor did I when I was with him. The boys collecting the toll were the very ones Bobby had gotten in trouble with the year before, so they all knew each other. Their leader, a kid named Jerzy Quinn who was a year older, had been suspended with Bobby, and for some reason that had made them cautious friends, as well as rivals. Jerzy liked to tease Bobby about being a wimpy Catholic who only hung out with girls anymore—a reference to my nickname, I knew immediately—and Bobby asked Jerzy if he wanted to be a singer like his father, a drunk who liked to sing at the top of his lungs before passing out in the gutter by the tannery.

The closest they ever came to actual hostilities was over me. At the beginning of the school year, the toll takers tried to shake me down, and one of them, Perry Kozlowski, put me in a headlock while the others went through my pockets. But Bobby said to leave me alone, that I was with him and didn't have to pay. He didn't question the authority of these boys to consider the bridge their own property, but did insist that I was exempt by virtue of our friendship. "Who says?" Perry wanted to know, as if there were rules governing such exemptions. They argued the fine points while I remained in the headlock, until Jerzy Quinn finally said, "Let him go. He's not worth it."

When they were gone I asked Bobby why he didn't have to pay, because of course that puzzled me. But Bobby just shrugged, as if I'd asked him to explain all the laws of nature. "Some people

25

just don't have to, Luce," he said. "Other people . . ." We both knew what happened to other people and that I fell into that category. Which was one reason I was so glad to have Bobby's friendship and also why, at the end of the school year, not long after Mr. Marconi got on full-time at the post office and they moved to the East End, I was so devastated.

THE FOLLOWING YEAR, with Bobby gone, I knew the public school boys would be on the lookout for me. Most days my grade got out on time, which meant I'd arrive at the bridge before they did, and once safely across I'd scramble up the bank and head for Berman Court. Sometimes, as I emerged from the trees and turned toward home, I'd see or hear them coming, hooting and jeering, a couple of blocks away, and if it was too obvious that I was hurrying, they'd laugh and yell "Run, Lucy, run!" and the words would make me do it. Then they laughed all the louder. We all seemed to understand that it was just a matter of time before my teacher would keep our class a crucial minute or two longer, or for some reason they themselves would get out early, and then there'd be a reckoning.

The day it finally happened, I had no one to blame but myself. I'd stayed late to help Sister Bernadette clap erasers, an honor, and when I started through the yard and along the path down to the stream, I caught a quick movement at the edge of the trees and thought I heard voices coming up from the green darkness below. I might, of course, have simply returned to the school and had Sister Bernadette call my mother to meet me, but as afraid as I was of the boys at the bridge, I was even more afraid of being a scaredy-cat. It was one thing to turn and hurry back to school *after* I'd seen the public school boys at the footbridge, a genuine threat, but it was another to run away from a shadow that might, for all I knew, be that of a first grader. My eraser duty had taken a good fifteen minutes, and then I'd talked with Sister Bernadette for a while, which meant the public school boys had probably come and gone by now. Or such was my reasoning as I continued along the path to the edge of the trees, where I stopped to peer down the bank into the darkness below, my head cocked, listening. There was the sound of the stream, of course, but was that all? Was some other utterance mixed in with or obscured by the burbling of the water?

I don't know how long I stood there before starting warily down the path, the trees and the darkness closing in behind me. In the middle of the footbridge lay a workbook. Public school workbooks were different from ours, used year after year, filled in with pencil and then erased at year's end, the answers still visible on the page, ghostlike, along with the checkmarks identifying incorrect responses. Was it possible for this workbook to be sitting there without its owner nearby? An urgent whisper slipped out of the trees. Still I stood transfixed, waiting, but it was quiet except for the sound of the water and the wind in the upper branches. Stepping onto the footbridge, I immediately heard a sound behind me and, turning, saw a grinning boy come out from behind a large oak to block my retreat. Ahead, two others materialized, then two more.

One was Jerzy Quinn, who grinned and said, "Hey there, Lucy-Lucy."

WE FOLLOWED the stream. Though it happened long ago, that afternoon's journey is still vivid in my recollection. I was flanked on both sides to prevent escape. With one exception they made it clear that I would remain their prisoner until they chose to let me go. When I lagged or showed any reluctance to get too far from home, they shoved me forward, hard, and took turns cuffing me on the back of the head and asking if I was a girl, since I had a girl's name. All except for Jerzy Quinn, who remained aloof from the fun. Each time I was pushed or tripped, he helped me to my feet, talking to me the whole time, explaining how I had public school kids all wrong, that they weren't such a bad

27

lot. How I was being treated in the meantime didn't seem to Jerzy to undermine his case in the least.

No, I was informed that he and his friends had started a charitable club, the purpose of which was to assist the unfortunate, cripples and widows and the like. The dues collected went to pay for their crutches and groceries and medical operations, and their club had already performed many good deeds. Did I know Janice Collier, the fourth grader in the wheelchair? Well, who did I imagine *got* her that chair? There was a good deal of smirking and snorting behind my back as all this was explained, then somebody tripped me again and I went sprawling in the stream, skinning the palms of both hands on the rocks, much to the delight of my captors. But again Jerzy Quinn helped me up and assured me that I was fine, after which he continued to recruit me for their club, as if he saw no reason I wouldn't want to join. In the event I needed further inducement, I should know that my old friend Bobby Marconi was also a member. "We're his best pals," Jerzy gave me to understand. "Those East End kids are all fags, so he comes down here to hang out with us."

"Are you a fag, Lucy?" one of the other boys asked.

"He doesn't even know what it is," said another, which was true.

What a strange downstream journey it was. The juxtaposition of the other boys' jostling ridicule with Jerzy Quinn's feigned friendship was what scared me most, that their behavior and his soothing words were at cross-purposes—the boys making it clear that they'd hurt me, even as their leader assured me that I'd come to no harm. Stranger still, while I knew his kindness was part of the cruel joke being played on me, some part of me believed him, or desperately wanted to. His pretend kindness, his urgent hope that I would admit I'd been wrong about him and his friends, were at some bizarre level almost convincing, as if just beneath the game he was playing lurked another boy who wished he *was* the boy he was pretending to be. Maybe that good boy was real. Maybe he wouldn't let the others harm me. I also wanted to believe he was telling the truth about Bobby, that when we got wherever we were going Bobby would be there, and then they'd find out who his best friend really was.

Eventually we came to a blighted place where the bank on both sides was very steep, spanned overhead by a rickety railroad trestle and a dark, tilting structure that opened onto a rock quarry. This, it turned out, functioned as their clubhouse. At the far end several sheets of plywood had been arranged across the beams, and in the center of one of these sat an old steamer trunk. There we paused, the other boys forming a circle, with Jerzy Quinn and me in the center. Jerzy regarded the trunk, then me for a long beat, as if expecting me to draw from its mere existence some weighty inference. When he grinned, I saw in his yellow teeth that I'd been wrong, that there was no good boy.

"So, you want to join our club?" he said, putting his hand on the back of my neck and squeezing hard.

Balanced as I was on my railroad tie, even a gentle nudge would have sent me over the edge of the plywood and down onto the dark, jagged rocks below. Fearing that either a yes or a no might have equally disastrous consequences, I said maybe. I'd ask my parents. See if it was okay.

Well, you see, that's the thing, I was told. Theirs was a secret society whose first rule was that no parents must ever learn about all the good deeds they performed. So I'd have to decide myself and if I joined I'd be made to swear a solemn oath never to tell anyone. It may have been then, seeing that in reality I had no choice, that nothing I said or did would change what was about to happen, that my eyes began to leak. Yes, I told them. Yes, I'd join.

"Look," one of the boys said, pointing. "He's so happy he's crying."

All that remained, they said, was the initiation. Did I know what an initiation was? When I said I didn't, they pulled up the lid of the trunk.

Inside, it was dark except for a thin crease of light at a seam,

29

and the air reeked of urine. "Hey, look who's here," I heard a voice say after the trunk's lid was fastened. Had somebody new just arrived? Was I about to be rescued?

"I just thought of something, Lucy." Jerzy's voice was confidential, mere inches away. "You *can't* join our club. Take a guess why."

I tried to stop blubbering but couldn't, because now that the possibility of membership had been withdrawn, I knew I should've agreed to join right at the start.

"Tell him."

Came the chorus, "*No girls allowed*," followed by much laughter.

Then Jerzy's voice again. "Guess what happens next."

That was when the sawing began.

WHEN I AWOKE, it was pitch black and the silence outside the trunk so profound that for a moment I wondered if I was home in bed, having dreamed my imprisonment. But my room was never this dark, the tree branches outside my window always reflecting the ghostly glow of the streetlamp in front of the building. Still, it was only when I tried to stretch out my legs that I knew I hadn't dreamed the trunk.

How long had I lain there in the dark? Probably not so very long, though upon awakening I remember feeling for the first time the dreamlike peace with which, over a lifetime, I would become so familiar. Exhausted from my earlier screaming and pleading, as well as from the panic of seeing sawdust filtering down through that thin crease of light, I'd waited in abject despair for the saw to finally come through the trunk's lid and rip my flesh. But then a strange thing happened. Realizing that my struggles were fruitless, I'd surrendered and simply gone to sleep. I remember thinking of this as an actual solution, that if I could somehow will myself into unconsciousness, then perhaps what was happening would cease by virtue of my not, in a sense, being there to witness it. While I didn't recall putting that plan into effect, I must have, because here I was, awake again, my ordeal apparently over.

Gradually I became aware of two things: time had passed, and I was alone. The sliver of light was now gone, from which I deduced that night had fallen and, from the complete silence outside the trunk, that my captors had vanished. Instead of being terrified anew, I felt an exhausted, inexplicable, yet very real sense of well-being. Through some act of will, it seemed I'd made my tormentors, their laughter, the ripping of the saw, all of it, disappear. But if true, this begged an important question. If I'd banished the boys by falling asleep, would I now bring them back into existence by awaking? Would the whole process start over again? Somehow I thought not, and just lay there quietly, sleepily content for each moment to pass without additional terror. True, I was curious how much time had elapsed and whether my mother and father were out searching for me. These considerations seemed remote, though. I was locked in a dark trunk, and it was possible, even likely, that I'd never be released, which should have terrified me but didn't. Rather, it seemed I'd simply entered a new, quite natural phase of my life inside the trunk, breathing the heady mixture of stale air and urine, some of which I understood to be my own, where I would await further developments. About these I felt more curiosity than fear, as if I'd already expended my entire store of the latter emotion.

I may even have drifted back to sleep, because when my eyes opened again, I heard singing, first far off, then nearer, and I remember not wanting the singers—for there seemed to be two voices, a man's and a woman's—to find me. Then, when their voices suddenly got louder, I realized they must have entered the covered structure.

The woman was laughing now, and there was a slapping sound. "Stop, stop, stop!" she urged her companion. "You don't know the fucking words."

"I know the words," the man said, then started up again.

Another slap. "Stop! You don't know—"

"Here's one thing I *do* know," the man said. "You hit me one more time and I'm going to knock you right on your ass."

"You wouldn't hit a lady."

"I don't know why you'd think that," the man replied. "I really do not."

"Give me."

A pause. "It's gone."

Some scuffling, and then the woman's voice, rich with disappointment. "It's all gone," she said.

"The fuck did I just tell you?"

Then the sound of glass breaking somewhere on the rocks below.

"You don't know the words," the woman repeated.

"Jesus. This again."

"It goes like this," she said, clearing her throat. She sang in a surprisingly pretty voice: "Then I kiss . . . your lips . . . and caress your waiting fingertips . . . and your heart—"

"And I kiss . . . your tits," the man warbled, "and caress your nipples with my lips—"

"No! No! No!" the woman objected, and there was another slapping sound. Two, actually, because she'd no sooner slapped him than he must have slapped her back, hard, I could tell, and then there was just the sound of her weeping.

"What'd I tell you?" the man said.

"You hurt me."

"Didn't I warn you not to hit me again?"

"That was just playing."

"Me, too."

The woman snuffed her nose. "You play too rough."

"You want nice, go back to that fat stupid fuck you're married to."

Kissing sounds now. They had to be standing right next to the trunk. "I don't want him. I want you," the woman said. "And I want you to be nice."

"People in hell want ice water."

Now more petulant sobbing. "I *am* in hell. My whole life is hell. I don't want to *be* in hell anymore."

"People in hell want ice water."

"Stop saying that! Stop being mean." More kissing. "Why does everybody have to be so mean?"

"People in hell—"

"Stop! I swear, if you say it again—"

"Come here."

Then the sound of a zipper and much fumbling. "I can't see you." The woman giggled.

"So what? You forget what I look like?"

"I want to look at you. Don't you want to look at me?"

"Not particularly."

"You're so mean."

Clothes were then tossed onto the trunk.

"Come here," the man repeated.

"*You* come here," the woman said, then immediately she yelped. "That's my hair, you son of a bitch. Don't yank my hair."

"Then do as you're told. Lie down on the blanket."

"You don't boss me. You're not my husband."

"Thank God for small favors."

"I shouldn't even let you fuck me, you bastard."

"Too late," the man said, and I heard the woman draw in her breath, then for a while there were just grunting, animal sounds. After that came a quiet so deep I wondered if they could hear me breathing.

"Why does everything have to be so horrible?" the woman finally said. When the man didn't respond, she added, "I hate him."

"He's not such a bad egg," the man offered.

"You're not married to him."

"Try not being such a cunt every minute of the day and night. Maybe he'll be nicer to you."

"You men always stick together."

33

I heard her rise, come back over to the trunk again and start getting dressed. Over in the direction of the man, there was the sound of a cap screwing off a bottle.

"I thought you said it was all gone," the woman said.

"It was. This is a new one."

She sat down on the trunk hard. "You should've taken me to a motel. What kind of man takes a lady to a place like this?"

Apparently the man didn't feel it necessary to answer this particular question, and in the silence that ensued I must have made a small noise, because suddenly the lid of the trunk was thrown open and the woman was looking in at me. Backlit, her face was little more than shadow, but even in the poor light I could see her darkly nippled breasts. She'd managed to pull her skirt on, though she was bare from the waist up. It took a moment for me to fully register with her.

Finally she looked back over her shoulder at the man and pointed down at me.

"There's a little boy in this trunk," she said.

"Right," the man said. "Tell me another one."

"A little boy," she said again, as if surprised that what she'd said before turned out to be true. She reached in and touched my cheek. "A real little boy."

"You're drunk," the man informed her.

While I watched, she put her brassiere on and buttoned her blouse over it. Then she leaned down into the trunk, so close that I could smell her breath and body. "He's mean," she confided, then lowered the lid of the trunk, surprising me almost as much as she had when she opened it.

"Where's my purse?"

"The hell should I know?" I could hear the man pulling on his pants and zipping his fly.

A moan now. "It fell," she blubbered.

"Fell where?"

"Down there."

Down between the ties was what she meant.

"Get it for me?"

"That's hilarious," the man said.

"I hate you," she said. "I hate you worse than my husband."

"Getting laid doesn't improve your disposition much, does it."

The voices were receding now. After a pause I heard the woman say, "There was too a little boy in that trunk." And then I didn't hear anything more.

I HAVE SCANT MEMORY of the journey home. My vague conviction that I now lived in some kind of dream was borne out by the nightscape. The Cayoga, which had run clear that afternoon, was scarlet now, which meant the night shift at the tannery upstream had introduced a new dye batch. The moon, nearly full, had risen, and it made the churning water look like blood, and twice, despite my care, I lost my footing on the rocks and splashed into the stream. I'd imagined we'd come a very long way—maybe a mile—from the footbridge, but in no time there were lights high up on both sides of the embankment, and rounding a bend, I identified the largest of the dark, looming shapes as the back of our own apartment house, clifflike, with my own lighted bedroom window impossibly high up its black summit. Many a night, awakened by the wind or the branches of the tall elms scratching the back wall of the building, I'd gotten out of bed and gone to that same window and peered down into the moonlit ravine, idly wondering what it would be like to be out in that ghostly landscape instead of safe inside.

When I caught sight of the footbridge, I immediately recognized the dark figure standing motionless upon it as my father. I was trying to find my voice to call out to him when he was gone again, the moon having slipped behind a cloud. Had I just imagined him there? Unsure now, I didn't call to him, but continued along the stream until I arrived at where he was staring sightlessly at the water running beneath the bridge, and I think he must have heard my step before he saw me. "Is that you, Louie?"

he said, as if he didn't trust the evidence of his own senses, and then I was in his arms, breathing him in. Feeling his big body quake with sobs, I began to cry again myself. How long we stood like that, shaking in each other's arms, I don't know, but his big embrace forced my detached dream-reality to retreat and allowed the necessary space for the old, normal world to return.

Berman Court was full of police cars and our neighbors were all out on their porches when my father and I emerged from the trees behind our building. My mother was talking to a policeman, and he first noticed our approach. "I found him, Tessa," my father called, his voice sounding strangely formal. "Our Louie's safe and sound. He's right here with me."

The horror on my mother's face when she looked up, though, caused me for a brief moment to imagine, as you sometimes do in a nightmare, that my mother didn't love me, that she had not wanted me to be found. It only lasted a second, of course—that look of horrified revulsion at the sight of me, a boy dyed vividly red. To her I must've been the embodiment of the fears that had grown worse and worse since my failure to return home from school that afternoon. But then her rationality returned, and she came toward us, her eyes streaming, as our neighbors began to clap and cheer on their sloping porches, glad to have been wrong, because of course they, too, had concluded I would never again be seen alive.

Even now, over fifty years later, I feel profoundly the miraculousness of these events, though explanation renders them mundane. In that trunk I experienced the first of the "spells" that have ever since haunted my life. The symptoms are familiar now—the sleepy exhaustion, the sense of detachment from reality, the feeling of having been "away," the odd, unaccountable, overwhelming sense of well-being that accompanies me on my return—but at the time all that was new. I had awakened not with a sense of having been victimized but ironically of having been given an invaluable gift. In captivity I had imagined a terrifying world, only to learn that I was safe in it after all, and that I had the power to vanish my tormentors. Having disposed of them, I had only to find my way home and into my father's embrace.

Though the police cars seemed staged for my dramatic return, I later learned that their presence had nothing to do with me. Rather, a fight had broken out at Murdick's, a nearby gin mill, and one of the combatants, who lived in Berman Court, had been arrested when attempting to sneak home and avoid arrest. My mother, hearing the commotion outside and imagining I'd been found, had rushed downstairs, only to be disappointed. She'd spent most of the afternoon and evening riding around the West End in a police cruiser, looking in vain for any sign of me. And while I looked like the survivor of a bloody adventure, in reality it gradually became clear that nothing awful had happened. Walking home along the stream, I'd realized what I'd been too frightened to grasp before, that the public school boys hadn't meant me any actual harm. After the man and woman had left and I'd finally climbed out of the trunk, the truth was obvious. What the boys had been sawing wasn't the trunk but one of the sloping rafters, from which the saw still dangled. Its significance came to me in stages too minute to measure, and only when I awoke in my bed the next morning did I understand what really happened and why it was that the louder I'd screamed in terror, the harder they'd laughed. Later, I learned that my tormentors had gotten a scare of their own when, opening the trunk, they couldn't arouse me from my catatonic state. Believing they'd scared me to death, they immediately fled the scene. Only after spending a sleepless night did two of the boys break down and confess what had happened. So in the end I'd been the victim of little more than a cruel prank transacted less than a quarter mile from Berman Court.

The only truly miraculous thing that night was my father's presence on the footbridge at two in the morning, where he'd been awaiting my return since dark and infuriating my mother, who viewed his stolid vigil as a mockery of reason. A West End boy roughly my age had disappeared the previous spring, abducted, many believed, by a stranger in a dark sedan rumored to be lurking in the neighborhood still. That I might have suffered a similar fate was now being whispered by neighbors and police alike. Why, my mother wanted to know, did my father insist on standing guard over the stream behind our house? Did he think we were living in a fairy tale and I'd just materialize there if he waited long enough?

Strangely, that was precisely what he seemed to be doing there on the footbridge as he stared down into the red, churning water—wishing me home and rescuing me from the trunk, from that parallel life I'd begun to imagine so vividly, by the sheer force of his will. When he called "I found him, Tessa," to my mind that pretty much summed up the situation. He'd found me. With my small hand safely locked in his big one, I *felt* found. "Our Louie's safe and sound," he told her, and me, and himself, thus making it true.

I MAY HAVE BEEN safe, but for some months after my ordeal I was not, to most observers, sound. Sister Bernadette noted that I was easily diverted from her lessons, staring out the window at nothing. "He just goes off someplace," the young nun explained. "I don't think even he knows where." I was equally abstracted at home. "Where were you just then?" my mother would ask, perplexed not just by my mental absence but also, at times, the expression on my face. "Can you tell me what you were thinking about?"

I could not. My mind seemed everywhere and nowhere. One afternoon, my mother came into my bedroom and found me staring out my bedroom window, the one that overlooked the stream. By then it was late November, and with the trees bare you could just make out in the distance the very top of the structure on the railroad trestle, the scene of my ordeal. I remember thinking how odd it was I'd never noticed it before.

According to my mother, I was in a trance she couldn't coax me out of. Unnerved, she was about to call the doctor when I suddenly snapped out of it and expressed surprise at finding her there in my room. She took me by the elbows, then, and regarded me so intently that I wanted to look away. "Where were you, sweetie?" she said, her now-standard inquiry. "You have to tell me. I can't help if you keep secrets from me."

But of course I couldn't answer. I didn't know I needed help and didn't *have* a secret, unless it was secret from myself as well. I had only my mother's word, and Sister Bernadette's, that something was wrong. Our family doctor believed I was still terrified, but I don't remember being afraid during the weeks and months that followed my abduction. If anything, the odd serenity I'd awoken with in the trunk, together with the sense of power I'd achieved by making my tormentors disappear, is what had persisted in the aftermath.

It's true, however, that I was seldom really happy except in my father's company, perhaps because he alone gave no indication that anything was amiss. His was the diagnosis—judging me safe and sound—that I clung to.

MY MOTHER SAID nothing to my grandparents about what had happened. Shortly after our move to Berman Court, they'd sold their house and relocated downstate, ostensibly to be closer to my grandmother's sister, who was ill, though there was surely more to their decision than that. By ignoring their advice and moving into town, my mother had sided with my father, just as she'd done in marrying him, and their moving away was intended to convey that she was now on her own. My grandparents didn't dislike my father, but neither had they ever made an effort to conceal their opinion that my mother had married beneath her station. There remains to this day in upstate New York a deep prejudice against anything rural, and in our valley the word "farmer" is used to explain everything from uncouthness to congenital idiocy. That my father had grown up on a farm, without city water, indoor toilets or electricity, and that his parents lost that farm to back taxes, ending their lives in the county home, made him, in their view, an unsuitable husband for the daughter of a white-collar worker.

That said, they'd welcomed him—and, of course, me—into their home, all of us living "in each other's laps" until we moved to Thomaston. Part of the reason my mother hadn't immediately told her parents about my ordeal was that she hoped to forestall their I-told-you-so's, spoken and unspoken. Moreover, my subsequent spells and abstractions had convinced her that we needed to move again, out of the West End this time, something we could not accomplish without their help. She had no choice but to swallow her pride.

This was our unstated purpose in boarding the train (back then there was daily passenger service downstate) to go see them. My father didn't accompany us, the official explanation being that he couldn't get time off from the dairy, but I think my mother had decided her prospects would be better if he remained behind. I wanted to stay in Thomaston, but my mother insisted I come along because there was no one to look after me when my father was at work. Besides, she needed me as a visual aid. Her task, after all, was delicate. She had to confess about what was going on with me, but in the same breath assure them there was nothing to worry about. Though in the end I'd be fine, right now my doctor was convinced a change would do me good. It wasn't that Thomaston's West End was dangerous, as my grandparents had argued, but rather that Berman Court reminded me—how could it not?—of what had happened, whereas in a new neighborhood I'd feel safe. A fresh setting would reinforce what I was being told, that nothing like that would ever happen to me again. I myself didn't subscribe to this logic because, as I said, I wasn't afraid, but I knew my mother did. Her certainty on this point made me wonder if it was possible for someone to be afraid and not know it. My mother had, more than once in my young life, suggested that she knew me better than I knew myself, so I supposed it was possible.

My grandparents met us at the train station, and I could tell right away that my mother had explained some of this on the phone, because my grandmother immediately pulled me to her and began to cry. My grandfather just seemed angry and shook his head at my mother, who didn't take it lying down. "It's not fair to blame me for this, and you know it," she told him, even before saying hello.

But if I seemed different to my grandparents, so did they to me. In the time since I'd seen them, they'd grown old. My grandfather had taken early retirement from his job selling insurance, and the ramrod-straight carriage I remembered was a thing of the past. My grandmother, always a slender woman, was now rail thin, and she'd developed a tremor in her hand. We would have to walk home, they told us, since they no longer had a car. My grandfather had been in a minor accident the previous winter, and they'd decided that both the car and its insurance were expenses they could live without. He picked up the heavier of our two suitcases, but a hundred yards from the station had to set it down on the sidewalk and bend over, hands on his knees, to catch his breath. Even with my mother and me carrying the suitcases, we had to stop twice more, and he leaned heavily on my grandmother's frail frame all the while. They looked not merely ill but scared, as if the world, including their own selves, could no longer be trusted. When we'd all lived together, it had been understood that it was because my parents needed their help, but now I saw, though I was too young to understand this exactly, that we'd provided them with something important in return. They'd weathered the Depression by drawing close, by tightening the inner circle, by trusting that all would be well if the family stayed together. With us gone, they now had one less financial burden, but that wasn't the way they'd looked at it. Our leaving had rent the fabric, left them somehow vulnerable to a suddenly hostile world.

41

They were now living in a dark two-bedroom flat not so different from ours on Berman Court. It was stuffed with the big, heavy furniture my grandmother had inherited from her family and couldn't bear to part with, though there wasn't enough room for all of it here. Her sister—the one they'd moved downstate to look after—had died several months earlier, and the spare bedroom my mother and I stayed in was stacked, floor to ceiling, with furniture *she* hadn't been able to part with. The room was so crowded we had to sidle around the bed in order to get in and out. I could see my mother's spirits sink as it became clear how her parents were living. We'd come in the hopes of borrowing money, but their shabby, overstuffed apartment, together with the fact that they no longer kept a car, demonstrated how little they themselves had.

Over the next few days, my mother would learn why. My grandparents' move downstate, done in part to punish my mother for her stubbornness, had been even more disastrous than our own move to Berman Court. My grandmother's sister had died without life insurance, so they'd had to pay for her funeral. Also, though this wasn't mentioned, they both had been ill, sick enough, in fact, to be hospitalized, she with pneumonia, he with a flare-up of his chronic asthma. The resulting medical bills had so far consumed more than half of the equity they'd garnered from the sale of their house. Realizing belatedly that he'd retired before he could really afford to, my grandfather tried to get his job back but found there was no chance of that. As a result they were now living on their meager social security and trying not to dip into what remained of their savings. They'd gone from a life with few emergencies, unless you counted us, to one in which emergencies were monthly events.

Yet when we boarded the train to return home, my mother had the money she'd come for, enough for a down payment, she hoped, on a modest East End house. She'd not wanted to take it, given how desperate they were already. But I was trump, as she'd known all along, and once that card was played the game was over. She promised, of course, to repay them, and since she'd recently landed another bookkeeping account, she could probably send them fifty dollars a month. My grandmother asked only that we take some of the family furniture to furnish our new home, and my mother agreed, promising we'd rent or borrow a truck and come down for it once we were settled. I think my grandmother knew that "settled" would be defined by my mother, just as she knew the furniture she couldn't part with was, in her daughter's opinion, old-fashioned and ugly.

My grandfather died first, a few short months after our visit. My mother again took the train south—I stayed behind with my father—to help with his funeral arrangements. Though he'd sold insurance all his life, it turned out he was himself under-insured, and the additional expense rendered my grandmother virtually destitute, though she declined my mother's invitation to come live with us. When she herself died a month later, my mother sold the whole houseful of furniture to an antiques dealer from the city, and saw in the man's greedy satisfaction that she'd been taken advantage of, that she'd failed to see the worth to others of something she herself thought unattractive. Had she undervalued her parents as well? I don't know that this possibility occurred to her, though I imagine it must have.

The other thing that surely became clear to her as a result of her parents' passing was that our safety net was now gone. We were on our own.

ALL WORM

NOONAN TOOK the vaporetto over to the Zattere. There he went to an outdoor café, ordered a cappuccino and waited for it to arrive before opening the manila envelope from Columbia University that Hugh had thrust at him on his way out the door, identical to the one that had arrived that summer and he'd marked RECIPIENT DECEASED: RETURN TO SENDER. Not a very good joke, now that he thought about it. Since then he'd turned sixty. His father had died at sixty, and it was beginning to look like sixty might just be Noonan's allotment of years as well, his troubles no longer coming singly but in . . . he tried to remember the quotation, what troubles came in when they left off coming one at a time.

The envelope contained, as he'd known it would, material touting the university's master of fine arts program. A cursory glance revealed that none of the painters, sculptors and visual artists pictured in the glossy brochure were people Noonan knew, but then they were mostly young and it had been a long time since he'd been in New York. As a younger man he'd tried to keep up with what was happening back home and elsewhere in Europe, but sometime during the last decade he'd realized that he didn't much care anymore. Lately, he even lacked patience for the local art scene. If he accepted Columbia's offer to teach next year, as Hugh was pressuring him to do, how would he ever summon the energy to learn who in the world his colleagues were, never mind the hypocrisy necessary to feign interest in them? It was dispiriting even to contemplate. His remaining time—the only true coin of any artist's realm—would be frittered away in the name of collegiality.

But wait. On the academic side of the MFA roster, he did recognize a scholar/critic named Irwin Popov—not a name one could forget—who'd written a long, labored and extremely unflattering review of his last New York show some thirty years earlier, accusing him of crude technique and, of all things, homophobia. Noonan was pleased to note that the supercilious little putz's career had ground to a halt at associate professor, and his most recent book had been published by an undistinguished midwestern university press. Tenured, Professor Popov was now insulated against professional anxiety, but not, thankfully, humiliation, as evidenced by the handwritten note stapled to the page below his mug shot. *Dear Bob (if I may)*, the note began. "You may *not*," Noonan, half a world away, replied emphatically, causing a nearby table of Japanese tourists to regard him curiously. *Advancing years offer the academic art critic many opportunities for regret. My little review of your show—what? three decades ago?—is one such opportunity, and I sincerely hope that its memory, in the unlikely event you* do *remember it, will not prevent you from doing my colleagues and me the great honor of joining our graduate teaching faculty. Indeed, I look forward to many bracing conversations on the subject of our shared passion with almost as much anticipation as your upcoming show next month.* It was signed "Irwin, the Contrite." How hard, Noonan couldn't help wondering, had the department chair had to twist the now-brittle Popov arm to procure *that* smarmy screed? *Little* review? The bloody thing had taken up a full third of the issue! And what shared passion? Did the mean-spirited little twit assume that Noonan, too, was a pederast?

Gathering up the brochure, catalog and cover letter, he shoved them all back into the manila envelope and consulted his watch. Half an hour had passed since he left Hugh alone in the studio to acquaint himself with the new canvases. He'd like them, Noonan knew. It was good work and for once there was a lot of it. In the past Hugh had chided him for laziness, but this time he'd have to find some other grievance. The *Bridge of Sighs* canvas, probably, even though it was unfinished and not intended for New York, or maybe any other show. What Noonan meant by painting it and why he continued to work on it so obsessively were two things he hoped to discover soon. Why his old man, long in the grave where he belonged, should start haunting him now was another. Finishing his coffee, he slipped some euros under the saucer and, placing his palms flat on the table, pushed himself to his feet. The pressure caused a dull throbbing pain in his wrist, familiar, somehow reassuring. He'd been in Europe when his father died, so he had no idea whether the old man had been felled by a single big problem or a legion of smaller ones. *Legions.* Was that what troubles came in?

BACK AT THE STUDIO, Noonan saw the mail had arrived, so he brought it upstairs and tossed it and the Columbia envelope onto the table next to his bed.

"Noonan, is that you?" Hugh's voice came ringing down from the studio. "Come up here. I need an explanation and I need it urgently."

Which meant that he'd taken the bait, just as Noonan had known he would. The finished canvases for the New York show he'd left in plain sight along the studio's outer wall, where the light was best. The portrait, though, he'd left draped on the easel, knowing full well that Hugh, of all people, would be curious. Childish behavior, he had to admit, wanting the painting to be seen but not ready to show it.

"I need you up here this instant, before I lose what's left of my sanity."

Upstairs, his old friend Hugh Morgan, notorious art dealer and international arbiter of taste, was dressed in the professional New Yorker manner—that is, for New York, and not for the place he happened to be just then. In Hugh's case, black designer jeans, black V-neck sweater and black blazer, as if he'd come to court a

Venetian widow. He'd ferreted out Noonan's small stash of good wine, opened a bottle and, as Noonan had predicted, now stood before the easel where the portrait sat undraped, his expression so full of revulsion that Noonan immediately saw the folly of not hiding the damn thing. Which was not to say that there wasn't also, he had to admit, a measure of perverse satisfaction.

"I was saving this Barolo, actually," he said, pouring himself a glass, then reluctantly joining his friend at the easel.

They'd come up in the art world together, having met in London in the seventies, expatriates avoiding military service. Hugh had a small gallery in Soho and gave Noonan his first real show. Later, with the amnesty, he'd returned to the States and opened a gallery in New York, then, over the years, in Paris and Rome. Noonan had remained in Europe, chasing women and commissions and good light—the right balance of conflict and ease—until finally settling in Venice a decade ago. Next month, when he went to New York, it would be his first trip to the country in more than twenty years.

Hugh regarded the painting, the painter, then the painting again. "Shouldn't you be getting younger?" he said.

"You don't like it?"

"Well, it's all worm, isn't it." It had long been Hugh's contention that Noonan's only subject, regardless of who or what he was painting, was the worm in the apple, the small, off-putting detail that registered in the viewer's subconscious and undermined the overall effect, the too-pale white spot on the skin that hinted at malignancy beneath. The result, in Hugh's view, of growing up in a place where everyone was being poisoned, to a greater or lesser degree, from an early age.

"We're all poisoned at an early age," Noonan was fond of reminding him.

" 'They fuck you up, your mum and dad. They may not mean to, but they do'?"

"I was thinking of original sin more than Larkin, but whatever. Anyway it isn't finished."

"Are you saying I'll like it when you're done?"

Noonan shrugged, then held the Barolo up to the light, squinting at it.

"I mean, Christ," Hugh said, waving at the painting as if to make it disappear. "Have you titled it? May I suggest *Portrait of the Artist as a Serial Killer*? *As Burn Victim*? Who paints something like this?"

Caravaggio, for one, Noonan thought. *David with the Head of Goliath*. Perhaps Noonan's favorite canvas. How long had it been since he'd laid eyes on it, that monstrous, severed head, Caravaggio's own, still full of rage, held aloft by a weakling for all the world to see? He'd like to see it once more before he died.

"My God," Hugh continued, "you look like you're poised to lunge right out of the canvas at prospective buyers. This troubles me, Noonan. I'm sorry, but I have to say this troubles me."

"Have you ever noticed that when people use the expression 'I have to say,' what follows usually needn't be said?"

"And what is *this*?" Hugh said, ignoring Noonan in his infuriating time-honored fashion, pointing at the dark rectangle on the wall behind the subject.

"A painting," Noonan explained. "That glint of gold is its frame."

"I know it's a painting. Of what?"

"Does it matter?"

"It looks like a fucking gallows."

It was the Bridge of Sighs, actually, or would've been, had Noonan allowed more of the picture into the light. Not that he saw any particular reason to explain. "Then it is."

"So what's it *doing* there?"

"I'm sorry. It's supposed to do something?"

"Oh, stop. You know what I mean. You're predicting you'll hang one day? Or saying you *deserve* it?"

"Stop being melodramatic. And where do you get burn victim?"

"That dark stain on the forehead? At the hairline?"

"The birthmark?"

Hugh poked him on the forehead with his index finger. "The point is, you don't *have* a birthmark."

Noonan covered the canvas again. "Do you have any feelings about the paintings you were actually supposed to look at?"

Together, Hugh rather reluctantly, they went over to the finished paintings along the wall. Next week they'd all be crated up and shipped to New York. Was it Noonan's imagination or had Hugh rearranged them? They now sat in chronological order. He didn't think that was how he'd set them, but who knew, maybe he had.

"It'll all sell, of course," Hugh conceded, as if this went without saying. But the "of course" implied a reservation or criticism of some sort, something he'd get around to expressing later, probably over dinner. "You were wise not to commit more than three pieces to that casino."

"That wasn't your advice at the time," Noonan felt compelled to remind him.

"Well, the money was good, wasn't it. And you needed it rather badly just then."

"As opposed to now?"

"I've often wondered, Robbie, what exactly it is that you *do* with your money."

Hugh was not alone in this. Noonan, together with his accountant, wondered the same thing quarterly. His father's military discipline had demanded that a person account for the whereabouts of every bent nickel, which of course went a long way toward explaining the vague pride his son always felt when his own money vanished without a trace.

"You live like a pauper," Hugh continued with a sweeping gesture, "yet you're hopelessly in debt."

" 'Hopelessly' might be a little strong," Noonan told him, "connoting as it does a lack of hope, of which I'm never wholly destitute."

"It *de*notes a lack of hope, actually," Hugh corrected. "You might as well tell me. Whom do you owe these days, and in what tragic amounts? The girls, I assume. Who else?" "The girls" were Noonan's ex-wives, who, for reasons best known to themselves, continued to grant him loans. Men generally knew better.

"I'd have to ask around," he sighed. In truth, his limited understanding of how much he owed pretty much paralleled his vague sense of where his money went. "My only real expense is this place."

"Don't get me started," Hugh said, flummoxed as always by his friend's militant, self-destructive inertia when it came to finding a new studio.

The Giudecca space had been affordable for most of the decade, but then the Venetian who owned the building, a man with whom Noonan had had an understanding, died and that understanding along with him. His son, having been informed that his renter was a famous painter, immediately quadrupled the rent. A cretin, to be sure, but on the plus side he lived in Milan and seemed not to mind terribly that Noonan was chronically six months in arrears, so long as he paid in cash, income that would never be declared. It was all very Italian. But for the past year Hugh had been trying, with the help of a local realtor, to locate less costly studio space, and Noonan was having none of it. "When I'm finished as a painter," he said, "I want to be able to throw myself into the lagoon." Which from the roof of the present studio he could, if he got a good running start. After New York, he now realized, he'd have a better idea of how close he was to finished.

"You *do* know that they're wetting themselves at Columbia over the possibility of your doing their residency? Did you even look at the material?"

Noonan nodded.

"A nice apartment comes with the gig. Also, I've been personally assured you'd have talented students."

50

"The worst kind," Noonan said. "They suck the very life out of you. Unless you tell them to fuck off and leave you alone, and then you feel guilty."

"When have *you* ever felt guilty?"

"Okay, so it's a theory, but one I've no desire to test."

"So you're broke."

Quite possibly, and perhaps even relevant. Still . . . "Then there's the IRS. If *they* discover I'm in residence, the bastards will garnish my wages for back taxes."

"If they discover you've visited, they'll take your gallery sales, as well," Hugh pointed out, not unreasonably.

"They're worried about terrorists now, not painters. Anyway, I think I'll stick to the original plan."

In and out in two days. An art day, with the obligatory Brie, overchilled white wine and endless obsequious introductions, until it all became insupportable and Noonan ducked out the back and into the nearest tavern for some serious drinking, then a diagnostic day, a full battery of tests at Sloane-Kettering before the very next flight back to Venice with no one the wiser, leaving the victim to await the reviews, sales, blood work and possibly biopsy all by himself. Exhausting even to contemplate. The plane out would be the worst of it, strapped into a seat, while trying in vain to anesthetize himself with free booze in first class—thank you, Hugh, for this, at least—and overcome the rising panic in the aisles, probably crawling out of his skin by the time they touched down. What if this experience was so bad he couldn't summon the courage necessary to board the return flight?

Feeling the dread rise, Noonan turned, half expecting to hear himself declare that he'd changed his mind and to hell with the show, but Hugh wasn't there. He'd gone back across the room, where he'd again undraped the painting on the easel. "Why paint something no one will ever buy, that's what I'd like to know. It's lunatic. You should stop painting this. I mean it. In fact, I forbid you to continue. Let's burn it right now, shall we?"

Like all art dealers, Hugh believed himself to be an integral part of the creative process. As if it would be foolish for any painter to embark on new work without first conferring with the man who would later sell it. He didn't really want Noonan to stop painting it, of course. Though unfinished, it was still the best canvas in the room, and Hugh had to know it. Even as he suggested the painting wasn't salable, he was busy coming up with a plan to do just that. What he was really after was the story behind it. People who bought art at these prices were hungry for backstory, gossip they could repeat to their friends. Here, Hugh could explain, was one of Robert Noonan's final canvases, begun when he'd first become aware of the illness that would eventually kill him. Ka-ching!

Talk. Vital to commerce. The end of art.

"Okay, I'll stop," Noonan said cheerfully, draping the canvas again.

Hugh didn't believe this for a second, but of course pretended to, clinking Noonan's glass with his own to make it official. "I can see why you didn't want to share this. It's excellent."

"I was just wondering if it was corked," Noonan said, holding the wine up to the light again. After so many years of working with chemicals, his sense of smell and taste had been blunted, though lately, for some reason, both had become annoyingly acute, and the list of foods to which he was suddenly averse had grown very long. Not true, alas, across the sensory spectrum, the intensity of his orgasms, not to mention their frequency, having radically diminished of late, a piss-poor trade-off.

"You're joking. I wish you had another just like it." Hugh allowed his gaze to fall directly on Noonan now, something he'd been careful not to do since he arrived. "So. How much weight have you lost?"

"Pounds, I couldn't tell you. A couple belt notches." Three to be precise. "Not all bad. I was getting fat."

Hugh looked serious. "And these night sweats?"

"Night terrors, actually." Suddenly wide awake at three in the morning, wild with rage and fear at he knew not what. So bad these last few months that he'd become nocturnal, painting by night until exhausted, then wandering the predawn streets and sleeping during the day.

"I have an idea," Hugh said, as if he'd just discovered a foolproof cure. "Let's dine at Harry's."

"That's the same idea you have every time you visit," said Noonan, relieved that the health issue could be tabled at least for the moment. Even though they were old friends, he disliked having such conversations with Hugh, who was by nature and profession a gossip. If his recent weight loss hadn't been dramatic enough to make him look gaunt, and if Hugh didn't have a physician's eye for medical detail, Noonan wouldn't even have mentioned it. "Dolce is right here on the Giudecca. Same owner, same menu, same food. Cheaper, too."

"I prefer Harry's."

"You mean being *seen* at Harry's."

"Can I help that?"

"Yes. People can help things."

Hugh cocked his hip provocatively. "Really? What things can people help?"

"Okay," Noonan conceded. "Not so many things." Not sexual orientation. And not cancer, if that's what the weight loss and night terrors were about.

"A person could choose *not* to paint gallows, I suppose," Hugh said, still looking at the draped canvas. "That much I grant you."

He obviously wanted to uncover it again, which told Noonan everything he needed to know and confirmed what his gut had been telling him for weeks. The pleasure of that knowledge put to flight the last of his dread, as in the end pleasure always did.

Troubles come not singly but in . . . what?

ARRIVING EARLY at Harry's, Noonan's least favorite restaurant in Venice, he nevertheless found Hugh already ensconced at the bar, surrounded by young Italian men and holding court in his flamboyant Italian, which was, in fact, far more fluent than his own. "I've had a perfect bitch of a time saving this table," Hugh informed him in a perfectly bitchy, insincere tone as the maître d' snaked them through the crowd of diners toward the most perfectly ostentatious table in the room. "Tell me, do you ever dress up?"

"Sure," said Noonan, who was wearing threadbare cords, a clean button-down denim shirt, a bulky sweater and boat shoes. "Now's a perfect example."

"I'm starting with the squid ink risotto, and you should, too," Hugh announced once they were settled. "I can't believe it. There's absolutely no one here. It's tragic."

Noonan understood that by "here" Hugh meant Venice, not the restaurant, which was full. And by "no one" he meant celebrities.

"There wasn't anyone on the plane either," he continued. "Everybody's still scared to fly."

Noonan snorted. "Afraid to fly, but not to live in a nation governed by an idiot."

"A duly elected idiot. This second time, anyway."

"Let's not talk politics," Noonan suggested. In addition to Italian, Hugh spoke fluent liberalese, which Noonan would've found tiresome even if he hadn't long suspected him of secretly voting Republican. "My stomach's iffy enough." Lately, that sour taste seemed to have moved onto the back of his tongue, yet another "trouble" to find out about in New York.

"I'm just the opposite. I'm like Audrey Hepburn in that movie with Cary Grant," Hugh said, his logic, as always, a quarter turn off. "The worse things get, the hungrier I am."

"It's true," Noonan agreed. "You *are* like Audrey Hepburn."

When the waiter came, Hugh ordered his squid risotto and Noonan the pasta *fagioli*, which elicited from his companion yet another personal observation—that he both dressed and *ate* like a peasant. To save further embarrassment, Hugh decided they'd both have the *branzino* and instructed the waiter to be certain that he, not his guest, got the larger portion. "Will I know it's a sea bass and not a sardine before I taste it?"

The waiter assured him that he would.

"I have my doubts," he said to Noonan, sotto voce, when the waiter retreated. "The Mediterranean is fished out. What they serve on this side of the Atlantic is hardly worth the effort of boning. Still, as long as my portion's bigger than yours, I suppose I'll cope."

Noonan broke off a hunk of bread. "How's Lady Brett's new work?" Anne Brettany was Hugh's other Venetian client, and he'd spent the morning at her studio in Santa Croce.

"Well, Anne is forever Anne, isn't she?" Hugh sighed, as if this were regrettable. "She thinks she's still in your shadow."

"She shouldn't. She's good."

"She says the reason I always visit her studio first is that I'm saving the best for last. When I ask how she'd feel if I came to see you first, she says then I'd be taking my clients in the order of their importance."

"You could've invited her to dinner."

"I did, and she accepted. Then she found out you were coming and suggested lunch instead. Over her fourth Prosecco the poor dear got maudlin and confessed she still thinks the two of you should be together."

Noonan couldn't help smiling at that, imagining skittish Anne trying to manage him in the throes of one of his bull-in-a-china-shop night terrors.

"She's between lovers, and you know how that makes her."

"I'll fuck her anytime she likes, if that's her problem."

Their first courses arrived at that moment, and Hugh used his hands to help waft the aroma of his risotto up to his eager nostrils. Hardly necessary, from where Noonan sat. Dead, rotting fish. His stomach turned over.

"Tell me," Hugh said, "do you really enjoy being an asshole?"

"Yes," Noonan said. His pasta and beans looked prechewed by

some earlier diner. "It's one of the few things I do enjoy, anymore."

"You and she are both going to be pleasantly surprised at the kind of money this new work brings. People are beginning to buy art again. Not everyone's, but they'll buy you. Anne will have to work harder, but then *she's* not averse to hard work."

"Here we go," Noonan said, pushing his bowl away, the food barely touched.

"Well, would it kill you to come to New York a week before the show? Do one or two interviews—don't look at me like that. Just the important ones, go to a couple of parties, allow yourself to be seen at the Four Seasons, that sort of thing? Maybe get a mention in 'Talk of the Town'?"

"Aren't you the one who's always telling me I misbehave in public?"

"In this instance misbehavior might not be so bad. It's been a long time. You still have your fans in the city, but a lot of people have forgotten what a bad boy you used to be. You could insult someone of my choosing. It wouldn't even have to be a new act. Your usual boorish routine would suffice to remind people of your vulgar origins, that dreadful little burg you hail from. Tanneryville."

"Thomaston."

"Create some buzz, is what I'm saying."

"God, you exhaust me. Less than twenty-four hours you've been here, and I swear I could sleep for a week."

"Your problem," Hugh said, his teeth and lips stained black with squid ink, "is that you think selling's beneath you. You're always in Tintoretto mode when you should be thinking Titian. Now *there's* a fellow who knew how to network. He had emissaries in every court in Europe, and they weren't pushing Venetian art either. They were pushing Titian."

Noonan leaned forward across the table so he wouldn't have to raise his voice. "The thing about Titian? He was Titian. And those paintings they were 'pushing'? Titians."

"Fine. You're not a careerist? Then do Columbia. Just paint and teach and forget the rest of it."

"Why? What possible reason could I have for leaving Venice? I'm getting more work done now than I did when I was forty. You saw for yourself."

"Yes, I did, and what I saw convinced me you need to clear out of here for a while. And don't go throwing up your hands. When you returned today, I bet you didn't even notice I'd rearranged your canvases."

So, Noonan thought, he'd been right. "I did, actually. You put them in chronological sequence."

"Well, that's not the organizing principle I had in mind, but it doesn't surprise me. I rearranged them so they went from dark to darker to darkest."

"Your point being?"

"And the darkest of all is that Dorian Gray number on the easel. One whole side of the face is in shadow and let's not even go into that thing on the wall, which we shouldn't be able to see, after all, given the light source."

"It's the Bridge of Sighs," Noonan said, expelling a sigh of his own.

"Oh, I feel *so* much better knowing that. It's not mortality that's troubling you, the possibility of a bad diagnosis. No, you're identifying with criminals making their final journey from the court to the dungeon, from which only death can free them. Thanks, that really cheers me up."

"It's a good painting."

"Good painting, bad painting. Who cares?"

"I do."

"What worries me isn't the quality of the work. It's that the painting is a lie. The rage, the self-loathing staring out from behind those dead eyes, that isn't you, Robbie. I've known you for a long time, and you're far from a saint. Truth be told, you've never been anything but a pain in the ass, but the face in that painting isn't yours. For better or worse, you've always been honest. You've painted what you saw, and if *that's* what you're seeing, something's very wrong." Hugh was staring at him, black lipped now, a rather gruesome sight, actually. And it was his turn to lean toward the center of the table. "I almost hope you *do* have cancer. Most cancers are treatable."

"More melodrama."

"You're in trouble, Noonan. I knew it as soon as I laid eyes on you. Your friends know it, too." He paused here to let this sink in. "You've become a recluse, and don't pretend you haven't."

Noonan snorted. "Who told you that? Anne Brettany? Please."

"You may be interested to know Anne said nothing, even under direct questioning. And you know how skilled I am in that regard."

"Who, then?" Noonan said.

Hugh seemed to be weighing whether or not to reveal his source. "The only time anybody's seen you in months, you were sobbing uncontrollably in some church. In the middle of the bloody afternoon."

Madonna dell'Orto, to be precise. Noonan remembered the afternoon. And now he knew who. Todd Lichtner, the prick.

"And another thing," Hugh said, on a roll now. "When was the last time you punched somebody?"

"A long time ago," Noonan said, pleased to be given this opportunity to prove his mental health. "I can't even remember, it's been so long."

"Exactly," Hugh said triumphantly. "I mean, what have you been for your entire life? I'll tell you. You've been a provocateur. A goad. An insensitive brute. At times a bully, a total dickhead. But here's the thing: it's always *worked* for you. Every time you got into a rut, whether it was a marriage rut or a work rut, you'd find somebody to piss you off, promptly break the fellow's nose, pack your things and move someplace new. And your very next painting would be great, your rut a thing of the past. Now? You're crying in churches. It's like all the fight's gone out of you."

"I'm closer to breaking *your* nose right now than you appear to realize," Noonan said, his wrist throbbing in anticipation. He expected Hugh to blanch at the threat, and so was surprised when instead Hugh leaned forward and offered his chin.

"Do it," he told him, and unless Noonan was mistaken, there were tears in his eyes. The room had gone quiet, and the other diners were watching expectantly. "Be a belligerent. And don't tell me you don't remember how, because we both know better." Grinning now, each tooth grotesquely ringed with squid ink.

"Go look at yourself in the mirror," Noonan suggested, bringing his companion up short.

"What?"

Noonan shook his head. "Nah, I'd hate to ruin the surprise."

It was a full ten minutes before Hugh returned from the men's room, his teeth gleaming white again. In his absence, Noonan had finished his pasta *fagioli*, the food suddenly tasting good. Could his friend be right, that the very idea of punching someone in public had improved his appetite?

The other diners had all gone back to their meals. "Battalions," Noonan said when Hugh sat down.

"I beg your pardon?"

It had come to him when Hugh was in the gents. Troubles come not singly but in battalions. Suddenly his spirits improved, along with his appetite.

When the sea bass was served, the larger portion was placed in front of Noonan, who gleefully dug in before the plates could be switched. Hugh just glared at him, finally saying, "So, are you going to tell me about it or not?"

"Tell you what?" Why he'd been crying at Madonna dell'Orto? That was the question Noonan had been expecting, and he was prepared with a glib answer. There were two damned fine Tintorettos in that church. Good enough to reduce any painter worth his salt to tears.

But what Hugh said was "What are you *really* afraid of?"

59

To that question he had no ready response. Still, Noonan was surprised to hear himself respond honestly. "Right this minute? Every little thing."

AND, STRANGELY ENOUGH, not the big thing. He wasn't—Noonan felt quite certain of this—afraid to die. If he had cancer, well, he had cancer. If it was treatable, then, as Hugh said, he would treat it. Cancer just was what it was. You weren't obligated to assign any meaning to it, especially if you hailed from Thomaston, New York, where the stream that meandered through town was a different color every day, thick with dyes now acknowledged to be carcinogenic. If it *was* cancer, he reflected, there was a kind of ironic symmetry to it—to have fled his hometown so long ago and never looked back, only to be felled in the end by some long-dormant, mutated gene.

Sure, cancer, if that's what it was, would mean fewer canvases when he'd have preferred more, but a decade hence, at seventy, that would still be true, as it would again at eighty. Nobody ever got enough, but if this was it, Noonan wouldn't feel cheated. He'd never imagined he'd be long-lived, nor did he particularly feel he deserved to be. There was no law that good painters got to live longer than bad ones or, for that matter, lawyers. He had little to complain about.

Okay, so forget cancer. It was the bouts of uncontrollable grief, even more than the occasional night terrors, that scared him. That mysterious sorrow, its source unfathomable. He was simply grieving. But for what, he couldn't say. Had some internal switch broken, slipping his emotions off their tether, out of their natural context? If so, why just sorrow? Why not joy? He hadn't had any sudden, inexplicable, overwhelming attacks of that. Or jealousy, or lust, or shame. One minute the grief wasn't there, the next it was, rising in him like nausea. The afternoon in dell'Orto he'd seen Lichtner coming toward him up the Fondamenta della Sensa, but by then Noonan was already

60

lost, utterly overcome. Pretending not to hear the man call his name, he'd ducked down a narrow *calle* and hurried into the church, where he'd knelt for nearly half an hour before Tintoretto's *The Last Judgment*, waiting for the waves of ridiculous, comic sorrow to subside. He knew from experience they eventually would, just as he knew he'd be left exhausted, mystified and, yes, frightened.

While he knelt there, the church's front door had opened several times, flooding the somber interior with soft light, but it hadn't occurred to Noonan that Lichtner had followed him inside. How long had the little putz observed him? And since that afternoon—what, five months ago? more?—how many people had he told about the incident at how many dinner parties and in what dramatic detail? He'd probably made a parlor game out of it. "You'll never guess who I saw sobbing his guts out in Madonna dell'Orto last week. I'll give you a hint. A local painter." Everyone would play along, of course, and the guesses, by the time the pasta course had been cleared, would have become increasingly far-fetched, until someone finally said, in disbelief, "Don't tell me it was Noonan." And Lichtner, triumphant, "All right, I won't tell you, but that's who it was, nevertheless." "Beneath *The Last Judgment*, you say?" one of the women at the table would offer. "Oh, I *do* like that. That's lovely. Who says there's no justice?"

"I've been telling you for months he's losing it," the hostess of the party would chime in then, and if Harvey Bellows was there, he'd recall how one morning, on his way to the Ferrovia at four-thirty, he'd rounded a corner and practically run into Noonan, who offered little more than a grunt for greeting or apology, hurrying off into the Venetian night as if the devil himself had been after him. Where could he have been coming from or going to at such an hour? Not the airport or the train station, the wrong direction for either of those; besides, he hadn't had any luggage. Probably visiting some married woman. Most of the women at the dinner party would have been married, and odds were good that at least one could testify from personal experience to Noonan's prowess in this regard.

"Weeping before *The Last Judgment*," that first woman would've repeated. "I *do* like that." Though she wouldn't say why, not with her husband sitting next to her.

At any rate, by now the tale had probably reached across the Atlantic. Venice's expatriate community of wanderers—writers, artists and visiting academics—was tight-knit, and Noonan could imagine how swiftly the story would have traveled. It also explained why, though he'd done his best to discourage it, Hugh had insisted on coming right before his show in New York. His excuse had been that he was worried about Anne, who was high maintenance, no doubt about it, so Noonan hadn't doubted him. Now it appeared that he himself was the true object of Hugh's concern. And maybe even *that* wasn't the worst of it. Maybe Hugh hadn't really wanted to visit at all. Maybe he'd just come to find out if Noonan was in any condition to proceed with the show. Having heard that something was wrong, possibly from a number of different sources, he'd decided to find out.

Declining Hugh's halfhearted offer of a nightcap at his hotel, he returned to the Giudecca at loose ends, having drunk too much to work but wanting to work anyway, and not knowing what he'd do with the night if he didn't. Undraping the portrait, he studied his father. Had he admitted this to himself before tonight, that the figure on the canvas was his father? He'd begun the painting a month earlier, as a self-portrait, then realized they were his father's eyes, not his own, looking back at him. In retrospect, reason enough to quit right then, but he hadn't. Over the next few days he found himself emphasizing the physical features they shared, minimizing those he'd inherited from his mother, marveling that as he did these things the man in the painting somehow became less his father and more Noonan himself, as if by subtracting his mother he was arriving at his own essence. The process wasn't unlike telling a police sketch artist "I think his nose was a little wider," except that he was making suggestions to himself that were based on distant, not recent, memory. He'd added the birthmark last, on a whim, the final damning detail, though for the life of him he couldn't decide which of them it damned. Nothing about what he was doing made any sense. How could giving the figure the features of one man make him more recognizably another? Was he losing his mind or going someplace new and exciting, where no other painter had ever gone before? Would the result be art or just creepy exhibitionism?

This, he now realized, was surely why he'd wanted Hugh to see the canvas. And his reaction—that the painting was a lie—was, in a sense, exactly what Noonan had hoped for. I am *not* my father. Yet hadn't Hugh, his old friend, recognized it as a self-portrait? The possibility that the man in the painting could be anyone other than Noonan himself hadn't even occurred to him.

Hugh *had* been right about one thing, though, much as Noonan hated to admit it. Given that the left side of the face was in shadow, what was over his left shoulder—the painting within the painting—shouldn't have been illuminated. Normally, there was nothing Noonan was more conscious of or meticulous about than light. How had he missed something so elementary?

"I don't know," Evangeline confessed. "How *did* you miss it?"

Intent on the canvas, Noonan hadn't heard her come in. Or, for that matter, realized he'd been speaking. "Hey," he said, trying to cover his surprise at her sudden appearance. She was dressed for the gallery, which, to judge by the time, she'd probably just closed. It had been a slow year, and she was staying open later. What he couldn't quite decide was whether he was glad to see her. "I didn't hear you come in."

"Or call up the stairs?"

"I guess not."

She came over to where he sat, put her hands on his shoulders and kissed the top of his head. When, he wondered, had he become the kind of man a woman could sneak up on?

"How's the Great One?"

"I assume you refer to Hugh?"

"No offense," she said, "but yes. I see you broke out the good wine." The empty Barolo still stood on the table next to the easel.

"He doesn't think I have cancer."

"Don't sound so disappointed. For what it's worth, neither do I. You're losing weight because you forget to eat."

"He thinks I'm depressed. Suicidal, even, except he didn't say that exactly." He'd come pretty close, though, over the zabaglione at Harry's. When Evangeline offered no response to this weighty diagnosis, he said, "Whereas *you* think . . ."

"I think you're just fucked up."

He couldn't help but chuckle. "Thanks. That's as close to a vote of confidence as I've had all day."

"People just slip into funks," she said wearily, as if she knew firsthand whereof she spoke.

"So this is just a phase I'm in? I wait for it to pass?"

She shrugged. "I don't know, Noonan. I really don't."

"That's the difference between you and Hugh Morgan. In the almost forty years I've known him, he's never once used that particular phrase."

She came around now, unbuttoning her silk blouse. "That's just one of the differences between us," she said, letting the blouse drop to the floor and sitting down gently on his lap.

"*This*, he claims," he said, indicating the portrait, "is a study in self-loathing."

Kicking her shoes off, she used her big toe to rotate the chair a quarter turn so she, too, could study the canvas. "Well, it's true you won't be accused of narcissism."

She'd seen it before and, like Hugh, assumed it was a self-portrait, though if she'd been repulsed by it, she never said so. And something else now occurred to Noonan, that his father, near the end, had apparently gone batty in his solitude. The neighbors reported hearing him inside the house, cursing at no one in particular, or perhaps everybody. When he did emerge, his hair uncombed, his shirt untucked, his fly unzipped, he always managed to give the impression it was only a supreme act of will that prevented him from punching everyone he passed on the street. When people tried to engage him in conversation, he just glared at them, as if he didn't trust himself to utter so much as a single syllable for fear that the dam would burst and swamp them in a torrent of abuse. Which made Noonan wonder. Late in life, long after he was gone, did his father also suffer episodes of inexplicable grief, or night terrors? And what would the cause have been? Something originating in the Cayoga Stream? Could it have been the *water*? If so, in what sense could anybody truly be blamed for anything?

Evangeline turned away from the painting and regarded him through narrowed eyes. "Either we drape that," she said, "or we drape me."

Noonan kissed her bare breast. "I was supposed to stop by the gallery, wasn't I."

"You were."

"I'm a shit."

"You are."

"But you love me anyway."

"I wouldn't go that far."

"How far would you go?"

"Downstairs. One flight."

As they started down to the bedroom, Noonan said, "I have a bone to pick with your husband. He witnessed one of my crying jags, and he's been telling people about it."

"Yeah, well, if he had clue one, he'd have a bone to pick with you, too."

THE ROUTE MEN

THE HOUSE my parents purchased on Third Street in the East End was plain and gray shingled. The residents of our new neighborhood were all working people, mostly Irish but with a healthy smattering of Italians and Poles and Slavs. Third Street was seven blocks long, anchored by Tommy Flynn's corner market at the lower end and Ikey Lubin's at the upper. Its single-family homes were modest and built close together on small lots, each with a thin grass terrace between the sidewalk and the street. Upstairs, typically, were two small bedrooms and a bath, downstairs the kitchen, dining room and living room, though, after the advent of television, most families wedged a dinette into one corner of the kitchen, thus converting the dining room into a TV-centered family room. The living room generally went unused, except when company came.

For each single-family home, however, there were two or three larger houses divided into upstairs and downstairs flats. Often, in terms of square footage, they were as large as the single-family homes, but after Berman Court we felt privileged not to be sharing our dwelling. My father liked to remark to our new neighbors that he couldn't live with somebody underfoot or overhead, though that was precisely what we'd *been* doing. My mother would scold him for such comments, but too gently to make much of an impression, so great was the pleasure he took in our change of fortune.

Of the three of us, I think he was the one most deeply affected by our move. My mother was glad to be out of the West End but wary, too, afraid of how much money she'd had to take from my grandparents, afraid that our little house on the corner of Third and Rawley might have come at too high a cost. The responsibility of ownership, of mortgage payments, of not having a landlord, frightened her, I'm sure, at least at the beginning. A leaky faucet or a running toilet worried her unduly, because they represented what just might turn out to be the tip of some terrible iceberg, or perhaps the first in a series of small but unrelenting expenses that couldn't be anticipated or, therefore, budgeted. Often I'd find her in the cellar worrying over a puddle of water that had formed after a hard rain, or up in the attic studying the roof for telltale signs that she'd done a foolish thing by putting every egg we had in this particular basket.

My father, having no such misgivings, couldn't get over how good luck had found us out so suddenly. His experience had been that houses were something people lost, as his parents had lost their farm, and the notion that he himself might own one someday hadn't occurred to him until it happened. That first year on Third Street, every minute he wasn't on his milk route he spent scraping and painting the trim, shoring up the collapsing garage (even though at that time we still had no car to put in it), or encircling the porch with bushes, adding small, inexpensive and, according to my mother, garish touches to the property. He'd have filled our tiny terrace with lawn ornaments had she allowed him.

He was in good spirits not just about us and our prospects but also about our country. Here, he reminded me proudly, anybody could become anything, and we ourselves were living examples of how America worked. Though I wasn't sure what we'd "become" by moving out of Berman Court and into the East End, I liked our new neighborhood and could see that while we weren't rich, we were better off. And I was especially comforted by my father's belief that we were living a story whose ending couldn't be anything but happy.

Interestingly, the nature and moral of that story began almost immediately to evolve. As we settled into the East End, our sudden good fortune seemed rooted less in luck than in the sober industry that I was being taught in school was the key to success in a free society. And for my father hard work and virtue were two sides of the same coin. The only families who were truly stuck in the West End, he now believed, were headed by dissolute men who couldn't manage to find their way past the gin mills after their shifts, gave their money to the bookies who haunted the tannery and spent their weekends at the racetrack while their wives and children went hungry. In America, he maintained, if you kept your nose clean, good things were eventually bound to happen to you.

Not surprisingly, my mother's take on our better life, as well as her estimation of America, was more complex and, to my way of thinking, far less satisfying. She never publicly contradicted my father's joyous outbursts, though later, when they were alone, she'd remind him that what got us out of Berman Court was not virtue but a loan from her parents, nor had hard work been much of a factor. True, he always worked hard, she'd grant him this much, yet that was no excuse to go around talking nonsense about good things happening to good people, because bad things happened to good people all the time. In fact, the bad thing that had happened to me was more responsible for our move to the East End than our industry and virtue combined.

On those rare occasions when she took my father to task, he always hung his head woefully and claimed she hadn't understood what he meant. "All I'm saying is, what if this was Russia? Over there you got no chance. You just gotta take what they give you." To which my mother would roll her eyes. "How much do you really know about Russia, Lou? Did you go to Russia once and not tell me?" Which would make him even more sheepish. "It's what they say," he'd reply lamely, which would elicit, predictably, my mother's trump observation, that she couldn't care less what "they" said. It was what *he* said that was giving her a headache.

None of which is to suggest that she was a pessimist. She

would concede that both our family and our nation were making progress. In large part that was due—speaking of bad things—to the war, which she said had made us all Americans first, Catholics or Protestants or Italians or Irish second. Much of the ethnic rigidity that had been common to Thomaston's neighborhoods when she and my father were children had begun to break down. Take St. Francis Elementary. Though still predominantly Irish, there were also kids with Polish and Italian last names, some of them, like me, the products of what were then referred to as mixed marriages. Thomaston was indeed the melting pot we were taught to be proud of in school, and its East End neighborhoods in particular were organized more by people's occupations and economic status than where they came from. If the West End was still primarily made up of more recent immigrants, that was because they happened to hold the poorest paying jobs in the tannery and nearby leather shops. More important, they *could* work their way out of the West End, as the Wilsons and the Lubins and the Gunthers and so many other East Enders had done.

As I say, my mother conceded this much. But about other things she wasn't so optimistic. At the economic extremes of Thomaston, she gave me to understand, there was little fluidity. If you were a Negro, of course, you'd remain in the two square blocks of the Hill, and if you lived in the Borough, that's where you'd probably stay. In America, my mother claimed, the very luckiest were insulated against failure, just as it was the unavoidable destiny of the luckless to remain thwarted. When I asked if we'd ever get to the point where we'd be one of the lucky ones, she said we already were. The middle, she said, was the real America, the America that mattered, the America that was worth fighting wars to defend. There was just the one problem with being in the fluid middle. You could move up, as we had done, but you could also move down.

I don't know why it troubled me so much that my parents disagreed about how the world operated, but it did, and when I intimated as much to my mother, she replied, "Really, Louie? Which of us should think differently? Your father or me?" I had thought that went without saying. My father's was a more reassuring interpretation of the known facts of our lives and a more elegant, satisfying story to boot. If you believed in America, then we would continue our ascent, and I wanted for all of us to agree that this was what would happen. From my vehemence on this point, my mother must have concluded that I was concerned about my own future, and she quickly conceded that after college I'd likely continue to rise even further, if that's what I wanted, as a doctor or maybe a lawyer (my relentless cross-examinations of everything she said may have suggested this latter profession). But in her opinion, she and my father were done moving up in the world. Getting out of the West End was about as much as you could hope for in one generation.

I still remember how much this upset me. It was our *family* I wanted to succeed, not me. There wasn't supposed to *be* any limit to the benefits of hard work and honesty, and her saying there *were* limits implied that she didn't believe in America, or, worse, in us.

And I was particularly troubled by my mother's notion of downward mobility. I wanted her to assure me that nothing of the sort would happen to us, not if we continued to do things right and follow the rules. "Oh, Louie," she said, giving me a hug I didn't want. "What am I going to *do* with you?"

THE HOUSE NEXT DOOR was one of those divided into upstairs and downstairs flats. The downstairs was occupied by spinster sisters, the Spinnarkles, both of whom worked at Montgomery Ward. They left the house together in the morning and returned together in the late afternoon. On Saturday nights they went to the movies. Neither, as far as we could tell, ever entertained a male visitor. They were fond of children, though, and seemed genuinely to welcome the opportunity to look after me on those rare occasions when my parents needed to be someplace else. When it was time to return me next door, they wished out loud that I was *their* little boy. I fear I must have conveyed in countless unsubtle ways how glad I was that this was not the case.

Nothing at the Spinnarkles' was even remotely interesting to a boy. They had no toys, no games, no books, no clue. There *was* a television set, but they always turned it off when company arrived, which struck me as downright rude. In our house, the TV we'd purchased shortly after moving to the East End was always on, at least when my father was home. He regarded this as one of the many fine things we had to offer visitors. He preferred a baseball game, if there was one, some other sporting event, if there wasn't. He gave me to understand that professional wrestling was fake, but this in no way diminished his appreciation of it. He wasn't much interested in the shows my mother liked—dramas like the *Philco Television Playhouse*—but offered no objection to her watching them, snoring peacefully in his armchair when she did.

That the Spinnarkle sisters should jump up and turn off their TV whenever anyone knocked at their door also struck my father as strange. "You ain't gotta turn that off," he'd say. "It don't bother me." To which the Spinnarkles, who always finished each other's sentences, would reply that they "weren't really watching" (Edith), "just passing the time" (Janet). When left in their company, I quickly assured them that the TV didn't bother me either, especially if *Tales of the Texas Rangers* was on, but the sisters had firm ideas about how guests should be entertained. "Let's converse," they'd suggest, smoothing their skirts down over their knees and looking at me hopefully. They rented their upstairs flat, coincidentally, to our old friends the Marconis.

Well, perhaps not coincidentally. When I discovered that one of the houses my parents were thinking about buying was next door to the Marconis, I lobbied hard for that one, and I could tell my father liked the Third Street neighborhood best. My mother had mixed feelings. She and Mrs. Marconi were friends, but she may have felt that having the Marconis so close by lessened the symbolic significance of our move. All-new neighbors were probably more what she had in mind. But she did feel sorry for Mrs. Marconi, who was pregnant again and seemingly every bit as trapped here in the East End as she'd been in Berman Court. "I'd forgotten how much I despised that man," I overheard my mother tell my father. Mr. Marconi had apparently come out onto the porch the weekend my parents first looked at the house, and according to my mother his expression had clouded over when he saw who was looking at the house next door, the purple birthmark on his forehead darkening.

"We're not buying that house unless you promise me to leave him alone," my mother said when they got home. "Do you understand? Mind your own business. You aren't in competition with him. He didn't like you before and he doesn't like you now. You're just going to have to live with it." My father opened his mouth to object, then saw the look on her face and shut it again. "I mean it, Lou," she told him, then fixed me as a witness. "What did your father just promise me?" she said. "Not to bother Mr. Marconi," I said, angry with her and not caring that she knew. I hated it when she made my father promise things, almost as much as I hated it when she made me promise things. She regarded us both dubiously, as if she knew better than to put much faith in either of us. "What'd I ever do to him, is what I'd like to know," my father said when she was gone.

In the end we settled on the Third Street house, Marconis or no Marconis. Its owner, desperate to leave Thomaston, came down dramatically on his asking price, so that was that. But the real reason, I suspect, was me, since I'd overheard a conversation my mother had with Doctor Boyer, who convinced her that Third Street was the best place for the simple reason that I'd have a friend there.

*

My father wouldn't have intentionally broken any promise to my mother, but I think even she knew he wouldn't be able to honor the one she extorted from him as a condition for buying the house on Third Street. It was like asking him not to breathe, or to stop loving me so much. If that was what she wanted, he'd try, but it ran contrary to his nature. What she was probably hoping for was to modify his behavior by small degrees. To her way of thinking he was like a puppy that chewed shoes. You probably couldn't break him of so rewarding a habit, but you could make him feel guilty, at least, keep him from doing it every time you turned your back, and that was something.

Until she made the point about my father and Mr. Marconi not being in a contest, it hadn't occurred to me that he might have seen it like that, but of course when I thought about it, it made sense. Weren't our families on parallel tracks, having both recently moved from the West End to a better part of town? Weren't the Lynches and the Marconis, despite our differences, both determined to take advantage of what America offered, a chance to prove our worth, to get ahead, to secure our future? Of course in Thomaston, as elsewhere, the Irish and the Italians often judged their progress against each other. So there was all of this, as well as one other potent comparison. Now that Mr. Marconi was a full-time letter carrier at the post office, they were both "route men" who owned a territory and were responsible for things getting done, for making sure people in their territory got what they needed. Men who moved throughout their world and became men of that world. This, I think, was what made my father even more interested in Mr. Marconi now than he had been before, and much more than he was in our other East End neighbors. They were both men of motion, of movement. Who would grab the brass ring?

Mr. Marconi had some advantages—not unfair advantages, my father never went that far. But in certain respects, he had to admit, the other man had it made. For one thing, the post office paid better than the dairy, and postal workers had government benefits that wouldn't quit. Also, letter carriers didn't have to get up nearly as early as milkmen. Except for the long summer days in June and July, my father always rose in the dark, and in winter he'd complete half his route before sunrise. Still, he confided to me more than once that he wasn't sure he'd have swapped jobs with Mr. Marconi even if he'd had the chance, not when you considered their respective routes. Mr. Marconi delivered his letters in the Gut, the very worst part of the West End, whereas my father worked the Borough, the plum route, proof of the high esteem in which his employers held him. He worried out loud about Mr. Macaroni's place in the post office hierarchy if the Gut was the route they gave him.

My father had begun referring to Bobby's father as "Mr. Macaroni" shortly after he'd promised to leave him alone, and he always nudged me to make sure I got the joke. I don't think he was aware of my mixed feelings. The joke was gentle enough, but since kindergarten I'd been called a name I wasn't fond of, so I was sensitive about nicknames. Of course with my father it was different. He wasn't calling the man a name to his face, and there was no ill will intended in any event, so I supposed it was all right for him and me to have a small private joke. My real fear was that he'd slip up someday when Bobby was around. And I suspect this was his response to the fact that my mother's injunction not to talk to Mr. Marconi had gradually broadened. By "leave the man alone" she apparently meant not just that my father shouldn't talk *to* the man but also that he shouldn't talk *about* him—that is, to quit bringing his name up in conversations. This extra weight, added to his already solemn promise, must have seemed particularly unfair, so he was glad to discover that he could expect a little more latitude if he referred to Mr. Macaroni, which occasioned a more benign, pained reaction. If I reported that the Marconis had purchased a television—they had, according to Bobby— my father was able to interrogate me by making the whole thing into a joke. Mr. Macaroni bought a TV? What kind of

TV did Mr. Macaroni buy, new or used? Did Mrs. Macaroni like the new Macaroni TV?

The questions were jokes and not jokes. Back when we'd all lived in Berman Court, my father had had a pretty good idea of our relative circumstances, but what had happened since we'd been separated? What had the Marconis acquired? How big were the economic strides they'd taken? How much had those strides been offset by two more little Macaronis? They were still renting, which meant something, but maybe they were saving for a down payment on a house. Were they close or still years away? My father had an inquiring mind, which he was now cruelly prohibited from using.

Therefore he had to rely on me for information. Did the Marconis drink Coca-Cola or the off brands that Tommy Flynn and Ikey Lubin stocked in their coolers and sold cheap? I never went into the Marconis' flat either, so I knew little more than my father did, and I told him so. "Ask him sometime," he'd suggest, meaning Bobby. "He'll do no such thing," my mother would reply. "It's none of our business."

She seemed to understand that eventually my father's curiosity would overpower his promise, so she kept a watchful eye on him those first few months after the move, especially if he found occasion to go out onto the front porch about the time Mr. Marconi finished his mail route and returned home. If she saw him start to sidle over and attempt to engage Bobby's father in friendly conversation, she'd fling the window open and call out that she needed something, and he'd have no choice but to return, hangdog, caught doing or about to do what he'd promised not to. "What do you need?" he'd grumble when he was back in the kitchen. "I need you to work on your memory," my mother would tell him. "What did you promise me if we moved here?" To which he'd shrug his big shoulders. "Saying hello to somebody ain't the same as bothering him, Tessa. We're neighbors, them and us. You can't not speak to people."

All still might have been well except that shortly after we

75

moved to Third Street Mr. Marconi bought a used Pontiac station wagon big enough to accommodate the entire clan, though they seldom used it except on Saturday afternoons to go to the supermarket. "What'd he buy it *for*, is what I don't understand. They don't go for no drives. They never go to the lake or nothing." These were things my father himself had always said we'd do as soon as we could afford a car. "It just sits there."

"You don't *need* to understand," my mother would remind him. "Guess why."

"I ain't sayin' it's my business," he replied, knowing where she was headed. "It just don't make sense, is what I'm sayin'."

One Saturday afternoon my mother was downtown doing errands when my father must have decided he'd lived with these Macaroni mysteries long enough. He'd seen the whole family pile into the Pontiac and head out to the A&P an hour earlier, so when the Spinnarkle sisters came out to sit on their front porch, he told me he was going over to see "the ladies" for a while, though I knew the Spinnarkles were a pretext, in case my mother came home unexpectedly.

He'd been sitting there for a half hour or so when the Pontiac pulled up at the curb. Pretending not to notice, my father stood and stretched and told the sisters that he'd better go back home and do some chores before his wife showed up and accused him of loafing. When Mr. Marconi got out of the station wagon and saw my father pausing on the steps to say hello, he just smiled knowingly and sent Mrs. Marconi on ahead with the children while he and Bobby unloaded the groceries.

"How's that wagon worked out for you?" my father wondered.

"Just fine," said Mr. Marconi, his tone suggesting that those two syllables conveyed the entire length and breadth of his thoughts on the subject, and perhaps all other subjects as well. Bobby saw me on our porch and waved. His father handed him a grocery bag.

"Price of gas and all . . . ," my father ventured, and getting no response to this, he continued. "I was thinking about a car myself," he said, rubbing his chin thoughtfully, "but then I figured what for? I can use the truck for free, so I decided against it."

Loaded down with grocery bags, Mr. Marconi and Bobby headed for the porch. "The dairy allows you to use their truck for personal business?"

My father shrugged. "You ain't really supposed to," he conceded, "but I know the old man real good, and he don't mind, as long as I stay around here. I give you a hand with them bags?" The station wagon's tailgate was down, two more bags standing right there.

"We can manage," Mr. Marconi said, brushing past my father and up the porch steps.

"I don't mind," my father said. "I ain't doing nothin'."

"We can manage," he repeated over his shoulder, and then disappeared inside with Bobby, the outer door swinging shut behind them. Alone on the terrace, my father regarded the last two bags with what seemed to me genuine longing. Had he been given permission to pick them up, he'd have been able to peer inside and see whether the groceries they'd bought were name brands or bottom shelf, cheap cuts of meat or expensive. Had he been allowed to help, the Marconis would've had to let him, however briefly, inside their flat, where he could've taken inventory. I could see he was seriously considering picking up those bags without permission, but just then my mother came around the corner and caught him.

"I was visiting the ladies, is all," he said when we were back inside our house. "Ask Louie."

My mother glanced at me, saw I was prepared to take my father's side as usual and went back to glaring at him.

"Or ain't I allowed to talk to them either?"

"Keep it up, Lou," she warned him. "Just keep it up and see what happens."

"It's him I feel bad for," he said later, over dinner. "All them

77

mouths to feed, another on the way." He was picking at my mother's hamburger casserole, normally one of his favorites. But I could tell by the look on his face that he was wondering what the Marconis were eating and that the food on his own fork had no taste.

WITH ALL THAT comparing going on, I was glad my father wasn't the sort of man to compare children, because Bobby Marconi had it all over me. Though half a head shorter, Bobby was a natural athlete, always first to be chosen when teams were picked, whereas I, despite my size, was among the last, at least on those rare occasions I allowed myself to be drawn into a game. My father enjoyed sports on television, but he'd grown up on a farm and had a farm boy's awkwardness when it came to handling balls of any description. Those meant to be caught he fumbled, those meant to be dribbled he'd end up kicking, an ineptitude he passed down to me. He hoped I might play Pop Warner football, something he'd wanted to do himself when he was my age, and given my size I suppose I could have managed one of those interior line positions that didn't require any ball handling. But my mother thought football was dangerous, so that was out, and in truth I was glad.

As an only child I was a voracious reader and did better in school than Bobby, but that didn't count for much among boys our age. Besides, I went to St. Francis, which everyone knew was easier than Bridger, the East End elementary school that Bobby now attended, and while he didn't distinguish himself, his teachers all agreed that he was one of their smartest students. When he felt like applying himself, they pointed out, he did fine. As I said, my father would never have compared me with Bobby. I doubt he would have known how, his devotion to me and pride in my accomplishments being as complete as mine toward him. But for some reason I felt certain that Mr. Marconi *was* the sort of man to compare sons and as a result didn't think much of me.

He never said anything, of course, but now that we were neighbors again, I had the impression he was just as happy that Bobby and I were going to different schools.

So the boundaries of our friendship, much to my disappointment, weren't very different from what they were on Berman Court. When I again pressed to expand them, I met with the same resistance and was offered the same unsatisfactory explanations I'd been given before. The Marconis were different from us. (How?) They preferred to keep to themselves. (Why?) Bobby wasn't allowed as much freedom as I was. (Why not?) Back then I'd had to content myself with a walk-to-and-from-school friendship. Now I had to be satisfied with a few hours on Saturdays. Even so, this might have been enough except for my vague sense that there was something I wasn't being told. Bobby was forever getting grounded, allowed to leave the apartment only to go to school or deliver his newspapers, and for some reason I got it into my head that these punishments had something to do with me, perhaps because whenever I asked what he'd done wrong, he said he couldn't talk about it. What could the reason be if it wasn't me? "Lou, look at me," my mother said when I floated this theory. "It doesn't have anything to do with you, sweetie."

"But what did I *do*?" I said plaintively, at the time unaware of how much I must have sounded like my father. ("What did I ever do to *him*, is what I'd like to know.")

She gave me a big hug. "Lou, sweetie. You're not listening to me. It has *nothing . . . to do . . . with you*." Then she added ominously, "There are things going on in that house that you know nothing about, but they have nothing to do with you—*or* your father."

What things, I asked, but she wouldn't say any more, just that they weren't any of our business. "And I don't want you quizzing Bobby either, do you understand?"

But it wasn't fair. Whatever was going on next door, my mother knew about it. If our families were estranged, this wasn't true of my mother and Mrs. Marconi. *Their* friendship, as far as I could tell, was exempted. True, it was largely clandestine. Mrs. Marconi was still supposed to stay in their flat and tend to Bobby's little brothers, but once her husband and my father were off on their routes, she and my mother could meet secretly, and I was pretty sure they did. When I returned from school, my mother would sometimes be on the phone and hang up as soon as she saw me, and later, after I'd changed out of my school uniform, I'd find her staring abstractedly out the living room window, and if she saw Mr. Marconi returning from work, his empty mail bag over his shoulder, her face would darken, and I suppose mine did, too. If she could have a secret friend, why couldn't I?

One day near the end of the school year, I came home and discovered my mother wasn't there. In our house, a window at the top of the stairs faced the Marconis' second-floor flat, and that day, thanks to an unseasonable heat wave, my mother had opened every window in the house, as Mrs. Marconi apparently had, and the houses were close enough that I could hear what I was pretty sure was whimpering, followed by my mother's soothing voice saying, "There, there, it'll all work out," and then I saw my mother's hand reach out and pat Mrs. Marconi's. A few minutes later, when my mother returned looking both shaken and angry, I asked her where she'd been, and she said down to Tommy Flynn's, but this wasn't a very good lie because she didn't even have any groceries.

That night, in bed, I heard a brief snippet of conversation between my parents float up through the heat register. "Just because she says it don't make it so," my father said. "That woman ain't right, you know."

"I know she's slow," my mother replied. "But that's no reason to treat her like a dog. He might as well chain her to a stake."

One morning later that month, my mother phoned her and was surprised when Mr. Marconi, who should've been out on his route, answered. There were children crying in the background. "What do *you* want?" he said when she identified herself, explaining that she'd called to see if Mrs. Marconi was feeling better. Now in her ninth month, she'd been ill with the heat and humidity.

"D.C. went to visit her sister."

"I didn't know she had a sister," my mother said.

"Why should you?" came his rude reply.

"Will you have her call me when she returns?"

"I'd just as soon you stayed away from her, actually."

"I don't think she even has a sister," my mother told my father over supper that night, still so upset she didn't try to conceal any of this from me. "Certainly not around here."

"How do you know?"

"Because if that woman had an option, she'd have taken it long ago."

My father opened his mouth to say something, regarded me, then shut it again.

"Plus," my mother continued, "she was in no condition to go anywhere."

My father considered this. "How come I gotta mind my own business and you don't?" he said, which was exactly what I'd been wondering. And if my mother had an answer to that, she wasn't sharing it.

A few days later, the Marconi station wagon pulled up to the curb with a dazed-looking Mrs. Marconi in the passenger seat. When her husband came around and opened the door for her, she just sat there staring up at their flat. "Help her out, you miserable son of a bitch," my mother said, watching from the front window and apparently not caring if I heard. "Help her, or so help me God . . ."

But now Mrs. Marconi was out of the car and waddling toward the porch, where she put one hand on the railing, the other under her enormous belly. Two days later she gave birth, yet another little brother for Bobby. As soon as her husband shouldered his leather bag and headed for the post office, my mother had my father give her a lift in the milk truck out to the new hospital so

81

she could pay her friend a visit. That night, over another hamburger casserole, she reported that Mrs. Marconi seemed to be feeling better, that whatever had been weighing down her spirits had lifted. She'd assured my mother she was fine, never better, that there was no reason to be concerned. In fact, she was anxious to return home and hated being away from her children. My father listened, apparently enjoying this hamburger casserole more than he had the last one. "See?" he told my mother. "You got yourself all bent out of shape over nothing."

I was glad, as I always was when it turned out my mother was wrong about something. Since the evening my parents had agreed so easily that Mrs. Marconi wasn't "right," I'd thought about her a lot, probably because, thanks to my spells, the same had been said of me.

"I also asked how her sister was," my mother told him, pushing away her own uneaten food, and the glance they exchanged told me that Mrs. Marconi, as my mother suspected, had no sister.

THAT WAS the summer I got my first serious bicycle, the kind that in those days were called "English," which meant it had three gears you could shift. It was an interesting gift, first because it was extravagant and second because I hadn't even asked for it. I'd mentioned that Bobby was saving his paper route money for one, so I suspect my father saw an opportunity to one-up Mr. Marconi. My mother, however, had different reasons. In her opinion I needed to "get out and expand my world." She'd always liked the fact that I was a reader, happy to while away hours in a book, but when she saw other neighborhood boys heading off to the American Legion Field with baseball bats over their shoulders, she worried that I stayed so close to home. I was putting on weight, and my mother said I was too young to be so sedentary.

But the real reason they got me that bike, I believed, was that they hoped it might help wean me off Bobby's friendship, or rather my continual dependency on it. For instance, his father knew someone in Parks and Recreation, and he'd enrolled Bobby in a free morning program and done it the last day you could sign up, so by the time I found out, it was too late. Afternoons, Bobby had to help his mother with the care and feeding of his little brothers, and early evenings he had his paper route. My mother didn't want me moping around the house waiting for him to show up, and if I rode around our East End neighborhood, maybe I'd make new friends. Such must have been her reasoning.

At first I was wary of both the bike and what I was meant to do with it. I knew how to ride, but felt odd about getting a gift I didn't particularly want or need when my best friend both needed and wanted one, so the first thing I did was offer Bobby the bike to use on his route. He thanked me but said his father wouldn't allow that. The following week, though, Mr. Marconi did get him a bike of his own, a used "American" one with bald tires, a torn plastic seat and a rusty chain.

For the first few weeks I used my new bike for little more than sidewalk circumnavigations of our own block, one after another, which worried my mother even more than my hanging around the yard had done. Riding on the sidewalk was technically against the law, and gradually I ventured out into the street and expanded my travels, first to the two or three square blocks that made up our immediate neighborhood, then to half a dozen and beyond. By midsummer I'd discovered Whitcombe Park on the outskirts of town, at the center of which stood Whitcombe Hall, a mere shell, which at the time was owned by the county. Most of the park's extensive grounds were surrounded by a tall wrought-iron fence that was maintained by a tiny Negro man named Gabriel Mock, who lived in a small outbuilding behind the Hall. Gabriel regarded the fence as his because it was his job to paint it, from one end to the other. Close to a mile of it, he claimed proudly. Officially, he was caretaker of the entire grounds, but what that meant in reality was the fence, since the county had no money to maintain either the Hall or the park. The only budget they had was for painting the fence, which Gabriel kept from rusting by applying a thick black lacquer to it each year. It took him all spring, summer and fall, and after an upstate winter it would be time to start all over again. His only other duty was to keep vandals off the property.

The day we met, I hadn't even seen him painting away a few feet from where I'd leaned my bike up against the fence. The word he used to describe how I was standing there, my chin between the black railings as I stared across the sloping lawn toward the Hall, was "forlorn," which he seemed proud to know the meaning of. "You the picture of forlornity," he elaborated, when I finally noticed him.

"How do you get inside?" I wondered.

"You don't. Can't let you in," he sighed, as if it disappointed him powerfully to have to deliver this sad truth. "Ain't nobody suppose to be on *this* side of the fence but me, and I ain't suppose to leave. That seem right to you? Maintain the darn fence and let history"—here he gestured over his shoulder in the direction of Whitcombe Hall itself—"go to rack and ruince."

I must have looked like I agreed with him, because he decided on the spot to let me in on a secret. "Thing is, though, the fence don't go all the way round the proppity. Stops just off yonder into them trees." When I followed along his thin index finger with interest, he may have suffered a misgiving at having told me so much, because he said, "Who you, anyhow?"

I told him my name was Lou.

"That don't tell me much," he said. "All kinda Lous. I know half a dozen of 'em my own self."

I told him my last name.

"Lynch," he repeated thoughtfully. "Your daddy the milkman?"

I said he was.

"Your mama Teresa?"

This tiny Negro man, I couldn't help reflecting, who looked almost thin enough to slip between the bars of the fence he was painting, knew an awful lot about us Lynches.

"Nice girl, your mama. Use to be, anyways. I expect she turn out good." He looked me over again, in light of my parents. "So, that make you Lou Lynch Junior."

Shaking my head, I explained that my middle name was Charles, after my mother's father, whereas my father's middle name was Patrick, after I didn't know who.

"Narrow escape," the little man nodded. "I'm Gabriel Mock Junior. No difference between me and my daddy, 'cept he's dead."

That seemed to me a distinction worth noting, and I said so.

"Still gotta go through life being Junior, though," he said. "Gabriel Mock Junior, even with him dead, whether I like it or don't. No Senior for me, ever. That seem fair to you?"

I said it didn't and on impulse confided that everybody called me Lucy, and he agreed that bad luck wasn't fair either. It occurred to me to ask if he had a son, and what he'd named him.

"Name him Gabriel Mock the Third," he said, and stopped painting to consider the decision. "Three's what everybody call him. All of us got crosses to bear, and that's the truth. A man's name the worst of it, he's doin' fine, I guess."

He returned to painting, and I climbed back on my bike. Before I could pedal off, he said, "Don't fall down no cave hole."

"What cave hole?" I asked.

"How my suppose to know which one you gon fall down?" Gabriel Mock Junior wondered back at me. "Whole proppity got caves under it, they say. Used to store liquor and gunpowder in 'em in the olden days, when all this here was England. That's how them people made their money," he explained, again nodding over his shoulder in the direction of the Hall. "Sellin' liquor and guns to the redskins. Get 'em all riled up so they go down and scalp people around Albany instead of right here. Rich people all rascals. You know that, don't you?"

This was the first time I'd ever heard that particular view expressed, and it seemed blasphemous, especially coming from a tiny Negro. After all, didn't we Lynches hope to be rich one day?

"You fall down a cave hole, ain't nobody gon hear you callin' for help neither. Don't expect me to come rescue you. I ain't climbing down into the earth till I been dead at least three days. No exceptions."

I promised I'd be careful, which I meant to be. The idea of the ground being hollow beneath my feet made me nervous.

"Drop by and say hello next time you in the neighborhood. I put you to work. I got all kind of brushes. Quicker I get done, the more time I got to howl. You like to howl?"

When I frowned, he said, "You prob'ly don't know what I mean by howlin'."

To illustrate, he pretended to drink something from an invisible container, then threw back his head and howled, and he continued to howl and cackle happily as I rode off down the fence. I'd already made up my mind to visit Gabriel Mock again, though for now I was more interested to see if I could find a cave without falling into it. As I said, the idea of hollow earth was disconcerting, but if the very ground beneath my feet was full of holes, I wouldn't mind knowing where they were.

WHAT I DISCOVERED I liked best about striking out on my bicycle was that the farther I got from home, the more interesting and unusual my *thoughts* became. I discovered I could think things in a new landscape that never would have occurred to me at home or in my own well-traveled neighborhood. I was just a boy, of course, and my thoughts were those of a boy and, as such, probably no different from the thoughts of thousands of other boys my age, but they were new to me and seemed as strange and unaccountable as the recent transformations of my body, which now required new shoes every few months. My mother had recently taken to buying my pants several inches too long, cuffing them thickly, then slowly letting them out as I grew. When I set out on my bike, it was usually with a sense of anticipation, not just that I might discover something new, like a cave in Whitcombe Park, or some*one* new, like Gabriel Mock Junior, but also I might *think* something new and unexpected, as if I were letting out my brain, its thoughts, much as my mother let out my pants' cuffs. And when returning home from my travels, I had the very pleasurable sense that I was a different boy from the one who'd left and half expected my parents and neighbors to notice the change.

But also this. If setting out into the unknown was thrilling, so, in a different but equally strange way, was coming back. I almost never rode home directly and instead wove a route through all the streets of our East End neighborhood, taking inventory of the houses and sheds and chain-link fences, to make sure nothing had vanished or been swallowed up by the hollow earth while I was away, that everything was in its correct place, as if to reclaim all of it as my own. It occurred to me that I was just becoming a route man, like my father and Mr. Marconi and like Bobby on his paper route, learning how intense the pleasure of the familiar can be, how welcome and reassuring the old, safe, comforting places of the world and the self.

Though my travels through Thomaston that summer were extensive, I stayed away from the West End. Just once did I venture back to Berman Court, which I was surprised to discover I could still locate. After I'd been away for so long the street looked almost as foreign and unexpected as Whitcombe Park that first morning I met little Gabriel Mock. The apartment house at the end, with its high windows overlooking the stream, had the feel of a storybook I'd lost, forgotten, then found again. Nothing had changed in any way I could put my finger on, yet it all felt completely alien, as if our ever having lived there was an implausible dream from which I'd awakened in our true home in the East End. Leaning my bike up against the footbridge, I followed along the Cayoga as far as the railroad trestle and covered bridge, which now looked even more abandoned and dilapidated. The sheets of plywood that had been scattered on top of the railroad ties were gone, and so, I thought, was the trunk, until I noticed it had fallen between the ties and broken on the rocks below. The only evidence of what had happened to me were the grooves sawed into the thick crossbeams, which were now eye level. I ran my index finger over them and discovered to my surprise that the terror I'd felt in the trunk had mutated into something almost pleasurable.

I don't remember how long I remained there on the trestle. I left only when I felt, or imagined I felt, the tracks begin to vibrate and heard, or imagined I did, the rumble of an approaching train.

BACK THEN most people paid the milkman by leaving money in the tin milk cases that sat on their back porches. If they wanted two quarts of milk, they'd fold a bill or two into an envelope or a piece of notepaper, and my father would make change and leave it in the box with the milk. On Saturdays he collected from those customers who preferred not to pay daily and resolved the disputes that inevitably resulted from this time-honored system. Seldom a week went by without someone remembering that the five-dollar bill they'd left in the box had in fact been a ten, or that they'd asked and been charged for two quarts of milk but received only one.

My father's route in the Borough was, as I said, the plum, in part because there were fewer collection difficulties there than in the West or East End, though my father maintained that the rich were more likely to try and pull a fast one. Recalling Gabriel Mock's observation that they were all rascals, I asked if he thought that was true, and he said no, but he did allow that the richer people were, the more carefully you had to watch them and the better your memory needed to be. In the West End poor people fell behind in their payments, which meant their route men had to either cut them off or "carry them" until they managed to pay. But West Enders seldom questioned your tally the way Borough people did.

There were no milk deliveries to residences on Saturdays, just to commercial businesses, and there were relatively few of these in the Borough. My father would finish his deliveries early, then swing by the house for Bobby Marconi and me so we could "surf the truck." The empty metal milk crates were by then stacked and roped off against the side panels to prevent them from sliding and bouncing around when he turned corners. His careful stacking left most of the back empty, and Bobby and I would stand in the space created, our feet planted firmly on the ribbed floor, and pretend to surf, our arms out at our sides to keep our balance as the truck rattled along the wide Borough streets. I always surfed in the forward position, an advantage because you could see the turns coming. Bobby, as athletic in the milk truck as he was elsewhere, surfed more or less blind behind me. Not being able to see what was coming made the game that much more fun, he claimed, though I did help him by calling out "Left!" or "Sharp right!" when a turn approached. The idea was to make it through these turns without grabbing the empty milk crates for balance or the rail that ran the length of the truck, my father chortling appreciatively up front in the driver's seat as we crashed about.

Of course my father wasn't supposed to take Bobby and me on his route, but the rules were lax and people did it all the time, was his thinking. There was no passenger seat, since there weren't supposed to be any passengers, so if my father braked hard, there was nothing to stop Bobby and me but the metal dash. My father would try to grab us as we flew by, and he was good at it, but you never knew what his big fist would grab hold of—an arm, your hair—and being saved from hitting the console sometimes hurt worse than colliding with it.

"No, you ain't gonna do no surfing today," he'd tell us first thing each Saturday. "Bobby's dad don't want him doing that no more." Mr. Marconi had made that pretty clear early on. Bobby had come home with a knot on his forehead, and his father had wanted to know why, so he'd explained how we always surfed the milk truck. It was fun, he said, and not really dangerous because my father never went fast. Which was true—you *couldn't* go fast in a milk truck if you tried.

But the next Saturday, when we pulled up in the truck, Mr. Marconi came out, too, and took my father aside. "Tell me about this surfing," he demanded, leaning toward him aggressively, his birthmark a bright purple. Lately, things had gotten a little easier between them, so much so that my father had remarked on it, even speculating that his neighbor had decided to bury the hatchet.

My father explained to him how devoted we were to our surfing on Saturday mornings, how we looked forward to it all week, how Mr. Marconi should hear how we laughed and shouted there in the back of the truck, how we hated it when he finally said that was enough. He said he was sorry about Bobby getting that lump on his noggin last week. "He don't like to grab on till the last second," he explained, which was true. It was Bobby's fearlessness, his refusal to grab on to the rail or the stacked crates to keep from going flying, that had caused the injury. "Don't worry," my father assured him. "I keep a pretty good eye on 'em."

"You better had," Mr. Marconi said. "Anything happens to my boy in that truck, you're responsible."

So the following Saturday, the new rule was No Surfing the Truck, but that made us miserable. There was no reason to be *in* the truck if we weren't allowed to surf. "Just a *little*," we pleaded. "Just five minutes? Just around this one corner? Pleeeeeease?" And so it was that we wore my father down. Over time we went from No Surfing to No Surfing Till We're Headed Back Home, thus limiting the amount of time for an injury to occur, to Be Careful, You Two, Because Bobby's Dad Will Skin Me Alive If He Gets Hurt, and If He Don't Your Mother Will, because, truth be told, she didn't like the idea either.

Why so much worry about us getting hurt? Well, because that's what invariably happened. Otherwise, how would we know the game was over? Of course our injuries were not serious—a jammed finger, a skinned knee, usually—and most Saturdays we surfed until I cried, because Bobby, when he was injured, refused to cry, so my father didn't know he'd been hurt and the fun could continue. I deeply envied Bobby his self-control and tried my best to emulate him, even as I suspected I'd never master the trick. Why he never cried was an even deeper mystery to me than why he never had to pay the bridge toll back when we lived on Berman Court. Every Saturday I'd tell myself that I wasn't going to cry, but when the time came and I went crashing into the side of the truck, and my father, hearing the impact, turned around in his seat to check on us, my resolution would dissolve, not so much because of the pain as from his expression, which suggested that he knew I was hurt, that I couldn't fool him anyway, so why try? And then the tears would just *be* there, brimming over, no holding them back.

Still, before long we'd forgotten all about Mr. Marconi's solemn warning, and why not? He had to know we were back at it. One or the other of us always got off the milk truck limping or rubbing an elbow, but we were also in high spirits, laughing and shouting and trying to get my father to promise we'd do it again next Saturday. Which wasn't hard work, since he enjoyed the whole thing about as much as we did. He never talked about his own childhood, but according to my mother it couldn't really be called a childhood at all, just an unrelenting series of chores, from sunrise to sunset, bleak and unending, which was why, she explained, he wasn't anxious for me to have a paper route like Bobby or to be overburdened with responsibilities around the house. I was to keep my room clean and study when I was supposed to, but otherwise I was simply to be the sort of boy my father never had a chance to be. The pleasure he took in our joy when we surfed his milk truck was purely vicarious, and his grin was ear to ear.

My own Saturday morning happiness was more complex. It's true that I looked forward all week to our surfing. As I said, it was about the only time Bobby and I got to spend together. But as the summer wore on I became troubled by the knowledge that part of me was waiting for, indeed looking forward to, my friend getting hurt. It had, of course, nothing to do with him and everything to do with my own cowardice and jealousy. The jealous part had to do, I think, with my understanding that Bobby's bravery meant he was having more fun, something that my own cowardly bailing out had robbed me of. Each week I told myself I'd be braver, that this Saturday I wouldn't reach out and hold on for safety. I'd surrender control and be flung about, laughing and full of joyous abandon. But every outing was the same as the last, and when the moment came, I grabbed on. Gradually, since wishing for courage didn't work, I began wishing for something else entirely. I never wanted Bobby to be seriously injured, of course. That would have meant the end of everything. But I did wish that just once he'd be hurt bad enough to cry, which would lessen the gulf I perceived between him and me.

And so our milk-truck surfing ended the only way it could. I didn't actually see Bobby break his wrist when he was flung against the side of the truck. I heard the bone snap, though. What saved me from suffering the same fate was my cowardice. I'd seen the curve coming and at the last second reached out and grabbed one of the tied-off milk crates. Bobby, taken by surprise, went flying.

He must've known that his wrist was broken, because he went very pale, and when our eyes met and he saw my shock and fear, he immediately sat down with his back to the panel, cradling his hand in his lap against the truck's vibrations. I think what my father heard wasn't the terrible crack of Bobby's wrist but only the silence that followed, and he immediately called back to us, wanting to know if we were all right. When Bobby refused to speak, I said that we were, but he knew better. If we weren't whooping and hollering back there, something was wrong, and more seriously wrong than what happened every other Saturday morning. He didn't just pull over and climb back into the dark interior of the truck, but instead got out, came around and threw the big rear doors wide open so the light could pour in. After one look at the angle of Bobby's wrist, the blood drained out of my father's face. While I expected him to get mad, he didn't, and when he simply closed the doors again, got back into the truck and turned for home, it wasn't Bobby but me who began to cry.

Mr. Marconi was sitting on their upstairs front porch reading a magazine when we pulled up at the curb, and he seemed to know something had happened even before my father opened the rear doors of the truck. On the ride back from the Borough, Bobby had gotten sick, and the front of his shirt now glistened with vomit.

When Mr. Marconi emerged from the house, my father began "It was an acci—" but Mr. Marconi held up his index finger, as if to say *Wait a minute*, except that he kept holding it there between them, which altered the meaning of the gesture completely. My father seemed to understand that he was being told to hold his tongue and, for the moment, at least, he held it. Mr. Marconi then reached up into the truck, lifted Bobby down and helped him into the station wagon. "I—" my father began again, but Mr. Marconi again held up that index finger and waited until my father backed up onto the terrace, allowing him to go around to the driver's side and get in next to Bobby, who was by this time slumped against the door, having finally passed out from the pain.

I was remembering what he'd said to me a few minutes before as we sat together in the back of the truck, everything quiet now aside from the rattling of the milk crates. "You didn't call the turn." He seemed less angry than curious, but it was an accusation just the same. I didn't know what to say, though as soon as he spoke those words, I realized they were true.

*

93

ODD, HOW WE MISREMEMBER the events of childhood, not just the sequence but also the cause and effect. It wasn't long after Bobby broke his wrist that the Marconis moved again. My own recollection, until I discussed this with my mother, was that what happened in the milk truck had somehow caused the Marconis to leave the East End. According to her, though, we'd known for months that they were moving. That entire summer I'd been dreading being separated from my one real friend, knowing all too well that our Saturday mornings were numbered. That was why they'd gotten me the new bicycle—to lessen the blow of the Marconis' leaving and to provide me, at least in theory, with a means of visiting them in their new neighborhood.

They were moving because the post office had unexpectedly promoted Bobby's father. Normally it took years to move up through the postal ranks, but that spring there'd been some sort of scandal that resulted in a general housecleaning. The new postmaster brought in from downstate had replaced most of the staff, including several senior letter carriers. Mr. Marconi had been promoted precisely because he'd remained aloof from everyone else and was thus untainted. Some people whispered that he'd ratted out his fellow workers.

According to my mother, the reason Mr. Marconi had been so livid about Bobby's broken wrist wasn't that my father had ignored his warning but that he suspected he'd done it on purpose, out of jealousy at their good fortune. This charge was ridiculous, of course, though it may be true that Mr. Marconi's promotion and his decision not just to move but to buy a house in the Borough—on my father's route!—may have upset their delicate equilibrium. My mother remembers that instead of simply congratulating him, my father let on that he didn't think we Lynches would ever move to the Borough even if we could afford to. We liked the East End just fine, he said, and guessed we had everything we needed right where we were. Mr. Marconi made no secret of his opinion that my father's attitude was nothing but sour grapes. This simmering animosity, according to my mother, was the backdrop to the surfing accident.

One thing was certain. Mr. Marconi's fury had not diminished a jot the next day. We'd seen Bobby return from the hospital that morning with his right forearm in a cast up almost to his elbow. My mother advised my father to wait before going next door, but he argued that would make it look like we didn't care. I suspected, though, that he was anxious to convey what he'd started to say twice the day before, when Mr. Marconi had held up his index finger. That he'd warned us over and over to be careful or somebody'd get hurt, that he hadn't been driving fast, that, hell, he never meant for nothing like that to happen, that a freak accident like that could just as well have happened to me as Bobby, that he hoped there wouldn't be no hard feelings—all the wrong things.

That there were going to *be* hard feelings was obvious from the moment Mr. Marconi opened the door and saw who was standing outside in the hall. Bobby was lying on the sofa, looking weak and pale, his cast resting heavily on his chest. He made no attempt to rise when he saw who his visitors were. I caught a glimpse of Mrs. Marconi's ashen, frightened face, peering in from the kitchen. I fully expected her husband to address my father insolently, with something like *What the hell do you want?* Instead, he looked him up and down, then me, then my father again. "Good, it's you," he said. "Wait here." Then he closed the door in our faces.

We didn't have to wait long before he returned. He had several sheets of pale green paper, and he handed these to my father. When he unfolded them, I saw the THOMASTON REGIONAL HOSPITAL letterhead, with a column of numbers down the right side of the page, and my father swallowed hard. "Hell, I'll take care of it, if that's what you want," he said, looking past Mr. Marconi to where Bobby lay on the sofa. I think the "if you want" reflected my father's surprise. It was this man, after all, who worked for the government and had such great medical benefits.

95

"Well, I should hope so," Mr. Marconi said.

"I ain't saying I can do the whole thing right now," my father admitted, regarding the long column of numbers sadly.

"Why's that?" Mr. Marconi said. "You're always going on about you're gonna buy this and that, and go here and there. To hear you talk, anybody'd think you could just take it out of petty cash."

"If they could work with me . . . ," he said.

"Work with you? Why would they do that?"

"I ain't saying they won't get their money. In a few months—"

"How *many* months, do you figure?"

My father shrugged, as if it was impossible to say, that simple subdivision was woefully inadequate to such complex financing. What he needed, of course, was to consult my mother, who could figure exactly how long it would take, but he wasn't about to say that. "If they'll work with me . . ."

Mr. Marconi grabbed the hospital bill back and shook his head in disgust. "Tell you what," he said. "Go home."

My father weakly held his hand out for the bill. "Hell, I ain't sayin'—"

"It's paid for," Mr. Marconi said. "It's all taken care of."

"You ain't gotta—"

"Just go home."

I wanted to, desperately, but he wouldn't. My father just stood there, looking about half his normal size. He still hadn't met Mr. Marconi's eye and was peering in at Bobby with an expression of terrible longing. He hated being on the outside of anything, and right now he wanted to be inside that flat, not out in the hall. What he couldn't figure out was how to get Mr. Marconi to, if not welcome him, at least step aside. What he'd planned on, I realized, was having the opportunity to talk to Bobby. He was good with boys, and in no time he'd have had him laughing and remembering how much fun we always had in the truck, and telling him it wouldn't be no time before the cast came off, and Bobby would admit it didn't hurt so bad now that the bone was set and immobilized. Before long, my father imagined, we'd all be friends again. Maybe we'd be first to sign Bobby's cast. He was an amiable man who believed in amiable solutions, who forgave easily and couldn't understand that other people derived pleasure from withholding the very thing he always gave so freely.

Which probably was why he didn't notice me pulling on his sleeve, trying to make him understand that even though we hadn't gotten what we came for, we should leave. It embarrassed me to comprehend so clearly what my father couldn't seem to grasp, that he could stand there forever and Mr. Marconi still wouldn't let him in, or take pity, or relent in any way. Even when the door finally closed, with the two of us standing there on the welcome mat, he didn't budge, and when he opened his mouth to speak, my first thought was that he hadn't realized Mr. Marconi wasn't there anymore. Because he just stood there staring at the closed door, I didn't immediately understand he was talking to me. "Don't never be like that, Louie."

I said I wouldn't.

"You ain't gotta treat nobody like that, is what I'm saying," he continued.

Anxious for us to be gone, I said I understood.

"Don't never treat people like you wish they were dead."

Afraid that my responses were rooting us to the spot, I said nothing this time, because I couldn't bear to stand there one more second.

Downstairs on the porch we met the Spinnarkle sisters returning from church. "Why, hello, Mr. Lynch. Good morning, Louie," they said in tandem.

"Isn't this just . . . ," one of them began.

" . . . the most glorious day?" the other finished.

They both beamed at us, neither registering that anything was wrong.

"Yes, it is," my father agreed, because he liked to agree with people, especially about the weather, or that people were mostly good, or that things were bound to work out okay in the end.

*

HE WAS QUIET the rest of the day and, after dinner, said he was going out for a while, something he never did on Sunday night, which was Ed Sullivan, whose show we watched religiously, though we rarely agreed on which acts were the good ones. My mother and I watched the show listlessly without him, and when it was over she got up and turned the set off. "So what happened over there?" she said, and I told her how mean Mr. Marconi had been, how when my father had offered to pay he'd snatched the hospital bill right out of his hand. None of which seemed to surprise her. When I finished, she was quiet for a bit, then said, "Your father . . . ," but fell silent again, apparently having thought better of whatever she'd been about to impart.

"When will he come home?" I asked, because he'd been gone a long time and I couldn't imagine where he might be.

"Oh, I'm sure that by the time you wake up in the morning, he'll be back. Don't worry. He just needs some time to make the world right again. Once he's got things back the way he wants them . . ." Her voice trailed off.

Normally such a remark would have sounded like a criticism, which I would've resented, but this time my mother didn't seem angry or annoyed, as she sometimes was, just sad about how things had turned out. And I thought I understood what she meant about him making the world right again so he could live in it. My own world had been out of kilter all day, and I knew why, though I didn't know what to do about it. Actually, I *did* know but didn't want to do it. All day I'd been picturing Bobby on that sofa, pale and sick and not at all like himself, and I couldn't help remembering how I'd hoped for something like this to happen, how jealous I'd been of his refusal to cry. He *still* hadn't cried, and now I felt even worse. And there was more. Finally, I heard myself say, "I didn't call the turn."

My mother regarded me seriously. "I don't understand."

"It was my fault," I said, and explained how Bobby always

surfed behind me, needed me to call out the turns so he could prepare, and how I always did, except this once. I told her I didn't know why I hadn't called that turn, that I never wanted Bobby to get hurt so bad, that it was all my fault and that he'd said as much, so now we'd never be friends again.

"Of course you will," she said, causing me momentarily to hope she was right, before realizing she wasn't. "He'll forgive you."

I shook my head. "No, he won't."

"He will," she insisted. "You forgave him, didn't you?"

"For what?"

She was looking right at me, and I couldn't meet her eye. "You know what."

"I don't," I said, barely able to speak.

"You don't *want* to," she replied, "but you do."

"I *don't*," I probably shouted.

"Okay," she said, looking away, disappointed in me. "Okay, Lou."

My father didn't come home that night until late. I heard him trip on the front steps, fumble through the door and finally lumber heavily up the stairs and into the bedroom next to mine. My mother was still awake, and I could hear them talking quietly in the dark, though I couldn't make out what they were saying. Probably she was just telling him to come to bed, that everything would be all right, that he needed to get some sleep, because in a few hours he'd have to get up and go to work. The other possibility was that they were talking about me.

The reason I was awake to hear my father return was that I was still turning over in my mind what my mother had said about what I knew but wouldn't acknowledge. And there in the dark I'd made up my mind. In the morning I'd tell her again that she was wrong, that there was nothing I knew and didn't want to know. I would keep on insisting until she had no choice but to agree that Bobby had *not* been there at the trestle and hadn't laughed with the others as I pleaded with them not to saw me in two. No, I had *not* forgiven him. Because there was nothing to forgive.

THE AFTERNOON the Marconis' possessions were loaded onto the bright yellow moving van, I watched morosely from the front steps, having been specifically instructed not to get in the way of the movers. I kept expecting Bobby to come over and keep me company, on our last day together, but my mother said it was probably his job to look after his little brothers while his parents organized the move. In the middle of the afternoon he appeared at an open window, and I waved, but he didn't wave back, and when his father passed by the same window a moment later, he drew the shade.

My mother had been right about one thing. Bobby apparently did forgive me for not calling the turn, or at least we never spoke of it again. That last month before they moved, he still came over to our house a few times, but it seemed he'd no sooner arrive than Mrs. Marconi would call and say to send Bobby home. And of course we never again rode in the milk truck.

Since the day Mr. Marconi made us stand in the hall, my father's good spirits had returned, but the two of them hadn't spoken. To my surprise, and relief, my father didn't try to insinuate himself back into his good graces, my mother having apparently convinced him it was a lost cause. During a stretch of hot, humid days when everyone had their windows thrown open, I heard Mr. Marconi remark, his voice suddenly very near, that in his opinion they were getting Bobby away from Third Street just in time. While there'd been no context for this remark, I couldn't help thinking that they'd been talking about us Lynches. As their move drew closer, I asked Bobby what his new phone number was, but he said he didn't know yet. As soon as they found out, he'd call, but something in his tone made me think he wasn't going to. I didn't even know where their new house was, except that it was somewhere in the Borough.

At any rate I must have looked pretty dejected sitting there all alone as they moved out, because when my father came home for lunch he suggested we go inside and help my mother, something we never did. Meals were her job, and our kitchen was tiny. She didn't like us in there, underfoot, until she had the food on the table. On this occasion, though, she seemed to understand his reasoning and stopped what she was doing to make us a pitcher of lemonade, remarking that the day was ferociously hot and she felt sorry for the poor moving men.

She set down two tall, sweating glasses in front of my father and me. "You and Bobby wouldn't be seeing that much of each other in another week or so anyway," she said. It was only one more week until Labor Day, and once school started, with me at St. Francis and Bobby back at Bridger, we'd have other things to occupy us. "Besides," she went on. "The Borough isn't the end of the world."

That's what it felt like, though. Since leaving the West End, we'd never once returned there to visit anyone, and the only reason Bobby would have for returning from the Borough to our neighborhood was me, and I was beginning to understand that I wasn't reason enough.

But my mother was right about life moving on. I had just that last week of August to mope around and feel sorry for myself, after which school started again. Such, at least, is my recollection.

What my mother recalls is the worst autumn of my young life, that after the Marconis left I remained militantly inconsolable. I also had several spells in September and October, and they lasted longer than the ones I'd had over the summer, leaving me both exhausted and despondent. The buoyant optimism and sense of empowerment that had accompanied that first one in the trunk were missing from these latest ones, which left me dull witted and lethargic for days. According to my mother, as soon

101

as I felt better, I'd hop on my bike and ride through the Borough streets looking for the Marconis' new home, determined to renew my friendship with Bobby. She even recalls getting a frightened phone call from Mrs. Marconi telling her that her husband was getting angry. Every time he looked out their front window, there I'd be, sitting on my bike and staring dejectedly at their house.

This last part simply cannot have been true. For one thing, had I indulged in any such behavior, I'd be unlikely to forget it, but for another, I didn't learn until the following spring exactly where the Marconis had moved because, as I feared, Bobby never called with his phone number and address. It's true I did ride my bike through the Borough that last week in August and early September, hoping I'd "accidentally" run into him or see him playing outside, perhaps with his new friends, so I suppose it's possible that Mr. Marconi may have looked out his front window one afternoon and been surprised to see me ride by, but the idea that I haunted them that autumn is ludicrous.

What my mother may be remembering is one Saturday afternoon when I was out riding. My own very vague memory was that I'd been visiting Gabriel Mock, and the most direct route home from Whitcombe Park was through the Borough. At any rate when I came around a corner I was surprised to see my father's milk truck pull up alongside. Since he would've finished his collections late that morning, my first panicky thought was that something must be wrong—either he was inexplicably angry with me or something had happened to my mother and he'd come to fetch me home. I must have appeared frightened, because when he stepped out of the truck, he looked as if in his mind he'd arrived in the nick of time.

"Louie?" he said—awkwardly, I thought, his voice not falling quite right, as if there were some other boy here in the Borough who was a dead ringer for his East End kid, and he didn't want to commit to anything until he was sure who I was. "Whatcha doin' way over here?"

I shrugged. Why *shouldn't* I be here?

"You want to ride home with me?" He opened up the back of the truck, and we lifted my bike inside, where I leaned it up against the tied-off crates.

As I said, milk trucks in those days had no passenger seats. Usually, if I was alone with my father in the truck, I'd tip a couple crates upside down and perch myself on top, to the right of the big stick shift that stuck out of a hole in the floor. That day, though, when I started to grab a crate, my father patted his seat cushion, and when I balanced myself on its edge he put his arm around my shoulder, and I felt good for the first time in what seemed like weeks.

"You know who lives in all these houses?" he said.

When I admitted I had no idea, he put the truck in gear and took me on a slow tour of the Borough streets that until recently Bobby and I had surfed on Saturday morning, pointing out houses on either side of the street and telling me what doctor lived here, what lawyer there, which one belonged to the owner of the Bijou Theater and where the Beverlys, who owned the tannery, lived. This was *his* route, the best route in town, and I could tell how proud he was to know all this. He said many of these people had so much money they didn't have to work anymore if they didn't want to, though I found this hard to believe. A few Borough residents waved to my father as we passed, which clearly pleased him. Others, though, failed to return his wave, didn't even appear to see us as we inched by, going slow, so he could keep his arm around me and not have to shift gears.

"Thing is, people are the same everywheres," he said, as if to explain the ones who didn't wave back. "They're just the way they are, and you can't do nothin' about it either." Was he thinking about Mr. Marconi, too?

I nodded.

"You know how some folks in our neighborhood don't like it when people from the West End come around?"

103

I knew what he was talking about, of course. The Spinnarkle sisters in particular were adamant in their disapproval of visitors who didn't belong there.

"People are the same way here. They see somebody who don't live in the Borough, and they say, *What's he doin' here?* Even if you ain't botherin' nobody. You understand?"

"I shouldn't ride my bike over here?" I said, thinking this was what he was trying to tell me.

"It ain't that exactly," he said, reluctant now. "This is America. You got a right to go wherever you want. Anybody ever tells you that you don't belong somewheres, you just remind them what country they're in."

I nodded, confused.

"Except sometimes it's better not to upset people. If they think you don't belong, the hell with 'em, is how I look at it. I mean, it's nice where we are too, right? Third Street?"

I said I thought Third Street was fine.

"Same with friends," he went on. "Better to be friends with people who want to be friends with you."

"Bobby wants to be friends," I said, knowing what he was getting at. "It's just his dad won't let him."

We'd come to the end of the Borough now, and my father turned left into the East End, our part of town. It occurred to me that in our leisurely tour we must have driven right by the Marconis' new house. It was on his route, after all, so he had to know which one it was. He no doubt put quart bottles of milk in their tin container twice a week, collected the money they left there and made change. Had they spoken to him, or he to them? Did Mrs. Marconi cower inside when he knocked on their door? Had he tried to get invited inside for a look? I'd been so absorbed in my own disappointment that it hadn't occurred to me to imagine the effect their leaving had on him. He could no longer think of himself as being in competition with "Mr. Macaroni." If it had been a contest, he'd lost. And he'd accepted the fact; that's what he was trying to tell me now.

"Them spells you get," he said, catching me by surprise. "Are you thinking about Bobby when they come on?"

I told him no, that I could be thinking about anything or nothing. My spells always began with things getting so fuzzy and remote that I felt almost sleepy. It wasn't a bad feeling, really. I wasn't scared. It was more like I was outside myself, an observer, like I was light enough to just float away. Actually, that part felt kind of good, as if I'd been released from something.

I'll never forget the look on his face when I explained this. "You wouldn't do that, would you, Louie? Just let yourself float away?"

I told him I wouldn't.

"Not ever?"

"Never," I promised, and this seemed to reassure us both. Because even though the sensation of floating away did feel good, so did returning. In fact, driving back to our East End neighborhood that afternoon in my father's milk truck felt a little like returning from one of my spells. Our house looked pretty small after our tour of the Borough, but for some reason, when we pulled up at the curb, it looked just right for us, for who we were. I *did* like our street, with Ikey Lubin's store at one end and Tommy Flynn's at the other. I liked living next door to the Spinnarkle sisters, even if they were quick to turn off the television when I visited. Only one thing bothered me.

"I just wish he'd do like he said," I told my father. "He said he'd call and give me his new phone number."

"They probably just kept their old number," he said, surprising me again. I'd thought that you always got a new number when you moved, and that whoever moved into the Marconis' apartment above the Spinnarkles would inherit their old one.

I didn't get a chance until later that evening, after my mother finished doing the dishes and joined my father and me out on the porch, where a cool breeze had sprung up. Once they both looked settled I went inside—to use the bathroom, I told them—

and quickly dialed the number I still knew by heart. Bobby himself answered on the third ring, but I hadn't thought things through. He must have said hello half a dozen times while I stood there, frozen, mute, trying to think of something to say. But how could I ask if his wrist had completely healed, if the cast had come off? Or say I was sorry I hadn't called the turn and that I wanted him and his family to move back to Third Street and for things to be the way they were. That this new arrangement might be okay for them, but not for me.

Only when Mr. Marconi took the phone from him and barked "Who the hell is this?" did I gently return the receiver to its cradle.

A SHOT TO THE HEART

"**H**ᴇʏ," Evangeline said. She was poking Noonan as one would a dangerous animal that looked dead but might not be. Fully dressed and standing next to the bed, she was clearly prepared to run should the need arise. "Talk to me, Noonan."

"About what?" he said groggily, rising up on his elbows. At the sound of his voice, modulated and sane, she visibly relaxed. Flight wouldn't be necessary after all.

So far she was the only person to witness one of his night terrors. This was now over a month ago, but the experience was still fresh in her mind. Half an hour after falling asleep, he'd awakened in a paroxysm of rage. When she made the mistake of trying to calm him down, he lashed out, not even recognizing her, really, and punched her in the face, hard. The resulting black eye had been hard to explain to her husband, and since then they'd agreed not to risk a repetition. They'd continued their sporadic, desultory sex, but when it was over either she or Noonan went home before postcoital sleepiness could descend. The last thing she'd done tonight before drifting off was ask him if he felt sleepy. He'd said no, thinking he'd be able to stay awake, but then fell asleep anyway.

"I suppose you could tell me what you're sorry about."

"I was talking in my sleep?"

She sat on the edge of the bed now, holding the back of her hand gently to his cheek. "You kept saying how sorry you were. Didn't sound like you at all."

"It didn't sound like my voice?"

"No, it was your voice, all right. Just not the sort of thing that comes out of your mouth, if you know what I mean. Sort of like Hugh Morgan saying *I don't know*. Anyway, I accept your apology, even if it was meant for someone else."

Noonan swung his feet out of bed. "I gather you're leaving?"

"It's almost midnight."

"If you can wait till I put my pants on, I'll walk you home."

"We really shouldn't be seen together," she said, but he could tell this objection was his to override.

As it turned out, they had both the vaporetto and the streets to themselves. Even San Marco was deserted, except for the last of the musicians putting away their instruments outside Caffè Florian and some waiters stacking chairs on a gurney.

"When does Todd get back?" he asked when they arrived in Campo San Stefano, off of which her gallery was located, their living quarters above.

"Tomorrow," she said. A failed novelist turned travel writer, Todd Lichtner was often away on assignment for one of a half-dozen magazines. "Speaking of which, will you see Hugh again?"

"It's possible. I got the impression he wasn't finished badgering me."

"Remind him he promised to stop by the gallery?"

"If he promised, he won't need to be reminded."

"I have one or two pieces I'd really like him to see."

"The Ponti?"

She nodded. "And Jean Nugent's new work."

Noonan shrugged. "The Ponti's good. Hugh might like it." Probably not, though. And he couldn't think of a single reason for Hugh or anyone else to like the Nugent.

Evangeline must have read his mind and, perhaps, even shared his assessment, because when she looked away there was just enough light from a nearby streetlamp to see that her eyes were moist. "I don't know how much longer I'll be able to stay open," she said, her voice full of terrible resignation. "Some days I can't even remember why I want to. Most of what I do anymore is just habit, starting with getting out of bed in the morning."

Getting *into* bed with him was another example, clearly—no need even to state it.

"People get into ruts," Noonan said. And ruts weren't always a bad thing. Maybe an artist's discipline, process and routine—habit, if you will—were just ruts with a purpose, and if you were talented and lucky they paid off in a kind of freedom, at least within the borders of canvas. Counterintuitive, granted, but there you were. The danger was that the purpose of your regimen would be lost, leaving mere habit to explain and justify itself if it could. And when it couldn't? Well, maybe you were done. Going through the motions, those motions a feeble prayer that was unanswered, unanswerable. Why had he become a nocturnal walker, taking the same route night after night? All five *sestieri:* San Marco, Castello, Cannaregio, San Polo, Dorsoduro, always in that order, never the reverse, gauging time by space and vice versa. In the end, how different was he from his father, whose strict discipline had never been rooted in anything more profound than a selfish need to be in control.

"I do love Venice," Evangeline continued, "but it's absurd living here."

"Where would you go?"

"Yes, well, there you are."

"What does your husband want?"

"Wouldn't it be nice to know? If I could figure that out, I could want the opposite."

"Try changing something small," he suggested. "Something that doesn't matter. See how it feels."

"I've been thinking about that, actually. The small thing I've been thinking about changing is you."

"If you're trying to hurt my feelings—"

"I'm not," she said, tears really starting to flow now. "I'm really not. I mean . . . did you enjoy it tonight? Us? Did it speak to you in any way?"

The question was fair enough. The exhausted orgasm he'd finally achieved, while pleasurable enough, had seemed remote, something happening on a parallel track, vibrations half absorbed by the ground, no danger of collision. Was it just age? The law of diminishing emotional returns played out in the flesh? "I'm glad you came over," he said, which was true, though it was also true he was now just as happy to return her to her husband and her life.

"Want to hear something crazy?"

"I guess?"

She wiped her eyes on the sleeve of her shirt, smudging it with eye shadow. "Here's what I seem to want from you, Noonan. I want to *not* see you again for a very long while. That's the first thing. The second is if Hugh comes tomorrow, I'd like you to come with him."

"I think you just summed up about forty years' worth of my relationships with women," he smiled. "It's not a new ambivalence. It's just new to you."

"Do you want to come up?"

"Now? Christ, no."

And then she was gone, the slamming door echoing out into the canal. He said her name, then tried the door, but it had locked behind her. Lucky that, for he might've followed her inside. He lingered a moment in the doorway, then stepped back a few paces to the water's edge and looked up, waiting for a light to come on inside, which eventually it did, reflecting off the shimmering water and the dark brick walls that framed the canal. A painting, Noonan recognized. And also a memory? A moment later Eve appeared at the window, reaching outside to pull the shutters closed. He didn't think she saw him standing in the shadows below, but then her voice came down, barely audible. "Go home, Noonan." With the shutters closed, the canal was dark again, the painting gone.

He had just rounded the corner and started to descend the three steps into the narrow *calle* that opened into Campo San

Stefano when something hit him in the chest, hard. Before he could make sense of that, there was the inexplicable sound of coins dancing on the stones at his feet. Todd Lichtner's pale face momentarily swam into view and, when Noonan blinked, was gone. He stepped back, rubbing his breastbone, the pain there the only thing he could be certain was real. Then he saw the other man again, gathering up the scattered coins as best he could in the dark and muttering, "What a rotten bastard you are, Noonan." It seemed not to occur to Lichtner that a truly rotten bastard might just kick Todd Lichtner in the head as he scrabbled around on his knees, and Noonan might have done just that if he hadn't been so puzzled by the coins. The punch and the simultaneous explosion of coins illogically suggested that his chest had been full of them, freed by the blow, like candy from a piñata. He would've preferred another explanation, but when he tried to form a question, he discovered he had no breath, that Lichtner had hit him harder and with more conviction than Noonan would have ever guessed he possessed. It was all deeply puzzling, so he sat down on the step to watch him grope around in the dark for coins he seemed to think belonged to him. One had come to rest between Noonan's feet, and he picked it up to examine it. Poor light, but he could have sworn it was an American quarter.

Finally Lichtner got to his feet and came over to glare down at him with a mixture of anger and, unless Noonan was mistaken, dawning embarrassment. Evangeline had apparently been wrong about at least one thing. Her husband *did* have clue one. Noonan handed him the quarter, which he promptly threw in the canal. "You shitheel," he said, still shaking, though his pique seemed to wane as his embarrassment waxed.

Noonan's breath was returning, and with it an idea. Lichtner must've had a roll of coins in his fist, to heighten the impact, but the blow had ruptured it. And with that realization, the world, which had momentarily tilted, righted itself. "You're home early," he said, his voice little more than a croak.

111

"Since yesterday," Lichtner said. "I've been staying in a goddamn hotel in case you're interested."

"Where were you before?"

"Las Vegas."

Noonan smiled, the roll of coins making sense now. He'd been playing the quarter slots. How perfectly Lichtner.

"I *knew* there was somebody. I *knew* it." He was still standing over Noonan, his fists clenched.

"If you punch me again, I'm going to throw you in the canal."

Lichtner took a step back. "Hey, I'm the one with the grievance here," he said indignantly.

"Nevertheless," Noonan said, still massaging his breastbone, "fair warning."

To Lichtner, Noonan's resolve not to be punched a second time seemed to limit the proceedings unfairly. Still, there could be little doubt that he'd carry out his threat, so he shrugged and said, "You all right?"

"I guess," Noonan said, though he wasn't sure and remained seated for the moment. His breathing was returning to normal, but it felt like the other man's fist was still inside his chest cavity, heaving and flexing. "That hurt, if it makes you feel better."

"Good," Lichtner said, offering him a hand. "I'm glad."

Noonan allowed himself to be pulled to his feet. "What now?"

Lichtner shrugged again, fully embarrassed now. "I don't know," he admitted. "This didn't go the way I imagined. I guess I didn't think much past punching you in the face."

"You punched me in the chest."

"You were on a step. My timing was off. I guess I was impatient."

Noonan went over to the water's edge, raised some phlegm and spat into the canal.

"I suppose we could go someplace and talk about it," Lichtner said, his hands now at his sides. "The bars over in Campo Santa Margherita might still be open."

"That's all students over there," Noonan reminded him. "Kids."

"What the hell," Lichtner said. "We're behaving like children, we might as well drink with them." He actually seemed disappointed that Noonan wasn't more enthusiastic. "I probably shouldn't go home yet. Not until I've calmed down."

To Noonan, he looked calm and then some, like a man more afraid of getting punched by his wife than of punching her. He seemed to comprehend utterly that he was good for about one punch a decade, and he'd thrown it not two minutes ago. "I thought you were staying in a hotel."

"Just the two nights. If I didn't find out who it was tonight, I was just going to ask her."

The bar they found in Campo Santa Margherita was, as Noonan predicted, full of university students, several of whom—recognizable by their outlandish costumes—were celebrating the completion of their final exams. They took a table as far from them as possible, which wasn't far enough. "*Dottore . . . dottore*," they chanted while a boy dressed as a penis chugged from a pitcher. Noonan ordered a beer, Lichtner a Campari. By the time the drinks came, some of the latter's indignation had returned. "I *knew* it had to be you," he said. "I just knew it."

"How?" Noonan wondered, curious about his logic. Evangeline, he happened to know, had had several lovers before himself. How had they been ruled out?

"You're the only man I know who'd punch a woman. That's repellent. I can't forgive that," Lichtner added, in case Noonan asked him to.

"That was an accident, actually. Ask her, if you don't believe me."

Clearly he did, though his resentment was such that he couldn't admit to it. "How about fucking her? I suppose that was an accident, too."

"Well, there was an accidental quality to the whole thing, now that you mention it. It's probably over, if that's of any interest."

113

"It isn't," Lichtner said petulantly. "It isn't of interest and it isn't over, not for me. I'm the one who has to imagine the two of you going at it. How can I stay here in Venice knowing what I know?"

Noonan was tempted to tell him this was just being silly, that if it wasn't him in Venice it would be another man in Paris, or London, or Davenport, Iowa. Lichtner's problem, or one of them, was that his wife was unhappy, a condition that, if not universal, was nearly so. She wanted more. More than Todd Lichtner, for one. More than Noonan, for another. Who the hell didn't? "Maybe you should divorce," he suggested.

Lichtner polished off his Campari with a sneer. "You'd like that, wouldn't you."

"Actually," Noonan said, summoning as much sincerity as he could muster, "I don't care one way or the other. Leave or stay. Divorce or stay married. Do what makes you least miserable."

"I never said I was miserable," Lichtner replied, his back up now.

"I'm sorry, I thought you did."

"Maybe right this second," he conceded miserably. "But Eve and I have weathered worse than you. Far worse."

"You aren't going to tell me about it, I hope."

"And it's not like I've been a hundred percent faithful to her," he added proudly.

"What percentage would you estimate?"

Lichtner ignored this. "I've never screwed the wife of a friend, though. That's where I draw the line."

"We're friends, you and I?" Noonan said.

"We're not?"

It was amazing to watch a man so all over the emotional map, each new feeling at war with the preceding as well as the subsequent, each important without being satisfying, sustainable or, for that matter, even reliable. Noonan couldn't be sure whether he was observing a person or a condition common to men their age. "It hadn't occurred to me, I guess," Noonan said. Not that it would have mattered.

"That day in church, you broke my heart, Noonan. I felt really close to you then."

"How close *were* you? How many pews?"

Lichtner shrugged, looking pitiful. "Hey, you don't want to be friends? Nobody's forcing you."

When the waiter came by, Noonan shook his head. A second drink would reinforce Lichtner's notion that they were friends, something he was determined to avoid. The other man took out some money. "I'm sorry I punched you," he said.

"Me, too," Noonan said. It still felt like the other man's fist was trapped in his chest.

"You're sorry you screwed my wife, or you're sorry I punched you?"

Just sorry, Noonan thought, no more able to pin it down now than he'd been earlier with Evangeline. Did you get credit for being sorry if you couldn't explain what you were sorry about? Noonan had spent enough time in catechism as a kid to doubt it. There you learned to diagram sins like sentences, and unless you could explain what you'd done wrong and why, forgiveness was withheld.

The students were still chanting when they rose to leave. "*Dottore! Dottore!*" they shouted. "Fuck yourself! Fuck yourself!" A girl dressed like a wood nymph chugged her flagon of beer, then set it down triumphantly. Nearby, the penis who'd been chugging when they entered was now slumped forward in his chair, flaccid.

Outside in the *campo*, Lichtner looked like he might cry. "I can't go home."

"Sure you can," Noonan said. He'd gone out for a drink with a man who'd just bushwhacked him because it seemed like the decent thing to do, but enough was enough. "Just don't punch Evangeline, because then you *will* be sorry. That I can pretty much guarantee."

"The thing is, I'm not supposed to be here. In Venice. My plane doesn't land until morning. How about letting me crash on your sofa? It's really the least you can do, if you think about it."

Noonan did think about it, and arrived at the opposite conclusion. Still. "How come you don't have a suitcase?"

"It's in a locker at the Ferrovia."

"Go get it, if you want. I'll leave the door unlocked."

"Yeah, right," Lichtner said. "Like I can trust you."

IKEY'S

I'M UPSTAIRS working in my study when I hear water running outside and realize Owen must be drawing water. And over at the window I see I'm right. My son is down on his knees, surrounded by gallon plastic milk jugs. (How appalled my father would've been by those!) His hair is thinning, as my father's did in that same spot on his crown, and so, of course, has mine. Owen is filling one of the plastic jugs at our outside spigot. When it overflows, he sets it down, screws the plastic cap on tight and places another under the stream. He's quick and efficient in his motions but doesn't bother to turn the water off between jugs, so the knees of his pants are soaked. I count seven one-gallon containers, a week's worth of water for drinking and making coffee and cooking spaghetti and potatoes or whatever.

He and Brindy, his wife, live just over the town line in a tidy, modest house not far from Whitcombe Park. They've recently discovered their well is poisoned, its water safe enough to shower in but definitely not potable. Sarah and I urged them to have this tested before they bought the place two years ago, but Brindy had fallen in love with the house, and they waived some inspections once they'd learned that another interested couple was about to make an offer. Apparently, their realtor advised them that in multiple-offer situations, sellers often take the "cleanest," that is, the offer with the fewest contingencies. Therefore, clean offer, dirty water. State-mandated inspections had already revealed lead-based paint throughout the house, as well as asbestos in the attic and marginally unsafe levels of radon, but Brindy, a West End girl from a large family, loved the idea of

117

living out in the country and couldn't imagine ever finding another house she'd love as much, so we gave them enough money for a down payment, and they signed on the dotted line. When the other offer never materialized, Sarah was suspicious. After all, the county's population has been in steady decline since the sixties. Every third or fourth house in Thomaston has a FOR SALE sign on its terrace and usually stays on the market for two years, even longer out in the country. So what were the odds that Owen and Brindy really had to compete for the place that caught her eye?

I myself had hoped they'd stay in town. Once our Third Street renters' lease was up, I could've put them in there rent-free. The house has been nicely renovated, and it was big enough, even if they had a child, as they were planning back then. And I'll admit it: I liked the idea of my son and his wife raising a family in the same house where I myself grew up—the symmetry, I guess. But as Sarah pointed out, it was my symmetry, not theirs. Owen grew up in our Borough house, of course, and never spent a minute on Third Street, so it couldn't possibly mean to him what it did to me. And the neighborhood isn't, alas, what it once was. I thought they might see the practical side of it, but I don't think Brindy warmed to the idea of being so close to the store. "It's their life," Sarah reminded me when she saw how disappointed I was. "Let them live it."

Still, when Brindy miscarried last winter, we blamed ourselves for not insisting on complete inspections. We could've made it a condition of giving them the down payment, but at the time that seemed unkind and manipulative. Besides which, everyone we've talked to since has agreed that while the arsenic discovered in their well might have contributed to Brindy's miscarriage, it's impossible to assign a single cause with anything like certainty. Find a well anywhere in the county *without* arsenic, was how one inspector, an old friend of my father's, had put it. Find a house over twenty years old *without* lead-based paint, or an attic that *wasn't* insulated with asbestos. Never mind the Cayoga Stream, the real culprit in our lives. Radon and low-level arsenic are the least of our problems.

If my son and his wife were foolish or careless in the purchase of their house, I understand. I do. I remember vividly my father's pride in our house at the corner of Third and Rawley. Sometimes, early on Sunday mornings, he'd wake up first, get dressed, cross the street and sit there on the curb and just look at the house, as if he couldn't wrap his mind around it without the necessary distance. Thinking about what I've written so far concerning his rivalry with Mr. Marconi, I wonder if I've done him a disservice. Like so many men of his generation, he was a creature of postwar optimism who looked around and saw things getting better and not a single reason they shouldn't continue to do so. Wasn't our move from Berman Court to the East End proof of how things worked, that such optimism was justified? Not that he'd been unhappy in the West End. I doubt he'd have been unhappy anywhere, as long as we were all together, he and my mother and me. But moving to the East End had changed everything.

Modest as it was, I think our tidy little house instilled in my father the notion that "getting ahead" was both possible and desirable, and so, without knowing exactly how or why, he entered into a paradox he never was able to resolve. On the one hand, he was content with what he saw as our great good fortune. Over the years, when he told me there was no reason I couldn't have a house in the Borough one day, I truly believe he was expressing as best he could what he imagined *I* might want, not something he himself yearned for or even necessarily wanted *for* me. That was the paradox. He discovered that embracing the notion of getting ahead trailed an unexpected obligation: to instill in me my right as an American to dream big, if that's what I had a mind to do. So he did his duty.

My point, though, is that my father already *had* what he wanted, and when he implied to Mr. Marconi that he didn't think we'd ever move to the Borough, it *wasn't* sour grapes. And that afternoon, when we returned to our own neighborhood and he said that the East End was the right place for us, I truly believe he meant every word. We don't always want what we compete for. Sure, he believed in getting ahead just as he feared falling behind, and believed he had every right to want more. He just couldn't imagine what *that* might entail. I don't doubt he hated losing any competition to Mr. Marconi, but that didn't mean he was jealous of the spoils with which the victor was crowned. Those grand Borough houses didn't make ours look small and shabby, not to him. I repeat: my father had what he wanted.

Below, Owen has finished filling his plastic jugs. As he stacks them in the club cab behind the seat of his pickup, I try to decide whether what I'm feeling is some vague disappointment, and I hope it isn't, because that would be terrible. More likely I just wish I knew him better. After all, he's not a complicated man, and often I know what he'll do or say next, maybe even before he does. I know, for instance, that before he drives off with his water supply, he'll come inside and help himself to milk from our refrigerator. He'll drink it straight from the carton, though his mother wishes he wouldn't, and feel mildly guilty when I catch him at it. I know him. I do. But if someone were to ask me what my son wants out of life, what he dreams of, what he fears, I wouldn't have a clue. I know he loves Sarah and me, and that he's devoted to Brindy. Nobody could've been kinder or gentler when she miscarried last year. And should they eventually have children, Owen will be a good, patient father. But there is and has always been a curious lack of passion in him, and that's what puzzles his mother and me. Years ago rental trucks had devices called "governors" that prevented speeding and reckless driving, and a similar mechanism seems to govern my son. Extremes of joy or anger or fear appear foreign to him.

Nor, when he was growing up, did his teachers know quite what to make of him, the way he waited so patiently for school to be over, for people to stop pestering him to read books that didn't speak to him, for the day to arrive when he no longer had to answer their odd questions or fill blank notebook pages with words he didn't believe. Though he invariably defeated their efforts on his behalf, I can't remember a single teacher who wasn't fonder of Owen than of their prize students. Sweet and resigned by temperament, he never rebelled against or challenged them. If he doubted the wisdom of their assignments or the relevance of their subjects, he kept his own counsel. Even as a boy he was quicker to blame himself than others. I once asked Sarah if she thought a truly gifted teacher like her father might've gotten through to Owen, burrowed deep into his core and forced the private boy out into the open, but she just smiled and kissed me and said no, he was his father's son. It's always been my wife's contention that I have a place deep inside me that is wholly mine, that it's fortified and unassailable, a place no one, even herself, has ever entered. This, she further believes, is where I go when I have one of my spells. Does my son have such a place? Don't we all?

Owen may have thwarted and frustrated his teachers, but not because he was lazy, and this, more than anything else, reassures me and makes me proud. From the time he was big enough to handle a mower, he tended our lawn as well as neighbors', and when snowplows piled the driveways high with heavy, compacted snow, Owen was there to dig us out, even when the drifts were taller than he was. He neatly folded the dollar bills he earned and deposited them at the Thomaston Savings and Loan and each month reconciled the bank's numbers with his own, pleased when they tallied exactly and when they grew, though he never seemed to be saving for anything specific. And of course, as soon as he was old enough, he worked at the store, fulfilling his duties there with care and diligence. Am I wrong to wish he loved the store as I do? To see it as I see it? Am I even sure he doesn't? In truth, I'm not, though I worry. When his mother and I are gone, will he and Brindy sell their inheritance? It's possible. Some years ago I learned, well after the fact, that Owen had his heart set on buying an old fishing camp up in the Adirondacks. The list price made it seem like a bargain, but the dozen or so lakeside cabins were so neglected that it would've been extravagantly costly to restore them. The remote location was a plus in the summer and fall, but after the first snow anyone living in the main house would be a virtual prisoner for the next five months, miles from the nearest store or doctor, hours to the nearest hospital or school, no place for a child. It was Brindy, I suspect, who made him see how impractical it was, but I was pleased to know that my son had wanted something bad enough to be heartbroken when he was denied it, even if he didn't share that heartbreak with me. It didn't seem fair, somehow, that someone who'd never known quite what to want should be refused when he finally discovered it. I tell myself he'll want something else, and that next time he'll be luckier. If he has to sell his inheritance to get it, so be it. To insist that he love what I love is asking too much. I know. I know.

In truth, I wouldn't mind if they sold the West End store on lower Division Street, which has no sentimental value to me. We purchased it after my father died, and while it outperforms our East End store, we've been robbed at gunpoint several times, and for a long time now I've had reservations about how revenue is generated there. We sell the usual convenience store items, of course—bread and milk and other things people run out of and don't want to run all the way to the supermarket for. But it's the Lotto machine that pulls them in. For the last several years Division has been one of the top-five stores in the entire state in terms of Lotto ticket sales. "Desperate people who can't wait to pay the taxes" is how my mother describes it. She's always considered gambling, especially the legal state-sponsored variety, to be a tax on ignorance, and Division's success may well be, as she claims, an accurate barometer of that ignorance. I'm not sure my father would've seen it in exactly those terms, but I know he would have been troubled not just by the robberies but also by the long lines of shabby people that form in front of the Lotto machine, especially late at night, after the bars close, waiting patiently for their luck to change. He wouldn't have felt much pride in owning the kind of store that had to hire an extra clerk just for the purpose of taking such people's last two dollars. Nor do I.

Of course if it's up to Brindy, it won't be Division they'll sell. Why sell the moneymaker, she'd say, and it's hard to fault her logic. It's the busier store, no doubt about it, and she likes to be busy, especially now. Since the miscarriage she seems a different young woman, though when I remarked on the change to my wife, she reminded me that this was to be expected. She's naturally sympathetic to Brindy, having herself miscarried, early in our marriage. "Don't you remember how long it took me to bounce back? We need to be patient with her." And I understand all that. I do. But I worry that their loss has driven some sort of wedge between herself and Owen, whom she treats coolly now, I think, as if he's constantly trying her patience or blocking her way and making her wait for him to move so she can do whatever needs to be done, though too many errors are born of this impatience, or so it seems to me. Naturally, I keep that opinion to myself. The house they bought out in the country, the one *she* wanted, she now claims is too isolated. She'd like to "unload it," so they could move back to civilization and have friends again. "Civilization?" my mother said when Brindy voiced that wish a few months ago. "Thomaston?" She's never made it much of a secret that she's not overly fond of her granddaughter-in-law. "You can take the girl out of the West End," she says, then lets her voice trail off.

"Pop," Owen says, when I find him with the carton of milk at his lips. "I didn't know you were home." He puts the milk back in the fridge and closes the door. "Sorry."

"Why don't you take what water you need from the store?" I ask, seeing what a mess he's made of his pants.

"That water costs money."

"What about your time and effort?" I say for the sake of

123

argument, though in truth I admire his frugality. "Isn't that worth something?"

"I guess," he says. "That's probably how I should think of it?"

You don't have to agree with me, I'd like to tell him. *You don't always have to give in.*

"Mom says you're writing your life story up there."

"Nothing quite so grand as that," I tell him, though it's true I've written far more than I expected to, having underestimated the tug of the past, the intoxication of memory, the attraction of explaining myself to, well, myself.

"Am I in it yet?"

"No, not yet. Your mother hasn't even shown up yet."

"Wow," he says, genuinely impressed, I can't be sure at what—that I had a life before his mother, or that there was so much worth recording before his appearance.

"Did you hear from your friend yet?" he says, amazing me, as he so often does, by tacking so easily from one thing to the next, almost as if he fears getting trapped with a single idea if he lingers too long with it. "The one who lives over there?"

"Not yet," I tell him.

"And you haven't seen him since . . ."

"Senior year of high school."

"Wow," he says. "And he really almost killed his father?"

And what's with this second "wow"? Wow, it's really been that long since I've seen Bobby? Or, wow, near patricide? "Who told you—"

"Mom, of course."

Writing about Bobby, I realize, has made me grateful that Owen has never lacked for friends. Easy and outgoing, he's both made and kept them effortlessly. Many have gone off to college and made lives elsewhere, but when they're in town for the holidays, visiting their parents, they always get in touch. Several of these boys from the Borough have done well, and now rent or own second homes on the Sacandaga Reservoir or even Lake George, to which Owen and Brindy are frequently invited for a long summer weekend. So far as I can tell, these friendships are rewarding and uncomplicated, untroubled and full of straight-forward affection. They've gone out of their way to welcome Brindy, too, though I gather from various things Owen has said that she's uncomfortable with them, probably because of who they were in high school and the relative ease of their present lives. She prefers her own West End friends. They're real, she claims. They don't put on airs.

"Who's minding the store?" it occurs to me to ask.

"Brindy," he says, surprising me.

"I thought she preferred Division."

He shrugs. "Did she tell you that?"

I try to remember. Maybe not. Maybe it's just my impression. "Did Mr. Mock make it in last night?"

Owen shakes his head. "He didn't look too good last time I saw him."

"I know," I say, resolving to investigate.

When Owen is gone, I go back upstairs and read over the last page or so of what I've written, reliving that ride through the Borough in my father's milk truck. How magical, how far away, those streets seemed to me then. And magical they still are in memory, though they're as familiar to me as the back of my hand, since I've walked them most of my adult life. Again I hear, my eyes tearing up, my father explaining who lives where along his route, though they don't anymore and haven't, with few exceptions, for a great many years.

Only one thing rings false. When I said my father had everything he wanted, that isn't true. He wanted one more thing. He just didn't know it yet.

WE HADN'T BEEN in the East End long before a brand-new A&P opened out on the highway bypass, and overnight, it seemed, the tin milk cases that once decorated every back porch from the Borough to the West End began to disappear. There

125

were rumors that my father's dairy was about to be sold and that the new owners would cancel home delivery. My father maintained that people buying their milk at the A&P was just a phase. Why, he reasoned, would they trek to the store to buy milk in waxy cardboard cartons when it could be delivered right to their door in bottles? He said Borough folks especially liked the convenience of home delivery. Maybe the dairy would do away with service to the West End, where people would want to save a penny or two at the supermarket. West Enders were famous for their willingness to burn a tank of gas searching out the lowest prices, as if gas were free, but my father credited East Enders and Borough residents with being smarter than that. My mother, predictably, saw things differently. Wanting to save a penny, to her way of thinking, was human nature, and she urged my father to prepare for a future that didn't include milk trucks or, for that matter, milk bottles.

As usual, she was right. "The Old Man," who owned the dairy and liked my father, swore he'd never sell, but then did so and promptly moved away. The new owner immediately curtailed deliveries in the West End and let it be known that our East End might be next. Publicly my father didn't waver in his stated belief that his lucrative route through the Borough was in no danger, but the milk boxes continued to disappear until finally there was no denying his route was shrinking. By midmorning he'd be back home, where he'd change out of his all-white uniform and head down to the Cayoga Diner for coffee with the seasonally unemployed men who loitered there, many of them laid off from the tannery. These were stoical men who went on unemployment every spring and patiently awaited the inevitable call back to work, a summons that came later and later each autumn.

Those days, talk at the diner was increasingly about the future of Thomaston and whether there was one. Many thought not, and my father took it upon himself to cheer up these defeatists. People had tanned leather in Thomaston since before the

Revolution, he liked to remind them, so he expected they'd continue awhile longer. These things ran in cycles, like the moon, waxing and waning and waxing again. Another year and everybody'd be back working full-time, even overtime, probably. Weren't famines followed by feasts? That he was willing to spring for a cup of coffee or float a small loan to a fellow who'd be good for it come the end of the week, along with his jovial good nature, made him popular at the lunch counter, where his optimism for the most part went unchallenged, except, ironically, for his younger brother, Declan. Uncle Dec always had answers for my father's rhetorical questions. What followed famine? Death. What followed death? Decomposition. In Uncle Dec's opinion, which he offered loudly whenever he ran into his brother in public, Lou Lynch would be next in the unemployment line. "I hope you've saved up, Biggy," he'd say, clapping my father on the back. He never called him by his name, preferring Big Brother or, more often, Biggy, which he knew my father hated. "You *do* know what happened to the dinosaurs, don't you?" Death. Decomposition.

   Much as my father enjoyed the company of men, he wouldn't step foot in the diner, the barbershop or the cigar store if Dec was inside. He had little use for his brother, who was constantly in and out of trouble, in and out of the newspaper, in and out of jail, giving us Lynches, my father said, a bad name. Though he was a year younger, Uncle Dec, at age sixteen, had left the doomed family farm and joined the army (from which he was later discharged for dealing in contraband), leaving my father trapped there until he finished high school and turned eighteen. According to my mother, he still resented his brother for escaping, and if he saw Uncle Dec holding court over by the diner's cash register, he'd just return home and take his ease on the front porch. If somebody down the block happened to be painting or doing repairs, he'd visit with them and offer advice, standing at the bottom of the ladder and carrying on a vertical conversation, or saunter down the street to Tommy Flynn's and shoot the breeze there. By midafternoon he'd finish his rounds and return to the front porch, where he and I would spend a contemplative hour or so, me with a book, my father with the *Thomaston Guardian*, which was always delivered about this time. Through the screen door, we could hear my mother starting dinner in the back of the house, and for me this was the most peaceful time of day, when everything felt right with the world.

But all was not right, and I knew it. As milk boxes continued to disappear from porches throughout Thomaston, my father became quieter and less social. He never changed his public stance, maintaining to all who would listen that his route was secure, but he was worried that the dairy's new owner, a man from Albany, didn't like him. The actual rules hadn't changed, but suddenly they were enforced. My father was no longer allowed to park the truck at the curb in front of our house when he finished his route, and its personal use was now grounds for dismissal, as was allowing unauthorized people to ride in it. Since each of these rules directly affected him, my father couldn't help wondering if they were imposed with him specifically in mind. Had the new owner heard about Bobby Marconi's accident? Or had Mr. Marconi himself reported it, hoping to get him fired? He couldn't inquire, of course, not without admitting to having broken the rule in the first place.

The continued uncertainty over his future definitely clouded our family planning. In Thomaston, junior high was seventh and eighth grades, and that year (sixth grade) one of the many things my parents argued about (they called their arguments "discussions") was whether I would remain at St. Francis or transfer to the public junior high. Unlike most of their "discussions," this one confused me, partly because each seemed to be arguing the other's point of view. My mother was the one who'd always wanted me in parochial school, not that she was committed to Catholic education but because the public schools were so rough. The boys who'd abducted me were good examples (though Jerzy Quinn was no longer a threat, having by

128

then landed in reform school), not that my being in St. Francis had protected me from them. I wasn't a scrapper like Bobby Marconi, and my mother didn't want me to become one. To her way of thinking, in public school I'd either be brutalized or grow brutal myself. My father didn't worry much about this. He'd been bused in to these same schools from the farm, and nothing terrible had happened to him, unless you counted being made fun of all the time, which my mother did. When we moved to the East End I assumed, as he did, that I'd be going to public school, but my mother put her foot down. I was doing well where I was and was being looked after—whatever that meant—and I would stay put until starting high school in the ninth grade.

But now my mother began wondering out loud if next year might not be the best time to leave St. Francis. All the public school kids would be in the same boat—that is, moving from familiar elementary schools into the new environment of the junior high. And Cardinal Fulton High, she hated to admit, would be out of the question. We simply couldn't afford both private high school and college, and the latter was more important. My mother had put her foot down about that, too. I was going to college, and that was the end of the story. No discussion allowed. My father could wonder all he wanted about where we'd ever come up with that kind of money, but every time he did so out loud she'd stop dead and stare at him until he relented and said sure, of course I'd go to college, he'd rob a bank if he had to. Only after she'd left the room would he grumble that robbing a bank was the only way he could see it happening. So it was strange to hear my father arguing that I should stay in St. Francis two more years.

Finally it dawned on me that they weren't discussing schools. This dispute was really an extension of their ongoing argument about whether my father was going to lose his job. My mother, who wanted me in parochial school, thought he was, which meant that the St. Francis fees, though not large, were a luxury we could no longer afford. My father, who'd always maintained that there was nothing wrong with public schools, remained adamant that he *wasn't* going to lose his job, which meant there was no reason I couldn't continue at St. Francis if that's what she wanted.

DIAGONALLY ACROSS THE STREET from our house sat Ikey Lubin's corner market, where it was well known that a man could play a number or daily double. In fact, Uncle Dec, who played both, was a regular visitor, though he never seemed to purchase anything. When he pulled up in front of the store, my father would invariably fold his newspaper and take it inside until he left, lest Uncle Dec spot him sitting there and saunter over to ask him if he remembered what happened to the dinosaurs, which he sometimes did anyway. My mother exhibited a weary tolerance for her ne'er-do-well brother-in-law, probably because he called her gorgeous, which she wasn't, and invited her to come find him if she ever got tired of that stiff she was married to. To this she always replied that she doubted she'd ever get *that* tired, to which Uncle Dec responded that you never knew.

I wanted to like Uncle Dec but distrusted him, mostly because he reminded me of the man at the trestle. It had been dark when I'd awakened in the trunk, and I'd never actually seen him, nor did I remember their voices being similar, but they did have several expressions in common, and whenever my uncle remarked that so-and-so wasn't such a bad egg or that people in hell wanted ice water, I couldn't get it out of my head that the two might be the same man. Also, Uncle Dec was forever promising to buy me something or take me someplace, and he never did. "That's your uncle in a nutshell," my father explained to me early on, after I'd gotten my hopes up and been disappointed. "Full of promises."

"He just likes to make people feel good," my mother said, her tone gentler than was customary. But then her voice regained its usual judgmental edge. "If he's a little short on results, well, he's a Lynch."

As the worrisome months wore on, I couldn't help noticing my father's increasing interest in Ikey Lubin's. It seemed like every time I raised my eyes from my reading, he'd be staring at the store over the top of the *Thomaston Guardian*, sometimes rubbing his chin thoughtfully, as if he were calculating how much people were spending inside by guessing the weight of the paper sacks they emerged with. His interest struck me as particularly strange because for our family Ikey's had long been a kind of joke. Weather permitting, Ikey liked to keep his fruit in bins under an awning out front, and my father and I often wagered on how many neighborhood dogs would stop in front of the store, cock a leg and pee on the cantaloupes. We were friendly with Ikey, but the only business we ever gave him was last-minute items that had slipped my mother's mind when she made out her grocery list. His market wasn't nearly as good as Tommy Flynn's at the lower end of Third, where we did most of our shopping, and it seemed only a matter of time before Tommy would put his nearest rival out of his misery. Of course, according to my mother, it was also only a matter of time before the A&P did the same to Tommy Flynn. The new A&P was what people called modern. You didn't have to wait there for the butcher to slap a pound of ground beef into a paper tub, then wrap it in pink paper and tie it off with string like Tommy Flynn did. At the new A&P, unlike the old smaller one downtown, it was already safely under cellophane, which people seemed to prefer.

By August my father was finding excuses to visit Ikey's every day. Sometimes I went along but more often not, because I got the feeling he didn't want me there. A knot of newly retired men who referred to themselves as the Elite Coffee Club loitered around the register keeping Ikey company—he was a dark little fellow, almost a dwarf—and telling jokes they'd break off in the middle of if a woman or kid came in. My father said they were the kind of jokes I didn't need to hear, that I was better off back on the front porch reading. But what I heard of them, they didn't seem so different from the ones that got told in the barbershop or the Cayoga Diner.

My mother had also noted my father's new interest in Ikey's, and one day after he folded his newspaper and headed across the street, she appeared at the screen door in her apron, drying her hands on a dish towel and staring rather malevolently at the market. "I swear to heaven," she muttered, "if he's betting horses over there, it'll be the last straw." She was always pronouncing one thing or another was the last straw, and there were enough of these, it seemed to me, to make a haystack big enough to lose the proverbial needle in.

OCCASIONALLY, whenever I found myself at loose ends, I'd get on my bike and pedal out to Whitcombe Park, where I'd help Gabriel Mock Junior paint his fence. Gabriel insisted on calling *me* Junior, though I'd explained several times that my middle name was different from my father's. "Don't care about that," he told me. "You look just like him. Talk like him. Act like him. Spittin' image."

It had been my impression, based on our first meeting, that it had been my mother he'd known when they were young, but apparently he knew my father, too. "Everybody know Lou Lynch," he added, making me feel proud to be so like a man everybody knew and wishing I *was* Lou Lynch Junior instead of Louis Charles Lynch, who was notable mostly for having a girl's nickname. The real reason Gabriel Mock called me Junior was that everybody called *him* Junior, a burden he felt should be shared. Early on I'd asked what I should call him, and he said he didn't care. "Any name you want," he said. "Call me something nasty, if that suit you. You can't hurt my feelin's no matter how hard you try. Anything 'cept nigger. Call me that, I'll have to cut out your gizzard. I got me a knife, too, don't think I don't."

I had no intention of calling him that, and I'm sure he knew it. "What's a gizzard?" I said, wondering if its similarity in sound gave it some mysterious connection to the word "nigger."

"A spare part," Gabriel explained unhelpfully. "Don't your mama feed you chicken?"

I said she did, lots of different ways.

"She prob'ly thown out the gizzard. Not good enough for white folks. Call me Gizzard, you want. Can't hurt my feelin's."

As soon as I showed up, he'd hand me a spare brush. "Slap that lacquer on good and thick," he always reminded me. "Don't be thin wit' it. Ain't gonna run out, don't you worry." Sometimes we painted along together, him on his side of the fence, me on mine. Other times he just stretched out on the grass and gave me instructions. "I be the job foreman today," he'd say. "I'm a rest my eyes while you work. Don't think I'm sleepin', 'cause I ain't." It seemed to both please and amuse Gabriel that I'd just show up like I did, ready to paint his fence. He said my helping him out gave him more time to howl. "You know what I mean by howlin'?" He asked me this question every time I visited, and each time I pretended not to. "Sneak out the house some night," he suggested. "Come by after the sun go down, you hear me howlin'."

He also wanted to know what I planned to do when I grew up, and I always told him I was still thinking about it. Apparently I was going to college, which meant I wouldn't be a milkman like my father. Probably I wouldn't live in Thomaston either, since according to my mother that would be a terrible waste of an education. Her idea was that I would venture out into the wide world, do things that people in Thomaston didn't do, see things that people around here didn't see. "Experience life" was how she summed it up. When I made the mistake of mentioning that maybe I'd return one day and live in a house in the Borough, as my father had suggested I might do, she looked at me hard. "You're *trying* to break my heart, right? *That's* why you say such things?"

133

"All women like that," Gabriel said, nodding. "They all got that go about 'em. Go here. Go there. Us? We stay put. Howl right where we're at. Twist the cap off that bottle, drink it down, howl at the moon. Moon's in the same place no matter *where* you're at. Now if you could go to the moon, *that* might be worth it. Look down at the whole earth from up there. I'd do that."

I wasn't sure about the wisdom or feasibility of that idea and said so. For one thing, I pointed out, if you were on the moon, you'd be looking up at the earth, not down. For another, you wouldn't be looking for long, because on the moon there wasn't any oxygen, which meant you'd asphyxiate before you had much of an opportunity to appreciate your privileged position. Gabriel conceded I was probably right about the air. He'd heard there wasn't any on the moon, but it didn't make sense that you'd be looking *up* at the earth. I tried to explain that down was all about gravity. On the moon, down would be the ground, where your feet were, and up would be the sky, same as on Earth. But Gabriel said it was more like a ladder. If you climbed up to the top and looked back at where you'd been, you'd be looking down. And if that ladder went all the way to the moon, you'd still be looking down.

I knew there was something wrong with his logic and tried for about an hour to convince him he was wrong, but he was sure he knew up from down and was having none of it. In fact, he thought I'd do well to stick close to home and not lead the wanderer's life my mother had in mind for me. Anybody who couldn't tell up from down had no business traveling very far. He wouldn't let go of the subject even when I stood up, handed him his brush back and said I was going to look for the caves he claimed were in the park. "Tell me this," he said as I climbed on my bike. "Suppose you walkin' along and you find one of 'em and you fall right in. You gonna fall up or down?"

More than a little peeved that he was laughing at me when he, and not I, was wrong, I conceded, not very gracefully, that I'd more likely fall down than up.

"Down's where I'll look then," Gabriel said. "If you was gonna fall up, I'd of looked for you in the treetops. But now I can concentrate my efforts on the ground."

I reminded him that on the day we met he warned me that he had no intention of looking for me if I fell into a cave.

"That was back before we was friends," he said, which both surprised and pleased me. I also felt bad that I'd gotten mad at him for being so stubborn. It hadn't even occurred to me that we *could* be friends. He was as old as my parents and as odd as anyone I'd ever run across, and that seemed to me to preclude the idea of friendship. This must have registered on my face, because he quickly added, " 'Less you don't want no brown-skinned friends." Which made me feel even worse, because that, too, had occurred to me.

Though my mother was anxious for me to explore my world's boundaries, she was surprised to discover how far I'd gone and whom I'd met. One night, when I said I'd spent half the afternoon helping Gabriel Mock paint his fence, she told me that at about my age he'd had a crush on her and hadn't understood this wasn't allowed. His father had explained things to him with his belt.

It was a disturbing story, and for that reason I wasn't sure I believed it. That Gabriel might've fallen in love with a white girl was plausible enough, but with all the white girls in Thomaston to choose from, how had he settled on my mother? And why would a man who'd given his son his own name then turn around and whip him for choosing the wrong girl?

When I raised these less-than-convincing points, my mother gave me one of those looks she reserved for similar circumstances, when she wanted to impress on me just how much I had to learn about the workings of the world. Of course Gabriel Mock Senior had first tried to explain, but the boy had been adamant. His father, she assured me, hadn't taken any pleasure in giving his son a licking. He did it so somebody else wouldn't have to, and do it worse, because there were white people in

Thomaston back then—and probably now, she admitted—who wouldn't think twice about visiting the Hill to teach the same lesson to every boy Gabriel's age, thereby ensuring they hadn't somehow missed the one they were after. No, Gabriel Mock Senior had strapped his son, and afterward he'd appeared, hat in hand, on her father's front porch with a swollen-eyed Junior in tow, so my grandfather would know he was being told the truth. Senior wouldn't look directly at my grandfather, and when he saw his son was looking past them at my mother, who stood just inside the door, he cuffed him sharply and said, "Don't you be lookin' in there. You got no business with nothin' in this man's house." To my grandfather, he just repeated, over and over, that he didn't have no cause to worry. All took care of. Boy knew better now. Nothin' to worry about. All in the past.

I could tell the incident was still fresh in my mother's memory, that young Gabriel Mock was standing right there in front of her with his swollen eyes as she relived the awful moment, and she would've let it rest there if I hadn't pressed her on the second point. "Why me?" she said, and shook her head. "Who knows?" What she wanted, clearly, was to be done with the subject, then I saw her change her mind. "Actually, that's not true. He liked me because I was kind. And do you want to know the oddest thing of all? It wasn't even him I was kind to. It was his sister."

I didn't even know Gabriel *had* a sister, and said so.

"She died of leukemia when we were in high school," my mother explained. "Lord, I haven't thought of her in years. Kaylene Mock. She was in my class. Gabriel was a year older. I remember in first grade all us girls were crazy to be in the Brownies, and I asked Kaylene if she was going to join. She just smiled and said she was already a Brownie, but later she admitted the real reason was that her parents didn't have the money for the Brownie uniform. The uniforms weren't even required, but Kaylene's dad didn't want her to join if she couldn't have what all the other girls had. I'd been saving my allowance, so I begged your grandparents to buy Kaylene a uniform when they got mine. We were the same size, so it would be easy. At first they refused, since the uniform cost more than I'd saved, but when they saw how heartbroken I was they said they'd make up the difference if Kaylene's parents said it was okay. I knew from the start they wouldn't hear of it, but I think they appreciated the gesture and remembered it, too. And the licking Gabriel got was so bad because it was me he kissed, not some other white girl."

"He *kissed* you?" I said, astonished.

"It was a very foolish thing to do. He came right up to me on Hudson Street, about half a block from the Four Corners, and kissed me, right in front of everybody."

"Why?"

"Because by then he was about your age. Because boys get crushes. Because his sister and I made fun of how little he was, and he wanted to show me he wasn't. All kinds of reasons, Louie. Don't just stand there frowning at me. Use your imagination."

Actually, I *had* been using my imagination. What I wanted was to stop.

"Think of it. Taking a belt to an eleven-year-old," she said, shaking the memory off. Then she looked at me again, and it was her turn to frown. "Also, you needn't look so surprised that someone other than your father might've wanted to kiss me, okay?"

"But—" I began, then stopped, realizing that no matter what I said, it would only make things worse.

ONE DAY, returning from Whitcombe Park, I found my parents engaged in what even they would have been hard pressed to call a discussion. In fact, they were so involved in it that they seemed not to notice, or care, that I'd entered the room.

"Well then, you're just going to have to return them *un*signed," my mother was saying. There was a thick sheaf of documents on the table between them. "I'm not risking this house, nor will I risk Lou's college."

For his part, my father looked like he had the morning when we returned Bobby Marconi to his father with his wrist broken. "So what do you want me to do, Tessa? If I don't do this, what am I *supposed* to do?"

That slowed my mother down, but it didn't stop her. "For a year I've been telling you this day was coming," she said. "*Over* a year."

"That ain't what I'm saying," he told her, even more hangdog now. "What I'm saying is, what's a man like me supposed to do? It's *us* I'm doing it for."

This slowed her even more, though of course she wouldn't give in. "But don't you see, Lou? You keep saying it's for us, and maybe you even believe that, but it's not true. This is about you and your pride. It's about being able to brag down at the diner, like you used to brag to Mr. Marconi, like you brag to everybody. What are you thinking, Lou? That you're the first man to lose a job? You'll find another. Losing a job doesn't mean you go out and risk everything we've got left on a doomed corner market that's really nothing more than a bookie joint."

"I ain't gonna make book over there, Tessa. You know I wouldn't do that."

My mother let out a gasp of pure exasperation, then let her head fall forward onto the kitchen table so hard that the salt and pepper shakers jumped. She let it rest there for several beats before finally raising it to look at him again. "Yes, Lou, I know you aren't going to make book over there. I know that. But the fact is that the book's the only part of Ikey's business that's *worth* anything. What do you think's kept him in business this long?"

"You know how sick he's been—"

"No, I don't," my mother interrupted. "Just because somebody says something doesn't make it true, Lou. Don't you *know* that? He's been telling you he's sick because he wants you to buy the store. He doesn't want you to know the truth, which is that he's not making a go of it because it can't be done. Tommy Flynn's been trying to sell his store for two years, and he's got twice Ikey's business. There used to be two dozen corner stores in Thomaston. More, probably. Now there's six. What happened to them? The supermarkets. Can't you see, Lou? Corner stores are going the way of milk in bottles."

Even I would've known better than to say what my father said next. Worse still was the silence that stretched between them, until he finally said, "Milk's better in bottles."

Then, to my surprise, it was my mother who was crying. "Oh, Lou, Lou," she sobbed. "Can't you see it doesn't matter what *you* think? People have decided. They want supermarkets. They want milk in cartons. Who cares which is better? When people want the wrong thing, they still want it. Usually they want the wrong thing more than the right thing. You've been outvoted."

It was only then, when she put her head on her forearms and continued to cry, that my father finally acknowledged I was standing there. "I bought Ikey Lubin's," he explained, unnecessarily. I must've looked frightened, because he added, "I don't want you to worry about it neither. I don't want you to worry about nothing."

LOOKING BACK, I think my father's purchase of Ikey Lubin's was a greater seismic event for our family than moving from Berman Court to the East End. Here again my mother and I remember things differently. As she recalls it, Ikey Lubin's was just one more thing she had to resign herself to, one more circumstance over which she had neither control nor choice. My own recollection is that my father's announcement set in motion a struggle that played itself out over many months, during which my mother was far from resigned. Right from the start she refused to enter the store, ever. What was done might be done, but she made it clear that Ikey's was my father's folly, not hers, and she wouldn't dream of giving up her bookkeeping accounts.

I was allowed to help out after school if I wanted to, on either Saturday or Sunday but not both. Yes, she'd do the books, but only if my father brought home the cash register receipts, vendors' bills and other documents she'd need. Otherwise, he was on his own. That he should've taken such a step without consulting her was . . . she didn't even know the word for it.

For many weeks my mother seemed to vacillate between depression and dark, inarticulate rage. In the grip of the first, it was as if she could see into the future and knew that what was marching inexorably toward us in the end couldn't be prevented, or that she and my father would have to see things the same way and share the same fears, something they'd never done. Other times her grim, mute fatalism turned into fury, and she would fire angry questions at him, one after another. "What *possessed* you? What is *wrong* with you? Is it so difficult to just *look* at things, Lou, and see them for what they are? Why do you always have to . . . ? Why must you be so . . . ?"

Here words would fail her, and when they did, the rage would slowly leak away. My father never argued back, just stood there waiting—silent, patient, hangdog, shrugging his shoulders, as if all this was as mysterious to him as it was to her. Eventually it became clear to my mother that he didn't intend to speak, ever again, if necessary. When I happened to be present, she'd study me, too, but if she expected me to take up my father's argument, to give voice to whatever he couldn't find words for, she was sorely mistaken. Then her eyes would fill and she'd look through the blinds at the darkening street outside, at Ikey Lubin's across the intersection, as if the only way she could control her emotions was to pretend that we were no longer in the room with her.

I was always glad when her rage morphed into grief, because I couldn't bear those despairing, unfinished questions. "Lou, Lou, why do you always have to . . . ? Why must you be so . . . ?" Try as I might, I couldn't help feeling they were addressed as much to me as to my father. Didn't we share the same name? Didn't I always see things with the same optimism? Was I not, as Gabriel Mock Junior had pointed out, his spitting image? If something was wrong with him, wasn't I equally to blame? Worse, I couldn't banish the fear that someday she'd finish one of those why-do-you-always-have-to questions she was forever trying to articulate and that when she did it would mean the end of our family. It was as if she knew, too, knew full well, that what she was about to say had the power to atomize us, and getting halfway there was terrifying enough.

Buying Ikey Lubin's had just as profound an effect on my father, whose life changed utterly as a result. Suddenly, for the first time in his adult life, he was no longer a route man. Accustomed to going out into the world armed with clear, simple duties, and with his own good nature as the primary tool of their implementation, he now had to stand still in one spot and trust that the world would come to him and also that, when it did, he'd have what was required. In the store he was like a man recently jailed without explanation and brutally interrogated on a subject of which he hadn't the slightest knowledge. Trapped behind Ikey's monster cash register, he bounced from one foot to the other, waiting for the next thing, whatever that might be. When a customer came in asking for something, he bolted from behind the counter like an escapee, sometimes doing two or three laps around the store before locating the item requested, then grimly returning to the register to ring up the sale and await his next fleeting liberation. Gone, he now realized, were the days he could stroll downtown for coffee and a doughnut at the Cayoga Diner or some joke swapping at the barbershop. He couldn't even leave his post long enough to stroll down the block and offer advice to roofers or painters or plumbers when they showed up unexpectedly at the Spinnarkles' next door or at the Gunthers'. He had no choice but to wait for those men to come to him on their lunch hour—that is, assuming they didn't buy their soda from Tommy Flynn's cooler down the street. Many of Ikey's regulars had, as expected, fallen away when they couldn't bet their number or daily double, and that first month or so my father sometimes waited an hour or more between customers. Uncle Dec came in just once, looked around, met my father's eye, shook his head and left without a word.

My parents had always argued over money, since no matter how hard they worked we came up short at the end of the month. My father wasn't a spendthrift, but saving for a rainy day wasn't in his nature. To his way of thinking, the sun was shining most of the time. My mother had inherited from her parents the exact opposite view. To her, a sunny day was a rarity. Tomorrow it would rain, and the only question was how hard. She didn't think we'd need an ark necessarily, but she favored spending money only on what we really needed. She was willing to spend larger amounts if whatever it was would last, if she could be assured she wouldn't have to buy it again next week. By contrast, my father had a great fondness for anything that sparkled, especially if it was cheap. If he went downtown with a pocket full of change, he'd spend a quarter here, a dime there and his last penny on a lemon drop, taking great pleasure in each tiny purchase. When it came to money, my mother maintained, he was like a tire with a slow leak; you couldn't find it and wouldn't even know it was there except that every third or fourth morning it was flat. Before Ikey Lubin's their disagreements, however heated they were, always got resolved peacefully. Once they'd both calmed down, they convened at the kitchen table, a pad of paper and a sharp pencil between them, and she would show him the consequences of what he'd done or wanted to do. She was left-handed, my mother, and my father always sat to that side of her at the table, watching the numbers appear in columns on the pad. After a while, usually in the middle of some calculation, he'd take the pencil from her and set it on the table and put his hand on top of hers, where it would remain, sometimes for a whole minute, while they agreed to say nothing, until finally he'd grin, as if to say it didn't really matter who was right, and give her back the pencil, which she always accepted with a sigh, as if to acknowledge that of course he was right, it didn't matter at all. How many times did I witness this ritual during my boyhood? Even now I can feel the sweetness of those gestures, of my father first taking the pencil from her, then giving it back.

But Ikey's was different. Sure, I knew my parents still loved each other, but what if they didn't love each other enough? What if the store made my mother love my father less, and that "less" was no longer sufficient to hold us together? "Divorce," an unheard-of word during much of my boyhood, was suddenly on everyone's lips, as familiar as cancer. Families, it seemed, could be dissolved. The real reason the Mulroneys down the street were leaving Thomaston, it was whispered, wasn't that he'd been offered a new job downstate but rather that he'd found a new woman in Amsterdam. My father's purchase of Ikey Lubin's brought home to me that my parents were now in a new conflict, that the stakes were higher, that the story of our family was being written without any guarantee of the happy ending I'd always taken for granted. My mother's anger and fear might be as powerful as her affection for him and even for me. What was happening to other families might one day happen to ours.

Rather than contemplate any of this, I absented myself by spending as much time as possible at the store, where I knew my mother wouldn't step foot. There I learned how to take deliveries, keep the storeroom organized and the dairy case rotated so the food in it wouldn't spoil, stock shelves and operate the big cash register. With so little business at first, my father could have handled all these chores by himself, but he liked having me around. He seemed to know that right from the start I loved the store as much as he did—its dry, warm smell, its crowded, sloping shelves and the fact that it was ours, though we kept Ikey Lubin's name to avoid having to spend money on a new sign. Strangely, with so much to worry about, I had fewer spells during this period, and never a single one when I was at Ikey's.

When I wasn't helping out at the store, I continued to explore on my bicycle, sometimes visiting Gabriel in Whitcombe Park, where I helped paint his fence and searched, without success, for the caves he insisted riddled the estate. That summer I also became a denizen of the Thomaston Free Library. Always a reader, I now borrowed six books every Saturday morning—the maximum allowable. At night I'd read until my mother made me turn out the light, then wake up early and read until it was time to bathe and eat breakfast and go to school. My father, who wasn't a reader, regarded my voracious habit with wonder and pride. "You couldn't hardly believe it," he'd report to anybody who happened into the store and showed the slightest interest, "the books he read just last week. Not skinny ones neither." If I happened to be there, he'd call me over and quiz me in front of his customers. "Tell 'em the books you read," he'd say, and I'd proudly tick them off—books by Jules Verne and H. G. Wells and H. Rider Haggard and Edgar Rice Burroughs. Sometimes the neighborhood men who congregated at Ikey's would be suspicious and ask questions designed to trip me up, but I'd read the books and they hadn't, so I had an unfair advantage. In the end they'd nod and agree that I'd done what I said, hard though it was to believe, and I'd bask in my achievement until the talk turned to baseball and stock-car racing.

My mother, true to her word, never ventured into the store, though she worked part of every Sunday on the books, shaking her head and rubbing her temples at my father's way of doing things. It was immediately clear that she'd been right about the nature of the business. What Ikey Lubin had been was a bookie, and the exodus of so many regular customers unnerved my father, who kept up a brave front for a while, shrugging his shoulders and saying, "Business is bound to pick up," to which my mother would reply, without looking up from the ledger, "Really, Lou? Why's that?" She knew perfectly well he couldn't explain why, because he had no idea. He was *hoping* it would, just as he was hoping she'd soon relent and take up the pencil and show him what he was doing wrong and how to do it differently. He'd already done what he shouldn't have done in buying Ikey Lubin's, and he'd done it without consulting her, knowing full well that if he *had*, she'd have advised him not to, probably forbidden it. What she was doing now was showing him the consequences of his behavior. He wanted to do things his way? Fine. He could just go on ahead and let her know how it all worked out. It was like she enjoyed watching him suffer.

What I didn't understand at the time was *her* strategy, too, was doomed to failure. She couldn't teach him this particular lesson, not really, for the simple reason that if *he* failed, we all failed. Even his suffering—and he did suffer, waiting for her to share her solution with him—was not his alone. Anxious for it to be over, we *all* became depressed. What was she waiting for, a sign from God? From my father himself? It seemed so to me, which was why I resented her so. Just as he was clearly waiting for her to tell him how to fix things, she appeared to be waiting for him to say some magic word, like the one that made the fake bird come down on the Groucho Marx show. He would say it, eventually, but it troubled me that I'd never know what that word was, because there were no bells and whistles, no descending bird.

Whatever the magic word was, it got said one Sunday afternoon a good two months later. He and I were sitting on the front porch while my mother worked on the market's books inside, receipts and invoices spread out all over the kitchen table. I was reading while he sat on the top step, staring morosely at the store, which was closed, this being the Sabbath. When my mother finally came out on the porch, she sat down beside him holding open the ledger, but he just looked away. "I guess people like Tommy Flynn more than me," he said with a sweeping gesture that took in the whole street.

"Oh, Lou," my mother said, her voice less harsh than it had been of late. "Why do you have to be so . . . ?" Her voice trailed off, like it always did. After a while, she tried again. "Look, it's

145

bad, but not the way you think. Tommy Flynn's a little ferret. People like you lots better than Tommy."

"Then how come they shop down to his store and not mine?"

My mother rubbed her temples. "Lou," she said. "Try to understand. Tommy Flynn's not your problem. The new A&P's your problem. It's going to bury you and Tommy Flynn in the same unmarked grave unless we can prevent it. Can't you see that?"

He couldn't. I could tell that much just by looking at him, though I wasn't sure what she was driving at either.

"How we gonna compete with superdoop prices?" he said, using his word for all supermarkets. "They buy in quantity. The vendors don't give us the same breaks."

"I know that. You aren't going to beat the A&P at what they do well, Lou. You're never going to be big like they are. You're never going to have wide aisles, and you won't be able to offer people lots of choices. Your only chance is to beat them at what *you* do well."

Suddenly, I found myself sitting up straight. I had no idea what we might be good at over at Ikey's, and I could tell my father didn't either, but he was listening carefully to find out, and so was I.

"You're small, Lou. You've got to find out how to make *small* a good thing."

My father glanced over at me. This was making sense to him, and he wondered if it was making sense to me, too. "How do we do that?"

I closed my book, got up from my porch chair and joined them on the steps and listened to my mother talk for the next hour. As she spoke, I found my anger at her leaking away. It occurred to me that what she'd been doing all these weeks, probably since the moment my father had announced his purchase, was figuring out how this foolish thing that he'd done could be made to work. In her initial fear she'd let it be known that the folly was his and his alone, but of course she'd known all along it wasn't, and so, perhaps without admitting it, even to herself, she'd devised a plan that she was now, finally, ready to share.

As she spoke, it became clear that while she was ostensibly addressing my father, she was also talking to me, his chief ally and helper, and every now and then she'd fix me with a look that suggested she was counting on *me* in this regard, usually concerning something she believed he'd forget or not be very good at. I recognized these gestures as votes of confidence in me, sure, but they also seemed like small betrayals of him, and I found myself looking down at the step I was perched on, ashamed, unwilling to acknowledge my father's shortcomings. I was embarrassed, too, of my suspicion that a mere boy might possess a deeper understanding of what she was explaining than he did, even though he obliged her by nodding enthusiastically at everything she said, occasionally even winking or grinning at me, as if to suggest that *this* was what we'd been waiting for, pardner, this right here, your mother figuring it all out. Now there'd be no holding us back.

The slender advantage we had at Ikey Lubin's, she explained, was that people could get in and out quickly, and time, she claimed, was just another form of money. When people went to the A&P out by the highway, they had to *spend* thirty minutes, whereas they could *save* twenty-five of them by darting into our little store. They wouldn't do it if Ikey's was a lot more expensive, so the trick was to convince them that the time they were saving more than made up for the marginally higher prices. Part of the brain, she admitted, would know this wasn't true, but this wasn't the part that counted. Also, it was imperative to remember that all items sold at our store were not equal. People would mostly go to Ikey's for things they'd run out of—milk, bread, toilet paper—and so these had to be priced within a few pennies of what the supermarket charged, even if that meant we didn't make any money on them. What we'd mark up were the things they *didn't* need and wouldn't make a special trip for, things they'd buy on impulse since, what the hell, they were already there. The entire store, she maintained, should be arranged so that whatever people needed most was located in the rear and they'd have to pass everything they didn't need both going in and coming out. The most overpriced items—candy, batteries—should be placed as near the register as possible.

It was also important to remember, she continued, that men and women were different. Women had money to spend but little time to waste spending it. No woman would want to enter Ikey Lubin's if she had to run a gantlet of indolent old farts lounging around the cash register swapping lies. She looked meaningfully at my father when she said this, knowing how much he liked having the Elite Coffee Club fellows in his store, even though they never spent any money to speak of. He felt they lent the place an air of commerce. If my mother hadn't suggested it now, it would never have occurred to him that they might actually be preventing commerce. "The Coffee Club don't hurt nobody," he said, defending their communal character. "If a woman came in, they wouldn't say nothing."

"I know that, Lou," my mother said. "They'd just stop telling their off-color jokes and stand there looking gutshot and wait for her to leave so they could start talking again." Which *was* pretty much what happened on those rare occasions a woman stopped at Ikey's.

"What do I do? Tell 'em they can't come in no more?"

My mother looked like she considered this an elegant solution, but instead she said, "Move them around to the other side of the center island. Put a coffeepot over there on the counter and make them buy *that*, at least."

"Charge them for coffee?"

"Don't put it that way. Say the first refill's free. The main thing is to keep them away from the door."

Across the street a mangy dog trotted by the market, stopping to lift a leg and pee into the produce bin where the cantaloupes would've been if the market were open. When he finished, the mutt glanced over at us with what, if I hadn't known better, I'd have sworn was a grin before trotting off up the hill. I watched him go while my mother explained the rest of it—how we were going to have to stay open later, maybe until ten or eleven at night, and after church on Sundays.

"I ain't afraid of hard work, Tessa," he said. "You know that. And Louie here's a darn good worker, too."

"After school only," my mother reiterated, before I could volunteer for greater servitude. "He's got his homework after supper. And only Saturday or Sunday, not both. This child needs to have a childhood."

"I'm not a child," I said.

"Says who?" she asked, smiling at me for the first time in forever. Telling us how everything had to be from now on out seemed to have cheered her up a little.

"Says me," I told her, smiling too, glad we were a family again and that I didn't have to be mad at her anymore.

"I almost forgot," she said, turning back to my father. "I bought you a present." She got up and went inside, returning a moment later with a black handgun, the long barrel of which she pointed at my father, who went pale. "I *should* shoot you for buying that store," she said, suddenly serious again. "You know that, don't you?" Then she flipped the gun in the air, catching it by the barrel and holding it out to my father, who regarded the thing as if it might be rigged to explode if he touched it.

"I don't think nobody's gonna rob us, Tessa," he said weakly.

I stared at the weapon, fascinated by how small the hole was that the bullet would have to squeeze out of.

"That's not what it's for," she told him.

My father and I stared at each other.

"It's an air gun," she explained. "It only shoots pellets."

At that moment, right on cue, the same dog came trotting back down the hill, flanked now by two other mangy curs. They trotted in formation right down the middle of the street, paying no attention when my mother rose from the steps and headed across the intersection to meet them. The lead mutt trotted right up to the same fruit bin, but when he lifted his hind leg this time, there was a muffled pop and he leapt like a circus animal, hanging there in the air, contorted, for a full beat. He returned to the sidewalk no wiser, though, frantically chasing his haunch and growling frightfully, as if whatever had bitten him might still be there with its mouth open. The other two dogs were surprised, but neither seemed to connect this sudden fit of madness to the object my mother held in her hand, now pointed at them. One of them watched curiously as the first continued to growl and chase his tail, then grew bored and lifted his own hind leg, whereupon there was another discrete pop and then there were two dogs dancing and spinning and yelping in front of Ikey Lubin's.

The third dog now regarded my mother and the gun with genuine suspicion. You could almost see the animal's thoughts scrolling slowly across his feeble, conflicted brain. On the one hand there was the very real need to pee, not to mention the deep and abiding habit of doing so in our fruit bin. On the other there was the fear born of recent, albeit secondhand, experience. He looked back and forth between his suddenly lunatic companions and my mother, started to cock his leg, then reconsidered, staring at this woman for a long time before trotting off down the block, checking over his shoulder every so often to see where she was. His companions followed along, deeply resentful at this inexplicable turn of events.

When they were gone, my mother returned to where my father and I sat on the porch regarding her, at least in my case, with new eyes. "Don't let anybody pee on your melons, Lou," she said. "That's my last bit of advice for today."

And with that she went inside.

AFTER DINNER that night we all watched Ed Sullivan together, like the family we used to be. When it was over, my father grew restless and took the transistor radio out on the porch to listen to the country music he favored. After a while we heard him turn the radio off, and then the porch steps groaned under his weight. I went over to the window and peered out through the blinds and saw him pass beneath the streetlamp on the corner, fishing his keys out of his pocket and letting himself into Ikey Lubin's. I waited for the lights to come on and was surprised when they didn't. I could tell my mother knew exactly where he'd gone without having to look.

"What's he doing?" I wondered out loud.

She continued to stare at the television screen. "Just looking at it," she said. "I suspect he's really seeing that store for the first time."

I didn't like her implication that my father didn't really see what was in front of him, and I felt some of my recently surrendered resentment return. I did want to know more about what she was thinking, though. "Will it be okay now? The store?"

"No," she said without hesitating. "It just won't fail as fast."

"I think it'll be a success," I said stubbornly.

"I hope you're right," she said, sounding like she meant it. "He doesn't know what else to do, anyhow, so I guess he'll have to do this."

"You could help," I said.

She looked at me hard, then. "I *am* helping," she said. "You must know that much."

"I mean help him," I said, knowing exactly what she was getting at, "at the store."

"I can't help him, Lou," she said. "I have to help *us*."

"What's the difference?"

"Please don't ask me to explain what you already understand," she said, meeting my eye. I was the one who looked away.

That night, in bed, I heard my father return, and shortly thereafter my parents' voices began to filter up through the heat register. I heard only part of what was said, but enough to know

151

that their conversation meant the end to the worst of their recent conflict. Their new covenant came at a price, though. Above the store was an apartment that Ikey had always rented to the sort of people who, according to my mother, belonged in the West End, people who saw nothing wrong with sitting out on their rickety porch shirtless on hot summer nights, who hung over the railing and hollered down to people who pulled up at the curb below, honking the horns of their ancient, rusted-out Buicks and Pontiacs. The flat was vacant now, unrentable to decent people until we could find the money to make repairs. "I'm not leaving this house, Lou. It was bought with my parents' money. They knew better than to give it to us, but they did anyway. I'm not moving in above that store. Not ever." When my father started to protest that he had no such intention, she stopped him cold. "Don't ever tell me it might be fixed up nice. That living above the store would be more convenient. That we could be happy there. Don't ever do that."

My father, of course, promised he wouldn't.

DIVISION STREET

MY FATHER'S LOSING his dairy job and buying Ikey Lubin's at least resolved the issue of where I'd go to school that fall. When he heard of our intention, Father Gluck paid us a visit and tried to dissuade my parents from taking me out of St. Francis, reminding them that it teetered on the brink and couldn't afford to lose good Catholic students like me. We had, he said, an obligation—to our faith, to the diocese, to the good sisters who taught us. He addressed these remarks to my father, perhaps in the hope that he was the one who required convincing. "*My* only obligation," my mother told him, deftly dispelling that misconception with a single pronoun, "is to this family. St. Francis will have to fend for itself."

"You don't mean that—" Father Gluck began, but my mother cut him off.

"But I do."

The priest, deciding on another tack, turned his attention to me. "You've done well at St. Francis." He was smiling benevolently, but I'd never liked the man, the way his eyes bored into you as if you'd done something wrong, or were about to. "You've been happy there? You like the sisters? Sister Bernadette takes good care of you?"

I allowed that all of this was true. A priest was saying it, so what choice did I have? And I did like Sister Bernadette, though it was also true I'd lately told my mother often that I'd be glad to get out from under her too-watchful eye and I was looking forward to public school. I suppose I might have repeated all of this to Father Gluck but, coward that I was, instead held my tongue.

"And you're feeling better now?"

I glanced over at my mother. Had I been feeling poorly? I saw her eyes narrow dangerously. My father looked as perplexed as I was.

"Those public school boys did a bad thing to you, didn't they?" Father Gluck said, his smile even more empathetic now, as if the incident at the trestle had been on his mind more or less constantly since it happened.

"Don't you dare try to frighten him," my mother said, her hands starting to tremble.

The priest regarded me for a beat before turning back to my mother, a pause apparently intended to suggest that he was unused to taking orders, particularly from a woman. If so, he must have been even more surprised when another command came right on its heels.

"And don't try to frighten me."

"Tessa," the priest said, now showing *her* his benevolent smile. "I'm not the enemy."

When my mother looked away, unable to meet his eye, I suddenly felt ill. She'd begged my father to call the rectory and tell Father Gluck not to come, after he'd cornered my father at Mass on Sunday—my mother staying home to nurse a cold—and explained that he wanted to discuss my leaving St. Francis with all three of us. "Tell a priest he can't come?" my father had said. "How am I gonna do that, Tessa?"

"Okay, fine," she conceded. "But I swear to God you better not take his side." So far my father hadn't said a word, but she now seemed to realize she was on her own, the poor woman. Raised Catholic, she had no reason except perhaps her own rebellious nature to believe she could do battle with a priest and win. I could see she was lost, an apology forming on her lips, when Father Gluck made an unexpected and welcome mistake. "We both want what's best for Luce—" he said.

I saw my mother stiffen. The man had started to call me by my nickname. Was it my imagination, or did the blood drain out of his face when he realized what he'd done?

"I have a small discretionary fund for emergencies . . . ," he went on, trying valiantly to regroup. "I'm sure we can find some compromise."

But my mother had risen to her feet. She crossed the room, took the priest's half-full coffee cup and stood looking down at him. She was trembling all over now, whether in rage or fear or a combination of the two I couldn't tell. I saw my father's jaw drop, and I suspect mine did as well.

When my mother spoke, though, her voice was surprisingly steady. "The compromise is this: we will continue to attend Mass on Sundays and drop the envelope we can no longer afford onto your collection plate. Unless you'd prefer we didn't."

Father Gluck turned back to my father, who made the mistake of looking up at that moment, and the two of them shared a look of devout commiseration.

"The compromise," my mother continued, "is that from time to time your housekeeper will stop at our store and buy a quart of milk." Then she went over to the front door, opened it and pointed across at Ikey Lubin's. "We're located on the same street as Tommy Flynn, so she shouldn't have any trouble finding us."

"Tessa," Father Gluck replied, reluctantly getting to his feet. "I'm disappointed—"

"Join the club," my mother told him. "We're disappointed, too. My husband was disappointed to lose his job. When we were living in Berman Court and *Lou* wanted to be an altar boy and you didn't select a single one from the West End, *he* was disappointed. As for my own disappointments, don't even get me started."

It took my mother about twenty minutes to stop shaking after Father Gluck had left. She paced back and forth between the kitchen and living room like a caged animal, stopping, opening

155

her mouth to speak, then closing it and pacing again. My father remained seated during that whole time as if he didn't trust his legs to support him just yet. "Don't look at me like that," my mother finally said, then shot a look at me. "You either."

"I ain't sayin' you were wrong," my father conceded. "It ain't that. It's just . . . he was offerin'—"

"A loan. It was a loan he was offering, Lou. We'd have had to pay it back. With interest, if I know him."

"I ain't sayin'—"

"He's lucky I didn't go get that gun."

At this my father's eyes widened, and he looked over at me as if I might confirm what he thought he'd heard her say. Who was this person who looked so much like his wife but was acting like a crazy woman? A few days earlier, when my mother had produced that pellet gun and calmly shot those dogs with it, he couldn't have been more astonished. Well, now it turned out that wasn't quite true. Here was that same crazy woman—an impostor, surely—expressing regret that she'd missed a golden opportunity to shoot a priest.

She took pity on him then, which would've been good except this meant it was my turn. "Laugh" was her suggestion to me.

I must have looked as confused as my father, because she looked up at the ceiling and muttered "Dear God" before fixing me again. "That's what you do when something's funny; you laugh."

It took me a moment to realize what she meant. The idea of seeing Father Gluck leap in the air like that dog had, with a cold steel pellet chewing on his big fanny, *was* funny, I had to admit, and part of me *did* want to laugh. It was a small part, though, and the bigger part was still too scared.

JUNIOR HIGH was where the lives of both West and East End kids began to merge with those of Borough kids. The school itself was located on Division Street, which ran perpendicular to

Hudson, our main commercial thoroughfare. The irony that it should represent the border between west and east in our asymmetrical town didn't strike me until I was an adult, but even then I knew that Division Street was real and to cross it meant something. The eight square blocks of downtown Thomaston were themselves considered neither one nor the other, but most businesses there, regardless of which side of Division they were located on, catered to either an East or West End clientele. (Borough residents tended not to shop in Thomaston at all but rather "down the line," as everyone referred to Albany and Schenectady.) We had two of everything. Two jewelry stores: a cheap one for West Enders, a slightly more upscale store for us. East End women like my mother generally shopped at Cheryl Lynn's House of Fashion, whereas West Enders had Elsa's Dress Shop. For men's and boys' there was Calloway's, which displayed in its window a tiny sign advertising the Botany 500 line my grandfather had always favored. My father hated to spend money on clothes and often snuck into Foreman's, the cheaper West End store, then told my mother he bought the shirt or pants in question at Calloway's, but she always knew better. That she could tell where he'd bought something after he'd removed the tags and thrown away the bags was akin to knowing which thimble the pill was under in a street scam. It was just the damnedest thing.

Thomaston's bars were similarly segregated. East End neighborhood bars, called taverns, were the sort of places where men met after softball games, where a woman could safely go with her husband, where even kids were welcome with their parents before sundown. You could order a hamburger at the bar, along with inexpensive tap beer, and on weekends a cold-cuts-and-potato-salad buffet was provided at no charge on long folding tables. The free food sometimes attracted shabby, hungry-looking West Enders who were generally received coolly, the bartender idly asking how things were "back home."

West End bars were rougher—gin mills, people called them—

and most of them were located down in the Gut, which was also
home to the pool hall and two pawnshops, both of which called
themselves music stores, an illusion fostered by the scarred
electric guitars as well as the odd accordion or trombone set up
in the front window. Into these gin mills West End women often
went unattended. At the diner I once overheard my uncle Dec,
one of the few men equally at home on both sides of Division
Street, talking about the previous Saturday night at a West End
dive, when a woman named Gina—odd how memory works, her
name racing back to me across five decades—entered, pulled her
blouse off over her head and spent the remainder of the night
with her bare breasts resting on the bar. Of course I immediately
pictured the woman who'd opened the trunk and peered in at me
that night so long ago, her naked breasts huge and pendulous.

"Yeah, you never know what's going to happen across
Division," Uncle Dec concluded, chuckling appreciatively when
the other men finally quit trying to get him to admit he was
exaggerating. "In her bra, you mean," one said in a last attempt.
No, Uncle Dec insisted, he could tell the difference between tits
in a bra and tits not in a bra, and these were the latter. So the rest
of them then lapsed into sullen regret at not having witnessed so
stunning an event.

It wasn't the Berlin Wall, of course. West End families that
had prospered, like ours, moved across Division into new and
better lives, just as families in reduced circumstances sometimes
found themselves slipping in the opposite direction. Most
families had cousins, aunts and uncles on both sides of Division,
but visiting them *was* like traveling to another town, even
another country, with its own set of customs. Naturally, such
separateness occasioned fear and mistrust, yet just as often
yearning. Take, for instance, the dime stores. We East Enders
had Woolworth's, which had wide aisles and bright, fluorescent
lighting as well as a lunch counter that specialized in toasted-
cheese and tuna-salad sandwiches and canned tomato and
chicken-noodle soup. Woolworth's catered to downtown shop

clerks who wore neatly pressed short-sleeved white shirts regardless of the weather and would leave the waitress a quarter or thirty-five cents under their plates. One of the front windows was always devoted to expensive toys, and here West End kids would congregate, pressing their runny noses up against the glass until their parents hustled them down the block to J.J. Newberry's.

This, the West End dime store, both attracted and frightened me. It was full of cheap plastic toys whose ruptured packaging was held together by Scotch tape. Newberry's aisles were narrow and crowded, its bins of tacky, exotic merchandise lit, at least in my memory, by little more than the light from the street outside. Most of the stuff I was attracted to there—lurid magazines like *Weird Tales* and motorcycle caps like the one Marlon Brando wore in the movie poster of *The Wild One*—was for sale at Newberry's and nowhere else. The whole store was permeated by the smell of the popcorn that cranked more or less constantly out of a stained, cloudy, antiquated machine near the front door, each kernel of exploded corn as bright yellow as a rabid dog's eyes. It didn't just look yellow, it *tasted* yellow. Needless to say, it was delicious, the reason being, according to local legend, that the machine was never cleaned, its oil never changed. When my mother and I passed Newberry's, she'd wrinkle her nose and say, "Lord, that *smell*." Little did she know how I yearned for the day I'd be old enough to go inside on my own and spend hours investigating its dark, delicious mysteries. Even then I seemed to know that all this would begin to happen in junior high.

So it was in seventh grade that all but the most sheltered of us began to share space and air with kids outside our own neighborhoods. Monday through Friday, from eight in the morning until three in the afternoon, kids from all over mingled in the halls—if not the classes—of the junior high on upper Division, but this was just the beginning of a new kind of social commerce that took place on weekends. Saturday afternoons, for instance, we all came together, trailing customs and baggage we were scarcely aware of, at the Bijou Theater. We East End kids would buy popcorn at Newberry's, and oddly enough the theater's management didn't seem to mind. Their own popcorn, in addition to being expensive, was fluffy and albino white, tasting of air. It was a point of pride among East End and Borough kids that we purchased our Sno-Caps, Jujubes and soda (no ice, we insisted) at the theater's concession stand, whereas West End kids filled their pants pockets with stale, off-brand candy stolen as often as purchased from Newberry's and generally went thirsty. Just from the detritus we left beneath the seats, the truth of those Saturday matinees would've been plain as day—that West End kids congregated on the left-hand side of the theater, we East Enders and Borough kids on the right. But the sticky floor would also have revealed another truth, because among the West End candy wrappers, there would be the odd Sno-Caps box, the shoe-flattened Jujube. We knew it was happening. As soon as the lights went down in the theater, shadows began to move stealthily along the bottom of the screen, left toward right, right toward left. And when the lights came up again, nervous new constellations had formed, though they held together only inside. Once we were out in the late-afternoon light, the separation would occur again, beads of oil scurrying on water.

If West End kids had to cross Division Street on Saturday afternoons to go to the movies, East Enders crossed it every Friday night to attend the junior high dances at the old YMCA on the edge of the Gut. The dances started at seven, by which time, on payday, the nearby gin mills were already revving up, and when their doors swung open, we heard the raucous revelry. By nine o'clock, when the dance let out, dark men would emerge from the bars—sometimes Uncle Dec among them—to leer at the more mature girls, West Enders mostly, since East End parents waited for their daughters in the parking lot of the Y rather than let them parade past the gin mills on their walk home.

Everything about these Friday night dances was dramatic.

Everyone was there. Not the black kids from the Hill, of course, but those of us with social currency to spend, a little or a lot (even we ourselves didn't know how much, though we were learning). Since the doors stayed shut until seven sharp, we were forced to mill about outside in the cold. In my memory, it's always winter, though dances were held throughout the school year. Inside, up on the third floor it was sweltering, the old gym packed to capacity with hundreds of jitterbugging twelve- and thirteen-year-olds. Nothing in my previous experience of life in Thomaston so completely subverted the social order as those dances at the Y, and it was this very subversion that was at once so thrilling and terrifying. As we gathered outside waiting for the doors to open—Borough kids with other Borough kids, with the East Enders and West Enders composing their own circles— the same social rules that governed the school lunch table still applied. But there was also an electricity, a sense that once the doors opened and we clambered up those six dark flights of stairs, the air redolent of nearby locker rooms and chlorine from the basement pool, anything could happen, that our strict conventions were about to be suspended. Inside, we were in a new world that resembled the old one, perhaps even paralleled it, but was also thrillingly, dangerously off-kilter. There were secrets to be learned, and it was here that we would learn them.

The terrible anticipation began on the stairs when, if someone tripped or an adult appeared on the first landing in an attempt to slow the throng surging upward like water through the damaged hull of a ship, the stairway would jam, desire and anxiety and unbearable hope momentarily thwarted, delaying by eternities our emergence into the gym, into Mystery itself, where the music—we could *hear* it there in the stairwell—had already begun to play. Once, stalled in this fashion, I happened to look at the girl next to me, and when our eyes met, I saw that hers were full of tears. Possibly she was simply afraid of being crushed. She'd been separated from her friends, and though we couldn't move forward, those below continued to press upward, causing

RICHARD RUSSO

everyone in the stairwell, our feet locked in place, to lean forward, our hands pressing for balance into the backs of those on the next-higher step. In a matter of moments we were stacked there like semitoppled dominoes.

That's one explanation. But I recognized this girl as a fellow East Ender and think now that her eyes had simply filled with pent-up anticipation. She was imagining her friends already upstairs, dancing without her, getting so far ahead that she'd never catch up. By the time she joined them, the boy she'd been thinking about all week, whose eyes she'd met across the crowded cafeteria, who was too popular—admit it—to be a realistic aspiration, would already be taken. We shared, all of us, a powerful sense that what was at stake on those crowded stairs was nothing less than the rest of our lives, that our every move in that gymnasium had an unimaginable significance, that we were being watched, judged, elected or damned. Slow down, we were being told at home and at school, you've got your whole lives ahead of you. But to get stalled in that stairwell was to understand how little time there was, and how fast it was wasting.

WHAT I MOST looked forward to about junior high was seeing Bobby Marconi again. Since homerooms were assigned alphabetically, there was a good chance Lynch and Marconi would be together. After the Marconis had moved to the Borough, I'd come to accept how unlikely it was Bobby and I would ever again be best friends. Mr. Marconi had probably made him promise that wouldn't happen, and my mother had warned me about getting my hopes up, but I did dare to hope that we might share the same lunch period and that I'd be welcome at the cafeteria table where he sat with his new friends. Being both shy and a Catholic school boy, I feared being friendless in a new, hostile environment.

Even armed with such scaled-down expectations, I was

162

destined to be disappointed. That first day of school, Mr. Melvin, our homeroom teacher, called Bobby's name and made a notation in his attendance book when no one responded. Was he ill? Would he be here tomorrow? Two West End girls I knew exchanged a look, though I wasn't able to decipher what it might mean. Maybe it had something to do with Mrs. Marconi. I was pretty sure my mother had kept in touch with her former friend because sometimes at night I heard her name come up through the heat register when I was supposed to be asleep. I was able to piece together that she'd gotten pregnant again, and Bobby had yet another little brother. And right before the baby was born, she'd apparently gone off on another unexpected trip, though it was possible I'd misheard this last part. I was always hearing fragments of my parents' conversations, but then the heat would come on and I'd have to fill in the blanks in the phrase, the sentence, the story. So it was possible my mother was just recalling Mrs. Marconi's previous visit to the sister whose very existence my mother had doubted. I distinctly remember hearing "turned up in Canada this time," but by then my parents may have been talking about somebody else. I'd grilled my mother on the subject of Mrs. Marconi more than once. Had she visited her old friend at her new house in the Borough? No. Did they talk regularly on the phone? No. Was there any news about Bobby? No. It galled me that she should be able to stay in touch with Mrs. Marconi when Bobby was off limits to me. Junior high, I hoped, would change all that.

Every day that week Bobby Marconi's name was called, and every day Mr. Melvin marked him absent on his attendance sheet. Finally, on Friday, Perry Kozlowski, who always lounged in the back row, looking bored, with his feet up on the desk in front of him, groaned audibly and said, "He's gone." Mr. Melvin seemed to have already concluded from Perry's slouch and dramatic boredom that he was to be neither trusted nor encouraged. Earlier in the week, when my own name had been read in homeroom, Perry had called out, "He likes to be called

Lucy," causing everyone to laugh, as expected. "Then *he* can tell me," the teacher said. "Or maybe you'd enjoy having him give you a nickname?" To which Perry had just shrugged. "He could try."

Mr. Melvin now regarded the boy with undisguised loathing. "And how would *you* know?" Meaning, probably, that Bobby and his family lived in the Borough, whereas Perry was a West End kid.

"Everybody knows," Perry replied, but did not elaborate.

I'd immediately swiveled around in my seat. Gone where? Had the Marconis moved again? Suddenly I could feel the blood pounding in my temples. I tried telling myself that Mr. Melvin was right. How would a boy like Perry Kozlowski know anything about Bobby Marconi? But I could tell by the smug look on his face that he *did* know something.

Halfway between us sat a thin Negro boy whose name— Gabriel Mock—was called next, and our eyes met briefly. Was it possible that even he knew where Bobby was? At the end of homeroom period we emerged into the corridor at the same moment, and I blurted out my question even before saying hello. Did he know where Bobby Marconi had gone? The look he gave me suggested I'd violated some rule by speaking to him, and I felt myself flush. "People call you Three, right?" I said, and I was about to explain how I, a white boy, happened to know his nickname, that I'd spent many a pleasant hour with his father, out at Whitcombe Park, when, looking straight ahead, Gabriel Mock the Third said, "I don't have a father."

MY PARENTS CLAIMED not to know anything either, and after interrogating both of them all that weekend I was convinced they were telling the truth. The following Monday, when roll was taken and Bobby's name wasn't called, I worked up the necessary courage to approach Perry Kozlowski and ask what he'd meant about Bobby being gone.

"You didn't hear?" he said, contemptuous of my ignorance. "You live where—in a cave?" Bobby, he told me, had been sent downstate to the Payne Academy, a military school known locally as the House of Payne. It was rumored to be worse than reform school.

"Why?" I said, instantly frightened for my old friend.

"You're telling me you didn't hear about the fight? Him and Jerzy?"

Having no public school friends was the equivalent of living in a cave, so of course I hadn't. I was to discover over the next few days that everyone else knew all about the fistfight between Bobby and Jerzy Quinn, an event so dramatic, so heroic, that its inevitable conversion from fact to legend was well under way. The details varied according to the teller, but its skeleton was pretty much the same as what Perry Kozlowski reported that day. The fight had taken place, amazingly, right outside the police station, with two uniformed cops looking on. What had occasioned the hostilities? Well, that was part of the story's romance, because there apparently *was* no reason. Every witness agreed that there'd been no preliminaries, no swapping of insults, no goading, no shoving, no gradual escalation, all of which were the traditional prelude to a Thomaston fistfight. But given how the two boys had come up to each other in the street, you'd have imagined they meant to shake hands. Instead, as if someone had said go, they'd simultaneously thrown punches, though neither landed flush. Within minutes a large, enthusiastic crowd had gathered, West End kids egging Jerzy Quinn on, East Enders and Borough kids cheering Bobby. Hearing the commotion, other cops came out of the station, and that normally would have brought the hostilities to a halt, yet not on this occasion.

How long the sidewalk battle raged—two minutes? ten? half an hour?—depended on who you talked to. But this was to be expected. Most of the kids recounting the story hadn't actually been there, though all claimed to have borne firsthand witness.

In the days following the fight other scuffles had broken out when some East End kid, in the throes of an enthusiastic rendering of the event, would be interrupted by a West Ender saying, "You weren't even there." No one wanted to admit to having missed so seminal an event. On another point, however, there was universal agreement, and that was the amount of blood spilled: *a lot*. Fights between junior high boys were fairly common after the Friday night dances at the Y and Saturday matinees at the Bijou, but rarely was blood actually drawn, and a fat lip or swollen eye was generally considered sufficient justification for calling it quits. Yet everyone who described the epic battle between Bobby and Jerzy Quinn agreed that by the time it was over, both boys—their faces, fists and shirtfronts— were a bloody mess. So much blood was on the sidewalk that it had to be fire-hosed off.

Young and inexperienced as I was, I didn't understand that the facts everybody agrees about, especially if they're lurid, are generally the most suspect. Hearing such details—a fire hose!— confirmed from one teller to the next convinced me they must be true. Nor did I understand how valuable I was as a listener, that a story is like a virus that can rage only for as long as there are new hosts to infect. The fight between Bobby Marconi and Jerzy Quinn, though drenched in glory, had about played itself out when school began. When it became known that there was a junior high boy who actually *hadn't* heard about it, I became the beneficiary of an unexpected day's worth of popularity. Here was a new receptacle, someone who could be *told*.

In addition to the blood, tellers of the tale, West and East Enders alike, agreed on one other fact. *Bobby Marconi had won*. This took my breath away. I wasn't surprised to learn that my old friend was a tough and willing combatant. After all, the reason his parents had once enrolled him in St. Francis was that he kept getting into fights. And I had good reason to recall his tolerance for pain. But while Bobby *could* fight, his opponent *was* a fighter. In the years since Cayoga Elementary Jerzy Quinn's reputation in this regard had only grown. He'd actually spent a year in reform school, where it was rumored he'd killed a boy in a knife fight. Gullible as I was, even I doubted this could be true, but that such a rumor would circulate about a boy was enough to give one pause.

And then there was his appearance. At thirteen, Jerzy was stick thin, so lean in fact that you could see his ribs through his T-shirt. Though he'd been held back and was nearly two years older than the rest of us, his height was about average, and his hungry, undernourished look might under different circumstances have made him the sort of boy who would be culled from the herd and made a victim of predators. Not so Jerzy. Even Perry Kozlowski, who was much bigger and always spoiling for a fight, wanted no part of him, and we all knew why. You had only to look at Jerzy to know that here was a kid with nothing to lose, and that was what made him so lethal. From adults—his teachers in particular—he'd learned that he had no future, a judgment he seemed to embrace wholeheartedly. His wolfish grin acknowledged as much, and you didn't want to see it directed toward you. That Bobby should have willingly fought him defied imagination. That he'd won defied reason.

But somehow he had. By all accounts they'd fought savagely—punching, kicking, some even said biting—like dogs trained for no other purpose, until fatigue and pain made it impossible to continue, yet continue they did, more slowly, perhaps, but with the same steadfast resolve to do each other lasting harm, until Jerzy finally lay flat on his back, his eyes glazed over, no longer completely present. Bobby, on top of him now, used his knees to pin his arms to the sidewalk and continued to pummel him. At this stage, the story went, Jerzy was no longer struggling, though his wolfish grin seemed to say *Don't stop now.* Eventually Bobby became so exhausted punching him with his right hand that he'd had to switch to his left. (With respect to this last detail I actually happened to know something even eyewitnesses couldn't have— that he must've reinjured the wrist he'd broken in my father's milk truck.) At any rate, one of the cops finally came over and lifted him off Jerzy's chest and said, "That's enough now. What're you trying to do, kill him?"

Apparently, Bobby'd had just enough strength left to answer that yes he was.

ODD, HOW OUR VIEW of human destiny changes over the course of a lifetime. In youth we believe what the young believe, that life is all choice. We stand before a hundred doors, choose to enter one, where we're faced with a hundred more and then choose again. We choose not just what we'll do, but who we'll be. Perhaps the sound of all those doors swinging shut behind us each time we select this one or that one should trouble us, but it doesn't. Nor does the fact that the doors often are identical and even lead in some cases to the exact same place. Occasionally a door is locked, but no matter, since so many others remain available. The distinct possibility that choice itself may be an illusion is something we disregard, because we're curious to know what's behind that next door, the one we hope will lead us to the very heart of the mystery. Even in the face of mounting evidence to the contrary we remain confident that when we emerge, with all our choosing done, we'll have found not just our true destination but also its meaning. The young see life this way, front to back, their eyes to the telescope that anxiously scans the infinite sky and its myriad possibilities. Religion, seducing us with free will while warning us of our responsibility, reinforces youth's need to see itself at the dramatic center, saying yes to this and no to that, against the backdrop of a great moral reckoning.

But at some point all of that changes. Doubt, born of disappointment and repetition, replaces curiosity. In our weariness we begin to sense the truth, that more doors have closed behind than remain ahead, and for the first time we're tempted to swing the telescope around and peer at the world through the wrong end—though who can say it's wrong? How different things look then! Larger patterns emerge, individual decisions receding into insignificance. To see a life back to front, as everyone begins to do in middle age, is to strip it of its mystery and wrap it in inevitability, drama's enemy. Or so it sometimes seems to me, Louis Charles Lynch. The man I've become, the life I've lived, what are these but dominoes that fall not as I would have them but simply as they must?

And yet not all mystery is lost, nor all meaning. Regardless of our vantage point, some events manage to retain their drama and significance. Bobby Marconi's epic battle with Jerzy Quinn seems to me just such an event. Picturing Bobby atop his adversary, punching him with every ounce of his remaining strength, yes, trying to kill the other boy, I'm filled with wonder. Who could have guessed that one day this same boy would become the most famous man to hail from Thomaston, New York, even more so than Sir Thomas Whitcombe himself? I can't help thinking that somehow Bobby actually managed to do what we all imagine we might back when we're young, before time and repetition erode and render mundane the mystery of existence. Bobby alone, it seems to me, invented both a life and a self to live it.

OBITUARY

"It's not a great couch," Noonan conceded when they arrived on the third floor of his place on the Giudecca. Lichtner was staring at the sofa gloomily as if he'd independently arrived at the same conclusion. "I'll get you a pillow and blanket."

When he returned, Lichtner was standing in his socks in front of the easel. Yet again the cloth had been thrown back. "It looks just like you," he offered.

"Thanks," Noonan said. "I think so, too."

Lichtner flopped onto the sofa, clearly disappointed that his insult, after landing flush, hadn't any discernible effect.

"I should warn you. I sometimes have night terrors."

Lichtner blanched. "You what?"

"That's how Evangeline got the black eye. Trying to get me to calm down. Which doesn't work."

Lichtner looked genuinely terrified. "What should I do?"

"Run like hell."

"Tell me something," he said when Noonan reached the stair. "Do you love her?"

"No," Noonan answered far too quickly, but the question had surprised him. "Do you?" When Lichtner just stared at him, he said, "You don't have to answer tonight. Sleep on it and tell me in the morning."

"I don't ever have to tell you."

"Get some sleep."

Downstairs, getting undressed, he glanced at the fat Columbia University envelope, thinking maybe he'd read through the

170

material again as a sleep aid, but he managed to knock it down between his bed and nightstand. Retrieving it, he found another piece of mail—unopened by the look of it—had fallen into the same narrow space. Its return address immediately made him wish he'd left the envelope where it was: 37 Elm Street, Thomaston, New York, USA. It had arrived a couple weeks earlier, maybe a month, and there'd been no need to open it, at least not right away, because all Lucy letters were alike. Invariably occasioned by either death or fatal diagnosis, it would contain an obituary from the local newspaper and a handwritten note that could be summarized in a single word: remember? Often that was the very first word. *Remember Scooter Walsh? Third Avenue? Well, his daughter has cystic fibrosis, and they don't have any medical insurance, so anything you could do . . . I know you're like me when it comes to kids, so . . .* Always there was that implied intimacy, as if he and Noonan had remained best friends down through the long years, sharing the same bedrock values. *Lou,* Noonan remembered replying to that one, *whatever gave you the idea I like kids?* He'd sent a check nonetheless, but just as often he refused. Once, many years ago, Lucy had written as chair of the committee raising funds to restore Whitcombe Hall: *Bobby, I know you haven't been back home since senior year, but Sarah and I hope you can help out. It's our history. Who will care if we don't?* Noonan had written back, *No one, I hope. I know I sure don't. Love to Sarah.* Apparently he hadn't been offended, as Noonan had half hoped he might be, because the appeals kept coming, at least one a year, usually on behalf of someone Noonan didn't remember, though the old, faded school photos Lucy often enclosed sometimes jogged the faintest of recollections.

He held the not-entirely-opaque envelope up to the light, shook it and saw a small square dislodge itself from the folded, lined notepaper inside: a school photo. There also appeared to be a narrow column of newsprint, the obligatory obit. But Noonan also noticed something that had escaped his attention back when the envelope arrived. The small neat hand that had addressed it was Sarah's, not Lucy's, and a guilty chill ran up his spine. Had something happened to Lucy? Noonan felt something very like fear at the idea that his boyhood friend—fussbudget and general pain in the ass that he'd become—had left this earth, that the photo contained in the envelope might be of him. Fortunately, an instant's reflection suggested how unlikely this was. Sarah would have contacted him immediately. No, the envelope might have been addressed by Sarah, but its contents were pure Lucy.

Tearing it open, he saw not one but two yearbook photos. He didn't expect to recognize their subject but immediately did: Jerzy Quinn. According to the obit, sixty-two-year-old Jerzy had been drunk when he crossed the median and hit the other vehicle head-on. For a moment, as Noonan read the lurid details, he was no longer in Italy, a grown man, but a boy in Thomaston, New York, kneeling on Jerzy's shoulders and punching him in the face, with his fist dangling from a broken wrist. That fight had been the first time he'd ever lost control of himself so completely, and he remembered marveling afterward at the intense feeling of liberation. It was as if he'd temporarily become another person. Only when he finally returned to his own body and his right mind did he realize he'd rebroken his wrist, the one he'd snapped like a twig in Lucy's father's milk truck. Now, halfway around the world, it was throbbing again with pain delayed a good fifty years. Massaging it, he read Lucy's note: *Remember the footbridge? Remember how I never had to pay when I was with you?* For Lucy, remarkably short. Usually there were a good dozen things he wondered if Noonan remembered.

He returned to the photos, examining them more carefully now. In the first, nine-year-old Jerzy was identified as a third grader at Cayoga Elementary, but he already looked like a kid who regarded the world with deep suspicion. They'd been secret friends back then. Of necessity, all Noonan's friendships had been secret. His father—who now stared out from the canvas upstairs—had been a rigid, angry man whose rigidity derived from military discipline, his anger from not having seen combat, or at least that's what Noonan now supposed. Arriving in Europe after the end of the Second World War, he'd been stationed in Germany for a year, most of it spent behind a desk. When he finished his hitch, he had no real choice but to return home to Deb Noonan, the East End girl he'd knocked up before he learned self-control. She'd been living with her parents while he was overseas, and by the time he returned she barely recognized him as the easy, charming fellow who'd talked her into bed. Grim and unyielding, he explained the discipline he now practiced in all things. It demanded that they be strict about both time and money, and he informed her as well about his newfound belief that sex between husband and wife was about procreation, not pleasure. He was severe with himself, with her, with the little boy who'd arrived in his absence. He was particularly vigilant in the matter of his son's friends. Jews, Negroes, Poles, Slavs and the Irish were all unsuitable. In his view they occupied the lowest rungs of society for a reason. Truth be told, he didn't have much use for Italians and Catholics either, though to his shame he was both.

The Quinns, who lived in an unpainted ruin of a house on lower Division Street, couldn't have been more Irish, of course. Their only talent seemed to be producing feral children they couldn't afford, one right after the other. Jerzy's father was a good-natured if maudlin drunk who was always getting tossed out of bars, not for fighting, like so many other denizens of the Gut (a term he'd forgotten until Lucy used it in one of his letters), but rather for singing. Early in the evening someone would suggest he give them a tune, and he'd oblige, then someone else would buy him a drink, which always made him feel like singing another. Before long people would be heckling him to shut the hell up, but by then he'd hit his stride and was convinced the majority wished him to continue. To ensure he could be heard above the din, he liked to stand on the bar and seemed never to recollect that climbing up there invariably resulted in his ouster, often rude and violent, from the premises. He usually arrived back home after the bars closed, sporting a fat lip, his chin scraped and oozing from a hard landing on the sidewalk, all the song gone out of him and in its place a heartbroken self-awareness. Waking his wife, he'd hand her a dull paring knife from the kitchen drawer and say, "Put me out of my misery, Peg. You and the kids will be better off without me." Which of course was true, but the woman apparently was susceptible to bathos because she invariably disarmed him and led him to bed, evidently with an eye toward filling the whole town, or at least the West End, with little Quinns.

The second photo, from junior high, looked to Noonan like an early Polaroid, the sort included in the yearbook only if its subject had skipped school both on the day the official photos were taken and when the reshoots were done. By now a transformation had occurred, the boy's eyes revealing not just suspicion but knowledge of both death and betrayal, and Noonan remembered the horrific story of how the boy's father had died. By then his wife had reluctantly come to share his conclusion that she and her brood were better off without him. He'd been living above the pool hall, but sometimes, when he was drunker than usual, he forgot this and returned home. That particular snowy night the door was locked, and he hadn't been able to raise his wife despite singing a love song directly beneath her bedroom window, which had been known to work, if not recently. However, he did raise a neighbor, who informed him the police had been called, whereupon the elder Quinn slogged around back through the deep snowdrifts to hide from them. When the cops were gone, he put his hand through a pane of glass in the back door, cutting himself badly in the process. When the door continued to resist entry, he apparently sat down on the step to consider his options, of which he was out, though he didn't know it. His wife and children found him sitting right there two days later, frozen solid and covered with snow, when they returned from visiting her parents in North Bath. In that condition the children didn't recognize their father, so their mother, thinking quickly, told them it must be a tramp, a lie they all believed, except for Jerzy. He must've been eleven, maybe twelve. Below the photo, his name was followed by a colon, then a chunk of white space where, presumably, you'd list extracurricular activities—CYO, the debate team, science club. There wasn't a single notation for Jerzy. Rather cruel, Noonan thought, to include that colon.

Their fight that day had been about far more than either of them comprehended at the time. In Jerzy's utter lack of fear and his total disregard for consequence there lurked the frozen "tramp" on the back porch and an understanding of a world in which that sort of thing could happen. No wonder something had hardened in him, causing the boy to navigate the world with red, cynical rage. No wonder he wanted to share it.

But hadn't the same been true of Noonan himself? This was the same summer his own hard education had begun, and he learned the reason for his mother's terrible unhappiness, the West End woman his father visited most days after finishing his mail route and before returning home to the Borough. He later learned that his mother had been aware of this since they'd lived in Berman Court. His father had made no great secret of the affair, nor had he been the least flustered the afternoon he looked out the apartment window in the West End and saw his oldest son sitting on his bike, watching from across the street. At dinner he'd fixed the boy with a dark look and asked what he'd been doing on lower Division Street, a place he had no business being. At that moment Noonan learned several valuable lessons, including the fact that right and wrong were beside the point, what mattered was power. His father's authority derived only from that. Otherwise, why would *Noonan* feel guilty under his gaze? It was his *father* who had no business on lower Division Street, but that simply didn't matter. And he'd also learned, to his utter surprise, that it was possible not to love your own father. To hate him, in fact, with a kind of purity that filled up the void of love's loss and gave purpose to your own life. A hate that gave you the necessary determination and patience to wait for the day when the power shifted, when you were old enough and big enough to usurp it and secure for yourself an authority equal to his own.

The West End woman's apartment was next door to where the Quinns lived, which was how Jerzy had come to know of the affair before he himself did, knowledge Jerzy likely wouldn't have shared until he heard that Bobby had talked his girlfriend— who happened to be Noonan's second cousin—into a game of strip poker. The idea that Noonan had seen his girlfriend's bare breasts, a sight he himself had not yet been treated to, was what their fight had ostensibly been about, but it was really about their fathers, the dead one wished alive, the living one wished dead, with no possibility of either wish being granted.

When the cops brought Noonan home and said he'd been in a fight, the first thing his father wanted to know was who started it. Noonan told him the truth, that he and Jerzy had thrown punches more or less simultaneously, and one of the policemen confirmed that this was what had happened.

"That Quinn boy's two years older than my son," Noonan's father reminded them.

That might be true, they conceded, but the fight had been so savage that they'd had to take the Quinn kid to the hospital.

"How come you didn't take my son to the hospital, too?" He'd noticed what the cops hadn't, that his hand flopped limply at the end of his broken wrist.

"Your boy won. He don't need no hospital."

His father grabbed Noonan's forearm roughly and held it up for their inspection. "A broken wrist doesn't qualify?"

That was the last thing Noonan remembered. He woke up in the hospital alone, with a lump on his forehead and his wrist in a cast. He didn't see either of his parents until they came the next day to take him home. In the car, his father announced that in the fall he'd be attending military school, where he might learn self-discipline. Somewhere his father had heard the fight had been about his second cousin. "What'd you do with her?" he said. Noonan, realizing that he was far angrier about this than about the fight itself, didn't want to answer. His mother was in the car, and he wasn't about to explain about the strip poker with her and his little brothers all piled into the backseat. "Nothing," he said.

"Nothing," his father repeated, nodding at the road ahead, his birthmark pulsing. After a moment he said, "Do you have any idea why God made women? Answer me."

He had no idea what his father was getting at, so he said no, he didn't.

"Then I'll tell you. God made women so we'd know how to go about ruining our lives. You don't believe it, just look at me."

But Noonan refused to. He, too, stared out through the windshield at the road.

"You got something to say, D.C.?" He adjusted the rearview mirror so he could watch her response. "You want to correct me, maybe? You got a different view you'd like to express?"

Noonan turned to look at his mother, and her eyes were full as she shook her head.

His father nodded in disgust. "Look at her," he told Noonan. "Take a good look. You want to end up saddled with something like that? That's your idea of a future?"

He looked down at the cast on his wrist, wishing it were bigger, heavier, and that he could bring it down on his father's head like a club. He wouldn't have cared if his father wrecked the car as a result. If they all died, even his little brothers, that would've been just fine with him.

"I didn't think so," his father concluded.

The last thing Noonan had wanted was to attend military school, but he'd gone willingly enough. The fight with Jerzy Quinn, the fact that he'd become that other person, had frightened him. How was it possible, he wondered, for a person to simply vacate his own body like that and then return to it afterward? Even scarier was his sense that such an ability might be a gift, one he'd have need of again in this life, perhaps often. To look at his father was to be reminded that the fight had exhausted neither his contempt nor his rage. Maybe being sent away from home would be for the best.

And there was another reason. If he went away, he wouldn't have to look—knowing what he knew about the West End woman—at his mother. Because when he'd turned around and looked at her in the backseat, though he didn't want to admit it, even to himself, he'd seen what his father meant.

NOONAN HEARD LICHTNER stirring around upstairs and hoped he wouldn't find an excuse to come down. Evangeline's scent, along with the stale odor of their sex, was still in the room. Only then did it occur to Noonan that perhaps it was a foolish thing to have left him alone in the studio with his canvases. How would he feel if he went up in the morning and found his guest gone, his paintings slashed, his New York show up in smoke? Would he *feel* at all? Tonight, watching Lichtner ricochet among his myriad emotions—rage, indignation, pity, affection, confusion —had been exhausting, but he'd been envious, too. That he himself had felt so little physical pleasure with the other man's wife didn't trouble him as much as that he felt even less emotionally.

Rising, he went barefoot to the base of the stairs to listen. For what, the sound of canvases being ripped to shreds? The muffled sound of weeping? But it was quiet above, suggesting that Lichtner had either fallen asleep or, more likely, was lying awake in the dark, brooding on the mystery of his marriage. Why he wasn't able to fill Evangeline's life to the brim, as he'd once surely hoped to. If he was honest, he was also contemplating why she no longer was sufficient to his own happiness. How had they managed to disappoint each other so? Was his decision to give up writing novels, something he apparently wasn't very good at, to do travel articles, at which he'd succeeded, the beginning of their troubles? Had she seen that as cowardice, a premature admission of defeat? And what of Evangeline herself? How had she disappointed him? By not being as beautiful as when they'd married? Was he *that* shallow? Or was it that she no longer needed him, that her passion now was her struggling gallery? If she could make a success of it, she'd be free of him. Was that what she was working toward so purposefully? Or had something else poisoned their affection, the miasma of Venice itself, too many summers spent breathing in toxic vapors from the canals? Blame, yet again, the water? Noonan found himself wondering what they'd been like as kids, and if what ailed adults could be traced back that far. Lucy, at least to judge from his letters, was the same as the boy he'd been, only more so, and Jerzy Quinn's drifting across that median had the feel of inevitability, the only surprise being that it had taken so long.

After their epic battle Noonan's path had crossed meaningfully with Jerzy's only once, during his senior year in high school. One of his part-time jobs that fall was as Sunday night bartender—the legal drinking age had been eighteen back then—at a West End dive called Murdick's. He'd just given last call when Jerzy sauntered in, his hair slicked wetly back in the same ducktail he'd worn in junior high. He'd dropped out years earlier, as soon as he legally could, and had been working nonunion construction jobs. Noonan occasionally caught sight of him on Division Street, filthy when he got off work, and they usually exchanged cautious hellos. Now he punched in an old Frankie Valli song on the jukebox and slid onto a barstool so gracefully that Noonan suspected it might become his defining adult gesture. He waited a beat before coming down the bar, not long enough to provoke his old adversary, but not exactly jumping to attention either. "How you been, Jerz?" he'd asked, keeping his voice neutral, neither friendly nor hostile, making it clear things could go whatever way the other boy wanted, though neither was exactly a boy anymore.

Jerzy said nothing for a moment, and in that brief silence there'd been an eloquent admission of just how little remained of what had been between them a few short years ago, of who they'd been but weren't anymore. "I'm still here," he said finally, and Noonan drew him the draft beer he asked for, along with a shot of cheap rye whiskey on the side. "How's life in the Borough?"

"I wouldn't know," Noonan said. A few weeks earlier he'd moved out of his father's house and was now living downtown, above the Rexall drugstore on Hudson Street. Dec Lynch, who knew everybody, had arranged with the owner that Noonan could squat there rent-free provided he didn't smoke in the building or have parties or allow vagrants inside. There was neither kitchen nor bathroom, which meant he had to shower at the Y, and he slept on the floor in a sleeping bag.

"Your old man cool with that?"

"I'm doing it. What he's cool with doesn't come into it."

Jerzy nodded, then took a drag off his cigarette. "Seen a couple of your games. Almost made me wish I didn't drop out. You could've used me."

Noonan said, yeah, they probably could, but for the life of him couldn't imagine it. "You'd have had to give those up," he said, indicating the cigarette.

"Fuck that, then," Jerzy said. "So, will you be graduating?"

Noonan admitted he probably would, and wondered if there was a note of wistfulness in this question.

Jerzy downed his shot of whiskey with one gulp. "Then what?"

He decided to be vague. College, maybe, if he got a scholarship. If not, probably enlist, though that would mean Vietnam.

"I tried to enlist," Jerzy said, "but I failed the physical."

He knew he wouldn't, though, and Jerzy seemed to know it, too. He gave Noonan one of his nastier grins. "You're with Nan Beverly now," he said. Not asking him, telling, just in case he tried to deny it. "What's she like?"

"She's a nice girl," Noonan said, no intention of saying anything more. The other boy pushed his beer glass forward for a refill. Noonan thought about saying no. It was past closing, but he poured him another shot of rotgut and refilled his beer. So far Jerzy had made no move toward his wallet.

"I'm married now," he said. "You probably knew that."

Noonan said no, he hadn't heard.

"She's a whore," Jerzy said, matter of fact, then told him her maiden name, which rang a vague bell, but he couldn't summon a face to go with it. "She's fucking somebody else for sure. Like I care," he added.

Noonan didn't know what to say to that.

"We got a little girl, though." Perhaps this was something he *did* care about. "They still talk about us, you know," he said, smiling now. "That fight we had? You hadn't got that first punch in, it would've been different."

"I don't remember much about it," Noonan told him, the absolute truth.

"Would've been different," Jerzy repeated, and for a moment Noonan wondered if he might be considering renewed hostilities. "It definitely would've been different. But you know what? It wouldn't have changed anything. You'd be right where you are, and I'd be right where I am. The shit that matters, you've got no say in."

"You could be right."

"Fuck that, I *am* right." And he downed his second whiskey by way of punctuation.

"Okay," Noonan said, "but I'm going to have to close up when you finish your beer."

Jerzy nodded, conceding this and every other lousy necessity in a world full of them. "Thanks for staying open. It's my birthday."

"I didn't know that," Noonan admitted, wishing him a happy one.

"Thing is, we never should have fought, you and me," he said,

then drained his beer. He still didn't reach for his wallet, and
Noonan guessed he wouldn't. It was, after all, his birthday. "I
never wanted to, really."

"Me neither," Noonan said.

"Hell," Jerzy said, sliding off his stool. "I knew that. Tell me
something, though. You ever see Karen anymore?"

His second cousin, the one he'd beaten at strip poker. Noonan
told him no, that he'd seen her a couple of times on the street
and said hello, but that was it.

"I should hope," Jerzy said. "She's three hundred pounds if
she's an ounce. We'd have to find somebody else to fight over if
we ever decided to go at it again."

Noonan told him he didn't see that happening, and Jerzy said
no, he didn't either, and they shook hands on it, Jerzy's grip
feeling strong in his bad wrist. When the door closed behind
him, Noonan locked it, and he never saw Jerzy again. How long,
he couldn't help wondering, had Jerzy been dead inside before
he finally allowed himself to drift across that median? Thinking
back on that night at Murdick's, Noonan could see that he'd
already been a fatalist, convinced there wasn't a thing you could
do about "the shit that matters." At twenty, the futility of the
struggle had come home to him powerfully. The girl you were
fighting over would weigh three hundred pounds in two or three
years, so what was the point? Which left the long second act
during which nothing changed. Like so many second acts,
Jerzy's seemed unnecessary, especially once you knew the first
and third. Sometimes you didn't even need to know the third.
Face it, Noonan's own second act was dragging a bit. Assuming
he was still *in* it and hadn't drifted, unaware, into his third. His
listless affair with Evangeline Lichtner certainly felt like second-
act stasis. Was it possible, he wondered sleepily, there'd been
more to Jerzy's second act than he knew? Maybe the daughter
he'd seemed fond of had unexpectedly given him a link to a
future he hadn't been able to imagine that night in Murdick's.
Fatalism was difficult to maintain in the presence of a child, so

182

maybe. He hoped so, and he hoped it had been an accident and not that Jerzy steered deliberately into third-act resolution.

Noonan stuffed the obituary and photos and note back into the envelope, wondering again how it had come to be addressed by Sarah when its contents were pure Lucy. A tiny mystery in the context of the larger one he still thought about from time to time—speaking of long, tedious second acts—what Sarah's life must've been like married for over thirty years to such a conventional, cautious man. Sarah, whose spirit at eighteen had yearned, every bit as much as his own, for adventure. Her mother had been a bit of a free spirit, Noonan recalled, and Sarah had admired that wildness, maybe even imagining she was the same way herself, deep down. But in the end she'd opted for stability and reassurance. And who knew? Maybe she was happy. Some people managed to be, despite all manner of ill fortune, just as a great many of the world's fortunates somehow contrived to be miserable. A sensible person, Sarah had probably made her peace early on. Even as a girl she'd been determined to take responsibility for the hand she'd been dealt, despite not having cut the cards, and the dealer a known cheat. Determined, also, to make the best of things, to see the glass as half full when it was three-quarters empty.

Had she married him instead of Lucy, a different sort of peace would have been required, one that would have ensured an even greater misery. True, she'd have been miserable in more interesting places than Thomaston, New York, and she'd have had more of the company that misery is said to love. She probably would've gotten on well with his ex-wives, who still got together every year without fail, like survivors, to wonder what there'd been about him that had attracted them, or any woman. "You're incapable of love," his second wife had once told him. She'd actually said this shortly after they'd finished *making* love, pretty damned successfully, as Noonan recalled, so the remark, not to mention its timing, had surprised him. Would Sarah have arrived at the same conclusion and said the same thing? It was possible, maybe even probable. One thing was for certain. He'd have minded it more, coming from her. On the other hand, maybe she'd have been just what he needed. Maybe she'd have been good for him. Noonan considered this possibility for about two seconds, then dismissed it. The best he had in him came out only as paint on canvas. To imagine a different life was to imagine a different self with which to live it.

Beside the point, in any case. Art, he'd come to believe, was little more than the principle of one thing leading to another, whereas love, insofar as he understood it, depended on a thing remaining forever what it was, which in Noonan's experience it militantly refused to do. What people called love was the perfect recipe for disappointment and recrimination at the benign end of the emotional spectrum, homicide at the malignant end. Like all the other women who'd had the misfortune to swim into his orbit, Sarah would have learned, when he finally betrayed her—when all was said and done, he was his father's son—to find comfort and solace in other men, much as Evangeline had done when she took stock of her marriage and life.

She'd avoided all that by marrying Lucy. Which meant that at least she wouldn't have to worry about things changing. With Lucy, one thing didn't lead to another. He would remain Lucy—steadfast, slow of movement, wit and tongue (precisely where Noonan was quick) and, yes, unfailingly kind. Dull virtues, all, but not nothing, especially to someone as deeply conflicted as Sarah. And what of Lucy's own drama? By the time Noonan had left Thomaston, Lucy, like Jerzy Quinn, had seemed to have arrived at resolution. In Sarah, he seemed to have more than he'd dared to hope for, and his second act was as difficult to imagine as Jerzy's. What was at stake? Where was the suspense?

Yawning, Noonan put the envelope back on the nightstand and turned out the light. A moment later he turned it back on again, aware that he'd solved one minor mystery. The envelope had been addressed in Sarah's hand because, at some point, it had contained a letter from her. It was powder blue, for one thing, and distinctly feminine for another, utterly unlike the sturdy business envelopes Lucy always sent his clipped photos and newsprint in. Had he steamed the letter open, read it, then replaced it with contents more to his liking? Speaking of unknowable second acts.

When Noonan turned off the lamp this time, he left it off, and fell asleep smiling.

LOVE

WHAT HAPPENS when the victor unexpectedly quits the field?

Had Bobby Marconi not been sent to military school, there can be little doubt he would've ruled Thomaston junior high. But his sudden, inexplicable retreat created a vacuum, and the boy who filled it was Jerzy Quinn himself. It didn't seem to matter that he'd been vanquished. Bobby's disappearance had the effect of first undermining, then mitigating and finally expunging his great triumph from the public record. It was a gradual process, of course, an evolution, but by the start of eighth grade, a year after their battle, Jerzy Quinn had carried the day, and Bobby's reputation lay in tatters.

Kids still remembered the fight, of course, and talked about it. Not even West Enders denied that Bobby had won, but there his disappearance was perceived as cowardice. No one said this so openly, at least not while there was a chance he might return, but there were whispers, and no one to contradict them. It didn't seem to matter that Bobby's father had banished him. His absence was all anyone needed to know. Yeah, sure, he'd won the fight, but Jerzy had never said uncle, never given in or admitted defeat. Even as he'd lain on his back on the sidewalk, face bloodied and eyes glazed over, his wolfish grin proclaimed, it was decided, that nothing had been settled. Round one had gone to Bobby Marconi, but so what? Next Friday night after the dance, or when the Bijou matinee let out on Saturday afternoon, Jerzy would have met him again, and this time, well, he could be taken by surprise once, but not twice. Some witnesses belatedly recalled

186

he'd warned that, when Bobby was pulled off him, it wasn't over between them, which explained why Mr. Marconi had sent him away. Probably Bobby had asked his old man to do it. Besides, he hadn't come home the next summer and over Christmas had remained holed up in his parents' house. Why? Because he knew what would happen if he showed his face on the street.

With history carefully revised, Jerzy Quinn's stranglehold on the junior high was even tighter than it would've been had he won the fight. All during seventh grade we East End boys held out hope that Bobby would return to defend his honor and ours, but finally, dispirited, we too saw the lay of the land and sadly began to have our own doubts. Though Bobby had fought heroically, his victory had been a fluke. There was really no other way to look at it.

And Jerzy was, in his own way, beautiful. Most every boy, including many of us East Enders, imitated him. His walk, for instance. He was always up on his toes, and we were forever mimicking the little hitch in his stride. Had our parents allowed it, we would've copied everything about him. Our hair would have been shiny, wet and ducktailed, hanging over our collars. Indeed, many of us left home in the morning with one hairstyle only to arrive at school with another. We'd have worn thin black cotton pants "pegged" tight, and white T-shirts under worn leather jackets like the boys in his West End gang. For us, these were "undershirts," made to be worn beneath the embarrassing plaid or checked shirts our clueless aunts and uncles had given us for Christmas, tucked into baggy, scratchy wool pants that flapped in the breeze, like our fathers' did. We're not raising hoodlums, our parents reminded us. We East Enders were almost glad Bobby was gone, since he looked so much like us.

Jerzy's girlfriend was Karen Cirillo—needless to say, a West Ender. Just as his gang was too cool for the Y dances, he was also too cool for a conventional relationship. Everyone understood that Karen belonged to him, since she wore his ring, as girls did back then, wrapped with masking tape until it fit snugly over her ring finger, but part of Jerzy's mystique derived from the fact that he seldom offered her even the slightest public affection. They were never seen kissing or even holding hands. To the rest of us, this could only mean one thing: they were "going all the way." Other junior high schoolers who "went steady" made a great show of necking in the Bijou, holding hands (strictly prohibited) between classes at school and dancing all the slow dances at the Y, her arms locked around his neck, his joined at her waist, in more of a slow-motion embrace, really.

Karen attended the Y dances with her West End girlfriends, their eyes so darkened by mascara that they looked beaten up, their dark hair helmeted by spray. Where Jerzy was, as I said, thin to the point of emaciation, she was voluptuous and, at twelve, already had the body of a woman, full bosomed beneath the same pale blue angora sweater she wore every Friday night, her voice husky and deeper than most boys', the most beautiful girl in town. Her only serious rival was a blond-haired girl named Nan Beverly from the Borough, whose father owned the tannery. Boys were always fighting over Nan, in the courtyard of the school, outside the Y or behind the theater, often in defense of her honor, after some overheard or imagined slight. Nan was always going steady. By the time we heard she'd broken up with her boyfriend, she'd already replaced him with somebody else. Still, she seemed completely artless, and the word we used to describe her, and girls like her, was "clean."

Nobody fought over Karen Cirillo. She had no honor to protect, for one thing, but more important, nobody dared. She was Jerzy's girl, and at the Y she jitterbugged only with her girlfriends until the much anticipated slow numbers, and then, when her girlfriends moved, one by one onto the dance floor, she stood alone while across the floor a hundred cowardly boys looked on with yearning, imagining, insofar as we were able, what it must be like to be Jerzy Quinn, who sometime later that night, we were certain, would slip his nicotine-stained fingers up under her soft angora sweater.

Jerzy's gang never appeared at these dances until late in the evening. The Cayoga Stream snaked behind the Y, and sometimes we'd catch sight of them down there among the trees where they smoked cigarettes and, according to rumor, drank whiskey. During most of the school year it was dark by seven, so we weren't able to actually see them, but we knew they were there by their eerie, distant laughter and the angry red glow of their cigarette tips. But during the last half hour of those dances, after the person stationed at the top of the stairs closed the cashbox, they began to filter in, cool and casual, as if to suggest they'd forgotten there *was* a dance until that moment. We'd spot one of them across the gymnasium, moving, wraithlike, through the crowd, and when we turned to share this thrilling news with whomever stood next to us, we'd discover that another grinning wraith had materialized at our elbow. *They're here.* You could trace this knowledge surging around the gym like an electric current. I wonder now what we were thinking. Did anybody imagine that this Friday would be different?

Even the music changed, or at least seemed to, becoming darker, more dangerous. There was a line dance the West End boys were famous for, called the stomp, which required a particular beat to execute. Certain records, we knew, were stomp songs, and the opening bars were all it took for Borough and East End jitterbuggers to clear the floor so that the stomp lines, exclusively male, could form. Usually, sometime during the first hour of the dance, whoever was spinning the records would give us East End wannabes such a song so we could practice, in hopes we might later join the line and thereby gain grudging acceptance when the real stompers appeared. But the step was intricate, its moves subject to continual innovation, its orders barked out by someone at the head of the line. If the call came too late it couldn't be carried out, if too early, then the rank broke down.

What the stomp resembled most was a military exercise, its dancers jackbooted in their aggressive precision, each move executed with a deadpan lack of emotion, fifty or a hundred boys all turning to face in a new direction on the downbeat. Turn the wrong way and you'd be facing an advancing army, then the jeering and laughter of the encircling crowd. At the heart of the stomp wasn't courtship, the basis of most dancing, but a tightly controlled rage. Its signature move was always withheld until the last few bars of the sequence, at which point every boy in the line, instead of simply turning on his heel in a new direction, brought that heel down hard on the floor in a thunderclap that shook the gym. There was no mistaking its intent. It was a declaration of war.

The last song of the night, though, was always slow, and the lights always came down, signaling, as if we didn't know, that time and opportunity were slipping away. Karen Cirillo, ever faithful, got her reward then as Jerzy Quinn, ever cool, would touch her elbow and wordlessly lead her onto the floor. Nan Beverly would already be there with whatever Borough boyfriend on whom she'd chosen to bestow her changeable affections. In my memory, if not in reality, the first verse of that last song belonged to these two most public of couples—the Borough pair radiant, laughing and touching discreetly, Nan tossing her blond head, her new boyfriend as happy as a kid can be who knows his days of grace are numbered, and their counterparts silent, nearly motionless, an angry, emaciated boy, drawing to him a seventh-grade girl who was already a woman.

How beautiful they were, both couples, and how beautiful this moment we'd been waiting for all week, the pairing off for that last slow dance. Two couples became four, four became sixteen, sixteen became thirty-two, we East End boys alternately eyeing lusty West End girls on one side of the gym and pristine Borough girls on the other, each group requiring a type of courage we didn't possess. Which was why we ended up asking a girl from down the block, someone we were pretty sure wouldn't say no. And who among us had any idea what was in that East End girl's heart? How many times in the last two hours—or the last two minutes—had *her* heart been broken?

Back outside the Y, the rule of law was quickly reestablished. In the parking lot the parents of Borough and East End girls flashed their headlights or tooted as their daughters emerged. Who was that boy you were with? Nobody. Well, he must be *somebody*. No, nobody. Then, as the cars dispersed, suddenly there'd be a rumor of a fight in the stairwell, and then flight—twenty, fifty, maybe a hundred seventh and eighth graders, roiling up Hudson and across Division Street, on the other side of which lay safety. Were we being chased? No one knew. Nor did anyone want to turn around to find out. Just run and keep running. Make it across Division. They wouldn't dare cross Division, not even Jerzy's gang would be so bold, except sometimes they did, so we kept on running, those West End wraiths in hot pursuit. In reality? In our imaginations? It was simply impossible to know.

Bobby could've told us. But Bobby was gone.

AFTER WE BOUGHT Ikey Lubin's it was a good six months before my father was able to rent the upstairs flat. The old tenants had moved out—skipped in the middle of the night, as my mother put it—before he'd even been able to talk to them about their lease. He told my mother not to worry, they'd get new renters soon enough. His mistake was in allowing her to inspect the premises. Apparently her refusal to set foot in the store didn't apply to the apartment, and my father agreed that she should look it over before they decided how much rent to charge. The expression on her face when she came back down suggested that the Great War over Ikey Lubin's had entered a new phase. "Did you even *go* up there, Lou?" she asked that night over dinner.

Well, yeah, he had, he said, but no, he hadn't really inspected it or nothing. It was the store that mattered, not the upstairs. Sure, he figured it would need a good cleaning. After all, they knew the last several tenants who'd lived there, West End refugees, so yeah, he'd expected it to be dirty. But he had some

191

leftover paint down in the cellar and would use that to brighten the place up.

"Dirty?" my mother said. "Paint? Lou, there's been a fire up there."

This was news to my father, I could tell.

"A fire? Where?"

"In the front room."

"I didn't see no fire."

At this my mother massaged her temples the way she always did when he voiced doubts about something she wanted him to understand. "Tell me, Lou," she said. "Did it strike you as odd that they left that big painting on the wall? They took everything else, including half the fixtures, but that they left. What does this suggest to you?"

"They didn't want it?"

"No, Lou. It suggests you should've looked behind the painting. That's where the electrical fire started, in the wall behind the painting." She allowed this to sink in. "Another thing. Did you raise the toilet lid?"

"No."

"Lucky you."

"What?"

"Two words. Black and full."

My father and I both stopped eating. "I'll go up and flush it," he said.

"I tried that, Lou, but maybe you'll have better luck."

"You're fortunate," the contractor told my mother the next day, after he'd examined the wiring in the wall behind the giant scorch mark. "Fortunate they didn't burn down the whole building."

"That's a matter of opinion," she answered, causing him to knit his brow in puzzlement. I knew exactly what she was getting at. If the former tenants had burned the place down, my father wouldn't have been able to buy it. "What would cause that kind of fire?"

"Off the top of my head, I'd say whoever lived here was tapping into the store's current, getting their electricity for free. Probably did the wiring theirself. Some people, huh?"

They went through the rest of the flat, the man jotting notes in a tiny spiral notepad. When they finished, he did some arithmetic and showed my mother the notepad. Whatever he'd written there shocked her sufficiently to make her sit down on the very commode that had so repulsed her the previous afternoon, whose condition had not materially improved overnight.

"Course that's if you do things right," he admitted. "Union plumbers and electricians." He paused here, as if trying to decide whether to go on. "Makes you wonder about the downstairs, too."

"Dear Lord" was all she could say.

"Well," the man said. "I like you, Tessa, and you've always done a good job on our books, so the inspection's free. You want to hire us, I'll give you every break I can, and you can pay in installments. I wish I had better news for you."

My mother continued to stare at the floor, as if she had X-ray vision and could see right through to the store below, where my father was chatting with the Elite Coffee Club. Finally, the stench emanating from the commode brought her back to reality, and we returned to the front room.

"Wasn't the place inspected when you bought it?"

She shook her head. "Knowing Lou, he probably waived that."

We stood staring at the scorch mark again. "That's what I'd take care of first," he said. "That wiring."

That night my mother found the inspection report in the packet of papers involving the purchase, and sure enough, every single problem they'd listed that afternoon had been duly noted. And as her contractor friend had feared, the wiring throughout the store was judged to be "substandard and potentially hazardous."

"It's why we got the place so cheap, probably," my father said when she finished quoting the concluding paragraph.

"You, Lou," she reminded him. "It's why *you* got the place so cheap."

I couldn't help noticing, though, that both their signatures were affixed to the bottom of the closing statement. My father's handwriting was straight up and down. I had to admit it looked like the writing of a child who was doing all he could do to stay between the lines. My mother's hand was small and graceful, professional in appearance. *Teresa Louise Lynch*, it said, surprising me. Until that moment, I'd had no idea what her middle name was, or even if she had one.

IT TOOK nearly six months to make all the necessary repairs, and I had no idea where my parents found the money. Finally, though, they got new tenants, and they were in the midst of moving in one gray, rainy November afternoon when I got home from school. That morning their possessions had arrived, not in a moving van but in a flotilla of pickup trucks and rusted-out station wagons. These were parked right in front of Ikey Lubin's, making it difficult for my father's customers to dart in and out like they usually did. Nothing was boxed up or organized in any way. It looked to my mother like things had simply been carried out of wherever the renters had been living and tossed into the beds of their vehicles. Some unloading had been done by the time I got home, but several of the trucks were still piled high with furniture and mattresses that had been tied down with old clothesline, this despite the fact that it had been rainy all day. "*The Grapes of Wrath*," my mother muttered, staring out from between the blinds.

The new tenant, Nancy Salvatore, was an old high school friend of hers, and the identically beer-gutted men who owned the curb-parked vehicles were her brothers. They took beer breaks under the sloping second-story roof every half hour, crushing their empty cans and tossing them, or trying to, into the bed of one of the pickups on the street below. They might have started out with pretty good aim, but by midafternoon the street near the truck was littered with flattened beer cans. According to my mother, they'd brought a case along with them, run out before noon and made a trip to the A&P for more, even though my father sold beer.

My mother would've been even madder if she hadn't been up a stump. She didn't usually feel sorry for anybody, but she did for Nancy, who worked at a beauty salon downtown and was having a hard time. She'd been divorced twice, and as a result had given up on marriage, if not men. She was raising her daughter with the help of a series of "uncles," the most recent a deadbeat named Buddy Nurt. It was Buddy, she told my mother, she was hoping to escape by moving into our flat.

My father hadn't wanted to rent to Nancy, who'd lived her whole life in the Gut. To him, it made no sense to spend good money fixing up the place only to turn around and rent to someone who'd have it looking and smelling like a tenement again in short order. My mother had talked him into it, and I could tell she was already regretting doing so.

When I went over to help out at the store, like I always did after school, my father had just about had it with the brothers, who at this pace would still be unloading soggy mattresses this time tomorrow. Leaving me to man the register, he went outside and started picking up the beer cans littering the street. He'd gathered up about half of them when one of the brothers called down from the upstairs porch, "Hey, leave them cans alone."

Apparently they were all drinking different brands of beer and keeping some kind of score, which my father was messing up. How could they figure out who had to pay for the next case? My father stood his ground, reminding the brothers that this wasn't the Gut, that East End people didn't toss empty beer cans into the street, to which the man responded that if this was true, then he was damn glad he didn't live here. But they took no further exception to my father's cleaning up, and half an hour later another brother came down to say they were sorry about how they'd been behaving, and to make amends they'd buy their next case of beer from my father. "How much longer you fellas think you'll be?" he asked.

The man shrugged, as if to say it was hard to predict given this many variables, but when he was gone my father ventured a guess that the job would be done when the beer was gone, along with the money to buy more.

He was wrong, though. The brothers evidently got the message, because they began working with renewed energy, lugging the last of the waterlogged mattresses and furniture up the side staircase. Half an hour later they all thundered back down again, hopped into their vehicles and careened away from the curb, their tires screeching and horns blaring, lobbing more empties at the store and hooting a drunken retreat at the top of their lungs.

MY FATHER HAD TAKEN my mother's advice on running the store, which now stayed open until ten o'clock on weeknights and midnight on Fridays and Saturdays. This meant, in effect, that our family no longer ate meals together. Some evenings, after my mother and I finished, she'd fix a plate for me to take over to my father, and he'd eat it standing up at the register. Other times, after he grew more confident of my abilities, he'd come home to eat in the kitchen while I minded the store. Early evenings were generally slow—it got busy again later—and sometimes during the half hour he allowed himself to be absent, I'd see no business at all.

For instance, the day the brothers moved Nancy Salvatore in upstairs, I had the place to myself. There was plenty of work to do, restocking and tidying the shelves, but my father had instructed me never to leave the register untended, so I usually brought a book along to help pass the time. I've always been the kind of reader who enters a trance, and that evening, when the bell jingled, I came up and out of my book drunkenly, reluctantly, until I saw who it was. She had on the same angora sweater she wore to the Friday night dances, and I caught a whiff of her perfume on the draft from the open door. Karen Cirillo, I thought, and right on the heels of this another thought: Jerzy's girl.

She seemed to take in both the market and me in one deft, appraising glance that suggested she had time to kill and no other choices. Sighing deeply, she came over to the register and picked a *TV Guide* off the rack, riffling its pages quickly and looking disappointed to discover they were mostly full of words. "Hey," she said, as if to the magazine.

When the magazine didn't respond, I said hi, my voice cracking, though she didn't seem to notice. She did look me over again, though, her close attention filling me with pride and fear. Karen Cirillo didn't look at boys twice. It was hard to know whether this was because she wasn't allowed to, being Jerzy's girl, or had no desire to, for the same reason.

"I know you?"

The answer was yes and no. We *were* in the same grade, and we saw each other every day, but there was no particular reason for her to have noticed me. "I'm in seventh, too," I told her. "We aren't in any of the same classes."

"You must be smart," she said, then, "That any good?"

This confused me. Did she want to know if being smart was all it was cracked up to be? Only when she held out her hand did I realize she was asking about the book I was reading, H. Rider Haggard's *She*. I handed it over, and she riffled through the pages with the same efficient lack of interest with which she'd examined the *TV Guide*. "Yeah, pretty good," I said, unable to tamp down my enthusiasm completely. What would she think if she knew I'd mentally cast her in the title role? "It's about this—"

"Don't tell me," she said, handing the book back. "I might read it someday."

197

I wanted to say she really should and to explain why, but realized this would involve telling her all about the book, which she'd just asked me not to do.

She noticed my hesitation. "What," she said, "you think I don't read? I read a lot."

That she cared in the slightest what I thought couldn't have surprised me more. "Like what?" I asked, genuinely thrilled by the possibility that I might have something in common with Karen Cirillo.

She shrugged. "Books," she said, her tone a challenge.

I stifled a laugh, realizing she was serious. "They're good . . . books," I said, inwardly cringing at how stupid this sounded.

"They're okay," she allowed, no longer much interested in pretending to be a reader and seeming to suggest there were other, better things than books that I wouldn't know anything about.

"How about a pack of Parliaments?" she said, nodding at the cigarette counter behind me. Again I hesitated. She wasn't old enough to buy cigarettes any more than I was old enough to sell them, and my father was strict about minors.

"It's okay," she assured me, her tone making it clear that she wouldn't rat me out, that we wouldn't get caught, that so far as she was concerned it was no big deal whether I did or didn't, that she knew plenty of places where she could get cigarettes, that nobody cared if she smoked, that I'd be a dork if I refused. I handed her a pack of Parliaments, and she peeled the ribbon off right there, thumbing the foil top open. "Want one?" When I shook my head no, she put them in her purse. "You don't smoke?"

"Not that often," I said, trying not to sound like the dork we both knew I was.

"You shouldn't," she said, surprising me. "Cigs are expensive. Also bad for your lungs." She touched a place on her sweater under her left breast, where she apparently believed her own lungs were. Why I shouldn't do what she herself did she didn't explain. "So," she said, looking me over yet again, squinting this

198

time, as if I'd managed somehow to go out of focus. "Your name is what?"

"Lou," I said, and then, when she kept squinting at me, I added, "Lynch."

"Nuh-uh," she said, squinting harder. "It's Lucy, right?"

"Right," I admitted, feeling the blood rush to my cheeks.

"How come?" she wondered. "How'd that happen?"

"Louis Charles Lynch," I explained. "In kindergarten, the teacher read my name as Lou C. Lynch."

"That's rough," she admitted, after carefully considering the matter. "You used to be Bobby's friend, right?"

I nodded, proud. Also a little nervous, unsure of what the consequences for such an admission might be if she reported back to her boyfriend. I hoped she'd remember the exact words she'd used—that I "used to be" Bobby Marconi's friend, which was all I'd admitted to. "You know him?"

"He's my second cousin, or some shit like that," she shrugged. "I guess we'll never see him again. Too bad. He was okay."

She was studying me intently now. I took her comment about never seeing him again to be a reference to Jerzy Quinn's threat to kill Bobby if he ever returned to Thomaston, a subject I thought it wise to navigate carefully, though I would've liked to agree with her that it *was* too bad and that Bobby was indeed okay. "They used to live over there," I said, pointing at the Spinnarkle house. But instead of turning around to look, she continued to stare at me, and I could feel myself glowing under her scrutiny. My knees were about to give out when I realized she wasn't looking at me at all, only at some unfocused point in the rear of the store. There seemed to be nothing to do but to continue talking, so I did. "I heard his mom's sick."

"Sick of living in this shithole, you mean." Karen snorted. "She tried running away, but they caught up with her."

That someone should express such an outrageous opinion so casually took my breath away. I'd never known anybody who didn't consider Thomaston a fine place to live. True, my mother often lamented that it didn't offer more opportunities, as well as the lack of what she called culture. But still, it was shocking that anybody could conclude it was a "shithole." Worse, the way Karen Cirillo was surveying Ikey Lubin's suggested that, in her opinion, if anybody needed additional evidence in support of her opinion, they need look no farther. What, I wondered, could possibly be the source of such a misguided opinion? The only explanation I could imagine was that as a West Ender, she was generalizing about Thomaston from her limited experience of its least prosperous sector. Which was what I tried to suggest, tentatively, by saying, "Yeah, but they live in the Borough now, the Marconis."

"Shithole," Karen Cirillo repeated, her tone even more bored and offhanded, her conviction apparently unshakable. So, I was surprised to discover, was my own contrary opinion. In the face of her insistence, I felt a sudden welling up of loyalty to my town and, in particular, our East End neighborhood—to the Spinnarkles and the Gunthers and the Bishops and, mostly, my own small family. Before I could offer anything in defense, though, the bell above the door jingled again, and I looked up, expecting, almost hoping, it would be my father, but it was Jerzy Quinn himself, and when he entered, the world wobbled even more dangerously than it had when Karen Cirillo intruded on H. Rider Haggard a few minutes earlier. About the only way I can explain this wobbling is to cite my profound sense that the presence of these two West Enders at the corner of Third and Rawley was not permitted. I had no concrete idea who or what governed what was permitted, simply that this wasn't allowed. A violation had occurred. A rule abrogated. A perimeter breached. Whatever immutable law kept Jerzy and his gang out of the YMCA dances until the last half hour, that kept West End kids out of the high-track classes made up of the Jewish kids and Borough kids and a few "gifted" East End kids, the same elemental force that caused everyone to cut a wide swath around Jerzy's bunch both in the school corridors and outside on the grounds—all of this was called into question by their mere presence in our little store, a dislocation of reality so profound that it left me mute. And as Jerzy came toward me with his signature little jig step, I was amazed that he had just sauntered through all the invisible barriers as if they didn't exist, when the three of us knew for certain that they did.

Since Jerzy almost never showed Karen any affection in public, I wasn't surprised that he didn't take her hand or anything. For her part, she seemed to know who'd entered the store without having to look. "Hey," she said, looking straight at me, but meaning, I understood, him. It was now, suddenly, two against one. That's what I remember thinking. A minute before, however improbable it might have seemed, I'd been on the verge of making a friend. Now I was alone again.

"Who's this?" Jerzy said, also looking at me. If he recognized me as a boy he'd once imprisoned in a trunk and pretended to saw in half, he gave no sign. What would I have done if he *had* recognized me? Sadly, I knew the answer to his question, for in the second or two it took him to join his girlfriend at the counter, I'd already begun to formulate a little speech about how, no, there weren't any hard feelings, it was a long time ago and hadn't been that big a deal anyway, that it wasn't like I still had nightmares or anything, or that when I came out of my occasional spells I sometimes imagined I was again locked in the trunk, a sensation so strong I could actually smell the urine. I even remember feeling guilty that he might've been worried about me all these years. Far from holding a grudge, I was anxious to set his mind at ease.

"This? This is Lou," Karen told him, surprising me with the news that I could be who I wanted. "He's a friend of Bobby's."

I felt the blood drain out of my face.

"Bobby who?" her boyfriend said, appraising the store like a potential buyer.

"Bobby who," she repeated with a snort. "The Bobby who kicked your ass. My cousin Bobby. *That* Bobby who."

My heart pounded in my throat and I felt my knees buckle, but then Jerzy did the strangest thing. He let out a nasty little chuckle and gave an almost imperceptible nod in Karen's direction as if to say *Girls. What're you gonna do?* As if the two of us—Jerzy Quinn and Lucy Lynch—were fellow sufferers. As if I had a girlfriend just like Karen Cirillo in the back room. As if I knew the score.

They were both regarding me now, curious, perhaps, to see whose side I would take, and if there'd been a trunk there behind the counter I'd have voluntarily crawled inside and pulled the lid shut over me.

"Lou's nice. He gave me a pack of cigs," Karen said, smiling at me now, challenging me to say the cigarettes hadn't been a gift, that in my father's store we didn't hand out free cigarettes or free anything. This, I intuited, was the price of being Lou and not Lucy, which meant the cigarettes *would* be free, just this once.

"Let's go," Jerzy said, then hooked his index finger into the waistband of Karen's slacks and gave it a gentle tug. When the material stretched, I could see that his finger was between her bare skin and her underpants—a gesture made even more staggering by the fact that she didn't seem to object. Sex, I thought, just that one word. That slender finger slipped down between her bare skin and panties meant sex. And during all of this she never once took her eyes off me.

"See you around, neighbor," she said, though I only half heard. Jerzy had pivoted, letting go of her waistband—the snap was audible—and was heading for the door. Karen followed, saying, over her shoulder. "Thanks for the cigs, Lou. You're a prince."

The front of Ikey Lubin's was all glass, and from behind the register I had a clear view of our house. At the precise instant Jerzy put his hand on the knob and pulled the door toward him, our front door opened and my father emerged, as if the two events were connected by a single cause, and I had the eerie sense that until the moment Jerzy opened the door, my father had been trapped inside our house, unable to come out onto the porch. Was it my imagination, or was there some urgency to his step as he came across the intersection?

"Who was that?" he wanted to know, shutting the door behind him.

"Who?" I said, lamely.

"Them two that just left," he said, glancing at the cigarette rack where the single packs were kept. For an instant I wondered if he'd counted them before leaving for dinner and now was counting them again. But a second later he was looking only at me.

"A couple kids from school," I said, meeting his gaze before looking down. If I told him their names, would he recognize Jerzy Quinn's? Had my father ever learned the names of the boys who'd locked me in that trunk so long ago? And what would he do if he made the connection across the intervening years?

He seemed about to say something else, but just then, on the other side of the wall, we heard the sound of feet pounding up the stairs to the apartment above. "They're back," I said, meaning the brothers, but I knew it wasn't them. No pickup trucks had pulled up outside, and though the noise of tramping feet was loud, it wasn't nearly as loud as they'd been all afternoon, big, heavy men pushing and shoving one another into the walls, pounding the uncarpeted stairs with their boot heels. Suddenly I understood what Karen had meant by calling me neighbor.

That night my mother regarded me suspiciously when I announced my intention to go to bed early, wanting to know if maybe I was coming down with something or felt one of my spells coming on. What I wanted was to be alone in the dark. For hours I lay awake, thinking it all through. Karen Cirillo and I would be neighbors. I would likely see Jerzy Quinn every day. If she became my friend, did it follow that he would? The idea was almost too thrilling to contemplate. Of course it troubled me that I'd betrayed my father by giving away a pack of cigarettes. In doing so, was I not hastening my family toward financial ruin? Mostly, though, I lay there thinking of how casually Jerzy had slipped his finger into Karen's waistband, and I tried to imagine myself doing something equally brazen and confident.

I don't know what time it was when I finally fell asleep, but I remember no longer minding so much that Bobby had moved away. If he and his family still lived above the Spinnarkle sisters, then I'd have to share Karen and Jerzy. And they now represented to me the embodiment of the mystery I'd come to feel was at the heart of everything, a mystery as deep and profound as why my parents loved each other, as why some people had to pay the footbridge toll while others did not, as why a woman like Mrs. Marconi felt the need to run away from her own family, all as inexplicable as the mystery of my own suddenly fluid identity. If I played my cards right, I could be Lou Lynch, like my father, not a boy with a girl's name. Wasn't that what Karen had implied when she introduced me as Lou? I considered again the possibility that my destiny wasn't etched in stone. The door to the future was suddenly wide open, and the light pouring through it, there in the darkness of my room, was blinding.

I could choose who to be.

FOR A WHILE it looked like things would work out as I'd hoped they might. Every night, when my father left me in charge of the store, Karen would appear and we'd talk, usually about school. Her belief was that all our teachers were idiots, an opinion I allowed her to imagine I shared. She was convinced they had it in for the school's dumb kids just because they were stupid. This wasn't an argument I'd ever encountered before, so it took me a while to get a grip on it. "Take us," she explained. "You're smart, I'm dumb. So they like you and hate me." When I protested, saying I wasn't that smart, she would have none of it. "Okay," she conceded, "you're not like a Jew or anything, but you're not dumb like me. And you're *way* smarter than Jerz," she added, apparently feeling no need to be loyal to her boyfriend. When I said that maybe the fact that I did my homework might have something to do with our teachers' unfairly high opinion of kids like me, she brushed this suggestion aside as well. She'd tried shit like doing her homework for a while, but it was counter-productive since she always did it wrong. Doing homework wrong, to her, was worse than not doing it at all, because doing it required time and effort and yielded the same result as not doing it, which required neither. Besides, our teachers had it all figured out in advance, she said, like who was going to get good grades and who'd flunk. "Ask Jerz," she concluded, without giving me to understand why I should value the opinion of someone she'd just admitted wasn't nearly as smart as I was.

That was the most curious thing about Karen's always curious logic. The way she saw it, stupidity didn't mean that a person's conclusions were necessarily unsound. She saw no reason to distrust her boyfriend's wisdom on most subjects, any more than she considered his being held back two grades indicative of anything. "Jerz knows stuff," she insisted, then added, "All *kinds* of shit," her rhetorical clincher.

I kept expecting him to join us, but after that first evening he didn't appear again, and I gathered from Karen that he'd recently come under some sort of house arrest, at least on weeknights. "He promised his old lady" was how she explained it. Karen was full of West End expressions like "old lady" for "mother." Apparently Jerzy's "old man" was dead, so it was just him and her and his brothers. Her own father wasn't in the picture either, which was why her last name wasn't the same as her mother's, and she seemed to have concluded that this, too, was normal. Jerzy's old lady was okay, Karen went on. She was just trying to keep him on the straight and narrow, because one more screwup and he'd be back in reform school for good and, after that, prison. So except for school and weekends, Jerzy was grounded. "You're my only friend, Lou," she concluded sadly. "How about a pack of those Parliaments?"

Though I continued to give Karen cigarettes, she was good about not lighting up in the store, for which I was grateful, because my father wouldn't have liked that, even if they'd been come by honestly. Nobody was allowed to smoke in the store except Uncle Dec, who did as he pleased in all circumstances, though he rarely visited us. When I casually let it drop that I was thinking about taking up smoking "again," Karen was adamant that I not. "Cigs give you cancer. Especially girls. They'll probably have to cut my tits off by the time I'm thirty." When she said this, she cupped a hand under each breast so I'd know which ones she was referring to. The word "tits," coming from Karen Cirillo's mouth, was nearly enough to make me faint, and when she cupped them, I don't know what kept me on my feet.

If I was, as Karen claimed, her only friend, you wouldn't have guessed it by school. Our paths crossed only in the hallways or on the property outside, but I quickly learned that our early evening friendship was something she had no intention of acknowledging publicly. I smiled a few times, maybe even waved, but though I was sure she saw me, her expression never changed. Karen possessed a special talent that I've seen in only one or two other people, the uncanny ability to look right at you and then, without appearing to shift her gaze, at some point over your shoulder. The change was so subtle that the only conclusion you could come to was that she'd never been looking at you in the first place, either that or you'd been there for a time and then disappeared.

At school Jerzy sometimes would be with her, but he never acknowledged me either. From being thus ignored, I learned a lesson: it might be true that I could choose who to be, but that didn't necessarily make me memorable.

*

THE THOMASTON FREE LIBRARY WAS LOCATED, seemingly out of fairness, on Division Street, at the upper end next to the cemetery. From the rear windows of the first-floor stacks you could see, at least in winter, the obelisk that marked the tomb of Sir Thomas Whitcombe, next to the flagpole at the cemetery's highest point. On Saturday mornings I generally rose early and helped my father open Ikey's, but by eleven or so he'd shoo me out, telling me to go do something fun. The money I earned at the store got put directly into my college fund, but on Saturday I was given an allowance to cover the matinee that day and my small weekly expenses. The movie started at one, so I usually spent the two hours in between at the library, returning the books I'd read the week before and checking out a new batch. During the school year I couldn't read as many books each week as I did in the summer, so I took more time making my selections. My habit was to take a dozen or so books over to a small table in the stacks and examine the plastic-sheathed back covers and inside flaps more thoroughly.

There, one Saturday, I thought I heard singing outside, and looking out the window I was surprised to see Gabriel Mock weaving down the path that led through the cemetery and into the library's rear parking lot, singing at the top of his lungs. I couldn't make out the words because they came too fast, but the refrain ran "no more, no more, no more, no more," and this was the part he bellowed loudest. He carried a bottle-shaped brown paper bag, and at the edge of the parking lot he stopped, put the bag to his lips and drank, his head thrown back, until whatever was in the bottle was gone, after which he stared at it, dispirited. Then something funny occurred to him and he resumed his singing with an even greater gusto—*no more, no more, no more, no more*—as if the unexpected dovetailing of song and circumstance was just the funniest thing ever. He continued his journey, unfortunately without noticing the shin-high metal guardrail that ringed the lot, over which he tumbled.

He went down hard enough to hurt himself, but was quickly

back on his feet and looking around to see who'd tripped him. The bottle lay at his feet, apparently unbroken, and he took it out of its bag and held it up to the light to make double sure it was empty, then turned it upside down and shook it like a ketchup bottle to make triple sure. "No more no more no more no more," he warbled, with somewhat diminished enthusiasm now, the joke having worn thin. Hearing the commotion outside, Mrs. Dirkus left the circulation desk, came over and peered out my window, shaking her head at the sight of a little drunkard singing in the parking lot, then, muttering, returned to her desk.

Gabriel was standing between two cars, one of which happened to be Jack Beverly's new Cadillac. I knew whose car it was only because I'd seen him and Nan climbing out of it just a few minutes before with an armload of books. Now they were standing at the circulation desk while Mrs. Dirkus stamped due dates on the little cards in the jacket sleeves, a task she approached with utmost seriousness, making sure each stamp sat squarely in the center of the next tiny rectangle on the grid. Other librarians stamped willy-nilly, but she countenanced no such slipshod work, and I admired that about her. The impatient look on Mr. Beverly's face suggested he didn't share my appreciation. Nan, peering down the long row of stacks, saw me in my window seat and smiled, causing me to look around to see if there was someone else she might be smiling at, and by the time I'd determined that her smile must've been intended for me, she and her father had picked up their books and turned for the front door.

I was contemplating all of this when I heard the sound of glass shattering outside and saw my fence-painting friend doing a little jig next to the Cadillac, the ground around it now glinting with broken green glass. "No more, no more, no more, no more, hit the *road*, Jack," he sang with renewed enthusiasm. The Caddy's rear window, I saw, now sported a diagonal crack. Gabriel must have heard the Beverlys approaching, then, because he darted off between parked cars, showing more speed and agility than I would've predicted in his drunken state. Just as he disappeared around one corner of the building, the Beverlys hove into view around the other, and Mr. Beverly stopped and put his hand on his daughter's forearm. His intention, I suppose, was to keep her from doing what she now did, which was run over to the car for a closer look, right through the broken glass. Her father stood where he was, gazing off in the direction where Gabriel had beaten his hasty retreat.

What happened next was perhaps the most surprising thing of all. Nan Beverly began to cry. Father and daughter were twenty or thirty yards from where I sat, but I was still able to read the bewildered, frightened look on her face as he took her in his arms and, I suppose, tried to explain why anybody would want to do such a hateful thing. At some point he noticed me watching, and after getting Nan calmed down and helping her into the front passenger seat, he came over. The windowpane was thick, so his voice was muffled, but of course I didn't need to hear much to know what he was asking. Had I seen who'd done it? I shook my head, no.

Back at Ikey's, after the matinee—which Nan, showing no sign of her earlier upset, attended with her boyfriend—I found myself still wishing I hadn't lied to Mr. Beverly. I told my father what I'd seen Gabriel Mock do, though I didn't mention lying to Nan's father, and he responded just as I'd expected, saying it wasn't right to damage other people's property. Maybe Gabriel had a reason, he wasn't saying he didn't, but that still wasn't no excuse. Because I continued to be fascinated by how differently my parents saw things, I later discussed the episode with my mother, going into even greater detail in describing how drunk Gabriel had been, shouting *no more, no more, no more, no more* before smashing the whiskey bottle on the rear window of the Beverlys' Cadillac. When she offered no immediate comment, I confided to her what I'd withheld from my father, that I'd claimed to have seen nothing. "You know," she said, "sometimes you make me very proud."

I thought about that before falling asleep. It was tempting to take pride in my mother's being proud of me. But with her, nothing ever came to you clean, and it occurred to me that if "sometimes" I made her proud, there must be other times when I didn't.

THE NEXT DAY, Sunday, I found Gabriel sitting with his back up against the Whitcombe Park fence, his legs splayed out in front of him. A recent cut cleanly bisected one eyebrow, and I didn't have to ask where that came from. He must've heard me ride up the gravel drive, but his eyes remained closed, and I wondered for a moment if he might be dead. Finally, when I leaned my bike against the fence, he opened one eye—the wrong one, since it caused the eyebrow to split open again and ooze tiny spots of blood.

"Junior," he said. "How you be doin' this fine morning?"

"It's afternoon," I said, sitting down next to him.

"Already?" he said. "Can't be. It's mornin'. I can tell by the sun."

I knew better than to argue when Gabriel was sure about something, but in this instance it was hard not to. "It's afternoon," I told him. "I can tell by my watch." I showed him, but he wasn't interested.

"Must be fast," he said, both eyes closed again. "You go on home and tell your mama you forgot to wind your watch. Tell her you don't know what time it is."

"If I forgot to wind it," I said, "it would run slow. Or stop. It wouldn't run fast. That's illogical."

"Junior, do me a favor? Go away. I don't have no strength to argue with stubborn white boys, not today, I don't. Normally I do, just not today."

I just sat there, annoyed, until he finally opened that same eye again, causing the cut to show pink and bubble a second time. "You still here?"

210

I said I believed I was.

"I believe you are, too. So tell me 'bout what all you did last night. You go out howlin' or what?"

Over the last month or so, Gabriel and I had agreed on the fiction that I enjoyed howling as much as he did. Sundays we'd each describe the howling we'd done the night before and express surprise that we hadn't run into each other when the howling was upon us. Gabriel guessed that we howled in different circles. Usually, it was fun trading these stories, but after what I'd witnessed yesterday I wasn't in the mood, so I said I'd stayed home.

"You nothin' but a ama-teur howler, is why," Gabriel said. "Bet you don't even know what last night was."

"What was it?"

"See? That's what I'm talkin' about. You a *ama*-teur."

"What was last night?"

"Last night be a full moon, Junior. A real howler would of knowed that. Best night to howl, full moon. You ama-teurs, you don't know your full moon."

Where we were headed, I feared, was yet another discussion that would end with Gabriel telling me I didn't know up from down. "Why do you like to howl so much?" I asked, since that's what I'd been puzzling about.

"I don't," he said, surprising me. "Up to me, I'd never howl. Drove to it, is what I am. You'd know that if you wasn't a ama-teur."

This was proving to be an even slower conversation than usual. As a general rule, Gabriel liked to talk but was never in a hurry to arrive anywhere. Two steps forward, one back, was the sort of dance he preferred. And the one step back was usually an insult of some kind.

"Don't know why I waste my time tryin' to educate white boys and ama-teurs. Specially you. You both a white boy *and* a ama-teur. No hope for you at all."

Though they were nothing alike and spoke a different

language entirely, at times Gabriel reminded me of my mother, both of them having concluded that I was a slow, reluctant learner. "What drives you to howling?" I asked.

"Pussy," Gabriel said. "What you think?"

I shrugged, instantly uncomfortable. I'd heard the word used in a similar context before and had a pretty good idea what it meant, and that I shouldn't be discussing it.

"Pussy make you crazy," Gabriel elaborated. "You still too young to know 'bout that."

I shrugged again, hoping to concede that he was right and thus open a new line of inquiry.

"You like it, though, I bet."

Yet another shrug.

"Don't you be shruggin' at me now. You old enough to know that much. You like it or you don't like it. Even amateur white boys know if they like it or they don't like it."

In that case, I said, I supposed I liked it.

"Ain't no suppose about it. Suppose." He snorted. "You a white boy if ever they was one."

I said fine, okay, I liked pussy.

"Watch your mouth now," he advised. "Your mama hear you goin' on about likin' pussy, you be in *big* trouble. Don't come to me for help neither 'cause I'll have to tell her the truth. How you told me your own self how much you like pussy. Be in trouble, then, won't you."

Gabriel's spirits appeared to be improving by the minute. He had both eyes open now, and his voice, thin a few minutes ago, was robust.

"Good news is, you prob'ly ain't gon have no brown girlfriends. Just as well, too, take my word. Start out, you all they need. That's what they tell you. 'Sugar, you *all* I need. You so sweet.' Then one day you ain't payin' attention, they find Jesus. Black girl find Jesus, she might as well sew it up with a needle and thread. Put a zipper on it, for all the good it gon do her *or* you."

I would have liked to change the subject, not because Gabriel's views on women were without interest but because something else interested me even more. Knowing what I did about his howling, I had no trouble understanding why his wife might be growing weary of his shenanigans. What I would've liked to know was what he'd done to cause his own son to say he didn't have a father. I tried to imagine what my own father could do that would make me deny his very existence that way, and failed utterly.

"Black girl find Jesus, the next thing she find is the devil. You know who the devil is?"

I had a pretty good idea. "You?"

"Damn straight. Now *you* the devil. Yesterday you sugar, you so sweet. Today you the devil. Turn you out so fast it make your head spin. Say 'Don't you be coming round here no more.' While back she like to howl just like you, but now it's 'Don't you be comin' round here with your howlin' ways. This child studyin' you,' she say, 'cause by now you got one, maybe two, if you ain't lucky. Pretty soon she got the child poisoned against you. Don't want you for his daddy. Want some other man don't have nothin' to do with him. Preacher, prob'ly. Somebody too good to howl. You stick to white girls, you know what's good for you. Older they get, the better they like it. Even the ugly ones. Nothin' better than a old ugly white woman. Grateful's what they is."

That seemed to be the end of the lecture. Gabriel closed his eyes again and was silent for so long I figured he'd fallen asleep. When I climbed back on my bike, though, he spoke again, eyes still closed. "So, you tattle on me yesterday, or what?"

"What do you mean?"

"Don't get cagey on me now. I seen you sittin' there in the liberry window watchin' it all. They must of asked you who done it."

"I said I didn't see."

He just nodded and said, without opening his eyes, "You look just like your daddy, Junior. Spittin' image. But you your mama's boy." He must have sensed me glaring at him. "You don't like me sayin' that, I guess."

"It wasn't very nice what you did," I told him. "Breaking that bottle on Mr. Beverly's car. He never did anything to you."

"How you know what he did and didn't do?"

He had a point, but I wasn't about to concede the moral high ground. "Okay," I said. "What did he ever do to you?"

He didn't reply at first, but finally he said, "Nothin'. Man never done nothin' to me. Truth is I'm ashame of myself, acting like God's own fool. Woman right, she don't want nothin' to do with me. Right to warn the boy against me, too. My own damn fault, the whole mess. There, you happy now, Lou Lynch Junior? Got it all straight now? Know up from down now, case somebody ask you?"

I wasn't happy, and I think he knew it. It was the first argument I'd ever won with Gabriel Mock, and it was worse than losing. It was true; I hadn't liked him saying I was my mother's son, even though he meant it, so far as I could tell, as a compliment. And when he'd called me Lou Lynch Junior I hadn't liked that either, sensing an insult. One or the other, it seemed, should've given me pleasure, but neither did, and in the end, pedaling away from Whitcombe Park, all I'd felt was guilty. Which didn't make any sense either. I wasn't the one who'd gotten drunk and smashed a bottle on somebody else's Cadillac. It wasn't me sitting on the ground with a hangover, oozing blood from a torn eyebrow, the embodiment of my own foolishness. He could be sarcastic all he wanted, but it *was* all his fault, just as he said.

Still, the closer I got to building an airtight case against my friend, the worse I felt and the more convinced that I *was* a slow, stubborn learner. Maybe I *didn't* know up from down.

In Thomaston, then as now, the only taxi service was Hudson Cab. Their ad in the Yellow Pages referred to a "fleet" of taxis, all clean and spacious, with courteous, punctual drivers—proof, my mother said, that you could claim just about anything and get away with it. Hudson Cab favored big rusted-out station wagons with torn vinyl upholstery and tailgates fused permanently shut by rear-end collisions. It wasn't unusual to hear one of these, its dangling exhaust system sparking along the pavement, before you saw it, and all the drivers looked as if they'd just that morning come off a four-month bender. Courtesy was hardly an issue for these men, who seemed incapable of any utterance at all.

It was just such a cab and driver that pulled up in front of Ikey Lubin's one day about a month after Karen and her mother moved into the flat above our store. The way the vehicle sat there, its motionless driver staring straight ahead, caused my father and me both to wonder if he'd in fact died at our curb, and the angle was such that we couldn't see whether there was a passenger in the rear seat. My father, who'd been about to go home for supper, was reluctant to leave until he knew what this was about, so he remained behind the register. Finally, there was a lurching movement in the rear seat, as of a man awakening from a dream so dreadful that the sour backseat of a Hudson cab represented a distinct improvement. Whoever it was went into a series of contortions, apparently searching for the fare. In vain, it seemed, because the driver's head rotated around on his thick neck so he could memorize what his passenger had looked like when he was still alive. From the rear seat a hand pointed vehemently at the store, and an unkempt, pear-shaped man got out. He was still going through his pockets as he came inside. I couldn't take my eyes off his hair. The man had the most amazing cowlick I'd ever seen, and my father, most days, sported a pretty fine one himself.

"Hey, big fella," he said to my father. "Lemme take a five-spot to get rid of this asshole driver. I'll pay you right back, I swear."

"How about watching your language," my father suggested, indicating me.

215

"Oh fuck . . . yeah, sorry," he said. Then he stood there, waiting, as if this apology had surely removed the last possible obstacle to a stranger loaning him money.

"What's wrong with that in your shirt pocket?" my father asked, since the corner of a bill was sticking out of it.

The man looked vindicated when he pulled it out. "*There* you are, you cock—" He stopped, remembering me.

And with this he turned on his heel and strode out to the cab, handing the bill in through the passenger-side window. Without further ceremony, the driver pulled away from the curb, deaf to the imprecations of the pear-shaped man, who clearly felt he had change coming.

I didn't think I'd ever seen anything more hapless looking than the man now standing on the sidewalk, though at that young age I didn't fully appreciate how hapless anybody looks when trying to summon a cab that has no intention of stopping. Especially when you're aware of being watched, your circumstance enjoyed. The man didn't turn around right away, and when he did he bent backward at the waist and gazed up at the Salvatore flat as if to commit its every unremarkable detail to memory. He seemed to wish there were some alternative, which there wasn't, you could tell. So he finally poked his head back inside and said, "How the fuck do you get up there?" Then, noting my father's expression, "How do you get up there?"

My father told him the entrance was around the side of the store.

"All right then," he said, this strange placement apparently agreeable to him, provided he was kept fully apprised of its location in the future. Glancing at our fruit bins, he said, "You sell flowers here?" Fruit and flowers being practically the same thing.

My father said we didn't.

The man nodded, as if used to disappointment, then again looked up at the apartment, considering. "Beer?"

My father indicated the cooler along the back wall.

Still the man remained where he was, standing in the doorway.

"You run tabs?"

"If you live in the neighborhood," my father said. "If I know you."

The man, cheered by this, came inside and let the door swing shut behind him. "Buddy Nurt," he said, offering to shake my father's hand, then bouncing from one foot to the other. What he seemed to be waiting for was confirmation that such a straightforward introduction had rendered him tab worthy. "I'll be living . . ." His head bobbed up at the ceiling. "Can't get much more in the neighborhood than that."

"With Nancy?" my father said, clearly displeased.

Buddy Nurt nodded like a man not unaccustomed to provoking displeasure.

"I'll have to get the okay from her first," my father said, and I could see how conflicted he was. On the one hand, he loathed trusting someone about whom he'd already heard so many unflattering things. On the other, he hated getting off on the wrong foot with a new customer. He glanced across the street at our house, as if my mother's advice would be radiating from it.

Buddy was eyeing the beer cooler with genuine longing. "She won't mind," he said, trying to sound casual. "Her and me, we . . ." He glanced at me and let his voice trail off, confident his coded message had been received.

Had it been me, I wouldn't have given Buddy so much as a stick of gum. His eyes were small and close together and darted from one object to another, refusing to settle anywhere. It made me tired just watching them. When my father shrugged a reluctant acquiescence, Buddy made for the case at a dead run, and he had two six-packs under one arm and was reaching for a third when my father called over that he was only good for one until things had been cleared with Nancy. So Buddy, clearly disappointed, put all three back and selected another, more expensive brand.

"Kinda steep," he remarked when my father rang it up. "Your prices."

"The kind you had before was cheaper," my father acknowledged.

Buddy shrugged. "What the fuck, right?" He grinned at me, clearly hoping he'd found someone who shared his personal philosophy, and then he recalled my father's injunction. "What the heck, right?" he corrected himself, pleased to have erased the bad word so completely.

"You gotta sign," my father said when he started out the door with the six-pack.

Buddy Nurt cautiously signed his name on the slip my father provided, as if this were the part that might trail unpleasant repercussions. "Got a . . . ?" he said, making a bottle-opener gesture.

My father handed him one from underneath the counter and he popped the cap off deftly, noticing that the opener was on a string only when he tried to slip it into his pocket. "Whoops," he said, putting it back on the counter. Then he drained off half the bottle right there in front of us, and this seemed to provide the courage necessary to brave the climb upstairs. We listened to his slow, heavy steps up to the apartment, heard him tap on the door and call, "Hey, babe?"

It was now safe, my father decided, to go eat his supper, but he hadn't even made it to the door, when we heard rapidly descending footsteps, and Nancy Salvatore burst inside and slammed the six-pack—well, the five-pack now—down on the counter. "Buddy Nurt doesn't sign for anything on my ticket, Mr. Lynch," she said, looking first at him and then at me, as if she suspected I might be the one who'd have to enforce this rule. "Not ever. He's the reason I had to leave all my friends and move here. He's why my life's a crock of shit."

My father looked scared, the way he always did around angry women. "Okay. It's just that he said—"

"Don't listen to him," she said, again fixing the two of us to make sure we understood. "He's a liar. You believe a word that man says, you deserve what you get." This statement seemed derived from experience both deep and profound. "Even if I change my mind later and tell you it's okay? It's not okay. It's not *ever* okay. I'm gonna hold you to that, Mr. Lynch."

My father nodded, confused but agreeable.

"How much for the one beer?"

When he told her, she took the coins from her purse and handed them over.

"My advice would be don't even let him in the store," she added. "On top of being a liar he's also a thief." I thought about pointing out that he'd already tried to pocket our bottle opener, but held my tongue. "In fact, have as little to do with Buddy Nurt as humanly possible."

"Okay," my father agreed. And when she looked over at me, I said okay, too.

She now calmed down a little. "I ought to have my damn head examined," she said, massaging her brow. "I don't know what comes over me with him. He's up there now, looking all hangdog. By tonight I'll be feeding him, by tomorrow I'll be loaning him money, and by tomorrow night. . . ." She studied me thoughtfully and apparently decided not to say what she'd be doing for Buddy Nurt then. "I had any sense, I'd shoot him. In ten years, I'd be out of prison, a free woman. Whereas now I'm looking at life with Buddy Nurt, no chance of parole."

More tramping down the stairs now. Nancy massaged her forehead even more ferociously, though it was already red from her previous exertions. "Here comes the other light of my life."

And sure enough, Karen came in and slammed the door shut so hard the glass rattled. You could see how furious she was, but I was still surprised when she pointed an index finger at Nancy and screamed, "This is *bullshit*, Ma!" I don't think I'd ever heard anyone my age yell at a grown-up before, certainly not in front of other people. In Karen's defense, I'm not sure she even knew we were there. That's how beside herself she was. Mother and daughter stood facing each other, a few feet apart, and Ikey Lubin's might as well have been a stage set. Karen's hands were clenched tightly into fists. Her mother's shoulders had slumped, most of her previous energy having leaked away, leaving her unequal to the task of waging this particular battle. "You *promised*, Ma!" Karen screamed. "You *said* never again. Don't pretend you didn't."

"Quit shouting at me, Karen," she said. "You make my head hurt. He only turned up this minute. I haven't made my mind up what to do yet."

"Then make it up now," Karen said.

"Karen—"

"Right *now*, Ma. I'm not going to wonder every time I take a bath if that shithead's on his knees outside the door with his beady little eye to the keyhole."

"Buddy wouldn't do that," Nancy said weakly, more to us than to her daughter.

"Don't *lie*, you stupid bitch! You caught him yourself. And what about that night I woke up and he was standing next to my bed?"

"He sleepwalks, Karen."

"Right. With that thing in his hand, straight into my bedroom."

"Karen—"

"Him or me, Ma."

This ultimatum stiffened her. "Where you gonna go, Karen?"

The question hit her daughter hard, I could tell, implying as it did that the decision had already been made.

"Who'd put up with you, besides me?"

Karen's eyes were suddenly full, but she refused to cry. "Besides you and Buddy, you mean?"

And just that quickly it was her mother sobbing. "I need *something* in my goddamn life, Karen. I'm sorry, but I do. Even if it's only Buddy Nurt. You'll understand that one day. Soon, probably, the way you're going."

"Fuck you, Ma," Karen said, a whisper almost. And then she was gone, this time leaving the door wide open. Her mother didn't move for a long time, while my father and I studied our shoes.

"Guess I'll take those other five beers after all," she said finally. When my father handed them to her, she studied me sadly. "Don't grow up," she muttered, then left.

Anxious as he'd been to go, my father now seemed reluctant to leave me alone in the store, even briefly. "I warned your mother something like this would happen," he said, putting Nancy's tab back under the cash drawer. There was no bitterness to the observation, though, not like there always was when my mother said her I-told-you-so's.

After my father finally went across the street, a truck driven by one of the brothers pulled up in front. Jerzy Quinn was with him. They went upstairs and returned a few minutes later with Karen, Buddy Nurt following at a respectful distance. There was no sign of Nancy. With the door closed I couldn't hear exactly what was being said, but Buddy seemed to be arguing that Karen didn't have to run off on his account. She was lugging an old cardboard suitcase, and when she tried shoving it behind the pickup's seat, the clasp sprang open, spilling clothes into the gutter. Only then did she begin to cry. When Buddy came over to help, she screamed at him to keep away. I couldn't tell if Jerzy and the brother felt the same admonition applied to them, or whether they just weren't sure she wanted them touching her underthings, but at any rate they just stood there watching her cram things back into the suitcase. When she was finished, of course, it wouldn't close, and she had to hold it shut as best she could on her lap. I hoped that maybe she'd remember I was there and look over at me, but she stared straight ahead as her uncle and boyfriend climbed in on either side of her. Buddy waved as the truck pulled away, though nobody waved back.

I actually felt kind of sorry for him, standing there alone at the curb, knowing, as he surely must've, that his mere appearance was enough to make people scatter. But then he turned toward Ikey Lubin's, and the expression on his face scared me. It wasn't anything like he'd looked when he was trying to borrow his cab fare. This face was sneaky and mean, and looking right at me. For a moment the irrational thought entered my mind that for some reason Buddy Nurt blamed me for what had just happened.

When he was gone, though, I went outside where he'd been standing, because by then it had occurred to me that he probably hadn't been looking at me at all. In the early evening it was still bright enough outside for the windows to reflect light. Was it possible that the cold, contemptuous and frightening expression was the one that greeted him every day in the mirror? This was somehow even scarier than thinking it was me he'd been mad at. My own face, I couldn't help noticing, had unconsciously mimicked Buddy's expression.

Heading back inside, I saw the three dogs my mother had shot at, loping up the street toward me. Inside, I found the gun under the counter and took it back outside with me. All three stopped in their tracks when they saw me, and when I raised the gun they turned and hightailed it back toward the West End. For all I knew they were East End dogs, but I thought of them that day as West End mutts and, because they had no business in our neighborhood, I filled the air around them with pellets.

THE NEXT EVENING my mother was working on her books, which she did when there was nothing good on TV and it was quiet and my father was at the store. Eyes fixed on her open ledger, her fingers flew over the keys of the adding machine she always set up in the middle of the kitchen table. At times like these her powers of concentration were so great that I suspected she wasn't really listening to anything I said, which was why I sometimes tried to slip in awkward bits of information—a poor performance on a math test, say, or a B on a science project—

when she was so engaged, though the strategy seldom worked. That particular night I had something on my mind, so I joined her there at the table. I'd been thinking about what Nancy Salvatore had said, how in no time, even though she knew better, she'd be loaning Buddy Nurt money and falling back into the very habits she'd hoped to escape by moving to the East End with her daughter. It struck me that anybody smart enough to figure out what the future held ought to be smart enough to avoid it. In Nancy's case it seemed merely an issue of self-control, a concept the nuns of St. Francis had famously drummed into us. If Nancy knew that Buddy Nurt was bad for both her and Karen, then it was simply a matter of acting upon that knowledge. Hadn't she sat right here in our kitchen the day after her brothers moved her in, proclaiming loudly that she'd finally learned her lesson and was done with Buddy Nurt, that if he ever showed up in the East End she wouldn't even let him in the door? What good did it do, I asked my mother, to talk like that if you were just going to give in without a fight later? I'd looked Buddy over pretty carefully and concluded that any woman in her right mind should've been able to resist his charms. In fact, I couldn't even imagine what his charms might be. My mother let me go on like this for some time before she stopped pounding numbers and regarded me critically.

"You're going to have to get smarter about people if you want to survive in the world, Louie," she said, so seriously that my feelings were hurt. "You don't really think just because some-body says they're going to do something, that means they're going to do it?"

"But why?" I said. "Why would she take him back?"

"You know the answer, Lou."

"I don't," I said, peevish now. In truth I was puzzled not just by Nancy Salvatore but by adult behavior in general. Though Gabriel Mock had expressed what I took to be genuine contrition about his drunkenness in the library parking lot, I'd seen him drunk twice since then, once outside the pool hall and again across the street from the Y after the dance let out. My parents' ongoing disagreements were annoying, too. If *I* could predict what each would say on any given topic, why couldn't they? Why did they feel it necessary to repeat themselves, to stake out the same positions time after time? Would I become like that when I got older, retracing my steps over and over, unaware that I was doing so or, worse, not caring?

My mother raised her eyebrow at me like she always did when she suspected willful incomprehension. "Look, when the Marconis moved, Bobby promised you he'd call, right? But he didn't. That wasn't very nice, and you were mad at him."

I shrugged, unwilling to admit that, yes, I *had* been mad at him.

"But if he showed up tomorrow wanting to be friends, you'd forgive him, wouldn't you?"

I shrugged again.

"Why?" she said, and when I didn't answer, she continued, "Because there's nothing worse than being alone. In your heart you know that's true, don't you?"

I nodded reluctantly. "But Buddy Nurt?"

She was having none of it. "What's worse, bad friends or no friends?"

I said I didn't know.

"Yes, *you do*. Don't be one of those people who go through life pretending not to know what they know." The implication was *Like your father*, who'd known for a full year he was going to lose his milk route but pretended not to. I wanted to object, but then the fingers of her right hand were racing over the adding machine keys, while those of her left tracked figures up and down the columns.

"Is that why you and Dad . . ." I couldn't complete the sentence.

"Your father and I are together because we love each other. Also because we love you."

That was the answer I'd been hoping for, of course, and to

hear the words made me feel good. Better, I think, than they made her feel, because when I got up from the table to head upstairs she said, "Don't go trying to figure out love."

I promised I wouldn't.

"And don't waste time wishing the world was different than it is. You aren't going to change it. Don't expect people to be something they can't. Or yourself for that matter."

"What can't I be?" I asked her, because lately I'd been thinking a lot about that very thing.

She looked up at me, and our eyes met. I had the distinct impression she was going to tell me something, but then she went back to her numbers, which always added up in the end.

Unlike love.

FACE VALUE

These days my mother likes to eat early. Lunch at ten-thirty, dinner at five. I understand. I do. She's rarely able to sleep much past five-thirty, when Owen arrives to open Ikey's, so everything gets pushed forward, including meals. Friday, though, is our regular luncheon date, and so she's willing to postpone the midday meal until eleven-thirty "to fit my schedule," though in truth that's when Dot's Sandwich Shoppe, downtown, starts serving. A new place, the Top Drawer Café, has opened out on Old County Road, not far from Whitcombe Park, and I've offered to take her there, but she prefers Dot's, probably because the food is plain and old-fashioned. We're usually the first ones seated, which means we get the window seat overlooking Hudson Street and the old Bijou Theater, the restoration of which is nearly complete. It won't show movies, as it used to, but instead will be used for concerts and special events. The grand opening is when Sarah and I are in Italy, and I'll be sad to miss it.

I arrive at Ikey's a few minutes early, so I decide to pop in and say hello to Brindy, who's at the register. "Hi, Pop," she says in that abstracted way she has, when my arrival is signaled by the same bell above the door that used to announce Karen Cirillo back when I was minding the till. I've lost count of how many new registers we've had during this span, this most recent a thin, light computerized model, but the little bell soldiers on heroically. "You all packed?"

"You'd have to ask Sarah," I tell her, taking a quick inventory and suppressing, or trying to, a smile of pure satisfaction. Good old Ikey's. I half expect my father to come in from the back room with a big box of toilet paper for me to shelve. What I wouldn't give.

"I wish it was me going," Brindy says.

"That makes two of us," I tell her. "Where's Owen?" I expect her to say he's in the back room, the door to which is open and shouldn't be, not if no one's in there.

"Down at the West End store," she says. "God, who doesn't want to go to Italy?"

"Sarah says I'll be fine once I'm there."

"Then you probably will. She knows you best."

"That's what *she* says." I know her observation is vaguely insulting in that it suggests a lack of self-knowledge, but I can't help smiling anyway. To have someone you love know you better than you know yourself is a compliment, I believe, and so did my father when people said the same thing about my mother. When someone knows your deepest self and still loves you, are you not a lucky man? Having spent much of the last month or so dwelling on the past, I'm particularly pleased to consider that there's someone who knows me so well and yet doesn't regret a lifetime spent in my company, much of it in this very store.

"Is everything okay down there?" I ask. The register hasn't been ringing out right lately, and Owen's thinking about firing the manager.

"Owen's the one who'd know," Brindy says, in a tone that gives me pause. For some time Sarah's been worrying that things aren't right between the two of them. I don't want to believe this is true. I'd rather think, as I have in the past, that my daughter-in-law's coolness is directed at me, or Sarah and me, and not our son.

"Have him call me if he needs anything," I tell her, and she says she will. These days, my job is to go wherever I'm needed in what Owen calls the Lynch Empire, which includes Thomaston's three remaining corner markets—"convenience stores" now—plus our video rental store and, in summer, the Thomaston Cone. I take uncovered shifts when someone calls in sick or has a problem with a child. In truth, I wish there were more of these shifts. The video store has its own manager and staff, and the tiny ice-cream store is seasonal, so sometimes I feel—what's the word that's so in vogue these days?—marginalized. But I do understand Owen's thinking. One day he'll oversee all three of our markets, whether or not I've prepared him for that responsibility. I have to allow him to do things his way and make his own mistakes. I'm determined not to meddle, either with him or Brindy, who's far more sensitive to interference. Which is why I won't go over and close the door to the back room, no matter how much I want to.

Upstairs, my mother answers the door a split second after I knock, and she already has her coat on and buttoned, which means she's been standing on the other side of the door waiting impatiently for my arrival. God knows for how long. I could ask, but I still wouldn't know, because she'd say she saw me pull up outside or heard me clomping up the stairs, both of which are no doubt true, though that doesn't mean she hasn't been ready for an hour, anxious, I fear, for this to be over. It would be different, more pleasurable, if Sarah were able to join us. My wife has been, lo these many years, an excellent buffer between my mother and me, somehow able to remind us, despite our many disagreements, of how close we are.

But on Fridays Sarah teaches at the junior high. She's been a fine teacher for over two decades now, cobbling together as many part-time gigs at the junior and high schools as our dwindling budget will allow. She has fewer classes this year, after her illness, and has rediscovered her old passion, painting up a storm in the junior high art room long after her students have gone home. Of course she denies it is or ever was a passion. Real painters, she says, become painters. That's what *makes* them painters. Nothing comes between them and paint. Not circumstance, not life. Like Michelangelo and Titian and Caravaggio and the other masters whose work we'll see in Italy; like Bobby, she sometimes adds, matter-of-factly. At any rate her Friday class leaves my mother and me to our own devices, devices that haven't changed, I sometimes think, since I was a boy. Maybe it's just how it goes with mothers and sons. Had my father lived, well, who can say?

She gives me a dry peck on the cheek and steps out into the hall, quickly closing the door behind her, but not before I glimpse the dark smudge on the wall behind her sofa where the fire was so many years ago. That wall's been painted half a dozen times over the intervening years, even wallpapered once, but eventually the faint outline of the old burn comes through, followed gradually by something darker and uglier. Original sin, my mother likes to call it, by which she means my father's purchase of Ikey Lubin's. A bitter thing to say, I've always thought, though she claims it's a joke. There's no denying Ikey's changed our lives, that it was a terrible risk my mother never would've taken. And it's true we had bad luck for a while when my father fell ill and we lost our house, forcing my mother to break her steadfast vow and move in above the store. But it's unfair to suggest that Ikey's was the first domino to fall against our family. All human events lead to other human events, and my mother's damning Ikey's is arbitrary. One could just as easily blame my father's illness, the polluted stream that caused it or the mountain of medical bills that resulted. Why not pin it all on the old dairy discontinuing home delivery, or the public school boys who locked me in that trunk? But for them we might never have left Berman Court. What would our lives have been like if we'd never crossed Division Street? There are a great many sins in the world, none of them original.

"Why don't you use the chair?" I suggest when I see how stiff my mother is today, but she immediately starts down the steep, narrow steps, clutching the banister grimly with her twisted fingers. I installed the mechanized chair two years ago, over her strident objections, when the arthritis started getting worse and the stairs were clearly becoming both a trial and a hazard. Her right foot turns in now, and her balance is not what it should be. I feared she'd fall but instead should have foreseen her stubbornness. "That damned contraption" is what she calls it, claiming the chair's dangerous, that it will come loose from the wall while she's aboard or its gears will strip and send her plummeting backward to the bottom of the stairs. I argued, of course, that it would restore her freedom, that she could come and go as she pleased, without waiting for someone to help her. "And where would I go?" was her reply. Which did make me smile at how the tables had turned. When she and my father got me that first bike, her idea had been to get me out of the house and into the world. "Where should I go?" I remember asking. "Out," she replied. "Away. Anywhere." Having paid good money for the chair, I'd have liked to say the same to her, though of course I didn't, and so it has remained, except on rare occasions, useless at the bottom of the stairs.

Which is where my mother says, "There." Which is shorthand for *I told you so*, for *I can manage the stairs just fine*, for *You wasted your money*. And, unless I'm mistaken, for *I enjoy my prison, the ugly smudge on my living room wall. Because some things in life can't be painted or papered over, or fixed*. Which is what, she maintains, I've never understood.

I help her into the car, where she sits staring down at her knees, refusing, as always, to look across the street at the house where we'd lived for most of my childhood. Five years ago, when it came back on the market, I bought it with the idea of showing her it wasn't lost after all, but she would have none of that. "What would I do," she said, "all alone in that big house?"

"Live?" I suggested. "Like you used to?"

But no. "It'd be too much work. I'm better off where I am." Then the clincher. "Besides, it's too late."

So, for now, a renewed tactic. "Would you like to try the new restaurant? The Top Drawer?" I ask her. "The food's supposed to be good."

As if I didn't know the answer.

AT THE CURB outside Dot's is a car whose bumper sticker sets my mother off. "Support our troops," she says, her voice oozing disgust.

This is a topic I'd rather avoid, because her opinions on impersonal matters of national and international scope have a way of becoming personal. She despises our president as a dishonest fool whose lies and stupidity have cost over two thousand American lives, but her deepest contempt is reserved for those who voted for him—her son, she suspects, among them, though I've never told her who I voted for. Sarah says my mother doesn't intend for her political observations to be so personal, but how many times as a boy did I hear this same withering sarcasm applied to my father and, by extension, to me? "Lou. Why would you believe such a thing?" Well, my father would reply, because this guy swore it was true. "You're telling me you believe it because he said it? That's the reason?" He don't have no reason to lie that I know of, my father would reply weakly. "Right. But he's got about a hundred you don't know of and will never find out about, because you take everything at face value. It's what's called being gullible, Lou."

Even more personal is her claim that our president's stupidity is apparent in his physical appearance, particularly his facial expressions. All you have to do is look at him, she claims. Here, no doubt, Sarah's right. I'm internalizing my mother's attack on the president, who does, I admit, bear a striking resemblance to Alfred E. Neuman. But in general I reject the notion that what's inside a person can be determined by his exterior. Large, slow-moving men like my father and me are often assumed to be slow witted as well, and in school it always took my teachers a while to realize I was bright. I'm the first to allow that my intelligence isn't quick, but I am observant and methodical and, I believe, fair-minded. To me, it's always seemed ironic that people who take the trouble to stop and think are often judged obtuse. When I was a boy, my mother had a habit of snapping her fingers when she asked me a question. "Come on, Lou, you're smart. You know the answer. Don't pretend you don't." That is, don't pretend to be like your father, which was what she always seemed to be saying, and this made me even more deliberate. Even if it were true that I'm smarter than my father, who had none of my advantages, would that make me a better man?

So I say, "Let's not talk about the president."

"Fine," my mother says agreeably. "If you'll admit you voted for him, it would give me great pleasure never to utter his name again."

It's tempting to give her the answer she wants, to confess to being who she thinks I am, but I can't and she knows it. She used to hound my father on the same subject, telling him sometimes directly, sometimes indirectly, whom he should vote for, and later badgering him to reveal whether he'd acted on her advice. I sometimes think that what he did in the voting booth was the sole secret of his married life, or at least the only one he was able to keep. He liked to try to sneak little things by her from time to time, like buying that cheap shirt in the West End store and telling her he'd gotten it at Calloway's, but she always knew better, which only deepened his respect for her powers of cognition. He knew better than to lie, so when it came to voting he simply refused to say anything, an example I've always followed. Indeed, I alone know what my father did in the voting booth. He confided it to me shortly before he died, one of his final acts of love. "Don't tell your mother," he said, unnecessarily. "Don't tell nobody," he added, his eyes filling with tears. By then he was in constant pain, the effectiveness of the drugs he was taking intermittent, at best.

"Fine," my mother says when I pretend to study my menu,

leaving her challenge in the air between us. "If you think you have a secret, keep it."

"I will, thanks," I assure her.

My mother orders what she always orders, a grilled-cheese sandwich and a cup of thin tomato soup. In addition to being inexpensive, the food at Dot's is bland, which she also appreciates. She suffers, like many women her age, from acid reflux, and spicy foods keep her awake at night. In turn, I order my usual burger and fries. For a while we eat in silence, until the clock strikes twelve and the shopkeepers and clerks from the few remaining businesses along Hudson and Division begin drifting in. Most of them like to sit at the counter where they can chat with Dot and each other, but many stop at our table to say hello. "I hope he's picking up the tab," they tell my mother, and she says she hopes so, too. It's a standing joke in town that I'm a skinflint who routinely loses his wallet in his deep pockets. "Has he taken you out to the Top Drawer yet?" they want to know, to which she responds no, not yet, feeling no need to elaborate. "Make him," they suggest. "Who else around here can afford those prices?"

When we've finished eating, I say "Will you be all right while we're gone?" and she says of course she will. "Owen and Brindy are right downstairs most days. One or the other."

But not both. My mother shares Sarah's fear that all is not well between them.

"And you've written down that cell phone number?" Sarah has rented one from a store in Schenectady, and the clerk, who she claimed looked all of fifteen, swore it would work on our trip. To each question Sarah asked, the boy had responded, "Absolutely." She pinned him down as best she could. Anywhere in Europe? "Absolutely." Italy is where we'll be. "Really? Awesome." And you're sure it'll work there? "Absolutely."

We'll see.

"I'll be fine," my mother tells me. "Will you?" She asks because last week I made the mistake of sharing my worry about having one of my spells in a foreign country, a concern I've not even mentioned to Sarah, though she's probably guessed.

When I tell her I'll be fine, that I'm more concerned about the long flight, she relents and reaches across the table to put her hand on mine, a gesture that makes a boy of me again. This may be why I told her in the first place. Whenever I'm in jeopardy, real or imagined, she allows herself to suspend judgment. In fact, I've suspected that our relationship has become increasingly contentious partly because it's been so long since my last spell. Odd that my old affliction should still be a trump card in our relationship—indeed, my only trump—and I realize how wrong and unmanly it is to play it.

Though it's not a lie, this fear I've confided. In advance of a spell I often feel slightly "off," as if at the periphery of my vision or awareness there's something I can't quite bring into focus, a fuzziness not unlike what I've heard migraine sufferers refer to as an aura. This has been especially true of those I've had as an adult, though this same effect was probably present when I was a boy, had I known what to look for. Back then my mother could predict an upcoming event when she noticed a remoteness, some part of me that couldn't be engaged, making me seem confused or conflicted. But neither one of us could ever be sure. Sometimes my abstraction was simply worry about a big math test or something I'd overheard or possibly misinterpreted in conversation between my parents as it came filtering up into my bedroom late at night through the heat register. A temporary worry, in other words, of the sort that would expire of its own volition, predictive of nothing and indicative only of the human condition.

Which may well be the case now. In writing my story I've brought myself back to that period when my spells were more frequent, and this may explain the aura I've felt of late, especially when I quit writing and return to my real, present life. At such times I can't help but wonder whether a spell is imminent, or if my slight disorientation is nothing more than the past colliding with the present, as they will when people my age attempt to see the figure in the carpet of their lives, which we can't help but do. The human condition, as I say, as opposed to the peculiar condition of Lucy Lynch. In confiding my fears about Italy, I guess I'm asking my mother if she's observed any of the old symptoms, if she still has the knack of knowing.

"I just don't want to ruin things for Sarah," I say. "You know how I am afterward. If I had a spell over there, she'd have to do everything herself. I just keep hoping we'll hear from Bobby before we go. That way if something happens . . ."

This is exactly the wrong thing to say, of course, since it makes me seem childlike, even more in need of reassurance. Saying his name out loud to my mother has the unintended effect of allowing the needy boy I was to creep back into my voice, an echo across the decades. All over again I'm telling her *I just wish* Bobby'd call with his new phone number like he promised, or *I just wish* he hadn't been sent off to school downstate, or *I just hope* he'll call during the Christmas break. And my poor mother, beyond exasperation, telling me for the umpteenth time that I have to stop depending on him, that my just wishing and just hoping are pointless, since I don't even know for sure that he'll be coming home for Christmas, or that his father will allow him to call even if he wants to. And finally, that if I don't stop worrying these same things over and over in my head, I'll end up having a spell.

So the sad look she gives me when I say I wish for my wife's sake that we'd hear from Bobby Marconi—who doesn't even exist anymore, at least not by that name—is the one I knew I'd get, the one that says I'm deluding myself, now as always. But kind, as well, as she sometimes was with my father when she took a break from trying to change him and accepted both who he was and even the fact that she loved him. She leaves her hand on top of mine, and it *is* a comfort, I must admit, though shameful. Is it a comfort to her as well? To be able to let go, however temporarily, of whatever unease has been between us, mother and son, for so long?

"Oh, Lou," she says, squeezing my hand so hard that it has to hurt her gnarled, arthritic fingers, "why must you be so . . ."

I can't say, any more than I can explain why I said that about Bobby writing back before we leave. Because I do know that's not going to happen.

I PARKED in the lot behind the movie theater, planning to fetch the car after lunch and save my mother the walk, but now she says she'd prefer the exercise, so we cross the street and walk slowly and silently up the alley between the Bijou and the now-abandoned Newberry's. For me this alley is one of the most haunted places in Thomaston. Here, though it's been nearly forty years since the last yellow kernel was popped, I can still smell the dime-store popcorn and Karen Cirillo's cheap perfume. Here, too, is the rusty fire escape leading up to the exit that was always chained shut for Saturday matinees to prevent West End kids who'd paid from sneaking up into the condemned balcony and letting their friends in for free. From the second step of this fire escape I witnessed one of the most shocking events of my youth, and I suppose I'll have to commit it to paper sometime next week if I continue writing my story. Even so many years later, I'm deeply ashamed to recollect what happened that afternoon and tempted to either skip the episode or put the whole undertaking aside.

We're halfway up the alley, each in our own thoughts, my mother clutching my elbow to steady herself, when I feel her stiffen and see a shambling, pear-shaped old man coming toward us. Backlit as he is, I don't immediately place him. He's dressed in ratty thrift-shop clothes, including a Thomaston High letterman's jacket with a faded blue wool body and gold leather sleeves that has to be over thirty years old. He's about my mother's age, sporting a full head of wiry salt-and-pepper hair. It's the cowlick I finally recognize.

It's a narrow alley, and Buddy Nurt has stationed himself foursquare in the middle. There's room for my mother to navigate around him on one side and me on the other, but that would involve her letting go of my elbow, something I can tell she has no intention of doing. We have no choice but to stop and regard Buddy as he's regarding us and apparently enjoying our predicament.

"I know you," he says, looking first at my mother and then me. "You got something for me?"

When I reach for my wallet, my mother says no, as much to me as to him.

He's seen my hand move, then stop moving, and now he's waiting to see if it'll start moving again. "Give me something and I won't tell," he says. This isn't really a personal threat, as my mother well knows. It's just how Buddy has greeted people ever since he went batty. All he wants is a dollar or two, which I usually give him, after which he says okay, he won't tell. I have no idea what he thinks he knows, or even if he actually recognizes either one of us. He's just convinced people will pay him to keep their secrets, whether or not he has any idea who they are.

"No one's going to give you anything," my mother tells him. "Will you kindly move out of our way? You smell."

Buddy waits a beat, then does as he's told. "You think I don't know about you, but I do," he tells her as we pass. "You think I won't tell, but I will."

"Keep walking," my mother says, reading my mind, because I'm tempted to go back and give the man a dollar.

"Lynch," he calls after us. "*That's* your damn name." And then he laughs his nasty old laugh, as if once upon a time he'd caught *us* stealing from *his* store, instead of the other way around, and that knowing our name proves he knows all about us, including every wrong thing we've ever done or imagined doing.

My mother and I don't speak until we arrive back at Ikey's. In the hallway she settles onto the lift chair and, with what appears to be her last ounce of will, presses the button that pulls the "damned contraption" upstairs. I follow, in case her irrational fears turn out to be real.

I DIDN'T SEE Karen Cirillo in school the next day, but since we had no classes in common, it didn't dawn on me until the end of the week that she was gone and not just from the flat over the store. On Saturday, when her mother came in for cigarettes, I had a chance to inquire.

I'd noticed that Nancy never visited my mother anymore and seldom came into Ikey Lubin's when my father was behind the counter because, I suspected, they'd recently had words. He'd learned from my uncle Dec, who knew such things, that she hadn't been exaggerating about Buddy Nurt, who over the years had been arrested on charges ranging from shoplifting to felony theft to attempted blackmail, though the latter charge had been dropped. Hearing this, my father certainly didn't like the idea of him living upstairs, and he especially didn't want him in the store, a message Nancy must have conveyed, since whenever she came in now Buddy loitered outside, trying to smooth his cowlick.

In the week since he'd moved in, Buddy had made no effort to find a job. He was a short-order cook by profession, but two of the three Thomaston restaurants that employed these were located out by the highway, too far to walk, in his view, and neither he nor Nancy owned a car. The hair salon where she worked now, on lower Division Street, was about the same distance from Ikey's as the highway, though somehow she managed to walk there every day. The Cayoga Diner was downtown, of course, but he'd already worked there on various occasions and been fired each time.

"She goes to school over in Mohawk now," Nancy explained, and she must've seen the disappointment on my face because her own expression became sly. "Don't worry, she'll be back," she added. "Karen don't like my sister any more than she likes me, and her uncle's no prize either. That Quinn kid gets sent back to reform school where he belongs, you could be next in line." Having voiced this possibility, she looked me over more carefully. "You one of the smart ones, like she says?" When I didn't deny this, she shrugged. "Your ma's smart, so I guess you come by it naturally."

"My dad's smart, too," I told her.

"I'll have to take your word for that," she said. "You get good grades and all?"

"Pretty good."

"B's?"

"And A's," I said, because it was true.

"Too bad. My daughter prefers idiots."

Outside, Buddy impatiently knocked on the glass, urging her to hurry.

"Speaking of things coming naturally," she admitted, reading my mind.

LATER THAT AUTUMN, my father became a hero.

It came about because he was doing as my mother advised, keeping the store open until midnight on weekends and, as a result, selling more beer between ten and twelve on Friday and Saturday nights than the rest of the weekdays combined. There was trouble sometimes, underage kids wanting to buy alcohol and getting belligerent when my father wouldn't sell it to them, and their peeling out from in front of the store angered the neighbors, who complained it had never been so noisy at Ikey Lubin's back when it was really Ikey Lubin's. Others still resented that my father had closed down the book that had operated so conveniently out of the back room. Ikey himself was in the hospital being treated for a lung tumor, and it was widely reported that he intended to buy his business back just as soon as he was cured. "If only," my mother remarked.

On the night in question, it was almost midnight, and my father was going over the day's racing form and listening to the recap of the harness races at Saratoga on the radio. He seldom bet the horses, but like almost everyone in Thomaston, he followed them, needing to be able to talk results with his regulars, almost all of whom wagered daily. I also happened to know he kept a spiral binder of imaginary wagers, dutifully noting which of his picks would've won and how much each paid, as well as all the losers, so he could tell how much money he saved by keeping his bets imaginary. Somehow Uncle Dec found out about this binder and ribbed my father unmercifully, claiming that everything he did was imaginary for the simple reason he was too cheap to spend the two dollars necessary to make it real. Which was why, my father replied, he always *had* two dollars, whereas his brother was always looking to borrow two.

Be that as it may, the print on the racing form was tiny, which meant my father had to wear his glasses, and it was in the corner of the lens that he gradually became aware of an orange flickering. At first he imagined this to be a trick of the store's fluorescent lighting, until he looked up and saw, across the intersection, a tongue of flame licking out from under a partially open window on the ground floor of the Spinnarkles' house. The upper flat, which the Marconis had rented, was still vacant.

What he did next was call my mother. I remember the phone waking me up, ringing there on the end table in the living room. My mother was downstairs reading, and with her back to the window, she had to rotate in her chair to pick up the phone, and that's when she saw. "Lou!" she said. "There's a fire next door!"

That, he informed her, was what he was calling about.

"Did you call the fire department?"

"You do it, okay?" he said. "I'll be right over."

241

This, of course, was in the days before 911. The fire department number was in the front of the phone book, but you had to look it up, then dial all seven digits. Further—how odd this seems now—the telephone was one of the things my father generally left to my mother. At home he always let her answer. If he wanted to talk to someone, he preferred to go see them, either that or say, "Tessa, call the plumber, would you?" There was a phone in the store, but he found all sorts of excuses for not answering it. One day my mother called and just let it ring until he finally picked up. "Don't tell me that," she said when he explained that he'd been too busy to get to it. "I'm standing right here in the front room looking at you. You're all alone in there."

"So, what do you want?"

"I want to know why you're afraid of the damn phone."

"I ain't afraid of it—" he started, but she hung up.

My own theory is that he was less afraid of the phone than the phone *book*. I never knew my paternal grandparents, but I'm pretty sure my grandmother was illiterate. Grandpa could read just enough to get by. As a result my father was so far behind by the time he started school that he never caught up, which was probably why he was so proud of how I devoured books and so embarrassed when my mother accused him of moving his lips when he read the newspaper. The Thomaston phone book was pretty slender, but I could tell that its long columns of similar names, the one he wanted buried among so many others, frustrated him. In an emergency, he might not have remembered that the fire department's listing was in the front, and even if he *had* remembered he'd have found at least a dozen other emergency numbers listed there and would've concluded the thing to do was call my mother.

When she hung up after calling the fire department, she saw that I'd come downstairs and was rubbing the sleep out of my eyes and staring stupidly out the window at the flames next door. By then you could actually *hear* the fire. "Get dressed, Lou," she said. "Hurry, in case the fire jumps."

"Where's Dad?"

"*Get dressed!*" she repeated, pushing me up the stairs. I did as I was told but apparently not fast enough, because a moment later she burst into my room and grabbed me by the elbow.

By the time we got out of the house, the neighbors were standing on their porches, pointing at the flames, which had spread to the second floor, and sirens were heading our direction. Across the intersection, the lights were all still on in Ikey Lubin's, but there was no sign of my father. Nancy Salvatore, her robe pulled tightly across her chest, and Buddy Nurt, in boxer shorts and a T-shirt, had come out onto their upstairs porch to view the proceedings.

"Where's Dad?" I asked again, but my question was drowned out by the fire engine screaming around the corner, and my mother just pulled me closer.

The flames were now dancing in the vacant windows of the Marconi flat. "Hurry up, before it jumps the roof!" one fireman shouted. Another connected a thick coil of hose to the hydrant conveniently located on our own terrace. I mowed around it every week, thinking of the plug as an inconvenience and wondering why it was there at all. "Is anyone inside?" I heard a fireman ask my mother.

She couldn't have taken more than a second to respond, but the question, together with the fierce hug my mother was giving me, was enough for me to understand that my father was inside the burning house.

"Two women live on the first floor," my mother said. "I think my husband's gone in after—"

Several windows exploded outward just then, causing us to move farther back and everyone along the street to gasp.

"Where are the bedrooms?"

In the back, my mother said, and two of the firemen started around the far side of the building.

"Wet this one down," one shouted to the big fireman operating the hose, which he then swung around to begin soaking our roof and back porch just a few feet from where the flames were licking at the Spinnarkle eaves, the force of the water dislodging a window screen that clattered onto the walk below.

"There!" someone shouted, and I saw that the front door to the Spinnarkles' downstairs flat was now open, black smoke billowing out. A moment later a child emerged.

That's what it looked like, though of course no child lived there, and it took me a moment to realize that this figure, doubled over choking, was one of the sisters. (I never could keep them straight.) She was blackened with smoke and soot and, I realized with a shock, completely naked. My brain immediately supplied a reason. The fire had burned her clothes off.

"This way, Edith!" she screamed back into the house (which made the screamer Janet). "This way, Mr. Lynch! Hurry!"

Several firemen ascended the steps now, and one of them threw a blanket around her, drawing her down the porch steps by force when what she intended, it seemed to me, was to go back into the burning house. Another fireman started in and then stopped in the doorway, reaching inside for Edith Spinnarkle's hand and pulling her, also sooty and naked, out onto the porch.

What happened next surprised me even more than their nakedness. Just as the fireman was pulling her out of the house, Edith was reaching back and pulling with her other hand. I fully expected that when my father emerged, he'd be naked, too. After all, if the sisters had had their clothes incinerated, it followed that he'd likely be in the same condition, and as I remember it now across the years, I think I was more worried about the fact that he'd be naked in front of all our neighbors than about the possibility that he'd been injured in the blaze. So I was very surprised when he emerged fully clothed. His white short-sleeved shirt was black with soot, of course, but it wasn't on fire.

"Lou!" my mother cried, bolting past firemen who were holding everybody at a distance, and I heard my father, blinded by the smoke and trying to locate her voice by sound, then bellow, "Tessa!" Now that he was safe, the tears started streaming down my face, and it seemed like I stood there forever, alone and forgotten on the sidewalk. I saw my parents embrace at the foot of the porch steps, then lost them in the encroaching crowd.

At this point the remaining windows of the Spinnarkle house exploded, glass raining down over the street. The entire structure was now engulfed in flame, and we were all herded to safety across the road. The firemen, cutting their losses, concentrated on trying to save the adjacent houses. As I pushed among the crowd of onlookers, I heard Edith Spinnarkle, hugging her sister close on a neighbor's porch, cry out, "Our home! Our home, Janet! Look! It's gone!"

I finally located my parents one porch farther down the block. My mother was clutching my father to her as one would a big, overgrown child. He was wrapped in a blanket and shivering violently, his tears leaving tracks down his sooty cheeks. Neither seemed to notice when I climbed the steps and sat down next to them. My father looked odd, and then I realized why. His eyebrows had been singed off. "Louie," he said, finally recognizing me and drawing me close, glad for somewhere else to look, because he couldn't bring himself to face the blaze. "Is our house going to burn down, Tessa?" he asked.

"No, Lou," she assured him, though she wasn't looking at the fire either, just at him.

"What'll we do?" he wanted to know.

"It's not going to burn down, Lou," she said. "You saved it. If you hadn't seen what was happening—"

"Is the store okay?" he said, causing me to glance over at Ikey Lubin's. Why wouldn't the store be okay, I wondered, since it was way on the other side of the street.

"The store's fine, Lou. The house is fine. You saved Janet and Edith both. You saved their *lives*, Lou."

My father looked over at them, huddled together on the steps of the porch next door, as if to ascertain whether seeing them there was full and sufficient evidence to warrant such a conclusion. "Then why is Louie crying?" he wondered.

"I don't know," my mother said, regarding me for the first time and laughing, which made me laugh, too, or rather to make some sound composed of relief and wonder and residual terror.

In twenty minutes the Spinnarkles' home burned to the ground, the whole neighborhood watching.

THE NEXT MORNING I woke up so exhausted that I wondered if I'd had a spell in my sleep, since these sometimes took the form of vivid dreams. But when I pulled back the curtain of my bedroom window, I was surprised to find myself looking at the Gunther house, which hadn't been part of the view until now. All that remained of the Spinnarkle house was the smoldering foundation and tipping chimney. My mother was in the shower, so I dressed quickly and went outside to inspect the ruins. It had rained in the night, and soot was draining in wide streams into the sewer grate. My father was already up and over at the store, where a police car at the curb didn't strike me as odd, given last night's dramatic events, though something did tickle at the edges of my memory. I tried to bring it front and center, but it wouldn't budge.

Our own house had sustained more damage than I'd thought. The heat from the blaze had bubbled the paint along the near side, and the roof and cornice of the back porch were badly scorched. The night before, despite the fears voiced by both my mother and the firemen, the idea that the fire might leap from the Spinnarkle house to ours had seemed far-fetched, but I now saw how close we'd come, which in turn made me remember Edith Spinnarkle whimpering, "Our home! . . . Our home!" What, I wondered, would happen to them now? I hoped they wouldn't be moving in with us, because that would be the end of our television viewing.

Thinking about all this I recalled the heat register conversation I'd heard late that night, after everything had finally calmed down and I'd been sent up to bed. "That's how I found them," I heard my father say. To which my mother replied, "Well, I'm not that surprised." I'd fallen asleep shortly after that, too tired from all the excitement to consider what my mother hadn't been that surprised by.

She was sitting at the table in her robe and staring into a cup of murky coffee when I went back inside. Seeing I was up and dressed, she said, "You should shower before we go to Mass." We hadn't been going to church much since my mother laid down the law to Father Gluck, but I understood why this morning might be different. God had looked out for us, so we'd go and give thanks. "Do I have to?" I said, prepared to be told to march.

"No."

I sat down across the table from her, suddenly remembering the police car.

As if she'd read my mind, she said, "The store was robbed."

"When?"

"While everybody was watching the fire. Your father never had a chance to lock up. . . ."

"How much money—"

"Whatever was in the till. Saturday's our best day, so . . ." She shook her head, as discouraged as I'd ever seen her. "What kind of person . . ."

The answer to her question came to me in the shower. When she and I had gone out into the street last night, I'd looked over at Ikey Lubin's, expecting my father to come bursting out of the store, but what I saw was Nancy Salvatore in her robe and Buddy Nurt in his boxer shorts and sleeveless T-shirt up on their porch. Later, when my father asked if the store was going to be okay, I looked there again and saw Buddy standing with his hands in his trouser pockets on the sidewalk out front. Which meant that in between he'd gone inside and gotten dressed. At the time I concluded, if anything, that he must've come down to the street for a better view of the fire. Except that made no sense. From their upstairs porch they already had the best view possible.

Buddy Nurt had robbed us.

THE FIRE OCCURRED late Saturday night, so it was Monday before my father appeared on the front page of the *Thomaston Guardian*. In the photo he's holding up his two bandaged hands for the camera and, as I mentioned, without eyebrows. Otherwise, his hair was basically unharmed—Brylcreem, apparently, didn't burn—and combed into his signature pompadour, which my mother must've done for him, given the condition of his hands. As a boy I always thought my father handsome, the sort of man people considered special in appearance as well as conduct, though I suppose this is how all boys regard their fathers. Now that he exists most vividly in my memory, the old newspaper photo sometimes catches me off guard, and I can't help thinking that while this man is perfectly my father, perfectly Big Lou Lynch with his broad, good-natured smile and his big, awkward body, the picture doesn't do him justice.

I still have the article, of course. Old and yellow and brittle, but safely under glass, it hangs on the wall in my study. At one point we had dozens of copies, because neighbors all along Third Avenue saved them for us. I remember the stack of newspapers in the corner of the living room, and also going through them, one after the other, proud yet disappointed, too, that the photograph and story were identical and thinking how much better and more just it would've been to have a different picture of my father in each copy, like baseball cards, so we could collect them all. By the next day, of course, there was other news, and that didn't seem fair either.

What I found interesting about the article, even at the time, was that the Spinnarkle sisters, who after all had lost their home in the fire, didn't feature in it all that much. They were named, of course, but there were no photos, even on the inside pages. Nor, apparently, was the Albany television station that sent a camera crew to Thomaston the following Monday much interested in them. It was my father they'd come to see. He was, at best, a reluctant hero, one who needed to be talked into giving interviews by my mother. His reluctance was born less of modesty than acute embarrassment over what had transpired inside the Spinnarkles' flat, which he feared was bound to come out if he talked to reporters.

For one thing, the Spinnarkles had as much rescued him as he them. By the time he managed to awaken them in the back of the house, their bedroom filling with smoke, he'd become disoriented. The sisters, of course, could've found their way blindfolded, which, with the black smoke billowing, was precisely what was required. And one of them apparently knew enough to get down and crawl along the floor. But somewhere my father encountered an obstacle of some sort, and one of the sisters actually had to go back to get him, and this was what shamed him.

"What if they find out?" he asked my mother, meaning the reporters.

"You saved their lives, Lou," she reminded him. "Who led who doesn't matter. If you hadn't gone in after them, they'd have burned alive."

"But they were the ones—"

"No, Lou. *You* were the one. That's why they want to talk to you. People want you to be a hero."

But his embarrassment had another source as well, though I was much older before I was able to piece together the surprising nakedness of the Spinnarkles when they emerged from the burning house, my mother's "I'm not that surprised" comment later that same night and the fact that afterward, instead of finding a new place in Thomaston, the sisters moved away. Because my father was in many ways an innocent himself, I've often wondered how much of what he'd witnessed he understood and how much my mother had to explain. A trusting man, he must've found it difficult to believe that people could not just *tell* but actually *live* so profound a lie. "Face value," she was always saying. "Why do you insist on taking things at face value?" Perhaps it was his innocence that I loved most, and the reason I've been reluctant, all my life, to hear a word spoken against him, and why I've not only kept that heroic photo safe under glass all these years, but also, when I show it to people, always explain that it doesn't do him justice.

KAREN CIRILLO'S MOTHER was right. A month after shoving her ruptured suitcase into her uncle's pickup, Karen was back. I was alone at Ikey Lubin's, immersed in a book, the front door propped open to catch a breeze, so I never heard her come in.

"So, Lou," she said, "did you miss me?"

"Sure," I said, setting my book facedown and taking her in. If anything she was more breathtakingly beautiful than before. Wearing her usual bored expression, she picked up my book, riffled through its pages as if to see how many there were, then set it back down, her curiosity completely satisfied, losing my page in the process, not that I cared.

"What?" she said. "I got a booger dangling?"

"No," I said, startled. This image was simply too incongruous to visualize.

"Why you looking at me like that?"

Having no idea what she meant, I said, "I'm not."

"Are too."

It was the kind of conversation she liked best, full of unresolvable conflict. If I continued to deny looking at her funny, she'd just keep saying "are too" forever. "Okay," I said, "you've got a booger dangling."

"Funny," she said. "Wait till I tell Jerz what you said." I must have blanched then, because she quickly added, "Don't piss yourself, Lou. I was just kidding."

"Oh," I said, "right."

"There's all kinds of shit I don't tell Jerz," she said, provocatively.

"Like what?"

"You know, secrets."

"What kind of secrets?" I said, my heart pounding at the possibility she might share one with me.

"Why would I tell you if I don't tell him?"

I had no ready answer for this.

"You're saying what? I could trust you?"

"I guess." I shrugged.

For a long moment, she seemed to consider this. "Okay, you first."

"Me first what?"

"Tell me a secret, then I'll tell you one."

"I don't have any."

"Everybody's got secrets. I bet you got a ton of 'em."

"Why?"

"You got the look," she informed me. "Okay, I'll start. Ask me anything, and I'll tell you the truth."

"How come you came back?"

"I missed you," she said, looking right at me, challenging me to deny the plausibility of this.

"I thought you were going to tell the truth."

"Know what, Lou? You got low self-esteem. I know 'cause I got the same thing."

"You?" I said, unable to disguise my surprise.

She shrugged. "Sure. I got these going for me"—she cupped her hands under her breasts here, giving them some additional loft—"but what else?"

Fortunately, this question appeared to be rhetorical. "What about . . . ," I started, glancing up at the ceiling, above which Buddy Nurt might or might not actually be. I'd seen little of him lately. He'd gotten a job driving the drunk shift for Hudson Cab, which did a brisk business in the Gut when the gin mills closed, and he slept during the day. He hadn't come into the store since the fire. Sometimes he'd stop outside and look in wistfully, before tromping upstairs, and a few minutes later Karen's mother would come down and purchase whatever he'd been tempted by, usually a six-pack of cheap beer or a pack of cigarettes. Other times, he'd come out onto their rickety porch, allowing the screen door to clap shut behind him. Shirtless, he'd scratch his belly thoughtfully, much as another man would scratch his head, then return inside, the screen door banging again. My mother said she fully expected him to unzip and pee right over the railing one day, but so far he hadn't. Now I was tempted to share with Karen my suspicion that Buddy had robbed our store. "I thought—"

"He tries anything, Jerz will kill him. Or maybe you. You'd do that for me, wouldn't you?"

I felt myself flush at this suggestion. "I don't think I'd *kill* him," I said, implying, I hoped, that I'd stop just short of homicide, out of mercy.

"So, you're saying you're not my friend?"

"No, I'm your friend, it's just—"

"Then how about some cigs? Give me a pack of Parliaments, and I'll let you slide on the other. Jerz would be way better at killing Buddy anyhow."

When I took a pack down from the rack, she opened her purse, and for a moment I thought she might actually pay, but she just slipped them inside. "And a pack of Camels for Jerz," she added without looking up.

"I really shouldn't. My father . . ."

She looked straight at me, her eyes smoldering. "Hey, it's okay. I thought we were pals, is all."

When I handed her the Camels, I saw she'd used her best trick on me. In the month she'd been gone I'd forgotten her ability to look right at me and then, seemingly at the same moment, at some spot over my shoulder. I could either be there or not, she seemed to suggest, according to her whim.

Halfway out the door, Karen paused as if something had just occurred to her. "Didn't there used to be a house over there?" she said, pointing at the empty space between our house and the Gunthers'.

"It burned down."

"No shit."

"My father rescued the two ladies who lived there," I told her, hoping one day to be just like him, even if it meant going through life pretending not to know things I knew.

"Jeez. I wish I'd been here," she said, not bored now, but as if she actually meant it.

LATER THAT NIGHT I realized that our thrilling, vaguely sexy conversation had really been about the cigarettes. Karen couldn't just come in and ask for them. She first had to establish that we were friends, that there was intimacy between us. I'd never suspected the whole thing was a cat-and-mouse game until it was too late, which meant that being smart wasn't the advantage it should have been. I *was* smart, as my mother was always insisting. Certainly smarter than Karen. But being smart wasn't much use if I could get suckered so easily.

Or maybe there were two kinds of smart, and Karen was the other, and maybe that kind was more advantageous than mine. I remembered my mother telling me that I had to get smarter about people if I was going to survive in the world, yet something in me rejected that notion, not so much because it was untrue but because it wasn't my preference. I preferred to think that Karen Cirillo was, or could be, my friend, who might one day need me to rescue her from Buddy Nurt. I preferred to think that her casting me in this role wasn't absurd. After all, I was my father's son, and he was brave enough to enter a burning building, so maybe I was braver than I knew. That night I spent most of my last hour before falling asleep trying to envision the complex set of circumstances necessary for me to become

Karen's rescuer. Jerzy Quinn, Karen's mother and my own parents would all have to be away somewhere. Alone in the store below, I would hear her cries for help. If I was afraid of what might be happening upstairs, and what might happen to me if I interfered, I'd swallow my fear and start up through the darkness. Maybe the pellet gun that put the fear of God into the mangy neighborhood dogs would have the same effect on mangy Buddy Nurt. I could almost form a mental picture of the rescue. Then it would vanish, and I'd be alone in the dark with only my mother's advice—that I needed to get smarter if I was to survive.

Ironically, that advice *did* make me suspicious, not of Karen Cirillo but of my mother. She, I realized, would've been one step ahead of Karen, not behind, as I'd been. She'd have recognized each devious ploy for what it was. Why? Because, well, she was sly herself. She was both kinds of smart—my kind and Karen's. Why then, I wondered, did I *not* want to be like my mother? Why did I know that the next time Karen wanted a pack of cigarettes, I'd give them to her, so I could keep believing we were friends?

Lying there in the dark, I tried over and over to visualize climbing those stairs and rescuing Karen from the pervert Buddy Nurt, my mother's voice echoing in my head with each upward tread. *Don't be one of those people who go through life pretending not to know what they know. . . . Don't waste time wishing the world is different than it is. . . . Don't expect people to be something they can't. . .*

THAT SPRING the Albany newspaper ran a series of articles about pollution in the Hudson, a river where salmon had once run but that was now contaminated by all manner of industrial waste. The paper had been critical of big polluters like General Electric but also cited smaller, particularly lethal ones that were poisoning the big river's tributaries. They'd even mentioned our tiny Cayoga Stream, noting there were no longer any fish downstream of the tannery and going so far as to call for a study to determine whether the tannery's chemical dyes had impacted our groundwater, hinting at a link to the county's alarming cancer statistics. The *Thomaston Guardian* responded with an editorial ridiculing the Albany paper and stopping just short of claiming the charges were a Communist conspiracy designed to undermine our only viable industry, a conclusion applauded by the majority of Thomaston residents.

But not long after the Albany series a FOR SALE sign appeared on the terrace of Jack Beverly's house, the grandest in the Borough, and this news roared through town like a tidal wave. It had long been rumored that the tannery would soon close for good, and it certainly employed fewer workers each year, the seasonal layoffs coming earlier and lasting longer. If the Beverlys were selling their house, then maybe the rumors were accurate. My father, true to form, was more optimistic. He doubted the tannery would close anytime soon, and in support of his hopefulness he marshaled many of the same arguments he'd used for why the dairy wouldn't discontinue home delivery. After all, leather had been tanned in Thomaston for longer than anybody could remember. Maybe things had been slow for a while, but they were bound to pick up again. Why? Because these things ran in cycles. Up follows down. Has to. He always saved what he considered his most powerful argument for last. "If the tannery closes," he'd say, pausing for emphasis, "what're people around here gonna do?" For him, the more disastrous something was, the less likely it would occur.

Often, after closing the store, he'd repeat these conversations to my mother, though he should have known she'd be a tougher customer. "If that tannery closes, what's Louie and all his friends gonna do for work around here?" he said one night when we were all watching the end of the Yankees game on TV.

Usually she just let him talk, but tonight she was in a foul mood after working on Ikey's books all afternoon. "Keep Lou out of it," she said, rising from her chair. "For one thing, he doesn't have any friends. Every minute he's not in school or doing his homework, he's helping you at the store."

What she'd said was true, and we all knew it. At the beginning the rules limiting my time there had been strictly enforced, but I loved Ikey's and my father's company, so they'd gradually eroded. I knew my mother disapproved of my hours at the store and was waiting for my grades to slip, if only a little, to lower the boom, but thus far they hadn't.

"And for another thing, Lou isn't going to work in that tannery whether it's open or shut, any more than he's going to work at Ikey Lubin's the rest of his life. He's going to college."

"I ain't saying that," my father said, surprised that she'd taken her stance right in front of his chair, coming between him and the Yankees, and was pointing her index finger at him.

"And why do you always say you aren't saying what I just heard you say?" she wanted to know. "You should've been a politician. You can't remember what you've said from one minute to the next."

"I ain't saying *Louie's* gonna work there," he explained. "I'm saying *people*. What're people gonna do around here if there ain't no work?"

"Starve, Lou," was her instant reply. "Either that or move to where there is work."

"They got houses here, Tessa. People all lose their jobs at once, how they gonna sell them?"

"They won't be able to. The banks will take them."

My father shook his head stubbornly. "They ain't gonna let that happen—"

"Who's 'they,' Lou? Just out of curiosity."

"The Beverlys and them," he said. "They got houses here, too. You got any idea how much them houses in the Borough are worth?"

"Not as much as the ones they've got in Florida. Wake up, Lou. The people you call *they*? *They'll* get out clean. *They* aren't stupid."

And you are was what she left unsaid.

Then she went upstairs, leaving my father staring at the TV, nodding at the Yankees as if their problems and Thomaston's were inextricably intertwined. "I ain't sayin' the tannery won't ever close," he conceded to me. "I'm just sayin' it don't have to be like your mother says. She don't know everything either." This last was spoken in a whisper.

We'd first heard about that sign on the Beverlys' front yard midweek, but it was Sunday morning before we saw it for ourselves. My father didn't say where we were going, just suggested we take a drive while my mother worked on her books, but I suspected what he had in mind. We parked across the street from the Beverlys' house, and my father turned the ignition off, though the engine continued to idle for a good ten seconds before finally shuddering into silence. We'd bought the car, a Ford, used, when the dairy clamped down on personal use of company trucks. But since we'd purchased Ikey's, it didn't get driven much. My father was always at the store, and my mother seldom drove, so it just sat out by the curb, unused, for weeks on end. She kept saying we should sell it and save the cost of insurance, but he didn't want to be totally without transportation. Besides, he was fond of joking about how we had the only car he knew of that liked to run so much it was reluctant to shut down. Today, though, there were no such jokes.

For a long time he just sat there staring at the house—pink and sprawling and all on one level, its backyard surrounded by a tall fence through the slats of which you could see the blue sparkle of a swimming pool. And sure enough, there was the FOR SALE sign everyone was talking about. I don't think my father completely believed it would be there, not until he saw it with his own eyes, and even then he wasn't sure of its meaning. I could tell by the way he was rubbing his chin that he was trying to come up with another explanation. I, too, found it hard to believe, though for reasons more rooted in my world than his. The Beverlys simply *couldn't* move away, because if they did, the perfect symmetry of my junior high world would crumble. Nan Beverly had to remain in Thomaston to counterbalance Karen Cirillo—the light girl and the dark. Could either exist without the other? I didn't see how. Even contemplating the possibility made me queasy, so while my father tried to come up with another meaning for the FOR SALE sign, I developed scenarios whereby Nan's parents would move and she'd stay on with an aunt and uncle I'd invented on the spot to take her in.

We were quiet for a while, trying to make our worlds right, until my father finally spoke. "How much do people gotta have to be happy, Louie?" he wondered out loud, as if he thought I might actually know the answer. "You lived in that house, wouldn't you be happy?"

I said I would, and meant it.

"Anybody would," he nodded, glad to have produced such a sensible kid. "How could you not be happy if you had all that?"

When my father and I were alone, sometimes I could hear my mother's responses to things he said, and now I heard her say, *You think people are geared to be content, Lou? And you came to this conclusion how?*

I was pretty sure this wasn't a skill my father possessed, or he wouldn't have said half the things he did. "When you're all grown up, if you live in a house like that, be happy. Don't let nobody tell you you ain't got it made neither."

I promised I wouldn't.

"You don't even need all this to have it made," he went on. "Your uncle and me? We grew up in a house didn't have no running water or electricity. You ain't gotta have everything to be happy."

Across the street, the front door opened, and Mr. Beverly emerged, followed by a slender, well-dressed woman I took to be Mrs. Beverly, then finally Nan herself, radiant and clean, her blondness highlighted in the morning sunlight. They were clearly on their way to church, and all three seemed to notice us at once, which made me want to slide down in my seat. How out of place we must have looked sitting there. Borough streets were extra wide, but ours was the only car visible on this one, the others all safely tucked away in their garages or on gleaming display in their double-wide driveways. I think my father also realized we didn't belong, and I felt bad for him because, as a route man, he *had* once belonged here, at least certain hours of the day.

If the Beverlys wondered who we were and why we were parked there, they gave no sign. They didn't stare at us like East Enders did at strangers who didn't belong, openly wondering who they were and who they might be visiting. Instead, father, mother and radiant daughter just got into their shiny Cadillac, the rear window of which, I noticed, had been repaired. I saw Mr. Beverly adjust his rearview mirror, perhaps to get another look at us but more likely to have the best view possible while backing out. When their Cadillac disappeared around the corner, my father looked stricken, as if they were leaving town for good, right that minute, not just going to church.

Reluctant as our Ford was to quit running, it was equally loath to start up again, but eventually it did. Though I figured we'd now head back home, we took another slow tour of the Borough, just as we'd done in his milk truck the day he told me which important people lived where. Probably he was just reassuring himself about how many prominent families there'd still be, even if the Beverlys moved, but I wondered if he was also puzzling over how to get here from where we were. Would a corner market, once we were better at running it, bring us here, or did Ikey Lubin's just mean we could stay where we were and not have to return to Berman Court?

When we'd exhausted all the Borough streets, we drove on out of town and slowed down at Whitcombe Park. There was no sign of Gabriel Mock. Beyond the fence the Hall looked both grand and decrepit, and I wondered if it suggested to my father, as it did to me, that my mother was right, that up wasn't the only direction you could go in America—that what was won could be lost again, that Gabriel's fence enclosed little more than a magnificent ruin. If it was true, as my father steadfastly maintained, that down was followed by up, then didn't it stand to reason that up was followed by down?

"I guess the fellow that lived there was about the first one to get rich around here," he said. "I don't know how he done it, but people must've liked him." In the end, that was how my father always measured things. If you were rich, it meant people liked you and wanted to do business with you and not some other fellow. Maybe it even meant God liked you.

Before returning home, we stopped at the Cayoga Diner. Usually we sat at the counter where my father could shoot the breeze with Stan, who worked the counter, and whoever else was idling there, so I was surprised when he steered us to an empty booth at the rear. We sat next to a window that overlooked the stream below, which was water colored today, the tannery being closed on Sundays, though the bank was rainbowed, as always, like the side of a trout.

"I guess I shouldn't've bought Ikey's," he said bleakly. "It don't make enough to live on, and we can't work no harder than what we're doing."

Trying to cheer him up, I said, "We'll get better at it. We just started, really."

I don't know why he should have valued my opinion in the matter, but he *did* seem to brighten up, then reached across the table to rub my head affectionately. "You know," he said, "you ain't gotta work in the store no more than you want to."

"I like it," I assured him, which was true, except my conscience was weighing on me. For many months now I'd continued to supply Karen Cirillo with free cigarettes, and earlier in the week a couple of her West End girlfriends that I recognized from the Y dances had come into the store when I was alone, I was pretty sure, to shoplift. They'd split up as soon as they entered, heading to opposite ends of the market. One got my attention by asking me a question while the other slipped something, I couldn't tell what, into her purse. I caught only a glimpse, but when my eyes met hers across the store, I was sure. They left without buying anything, including the item the girl had asked me about. Later it occurred to me that Karen had probably put them up to it, explaining when I was usually there by myself.

And a couple of weeks earlier, before falling asleep, I'd overheard snatches of a late-night conversation between my parents. "Then you explain it, Lou. Tell me how stuff that comes off the truck just disappears. It's right there on the inventory, and then it's gone. If you sold it, it'd be in the register." No wonder Ikey's was failing. Not only did my father have a known thief living right above the store, but on those rare moments he wasn't running it himself, he turned Ikey's over to a Judas.

I knew he would've suspected himself of stealing in his sleep before he'd have suspected me, which was why I felt particularly wretched. His confidence in me was so complete, so unquestion-ing, that I wasn't even sure he'd believe me if I confessed outright. Even if I could manage to tell him, and I didn't think I could, he might just sit there and look at me expectantly for the part of the story I'd left out and without which no valid conclusions could be drawn. How could I tell him that Karen Cirillo was a fantasy I simply hadn't the strength to resist?

"So I guess she must be about the cutest one, huh?"

I was so surprised to discover he'd been eavesdropping on my thoughts there in the diner that it was all I could do to croak out my assent. He and I had never talked about girls, and I always imagined that if we ever did we'd go slow, the subject being as terrifying to him as it was to me. Now here we were admitting that Karen was the fairest of them all, which meant that my father had also registered her dark attractions.

"You and her in the same grade?"

I was about to remind him that he knew perfectly well that Karen and I were both eighth graders when it suddenly occurred to me that he wasn't talking about her at all. He was talking about Nan Beverly, whom he'd just seen climb into the family Cadillac.

"She a nice girl?"

My relief must have been palpable. Nan Beverly was a girl we *could* talk about, so I did, explaining that she was the most popular girl in the whole school, so popular in fact that boys got into fights over her outside the Y on Friday nights. At this he nodded sadly, as if his memory had been jogged. Had the same sort of thing happened when he was my age, his friends getting into fistfights over the prettiest girls? Maybe over Nan's mother? Had my father been such a boy? It was hard to imagine him in love. I knew that he and my mother must have once felt passion, since that was what love entailed, but I was grateful that over time the madness had evolved into something more like friendship or a business partnership, something I myself could be an integral part of. Even seeing my father recollect passion was disconcerting.

"You and her dance partners, down there at the Y?"

I shrugged and said, "Sometimes," which amazingly he believed, making me feel even worse. One more lie on top of all the others.

Our burgers and milkshakes arrived then, along with a big platter of fries drenched in brown gravy. My father didn't like to talk when there was food around, so our awkward conversation would be put on hold for a bit, and I wouldn't be obliged to lie while we ate. But after my father had mopped up the last of the gravy with the final greasy french fry, he said, "She ain't gotta be the cutest one. You know . . . the one you like?"

I felt what I'd eaten shift in my stomach. Though I knew it was true, I didn't want him to say my mother hadn't been the cutest.

"The one you're looking for," he went on, "is the nicest."

I knew I was supposed to comment, so I agreed.

"The one you want, she's gotta like you, too." I couldn't help noticing that he'd broken out in a sweat from this emotional heavy lifting, and I wondered why he thought it was necessary. "It's not just about you liking her. You gotta like each other."

This sort of conversation required all of our concentration, which was probably why we didn't see Uncle Dec come in, or notice him until he was right there at our booth, telling me to shove over, Bub. He sported his usual rich three-day stubble, and when he slid in next to me he made the dry, concussive little sound I always associated with him, as if he had a tiny fleck of tobacco on the tip of his tongue that he was determined to expel. Every time he spat, I followed what I imagined to be the trajectory of whatever he was trying to expectorate, but nothing ever landed. "What," he said, looking at me. "You couldn't save me one lousy french fry?"

"You could order a plate of your own," my father said. "They ain't that expensive."

"I don't want my own. I eat like you, pretty soon I'll look like you," my uncle told him, still regarding me. "Speaking of which, *you* look more like your old man every day. You both got the same pointed head." He rapped a hard knuckle on the top of mine so I'd know the spot he was talking about.

"You ready to go, Louie?" my father said.

"What's your hurry?" Uncle Dec wanted to know. "Relax. Have a cup of coffee. I'll spring, if it'll make you feel any better."

My father was half out of the booth, but since his brother hadn't moved I was trapped on the inside, so he sat back down.

"Have some ice cream," my uncle suggested to me. "I'll spring for that, too."

"He just had a milkshake," my father told him.

"So what?"

Our waitress brought two coffees and a dish of vanilla ice cream for me.

"You hear Manucci's closing?" my uncle said, still looking at me, though this was clearly directed at my father, who blanched at the news. Manucci's was an old West End market, three times the size of Ikey Lubin's. For the last year my uncle had been working there as a butcher, which was what he did when he wasn't roofing or tending bar.

"How come?"

"The asshole son, what do you think? Likes to pretend he's a high roller. He could lose the old man's money slow, but he prefers fast. Before he goes to the track he comes in the store and takes what he needs right out of the till. All this while the old man's dying. Weighed about ninety pounds the last time I saw him. It's all he can do to raise his right arm, then he has to take a nap afterwards he's so exhausted."

My father shook his head. "West End."

"West End, East End . . . what the hell difference does it make? The kid's a bum." Now he was studying me again, as if he suspected I might turn out to be the same kind of son. "Anyhow, you know what that means, don't you?"

You're next was what he was getting at. *You know what happened to the dinosaurs, right? Death. Decomposition.*

"I guess it means you're out of a job," my father said, which I considered a pretty good comeback.

"Yeah, but what else?" He was grinning at my father now. "I'll just sit here and count while you think," he said, sticking out his left hand and beginning with his thumb. "One. Two. Three."

"I ain't gonna—" my father began.

"Tessa got it right away," my uncle interrupted, his fingers snapping to attention, four, five. "She explained it to me as soon as I told her Manooch was history." Right hand now, six, seven, eight, nine, ten.

"When did you see Tessa?"

Back over to his left hand, eleven, twelve, thirteen. "Just now. She told me you were probably down here eating french fries and gravy." Right hand, seventeen, eighteen, nineteen.

It means he wants you to give him a job. I tried to send my father this telepathic thought, as my uncle's cruel fingers continued to stiffen. I thought for sure he was going to start over again a third time when he got to twenty, but he just shook his head at my father. "We'd still be sitting here an hour from now, wouldn't we?" he said. "What it *means*," he said, lowering his voice now, "is that all your rich friends in the Borough have no place to buy their crown roast for Sunday dinner."

"How about the A&P?" my father said.

"They slice pork chops with a band saw, is what they do," Uncle Dec said with contempt.

"We don't have none of what we'd need," my father said. "A meat case. Slicer. Scale. I don't know what else. All them things cost."

"They're expensive new," his brother conceded meaningfully.

"Where you gonna find good used ones?"

Uncle Dec just stared at my father for two good beats, then swiveled to regard me. "Okay," he said. "You got the same pointy head as your old man, but I'm gonna go out on a limb here and guess you've got that figured out."

I hated taking his part against my father, but I *did* have it figured out, and I just couldn't pretend I didn't. "Manucci's?" I ventured.

"And you're *how* old?" he said, looking back at his brother, who at the moment was beaming at me, full of pride.

"Thirteen."

"Thirteen," he repeated. "Okay, I gotta go. Tessa can explain the rest of it to you. Truth? I don't care if you do or you don't. I know how to cut a crown roast, but I can also cut pork chops with a band saw. The A&P's been trying to get me to come work for them for a year, so do what you want."

"I'll think about it," my father said, regarding him suspiciously as he slid out of the booth.

"Fine. Think all you want. You don't have much time, though, so I don't recommend your usual pace."

"No way," my father said when he was gone. "I hire him and before I turn around he's making book and running numbers out the back door."

Actually, I thought this could be one time when my parents

265

might actually agree about something, given how undependable Uncle Dec was. It would be just like him to get us to spend money we didn't have and then back out at the last minute, leaving us in the lurch. But I could tell my father was thinking it over. Despite his brother's relentless teasing, he had often remarked on his brother's overall shrewdness, how he always managed to land on his feet, prospering about as well as a man with no ambition possibly could.

At the cash register, though, we discovered that Uncle Dec had paid for neither the coffees nor my ice cream. "This right here," my father said, holding up the unpaid check, "is why we don't want nothing to do with him."

WHEN WE RETURNED HOME, the kitchen table was still crowded with the apparatus of my mother's bookkeeping—the adding machine with its long scroll of paper, the spiral tablet with its columns of numbers, the stack of worn ledgers from True Plumbing and Supply, Angelo's Pizza, Bech's Flowers—but she herself wasn't there. For a frightening moment I remembered Mrs. Marconi's serial disappearances. I didn't think my mother would do anything like that, though I also had the distinct feeling she hadn't just stepped out either. My father called her name and went upstairs to see if she might be taking a nap, but I knew she wasn't up there, just as I knew she hadn't gone to visit a neighbor. She hadn't even turned the adding machine off, which suggested that she'd interrupted one important task to attend to something even more important.

When my father reappeared at the foot of the stairs, he stopped and scratched his head thoughtfully, a gesture that just then annoyed me, perhaps because Uncle Dec had lately referred to us both as having pointy heads, and here he was scratching the very spot where the point would've been, had there actually been one.

"She's over at Ikey's," I told him, suddenly sure that this was true, whether it made sense or not, and I could tell that possibility alarmed him as much as it did me. Having sworn never to set foot in the store, my mother had been good to her word all this time. If she needed to speak to my father during the day, she'd either telephone or cross the street, open the door and summon him outside. Which meant that if she *was* over there now, she must have a pretty good reason, and I could tell that whatever that reason might be worried him.

We found her standing in the middle of the store with a tape measure. "That's the wall that'll have to come down," she said when we entered, pointing at the one she had in mind. "You'll lose a parking space. Maybe two."

She was planning where the meat counter would go. My father understood that much.

"We don't want nothing to do with Dec," he said. "You can't depend on him." To illustrate his point, he told her about the diner, how he'd offered to buy the coffee and ice cream and then stiffed us.

"But don't you see, Lou? Your brother *is* dependable. You can depend on him to do exactly what he always does. In his own way, he's as dependable as you are. You're always you, and your brother's always your brother. There isn't a nickel's worth of surprise in either one of you."

I thought about pointing out that my father had certainly surprised her when he bought Ikey Lubin's, then decided to hold my tongue.

"But I don't want him here, Tessa."

"That's the good news," she said. "In six months he won't be. When have you ever known Dec Lynch to stick with anything? That gives us six months to learn what he knows."

I noticed the pronoun right away, but I'm pretty sure my father didn't. He was too chagrined by the direction she was taking us. "He comes in here, people will think it's his store, not mine."

267

"Right now your problem is that Buddy Nurt thinks it's his," my mother said, confusing him further. She motioned for us to follow her into the back. The storeroom was dark, lit only by one small, high window, but when my father went to flip the light switch, she turned on a flashlight instead. I started to say something, but she held a finger to her lips. "I found our leak," she whispered, shining the beam on a door I'd always assumed must lead down into a cellar. Directly in front of it sat a couple of crates, blocking access. "Guess where that leads."

As soon as she said it, I knew. It didn't lead down but up, into the apartment. My father also saw what she was driving at. "It's locked, Tessa," he said, leaning around the crates to give the padlock a tug.

"Shhhh!" she said, motioning for him to step aside. Handing me the flashlight, she went over to the door, pressed her ear against it and listened. In the silence, we could hear muted voices—Karen's, I thought, and her mother's—and footfalls from the apartment above. Finally, when she was satisfied, my mother, to our astonishment, *swung the door open.* Not how you'd expect, of course, because it *was* padlocked, but rather on its hinged side, just wide enough for a man to slide through. The crates, I realized, weren't directly in front of the door, as I'd thought, and they blocked the door only if it opened as it was designed to. This other way, the crates didn't even come into play.

Taking the flashlight back, she used its beam first to locate the two pins that had been removed from the hinge where they lay on the first step, then the makeshift handle attached to the door so it could be opened and closed from the inside, finally the footprints leading up and down the dusty stairs and the wood shavings on the floor and lower steps. My father and I watched slack jawed as she closed the door again, the upper and lower sections of the hinge sliding neatly into place. If you looked close, you could see that with the door shut they didn't line up exactly, but why would you?

"He must've taken the door off at some point so he could plane it," my mother explained when we were back in the store. "The only thing we can't figure is how he managed to take the pins out to start with. That could only be done from this side. He must have slipped in during a delivery, when you and the driver were both in the front."

This time my father caught the pronoun. "We?" he said.

"It was your brother who figured it out, not me," she told him.

I couldn't tell whether my father was more discouraged that Buddy Nurt had been systematically stealing from us or that it was his brother who had figured out how. He sank heavily onto the stool he kept behind the counter. He said nothing for a long time, and my mother seemed content with the silence. Finally, he said, "What do we do?"

"That," she told him, "is the part *I* figured out."

THAT VERY NIGHT Buddy Nurt paid us his last visit. At dawn I awoke to the sound of what could only have been a Hudson cab idling somewhere nearby. I woke up again at six when my father overcame his aversion to the telephone and called my mother. He'd gone over to Ikey's to open the store as usual and found the door leading up to the apartment wedged open. Buddy must have been pretty surprised when he pushed on that door. Too late he must have felt the shim my father had nailed to the floor, the bottom of the door riding that smooth, gentle incline before dropping down an inch into a groove, immovably ajar. He then must have panicked, because you could see where the door had splintered when he tried to pull it shut again by force.

It was my mother who called the police and explained how we'd caught him red-handed. When they arrived at the store, my father looked embarrassed, like *he'd* been snared in her trap, not Buddy. I knew how he felt. I despised Buddy, but there was something especially humiliating about getting caught in the act,

269

and realizing that for all your care and stealth and cleverness—and Buddy's thievery *had* been clever—somebody out there was smarter than you were, and now the whole world would know you for what you were. That, I thought, must have been what Buddy Nurt couldn't face, what caused him to bundle his belongings into the backseat of a Hudson cab, and rattle away, leaving sleepy-eyed Karen and Nancy to answer the door when my mother, flanked by two burly policemen, knocked.

While this transpired, my father and I remained in the store below, too cowardly to bear witness to what was happening upstairs. When the early morning coffee drinkers began filtering in, I didn't even have the stomach to listen to my father's explanation of the police car out at the curb. I retreated into the back room to take charge of the morning's deliveries of bread and milk.

Try as I might, I couldn't stop thinking about Buddy. He had been, for most of his adult life, a sneak and a thief, and the worst moments of his sorry life were surely the result of being exposed for what he was. Why didn't he just stop? To my surprise, I no sooner asked the question than the answer came to me. Buddy Nurt wasn't a thief because he stole; he stole because he was a thief. Each time he got caught, he added that mistake to the growing list of those he wouldn't make again, but it wouldn't occur to him to stop stealing. The solution, he imagined, would be to get better at it. That first day he'd arrived at our store in a Hudson cab and studied his reflection in the glass, what I'd seen there was the real Buddy Nurt, a man who simply did what he did, because of who he was. What I'd recognized in his expression was self-loathing, but there was also something I'd missed: the futility of struggling against his fundamental nature. The man he saw reflected in our storefront that day would continue doing the very things that had brought him to this point in his life. And he must have known, too, what the consequences would be, that before long another Hudson cab would arrive, this time in the middle of the night, to bear him away to further misadventure and disgrace. That's what his terrible grin had meant—surrender to the inevitable.

Even more chillingly, I recalled going outside myself and studying my own reflection in the glass, and being startled to see Buddy Nurt's terrible self-loathing mirrored in my own features. What, I now wondered, if we all just were who we were? What if we were kidding ourselves if we believed otherwise? Was that what my mother had wanted to convey when she said I needed to get smarter about people if I was going to survive in the world? Did she want me to understand that we have little choice but to slog forward through life, repeating our worst mistakes without ever learning from them or, worse yet, without being able to use what we'd learned?

Before I was able to resolve these issues, my mother came back downstairs with the two policemen. All three stood talking outside Ikey's until one of the cops, glancing at the apartment above, shrugged as if to say *Fine, if that's how you want to play it.* When they got back in the cruiser and pulled away, she came inside and regarded my father's coffee drinkers darkly until they became self-conscious and left. Then she turned her attention on me, studying me so intently that I wondered if I was supposed to leave, too. I still wasn't used to seeing her in Ikey's, and I could tell my father didn't quite know what to make of her presence either.

"Well," she finally said, "at least he's gone."

"What about the money?" my father said, referring, I supposed, to the cost of all the stolen beer and cigarettes.

"Think of that as gone, too, since it is."

"Maybe they'll catch him," I ventured. Buddy didn't strike me as the sort of person who'd have much luck evading the police.

"What good would that do?" she said. "You'd sooner get blood from a turnip than restitution from Buddy Nurt."

"What about her?" my father said, nodding at the ceiling.

It was my mother's turn to shrug now. "She claims she had no idea what he was up to."

271

Outside, the dogs my mother had shot with the pellet gun came trotting up the street. When they got close, all three actually crossed the street and continued to watch the store nervously out of the corners of their eyes, a sight that seemed to cheer her up, and I have to admit it cheered me, too. Thinking about Buddy, I'd just about concluded that everything was pretty pointless, but these dogs suggested otherwise. Their behavior had changed as a direct result of their experience. True, they were probably smarter than Buddy, but still.

"Anyway," my mother said, turning to my father, "you wanted a partner in this venture. I guess you got one."

My father looked like he might cry. "How come he has to be my partner? How come I can't just pay him, like they do down at Manucci's?"

She rubbed her temples vigorously. "I'm not talking about your brother, Lou. I'm talking about me."

AFTER LUNCH I was left in charge of the store while my parents went to the West End to look over Manucci's meat case and the other equipment we'd need if we were going to install Uncle Dec as our new specialty butcher. The next day they'd meet with a contractor to discuss how much it would cost to expand into the parking lot.

Early afternoon was usually the slowest time of the day at Ikey's, but I kept busy with the steady stream of neighbors who ostensibly came in for a half gallon of milk but were actually curious about the police cruiser that had been parked outside for so long that morning. Around two, a battered pickup truck squealed to a halt at the curb out front, and then another, and then a third, the brothers all piling out and lumbering up the stairs to Nancy's apartment. Ten minutes later a crushed beer can rattled into one of the truck beds and bounced out onto the street, followed by a second that managed to stay in and a third that missed altogether. Fortified in this fashion for physical labor, they began hauling down the same possessions they'd hauled up to their sister's apartment less than a year ago. Nancy herself came down to supervise and, seeing I was alone in the store, came in to buy a pack of cigarettes. Her eyes were red and swollen, but she'd clearly made a successful transition from shame to anger.

"I hope nobody thinks it's gonna break my heart to leave," she said, as if she suspected I might be such a person. "People around here seem to think their shit don't stink."

I gathered that by "here" she meant the whole East End, not just our immediate neighborhood. As to our shit not stinking, it was my impression we just thought ours probably didn't stink as bad as Buddy Nurt's, but I held my tongue.

"I could tell you a thing or two about that mother of yours if I felt like it," she continued, "but I don't. You think my Karen's wild? You should've known your mother back when. Your father never knew what hit him. He wasn't the only one either, just the least prepared. You don't believe me, ask your uncle."

But then she made a zipping motion across her lips to suggest that she'd said too much and I couldn't get anything further out of her. She went over to the door and shouted at her brothers, who were balancing her box spring and mattress in the back of one of the pickups, "You're joking, right?"

I was surprised to see the fattest of the brothers turn around and *un*zip an imaginary zipper of his own, this one at his crotch, from which he yanked an imaginary penis and began stroking it feverishly.

Nancy seemed to make no connection between the two zippers and turned back to me. "Then on top of it she's got the nerve to make out like I knew Buddy was stealing beer and shit from this so-called store. Like I didn't tell her from the start he was a thief. Like the whole town doesn't know Buddy Nurt's got magic fingers. Like my own damn purse doesn't come up light every other morning."

Listening to Nancy Salvatore, I began to understand where
Karen's curious logic came from. If I understood her correctly,
Buddy Nurt was, or should've been, a shared burden. Sure, he'd
been stealing from us, but in refusing to let him continue we
were shirking our fair share of the responsibility, which meant
she'd have to shoulder her share and ours, too.

"Buddy Nurt," she spat contemptuously. "If you know what I
did to deserve that asshole, I wish you'd tell me. It must have
been in another life, that's all I can say."

Outside, the brothers had finished tying off the tippy springs
and mattresses with an old clothesline. "Yeah, right, that's
secure," Nancy muttered, then looked at me. "You don't have no
brothers, do you."

She knew full well I didn't but seemed to be waiting for an
answer, so I admitted to being an only child.

"Lucky you," she said, and left.

Where Karen was during all this I have no idea. I kept watch
out Ikey's front window, expecting her to appear, but she never
did. Since I was by myself in the store, I figured she'd come in
and say goodbye, maybe con me out of one last pack of
cigarettes. But she probably felt guilty about Buddy and
decided to let me off the hook. Around midafternoon, the
brothers piled back into their pickup armada and sped off. The
last truck took the corner too sharply, and the clothesline
broke, allowing the box spring to tumble out right in front of
our house. Our Ford was parked at the curb, and the
cartwheeling box spring sheared off its side-view mirror, neat
as could be, then came to rest up against the front bumper.
When my father returned, I told him what had happened, and
we waited the rest of the afternoon for the brothers to come
back for it, so we could demand that they pay for the damage to
our car, but they never did. When it began to rain, my father
said, "Good," and we let the box spring soak the rest of the
afternoon. By evening it was so waterlogged we had all we
could do to carry it around to the back of the house, where we

274

decided to leave it until garbage day. The next morning, to our amazement, it was gone. "West End," was all my mother had to say on the subject.

Later that day, she and I went up to inspect the apartment, none too sure what we'd find. Evidence of another fire? Another full, black toilet? My mother had said barely two words since breakfast. After sleeping on her decision, she seemed to be having second thoughts about throwing herself into Ikey Lubin's. But things in the apartment were better than she feared. Buddy may have been a slob, but Nancy had kept the place clean, and there was no evidence of further damage, so I was surprised when my mother's dark mood didn't improve. Maybe she was just feeling bad for her old friend, who'd now have to move back to the Gut. Once you knew something better, my mother always said, it was hard to go backward in life because even if you'd once been happy with less, more—the knowledge of more—was always with you.

Or perhaps she was contemplating the possibility of her own diminished future. By tearing down the financial and psychological firewall she'd erected between herself and the store, she now realized just how vulnerable we all were. She was determined to keep as many of her bookkeeping clients as she could, so we'd always have that income to fall back on. But she'd now committed herself to making Ikey's succeed, even though she'd told me long ago that it *couldn't*, that the best we could hope for was that the market would fail slowly, providing us with a marginal living until the inevitable time we'd be put out of our misery by the A&P or whatever came next.

Her reasoning must have been that by becoming a fully vested partner she could forestall that fate awhile, maybe until I finished college. If she was in the store, seeing things firsthand, she'd have more influence. She could watch our inventory, making sure we were ordering the right quantities and that slick salesmen weren't talking my father into anything, that we weren't being given what was left over on the back of the truck.

She'd often voiced her suspicion that his fear of women dis-couraged female customers from returning to Ikey's once they saw how flustered they made him. Her presence would alleviate that problem and also give him some much needed time away. The clincher, though, was her belief that for Ikey's to succeed, we had to be special, to give people something they couldn't get at either the A&P or other corner stores. Like a good crown roast.

What I didn't realize at the time was that in order to expand Ikey's along these lines, my parents not only took out a loan from Thomaston Savings but also put a second mortgage on our house. Had I known, of course, I would have applauded their decision, because I loved and believed in Ikey's as much as my father did and wanted my mother's complicity in the venture. I wanted for us to be a family and to be devoted to the same cause. I was even willing to expand my definition of "family" to include Uncle Dec, if that's what it took, especially since, as my parents agreed, he likely wouldn't last.

That the cause we were now to be united in might be the wrong one didn't really register with me. Despite my mother's palpable fears, and even after witnessing in the person of Nancy Salvatore how swiftly reversals of fortune could happen, it never occurred to me that we wouldn't succeed in the end. After all, no Buddy Nurt was dragging us down. Our move from Berman Court to the East End had seemed only natural, progress that one day might carry us all the way to the Borough, if we were fortunate. Sure, there'd be setbacks. But ultimately we would prevail.

Despite her innate caution, my mother must have shared this desperate conviction, this blind faith, at least long enough to sign for the expansion loan and the second mortgage. I doubt she seriously feared we'd ever have to return to the West End like her old friend. Rather, the fate she feared was the apartment itself, and as we stood there in its small, dark, empty rooms, I think now that my mother may have had a premonition, envisioning the day when our luck would fail utterly and the little house she'd purchased with money borrowed at such a heavy cost from my grandparents would be lost, as well as her argument with them. They'd not wanted her to marry my father or, for that matter, anyone from Thomaston. They intended for her to go away to school and meet a better class of boy, a more suitable mate who'd take her to live in a place where the streams and rivers were the color of water, not blood. But she'd sided with my father, and in doing so had broken their hearts. Now here she was, years later, reaffirming that decision, siding with him yet again in a venture she'd once believed to be foolish, this time risking everything.

What was *I* doing while my mother contemplated our future? Brooding over the past. Hers. Or rather Nancy Salvatore's version of it. Could it be true what Nancy had said, about how wild she'd been? I remember trying to square all this with the woman I'd known only as my mother, with my own very different version of my parents' history. I'd never thought about their courtship before. Somehow I'd always imagined my father's asking her to marry him as the beginning. He'd simply shown up, a stranger on her doorstep, and asked her, and of course she'd said yes, just as any other Thomaston girl would've done if she'd been lucky enough to be asked by a man everyone knew and liked. *She* was the one who hadn't known what hit her.

This was what I was mulling over when I heard footsteps on the back stairs, and as my uncle appeared in the doorway I knew who our new renter would be. Maybe it was the surprise, especially since I should've seen it coming, that made me aware of the aura—the fuzziness at the perimeter of my vision, the tingling of my extremities—I'd been ignoring since yesterday. This was no new phenomenon, of course, nor was the fact that when I saw my uncle standing there, I again had the irrational thought that he was the same man I'd heard when I awoke in the trunk so long ago. What *was* new this time was the sudden

277

certainty that the woman who'd been with him, who'd opened the trunk and stared in at me, was my mother.

Even now I marvel at our ability, at certain odd moments, to embrace the most contradictory logic, as if truth and falsehood were not the opposites we know them to be but rather sly brothers under the skin. In my mind's eye I could still see the woman who opened the trunk that night and gazed in at me with such innocent, drunken astonishment: "It's a little boy!" I'm sure I needn't state here, though I do, emphatically, that this woman was *not* my mother. Though backlit, she had been large and pale and fleshy and blond, and their voices had nothing in common. Why, then, when my uncle appeared, did a tiny door open in my brain and allow so bizarre a notion to enter? And why, in view of conclusive evidence to the contrary, was it so difficult to dispel?

"What's the matter, Bub?" my uncle wanted to know. For some reason he wasn't standing in the doorway anymore but next to my mother, both of them staring at me curiously. I guess I must have been staring at them, too, or perhaps at nothing at all. Realizing that I'd just suffered one of my spells, I tried to say something, but as was so often the case when I "awakened," my disorientation was too profound, and I couldn't find the right words. Sometimes, if I tried to speak too soon, unable to form the right combination of sounds to make familiar words, I'd spout gibberish. Less severe episodes would leave me in possession of the right words but no sense of how to arrange them in the right order, which was almost as frightening. Usually I was able to gauge the severity of a spell by studying the people who'd witnessed it, and I was pretty sure this one hadn't lasted very long because Uncle Dec was standing just a few feet away from where he'd been before and my mother's posture suggested she'd only this moment become aware that something was wrong. She squatted in front of me and took my hand, saying, "Lou? Are you back?"

I nodded, unwilling to trust language just yet, not with Uncle

Dec there. He'd never witnessed one of my spells, and he now regarded me suspiciously, as you might if someone pronounced dead at the scene of an accident suddenly sat up and started looking around.

"You're cold," my mother said, rubbing my hands together in her own. "You want to go downstairs and see Dad?"

This was what I always wanted after a spell, so she wasn't surprised when I nodded again. As usual I was exhausted and thirsty, as if I'd been walking along a dusty road for days, so tired I wasn't sure I could make it down the stairs, but I didn't want to be carried or even helped, especially by Uncle Dec. "This is pretty weird, Bub," he remarked as we descended. "You know that, don't you."

"He'll be all right," my mother assured him. "He hasn't had one of these in a while."

In the air outside I could feel the vagueness begin to dissipate, though I still felt stupid and uncertain. My father knew what had happened as soon as we entered the store. "You have a spell, Louie?" he said, more an acknowledgment than a question. I closed my eyes, allowing the sound of his voice to soothe it all away. Not much remained now but the tingling in my fingertips and toes, that and the thirst. He got me settled on the stool next to the register. "You want a soda?"

"Me," I said, the word "yes" not yet where I needed it to be.

"Shouldn't—" Uncle Dec began. I knew how he would've finished, too. Shouldn't I see the doctor?

"No, he just needs to sit quiet a minute, don't you, Louie?"

I was determined to say "yes" and tried hard to do so, but again all that came out was "me."

"Me, right," Uncle Dec repeated, rolling his eyes.

Unwilling to speak again, I focused on my father's white shirt as he went over to the cooler, returning with a bottle of grape soda. I drank half of it down in one huge gulp, then closed my eyes and concentrated on the big, gentle hand my father had placed on my shoulder. When I opened my eyes again, I saw that it was over. My uncle was just my uncle, not the man outside the trunk, and my mother was just my mother. And I was myself again: Louis Charles Lynch.

CROSSING THE LINE

"THAT'S PITIFUL, really. He shouldn't even be on the street," Sarah says when I tell her about our encounter with Buddy Nurt. I wouldn't even have mentioned it except she's already observed that I seem out of sorts, and I'd rather have her blame Buddy than my mother, whom she'll now question about it, though I wish she wouldn't. Saturday is Sarah's day to look in on her, to gauge what she'll need for the week. She'll pick up the few things we don't stock at Ikey's, plus whatever she needs from the drugstore and Kmart, a bigger list than usual tomorrow because by next Friday we'll be on a plane for Italy and my mother won't want to trouble Owen.

"I'm not sure I'd bring it up," I tell Sarah. "I think the whole thing upset her."

Another untruth, or half-truth. I don't *think* the episode upset her; I know it did. Upstairs in her flat, she collapsed into her reading chair without taking off her coat and just sat there staring at the dark smudge on her wall as if it had suddenly taken on new meaning, leaving me to make tea, a task I'm usually not allowed. My mother doesn't like anyone in her kitchen, which is why it took me longer than it should have to find what I needed. By the time I returned to the front room, she'd taken off her coat and composed herself. "I was going to throw this away unless you want it," she said, handing me a photograph.

I set her cup down and took the photo, immediately perplexed. In it, my mother's seated playfully on the counter of Ikey Lubin's, my father and Uncle Dec standing behind her. All three are smiling at the camera, and I'm struck by how different their

281

smiles are. Uncle Dec has his usual, knowing smirk, entirely in character. My father's in character also, his smile too broad, too unguarded—a smile that reveals the fact that he has everything he's ever dreamed of and is at a total loss to explain how he got so lucky. The smile that unkind people so often described as "goofy," and one I'm said to have inherited. My mother's smile is the most intriguing. The fact that the three of them were together in the store dates the photo as being taken shortly after she'd broken her vow and joined my father in his venture. I remember it as a happy time, but I have no idea what, specifically, would have provoked such a playful attitude. Who talked her into climbing up on the counter and posing like a calendar girl, with one knee over the other? Her smile suggests not only that she'd laid down some burden but also that she'd just been told she was beautiful and believed it. Out of character, in other words. Usually my mother refused to be photographed at all, and on those rare occasions when she did agree she seemed to be trying to make herself disappear and mostly succeeding.

And where was I? Holding the camera? That would make sense, but I don't recollect the incident, even though my memories of the period, as my little history suggests, are encyclopedic. "I don't think I've ever seen this before," I told her. "Of course I want it."

"I was going through an old album," she said.

"I hope you wouldn't ever throw anything like this out without asking me," I said, to which she replied, "I *did* ask you. Didn't I."

This gifting process troubles me. It began a couple of years ago, my mother producing some item that belonged to my father and asking if I had "any interest" in it. Some of this I could understand. My father was a pack rat. For thirty years he brought stuff home from flea markets and yard sales, even the dump. "Wonderful. More crap," my mother would say when he arrived home, telling her to come look at what somebody was going to throw out if he hadn't happened by. But eventually even she admitted he had a good eye for the kind of thing somebody'd pay money for, maybe not today, but someday: the right baseball card, an old campaign button. And later, when he was ill and it looked like we'd lose everything, we sold many of his treasures to help with costs, which left only the junk he'd been wrong about, that cost a quarter or fifty cents twenty years ago and was still worth a quarter or fifty cents. After he died, I put box after box of flea market bric-a-brac in storage, unable to part with it, especially if I recalled the day he brought it home or his explanation of why it would one day be valuable. I still go through this stuff from time to time. Now it's boxed up in our cellar, where, one day, Owen will find it.

It's hard to know what my son will make of items like the frogs. My father had little use for dirty jokes or anything pornographic, but one evening when I came into Ikey's to relieve him on his supper break, he asked if I could tell the difference between a male and a female frog, and pushed two ceramic figures across the counter at me. I was at the age when any question having to do with sex made me apprehensive, not wanting to appear stupid on so important a subject, and I remember looking at the identical frogs with genuine misgiving. "It ain't that hard," he said when I confessed I had no idea, then turned them over to reveal their pale undersides, one of which sported a penis, the other breasts and a tiny vagina that looked like a grain of barley. The frogs had been a gift, I later learned, from Uncle Dec, who'd gotten a lot of mileage out of my father's inability to tell the difference either. Owen, no doubt, will toss it all, but better him than me.

I understand why my mother might want to divest herself of such dubious possessions. I do. Still, it occurred to me one day last year how little was left in her apartment to remind her of him, or even their marriage. Was she trying to erase him? Many times over the last eighteen months she has offered me something with the excuse of having no room for it but which, like this photograph, takes up no room at all. It's as if the dark smudge over the sofa is full and sufficient reminder of their lives together, and this possibility, I admit, has made me increasingly bitter.

Which may be why, when she asked if I had "any interest" in the photo of her and my father and Uncle Dec, I felt my resentment rise up, like bile. I told myself to swallow it as I always do, today of all days, so soon after the upset of Buddy Nurt and less than a week before Sarah and I leave for Italy. My mother is old and frail and she has her reasons, not all of which can be known to me or, for that matter, even to herself. Maybe it has less to do with my father than her own mortality, and this gifting is her grim acknowledgment that we don't in the end get to take anything with us. Still, I heard myself say, "Mom, does it ever seem to you that no matter what we're discussing, we're always arguing about Dad?"

When she didn't immediately respond, it occurred to me that perhaps she'd been thinking the same thing, maybe for years. "Why," I went on, "is it so important to you that I remember him as you do? That I not love him?"

And just that quickly she was trembling with rage. "I *never* wanted you to not love your father," she declared. "I wanted you to love *me*."

Did I speak then? I don't remember. I think probably not.

"Did it ever occur to you, even once during all those years, that you might have taken *my* side? That *I* might have needed a friend?"

How long did we sit there staring silently at the smudge above the sofa, both aware that we'd crossed a new line? Finally my mother said, "Go home, Lou." As quickly as it had come, her rage had leaked away, and left her hollowed out, almost as if she'd had one of my spells, and of course I wished that I could take back every word. "Sarah will be missing you."

"You'll be all right?"

"My life is what I made it," she said. "No fault of yours. I wish it were."

At the door I said, "I'm sorry I've disappointed you," and I'm sure I said this partly to give her the opportunity to deny it.

"I did hope," she admitted, "you'd see things differently after your father died. Instead, all your beliefs have hardened. But I never wanted you not to love him."

Do I believe this? I suppose I do. I know I do.

And have I, over time, become stubbornly calcified in my beliefs? That, I suppose, is also true.

AFTER SARAH AND I FINISH the dinner dishes, I go into my study and read over the last few pages of my story, trying to square the past as I remember it with today, this day. Should I continue writing? Is the urge to relive the events of my childhood rooted in the desire to see things clearly, just as my mother has always claimed she wants me to do? Or is my intention merely to etch my hardened conclusions into stone? How does one know? And in the end, what difference does it make? Who cares about a single life beyond the one whose task it is to live it? Am I not as entitled to my life as my mother is to hers? Must there be a version that reconciles all the versions, large or small? *Can* there be?

But her accusations trouble me, in part because they're not new but also because I feel their truth. I wish I could deny that I've missed opportunities to be my mother's friend. And of course I *have* chosen my father's side. But at the core of her accusations is the belief that I'm willfully dishonest, always seeing what I want to see rather than what is. My father never once thought this. Did I choose him, his side, because he thought better of me?

At this particular moment, as I review the events of this day in the dark of night, I incline toward her assessment. There is, after all, recent evidence. Over dinner I told Sarah about our encounter with Buddy Nurt and how it upset my mother, but I said nothing about how we'd argued, nor did I repeat her accusations. I've kept them secret because I know my mother will never tell a soul, not even Sarah, of whom she's extraordinarily fond. They will remain locked safely away unless I myself decide to reveal them, and I've already decided I will not.

It is the nature of some things, I believe, to remain locked away for the simple reason that revealing them serves no earthly purpose. For instance, I've never told anyone, even Sarah, what my father confided to me when he was ill. I've wanted to. His secret has weighed heavily on me, especially these last few years. I tell myself that he didn't mean I shouldn't tell Sarah, whom he loved and whose kind heart he trusted. But his instructions were "Don't tell nobody," and so I haven't. I've told no one that when my father entered the voting booth each Election Day, he stayed there for as long as he judged it would take to complete a ballot, then returned his to its protective sleeve, unmarked. Unable or unwilling to follow my mother's advice, he wasn't confident enough of his own conclusions to act on them. He felt the burden of democratic responsibility and believed that decisions of such magnitude should not rest with men like him. Because he was a proud American, he knew he had the right to vote. But he also knew he had the right not to, and he exercised both of these rights each Election Day.

Have I kept his secret so long because I'm ashamed of him, as my mother would've been if she'd known? Or because it would break Sarah's heart to hear it? Or because it broke my own, to know that he considered voting to be something for my mother, and later for me, but not for him? I don't know, but his secret is mine to keep, and so I will. I am not Buddy Nurt. I don't mine humiliation for gold. That said, what then can be the point of telling my story? Why scan the past for the shapes and meanings it surrenders so reluctantly if you mean to suppress some and exaggerate others?

But is the living of life so different from the telling of it? Do we not, a hundred times a day, decide *not* to bear witness? Do we not deny and suppress even at the level of instinct? Today, for instance, my mother and I both saw something in that haunted alley that was almost certainly responsible for our bitter quarrel over my father, though neither of us acknowledged it then or afterward. My mother may be old, but her vision remains sharp, and I'm sure she noticed the old moth-eaten varsity jacket Buddy was wearing, saw that the threads used to stitch the original owner's name below the cloth collar had been removed, leaving behind a ghostly reminder like the smudge that manages to seep through repeated paintings of the wall behind her sofa—that the jacket had once been the proud possession of someone who announced himself to the world as BIG LOU. Are we not complicit in each other's secrets?

I will have to make a concerted effort not to brood about the fact that Buddy's walking around Thomaston in my father's old coat. After all, things like this happen all the time in small towns. When I was growing up it wasn't difficult to trace the provenance of a particular item of clothing. A blue blazer, for instance, might be purchased for a junior high or high school boy by his Borough parents; by the following summer he would have outgrown it, and the blazer would then be donated to their church's clothing drive, after which it would reappear on the back of some East End kid, whose parents would take it the following year to Goodwill, where a West End mother would purchase it for her son. Nor will I ever forget the senior prom when a Borough girl, a friend of Nan Beverly's, came over specifically to tell Sarah how pretty she looked, that the dress she was wearing really looked much better on Sarah than it had on her at last year's junior prom.

Is it any wonder our adult lives should be so haunted? Over and over we go up and down the alley between the theater and the dime store, as my mother and I did today, moving through space, yes, but also through time, meeting ourselves, as Owen always says, coming and going. How beautiful Sarah looked in that dress. How important it must have been to that Borough girl, who wasn't pretty, to undermine her beauty. How she must have wanted to tear the dress right off her.

When I see Buddy Nurt again, I'll offer him money for my father's jacket. I don't want him wearing it.

ONE SATURDAY AFTERNOON a month or so later I was standing in the popcorn line at Newberry's when I felt something pillowy soft on my elbow and heard a familiar voice say, "So, Lou, do you miss me?" The pillow, of course, was Karen Cirillo's breast. She was accompanied by the two girls who'd shoplifted at Ikey's—pale, skinny apparitions compared with Karen, who was voluptuous as ever. I was amazed she'd acknowledged me in front of them, and in Newberry's of all places.

I stammered that, yes, I did miss her, which was true, though it was also true I didn't miss her cadging me for free cigarettes. Now that Buddy wasn't stealing from us anymore, Ikey's was doing better. The renovation was well under way, and next week we'd close for a couple days so the old exterior wall could be knocked down and the meat cases from Manucci's installed. My uncle was supervising, to make sure it was all done right, claiming things had always been messed up at Manucci's. Then, my mother said, we would reopen with a flourish.

So far, to my surprise, Uncle Dec had been dependable, showing up on time—no great challenge, now that he was living upstairs—and prepared to help out. I hadn't expected him to be a good worker, but he was. He still referred to my father as Biggy and me as Bub, though otherwise he'd toned down the relentless kidding. For his own part, my father seemed to have drawn a mental line down the middle of the market, granting each of them a separate realm of responsibility. While he was still distrustful, I could tell that he, too, was impressed by how seriously his brother was taking things, and he appreciated it when he consulted my mother on important matters, even if that courtesy was seldom extended to himself. They seemed to have agreed that she was the brains of the operation, as well as a natural go-between.

My uncle continued to regard me warily. I'd had two more spells since the first one he witnessed, and it was as if he'd concluded I was having them on purpose, to gain attention. At the very least I was shirking my duty to figure out what was causing them. I'd have gotten about as much sympathy if I'd been a bed wetter. "Quit drinking out of the crick, Bub," was Uncle Dec's advice each time he learned I'd had another episode. "He's fine," my father would assure him. "Don't you worry none about our Louie." To which my mother would add that the Cayoga was poisoning everyone in town, not just me, and then the subject would turn to cancer and who else had been diagnosed recently. The Albany newspaper was running cancer stories every week now, articles our local paper continued to dismiss as rabble-rousing.

Karen took the Jules Verne book I'd been reading in the popcorn line and quickly scanned its pages, pausing briefly at the illustration of the giant squid, then handed it back to me, her curiosity, as always, completely satisfied. "You going to the show?"

I said yes and asked if she was, too.

"Probably," she said. "You want to sit with me, Lou? I'm all alone." I glanced at her girlfriends, puzzled. Weren't they going to the show? Neither seemed to object to Karen's rather loose definition of solitude, though it struck me as vaguely insulting. And where was Jerzy? Had his house arrest been extended to weekends now? Or had the two of them broken up? When I offered to buy Karen's popcorn, she said, "Sure, Lou," like she wondered why it had taken me so long to offer. "Them, too?" she said, indicating her girlfriends. When I opened my wallet to take out another dollar, I felt the pillowy softness at my elbow again and saw that she'd leaned forward to see how many other dollars might be in there. "Lou's rich," she told her friends. "He works like a hundred hours a week."

Popcorn in hand, we headed next door to the theater, joining the long line there. "You gonna pay for me, Lou? Like on a date, or some shit like that?"

I did a quick calculation and was relieved to conclude that I had just enough, though I wouldn't be able to get the soda I'd counted on. A small price to pay. That I might actually be "on a date, or some shit like that" with Karen Cirillo took my breath away.

"Them, too?" she said, again indicating her girlfriends.

I said no, I had just enough for us, feigning greater regret than I felt, because being on a date with all three of them was a far lesser thing than being with Karen alone. Only when I showed them did they reluctantly dig into their purses.

Preferring not to watch them fish for quarters, I turned away, just in time to see Perry Kozlowski, Jerzy Quinn's best friend, come slouching up the street toward us. Only now, seeing Perry, did it occur to me that my being with Karen at the matinee would be reported to Jerzy. I turned back to my companions, but not before noticing an odd thing. Perry seemed to be talking to someone who wasn't there, a fact he himself seemed to realize at that same instant. Stopping in his tracks, he retreated a few steps and appeared to study something in a shopwindow with urgent interest. I might have accepted all this—"at face value," to use my mother's favorite expression—had the window in question not belonged to a dress shop.

Inside the theater, I followed Karen and her girlfriends to the very back row, where she and Jerzy always sat. It was understood that this row was reserved for them and that once the lights went down and the movie began you weren't permitted to turn around and watch them make out. As I said, Jerzy seldom showed Karen any sign of public affection, but the dark theater on Saturday afternoons was the exception. The speculation about just how far those two went in that back row was endless, but nobody dared more than glance. Nan Beverly and whatever boy she was with always sat down front and when their heads

290

came together for their first kiss there were as many interested spectators as there were for any kisses enacted on-screen.

We were no sooner settled in the back row than I noticed we'd drawn the attention of kids throughout the theater, who were turning around in their seats to stare. Was that Lucy Lynch sitting with Karen Cirillo? The envy of the East End boys would have been deeply pleasurable had it been envy alone, without the fear I also recognized in their expressions. One East End boy actually got up and came over to where we sat, leaning down the row and whispering, loud enough that Karen and her friends could hear as well, "What're you *doing*, man?"

"Nothing," I said, adding weakly, "we're just friends. She used to live upstairs over our store." And I was glad now that I'd bought popcorn for all three girls, not just Karen. That was the point I'd emphasize if anyone misunderstood. Still, I thought it might be wise to ask where Jerzy was, which I did now, trying to sound casual, like I was hoping he'd show up, in which case I wouldn't mind moving down the row to sit between Karen's girlfriends.

"Who knows?" Karen said, like it wasn't her job to keep track of her boyfriend. "Why? You afraid he'll show up and find us here alone?"

The girlfriends were leaning forward to grin at me now, and again I marveled that they seemed not to mind that their physical presence counted for so little.

"Big guy like you," Karen went on. "I bet you could take Jerz, no problem."

Replying to this comment was tricky, of course. If I gave the slightest indication I agreed with her, by Monday morning everybody in school would know I'd claimed I could whip Jerzy Quinn, and then there'd *have* to be a fight.

"So, where are you living now?" I said, pretending the subject of who was tougher didn't interest me.

"Some dump," Karen confessed cheerfully. "You wouldn't know the place."

"I might," I said, though I thought she was probably right.

"You know Berman Court?"

I sat up straight. "I used to *live* on Berman Court. Number seven."

Now Karen turned to regard me, as if curious why I'd lie about a thing like this. There was no doubt she was looking at me either, not some point over my shoulder. "That's where *we* live," she said. "Seven Berman Court."

I felt a chill, like you do when you encounter a coincidence that doesn't really feel like one. I was almost afraid to ask the next obvious question. "Ours was the flat on the third floor."

"You're shitting me," she said. "Which room was yours?"

I described my old room, with its small, high window overlooking the stream below.

"That's the one they gave me, too. Kids always get the worst one."

The idea that we'd both been naked in the same room and now were sitting together in a dark theater caused my heart to skip a beat. It was all incredibly intimate and scary, and I again felt the need to change the subject. "Who's 'they'?"

"Buddy and my old lady. Who else?"

"Buddy's back?" I said, astonished.

"He went someplace?"

"I thought he went away. The police—"

"Buddy won't be gone till he's dead."

Just then the lights in the theater began to dim, and when I faced the front I became aware, to my surprise, that the seat on my right was now occupied.

"You remember Lou?" Karen said, leaning forward so she could talk directly to her boyfriend. "From the store?"

Perry Kozlowski must have stopped at the snack bar for a soda, because he now sidled down the row in front of ours, stopping at the seat directly in front of me. Handing the soda to Jerzy, he knelt in the seat, facing me. "How come you're sitting next to Karen?" he said. "She's not your girlfriend."

"Lou bought my ticket," Karen said, sounding bored. "Also my popcorn. Which is more than I can say for some people."

The coming attractions were on now, and Jerzy, the apparent object of Karen's remark, seemed totally engrossed in them. He took a sip of soda, then passed it across me to Karen, who took a sip and passed it back, ignoring her girlfriends. I knew better than to take a sip myself, though the popcorn was suddenly dry as dust in my throat.

"So you think if you buy her ticket, she's your girlfriend?" Perry said.

I told him no, that wasn't what I thought.

"You think if you buy her a bag of popcorn, she's gonna what? Let you feel her up or something?"

I assured him that this wasn't what I thought either. I was hoping Karen would come to my defense, but she also seemed engrossed in the coming attractions, so for the longest time Perry just knelt there staring at me.

Karen finally said, "Lou's not that kind of guy."

"That true?" he said, smiling at me thinly. "What kind of guy are you?"

"I don't know," I told him, the safest reply I could think of under the circumstances.

An usher appeared in the aisle then, fixing Perry in the beam of his flashlight and motioning for him to turn around in his seat, which he did until the usher left, then he resumed his former posture. "Let's you and me take a walk, Lucy."

"See you later," Karen said, without actually looking at me, when I got up. "Thanks for the popcorn."

Jerzy stood to let me by, his attention still on the screen, then settled into the seat next to Karen. Perry motioned for me to follow him, which I did, figuring he intended to take me out into the alley, but instead we went out into the lobby. There he lifted up the velvet rope, with its keep out sign dangling, and led me up to the balcony, then down to the front row of the creaky, condemned structure. From our perch we could track the usher below by his flashlight. Directly below us were Jerzy and Karen, her girlfriends also having moved off somewhere. He was holding Karen's hand, and the two had slumped down in their seats, but to my surprise they weren't up to anything. Perry noticed where I was looking and elbowed me. "If you're still thinking about Big Tits, forget it," he said, his voice low, confidential, almost friendly. I'd just about concluded he meant this to be a warning, then he added, "Nobody home."

Below, in the company of his West End friends, Perry had been all menace. Now it seemed we were suddenly pals. After a moment he chuckled, at something on the screen, I thought, though nothing funny had happened there. "Damn," he said. "I thought you were going to pee in your seat down there."

"Why were you so mad?" I said, which in truth was only half of what perplexed me. The other half was *Why wasn't he mad anymore?*

"Who, me? That was for show. Like I care if you feel Karen up."

"Then why—"

"You crossed the line."

"What line?"

"What do you mean what line? The line."

"I didn't—"

"You didn't know? I could tell that. Now you do, right?"

Actually, I wasn't sure. Had I crossed the line by paying for Karen's popcorn? Her ticket? By sitting next to her instead of between her friends, where apparently a person could sit and still be alone? Or was it the row itself I wasn't allowed in?

"It's like Division Street," Perry explained. "You gotta know where you are. You gotta know *who* you are. Anyhow, it's over. Forget it. And like I said, Cirillo's all tease. You don't believe me, ask Jerzy."

As if I would. "Why doesn't he—"

"Dump her ass? 'Cause he's pussy-whipped, is why." He shot me a sidelong glance. "You know what pussy-whipped is?"

I'd heard the expression before, maybe at Ikey's or the Cayoga Diner. It was the sort of thing a man would say if somebody said he had to go home or his wife would get mad. The sort of thing Uncle Dec might say about my father if he was in one of those mean, kidding moods. So I nodded. Yeah, sure, I knew what pussy-whipped meant.

"Here's something I bet you *don't* know," Perry continued, his voice still barely audible, though the theater had grown quiet now that the feature had started. "The girls that come across usually aren't the ones you figure. I could tell you which ones put out, if you're interested." What did he have in mind? I wondered. To name them? Point them out in the dark theater below so I'd be able to recognize them by the backs of their heads? "It's usually the tweenies," he continued. "You know what I mean by tweenies?"

Unlike "pussy-whipped," I hadn't any idea what a tweeny might be, but I said sure, I knew what he meant.

Which elicited a lip fart. "The hell you do," he said. "I made it up."

I told him I meant that I sort of knew.

"Okay, tell me what a tweeny is."

I took a wild stab. "An in-between?"

He looked at me in astonishment. "Right," he admitted. "Not that pretty, not that ugly. An ugly girl? She just gives up, 'cause nobody wants to do it with her anyhow. If she's real pretty like' Nan, or she's got tits like Karen, she doesn't have to put out, 'cause guys are gonna drool anyway. Tweenies are the ones gotta give you something. Otherwise they might as well be ugly, am I right?" When I couldn't fault his logic, he went on. "Something else you wouldn't necessarily expect. East End tweenies put out the most, 'cause they're tweenies twice. Not ugly, not pretty, not West End, not Borough. They don't know what the fuck they are, so they gotta put out."

I could tell he was proud of his careful reasoning, and also glad to have an audience. What I couldn't tell was whether Perry was just a theorist or if he was speaking from experience. His face was full of purple acne; Perry was not a handsome boy.

"You live in the East End, right?" I said I did, and he nodded. "Hell, you could be getting laid all the time if you wanted," he said. "Talk about crossing the line, do you believe that shit?" He leaned close so I could sight along his index finger.

At first I couldn't tell what I was supposed to be looking at, but then the movie went from a night to a day scene, and I saw he was pointing at a Negro boy. That in itself wasn't so surprising. There were usually Negroes present at the Saturday matinee. They sat together in two rows down in front on the far left-hand side, where the angle at the screen was bad. Behind them a buffer zone of another couple rows was always left empty, the white kids not wanting to get too close. From the balcony those rows looked like a wide aisle, as if the seats themselves had been removed to allow for better access to the exit.

The boy Perry indicated wasn't sitting with the other Negroes, but rather on the opposite side of the theater, where the Borough kids usually congregated, and the girl sitting next to him looked white. Not surprisingly, they were the only two in that row. Another buffer zone, smaller than the one where the other black kids sat, had been created in deference to this one boy.

Perry shook his head in a kind of weary, grudging admiration, or so it seemed to me. "Fucking Three. That boy's always been crazy."

Three. Of course, I thought. Gabriel Mock the Third. Who'd told me, the only time we'd ever spoken, that he had no father. At the time this had struck me as something akin to blasphemy, and I remembered it now with a chill, because here was a boy who not only *had* a father but was also repeating his father's mistake. I also recalled the words the boy's grandfather had spoken when he dragged his son up my grandfather's front porch steps to apologize. "All took care of," he'd kept repeating. "All in the past." What I had no way of knowing, of course, was

296

whether *this* boy had any idea that his father had kissed a white girl and gotten punished for it. Had he, like me, little or no understanding of the line he'd crossed, of where exactly he'd crossed it? Was he sitting next to this white girl on impulse, like I'd done with Karen Cirillo, realizing only when people turned to stare what a foolish and dangerous thing he was doing? Or was he perversely determined to do exactly what his father had done before him? And what of the girl? Was she just foolish and kind, like my mother had been, or was she actually his girlfriend?

"I mean, he's gotta know, right? *That* kind of shit you keep secret, man. You bury it with a shovel, then you bury the shovel. Out there in plain sight? You're *making* people give a shit. Maybe all they want to do is mind their own business, if you'd let them, but you don't."

I would have liked to hear more about this, but Perry abruptly lost interest in the subject. "So, you live where in the East End?"

"Third Street?"

"Near Ikey Lubin's?"

"We own Ikey Lubin's."

"No shit. Hey, we might end up being neighbors," Perry said, sounding more pleased than I would've predicted. "My old man got on at GE."

He didn't have to explain the rest. A job at General Electric in Schenectady meant your ticket out. Out of the tannery. Out of perpetual low wages. Out of the Gut. Out of the whole West End.

"This time next year I'll be wearing plaid shirts, I guess," he said with great sadness, indicating my own. He himself was dressed in his West End uniform: pegged black pants, thin white T-shirt, worn black boots. "Probably get promoted into the advanced classes, too."

I didn't think there was any danger of that, but didn't say so. I'd come to understand that Karen's most cherished conviction —that our teachers had our fates all worked out in advance, based on who had money and who didn't—was widespread in the West End. The idea that Perry's teachers might suddenly find him worthy of their attention because his family moved across Division Street struck me as comical, but he seemed to think it followed as naturally and unavoidably as the necessity of wearing plaid shirts. There was more to say, of course, but the movie caught our attention, and we fell silent until, with about fifteen minutes left, Perry announced he had to visit "the shitter." When he was gone, I took the opportunity to peer over the railing at Karen and Jerzy below. They were still holding hands, and she leaned over to whisper something in his ear, but otherwise nothing was going on. Down front, Nan Beverly's head was resting on her boyfriend-of-the-moment's shoulder, and I cocked my head to see what it was like to view a movie sideways.

Nan's presence at the matinee each Saturday afternoon was enormously reassuring. The FOR SALE sign was still up outside the Beverly home. My father and I drove out to the Borough to check every Sunday. He never said that's what we were doing, but I knew. We didn't park across the street, and he never commented on the sign again, but when we rounded the corner I could see his eyes search it out, anxious and relieved at the same time when he saw it was still there, which was bad, but no sold sign attached, which was good. "Who around here can afford a house like that?" he was fond of asking his coffee drinkers at Ikey's. Answer: nobody, he hoped.

That very week Mrs. Beverly, the slender woman we'd seen getting into the Cadillac, had come into Ikey's, and Uncle Dec had cut her a standing rib roast. "Now let's hope she knows how to cook it," he said when the door swung shut behind her. "If she leaves it in too long, it'll be our fault and that'll be the last we'll ever see of her or her friends." When I asked why that should be our fault, he just looked at me, and I understood now that he'd been trying to tell me pretty much the same thing Perry was saying in the balcony—that things just were the way they were and that it was your job to figure out *how* they worked, not why.

Speaking of Perry, I noticed he'd slid into the back row next to Karen and Jerzy, who shrugged at whatever he was whispering to him. Then both boys rose half out of their seats and Perry pointed in the general direction of Three Mock and the white girl. An on-screen gunshot drew my attention to the movie's climax right then, and by the time I looked back Perry had moved over to the other side of the theater. His lips were moving, but I saw it was himself he was talking to, his body rigid, his hands balled into fists. He gave the impression of somebody talking himself into something.

When the credits began to roll and the lights came up, he strode purposefully toward the couple. Kids were spilling into the aisles now, but quickly stepped back into the row when they saw him coming. I saw, rather than heard, Perry shout something down the row, then a surprised Three Mock turned toward him and shook his head. The white girl, who was standing between them and looking scared now, said something— maybe *Go away!*—but Perry paid no attention, lunging across her and shoving Three Mock, hard.

A chant went up then, like it always did—"*Fight . . . fight . . . fight*"—and I saw the usher pushing through the throng. Perry and the black boy were scuffling now, right in front of the white girl, who got knocked back into her seat, clutching her nose. When the usher finally arrived, he pulled the boys apart and pushed them out the side exit into the alley, then closed the door, as if what happened out there was none of his business. The Negro kids, I noticed, were standing on their seats to see what the fuss was about, and I could tell by the way their heads went together that they knew one of their own was involved. Wondering what Jerzy's reaction to all this might be, I glanced down to where he and Karen had been sitting, but they'd disappeared.

In order to avoid being seen coming down from the balcony, I had to wait until the theater emptied. The usher had positioned himself at the foot of the stairs, on the other side of the velvet rope, flexing importantly at the knees until the last kid (he thought) was safely out the door. Only when he disappeared back into the theater—presumably to start cleaning up the mess left behind by a hundred-plus heedless junior high schoolers— did I dare steal down the staircase and around the rope. Heading outside, I noticed that the door marked office was partially open and a girl was sitting there with her head between her knees. Her dark curly hair hung down, so I couldn't see her features, but I knew it had to be the girl who'd been with Three Mock. She was holding a bloody handkerchief.

A voice from behind the door said, "Still no answer," followed by the sound of a phone being hung up. "Is there someone else we can call?"

"It's okay," the girl said, her voice weak and frightened. When she raised her head to speak, I could see that her nose was crusted with dried blood and her eyes swollen from crying. Even so, I recognized her as Sarah Berg, an eighth grader, and I think she recognized me, too. "I'm better now," she said, but then lowered her head again, and I went out into the street.

Fights in the parking lot behind the theater on Saturday afternoons were not unusual, but they had a lazy, obligatory feel to them. Often they seemed to originate in the lurid melodramas of the movies themselves. So many teenagers crowded into a theater watching a story of passions run amok invariably created an excess of energy. The result was usually just a shoving match, the combatants taunting each other, calling names, without any real fear of escalation. After all, the police station was just a couple of doors down, and Mount Carmel's church and convent were right across the parking lot. Even a noisy throng of excited spectators wasn't often able to produce any real hostility, and this was the sort of flaccid conflict I expected to find when I joined the crowd that had gathered there today.

But halfway down the alley I sensed that something was different. Perhaps it was the relative quiet. The circle of kids surrounding the combatants was three or four deep, so at first I couldn't make out exactly what was going on, but then I noticed the theater's fire escape was down, and I climbed the bottom two rungs for a better view. Three Mock was just picking himself off the pavement, and he had a split lip, the red of it contrasting vividly with his dark skin. Something about his manner suggested that this wasn't the first time he was picking himself up. Perry had probably begun by shoving him, hands to the chest, but apparently the most recent shove had been to the face. The boy ran his tongue over his busted lip and must have tasted blood because he spat—nowhere near his adversary, though Perry chose to interpret this differently. "You think you can *spit* on me? Is that what you think?"

The boy just stared at Perry darkly, his arms hanging limp at his sides. He was a skinny kid, much taller than his father but no match for Perry, who shoved him again. Though Three Mock tried hard to keep his balance, he went down anyway and for a moment just sat there examining his gravel-scraped hands. Perry stood over him, fists clenched.

"Fuck it, Perry," Jerzy Quinn said. He was standing at the inner ring, with Karen at his elbow, looking bored as usual. "Let it alone. What do *you* care?" But if Perry heard this advice, he gave no sign, and Jerzy seemed disinclined to interfere more forcefully. Everybody knew that he was just one fight away from returning to reform school, which is why the rest of his gang had been delegated so many responsibilities.

"Tell me why this is happening to you," Perry told Three Mock. "I know you know." When the boy tried to rise, Perry planted a big foot on his shoulder and sent him sprawling. "Sit there till you tell me what I want to know."

Some distance off, maybe a half-dozen Negro kids clustered together. You could tell they didn't like what was happening, but they kept their distance. Probably they'd warned Gabriel Mock the Third about his foolishness, but he'd persisted, so now he was alone. Even from where I stood on the fire escape, I could see there were tears in his eyes, but determination as well.

301

"You're doing what I just told you not to do," Perry said when the boy scuttled backward like a crab and got to his feet again, his arms still at his sides. "You gonna tell me why this is happening to you?" When Three shook his head, you could tell he was preparing himself for another shove, but this time Perry hit him right in the face. The blow surprised everybody, not just Three. It wasn't only that fights out back of the theater in broad daylight seldom went this far. It was also that the boy who'd been struck neither flinched nor tried to avoid the blow, accepting Perry's fist as if he'd been receiving punches like this one all his life and understood they couldn't be avoided. His head snapped back, and he sat down hard on the pavement, his nose gushing an astonishing amount of blood down his white shirtfront. Everyone gasped at the horror of it, and a girl— maybe Nan Beverly—said "Make them stop" to no one in particular, as if she held both boys equally responsible. It was clear that even those who'd crowded in so eagerly had now taken a step back, wanting no more of this. You couldn't really even call it a fight. It was just one boy punching another. Three Mock might as well have had his hands tied behind his back. I'd not been there to witness Bobby Marconi's legendary battle with Jerzy Quinn, but I knew it couldn't have been anything like what I was witnessing now. That fight had been drenched in glory, whereas this one offered only blood.

Three now sat blinking on the pavement, shaking his head, probably trying to clear it, an effort that sprayed blood left and right, causing another gasp to run through the crowd. The other Negroes began to stir now. The boys seemed to know it was their duty to intervene, but they clearly feared what might happen if they did. The girls whispered to them to do *something*, though no one seemed to know exactly what. They weren't alone in this. Perry himself didn't seem to know what to do next. He was still standing over the boy with his fists clenched, but when he spoke again, his tone was different.

"Tell me why this is happening," he repeated, but this time

there was a plea in his question, as if he desperately needed to know how things had come to such a pass. I recalled what he said in the theater about how people who wanted to mind their own business sometimes just couldn't. And when Three, still wobbly from the blow, began to struggle to his feet again, I saw Perry steal a glance at Jerzy, who said, "Let it go," his voice barely audible, and I could tell from the slump of Perry's shoulders that he'd have liked nothing better. Three was now on his feet again, swaying, his eyes glassy. "You did something wrong," Perry reminded him, coaching him, really, toward the correct answer that would make further punishment unnecessary. "Tell me what it was and I won't hit you again."

The boy blinked, turned his head away and again spat blood, then turned his fixed, glassy stare back on Perry, who waited a beat, in case he was mistaken and Three intended to speak, before punching him again. This time it was his tailbone that hit the pavement first, then, with a sickening sound, the back of his head, after which he lay perfectly still. But for the blood, he might have been taking a nap.

Now, at last, other boys from the Hill found the courage to come over, the white kids stepping aside to let them into the circle. "Three," I heard one of them say. "Wake up, Three." But Gabriel Mock the Third didn't stir, and one of the Negro girls began screaming, "He's dead! Y'all killed him!"

And for a long moment, I think everyone believed her, including Perry, who looked stricken, as if he were about to curl up on the pavement himself. But then Three's foot twitched, and we saw him blow a blood bubble. "That," somebody remarked, "is one dumb jig."

If anyone had a different benediction to offer, it remained unspoken, and I felt ill when I realized that this was the story that would be told in the corridors of the junior high come Monday morning. Perry Kozlowski's terrible beating of a boy who'd offered no resistance would not feature in the narrative, whose thrust would be about the stubborn stupidity of a Negro who didn't know enough to stay seated on the pavement, who'd been given every opportunity to avoid the beating he took, who'd brought the whole thing on himself. The dumbest white boy in the school wouldn't have been *that* dumb.

By now a couple of policemen had come out of the station and were trotting over, ordering the crowd to disperse. Jerzy, I noticed, was squatting in the midst of the Negro kids and saying something to Three who still wasn't stirring. Perry had disappeared. I didn't notice Karen standing next to the fire escape until she spoke. "Cheer up, Lou," she said, sounding bored even now. "Could've been you, right?"

THE NEXT MORNING, Sunday, I awoke with the vague notion that Uncle Dec had been in the house, that his voice, along with my parents', had come up through the heat register while I was asleep. Whether he'd been there last night after I fell asleep, or this morning just before I woke up, I couldn't be sure. Maybe I'd dreamed this. After all, he liked to close the bars on Saturday nights, and it would've been out of character for him to be up and about on a Sunday before noon, and more unlikely still for him to pay us a visit when all he had to do was wait for us to show up at Ikey's.

Downstairs, there was a note from my mother telling me she'd be back later in the morning. My father was already at the store, getting ready to open. I poured myself a bowl of cereal, wondering sleepily if something had happened but still too groggy to imagine what that something might've been. I was staring into the shallow pool of milk at the bottom of my cereal bowl when I heard my mother return, making so much noise I could tell she was angry. In the kitchen she paused at the sight of me, as if I might be the cause.

"You're just getting up?" she said, glancing at the clock above the fridge.

I nodded, not realizing until that moment how late it was.

"You slept twelve hours," she said, examining me more closely now. "Did you have a spell?"

"No," I told her.

She nudged my empty cereal bowl. "Are you finished, or do you want to stare at this some more?"

"I'm finished," I told her. "What are you mad about?"

"I'm mad at this stupid town we live in."

I was glad it was the town and not me, though as a resident I still felt implicated.

"I should've listened to your grandfather. Stupidity, ignorance and violence. The Thomaston Trifecta, he called it." And with this she dropped my bowl into the sink where it shattered. "There," she said, almost pleased, it seemed to me. "Perfect." She commenced picking the larger shards out of the sink and dropping them into the trash. "That movie you went to yesterday," she said when she'd finished. "There was a fight afterward. Did you know about that?"

I was awake now. I acknowledged, warily, that I did.

"Were you there?" she wanted to know. "Did you see it?"

I nodded again, confused.

"That boy's in a coma," she said. "He may die."

I tried to swallow but couldn't. Again I saw Three lying on his back, still except for his twitching foot, a blood bubble pulsing at his lips.

"My *God*, Lou. Didn't anybody try to stop it? What did you all do, just stand there watching?" When I looked out the window, pink with shame, at where the Spinnarkles' house had once stood, she said, "How many of you were just standing there?"

I shrugged, as helpless now as I'd been the day before. "All of us," I said. "Everybody."

"Everybody," she repeated. "So it's okay, because everybody was there?"

"No," I said, choking on that single syllable, the full force of my cowardice pressing down on me.

305

"I know that boy's *father*, Lou," my mother said, and what entered my mind, unbidden, was He Kissed You.

"I'm sorry," I said, tears spilling out now.

Of course, when she saw that, she took pity, sitting down across from me and taking my hand. "I don't mean you had a bigger responsibility than anybody else," she said.

But her kindness was somehow worse than her fury had been. "Dad went into the Spinnarkles'," I said. "It was on *fire*."

"Lou, listen to me," she said, her brow furrowing and her own eyes filling. "Your father's a man. You're a boy. You can't compare what a man does with what a boy does. Don't worry. When you're a man, you'll be brave."

"Why?" I said, wondering what there was about me that made her think I'd be brave later when I wasn't brave now.

"Look, your father isn't brave because he went into a burning house. He's brave because . . ." She paused here, momentarily at a loss, it seemed, at how to explain my father's courage. Then, when I'd just about given up on her ever completing the thought, she said, "It's hard to believe in things, Lou, day in and day out. It's hard to believe in Ikey's every day, and it's hard to believe in the town or the country you live in. You know how your father is, how he loves things? How sure he is that it's better right here than all the other places he's never been to? How he never doubts?"

I nodded, thinking that one of the things he'd never doubted was me. "Louie's okay," he was forever saying, and his saying so made me believe it, too. That was why I needed him when I came out of one of my spells, needed him to put his big hand on my shoulder and say, *Don't you worry none about our Louie.* Because until he said it, I knew deep down that I was *not* fine and never would be, not without his help.

"I gave Karen Cirillo free cigarettes from Ikey's," I told her. For some reason I wanted her to know the truth, that I was a coward, not just yesterday but every day.

But instead of making her even more unhappy, she just smiled that sad smile of hers, the one I always hated because it meant she knew the truth. "Oh, sweetie, of course you did."

Which did make me feel a little better. "Does Dad know?"

"No," she said. "That's what I've been trying to explain. Your father prefers to see things a certain way. How they really are doesn't come into it."

When she let go of my hand, I said, "Will he die?"

She looked startled, then realized what I meant. "The Mock boy? I don't know."

"What will happen to Perry Kozlowski?"

"I don't know that either," she said, rising from the table.

"He didn't want to do it," I told her, recalling Perry's gloomy sense of duty. "He wanted to stop. But with everybody watching, he didn't know how."

I didn't expect my mother to understand this, not having been there, but apparently she did. "Oh, God," she said. "If you're trying to cheer me up, just quit, okay?"

LATER, at Ikey's, I learned that the fight had led to other events that night. Gabriel Mock Junior, "drunk as a lord," according to Uncle Dec, had turned up at Murdick's, the West End gin mill, hunting for Perry Kozlowski's father, who was seated at the far end of the bar and wondering out loud whether his son would have to go to jail for being the only boy in Thomaston willing to stand up and defend the honor of a white girl. The terrible injustice of this became clearer with each gin and tonic. Murdick's bartender, hearing that Gabriel Mock was waiting outside and perhaps wearying of the maudlin Kozlowski, went out and found Gabriel leaning against the railing for support. "Go home, Junior," he told the little black man. "I'm sorry about your boy, but you can't come in here. You know why, too, so don't make me explain it to you."

"Damn straight I know why," Gabriel replied. "Same reason my boy ain't allowed into the movies."

"That's not true," the bartender said. "That's not what got your boy in trouble. A good dozen of your people were in that movie house, and nothing happened to any of them. So go on back to the Hill now."

"I ain't goin' nowhere," Gabriel Mock assured him.

"You better had, Junior. I mean it, too."

"Send him out here so I can cut out his gizzard," Gabriel said. "Then I'll go home."

"Who?"

"Johnny Kozlowski. Who you think?"

"Johnny Kozlowski didn't do anything to your boy."

Gabriel Mock said he knew that. But what was he supposed to do—cut the gizzard out of a thirteen-year-old boy?

"What you're supposed to do is go home, before a bad thing turns into a worse thing."

"My boy's lyin' in the hospital," Gabriel told him. "Can't talk. Can't even open his eyes. Just lays there like he ain't even inside his own body no more. Only thing could be worse is if he dies. Somebody got to pay, so send the man out."

"Go home, Junior," the bartender repeated. "I like you personally and I don't want to call the cops after what just happened to your boy, but we can't have this sort of behavior, so just go on home now."

"Send him out," Gabriel insisted.

An hour later the scene at Murdick's had turned festive. Every time a patron entered or left, Gabriel Mock would be framed in the doorway, saying to send Johnny Kozlowski out. The sight of him out on the stoop, according to Uncle Dec, struck people as comical, so if ten minutes went by without anybody entering or leaving, somebody would go open the door to make sure he was still there. "*Send him out,*" Gabriel Mock would call in, which also struck people as comical, so when the next person entered or left, everyone at the bar swiveled on their stools and shouted, in a mocking chorus, "*Send him out?*" To which Gabriel, who seemed not to mind being a figure of fun, would answer "Send him on out. I'm waitin'."

Uncle Dec had actually been drinking in another gin mill until he heard about all the fun down at Murdick's. "Hi, Mr. Mock," he said to Gabriel, joining him on the top step. Not many men had a better rapport with Thomaston's Negroes than Uncle Dec. "I'm sorry you've had such a bad day."

Perhaps because he'd been addressed with respect, Gabriel looked down at his shoes and spoke almost in a whisper. "Send the man out." Uncle Dec said he appeared to be on the verge of tears.

"Send who out?"

"Johnny K.," Gabriel told him.

"He's not even in there, Mr. Mock," my uncle told him, though he couldn't have known that, having not stepped foot inside. "How about I give you a lift home? My car's right here."

"He's sitting down there at the end of the bar," Gabriel said. "You can see the man from here."

The door opened just then, allowing some inebriate to stagger out, and sure enough, there was Johnny Kozlowski, right where Gabriel had said. "*Send him out?*" came the chorus from inside.

"That's not Johnny K.," my uncle said, apparently in earnest. "That's his brother Jerry. You've had so much to drink you can't tell 'em apart."

But Gabriel Mock was having none of this. "Jerry K. lives down to Atlanta. Moved there last year."

Uncle Dec had either forgotten this or never known it. "Really? He did?" It was disappointing and mildly embarrassing to have invented such a fine lie under duress, only to have it exploded so effortlessly by a tiny drunk Negro. He'd been confident of his ability to convince Gabriel that Johnny Kozlowski was his brother Jerry, since the two men did look a lot alike, but not if the latter now resided in Georgia.

Apparently Gabriel didn't hold this attempt to confuse him against my uncle. "What kind of place we livin' in, where a

Negro boy, all by himself, gets beat half to death and nobody does nothin'?"

"People are no good," my uncle conceded. "They *enjoy* shit like this."

Gabriel shook his head in wonder. "Enjoy seeing a Negro boy beat into a coma for goin' to a movie?"

My uncle nodded agreeably. "And in about five minutes, when the cops come and shoot you, those people in there will enjoy that, too."

"Let 'em come. I'll cut their gizzard out."

Then he showed him the knife he was planning to use, and Uncle Dec pretended he'd never seen a switchblade before. When Gabriel pressed the button and the blade flew open, locking into place, he said, "Hey, do that again."

Gabriel, proud of the knife, obliged, folding the blade back into the handle expertly, after which my uncle took it from him. "Give that back here," Gabriel said, astonished that a man who'd just admitted people were no good would do him like this.

"I tell you what," Uncle Dec said. "Let me hold on to it for a while. You can have it back in the morning."

Gabriel blinked at him. "How my gonna cut his gizzard out with my knife in your damn pocket?"

Two police cars pulled up at the curb just then, disgorging angry cops, and a moment later they had the little black man facedown on the concrete, his hands pinned behind him. "Careful," one of the cops said, "he's got a knife."

"No, he doesn't," Uncle Dec told them.

But the cops had been warned about the knife and couldn't be dissuaded. They pulled his pants down around his ankles so they could inventory the contents of his pockets, and Gabriel was not, according to my uncle, wearing underwear. By then Murdick's patrons had begun spilling out onto the sidewalk. "I thought them people were all supposed to have big dicks," one man said when Gabriel was pulled to his feet before the assembled crowd.

One of his front teeth had been knocked out in the struggle, and blood dripped down his chin, onto his shirt.

Uncle Dec suggested that the speaker drop his own pants for the sake of comparison, but the man demurred. The only person still inside Murdick's was Johnny Kozlowski, who took the opportunity to make himself a free gin and tonic, after which he sat back down on his barstool until last call, growing more and more convinced that the world was rank with injustice.

THAT SUNDAY AFTERNOON I rode my bike out to Whitcombe Park, hoping Gabriel might be there, but of course he wasn't. I knew he'd been arrested but thought he might be out of jail by then. I knew the small outbuilding where he kept the thick black lacquer and found the section where he'd left off, and I set to work painting, first one side and then the other, imagining Gabriel's surprise when he returned. If he thought about it, he'd figure out who'd been helping and be grateful.

But by midweek he still hadn't returned, and on Friday when I arrived home with black paint on my clothes, my mother asked what I'd been up to. Normally, I went straight to Ikey's after school, but this week I'd barely put in an appearance. When I told her I'd been painting Gabriel Mock's fence while he was in jail, she sighed and said she wished I'd said something sooner. Gabriel had been let go from his job on Monday, so it wasn't even his fence anymore. When I asked why, she said, "Because black men don't threaten white men with knives."

"But Uncle Dec had it," I protested. "When they searched him—"

"People saw it, Lou. He'd threatened a white man."

"But that's not fair," I said, feeling young and helpless and stupid.

"Of course it isn't," my mother said. "Do you think it's fair that man should spend his whole life painting and repainting a fence that belonged to a white man who owned slaves? Do you

311

think it's fair that if we hired Mr. Mock to work at Ikey's people would stop coming to the store?"

The way she said this made it clear that she and my father had already had a conversation about this, one I had no difficulty reconstructing. She would feel more deeply than he about the injustice done to Gabriel and his son, and she'd want to help if she could. But she was also what she liked to call a realist, and she, not my father, would've calculated the cost of offering a job at Ikey's to a Negro. To some of our neighbors, it wouldn't matter. Others would claim it didn't, but then would quietly take their business to Tommy Flynn or drive to the A&P when they ran out of milk or bread. Despite our renovation, my mother knew Ikey's was still a marginal business, and she understood just how little it would take to tip us out of slender profitability and into red ink. A tiny black man could maybe do it.

Naturally, my father would disagree with her reasoning on both counts. In the face of her fury, he'd admit that Three and Gabriel had been victims of injustice, but for him it didn't necessarily follow that it was our particular responsibility to find a remedy, however partial. People like us were responsible for our own families, not other people's. Sure, the Negro kids had every right to go to the theater on Saturday afternoons, to sit wherever they wanted, next to whomever they wanted. But his more deeply held conviction was that people should get along and not start trouble that could easily be avoided. That had been the heart of what he'd wanted me to understand so long ago when he'd taken me on that milk-truck tour of the Borough. Yes, I had every *right* to be there. This was America, and I was an American. To him, though, it wasn't a question of rights or privileges. It was just better all around for a person to know where he belonged. He wanted me to understand that the East End was a good place and ours a good family. Sure, you had a right to want something different, or something you believed to be better, but that right shouldn't spoil what you already were lucky enough to have. He wouldn't dispute Gabriel Mock the

Third's right to want what he wanted, but the desire itself would mystify him. What about all those cute little Negro girls? he'd ask my mother. What's wrong with them? What would possess the boy to *want* so foolishly? What good did it do you to want what was bad for you?

But he'd also doubt my mother's pessimistic view of our neighbors. "They ain't gonna care," I could hear him say, shrugging his big shoulders in incomprehension. When he was a younger man, before he'd been given his Borough route, he'd delivered milk on the Hill, and while he didn't have his brother's ease with the Negroes who lived there, he knew and liked many of them. Some still spoke to my father when they met on Division Street, and I couldn't see where his conversations with these men were all that different from those he had with white men he met at the diner or the barbershop. A Negro man, asked how he was doing, might mention he'd won a daily double last week or quit playing a number he'd been betting for the last two years only to have it hit yesterday, and my father would commiserate and say he should've stuck with it one more day or ask the man what he did with his winnings, to which he'd reply, *I spent it, whatchu think?* I'd noticed my father didn't shake hands with these men the way he did at the diner or the barbershop, but this reserve seemed to me as much theirs as his. He believed in polite behavior, and so did they. If people would just treat each other decent, he was fond of saying, there wouldn't be near as much trouble in the world.

"You ain't gotta *love* each other," he'd say.

"Really, Lou?" my mother would interrupt. "Didn't Jesus say that's exactly what we're supposed to do?"

"Just act polite," he'd go on, talking to me now, not her. "It don't cost nothin' to be nice to people."

He believed that people were basically good, and to prove his point he'd name half a dozen or so, some from the neighborhood—old Mr. Gunther, say, who was so sick with cancer but never complained—and others who were famous, like Mickey

Mantle or John Wayne. Which always caused my mother to rub her temples and wonder out loud why she even tried.

THE QUESTION of whether or not to hire Gabriel Mock turned out to be moot, because after his arraignment on a charge of criminal threatening, he packed a small bag and called Hudson Cab, whose driver, Buddy Nurt, after determining that Gabriel had the fare, drove him to the train station in Fulton, which left me even more friendless than ever. I saw Karen Cirillo from time to time at school or the Saturday matinee, but she almost never acknowledged me. Sometimes I'd think she was going to, only to have her play that trick with her eyes and make me disappear. Once we found ourselves pressed together on the stairs of the YMCA, waiting for the gym doors to open, and I tried to strike up a conversation by asking how things were over at Berman Court, reminding her that I'd once lived in the very apartment she now occupied with her mother and, I presumed, Buddy, but all she did was regard me strangely and say, "You're *weird*, Lou. You know that?" Only after offering this personal observation did it occur to her to ask if I had any money. She and her girlfriends weren't sure they had enough to get into the dance. I did but claimed I didn't, feeling something shift inside me with that lie. I was glad not to have given her money— besides, she and her friends did discover the means to get in— but I felt dispirited, too. My weakness, my inability to deny Karen what she wanted, I knew, was my only connection to her, and strength, if that's what my lie represented, pretty much removed any hope of reestablishing our old Ikey's intimacy. She was, as she'd always been, Jerzy Quinn's girl.

During this same period, the second half of eighth grade, Jerzy himself became even more of a phantom, disappearing from view for weeks at a time. It wasn't unusual for him to be absent from school, of course. He often skipped or left by the gym door after attendance was taken in homeroom, behavior that sometimes, perversely, resulted in suspension. But he was also less visible around town. He still commanded his army of pale wraiths, but they often congregated outside the pool hall or along the banks of the Cayoga without him. He'd been only tangentially involved in what happened to Three Mock, who remained comatose for weeks after his beating, but he'd taken some of the blame for it, perhaps because he was the one the cops had found kneeling beside him there in the parking lot. Even at the time I found it ironic that he should emerge victorious from the whipping he'd taken at the hands of Bobby Marconi, only to be undone in the end by a skinny Negro who'd never thrown a punch. Overnight, it seemed, everyone understood that Jerzy and his gang were a junior high phenomenon that could not survive the transfer to high school, where thick-necked football players ruled.

Not long after the fight, the Kozlowski family did move to the East End, just as Perry predicted. For some reason I'd concluded that as a natural consequence of those events they wouldn't be permitted to cross Division Street, but one Monday morning Perry showed up in school wearing a plaid short-sleeved shirt. His new uniform drew immediate derision from a boy in Jerzy's gang, but Perry grabbed him by the throat, lifted him off his feet and offered to put him in the hospital bed next to Three Mock, and when the boy said he'd just been kidding, Perry let him go. For days after this incident we expected to hear that Perry's former friends had caught him alone somewhere and showed him who was boss, but it never happened, further evidence that Jerzy's reign of terror was coming to an end. No sooner did we imagine it *could* end than it did. Thinking back on it, we seemed to recall almost weekly beatings and humiliations, but how many had there actually been? When we tallied them now, the number wasn't large. And how many gang members were there? Too many to count, it had seemed a month earlier, until we counted them, and again the number wasn't so large. It had been well known that all the West End boys who had sworn allegiance to Jerzy carried knives, but had we ever seen one?

Then, in late May, with summer vacation just a few weeks away, a rumor that explained Jerzy's mysterious absences began to circulate. He was sick. He needed to have an operation. When he showed up on the last day of school, he looked so thin and weak that we knew it had to be true, which aroused a new fear. It had never occurred to any of us East Enders that illness would have the temerity to attack Jerzy Quinn or, if it dared, it would make headway.

Without school to foment rumors, and with high school and its new terrors to consider, Jerzy disappeared from our collective consciousness that summer. I know he hadn't crossed my mind in a month when, in late July, Perry Kozlowski stopped in at Ikey's for a soda. "You heard about Jerzy, right?" he said. And when I confessed I hadn't, he shrugged. "The doctors cut his left nut off. I guess he's not so tough anymore."

INSTALLING MY UNCLE as the butcher of choice for Borough housewives did draw shoppers from beyond our East End neighborhood, but it had some unintended consequences as well. With a larger store and longer hours, we found ourselves stretched thin. My father didn't like to leave Ikey's when there was work to do, but there always was, and he couldn't be there every minute, not seven days a week. He opened the store in the morning and closed up at night, but my mother insisted he get out for a while in the middle of the day. Sometimes he'd just go across the street and make himself a sandwich and read the paper on the front porch. Or he'd head down to the Cayoga Diner or the Thomaston Grill for a hamburger or a chili dog, over conversation with men who'd been laid off. The tannery was down to one shift now, but so far it hadn't closed its doors completely.

Having overcome her reluctance to enter Ikey Lubin's for any purpose, my mother now worked almost as many hours as my father. In addition to handling inventory, she took Uncle Dec's advice and started making salads—just potato and macaroni and three bean at first—to fill out the meat case, and she was pleased when Borough housewives preferred hers to the vinegary offerings at the A&P. She kept her bookkeeping clients as well, and when my father came home around midnight after closing the store, she often would be staring at a ledger, her fingers rattling over the keys of the adding machine, a pencil clenched so hard between her teeth that the bite marks pierced right down to the lead. He'd urge her to call it a day, and she'd say yes, she'd join him in a minute, though it was often another hour or more before I'd awake to the whisper of her slippered feet on the stairs. Most days she left the adding machine set up on the kitchen table, so we cleared space around it when we ate, usually just one or two of us at a time, family dinners long since a thing of the past.

Uncle Dec continued to be more of an asset than I ever would've predicted. He had an easy, flirtatious way with the Borough women, who stepped into the store as if determined to spend as little time there as possible, often leaving their cars running outside at the curb, but they couldn't hurry Uncle Dec. "Janice," he'd say, "I know you think I should cut my thumb off just because you've got your knickers in a twist, but I'm not going to." To which this Janice would say, "What do you know about my knickers?" "Just what I hear," he'd reply, "I could tell you, if you're interested." Well, I'm not, the woman would insist, but you could tell she enjoyed the exchange. "Slow down, Bev," he'd tell the next impatient customer. "I know the stiff you're married to, and there's no reason for you to be rushing home all the while." "You are the slowest butcher in all creation," Bev would inform him, and then she'd be told that people in hell wanted ice water. When he finally handed these women their crown roasts, he'd say, "Thanks, beautiful," whether she was or wasn't, thought she was or knew damn well she wasn't. "I live right above the store, you know. In case you want to visit me some night." My father, overhearing such banter, wasn't sure his brother's behavior was appropriate here in the East End, but my mother disagreed. "He's just making those vain, foolish women feel good. I know, because he treats me the same way, and it makes *me* feel good. I'd have him give you lessons if I thought you'd be any good at it."

"If they tell their husbands—" he began.

"They're not *going* to tell their husbands," my mother said with the sort of conviction I knew he found disconcerting.

Once school let out for the summer, I worked long hours, too. My mother's, father's and uncle's duties were well defined, whereas I was used as needed, according to the time of day. Late morning and early afternoon were when my uncle got busy, and sometimes he needed me to clean the slicer or tidy the meat case or replace a roll of butcher paper or the spool of string. I could handle the basics at the meat counter, a pound of ground beef or half a dozen precut pork chops, while he took care of complicated orders and difficult customers. Early mornings, it was my father who needed help, so I manned the register while he took deliveries, then, after he returned, broke down the cardboard boxes in the back room and stocked the shelves and cooler cases, pushing the dated items up front, placing the ones just delivered in back, though this didn't prevent Borough women from reaching in up to their armpits for the half gallon of milk farthest back. Late in the afternoon, I made small neighborhood deliveries on my bike, and in the evenings I'd help my mother prepare salads. By the end of the summer I was better at these than she was, because her attention was frequently divided between her bookkeeping chores and whatever was on the stove. One evening I came in and saw our largest sauce pot glowing bright red and dancing on the stove over high heat. My mother had filled it with water and then forgotten all about it, allowing the water to boil off. "Don't," she warned me when I started to chide her for such dangerous inattention. "Just because you're invaluable doesn't mean you're . . ."

"Doesn't mean I'm what?" I said, amused that she'd begun a sentence she couldn't complete.

"I don't know," she admitted, her eyes suddenly moist.

I wasn't officially on the payroll, but the tips I received for deliveries gave me walking-around money, and my mother had opened an account at Thomaston Savings and Loan in my name—my college fund, she called it—into which she deposited, every Friday afternoon, the money I would've earned if I'd been an actual employee. She wrote all of Ikey Lubin's checks, paying not just the vendors but also my uncle, my father and, when we could afford it, herself. "God only knows what the IRS will make of this," she'd say after writing them out each week. "If they ever take us to court and put you on the stand," she told me, "you *don't* work for us."

"What if they make me swear?" I asked.

"Call 'em any names you want," she said. "Just don't tell the truth."

THOMASTON CONGREGATIONAL'S HALL was located on upper Division Street. The church itself had been razed a decade earlier, but its bell tower, deemed to be of historical significance, still stood. Ironically, it was the bell that had caused the church itself to be condemned when the rotting timber that held it collapsed one Sunday at the conclusion of services, the bell crashing down with a sound so richly horrifying that several parishioners were converted in that ringing moment to Catholicism. A subsequent inspection concluded that the entire structure was unsound, so the Congregationalists found a site across town and immediately broke ground for a new church. Now permanently padlocked to prevent high school kids from climbing up into the belfry for drinking and sex, the tower stood alone on the lot, looking every bit as foolish as people had predicted it would. Though the Congregationalists planned to build a hall next to their new church, they'd run out of funds and were still using the old one for church-related socials and renting it for civic functions like the annual art show.

The latter always occupied both levels of the hall. Upstairs featured the work of the adult artists of greater Thomaston County, while the basement exhibited student artists, grades one through twelve, who'd been coerced into submission by their teachers. That year, my last in junior high, I'd submitted a pencil drawing of Ikey's that I'd slaved over for the better part of a week. I'd started out thinking it was going to be good, but the more I worked on it, carefully shading, darker here, lighter there, the worse it had gotten, though I couldn't say how or why. My father said it looked just like the store, which made me feel good, and my mother agreed, but I could tell she harbored misgivings she couldn't put into words either, which made me resentful. I'd hoped to be present when the awards were handed out, but I'd been needed at the actual store, so the following day was my first chance to see if the judges had given my drawing a prize.

The sign on the door of the church hall said the student exhibit would remain up for the rest of the month, and I expected plenty of curious people would be milling around admiring our efforts, but the room I entered was empty. A few paper plates with cake crumbs and plastic Dixie cups from yesterday's festivities remained on folding metal chairs. The room, windowless and low ceilinged, was lit by bright fluorescent bulbs. The outer walls, along with several temporary cork partitions set up in the center of the room, were crowded with first-, second- and third-place winners, plus honorable mentions for all twelve grades. I could see at a glance that my drawing of Ikey Lubin's hadn't placed in the eighth grade, and I probably would've left right then if I hadn't noticed the bins marked OTHER along the far wall. These, too, were arranged by grade, and I found my drawing halfway down the stack. In the harsh fluorescent light it looked smudgy, and all at once I was sick with embarrassment.

Technically the drawing wasn't that bad, especially compared with those done by other boys in my class, most of whom had drawn New York Giant football players or stock cars. But there was something "normal" about their efforts that I envied. After all, what kind of thirteen-year-old boy drew a picture of his family's corner market? I remembered Karen Cirillo's remark— "You're *weird*, Lou. You know that?"—and felt the full force of her judgment. Worse, I'd made our store look exhausted and drab. It was as if, without meaning to, I'd managed to document why more people didn't shop there. Suddenly grateful it hadn't won, I wanted desperately to remove the evidence from public view. The OTHER bin wasn't going to attract a lot of attention, but even so I was about to fold up the drawing and put it in my pocket when a voice at my elbow said, "It's good."

I hadn't heard her come in but immediately recognized the speaker as Sarah Berg, the girl who'd been sitting with Gabriel Mock the Third at the movie. In the weeks that followed the incident I'd seen her in the corridors at school, always alone and frightened looking, as she was now. The elbow to the nose she'd taken in the scuffle had resulted in two black eyes, and now, over a month later, one cheekbone was still a faint, greenish yellow.

"You should trust your lines, though," she said, taking my drawing from me and studying it critically. Perhaps because I didn't understand what she meant by "trust your lines," the remark irritated me, and I wished I'd been quicker about hiding the drawing. "You shade everything. It's as if you're afraid of the white."

Her index finger traveled over the surface without quite touching the paper, pausing here and there so I could see what she meant. And it was true. I *had* shaded everything right out to the edges, and this was responsible for what I'd earlier identified as the drawing's smudginess. Strange, too, because when I'd been working on it, the subtle variations of the shadings, rendered so carefully with the side of my pencil, were what I'd been most proud of. What I'd thought of as the drawing's

321

principal strength I now saw was its primary weakness. I'd been blaming myself for not working on it harder, for somehow betraying Ikey's, but I suddenly realized another hour or two or four would only have made it worse. That this should be true was disconcerting. Working hard at something, I'd learned in school, usually paid dividends.

"It's not cheating to leave some white," Sarah Berg explained. "It shows where the light's coming from. Some drawings can be mostly white, if the lines are good."

"It's my dad's store," I said, apropos of nothing.

"Ikey Lubin's," she said. "I recognized it."

Of course that's what the sign above the door said, so . . .

"I mean I *would* have recognized it, even without the sign," she said, flushing bright red. "That was stupid. *I'm* stupid."

"No," I said urgently, surprising myself. "It's the drawing that's dumb."

"The judge gave it two checks," she said, pointing out two pencil markings in the upper-right-hand corner that I hadn't noticed.

"Is that good?"

She nodded. "Three checks is highest. Most have just one."

We went through the trough again, and she was right. The majority had just one check. Four or five, like my drawing of Ikey's, had two. I couldn't find any with three. "I guess our class isn't very talented," I said, annoyed that the judges should've reached so unflattering a conclusion.

"Two of the winners got three checks," she said, indicating the cork wall across the room. "Third place and honorable mention got two checks, which means yours was as good as those . . ." That would have cheered me up if she hadn't added, as if compelled by scrupulous honesty, "Almost."

It occurred to me that she had a lot of knowledge. "Did you . . . ?"

She shrugged apologetically. "It's the only thing I'm any good at," she assured me, lest I peg her for a braggart. After an awkward pause she said, "I could show you mine."

"Sure," I said, and to my astonishment she took my hand and led me across the room, as if I might not be able to find her drawing otherwise. Her hand was slender and warm, and it fit into my own like it belonged there. I remembered how Jerzy had slid his index finger into the waistband of Karen's slacks, how thrilling that gesture had been to observe and interpret. This was less suggestive of sex, but it was also better in some way I couldn't define, and I could feel myself flush with a heady mix of pleasure, surprise and affection. Was this what Karen's mother had meant when she said my father hadn't known what hit him? Was what my mother had done this simple? Had she just taken my father by the hand, led him across a room and placed him before something she wanted him to look at? Had the frailty and warmth of her hand opened something in my father's heart that he hadn't known was there?

Sarah's entry was a pen-and-ink drawing of a boy who looked to be six or seven years old, and you could see why it got three bold checks in the upper-right-hand corner. True, it looked like there might be something wrong with the proportion of the boy's features. One eye seemed slightly larger than the other, and they appeared not equidistant from his nose. But they were alive, those eyes. She wasn't drawing how the boy's eyes looked. It was like they were real, that he was using them to see with. They made you wonder what he was looking at. You could tell right away that it was located just off the edge of the drawing and also that it worried him. And you could tell where the light was coming from. Sarah's name appeared in the lower-right-hand corner, printed impossibly small, as if whatever confidence she'd had went into the drawing itself, with none left over for a signature.

"My little brother," she said. "He died of leukemia. I draw him all the time. We've got lots of photos, so I draw those. When I try to draw him from memory, it never looks like him."

323

"I'm an only child," I told her, feeling inadequate for having nothing to say about the dead boy.

"Me, too," she said. "Now, I mean. It's just my dad and me."

"What about your—"

"They're separated. After Rudy died, she didn't want to live here anymore. I live with her summers. My dad teaches at the high school."

"Mr. Berg," I said, making the connection. Even in junior high, we'd all heard about Mr. Berg. Everybody tried to stay out of his English classes. "I hear he's strict," I said, hoping to imply that this was why kids didn't like him, not that he had bad breath or body odor. I waited, expecting Sarah Berg to confirm or deny her father's strictness, since she was in a position to know. When she didn't, I noticed that her drawing of her little brother had taken second prize, not first. Nan Beverly's watercolor of a spaniel puppy had won first, but I noted an odd thing about the three checks in her margin. Two were identical, in black ink, whereas the third looked different, in blue ink, as if someone had added it after the fact. Had Sarah noticed this? Though I decided not to ask, that third check mark reminded me of Karen Cirillo's unshakable conviction that our teachers had everything worked out in advance, the Borough kids catching all the breaks. Looking Sarah Berg over more closely, I was surprised to discover she was pretty, something I hadn't noticed before. Also, that she had eyes like the boy in the drawing, one slightly larger and lower than the other. After leading me across the room, she'd dropped my hand, but I could still feel the warmth of hers and wished there was someplace else for her to lead me.

"You should've gotten first," I told her. "Yours is a lot better." I said this last quietly, even though we were alone in the room. It was the sort of statement that, if overheard, could lead to a fight in the school yard.

"Nan's is good, too," she said, and I could tell she liked having a reason to say her name, as if that might make them friends. Which made me like Sarah Berg even more.

324

I was still holding my drawing of Ikey's, and this gave me an idea. "Maybe *you* could draw Ikey's someday," I suggested, immediately feeling foolish. Why would she want to draw that? "You could show me which parts should be white." Dumber and dumber.

But she smiled, as if the only thing holding her back was just such an invitation, and when our eyes met I half expected Sarah's to shift to some point off in the middle distance, like Karen Cirillo's always did. But they didn't. They stayed right on mine.

Which must mean, I concluded, that I was still there.

THE VERY NEXT DAY Sarah Berg appeared with her sketch pad. I'd been working in the back room, and when I came out, there she was, sitting Indian style on the terrace across the street. "You'll never guess what that girl's doing," my father said, staring out at her in wonder.

"Drawing the store?" I said.

"She's drawing the store," he said, apparently not having heard me. "You should see her go with that pen."

I'd only been in the back room for about twenty minutes, but evidently that was long enough for Sarah to begin half a dozen drawings, now scattered on the grass next to her. Some had just a few lines, while others looked half done, and I couldn't tell what it was about any of them that had caused her to stop and start over. Even the ones she'd abandoned after a few lines looked more promising than the drawing I'd worked on for a week. The one she was working on currently was the best. She'd done the outline of the whole store, dividing it into quadrants, and now appeared to be working from the center out, though for some reason, every now and then, she'd quit the section she was working on, as if an idea had occurred to her, and she'd squint at Ikey's, then at her sketch pad, and draw a few lines in an adjacent quadrant before going back to where she'd been. "Your dad's nice," she said without looking at me. "All the way down. Most nice people are nice just partway."

She herself seemed nice "all the way down," and I searched for the courage to say so, but it took too long and I gave up. I was glad to see her, though, glad that she hadn't forgotten her promise to draw Ikey's, glad she'd come by the very next day, glad she still seemed as at ease and comfortable as the day before. After the art show we'd gone for a Coke at the Woolworth's lunch counter, and in the middle of the afternoon we had the place to ourselves. Accustomed to Karen Cirillo, I expected to pay, but Sarah said no, it had to be Dutch treat. Even before our Cokes arrived, she'd launched into a personal history. Her family was Jewish, she said. They didn't practice the religion but instead something her father called humanism, which was more of a belief system. They didn't go to church, just put their faith in what her dad called the fundamental nobility of man. They ate pork chops like we did, Sarah gave me to understand, and also celebrated Christmas, at least as a season of fellowship, even if they didn't, as humanists, subscribe to the notion of Jesus being God or anything like that. That he was *good* was full and sufficient. People who believed that good wasn't good enough, that Jesus had to be *God*, were the ones who gave us the Crusades and the Spanish Inquisition and the Holocaust. All of these confidences came out in a rush that inspired me to offer intimate revelations of my own. We were Catholics, I told her, though she seemed already to have guessed that much. Nor did she seem that surprised that I'd gone to St. Francis until junior high, which meant we believed that Jesus *was* God, though we probably agreed that the Crusades and the Spanish Inquisition— which I looked up later—and the Holocaust were bad things. If I understood Mr. Berg's humanism, I suspected we were listing in that direction ourselves. Ikey's was open on Sunday, a point Father Gluck had raised with my mother and was told, for his trouble, to mind his own business, after which we hadn't gone to Mass for a month and now ate meat on Fridays, ecumenical behavior that put us on a par with the Bergs eating pork chops, at least so far as I could see.

The Bergs had moved to Thomaston from Long Island when she was in second grade, for reasons that weren't entirely clear even to Sarah. Her father had been a high school teacher there as well, and from what she said, or didn't say, I got the impression that he'd gotten into some kind of trouble that required him to look for a new job. He hated Thomaston, Sarah confided, because our town sorely tested his belief in the fundamental nobility of man, and because you simply couldn't get a decent bagel, with or without the lox to put on it.

Also, this. It had been her father who insisted she accept young Gabriel Mock's invitation to the fateful movie. As a rule he didn't let his daughter go out on dates, but here was a chance to make a statement. In Mr. Berg's opinion, Thomaston's Negroes had been ghettoized by people who, when it came to bigotry and ignorance, rivaled the citizenry of Birmingham and Selma. And why not? Did we not descend, at least symbolically, from Sir Thomas Whitcombe, like Thomas Jefferson a slave owner? No doubt both believed that all men were created equal, if by men you meant white landowners. All American patriots, in Mr. Berg's view, were hypocrites by definition.

"My father has a lot of opinions." Sarah had sighed, sucking the last of her soda noisily through her straw, and I had to agree with her. When I said, hoping to impress her, that I might take a class with him anyway, she warned me that he wouldn't like me. "You like it here in Thomaston, so he'll think you're a fool. Besides, he only likes angry people."

"You're not angry," I'd pointed out.

"I don't count," she'd shrugged, and at first I assumed she meant that of course he loved her anyway, since she was his daughter. But something about her tone suggested another possibility—that her father really didn't think of her as someone who counted.

Back when her little brother was alive and Sarah's mother still lived with them, the Bergs had rented a house on Seventh Avenue, near the Borough. But now that it was just the two of them, they rented a smaller, less expensive house a couple of blocks from Division Street, technically in the East End, but close to the gin mills and the YMCA. Until recently, her best friend had been a girl named Sally Doyle, who lived next door, and they'd always gone to the dances and Saturday matinees together. But after young Gabriel Mock showed up at the door to take Sarah to the matinee, the other girl's mother didn't want them to be friends anymore, which seemed to please Mr. Berg, who saw the whole experience as a teaching opportunity. His daughter would have lots of friends, good ones, he told her, once she got to college. They'd be different, by which he meant better. (Though I didn't say so, I was reminded of my grandparents, who'd had a similar ambition for my mother.) Sarah would then go to Columbia University, it had been decided, where Mr. Berg had himself spent two years before transferring to the state teachers college, where he'd met Sarah's mother. His reason for leaving Columbia, he maintained, was that his family had suffered a financial reversal, though Sarah's mother claimed he'd been asked to leave to avoid the indignity of flunking out.

I told Sarah that my mother was adamant that I attend college, too, though we hadn't decided where, as well as my father's doubts that we could afford it, an opinion he was not allowed to voice openly, which made Sarah smile. And, so she wouldn't feel so bad, I told her I'd also lost my best friend. I described how Bobby Marconi and I had surfed my father's milk truck on Saturday mornings, and I must have done a pretty good job describing Bobby, his courage and his refusal to cry even though his broken wrist hurt so bad he'd thrown up, and when I finished she said it was too bad she'd never have the opportunity to meet him, and I admitted I sometimes still missed him, though of course that wasn't nearly as bad as having your little brother die or your mother move away, so I supposed I was pretty lucky. I'd meant this observation to be sympathetic, but knew it was stupid when Sarah's eyes filled with tears. I'd walked her home, then, trying to make the conversation easy and fun again, but it was like her dead brother and departed mother were there with us, and walking back to Ikey's I kicked myself for saying the wrong thing. Now she wouldn't ever want to draw Ikey's or go out Dutch treat at Woolworth's again.

But here she was, scratching away with her special pen, a gift, I would later learn, from her mother, who was herself some kind of artist. Her good spirits had returned, and Ikey's was coming to life on the page. She was just about done when my mother came out of the house with two stainless-steel tubs of macaroni and potato salad for the store. I met her on the sidewalk and took one of the bowls, then helped her fit them into the far end of the meat case next to the ground beef. Sarah was tearing the completed drawing out of the sketch pad when my mother and I arrived back at the curb.

"This is my friend Sarah," I told her, glad that I could say this without fear of contradiction. I wouldn't have dared say such a thing about Karen Cirillo, who probably would've said, *We're friends, Lou? When did that happen?*

"She won second prize in the art show," I continued.

"I *see*," my mother said, amazed, like anybody would be, at how good the drawing was. Ikey's looked like a place even my mother would be proud to own, the kind of store that wouldn't make a pauper of you the first moment your attention slipped.

"You can have it," Sarah said, "if you want."

"But you worked so hard on it," my mother objected.

"It's your store," Sarah said.

My mother must've seen that Sarah was proud of the drawing and also that she wanted us to have it. "How about we put it in a frame and hang it up by the register where everybody can see it? That way, when you visit, you can see it, too."

The store got busy then, so it was later that afternoon, long after Sarah was gone, that I finally had a chance to inspect the finished product and see that she'd added people to the drawing.

A female figure, clearly my mother, could be seen bending over to slip a salad bowl into the meat case, the door to which was held open by Uncle Dec, recognizable by his shiny black hair. The man behind the register, by the bearlike slope of his big shoulders, was obviously my father. Also, she'd given Ikey's some business, an idea she probably got from me. The day before, sitting at the Woolworth's counter, I'd confessed our continuing anxieties that Ikey's might fail, so she'd given us three customers. The nearest, his back to the viewer, was about to enter the store, and his opening the door gave us that privileged glimpse inside. The two people at the register, a boy and a girl, seemed to be completing a purchase. Only when I looked closer did I realize they were Sarah and me. I was identified with a few tiny strokes expertly representing the plaid shirt I was wearing that day, whereas Sarah, half a head shorter, was identifiable by her dark, curly hair. On closer inspection, I saw that we were holding hands.

She had drawn us together. Which was how I learned that we were.

THAT DRAWING STILL EXISTS. As promised, my mother got it framed, though my father insisted that mine be framed as well, so people could compare. He thought mine was every bit as worthy, a minority view. Both renderings hung above the register at Ikey Lubin's for years, and Sarah and I have marveled more than once at how she captured in an hour or two our world as it then existed. After the fact, of course, it seemed not just a drawing but a prophecy. In her innocent depiction, Ikey's seemed prosperous, and for a while it was. For most of the next four years, it appeared our store would succeed, an illusion fostered in part by the failure of so many other neighborhood markets, among them Tommy Flynn's, whereas we had found our niche. I always maintain that Ikey's never failed, not really. It was our luck that did, and that only for a time.

Sarah's drawing of this happy, cheerful, hopeful place also marked some sort of passage, at least for me. More than anything else, it meant the end of junior high's worst terrors and social anxieties. I wasn't the only one who felt this change. The first time I ever really saw Sarah was in the theater manager's office, where she had been the very picture of fear, and I sometimes think she began to conquer that fear the day she drew herself as a member of our family, for that was what she quickly became. No surprise, she was a favorite of my father's. I remember his eyes filling when I told him what Sarah had said about him—that he was good all the way down. Uncle Dec teased her unmercifully, like he did every female, reminding her that he wasn't as old as he looked, and one day, who knew?

I could tell my mother was fond of Sarah, too, though she was also wary. We were young, she reminded us all through high school. It was great that we were such good friends, but the world was large and we shouldn't discount that just because we as yet had no notion of it. Sometimes, when Sarah and I were together, I caught my mother studying us—or was it just me?—with perplexed concern. I couldn't imagine what caused this, which may be why it troubled me. Sarah's father never overtly objected to our friendship, but I could tell Sarah had been right. He wasn't fond of me. When I told my mother, she said it was probably nothing personal, that no boy would ever be good enough for his little girl. He was a Jewish father, and I shouldn't let his opinion worry me. Somehow, though, he'd learned my nickname, and he enjoyed calling me by it, always in an ironic, joking way, but still.

By the end of eighth grade Sarah and I were, just as she'd portrayed us, together and inseparable. It was my mother who noticed the other thing, the significance of which had escaped even me—that since meeting Sarah I hadn't had a single spell. "Grown out of them is what happened" was my father's optimistic assessment. "There's nothing wrong with our Louie," he said, beaming at me. "There never was." Because I wanted

331

desperately for that to be true, now more than ever, I made no mention to Sarah of the spells that had punctuated my childhood and early adolescence. Nor did I tell her about my ordeal in the trunk, an event that at long last was receding into insignificance. If I was well, what difference did it make?

At the time I paid no attention to the third customer in Sarah's drawing, the one about to enter the store. It was the most generic figure in the drawing. Though I'd always assumed it was male, you couldn't really even be sure of its gender. Years later, when my father was diagnosed, I came to think of the dark figure as representing that illness on our very doorstep, with us still unaware of its presence. I don't remember how old I was, or even if Sarah and I were married yet, when I asked if she'd had anyone particular in mind. The figure had a curiously wide stance, as if he needed to hold on to the open door to keep from losing his balance. I'd expected her to say that, no, she'd just imagined a random customer, so I was surprised to learn that she had placed in the foreground a person she'd never seen but had heard me speak of so vividly that she hoped one day to meet him.

Bobby Marconi.

GHOST IKEY'S

WHEN OWEN COMES into the store, he finds me staring at his mother's drawing of Ikey Lubin's on the wall behind the register, yellowing and brittle now, behind glass. Sunk deep in reverie, I didn't hear the old bell above the door, which is just as well because I'd likely have turned around expecting to see a young Bobby, or Karen, or Uncle Dec. Even my father.

"Pop?" Owen says, startling me. "You having a spell?"

Trying not to sound irritated, I tell him no, I'm not. I'd have spared my son all knowledge of these episodes if I could, but at least I wish he'd react to the possibility more appropriately. Had I actually been having a spell, asking me would've been useless. Better to just go away and come back in half an hour. But it's unfair to get annoyed about this. In his entire life he's only witnessed two or three, and it was so long between them that he can be forgiven for forgetting what to do, or rather that there's really nothing to be done. Only two people—my father and my wife—have ever had much influence over the severity or duration of my spells. Poor Owen, who knows better, or would if he thought about it, can't help thinking he should do something.

"Your eyes are all red," he says when I turn around. He studies me carefully, which gives me the opportunity to study him back. My son looks like me, more with each passing year, though I don't know how he feels about the resemblance. As a boy, being told how much I resembled my father was a source of pleasure and pride to me, and later in life I enjoyed being mistaken for Big Lou Lynch on the street. Apparently Owen was recently mistaken for me, and my impression was that he didn't feel complimented.

Be that as it may, he's clearly embarrassed to have caught me gathering wool. "Mom's going to be fine," he assures me. "I was just out at the house. She looks great."

"I know," I tell him.

"They got it all," he continues, as if I've disagreed with him. "There's no reason—"

"I know."

Tomorrow she and I meet with the oncologist to confirm this and, assuming there are no surprises in the blood work, we'll be officially cleared for international travel. There can be little doubt that the promise of Italy has accelerated Sarah's return to health and contributed significantly to her renewed sense of general well-being. Her physical strength and stamina improve daily, so much so that my warnings not to overdo now seem more grumpy than caring.

I probably should tell Owen that he's mistaken the cause of my melancholy, but concern for his mother's health is a far better excuse for my puffy eyes than the actual reason, which I'm not sure I could explain anyway. Owen's as good-hearted as they come, though he's impatient, as the young are, with emotional complexity. Not that he's so young anymore, as Sarah is always reminding me. Anyway, I let it go.

What I doubt I could explain is how his mother's drawing amplifies my profound sense, much aggravated of late, that another, alternate version of my life exists, that I'm trapped in this one when I really belong in the other. My alternate life, though ethereal, is somehow truer than the one I know to be factual and real. The shadow version contains everything that *should* be there—Ikey's itself, my father and mother, my wife and me, with Bobby poised outside, about to enter. Since Sarah drew our world so long ago, two things have happened that shouldn't have. My father died of cancer, and Bobby fled Thomaston for the wide world, never to return.

334

"What do you mean?" Sarah said, genuinely puzzled, when I asked not long ago if she, too, ever sensed another reality where things existed as they were supposed to, where providence hadn't been thwarted. "People lose their fathers, Lou. And what would have happened to Bobby if he hadn't left when he did? You don't really think he'd be with us here at Ikey's?"

Which did make me smile. When Sarah uses that particular tone with me, I'm reminded of my mother's attempts to straighten my father out when she caught him meandering hopelessly in the labyrinths of what *should* be, a world where milk still comes in bottles, where meat's still wrapped in butcher paper, not cellophane, and tied off with string. And of course my wife's right. It was thoughtless of me to give the impression that *my* loss was special, or that I alone should've been exempted from something so universal as the loss of a parent. After all, Sarah lost both her parents, and her little brother, too. Nor had I meant to suggest that Bobby could or should have remained in dear old Thomaston when fame and fortune awaited him elsewhere. Embarrassed, I must've looked just as sheepish as my father always did when my mother shredded his logic, shining the light of reason on his foolishness. I remember vividly wishing she wouldn't do that, that she'd let him arrange his thoughts and feelings the way he wanted. After all, how does one invalidate a powerful feeling? Not with logic, surely.

Still, who *doesn't* suspect that providence has somehow been thwarted, that the true narrative of one's life is proceeding merrily along but on a strictly parallel track and therefore inaccessible? What I was trying without success to explain to Sarah was not that I think my father *shouldn't* have died, but rather that he *didn't*, that he lives on, as full of life as ever, in some other Ikey's, the *real* Ikey's, truer than ours for the simple reason that he's there, a part of it. He's aged, of course, in that next-door world, and the rest of us worry about his health. It's not a *perfect* world, this alternate one. Nothing in it is idealized. He could be diagnosed with some terrible malignancy tomorrow. As it is, he has good days and bad. He's failed, as people do, as even my mother has. Some days he's more of a hindrance than a help at the store, wanting to do everything like he always has, jotting notes on scraps of paper and stuffing them under the cash register drawer, refusing to do his inventory on the computer and thereby causing no end of confusion. And of course he's never come to terms with the Lotto machine that saved Ikey's and enabled us to buy the other two markets. When my father purchased Ikey's all those years ago, he promised my mother he'd never make book or sell numbers there, and even though betting horses and playing Lotto numbers is now not only legal but state sponsored, he sometimes feels like he's broken that promise.

If this narrative seems whimsical simply by virtue of its being untrue, all I can say is that it's more *realistic* than the truth, and Bobby's presence heightens that realism even further. When the bell above the door jingles and we see it's Bobby entering with his new girlfriend, where's the implausibility? Of course he, too, has aged. He's got a bit of paunch now, his former athleticism having yielded to years of high living. He sports some gray at the temples but still has a full head of hair, and he has a way with the local girls, women now, all of them. He brings a different one to the store every week, and each of them understands that she's auditioning for a foursome—Sarah and me, Bobby and this new woman—and also that it won't work out, that we're naturally three and there's nothing to be done about it. He's still hot tempered, of course, still willing to mix it up, and even men my son's age know better than to trifle with him. Though they know nothing of his legendary battle with Jerzy Quinn, they have only to look at him to know he's brave and willing, a dangerous combatant.

I don't *dwell* in this alternate world, or even on it. I'm not crazy. But at odd moments I do sense its existence, and more frequently of late, I'll admit, but for a very good reason. I've been living in the past these weeks, working long hours to write my story, and Bobby will return to it soon, if I continue. I'd hoped to be finished before we left for Italy, but I'm not sure that's possible.

My point about the alternative Ikey's is that, as a narrative, it holds together. It makes sense. Though untrue as regards its facts, it has the *ring* of truth—Bobby still here, swinging by the store after work on Friday with a hearty "Hello, you Lynches" and introducing the new girl to my father, who jokingly warns her against him. By contrast, it's reality that feels far-fetched—Bobby running off like he did, taking his mother's surname, drifting and brawling his way from London to Paris, Barcelona to Rome and, finally, to Venice, through a maze of marriages and affairs, finding fame and disgrace in equal measure and (to me the strangest part) never returning, not once, to those of us who cared for him. How plausible is that?

I'm not sure what I was thinking when I tried to explain all this to Sarah. I certainly didn't expect her to believe literally in this other Ikey's. I guess I just hoped she'd see the story's inner truth and beauty. Even taken as pure whimsy, wouldn't my Sarah have as much reason as I to indulge it? Seen in a certain light, didn't Bobby hijack a destiny that was rightfully hers? It was she who went off to study art at Cooper Union in New York, all expenses paid; she who got scholarship offers from so many universities; she whose talent was so large, so full of the most extraordinary promise. When Bobby fled Thomaston, he'd put neither pencil to paper nor brush to canvas. What would be more natural than for Sarah to look at our old friend's life and conclude that somehow their destinies had been switched, like babies in adjacent bassinets? But as Sarah was quick to point out, once a thing has happened, the *odds* of its happening become moot. Realism and plausibility aren't reality's poor cousins. No doubt this was what all those arguments between my parents were about. No wonder my father lost them all.

"What happens in this story you're writing?" Sarah asked me earlier this week as we lay in bed, catching each other up on our day. I could hear the worry in her voice. "Does Lou-Lou live?" Lou-Lou. Her fond name for my father.

"No, he dies," I assured her. Our bedtime conversations are mostly playful and tender, and this was the tone I adopted, or tried to. "Bobby leaves and never returns. He becomes a famous painter and lives in Venice. We visit him there. Except I haven't gotten to any of that yet."

She seemed relieved to hear that I'm sticking to the facts, though still worried about something, probably that I'm obsessing about my story despite my promise not to. It's true I've already spent more time than I ever imagined would be necessary to recount the particulars of a life as uneventful as mine, and also that I've far exceeded the hundred pages I judged would be sufficient to my purpose. I go into my den and close the door behind me so I won't hear the telephone or the TV. Sarah can't help recalling what we now refer to as my Map Days, and they were dark indeed. I've tried to reassure her that this is different, but I can't blame her for worrying. My surprising devotion to this enterprise probably also reminds her of her father, the poor man. Forever writing a story with no ending, a story that consumed instead of enriching. But of course I don't have her father's ambition. He thought his story was important, that fame and fortune would be its natural consequence, whereas I'm doing this only for my own amusement and edification. For Sarah's father only the grandest dreams were worth the effort of dreaming. Ikey's wouldn't have counted. Moreover, far from making my mind uneasy, my narrative journey has proven therapeutic, I think, a welcome diversion. "I'm just passing the time until we leave. I need to remember it all. I don't want to be confused."

"About what?"

"Our lives. What happened to us. Why we've lived as we have, instead of some other way."

"Oh, Lou," my wife said, taking my hand. "I wish you wouldn't take things to heart so."

Exactly what my mother always said to my father.

"If we don't hear from Bobby soon—"

"There's still time," I told her, though my heart sank to see hers so set.

"His studio's here," she pointed. The map of Venice was spread out on our bed. "Somewhere around here." Her index finger traveled lightly over the whole of Giudecca Island, suggesting—sadly, I thought—that Bobby could be anywhere, that without explicit directions we'd never find him.

BACK IN IKEY'S—the real one—Owen says, "You're driving Mom nuts. You know that, right?"

"I am?"

"She's all packed. You haven't even started."

"It won't take long."

"Is it true you threw your passport away last week?"

"It came in an unmarked envelope. I didn't know what it was."

The look he gives me implies he isn't buying that explanation any more than his mother did. "You think I threw it away on purpose?" I ask once again. "Why would I do that?"

What have I done to merit such unkind suspicion? We have our airline tickets, our hotel reservations, all of it paid for, a small fortune.

"It's not something you'd do up here," Sarah had conceded, kissing the spot on my forehead that didn't worry her. "It's what goes on back *here*," she explained, playfully fixing with her thumb the very spot on my skull beneath which I've always imagined my spells originate, small and dark, a single bent gene at first, then a cluster of twisted cells growing like a migraine until they overload and shut me down. "It's the part you don't have access to, that I'm keeping an eye on." My son, too, apparently.

He and I switch places now, Owen coming around the counter just as my father and I used to, and the pleasure of this simple act is so overwhelming, so intense, that I'd like to share it with him.

But I know I should control this impulse, and so I do, though it leaves me momentarily without purpose, on the wrong side of the counter, while my son opens the register and checks the drawer to make sure he has everything he needs. He does. I made sure.

"Have you been to the studio?" he says, lips continuing to move as he counts.

"The where?" I say, remembering how his mother's fingertips floated over Venice in search of Bobby's studio.

"The art room. At the junior high. Mom's finishing a new painting, and it's pretty good. You should stop by."

I tell him I will and make a mental note to follow through later today. It will please Sarah to know I've taken the trouble when I could've just waited for her to bring it home. Earlier in the week she said something about "the painting going well," and I'm afraid I looked blank for a second, trying to guess what she meant. I was thinking of rooms, of course, one of ours in the Borough or maybe the Third Street house or one of the West End apartments. I covered my mistake as quickly as I could, but not quickly enough, and I saw the hurt register, just a flicker, across her face. So later today I'll not only visit the studio but also take time to memorize this new work, so we can discuss it in detail over dinner.

"Where's Brindy?" it occurs to me to ask. She's listed on Ikey's schedule for today, not Owen.

"She's in Albany," he explains, or half explains, telling me where she is but not why. Perhaps consulting the doctor who told her she was unlikely to get pregnant again. Or maybe a specialist who can tell her something different. Or else she just went shopping.

"Does she dislike me?" I hear myself ask. Owen's still counting, the change now, and it takes him a while to respond.

He squints at me, and I can't tell if it's the oddness of the question or just that it's come out of left field, surprising even me. "Why would she dislike you?"

"She just seems impatient sometimes. I try not to meddle, but—"

"That's just her way, Dad," he reassures me. "You should know by now. You should see how she is with me."

Not the response I was hoping for. "Do you think she's unhappy?"

"About what?"

I shrug. "I don't know."

"It's probably just from before," he says, meaning the miscarriage. "It got Mom down, right?"

"Yes," I say, remembering.

"But she got over it."

In fact it was Owen's birth, as much as anything, that got her over it, though I can hardly say this to my son, not if Brindy can't conceive again. "You'll tell me if there's anything I can do?"

"Sure, Pop," he says, "but there isn't."

He sounds very sure of this, and I wish he wasn't. I open my mouth to tell him so, then close it again. He has resumed counting.

GABRIEL MOCK LIVES in our Berman Court building in the small ground-floor apartment below the one the Marconis once occupied. He's lived here rent-free for over a decade, in return for which he acts as caretaker. He's old now but still spry and useful with a wrench or a paintbrush, and to observe him, you'd never guess he was older than my mother. He also helps out at our West End market, though according to Owen he hasn't been by in several days, which is why I'm anxious to make sure he's all right. I'd call, but he doesn't have a phone.

Though it takes a while, Gabriel finally answers my knock. "Junior," he says, his red eyes spiderwebbed and dull. He opens the door wide so I can enter, but I remain in the hall. It troubles me that Gabriel seems to think I have a right to enter his home on a whim, just because I own the building. I've tried to explain that it's his apartment and he has as much right to tell me to go away as he would anyone else, but he sees it differently. And he's as stubborn in his advanced years as he was back in the days when we argued about up and down.

"Mr. Mock," I say. Over the years I've settled on this mode of address, though he insists he doesn't care what I call him. Call him Gizzard, if I want to. "I was just checking to see if you're okay."

"Be back at work tomorrow," he assures me. "Had me a little setback, is all."

I can smell his humid solitude even out in the hall, and also the fact that he hasn't left the apartment in days or even opened a window. Gabriel doesn't drink anymore ("Done howlin'. My howlin' days is all in the past. You got to howl for the both of us now, Junior. Even though you still a ama-teur."), except when something reminds him of his son: the boy's birthday, perhaps, or news of some black kid from the Hill getting roughed up behind the new YMCA. These setbacks usually last a few days, but Gabriel emerges none the worse for wear, and he seldom misbehaves in public anymore, even when egged on. Seeing him on the street, some Thomaston wags still shout "Send him out!" though most of them are too young to remember what happened at Murdick's that night. There's a story attached to it, but they don't recall what it is. Other people ask Gabriel for matches, a half-joking reference to the commonly held belief that he set the fire that burned down Whitcombe Hall so many years ago.

"Is there anything I can do?" I ask him now, though I know there isn't.

"Just leave everything go," he tells me, meaning whatever has piled up in his absence here at Berman Court and at the market. "Be back in the mornin'."

"Are you sure you don't need to go to the doctor?"

"What for?" he says. "She just inform me I'm stupid. Tell me somethin' I don't already know, I might go see her sometime."

"You're an original, Mr. Mock," I tell him.

"Not me," he says, suddenly, unexpectedly adamant. "I'm just a copy. You, too."

Which makes me smile.

"In fact, you a bigger copy than me. You your daddy all over again. Big Lou Lynch in the flesh. Big Lou Junior. You gonna grin at me like that, go on away. You makin' my teeth hurt."

I stop grinning.

"Your mama doin' okay?"

I tell him she is.

"Good woman, your mama. Prob'ly don't remember me."

"Of course she does, Mr. Mock. She often asks after you."

"Woman like that enough to make a man good an' ashamed of hisself. You married to another one, so you know what I mean. There you go, grinnin' again."

And with that he shuts the door.

Since I'm here, I make a circuit of the property to check for trouble, particularly in the foundation. I've been warned that some rainy spring the whole building could tumble down the steep bank into the stream. Probably not in my lifetime, though, which means that's another thing Owen can deal with. It's ironic, I suppose, that the other structures up the street are in less danger of collapse, despite the fact that their owners have let them decay, one rotten clapboard at a time, while we've spent money. Foolishly, some would say, and it's true that Berman Court never made much sense as an investment. According to my mother, I'm attempting in vain to "own my life." Otherwise, why throw good money at Berman Court or, for that matter, the Third Street house I can't convince her to move back into? The answer she stubbornly refuses to credit is that while the house where Sarah and I now live is in the Borough, I consider myself not only a resident but also a product of the whole town. Why shouldn't I invest in all three sectors? I have a convenience store in each, why not a house? I'm not trying to own my life, just acknowledge it, as well as the narrative of our family, its small, significant journey. Is this not an American tale? Are we not the most typical of postwar Americans? That's how my father would see it, so of course it makes sense that my mother would adopt the opposite view.

At any rate, I'm proud that these Berman Court apartments are in better condition now than when the Marconis and we Lynches lived here so long ago. The rent we charge is modest, not even enough to cover expenses some months, but over time we've found good tenants, most of whom are getting on in years and respectful of the premises and each other. Despite the neighborhood, our building always has a waiting list.

Nobody's around, so I lumber down the bank to where the footbridge used to be. Since St. Francis closed, there's been far less pedestrian traffic there, so the bridge was allowed to gradually fall victim to our long, difficult winters. Downstream, the old trestle was condemned and torn down years ago, and the gravel pit into which the braver boys leapt from the trestle's edge is now infested with weeds. Despite signs posted all over the property, people use it as an unofficial dump, thereby avoiding the fees charged by the county landfill. Given what they represent, there's no reason I should miss either the footbridge or the trestle, but in truth I do. The loss of a place isn't really so different from the loss of a person. Both disappear without permission, leaving the self diminished, in need of testimony and evidence. *This happened. I was there. Once upon a time there was a footbridge. My father stood just there.* This story I've been composing so faithfully, now I think about it, probably is little more than my poor attempt to restore what was and is no more. Is this why Bobby paints? To leave his paintings as evidence?

Half an hour later, I'm sitting at a traffic light in wet, squishy shoes, having somehow slipped into the stream. Trying to imagine how I'll explain this clumsiness to Sarah, I see Brindy and a man I don't know emerge from a lower Division Street duplex. She's wearing a jacket, but the man, despite the chill in the air, is in his shirtsleeves, his hair mussed. The nonchalant way he leans in the open doorway reminds me of Uncle Dec, though he's been dead some years now. Brindy's a head shorter than whoever this man is, and when she turns back to face him, I almost expect her to rise up on tiptoes to kiss him, but she doesn't. When the traffic light changes, the car behind me toots and she turns around, her face flush and radiant until she sees me, but her expression changes before I can look away and pretend not to see what I've seen.

HOMECOMING

TWO THINGS AMAZED Noonan about his mother's final flight—that she'd gotten so far as Jacksonville, Florida, and had been gone for so long, almost two months. He hadn't heard about it until after the fact, when he was downstate, with one more year to go at the academy. If he managed to graduate, which, given the turmoil of his junior year, was by no means a certainty, nothing much awaited him but the draft and, almost certainly, Vietnam. If he got tossed out before graduation, Vietnam that much sooner.

Of course his mother had been running away since he was a boy, but only later, after he'd returned home, did he understand the sad truth—that she'd finally made the clean getaway she'd been dreaming of for so long. Instead of staying lost, though, as he would've advised, she'd called his father from Florida and told him that, yes, she'd consider returning, but only if Noonan could return as well. Which was how he came to spend his senior year at Thomaston High, how he came to meet Sarah and how his conflict with his father came to a final, brutal resolution. He would often wonder if, had his mother imagined the sequence of events she was putting in motion, she still would've brought him home.

THE FIRST TIME he'd been—what, six? They were still living at Berman Court, and her husband was working at the hotel then, but she forgot that Fridays were different, that on that day he worked as a letter carrier. She'd turned a corner, suitcase in

346

hand, and practically run into him coming out of an apartment house. Had she just lowered her head and kept going, she still might've made it, because he was riffling through a fistful of letters as he walked. Instead, she'd let out a little squeal of surprise, and when he looked up, that was that. Grabbing the suitcase, he tried to open it on the spot, but she'd locked it with its tiny key, so he smashed it open on a nearby brick wall and tossed her clothing into the street, flinging the case over a nearby culvert and down the bank. Shaking, she started down after it, thinking that this was to be part of her punishment, but he told her no, leave everything right where it is, the clothes, too, even her underthings, and get on home where she belonged. But they couldn't afford new, she objected, to which he replied that she should've thought of that before. Now she could do without.

Even before his mother left, Noonan, young as he was, had known something was wrong. She'd told him not to worry, that she was just going away for the day, that he should look after his little brothers until his father got home from work. If there was an emergency, he was to go upstairs and get Mrs. Lynch. He knew she was lying, that she wasn't just going away for the day, so he was surprised when she returned so soon. When he asked where the suitcase was, she said it was gone and started crying. Finally, she told him what had happened. She didn't want him to go fetch her things, and he knew that his father wouldn't want him to either, but he did it anyway, never mind the consequences. It was the beginning, as Noonan now saw it, of a seemingly ceaseless contest of wills with his father.

When he arrived on the scene, his mother's clothes still lay scattered in the street. Some of them had been run over by cars. People came out onto their porches to watch him, just a kid, gathering up these items, and it felt particularly awful to retrieve her panties and bras, things he knew he shouldn't be touching. The suitcase, its hinges sprung, lay at the edge of the stream below, but he fetched it and stuffed the clothing inside, after which, of course, it wouldn't close. Hard as it was to carry in that condition, he'd made it back the few blocks to Berman Court. His mother was still sitting in the chair where he left her, one hand over her mouth, the other over her swollen stomach, with his little brothers at her feet, behaving for once, having somehow intuited the gravity of the situation.

Over the years she got better at fleeing, just never good enough. On her second attempt she got as far as the cigar store at the corner of Hudson and Division where the Greyhound bus stopped, but the man at the ticket window knew her husband and called him at work. The time after that she called a Hudson cab and took it to the train station in Fulton, where she bought a ticket to New York. Her plan was to get off in Fordham and take the local into the city, in order to fool Noonan's father, but she'd been so exhausted by all the planning and the sleepless nights preceding that she'd fallen asleep. The conductor woke her in Grand Central after everyone else had gotten off the train. He had two men with him, one of whom took her by the elbow, the other carrying the suitcase she'd purchased used the week before and hidden in the back of the closet. She half expected the men to open the suitcase and toss her clothes onto the tracks, but all they did was put her on another train headed back north. She might have gotten off, say, in Poughkeepsie, and simply resumed her journey, but by then her respect for her husband's power and reach was too great, as if he'd managed to convince her that he had a network of spies and accomplices as vast as the U.S. Postal Service, all of them devoted to making sure she stayed where she belonged. He and their three sons were waiting for her on the platform back in Fulton. "Welcome home, D.C.," he told her. "You have a nice trip?" In the station parking lot he tossed her suitcase into the metal dumpster.

Though she became more sophisticated with each subsequent attempt, Noonan's father also got better at anticipating her flight. Everything was against her. For one thing, she always bolted when she was pregnant. Of course she was pregnant most of the time, but still. If she'd fled as soon as she *got* pregnant, she'd have been in better shape and also less easily identifiable to her pursuers. Yet it was always in the seventh month that her despair peaked, when it occurred to her that she couldn't bear to continue here. By the age of ten, Noonan himself could see it all coming as clearly as his father, and as the time approached he kept an eye out for another new suitcase.

Her husband couldn't watch her every minute of the day, not while holding down his job, so his strategy was to keep her poor, thus making flight more difficult. He gave her only as much money as she needed for the week's groceries and warned nearby markets not to allow her to set up charge accounts without his approval. No matter how little he gave her, though, she somehow managed to squirrel away bus or train fare. Returning from work each day, her husband took careful inventory to make sure none of their possessions was missing, and he also alerted the owners of Thomaston's two pawnshops that she soon might appear, hoping to unload their valuables.

The deck was stacked against her, but the run she made when he was in sixth grade had nearly succeeded. Someone—Noonan suspected Mrs. Lynch—had given her a ride to Albany, where she'd purchased a train ticket to New York, but then, instead of getting on, she'd taken a taxi to the bus terminal and boarded a Greyhound for Montreal, trusting that her husband's reach wasn't international in scope. At the border, probably because she looked terrified without apparent cause, she'd been taken off the bus and questioned, and her answers were, of necessity, vague. She had no idea where she'd be staying. How long would she remain in Canada? Until her husband located her and brought her home. How much money did she plan to spend? She had fifty dollars in her purse, and unless she was mistaken, she'd have to spend all of it. Evasive answers led to further questions, which led to suspicions that she could read in their faces. These men clearly knew her husband, and they had no intention of letting her into Canada. She sat in the tiny room where they questioned her, staring out the window at the bus, the other passengers fidgeting in their seats and blaming her for their delay. For how long? She glanced up above the door at the round clock, which was there and then wasn't there, and then nothing was there.

When she awoke on a cot with an IV in her arm, she was told not to worry. Her baby would be fine. Everything would be fine. They'd gone through her purse and found a library card, then called information in Thomaston and gotten her phone number. Her husband was on his way.

Noonan had known he was going to catch it. It had taken his old man no time at all to find out about the train ticket she'd bought for New York, so he was surprised to get the phone call from a hospital on the Canadian border. Where had she gotten money for both a train and a bus ticket? When he hung up, he studied his son suspiciously, and Noonan made the mistake of looking away guiltily.

When they returned, his father was no sooner in the door than he fixed Noonan with that same stare, just to let him know that the ten hours it had taken to fetch his mother home hadn't interrupted his focus a bit. "Welcome home, D.C.," he said. His mother stood in the doorway, one hand beneath her enormous belly, looking down. Noonan heard her murmur what he thought might have been "Please."

"What's that, D.C.?" his father said. "You have something to say to your family?"

"Please," she said, audibly this time, though just barely. She was peering out from behind her husband at Noonan, who knew she was beseeching both of them with that single syllable, begging her son not to further antagonize his father, begging her husband not to punish his son for what she'd done.

His father came over to where he stood shaking with fear. "Well," he said, "you've had time to think about it. Where do you suppose your mother got all that money, Robert?"

"I saved it," his mother said.

"The hell you did, D.C.," he told her. Not once since the moment they entered had he taken his eyes off Noonan. "A train ticket you didn't even use? A bus ticket to Montreal?"

"I put a little aside every week," she said. "I did . . . I promise."

"When I call the bank tomorrow," he said to Noonan, "and ask how much is in your savings account, what are they going to tell me?"

Noonan's eyes met his mother's then and saw how pointless it was to lie. He'd emptied the account containing five months' worth of paper route money last week, the same day he discovered another strange suitcase in the back of the hall closet, right where his mother always hid them. It had been *his* idea to buy the train ticket but not use it. Let his father look south while she was heading north. He remembered the look on her face as he explained how to do it, at once frightened and proud of his gift for deception and strategy. One day he'd be a match for his father. Before long he'd be a man, ready for whatever the world threw at him.

But not *this* day. Today he was still a boy, and he was quaking violently now, waiting, as he had been for ten hours, for what would happen next. He wasn't stupid. He knew the thing to say was *I'm sorry*. For his own good as well as his mother's. *I'm sorry.* Say he didn't know what she wanted the money for. She'd back him up, no matter what he said. Though his father wouldn't believe either of them, that's what he wanted to hear, and once he did then things would gradually get better. *I'm sorry* was the right thing to say, the only thing, really. Instead he heard himself say, the words nearly lost in his sobs, "*You're* why she runs away. If you were nice to her, she wouldn't want to. It's *you* she hates."

As he said this, his father stood over him flexing his big fists, the birthmark along his hairline dark purple now with rage. Scared as he was, Noonan remembered thinking, almost with relief, All right then. This was the day the terrible blow would finally come. By now his brothers had begun to cry, and his mother was pleading urgently on his behalf, imploring her husband not to strike him, telling him he was just a boy, that he hadn't had any idea what she wanted the money for, that he didn't mean what he'd just said. And besides, it wasn't true. She didn't hate him and didn't want to leave her family, not really. It was just that sometimes she got so tired and confused that she was afraid she'd just start screaming in front of the children. "He'll apologize," she said. "Bobby will apologize right now. You will, won't you, sweetie?" She'd come over to where he stood and gotten down on her knees. She'd taken his hand and was kissing it, wetting it with her tears. How ugly she was, he remembered thinking, her face contorted with need and fear. "Tell him you didn't mean what you said, okay? Do that for Mommy?"

Noonan hadn't yet learned that his father would not strike him. That understanding would come to him years later at the academy, a blinding, utterly transformative revelation. For all his threats to thrash the boy within an inch of his life, he'd never once struck him or, now that he thought about it, his mother. Why hadn't it occurred to him that adults could be like school-yard bullies? Sure, his father was a holy terror when it came to inanimate objects. Earlier that year he'd taken a Pyrex dish containing a casserole his mother had scorched and scraped the food directly into the trash, refusing to let anyone taste it. Then, to make his point—that the dish itself was ruined—he smashed it on the edge of the counter, in the process slicing open the web of skin between his thumb and forefinger, and a look of horrible satisfaction had come over his features as the bright blood pumped into the sink. "See?" he kept saying, showing the wound first to his mother, then to Noonan. "See?" *Sure, the blood's mine*, he seemed to be saying, *but next time it could be yours. Next time, if you aren't careful, it* will *be yours.* For years Noonan had watched his father kick trash cans, rupture suitcases, throw bottles across the room so they smashed on impact, their contents oozing down the wall.

But what his father had always wanted him to fear was the day he'd lose control, when the blood would really flow. His mother's surely, and probably his own. Maybe even his little brothers'. Noonan's realization at the academy, that his father would run a bluff with his own blood, was liberating, though it came at a price. If he could figure this out at fifteen, what was wrong with his mother? Why had the penny never dropped for her? After all the years of cowering, had it never once registered that she was married to not just a bully but also a coward? How could she, a grown woman, fall for the same trick day after day, year after year?

And why hadn't *he* realized then, the day his father stood over him clenching his big fists, that he didn't have to say the words, that nothing would happen if he didn't? How could he have been so stupid? In his room at the academy he remembered the terrible quaver in his voice when he did what his mother had asked and said, "I'm sorry, Daddy." In that moment he felt something harden inside him, and in time he'd recognize it for what it was—a resolution. To be more like him than her.

HIS MOTHER HAD farther to travel, coming from Jacksonville, Florida, so he arrived home before she did. His father took the opportunity to lay down some ground rules. "You want to stay here, you turn over a new leaf. You do what I say, when I say it," he said, holding his index finger an inch from Noonan's nose, his brothers looking on. "I say jump, the only question you ask is how high. You understand?"

"Yes, I do," Noonan said. It was a strange sensation to be threatened by a man he'd feared all his life but no longer did. Though it was tempting to grab the finger and snap it back, he didn't. It was true he'd had his troubles at the academy, but one of the things he'd learned there was the difference between what was worth fighting over and what wasn't. For his own part, his father seemed to understand that something had changed, even if he wasn't quite sure what. It wasn't that his son was suddenly two inches taller than he was. No, he had a new calmness about him. Was it docility? Had the boy's stubborn spirit finally been broken? Noonan could see his father's mind working, observing, weighing evidence, trying to form a valid conclusion, but not guessing, at least not yet, the unthinkable truth.

The next afternoon Noonan drove to Fulton to meet his mother's train. "I almost didn't recognize you, you've grown so," she said when he took her, big as a house, into his arms. The journey had been arduous, and she looked pale and weak. "I forgot you have your driver's license," she told him. "I thought I'd have to wait here until your father got off work."

He took her suitcase, and when they passed the dumpster in the parking lot he said, "Dad told me to toss this in, but to hell with him." When he realized she'd taken him seriously, he added, "That was a joke, actually."

"You shouldn't say such things," she told him.

"Why's that, Mom?" he asked, genuinely curious as to why he should exercise such caution when it was just the two of them.

"You shouldn't provoke him. You know how he is."

"Yeah, I do," he told her, thinking about what he now knew, and what she still didn't and probably never would.

When she told him she'd run out of money and hadn't eaten since the day before, he insisted they stop at a drive-in on the outskirts of Thomaston, where she inhaled a burger, a bag of fries and a big vanilla shake. Between bites, she told him why she thought things would be better now. His own return to Thomaston hadn't been her only condition. When she delivered this baby—of necessity by Cesarean section, since that's what the last two had been—she meant to have her tubes tied. "I made him promise," she said, proud that she'd stood her ground. In return for this long overdue consideration, she agreed not to pester her husband about that woman anymore. Noonan hadn't been aware she ever had even acknowledged the other woman's existence, but she admitted she'd pestered him plenty, especially when she was pregnant. But now she wouldn't be pregnant again.

"And you trust him?" he asked, the question catching her off guard.

"He promised," she said. "He's never done that before. He's never promised me anything."

It stayed on the tip of Noonan's tongue that once upon a time his father had promised to love, honor and obey.

By the time they arrived, Noonan's brothers were home from school, his father from work. The boys, while glad to have their mother home, were muted in their welcomes, perhaps because she looked so unwell or because they knew better than to be too effusive in front of their father, who neither rose from the table nor looked up from his newspaper, though he did say, "Welcome home, D.C.," as was his well-established custom on these occasions.

This, the moment of his mother's homecoming, had been what Noonan had been waiting for. He'd spent the whole morning and early afternoon cleaning the house. He'd actually started the night before, but his father had told him to leave it. Whenever his wife fled, he was adamant that nothing be done in the house, so that when she returned all of her work would be waiting—the dishes accumulated in the sink, dirty clothing mounded on the laundry room floor, the garage stinking of garbage. But as soon as his father had left for work that morning, Noonan had started in and worked right straight through until it was time to meet his mother's train. He hadn't been able to do everything. She'd been gone too long and the squalor was too great, though he'd done most of it and found the work powerfully and unexpectedly pleasing. Cleaning up after his father had forbidden him to was disobedience bordering on rebellion, but he'd known instinctively that the old man couldn't call him on it because he could claim to be turning over that new leaf, as promised. That defiance and contempt could be cloaked so completely in apparent virtue made the housework doubly satisfying.

Yet when he turned to his mother, hoping to enjoy her surprise and pleasure at returning to a clean house, she'd stopped in the doorway with one hand under her abdomen, the other clutching the doorframe and her eyes clenched tightly shut. "Mom?" he said.

"It's wonderful to be here," she told them, after the contraction passed. "And I'm sorry I can't stay, but I have to go to the hospital now."

She had the baby by natural childbirth half an hour later, before her doctor could get to the hospital. After the fact, he took Noonan's father aside to tell him about the damage that had been done. "You have to understand," Noonan heard him say, "that it would be catastrophic for your wife to become pregnant again."

Later, when his brothers were in the nursery admiring the littlest Marconi, leaving him alone with his father, he took the opportunity to lay down some ground rules of his own. "I'll do what you say, when you say it," he promised his father. "You tell me to jump, I'll ask how high. Just know this. You ever get my mother pregnant again, or call her D.C. in my hearing, I'll kill you."

That was the other realization he'd come to at the academy. His mother's first name was Deborah, but her middle name was Margaret, so why D.C.? He'd asked his father once, in her presence, and had never forgotten the look on her face. "Your mother knows what it means," he'd chuckled. "She can tell you herself sometime, if she wants."

He'd awakened in his dorm room in the middle of the night, suddenly knowing. Dumb Cunt.

NOT LONG after returning home, Noonan got a call from his old friend Lucy Lynch, who'd heard, somehow, that he was back in town. Noonan had been expecting the call, dreading it, really, because he could think of no good reason to renew their friendship, which had always been based, it seemed to him, on their mothers' secret friendship and Lucy's terrible neediness.

Since confronting his father, though—his brow had darkened, but he'd just smiled at his son's threat—he'd decided to focus on his future, whatever that might entail. His senior year, he understood, was a trial to be gotten through. Once he turned eighteen and had his high school diploma, his father would have no further control over him. He could head out west some-where, get a job, take some night classes and begin some sort of life far from Thomaston, New York. Toward that end, he'd do well to keep busy and stay out of trouble, the latter always a challenge. He'd already decided to try out for the football team, which would provide both structure and the release of pent-up energy and animosity. And he planned to get as many part-time jobs as he could handle so he'd have some money saved for when he left town and be financially independent in the meantime. He was determined to ask his father for nothing.

But he also felt an equally strong impulse to remain in Thomaston at least until their conflict reached a satisfying con-clusion. His loathing of the man had deepened at the academy, distilling itself into a pure and satisfying essence, a reason for being that would vanish if he lit out for the West after graduation. He supposed it was possible this intense loathing was just the affection he felt for his mother turned upside down. After all, didn't he have an obligation to protect her from further harm? And was it fair to abandon his brothers to the old man's bullying? Attractive as these rationalizations were, the ugly truth was that his black hatred for his father was far more satisfying than the affection and obligation he felt toward his mother, which, though real enough, was also tinged with pity and, face it, something like the contempt one feels for a dog that continues to love the owner that beats it with a stick.

The thing was, renewing his friendship with Lucy Lynch fit with neither the impulse to flee nor the one to stay. If the plan was to leave at the end of senior year and stay busy and out of trouble in the meantime, then friendships of any sort were probably counterproductive. If the plan was to stay until the conflict with his father was resolved, whatever that meant, then it was important to stay focused on that goal. Friendship, in all likelihood, would be a distraction. So when Lucy called and invited him to stop by his parents' market—still called Ikey Lubin's after they'd owned it for five years, its previous owner now dead of cancer—Noonan made an excuse, saying he had a job interview.

"Too bad," Lucy replied, surprisingly restrained in his disappointment. When they'd been boys and Noonan hadn't been allowed to go next door and play, Lucy had always been inconsolable. "Why *not*?" he'd whine, never satisfied with "My dad said no." Always demanding to know *why* he'd said no.

"Maybe another time," Noonan said, and thought to himself, Or maybe not.

"I just wanted you to meet my girlfriend," Lucy explained.

Lucy had a girlfriend? Noonan couldn't help being intrigued.

Her name was Sarah Berg, the boy told him proudly, and she was leaving the next day to spend the summer with her mother. Her father, he continued, was a legendary Thomaston High English teacher. "She's anxious to meet you," he added, "but she'll be back on Labor Day."

"Why would she want to meet me?" Noonan wondered.

"She drew you."

Drew him?

"Back in junior high, actually," Lucy said, explaining that Sarah was an artist who, when they first started dating, had drawn the Lynch market, including his old friend. "Stop in sometime, I'll show you. It's cool."

Again, no pleading. By midafternoon Noonan's curiosity, together with his need to get out of his parents' house before his first part-time job began the next day, had gotten the better of him. It was a nice, warm afternoon, and the walk from the Borough to Third Street was pleasant, though it struck Noonan that he was going to need some kind of wheels and soon. One of his summer jobs was downtown, the other two over a mile away on the arterial highway. A car was out of the question if he meant to save money. A bike would be better than walking, but not a lot. Maybe a used motorcycle?

He hadn't been back to the old neighborhood since his family had moved, so he was surprised that the house they'd lived in wasn't there anymore. Ikey Lubin's, by contrast, had expanded. Otherwise, the neighborhood seemed unchanged. When he entered the market, Big Lou Lynch, at the register, looked just the same, except he wasn't wearing his milk delivery whites anymore. Noonan recognized the man behind the meat counter as his brother, Declan. Clearly, neither one had any idea who he was.

"Didn't there used to be a house over there?" he asked Lucy's father, pointing across the intersection.

"Burned down six years ago," the man said, smiling, for some reason, at the memory.

Noonan nodded, trying to remember if he'd ever been told about this. "Then I guess we moved just in time," he said, expecting him to put two and two together.

Big Lou blinked and studied him, on the very precipice of comprehension, but only when Noonan assumed his old surfer's stance, feet wide apart, arms out for balance, did he break into his wide, goofy grin. "Well, I'll be," he said. "Louie! Look who's here!" He didn't take his eyes off Noonan, as if he feared he might be an apparition.

"I see him," Lucy said, coming in from the back room with the identical goofy grin. "Wow," he said. "You're different."

"Well, you've changed, too." Noonan chuckled, and they shook hands. Actually, Lucy looked pretty much the same, except bigger. He was almost as big as his father now, still soft looking, though more comfortable in his skin, somehow.

"I thought you said you couldn't come by," Lucy said, just a hint of the old whining and grievance coming through.

"I got the job, so . . ."

Big Lou leaned across the counter and gave his hand a vigorous shake. "How's that wrist?" he said, as if the injury had occurred just last week and been on his mind ever since.

"It healed," Noonan said.

"How's your dad?"

"The same," Noonan told him, hoping that would be the end of the subject.

"He done good down at the post office, didn't he," Mr. Lynch said. "People must like him there."

"You going out for football?" Dec Lynch interrupted.

"I plan to," Noonan admitted.

"Can you block or tackle or hang on to the damn ball? Or will you be like the rest of the team?"

"I guess we'll see."

"Talk your buddy here into going out. He could use some toughing up."

"Come out from behind that meat case," Lucy said, to Noonan's surprise, "and we'll see who's tough."

"Watch yourself now," his uncle advised. "Somebody's about to come through that door who's tougher than the both of us. Meaner, too."

The bell above the door tinkled then, and Tessa Lynch came in carrying a big stainless-steel tub of what looked like potato salad. She recognized Noonan immediately, and the thought crossed his mind that, unlike his own mother, it would have taken Lucy's about two seconds flat to peg his old man for the bullying coward he was. On the other hand, she'd married Lucy's father, so go figure.

Only when Tessa Lynch stepped aside to hold the door did he realize there was a girl his age standing behind her, also holding a salad bowl. She too took him in with a single glance and broke into a wide smile. "Well," Sarah Berg said, setting the salad down and giving him an unexpected hug. "It's *about* time."

Noonan was more than a little embarrassed to be hugged by

Lucy's girlfriend, especially with him standing right there, looking on with that goofy grin as if this were precisely what he'd been hoping for.

"About time?"

Sarah Berg went around the counter, took a framed drawing off the wall and handed it to him. "I drew this *four years ago*. That's you, about to come in. It took you four years to go two feet. That's what I call taking your own sweet time."

Noonan smiled, enjoying her game. No doubt Lucy had told her all about his being shipped off to the academy. By portraying him as a stubborn ingrate, she'd spared him the necessity of explaining his years in exile.

"We've all been covering for you," she went on, putting the drawing back on its hook. "Doing our own work and yours, too, and not a single thank-you."

"I was wondering if I could have tomorrow off?" he said.

She'd gone over to Lucy now and was giving him a hug, which he accepted with obvious if awkward pleasure. "He's got other, cooler friends he wants to go see," she told him. "It took him four years to come visit us, and now he's leaving again."

"I'll take one of them hugs," Big Lou said, clearly impatient with this difficult-to-follow conversation.

Sarah went around the counter and gave him what appeared to be a heartfelt one.

"How about me?" Dec Lynch called.

"No hugs for you," Sarah told him, still clinging to Big Lou. "You lost the bet." Turning to Noonan she explained, mock seriously, "He said you were gone for good."

"But you knew better."

"Yup," she said. "I only draw true things." And she fixed him with a smile and her dark eyes, amounting to a challenge. The Lynches were all grinning at him, too.

And in that moment it occurred to Noonan that his options had just narrowed. He might leave Thomaston after graduation and head out west somewhere, just as he'd planned, but he wasn't going to be able to remain aloof. That option had evaporated when he walked through the door at Ikey Lubin's, making Sarah Berg's drawing come true. His presence had completed something, though he wasn't sure what. It felt dangerously like he'd just gotten a new family. It felt good.

LATER, when they were in the back room tearing down a mountain of cardboard boxes, Lucy said, "So, what do you think?"

About his having a girlfriend? Or about Sarah? Noonan decided he must mean the latter, but in truth, he didn't know what to think about Sarah Berg. She was no great beauty, though neither was there anything obviously wrong with her, as he'd feared there might be. Back in the front of the store the girl had somehow commanded his attention, whereas now he couldn't imagine how she'd done it. Bony and angular, she wasn't the sort of girl he normally looked at twice, and now that she was gone he had a hard time remembering her facial features. It was her attitude, her sense of play, that lingered like a sweet scent in the air. She'd seemed almost to be laughing at him, and girls didn't usually do that. She also had a natural grace that wasn't particularly feminine or studied, and a forthrightness and vulnerability that had made him feel protective, though he couldn't imagine what she might need protecting from. Without being able to put his finger on why, he was disappointed she was leaving tomorrow, sorry that he wouldn't be seeing her again until September.

"My father offered her a summer job here at Ikey's," Lucy explained, "but she's saving for college and she'll make a lot more money babysitting for summer people on Long Island. Plus it's the only time she gets to see her mother. Her parents have been separated for years, and now her mother's filing for divorce." This last he said as if it were an unspeakable tragedy.

"Good for her," Noonan replied, thinking of his own mother.

Then, when he saw the stricken look on Lucy's face, "Why stay together when everybody's miserable?"

"I don't think Sarah was miserable," Lucy said. It was the death of her brother, Rudy, he believed, that caused their separation. Her mother had moved back to Long Island, where she hustled work as a freelance commercial artist, while looking for long-term projects, but mostly settling for scraps—designing logos and pamphlets and restaurant menus. Her father had predicted that in the end she'd fail and have no choice but to return, and they'd all be a family again, but so far that hadn't happened. Her mother was making a go of it. Sarah's father, in addition to being the town's eccentric English teacher, spent his summers working on the novel he'd been writing for over a decade. His book was another reason Sarah couldn't stay there for the summer. It required the deepest of solitudes.

As they tore down boxes, Lucy chattered on, bringing Noonan up to speed on all things Thomaston, all things Lynch. He explained how they'd come to buy Ikey Lubin's, and then to expand it, how his mother, who'd been reluctant at first, became a partner and why they'd brought his uncle Dec in. He told Noonan that his second cousin, Karen Cirillo, had lived upstairs for a while, and how Jerzy Quinn had ruled junior high, and what had happened to Three Mock and how he'd come to meet Sarah. And he wasn't having his spells anymore, which was really great. He told Noonan his father had become a hero for rescuing the Spinnarkles and that he'd had a small cyst removed from under his right arm last year. Everybody had been alarmed, but the biopsy had proved negative. Some of the cells didn't look quite right, though, and the fact that the cyst was so near the lymph glands had worried the Albany oncologist. As did the fact that his patient lived in Thomaston, so now Big Lou was getting blood work done every other month, just to be sure.

As Lucy rattled on Noonan felt some of the ease of their old friendship return. Odd, how he'd vividly remembered every one of his irritating habits and forgotten his virtues entirely. Always

363

good-hearted, he now seemed less needy, not so inward gazing as before, which was good. If the Lynches were determined to adopt Noonan this summer, at least it wouldn't be painful. In fact, he was glad he'd stopped by. Noonan kept hoping Sarah might join them, but Lucy told him today was salad day, which meant that his girlfriend was busy helping his mother make fresh salads to stock the deli portion of his uncle's meat case for the weekend. The weather was supposed to be good, so half the East End would be stopping by the market on the way to the lake to stock their picnic baskets with Tessa Lynch's salads and Dec Lynch's smoked pork chops.

When they finished with the boxes and returned to the front of the store, everyone was there but Sarah, who was across the street putting the kitchen back in order. Mrs. Lynch remarked that Noonan looked hungry and handed him a heaping plate of salads—potato, macaroni and egg. In fact, he was famished. His father was as stingy as ever with grocery money, and he felt as if eating there was taking food out of his brothers' mouths. "Damn," he said, swallowing a too-large forkful of macaroni salad. "This is good."

This seemed to please Lucy's mother. "You got a summer job lined up?" she asked.

He told her he was busing tables at three different restaurants, half expecting her to offer him another at Ikey's.

"I guess we won't be seeing much of you, then," she said, glancing over at Lucy, who rather peevishly refused to meet her eye. It was an odd moment. Did she mean to prepare her son for disappointment? Had Noonan been wrong in concluding that his old friend was less needy than before?

Noonan was finishing the last of his plate of salads when Sarah returned and came right over to where he sat at the small table by the coffeepot. "So, what do you think?" she said, pulling up a chair.

"About?"

"About what you just finished eating."

"Good," he said. "Really good."

"Which was your favorite? And be careful how you answer. I made one of them. Tessa made the other two."

"I liked all three."

"Coward."

"The macaroni was my favorite."

"I made the egg," she said. "Maybe we'll get along better when I come back in September."

"You're really going away for the whole summer?"

"You can keep Lou company."

Lucy came over then. "He's got three jobs lined up."

"You'll wind up working here, too," she warned. "Just you wait. Ikey's is addictive."

Dec Lynch was in the process of cleaning up. The store would remain open until midnight, but the meat and deli section closed at six. "How long will you be at the doctor tomorrow?" he asked his brother.

"I'm thinking maybe I'll cancel," Big Lou told him. "Why lose half the day drivin' down there and sittin' in that office when we got so much work to do?" he said. "Hell, I'm feeling good."

"You're going," Tessa Lynch said.

"All damn foolishness," Big Lou whined, though he did seem to understand that his wife had just spoken the last meaningful word on the subject. "Ain't nothing to worry about no more. The tannery's been closed goin' on two years."

"The poison's still there, Lou," she reminded him. "If I put a grain of arsenic in your coffee every morning for thirty years, it wouldn't disappear from your body just because I started making tea."

"I ain't sayin' that, Tessa," said her husband, apparently more worried by his wife's analogy than poisoned groundwater. "You read that story in the paper? They say fish are comin' back to the stream. They wouldn't live here if it wasn't good for 'em."

"Why not?" his wife responded. "We do."

"Tessa's right as usual, Biggy," his brother piped up. "I saw the trout that guy caught last week, and it had a tumor the size of a golf ball under its gill. In fact, right where it'd be if *you* had a gill. Have that specialist check under there, Tessa. Make sure Biggy doesn't have a gill growing under his armpit."

"I wish he did," said Mrs. Lynch. "We could charge money to see it."

Sarah rose to her feet and went over to give Big Lou a hug and kiss goodbye. "People sure are mean to you, Lou-Lou," she said.

"I know it, sweetness," he said, folding her in a great embrace. "They enjoy being mean, I guess, or they wouldn't do it. That's a long train ride you got tomorrow. Can't your dad go along to keep you company?"

"No, by tomorrow he'll be at his typewriter, and he won't stop until Labor Day."

Clearly, this didn't sit well with Big Lou. "What's that book of his about, anyhow?" as if its subject matter might reveal whether it was important enough to justify not accompanying his daughter to New York.

"Right now it's about a thousand pages, single spaced," Sarah told him.

Which only added to Big Lou's original argument. "One day wouldn't hurt none," he said.

"How would you know, Biggy?" his brother chimed in. "You haven't even read a book, much less written one."

Big Lou ignored this insult, just as he did most of what his brother had to offer. "He could ride down with you, meet your ma and ride right back again."

"But then they'd have an argument in Grand Central. Don't worry, Lou-Lou. I meet my mom in the same place every year. She's always there." Taking him by the elbows, she said, "Promise me you'll keep your appointment."

"*I* promise you," Tessa Lynch said.

"I just wish you didn't have to go," Big Lou said, his eyes, to Noonan's astonishment, filling with tears. "You could work here this summer."

"Cut it out, Lou," his wife warned him, pulling open the door to the walk-in. "We've been through this. Sarah's doing what she needs to do."

"I ain't sayin' that—"

"Yes, you were, Lou. We all heard you. *Don't go.* That's what you were saying."

"I'm just saying I wish she didn't *have* to," he explained, wiping his eyes with the back of his hand.

"Well, she does have to," Tessa said, and disappeared into the walk-in.

"I know," Big Lou conceded, more to Sarah than his wife.

"I'm going upstairs," Dec said, though he made no move to go anywhere. "I've enjoyed about as much of this conversation as I can stand."

Sarah pulled on her jacket. "You two can walk me home if you like," she said, meaning, apparently, Lucy and Noonan.

Noonan would have liked to, but he assumed that neither one of them probably wanted him along to witness their goodbye, so he was surprised that both Sarah and Lucy seemed disappointed when he declined.

"You have a good summer, sexy," Dec said, coming over for his own goodbye hug. "I'm not as old as I look, you know. A lot of girls your age think I'm cute."

"Name three," Sarah said, making Noonan smile at the ease with which she handled him and, really, all of the Lynches.

"That'd be bragging."

Tessa Lynch returned from the walk-in then, carrying a heavy tub of potato salad and regarded her brother-in-law with chagrin. "Quit fondling that girl and open the case, will you?"

"Yes, ma'am," Dec said, going back around the counter to help her.

"Most women my age think you've seen better days," Tessa told him.

Was it Noonan's imagination, what he witnessed then? The

glass of the display case was thick and curved, magnifying and distorting the purple roasts and troughs of ground meat within, so probably it was just a trick of the eye. Yet when Tessa Lynch stepped away, it seemed to Noonan that Dec Lynch reached out and grazed the back of her hand with his.

LATER, walking home, he talked himself out of it. The fact that his own parents' marriage was a tangle of deceit didn't mean other people's marriages were similarly flawed. In truth, he was quite taken with the world the Lynches had created for themselves and how easily they all moved within that sphere. Not just them—Sarah, too. It was clear she loved not only the Lynches but also Ikey Lubin's, as if the store satisfied some deep craving, and everything she could ever imagine wanting was right there on the shelves, whereas all the things she didn't want or weren't good for her had been thoughtfully removed. Though Noonan was pretty sure that much of what he himself wanted out of life was not for sale at Ikey Lubin's, he had to admit the attraction of the place, its warmth, camaraderie and generosity. Would he have felt that way if it had been just the Lynches, if Sarah hadn't been there? He supposed the coming months would tell.

He was halfway home, dusk falling, when a horn tooted, and the Lynch station wagon, Lucy's mother at the wheel, pulled alongside the curb. "Get in," she called across the seat, "and I'll give you a lift."

Since her phrasing was more an order than an offer, he did as he was told, sliding onto the big bench seat and closing the door. He'd never been alone with Mrs. Lynch before, and while he had no particular reason to be uncomfortable, he was. Had she followed him, and if so, for what purpose? To warn him away from their world, from Ikey Lubin's, from her son? He thought again of Sarah's drawing, where he was pictured outside, about to enter. Was Tessa Lynch there to tell him that outside was where he belonged? He was relieved when she spoke, revealing another agenda entirely.

"How's your mother?" she asked, taking her eyes off the road to watch him answer.

"Okay," he said. "You should give her a call sometime."

"I went out to the hospital," she said, "but your father sent me packing. I called the house last week, but apparently she promised him not to talk to me."

Noonan nodded but offered no comment. Had he wanted to talk about his parents, Mrs. Lynch wouldn't have been a bad person to confide in. But he *didn't* want to talk to anybody.

"You don't have to say anything," she said, apparently reading his reluctance. "I want you to promise me, though, that if things get bad you'll tell me. Your mother's endured about as much as she can, and I might be able to help. Don't tell my husband or Louie. Tell me."

"Nothing's going to happen," Noonan assured her.

"Really? And why's that?"

"I'm home now."

She turned to look at him again. They'd come to a stop sign and were about to cross the Boulevard, which unofficially separated the East End from the Borough. They were just a couple blocks from the Marconis' home, but Mrs. Lynch put on her blinker and turned right, heading out of town. "Look, I know you're game," she said after a few moments' silence, "and I'm sure you'd try your best—"

"Where are we—?"

"—but you're only seventeen, and you might not have the kind of help your mother needs."

"Like what?"

"Like someone to talk to. She and I have been good friends since Berman Court. You probably didn't know that."

"What good has talking done her?"

"A lot. More than you know. Not just her. Our talks go both ways. We listen to each other."

Noonan thought again about what he'd seen earlier, or imagined seeing, Dec Lynch's hand grazing hers.

Suddenly she looked concerned, almost frightened, as if considering something that had until that moment escaped her. "I hope you don't think there's a solution to your mother's problems," she said, glancing down at his lap, where Noonan's hands, to his surprise, were balled into fists.

He quickly relaxed them before speaking. "Why shouldn't there be?" After all, he'd been congratulating himself that the solution had already been found. He'd served notice to his father, hadn't he? The old man knew he was onto him. Things were already different.

"Because people don't change. You *do* know that, right?"

Noonan shrugged, not wanting to disagree openly with something she clearly was adamant about. But people *did* change, didn't they? He himself wasn't the same person he'd been five years ago, before going to the academy. And a couple of hours in Lucy's company suggested that he'd changed, too, as much as Noonan or even more.

"Don't confuse growing up with changing," Tessa Lynch said, reading his mind again. "I'm talking about what's inside, not the fact that you shave your chin."

That seemed to Noonan an uncomfortably personal observation. What was Lucy's mother doing looking at his chin? Suddenly there was an undercurrent of electricity in the car, and it was amped up a moment later when she turned onto the gravel drive and stopped at the main gate to the old Whitcombe estate, a spot that served, unless things had changed, as a lovers' lane. It was almost full dark now, and the headlights sliced through the night, illuminating the dark outline of the Hall in the distance. He was relieved when Mrs. Lynch put the wagon in reverse, suggesting she just meant to turn around and head back.

But then she thought better of it, put the car in park and turned to face him. "Tell me what you mean to do," she said, fixing him.

"Do? What do you mean, in the future?"

"Okay. Start there if you want. We can work backwards."

"Graduate. After that, maybe move out west. I don't know."

"You plan to bring your mother out there with you?"

"No!" he blurted, the word escaping like a hiccup.

Mrs. Lynch smiled, not unkindly. "Right. So when you said there was nothing to worry about because you were home, you meant for the next year."

"That's not—"

"What about college?"

"Maybe. I'll apply."

"You've heard of Vietnam, right? You know what a word like 'maybe' means in that context? It could mean finding yourself in the jungle on the other side of the world for no good reason." When he just shrugged, she forged ahead. "What about Lou?"

Was the woman insane? What *about* Lou? Was this a new subject or the same one? Was Lou going to college? Did he plan on enlisting for Vietnam? How should *he* know? "I don't—"

"Why did you come to the store today?"

"He invited—"

"Don't lead him on, Bobby. If you want to be friends, fine. If not, find a way out now. You know how he is."

"He seems really good," Noonan told her, a little ashamed that his friend's mother should talk about him behind his back like this. "Happy, I mean. He's changed a lot—"

"No, he hasn't. You weren't listening before. *People don't change.*"

"He's not having those spells anymore," Noonan said, confident that he had her on this count at least.

"That's a circumstance," Tessa Lynch said, "and those change all the time. Today you're healthy; tomorrow you discover a tumor. But who you *are* stays the same. Lou hasn't changed any more than you have. You're still the same boy you were that first time your mother tried to run away, the same boy who went out

371

and gathered up her things off the street and stuffed them in that suitcase and lugged it home, fully expecting to get a whipping for your trouble. You didn't think I knew about that, right? You thought you'd solved her problem then, too."

"Actually, I think I've changed a lot since then," Noonan said, feeling suddenly raw and exposed.

"I know you do, but you're wrong. And now there's Sarah."

"I'm not interested in Sarah," Noonan said, pretty sure he knew where all this was heading.

"You will be, when you get to know her."

"I don't think so. Besides, she's Lucy's girlfriend," he said, correcting himself quickly when he saw her flinch, her eyes narrowing. "Lou's girlfriend."

At that moment there was a loud rap on the driver's side window, causing both of them to jump just about out of their skins. Lucy's mother was the first to recover, and she rolled down her window. A tiny black man, vaguely familiar, was grinning in at them. Completely wrapped up in their conversation, neither had heard the man approach.

"Teresa Lupino," he said. "You come out here to howl wit' me?" He set a half-empty bottle of whiskey on the edge of the open window.

"No, I didn't, Gabriel," Mrs. Lynch told him. Gabriel Mock, Noonan thought, remembering him now. "As I'm sure you know."

"Why's that?" he said, peering around her at Noonan.

"You're way too short for me," she told him. "I only howl with tall men. Six feet at least."

How tall was Dec Lynch? Noonan wondered. Not six feet, but close.

At this Gabriel Mock threw back his head and laughed so hard he nearly lost his balance. "*Short?*" he said. "That's what it is? I'm *short?*"

"Also, I'm married," she said.

"You married and me short," he said, wiping his eyes with his shirtsleeve. "Thank the Lord it ain't nothin' else. Wouldn't want there to be no other obstacles. Who's this here?"

"This is a friend of my son's. I'm trying to talk some sense into him."

He studied Noonan with bloodshot eyes. "You smart, you'll do like this woman says. She's smarter than you by a mile, and I don't even know who you are. Don't *care* who you are. You want a sip of this howlin' juice? You ever howl?"

"No, thanks."

The little man returned his attention to Lucy's mother. "*Po*lite," he said. "Don't know who he is, but he's polite. Give him that much. But stupid, huh?"

"Not completely," Tessa Lynch said, far from a ringing endorsement, though it pleased Noonan anyway.

Gabriel regarded him again. "NCS. I see you again, that's what I'll call you. NCS. Not Completely Stupid. You and me'll know what it stand for. Call me what you want. Call me Gizzard if that make you happy. I don't care. I'm a call you NCS, whether you like it or not. Come out here some night, you feel like it. I live right over there." He waved in the general direction of a small outbuilding, its silhouette just visible in the dark. "Bring a bottle of juice and you be welcome. Bring Junior with you. You know who I mean?"

Noonan nodded.

"Lou Lynch Junior, who I mean. He's a ama-teur howler, like yourself, I 'spect. Maybe I start callin' him NCSE. Not Completely Stupid Either."

"Neither of these boys is going to come out here and get drunk with you, Gabriel, so you can put that right out of your mind."

"Why not? Maybe they not like you. Maybe they ain't prejudice against short people."

"They're underage. You supply them with alcohol, you go to jail."

"Supply *them*?" Gabriel Mock seemed to think this was about

373

the funniest idea he'd ever heard. "They supply *me*, the way it gon work. Besides. Who my suppose to howl wit' out here? Tell me that. Man don't like to howl by hisself all the time. Gets lonesome."

"I imagine it does," Mrs. Lynch conceded. "How's your boy doing, Gabriel?"

"Don't know," he said, straightening up, suddenly sober. "Never say a word to me."

"It was a terrible thing."

"World full of terrible things. Maybe you noticed."

"Oh, I have, Gabriel. I have," she said. "I still remember the day you and your father appeared on our front porch." Her eyes, Noonan saw, were glistening.

"Wadn't your fault, none of it," Gabriel told her. " 'Cept for not likin' short people, you all right. Always was. Shouldn't pay that day no mind. All in the past." He paused, staring off in the dark. He was still holding the bottle, but he'd yet to bring it to his lips. "Guess that teacher lookin' after him now. Thinks he's the boy's father or some such. Talks to him, people say. Converse, the two of 'em. Teacher observe somethin' and my boy tell him he agree or don't agree. What you make of that?"

"I think any son of yours would be foolish not to talk to his father."

Gabriel shook his head, but seemed to appreciate her vote of confidence. "Nah, I don't know nothin', come right down to it. Guess he figure that out and decide not to waste his time talkin' to a man who don't make sense, that waste all his time howlin' and other nonsense. Anyhow, good night, Teresa. Okay if I call you Teresa?"

"Call me Gizzard if you want." Mrs. Lynch smiled, putting the car in reverse. Only when they'd turned around and she put the car in drive did the little man lift the bottle to his lips.

Back on the highway, heading into town, Mrs. Lynch shook her head and glanced over at him. "Look in that man's eyes sometime and tell me the world's a good place." But then she chuckled. "Teresa Lupino. My maiden name. Nobody's called me that in twenty years. It might as well have belonged to another person entirely."

"Wasn't it you who just said people don't change," Noonan reminded her, pleased to be able to lob her own conviction back at her.

"Touché," she said, shooting him a wry smile.

"What happened on the porch?" Noonan thought to ask.

"Oh, maybe I'll tell you someday when I'm not feeling so blue. I don't need to remember that tonight." She *was* remembering it, though, he could tell. By the time they pulled into the Marconi driveway, a full moon had risen, illuminating his mother where she stood, pale and ghostlike, at the front window, looking out into the street. Waiting for Noonan? His father? Mrs. Lynch rolled down her window and waved, but she must not have recognized who it was because she didn't wave back.

OVER THE SUMMER Noonan found himself spending more and more time at Ikey Lubin's. In the beginning he went there to avoid going home, but in truth the place had grown on him. He discovered, as Sarah apparently had before him, that you couldn't have a relationship with just one Lynch, and she seemed to have a deep affection for the whole clan. It was like she was going steady with Ikey Lubin's, with the entire Lynch family, and they with her. She completed them, somehow. That's what her drawing of the market seemed to mean, not just to her but to all of them.

And now, as the drawing had predicted, Noonan himself had rung that tiny bell over the front door and entered Lynch World, as he'd come to think of Ikey Lubin's. By now he'd discovered that it didn't really matter whether Lucy was working or not, since he hung out at the store regardless. "Bobby Macaroni," the ever jovial Big Lou would announce whenever Noonan appeared on the premises, even if it was for the third time that day. This, to him, was the best joke ever. "Have your dad drop by sometime," he suggested at least once a week, as if the Lynches and the Marconis had remained the best of friends down through the years, without so much as a cross word between them. "You don't never see him around anywhere." By "anywhere" he apparently meant Ikey Lubin's, which Big Lou seldom left.

Dec also seemed to enjoy having Noonan drop by, especially after football practice started in August. A born gambler, he bet the horses and the daily number religiously, but his first love was sports—professional, college, even high school—so he quizzed him hard about how Thomaston's team was shaping up. And when he heard that Noonan was thinking about a used motorcycle to get back and forth to his various jobs, he took him down to a West End garage across from the gravel pit where he stored his beloved old Indian. He'd given up riding it over a decade ago, but loved the bike too much to sell it. "Cost you a few bucks to bring it back to life," he said, "but it'd be yours to use. Just keep it running good and don't blame me when you get killed on it." Noonan, falling in love with the Indian on sight, promised he wouldn't. Lucy made him a loan for repairs and insurance so he wouldn't have to ask his father.

After that first night, when she quizzed him about his intentions, even Tessa Lynch seemed disposed to cautious affection. Aware that he was always hungry, she'd fix him a plate of food as soon as he entered Ikey's. There was always work to be done at the store, so he gave as good as he got, but still. It was as if she'd intuited what his life was like at home, and they'd agreed that the less time he spent in the Borough house, the better for all concerned. She still didn't seem entirely to trust him but rather to have arrived at the calculated decision that his presence posed less of a threat than his absence.

The unspoken understanding was that his real role at Ikey's was to see Lucy through the summer in Sarah's absence. While Lucy had told Noonan his spells were a thing of the past, his mother wasn't convinced. True, he'd only had one relatively minor episode in the last couple of years, but it had occurred the previous summer when Sarah was away. Ever the optimist, Big Lou believed Lucy had simply outgrown the spells. Lucy's doctors—who had no idea what they were or what caused them—apparently had predicted as much. Mrs. Lynch didn't openly disagree, though Noonan could tell that she credited Sarah and her calming, grounding effect. If true, that meant that she was hoping Noonan might serve the same purpose.

As the summer wore on, Noonan also became less certain that his friend was cured, and he often recalled Mrs. Lynch's mantra—that people didn't change. Though more squared away and less needy, Lucy was in some ways stranger now than he'd been before. Seemingly incapable of imagining a world or a life outside of Thomaston, he exhibited no curiosity about Noonan's experience at the academy, almost as if he didn't believe the place really existed or believed that his friend hadn't existed during his time there. It was understood that Lucy would be going off to college right after high school, but he refused to apply to any school more than two hours away, so that he could come home on weekends to help out at the store. It didn't seem to trouble him that Sarah, who was applying to colleges in New York City, *wouldn't* be coming home on weekends, nor did he seem excited about visiting her there. What Noonan had been hearing about the city—the great jazz clubs, the exciting times to be had in Greenwich Village and, if you were bold enough, Harlem—didn't interest Lucy at all.

No, rather than contemplate the future, Lucy seemed fixated on the past. At seventeen, he was already as backward looking as an octogenarian. He'd begin every other sentence with the same word, "remember." "Remember how all us boys were in love with her?" he asked one day when they passed Marie's Beauty Shop, where Karen Cirillo, who'd dropped out of school, now worked. Noonan had no idea he'd ever been keen on Karen, his second cousin, any more than Lucy knew he'd deflowered her when they were twelve. She'd been lush and voluptuous back then, it was true. Now, though, four short years later, she looked about thirty-five, completely gone to seed. And for some reason Lucy seemed to take Karen's decline personally, as if some foundation had been weakened, and it was his duty to shore it up. "She just needs to lose some weight," he said hopefully, anxious, Noonan could tell, for him to agree. "That and the mustache," he'd replied.

To Noonan, his friend's obsession with the recent past made no sense. After all, he'd just completed three reasonably happy, well-adjusted years in Thomaston High. Why would anybody, much less Lucy Lynch, feel nostalgic for junior high, with all its skewed symmetries? There he'd been a miserable loner, whereas now he had Sarah, and the two seemed happy together. Why pine for Karen Cirillo? *Because*, he could hear Mrs. Lynch saying, *people don't change*.

AT THE MARCONI HOUSE, everything had changed. His father was rarely there, even in the evenings. He claimed to be working longer hours at the post office and traveling around the region as a consultant to support his growing family, but Noonan was sure he was spending most nights with the woman on Division Street. Which was fine. His mother, strangely blissful now, a new infant at her breast, seemed content that peace and quiet should reign. His little brothers, most of whom weren't so little anymore, had the look of pale, exhausted victims of the blitz, climbing up out of underground bunkers at the all-clear signal, blinking at the light and wondering if the bombing would resume. With Noonan working long hours and hanging out at Ikey Lubin's, he himself was seldom there either. Occasionally, late at night or early in the morning, he'd run into his father at the refrigerator, and then there'd be a wary, wordless little dance of courtesy. Amazingly, his mother seemed to conclude that her husband and eldest son were in the process of reconciling, putting their long, virulent animosity aside. Only once did she regard Noonan curiously and ask if he'd said something to his father back when she was in the hospital. Noonan, seeing no reason to trouble her, had lied.

It was the middle of July before he noticed the tiny pill she took with her orange juice first thing every morning and again before going to bed at night. Nor was he quick to connect that pill with the fact that this baby—alone among Marconi infants in this respect—never seemed to fuss, instead smiling blissfully at the world as if it had no father and no need of one.

WHEN SARAH RETURNED to Thomaston at the end of the summer, Noonan barely recognized her. Suddenly she was no longer a girl, but rather a young woman. Lucy had invited him to come along to meet her at the station—he couldn't help wondering why—and waiting in the parking lot, he saw the hug she gave Lucy when she got off the train. Did it differ from the one she gave him a couple minutes later? He didn't think so.

"How come you never wrote me?" she demanded on the drive home. They were sitting three across in the Lynch station wagon, and she elbowed him in the ribs, hard, when she asked.

"You never wrote *me*," he pointed out.

"Untrue," she said. "I addressed every one of my letters to Ikey Lubin's, which includes you. Everybody else wrote back. Even Dec sent me a dirty postcard. First you show up four years late, then you don't write. Are you going to be a crappy friend?"

"I guess we'll see."

"I hear you bought a motorcycle."

"Not exactly. Dec's letting me use his."

"So who do I ask for a ride, him or you?"

"Ask your boyfriend."

Now she elbowed Lucy, just as hard. "Can Bobby give me a ride on Dec's motorcycle?"

Say no, Noonan thought.

"Sure," said his friend. "Why not?"

Noonan could have told him. Should have.

WAS IT POSSIBLE to miss somebody you'd met only once, someone you didn't really know? Probably not, but that was what it had felt like having Sarah back—like he'd been missing her all summer without knowing it. He lay awake that night, remembering the hug she'd given him there in the parking lot. Never having received such an unself-conscious embrace from a girl his own age, he didn't know what to make of it. By seventeen, most girls were physically aware, and they angled their bodies accordingly. Sarah had hugged him like an older sister would, unafraid that he might misinterpret it. Did that mean she had no more interest in him than a sister would? She was Lucy's girlfriend, after all. Still, Noonan couldn't quite decide whether her embrace suggested confidence or a complete lack thereof. Was she unable to imagine a boy like him being attracted to a girl like her, or was she placing her trust in *him*, in his virtue, as Lucy's friend? A mistake, if the latter.

To Noonan, it was unsettling to be so confused. He could read most girls, whose level of interest in him was like a visible aura. They could be as coy as they wanted, but he still knew. It was almost cheating, really, like shooting fish in a barrel. With Sarah, though, it was different. She made no secret of how glad she was they were friends. That should've clarified matters, but instead it confused them. Could it be that her undisguised affection was the *source* of his confusion? It was possible. Most of the girls who were drawn to Noonan didn't like him very much. At the beginning they didn't know that, which was good, and even after they learned it, they sometimes forgot, which could be nice, too. Was it the fact that Sarah actually *liked* him that muddled things?

The other possible explanation was even more distressing. What if it had nothing to do with her affection for him, but rather his for her? Tessa Lynch, damn her, had warned him that he'd be interested in Sarah once he got to know her. Had he fallen for her? He'd been attracted to lots of girls before without ever really falling for one. The solution was obvious. He simply wouldn't fall for Sarah Berg. It shouldn't even be that difficult, now that he'd made up his mind. Maybe she wasn't the bony, angular girl who'd left in June, but she wasn't exactly a ravishing beauty either. And besides, she was Lucy's girlfriend. There. It was settled.

Still, he looked forward to school starting and wondered if they'd have any classes together. Probably not. His academic record at the academy hadn't warranted advanced placement, which was why, when Sarah advised him on the drive back to Thomaston to drop Mrs. Summers and sign up for her father's honors English class, he'd feigned uninterest, not wanting to admit he wouldn't qualify. With any luck, Sarah had a weak subject herself, maybe math, that would land her in one of his regular-track classes. Or else he could elect an art class. He'd never taken one—art hadn't even been offered at the academy— but how hard could it be? During the summer he'd often studied Sarah's drawing of Ikey Lubin's and even wondered what role it might've played in pulling him, against his better judgment, into Lynch World. Would he have enjoyed Ikey's as much if he hadn't seen it through her eyes? He liked the idea of getting people to see things as he did without them even being aware of what he'd done. Now *that* would be a trick worth knowing.

A DREAM OF FISH

MRS. SUMMERS, Noonan's homeroom teacher, regarded him blackly over the top of her bifocals, her mouth drawn into a thin line. Was it possible she disliked him already on the basis of how he'd said "Here" when she called his name? "See me before you leave for first period," she told him, eliciting a nasty chuckle from Perry Kozlowski. Ten minutes into the new school year and Marconi's already in trouble, the chuckle seemed to signify. Same old Bobby.

"There's been a change in your classes," the teacher informed him as the other students filed out of homeroom. "You've been added to Mr. Berg's roster." She was holding what he assumed was his revised schedule.

"Really?" he said, surprised, then thought: *Sarah*. So, even as he'd been hoping they might have a class together, she'd been doing the same thing. At last, a clear signal.

"I don't blame you for being surprised," Mrs. Summers said, clearly annoyed, though apparently not at him. "Honors is supposed to be reserved for our best and brightest students."

"Right," he said, half expecting her to realize she'd just insulted him and apologize.

"That man thinks the rules are for other people," she went on, growing red faced. "That *he* is exempt."

"Well," Noonan said, holding out his hand for the schedule, then dropping it again when he saw it wasn't forthcoming.

"It's not *bad* enough I have to spend my summer explaining to every Jewish mother I meet on Hudson Street why her child wasn't selected for honors English, while he hides at home pretending to write that stupid book," she told him, clutching the schedule close to her massive bosom. She seemed to understand that it was the only thing that held him there and after surrendering it she'd be talking to herself.

"If—"

"It's not *bad* enough he hogs all the honors classes for himself, as if the rest of us were unqualified. It's not *bad* enough—"

"Uh . . . I'm going to be late?" he ventured. He wasn't sure how many more "bad enough's" there might be, but he guessed quite a few.

Reluctantly, she handed over the schedule. "I've got my eye on you, mister," she warned him.

Outside in the hall, Lucy was waiting for him, beaming. "Mr. Berg's honors?"

Noonan nodded, feeling guilty that his friend should be so pleased on his behalf. Anybody but Lucy would be suffering a pang of jealousy, or at least vague misgivings, that his girlfriend was pulling strings for another boy. Hadn't it dawned on the poor bastard why she'd done it? "What do you have for first?" he asked, trying to conceal his elation.

"Calculus. You?"

"Geometry. See you in third."

"Be prepared," Lucy said. "He's pretty weird."

Two periods, then, before he'd see Sarah. He thought again of her drawing, the meaning of which had now subtly shifted. Instead of being about to enter Ikey Lubin's and Lynch World, he now saw himself on the verge of entering Sarah's affections.

Two hours later, though, he would conclude that Mrs. Summers had been right. He *wasn't* one of the brightest kids in the school. Why in the world had he assumed Sarah would be taking her father's class? Sure, she was smart and industrious, an honors student, but the class was being taught by her *father*. Of course he couldn't select his own daughter. What had Noonan been thinking? And that wasn't even the worst part. Sarah, it turned out, was in Mrs. Summers's class. She'd moved him out of the one class they otherwise would've shared. Speaking of clear signals.

HIS HOMEROOM TEACHER HAD BEEN right about something else, too. The best and brightest of the senior class seemed to have been purposely excluded from Mr. Berg's honors seminar on the American Dream, which resembled some weird social experiment whose purpose wouldn't be revealed until the study was concluded. A case might be made for Lucy, Noonan supposed. He had good grades, and he was a reader, though his taste in books tended toward the juvenile. Worse, his thinking was relentlessly conventional. He had not only been taught by nuns, he'd actually listened to them.

But what was *Nan Beverly* doing there? Had her old man pulled strings? It was possible. Nan was good-looking, but there was also something a little bit off about her—something green, unseasoned—that Noonan couldn't quite put his finger on. She had a good body, so that wasn't it. What, then? She'd dated every eligible boy in town, some two or three times, and not one, if the rumors were true, had gotten anywhere with her. But that, he guessed, might have less to do with her than them. Pretty girls who had rich daddies often inspired cowardice in their social inferiors, which in Nan's case was pretty much everybody.

Just as he arrived at this conclusion, she glanced over and met his eye, then looked away with indifference, feigned, he was certain, because her aura told a different story. If she looked at him again before the end of the period, he'd be sure, and he was already sure. She'd make an excellent diversion, he decided, and he was going to need one now that he'd come a cropper with Sarah. Green or not, Nan was the prettiest girl in the school. He wondered if she expected his courage to fail him, as it had her other boyfriends. For her sake, he hoped not, because it wouldn't.

But of all the kids in Mr. Berg's honors class, Perry Kozlowski was the most inexplicable. He wasn't so much dumb as sullen, a boy who seemed to embrace his reputation as a lout. Noonan supposed his attitude had something to do with the lush garden of acne on his face, in full bloom at the moment, zits on top of zits, crowding each other angrily for space, their tendrils tapping into some deep reservoir of pus. According to Lucy, the experience of nearly killing the Mock kid had briefly chastened him. Public opinion, in the weeks and months that followed, had unexpectedly turned against the Kozlowskis. To get Perry out of town and away from social scrutiny, they'd enrolled him in a Catholic summer camp. Mr. Kozlowski had been against so drastic a measure, unwilling to make a mountain out of the Three Mock molehill, but their buttinsky parish priest had told Mrs. Kozlowski that their son had committed a mortal sin by beating that colored boy into a coma, and damned fool that she was, she'd believed him. "Let *him* pay for camp, then," her husband said when he found out how much it cost. Wasn't it just like a priest to come up with a penance that put money into the church's coffers? "What do you wanna bet he gets a cut?"

To their surprise—again, according to Lucy—Perry actually liked the camp and learned from the Brothers who ran it the seriousness of his offense and how lucky he was not to have committed it against a white boy, which would not have been a summer camp matter. After six short weeks he returned to Thomaston sunburned and rehabilitated, actually thinking he might have a religious vocation. The Brothers were big, robust men with florid faces and a fondness for brutal full-court basketball, played outdoors in the noonday sun. They employed sports metaphors to explain faith and morality to teenage boys who hadn't much interest in either one. They also liked to drink and intimated they'd have been ladies' men, too, had women been allowed. The Brothers were, in short, the antithesis of every wimpy, pansy-ass priest he'd ever encountered. Brother Jacob was his favorite, perhaps because he was built powerfully and low to the ground, like Perry himself, and his rugged fifty-year-old face bore the pockmarked ravages of Perry's own affliction. But what he'd liked most was the man's attitude, his willingness to admit that some things could neither be helped nor changed. His favorite expression was "That's the way it goes. First your money, then your clothes." Returning from camp that August, the whole Three Mock incident a distant memory, all Perry Kozlowski could talk about was Brother Jake, and even now, years later, he never missed an opportunity to remind people of how things went: money first, clothing afterward.

In the long run, though, he'd decided against the priesthood. In high school he discovered that football offered many of the same advantages as religion—structure, unlimited zeal, a uniform. Much as he'd enjoyed the Brothers' hard-hitting brand of basketball, football was even better. Here, within clearly defined parameters, you could stick people as hard as you wanted and get praised for so doing. Instead of people looking at you like you were some sort of criminal, they applauded your better efforts and shouted gratifying things like "Hell of a shot, Koz!" If the boy you stuck gave you attitude, you kept sticking him until he got tired of it, then the two of you were friends and teammates. Some different from the situation with Three Mock, to whom he'd apologized—"No hard feelings" were his exact words—and been given a blank stare in return, as if the kid imagined it was easy to humble yourself to a Negro who'd brought everything on himself to begin with.

Perry Kozlowski in honors?

Then there was Noonan himself, whose history was only slightly less violent, his claim to fame being sent away to a military reform school. With a mother who tried to flee her family every time she got knocked up, and a father who made no secret of the woman he kept on lower Division Street. What must his classmates think of *his* inclusion? He could imagine Nan Beverly telling her parents over dinner, "You'll never guess who they let into honors English. Robert Marconi. I'm not kidding." Maybe that in itself was reason enough to tough this out.

LUCY HAD TALKED about Mr. Berg all summer long, but even if Noonan hadn't heard a word, he'd have known at a glance that the man was batshit. He arrived in class cave dweller pale, looking like he'd sworn off both sunlight and solid food for the entire summer. His belt had additional holes punched in it, inexpertly, with an awl, but even so his trousers rode dangerously low on his nonexistent hips. He held his scuffed, boxy briefcase to his chest, and when he set it down on the desk Noonan saw why: its handle had apparently snapped off. What sort of man didn't buy himself a new briefcase or just fix the old one?

Three Mock, whom he had heard was Mr. Berg's constant companion, slipped in behind him, silent and vacant as always. The teacher's interest in the Mock boy was a matter of considerable speculation. Having reluctantly come to terms with him as a tragedy, most people were taken aback when he abruptly awoke from his six-month coma, much of it spent in a facility in Schenectady. Peacefully asleep in another town, he was someone they could feel bad about, whereas shuffling through the streets of Thomaston he was a constant accusation. Then, when Mr. Berg took him under his wing, hiring him to do odd jobs and helping him enroll in vocational night classes, many imagined it was because he felt responsible, as well he might. Had he prevented his daughter from going to that matinee with a colored boy, the whole unfortunate incident never would have happened. Others—Mrs. Lynch among them—had a different interpretation. Far from feeling guilty, Mr. Berg took perverse pleasure in parading Three Mock around town, enjoying the effect he had on people. The whole town, in Mr. Berg's view, was responsible for this outrage. Maybe the Kozlowski kid had administered the actual beating, but he'd done so with the town's implicit blessing, indeed with half of Thomaston looking on. That no charges were ever filed served as the community's final benediction. It was simple justice, as Mr. Berg saw it, for the victim to remain in full view of his victimizers. It was even rumored that the assault on Three Mock was a central event in Mr. Berg's novel.

What, Noonan couldn't help but ask, did the boy himself think about being put to such ironic use? If he had any views on the subject, or indeed any other subject, he gave them no voice. While no actual tests had been run, because of his slowness of speech and manner it was generally conceded that brain damage had occurred, though with a Negro you couldn't be sure. He did follow instructions well enough, had no trouble completing simple tasks and seemed to have an aptitude for anything mechanical, the very sort of thing Mr. Berg himself had little patience for. Some people were convinced the boy liked to hang around the Berg house because of Sarah, but according to Lucy, he was oblivious to her presence and never even looked at her. No, if the boy loved anybody, it was the girl's father.

Today, he was carrying a portable record player, which he went about setting up while Mr. Berg wrote a poem—at least Noonan supposed that's what it was—on the portable blackboard that had been wheeled in on casters earlier.

> He rose up on his dying bed
> and asked for fish.
> His wife looked it up in her dream book
> and played it.

Was Mr. Berg himself the author of these lines? Noonan wondered. If so, had he written them out from memory or composed them on the spot? Noonan sort of liked the poem, though it didn't make much sense. Why would a dying man want fish? Who had to look that word up and how had the wife played it? Like a song on a piano? Had Mr. Berg left out a word? Was she supposed to play "with" it? Feeling Lucy's eyes on him, he glanced over, and sure enough, his friend was grinning at him as if to say *Pretty weird, huh?* Noonan raised an eyebrow. *Yup, pretty weird.*

Their classmates were also studying the poem, with expressions ranging from confusion to alarm. Noonan had little trouble reading their thoughts, since they weren't that dissimilar to his own. Was it too late to drop honors and return to Mrs. Summers's class? She was beyond dull but at least, by Thomaston standards, sane. She was also his homeroom teacher and by returning to her own class he might get back into her good graces. Outweighing these considerations, though, was the difficulty of explaining such a decision to Sarah.

Mr. Berg stepped back and examined what he'd written, then slashed the word "hope" onto the board with such force that the chalk broke. Was that the poem's title? And what did these lines have to do with hope? Three Mock, who'd plugged in the record player, now turned the power on and placed the arm on its rest, awaiting further instruction.

"Take a seat," Mr. Berg suggested. When the boy started toward the back of the room, he added, "No, right up here in front. This isn't a Birmingham bus, Mr. Mock. You can tell, because it's not yellow and it doesn't move."

This, Noonan guessed, must be a joke, because then he smiled, his mouth full of thin, wolfish teeth the same shade of yellow as the inside of his collar and the underarms of his otherwise grayish-white short-sleeved shirt. *This* was Sarah's father? He searched Mr. Berg's features for genetic resemblance, half hoping to find some. Meeting a girl's parents was like getting an unauthorized glimpse of the future. If he looked at Sarah and saw her father, or vice versa, that would be enough to banish her attractions for good—whatever those attractions might be, since he hadn't figured them out yet.

Three Mock did as he was told, taking a seat near the door. Perry Kozlowski, who apparently expected him to leave once he'd set up the record player, cast a sullen, resentful look in the teacher's direction. "Mr. Berg?" he said, still staring at the boy.

But the man was shuffling through the stack of records he'd brought, finally slipping one from its sleeve and balancing it on the spindle. When the record dropped onto the turntable and the tone arm lowered gently onto the vinyl, there was a loud hissing. The record had clearly been worn scratchy, a problem Mr. Berg seemed to believe could be remedied by turning the volume up, causing everyone to wince. Spreading his feet wide, he began snapping his fingers to the beat, bobbing his head and grinning his yellow grin. Was this another joke? Nobody seemed to know.

"Mr. Berg?" Perry repeated, still eyeing Three Mock. Noonan assumed he was going to ask why the boy hadn't left, but he was mistaken. "How come we're meeting in *here*?" Kozlowski asked instead.

They'd all assumed the room assignment on their printed schedules was a mistake until the office secretary informed them that, no, Mr. Berg had specifically requested the stale, dusty, windowless former storage room, though why he should prefer it to the bright, airy plum of a room set aside for honors classes remained a mystery.

Mr. Berg grinned unpleasantly at Perry Kozlowski. "Which answer would you prefer?" he said finally.

"Which answer?" Perry repeated, glancing around to see if the question made any more sense to his companions than it did to him.

Mr. Berg nodded. "In your other classes you're used to getting one answer, usually a lie. In this one you'll get two or more, depending on the question. Among these answers you will search for the truth and mostly not find it."

"You're going to lie to us?"

"For instance, I could tell you I've selected this room so we could listen to loud jazz without disturbing other classes, and that would be true, though it wouldn't be the whole truth and nothing but the truth. Not so help me God." He was now fishing around in his jacket pocket, from which he extracted a crumpled pack of cigarettes and a tarnished silver lighter. "It might also be true that I selected a room far from all other classrooms because"—he lit up, inhaled deeply and exhaled into the room—"I like to smoke." Nan Beverly wrinkled her nose.

"That's against the rules," Perry pointed out.

"Yes, it is," Mr. Berg conceded, filling his lungs a second time, exhaling through his nose. "But I really do enjoy smoking, don't you?"

"If I get caught with a cigarette, I'm off the football team."

"And you're afraid I'll report you?"

"You're supposed to. You're a teacher. Or somebody else could."

"Who do you imagine might betray you? Mr. Mock, perhaps?"

Perry was clearly startled by this reference to Three Mock, who seemed to register that his name had been spoken, but gave no other indication of following the conversation. "Maybe." Perry shrugged. "How do I know? Marconi, maybe."

"You're suspicious of Mr. Marconi?"

"I said maybe. I don't know."

Mr. Berg turned to Noonan. "Do *you* like to smoke, Mr. Marconi?"

"Yes," said Noonan, whose repeated violations of the prohibition had often gotten him in trouble at the academy, though he saw no reason to volunteer this information. He'd also been written up for drinking and brawling with townies, where he'd again broken his wrist. No reason to volunteer any of that either.

"Here, have one," Mr. Berg said, tossing him the pack.

"He's on the team, too," Perry said.

Noonan surprised himself by taking out a cigarette and lighting it with the lighter Mr. Berg held out to him. He felt Lucy's amazed eyes on him.

"There," Mr. Berg said, again addressing Perry. "Now you

don't have to worry about Mr. Marconi. He can't betray you without betraying himself."

"Somebody else might, though."

Mr. Berg leaned forward, lowering his voice in mock confidentiality. "Miss Beverly, for instance?"

Nan started at this suggestion.

"No, not her," Perry said quickly.

"Why not?"

"She just wouldn't."

"She's too blond?"

Perry grimaced. "What?"

"She's very blond, isn't she."

"So what?"

"It's dark people who do dark deeds, right?"

Perry looked around the room for an ally. "That's crazy."

"Or do you think she's secretly fond of you?"

Now it was Nan's turn to grimace.

"No."

Mr. Berg nodded. "You're probably right." Perry's face darkened and he added, "Right to be suspicious, I mean. Most people *are* up to no good, isn't that true?

"I guess."

"I don't mind telling you, *I'm* worried," Mr. Berg continued in a tone that made it impossible for Noonan to take anything he said seriously, though most of his fellow students seemed to. This was a game, and the referee was crazy. Which meant there was nothing to do but relax and enjoy it. "I could be fired for giving Mr. Marconi a cigarette, and he could be kicked off the team for smoking it. As you point out, it's against the rules, so maybe this means the end for Mr. Marconi and me. And yet the fact remains, I love to smoke and so does Mr. Marconi here, I can tell. We're mighty glad, he and I, that the principal isn't likely to walk in on us, not all the way over here, which may have been another reason I chose this room. Far away from prying eyes and malicious gossip. My inference is—and you may be interested to hear this, Miss Beverly—that if nobody rats out Mr. Marconi and me for smoking, maybe we'll break some other rules, too. Does that possibility frighten you?"

"What other rules?" Nan asked warily.

"Are you sure you wouldn't like a cigarette, Mr. Kozlowski?" That Perry would have loved one couldn't have been more obvious as he regarded Noonan with longing and hatred. Who, in return, stretched out and smiled back, exhaling languorously out the side of his mouth.

"I really wish you would," Mr. Berg said. "Then I'd be less worried about losing my job and getting Mr. Marconi kicked off the football team. Both of those possibilities trouble me greatly." In actuality, Noonan felt certain he couldn't care less about either one, though Perry seemed not to grasp this essential fact.

"I better not," he said glumly.

Mr. Berg shrugged. "Of course the real reason I selected this room may have nothing to do with cigarettes. Maybe I've located us all the way over here not so much because we could *do* things as *say* things. Things we might not want to say over there." He was again talking to Nan Beverly in that same mock-confidential tone. "Things we might not want overheard."

"Such as?"

"There is no God," said Mr. Berg, then clapped his hand over his mouth. "I shouldn't have said that. Wow. If somebody heard me say that, I could be fired. Just like for smoking."

"Are you saying there *is* no God?" Perry Kozlowski said.

"No, that just slipped out. It was only a thought. But it's a good thing we're over here, isn't it? Not the sort of thing you'd want our principal to overhear. I believe he attends the same church as Miss Beverly, and in faculty meetings I've heard him speak about God as if they converse regularly, so I know he'd be very displeased to hear something like I let slip. Which he might just do in that honors room, right next to his office. Have you ever noticed how sneaky he is? How he likes to loiter in the hallways and listen to what's going on in the classrooms?"

RICHARD RUSSO

"He could still do that here," Perry pointed out.

"But he's also fat and lazy," Mr. Berg said. "He wouldn't come all this way. And if he did we'd probably hear him because that's how fat and lumbering he is, though I probably shouldn't be saying such things. He *is* our principal, after all. The only reason I mention that he's fat and lazy is because it's true, which is different from saying something just to be unkind, don't you think?"

"Yes," Noonan volunteered.

"Yes," Mr. Berg repeated. "Mr. Marconi agrees. I expected as much. But Miss Beverly, here's something I've been wanting to ask you. It's about our country. People say it's great, indeed the greatest country of all. Do you agree?"

"Yes?" she said, herself glancing around for support.

"Why?"

She thought about it for a moment, then said, "Because we're free? Because we can be whatever we want?"

"Are those statements or questions?"

"Statements?"

Mr. Berg sighed. "Oh. I thought perhaps your lilting inflection suggested a reservation. But maybe by the end of the term you'll be able to speak in the declarative. Does that strike you as a possibility?"

"Yes?"

"Mr. Marconi has his doubts," Mr. Berg said, responding to the guffaw Noonan wasn't able to suppress. "Are you an agnostic in general, Mr. Marconi, or only where Miss Beverly is concerned?"

"In general," Noonan said, careful to sound very certain.

"Are there other agnostics in this class, or is Mr. Noonan our sole practitioner?"

No response.

"How about you, Miss Beverly?"

Nan started again. Having been called on once, she clearly didn't expect to find herself in the crosshairs again so soon. "I don't know?"

394

"What don't you know?"

"What an agnostic is." She was looking more alarmed by the moment.

"I don't understand you at all, Miss Beverly. When you know the answer you make it sound like a question, but when you have an actual question—what is an agnostic?—you don't ask it. Is it that you don't want to know what an agnostic is? Or are you afraid you won't like the answer?"

"How come you're picking on her?" Perry blurted.

"Now *there's* a question in its true form," Mr. Berg replied, as if Kozlowski had offered his comment with no other purpose than to be helpful. After a beat he turned to him again and said, "Which answer would you prefer?"

"I don't—"

But Mr. Berg had already redirected his attention to Nan. "A doubter, Miss Beverly. An agnostic is a doubter. Someone who questions things, especially authority." As a visual aid, he now pointed at Noonan, in case anyone had forgotten who was being alluded to. "Mr. Marconi claims to be one, and I believe him. How about you? Is he convincing on this point, or do you think it's merely a pose?" Again he lowered his voice and leaned forward, as if this were just between the two of them. Nan Beverly leaned back in her seat, while everyone else leaned forward. "People adopt poses, don't they? Pretend to be what they aren't?"

"I don't—"

Then just as quickly he was done with her. "What's the opposite of an agnostic, Mr. Lynch?"

Noonan looked over at his friend, expecting Lucy to be paralyzed by the sudden spotlight and relieved to discover he wasn't.

"A believer?"

"Another answer in the form of a question. You and Miss Beverly should marry and have children," Mr. Berg said, a suggestion that caused Lucy to blush deeply. "And which are you, Mr. Lynch, a doubter or a believer?"

"I guess I'm a little of both," Lucy said.

"An equivocation, surely," Mr. Berg replied, then regarded Nan rather pointedly.

It took her a moment to realize what he might be driving at. "What's an equivocation?" she finally said.

Mr. Berg applauded. "Bravo, Miss Beverly. I take back everything I said about you. Except the part about being blond. You're very blond."

"What's wrong with that?" Perry wanted to know.

"Which answer would you prefer?"

"Why do you keep asking me that?"

"Because I haven't yet received a satisfactory answer. Or even an unsatisfactory one, come to that. The good news is that we have the whole semester, so I'm not discouraged by our lack of progress thus far, and I hope you aren't either. Now, Mr. Lynch."

"Yes, sir."

"Why do you suppose you're a bit of a doubter and a bit of a believer?"

"I'm still learning?"

"Not a bad answer, Mr. Lynch, even if stated in the form of a question, though I don't believe it's true. Do you want to know why? Yes, *excellent*, I knew you would. You may still be learning, as you say, but you aren't learning much. Which is to say, you aren't learning at the rate you were when, say, you were two or three years old. That's when the real learning takes place. By the time we're seventeen or eighteen our characters and attitudes are mostly formed. We're basically looking for evidence in support of conclusions we've already arrived at regarding the world and our place in it. We like the *idea* of change even though we know it's an illusion. We keep hoping for new experiences, but we're frightened, because the next really new experience for us will be death, and we aren't likely to learn much from that, are we? That little item's pretty much the end of our education, though it will answer the question whether it's better to doubt than believe, which reminds me of my original question, Miss Beverly. You and Mr. Lynch have so much in common—I speak here temperamentally—that I wonder if you can think of any other reason why he should be a bit of a doubter and a bit of a believer?"

"Who cares?" Perry said, hoping for a laugh but not getting it.

"Which answer would you prefer?" Noonan said, taking one last mock-thoughtful drag on his cigarette and getting the very laugh that eluded the other boy.

Mr. Berg turned to him, apparently delighted that Noonan had seized upon the sense of play. "You're Mr. Lynch's friend, are you not?"

Noonan nodded. "Yeah."

"You say you are, but there was a slight hesitation to your answer. What made you hesitate?"

"You," said Noonan, winning another laugh.

"Me? Good heavens. Am I making you nervous?"

"You're making everybody nervous. About giving the wrong answers."

"Oh, nonsense. I'm making Miss Beverly nervous, I admit. She's unused to confrontation, but you, Mr. Marconi? Come now, you wouldn't shit a shitter."

Everyone else in the room gasped at this.

"I said we're friends. I think I know if somebody's my friend or not."

"I think you do, but here's the question, Miss Beverly," he said, turning abruptly away. "Don't be nervous. We'd simply like to hear your opinion. Who do you think understands Mr. Lynch best, Mr. Lynch himself or his good friend Mr. Marconi?"

Was it Noonan's imagination, or did Mr. Berg give the word "good" an odd emphasis that cast some doubt upon whether they were friends at all?

Perry interrupted. "How come you ask the same four people all the questions?"

397

Mr. Berg raised his arms like a conductor, and the entire class responded in a chorus, led by Noonan, "Which answer would you prefer?" Perry seemed on the verge of spontaneous combustion.

"Bobby," Nan said, her eyes meeting Noonan's directly. Ah, he thought. She's caught on and is fighting back. Also, her aura was ablaze.

"You could be right, Miss Beverly. Like you, I wouldn't sell Mr. Marconi short. No fool, our Mr. Marconi."

"Are you going to play favorites?" Perry now wanted to know.

"I'd like to say no, but that would be a lie, wouldn't it? We all have our favorites. I'm just like you in that respect. I like some people and don't like others. For instance, you don't like Mr. Marconi, am I correct?" He waited now, grinning, and Noonan had a pretty good idea what for.

So, apparently, did Lucy, who nudged Perry and whispered, "Which answer would you prefer?"

"Ah, Mr. Lynch, welcome aboard," Mr. Berg said, then quickly turned his attention back to Noonan. "But Mr. Marconi, I really must insist you tell us why your friend's a bit of a doubter and a bit of a believer."

He shrugged. "His dad's a believer and his mom's a doubter."

"Ah," Mr. Berg sighed theatrically. "What they call a mixed marriage. True, what your friend alleges, Mr. Lynch?"

Lucy allowed that it was.

"And exactly what does your father believe in?"

"America," Lucy said. "Our town. Our family. That people are basically good."

"And your mother has her doubts?"

"Not really. She just—"

"Has her doubts, yes, I understand. Thinks people are basically up to no good, as Miss Beverly and I agreed earlier. I hope we aren't boring you, Mr. Kozlowski," he said, noting that Perry was sulking in his chair, "since we're closing in on the subject of our seminar, and I'd hate to think you're losing interest already, because I, for one, am very, *very* excited."

THAT EVENING Noonan's head was still reeling. After football practice he stopped at Ikey's, where Lucy was manning the register. They took one look at each other and burst out laughing. When Dec Lynch tripped down the back stairs from his apartment, they tried to compose themselves, but it was no use.

"You two giggle like a couple girls," Dec observed, his head in the meat case, from which he extracted two thick pork chops and a small boat of potato salad for his dinner. "The hell's wrong with you?"

"Which answer would you prefer?" they said in unison, and cracked up all over again, while he just stood there glaring at them. Finally, they became self-conscious enough to stop.

"Just tell me one thing," he said, fixing Noonan. "And I want the truth. Do we stand any chance against Mohawk next Saturday?"

It was tempting to give him the Berg response all over again, but Noonan could tell the man was serious. A gambler, he wanted the inside scoop. "Hard to say," he told him.

"I know it's hard to say," Dec countered. "If it was easy, would I be asking *you*?"

"I don't think they're any better than we are. They're at home, though."

Dec Lynch snorted derisively. "Home?" he said. "Ten miles upstream, you mean. A fifteen-minute bus ride, assuming both traffic lights are red. Hell, it's the same damn gene pool. If we were any closer there'd be nothing but harelips on both sides of the ball. Is anybody hurt, is what I'd like you to tell me."

"Perry Kozlowski got his bell rung in practice today," Noonan told him. Which was the truth but not, to quote Mr. Berg, the whole truth and nothing but the truth. Rather, it was the answer he preferred, since he himself had met Perry helmet to helmet on the fifty-yard line, their collision leaving the other boy dazed and disoriented. Noonan had taken a handoff and run between the tackles, the secondary opening up in front of him. Had he continued left, he might've made it all the way to the end zone, but instead he lowered his head into a surprised Perry, the team's captain and middle linebacker. Noonan's own fingers and toes were buzzing for the next hour. Coach took him aside after the play. "What is it with you two?" he wanted to know. Noonan just shrugged, not knowing quite what was between him and Perry, or why he thought it might be fun to pin him to the ground with his knees and pop his zits, one by one. Worse, at the satisfying moment of impact, he'd felt some diminishment in the more important loathing he harbored for his father. Was it possible that a person possessed a finite amount of such a valuable commodity?

"Terrific," Dec said. "The one guy on our team who can tackle. I may have to buy a disguise and drive up to Mohawk and watch them practice." Before heading back upstairs, he stopped at the cooler and grabbed a beer, letting the door swing shut with a soft thud, and Noonan wondered how having Dec Lynch living above Ikey's represented an improvement over Buddy Nurt. Hadn't they just replaced one slow leak with another? According to Lucy his uncle paid no rent and took whatever he needed or wanted from the store. On the plus side, he was paid little more than what he needed to cover his weekend carousing, and that was under the table, so he could still collect unemployment.

"So," Lucy said, once he'd left, "you going to stick it out with Berg or switch to Summers?"

"Berg," Noonan said, with no hesitation. "He may be nuts, but he's not dull."

In fact, the class had been nothing short of exhilarating. When they'd finally gotten around to discussing the four-line poem on the blackboard, Mr. Berg had unfolded it the way the sun opens a flower, patiently, one petal at a time. The class began by agreeing the words made no sense, that something must be missing or wrong with the poem, so they were shocked to hear that in Mr. Berg's opinion the poem was perfect as it stood. Indeed, he'd gone so far as to suggest there might be something wrong with them.

"Okay," Perry challenged him, "then tell us what it means."

Grinning, Mr. Berg asked a question instead. "What's a dream book?" They'd all looked at one another. "Nobody knows what a dream book is?"

Clearly nobody did, and Noonan was surprised when a voice said, "It's where you look it up."

Everyone had forgotten Three Mock, who, unless there was a ventriloquist in the room, had actually spoken. He sat motionless, as before, still facing the front. To look at him, you wouldn't have guessed he was wired to any external reality.

"Thank you, Mr. Mock," Mr. Berg said, apparently not surprised at all. "Would you be willing to elaborate? It's where you look *what* up?"

"What you dreamin'."

"So, if I dream of a fish," Mr. Berg said, "I can look it up in this book?"

The boy nodded.

Berg turned back to the rest of the class. "Interesting. How is it that Mr. Mock knows what a dream book is and the rest of you don't? How could we account for that?"

"Easy," Perry said. "You told him before class. To make the rest of us look stupid."

"Ah," Mr. Berg said. "The people-are-up-to-no-good thesis again. Mr. Mock, did I tell you what a dream book was before class?"

All eyes now on him, Three Mock shook his head almost imperceptibly.

"Do you believe him, Mr. Kozlowski?"

"No," Perry said.

401

"How about you, Mr. Lynch?" When Lucy hesitated, he moved on, "Mr. Marconi?"

"Yes," Noonan said, partly because he did, but mostly because he wouldn't agree with Kozlowski unless he had no choice.

"Our resident agnostic believes him." Mr. Berg chuckled, turning again to Nan. "Funny how that works out sometimes, no? Doubters believing. Believers doubting."

"What difference does it make?" Perry Kozlowski demanded. "Everybody knows what a fish is. Why would you look it up?"

"Mr. Mock?"

"Dream book give you a number," he said, and Noonan felt some inner door swing partway open on an unseen hinge, allowing a breeze to blow in. He glanced over at Lucy, who'd felt it, too.

Not Perry, though. "What good would this number do?"

"You could play it," Lucy said, a little breathlessly, like this sudden realization had left him weak. "You could bet your dream."

Mr. Berg just grinned his wolfish grin, and the bell rang. As if he'd planned that, too.

"HE MUST BE TRYING to get himself fired," Tessa Lynch speculated.

She'd come into the store with two big tubs of macaroni and potato salad a few minutes after Dec Lynch went upstairs. Taking one look at Noonan, she scooped a generous portion from each into a paper boat, handing it to him along with a plastic spoon. He didn't bother denying he was famished, as usual. After practice he was always hungry, and he just dug in.

"Nobody feeds you at home?" she said, watching him and looking pleased.

"My mother usually tries to save me something," he said, which was true. His little brothers had the appetites of young dogs, though, and if he got home late, they'd have grazed through whatever she'd set aside for him. From upstairs came the smell of Dec's pork chops frying—it would've been nice to have one of those to go with the salads—and the sound of the ball game he'd turned on. "Why would he want to get fired?" Noonan said.

"Right off the top of my head, I can think of about a dozen reasons." Mrs. Lynch gazed around the store. "There's times I wish somebody'd fire me."

Noonan noticed his friend's face cloud over when she said this.

"It'd make sense. He's always hated it here, and after Sarah graduates there won't be any reason for him to stay. Sarah says he's close to finishing that book of his."

"I'd like to read it," Noonan admitted after she left, but Lucy appeared not to have heard. He was watching his mother cross the intersection, his expression troubled. He hated the very idea of change, Noonan knew, and its inevitability was what his mother was trying to prepare him for. "Part of it, anyway," he added, trying to draw him back. "Just to see what it's like."

Lucy's focus returned. "You're his favorite," he said, a little enviously, Noonan thought.

As the class had progressed, Mr. Berg continued to focus on Nan and Perry. If anything, his comments and questions became even more probing and personal, Noonan's suspicion that he was conducting some sort of bizarre experiment deepening. And he knew a lot—too much, really—about every kid in the class. It was almost as if the books they'd be reading were really just for show, and the actual subject of the class would be themselves, the fifteen students handpicked to investigate the American Dream. And not only them either, but also their parents and the rest of Thomaston. It occurred to Noonan that he hadn't even taken roll, that he already knew who each student was. Of course he might've had some of them in other classes, and he knew Lucy through Sarah. Still, he'd never met Noonan before today, yet he somehow required no introduction. Had Sarah been talking about him? Was he hastily being written into the famous novel?

They now heard Dec on the stairs again. He came in wiping his mouth on a paper napkin that he wadded up and threw at Lucy, who ducked, picked it up off the floor and dropped it in the trash pail behind the counter.

"What worries me is those Puerto Ricans," he told Noonan, apparently confident the subject hadn't changed since he left the room half an hour earlier.

Ten years ago, a dozen Puerto Rican families had moved to Mohawk to work for a company that manufactured cheap plastic wading pools. The temperature on the factory floor was routinely over a hundred degrees and the air liquid plastic, which people said reminded them of home.

"They're speedy little bastards," Dec said, "and if they ever get loose in our secondary, it's all over."

"We've got some speed," Noonan said out of a loyalty he hadn't known he felt until the words were out of his mouth. He, too, had heard the Puerto Ricans were quick.

"Coach should be recruiting some of those Negro kids from off the Hill," Dec said. "They can run, at least the ones that haven't been beat up to the point of brain damage. I'm guessing even in his present state that Mock kid could run circles around you and Kozlowski."

"You should bet on Mohawk," Noonan suggested, "if you think they're so much better."

"I might," he said. "But that's assuming I could find somebody to bet on you."

MR. BERG'S NEXT CLASS was even more disconcerting. The same poem was still on the blackboard, and he picked up right where they'd left off, with Lucy's brainstorm about the wife betting on her husband's dream.

Perry still refused to see it. "That's stupid," he said. "Why would she bet on somebody else's dream? Besides, the guy's hallucinating. The whole thing's crazy."

"Who remembers David Entleman?" Mr. Berg asked, and evidently Noonan was the only one who didn't. The Entleman family, he learned later, had moved into a house in the East End shortly after he'd been sent to the academy. One morning about a year later, Mr. Entleman had gone into the garage and found his son David dangling from a rafter. The next day everybody had picked the day/month/year of his suicide as their number. Had it hit, local bookies joked, they'd all have had to join that fucking kid on the rafter.

"Your father never bets the number?" Mr. Berg asked Perry.

"He used to, back when he worked at the tannery."

"Not anymore?"

"You can't bet at GE," he said.

"Why not?"

"It's not allowed. They don't let bookies in."

"Why not?"

"It's against the law."

"But wasn't it also against the law at the tannery?"

"People want to bet. They enjoy it."

"Like smoking," Mr. Berg said, taking this opportunity to light up. He again offered the pack to Noonan, who this time declined. "So if you really enjoy something, it's okay, even if it is against the law."

Perry shrugged.

"How do you think the bookies got into the tannery?"

Perry snorted. "They walked in. They made the rounds every day. Everybody knows."

And Mr. Berg again leaned forward, crooking his finger for Perry to lean toward him, which he reluctantly did.

Noonan was beginning to recognize this as part of the game they'd all embarked on. It was like Hamlet, alone onstage, addressing his innermost thoughts to the audience in the form of a monologue: *To be, or not to be . . .*

405

"Even . . . Miss Beverly's father?" Mr. Berg whispered, just loud enough for everyone to hear.

Perry snapped back in his chair. "How would I know?"

"No idea?"

Perry shrugged, torn between loyalty to a pretty girl who'd never given him the time of day and his desire not to appear stupid. "It's his factory."

Mr. Berg nodded thoughtfully. "His business to know," he said, as if it pained him greatly to acknowledge this. "I see what you mean." Then he looked over at Nan, whose eyes, Noonan noticed, had filled with tears. "Want to know a secret?" he asked her, his voice full of sudden, alarming good cheer. "I never even knew what *my* father did for a living."

"Come on," Perry said, though the man was no longer talking to him.

"I shit you not," said Mr. Berg, still looking at Nan, like he was about to reach out and take her hand.

"You never asked him?" Perry said.

"Claimed it was none of my business. Acted like I had a hell of a nerve to ask. Said there was food on the table and that was all I needed to know. Mr. Mock here knows more about his father than I knew about mine," he said, turning to the silent boy. "What's your father do, Mr. Mock?"

"Paints the fence."

"See? Mr. Mock knows what his father does. He paints the fence around Whitcombe Hall. And what's he do when he finishes, Mr. Mock?"

"Paints it again."

"So your old man was a hoodlum or something?" Perry interrupted—anxious, Noonan thought, that they linger on the Mock family no longer than absolutely necessary.

"It's a mystery," Mr. Berg said, throwing up his hands dramatically. "That's what our parents are. The first mystery we encounter in a mysterious world. We see them every day as they go about their business. Painting the fence. Painting it again.

406

But who are they? Why do they paint that fence? One thing's for sure, they aren't telling us. Isn't that so, Mr. Lynch?"

Noonan turned around to look at Lucy, who was sitting directly behind him, and saw he was wearing a strange, distant, almost fearful expression, as if he'd just remembered he had a major exam next period and forgotten to study for it. He hadn't even heard Mr. Berg's question. "Hey," he said. "Lucy?"

The boy's eyes flickered.

"Lou," Noonan said, worried he was having a spell.

This time Lucy looked back at him.

"Mr. Lynch," Mr. Berg said. "Welcome back."

Lucy looked around, red faced, surprised to see everybody staring at him.

"The subject is parents," Mr. Berg continued, "and we're anxious to hear your opinion. Do you know who they are, your parents?"

"Sure," Lucy blinked. "They're my parents."

"You know all their secrets? What they're thinking? What they do after you fall asleep?" This occasioned some snickering. "Do you know who they were before you came along?"

Noonan couldn't be sure, but unless he was mistaken, his friend was angered by this question.

"I know who they are now," he said, his jaw working.

"You do. Excellent. How well, though, I wonder? Would you say you know them as well as you know yourself?" Lucy didn't answer, and his silence was rewarded with one of Mr. Berg's yellow grins. "And how well would you say you know yourself?"

Again he was silent, but this time it didn't matter because Mr. Berg had pivoted back to Nan. "You want to know another secret? I don't want to frighten you, Miss Beverly, but I don't know myself any better than I knew my father."

"How can you not know yourself?" Perry said.

Mr. Berg threw up his hands in mock despair. "Too much evidence. Too much information. Most of it contradictory. Evidence here suggests one thing; other information suggests the opposite. No clear picture emerges. Won't hold steady. I like jazz music, I know that about myself. And I like to smoke. But then sometimes I think to myself, Do I really like jazz, or do I just think I do? Do I like to smoke, or just the idea that smoking's forbidden? What if I wake up tomorrow morning hating Louis Armstrong? Who would I be?"

"The same person," Perry said, confident, yet exasperated. "If I woke up tomorrow liking Marconi, I'd still be me."

"Except smarter," Noonan said, eliciting a smile from Nan.

"Mr. Berg?" It was Lucy. "I think I need to see the nurse."

Noonan thought so, too. Every bit of blood had drained from his friend's face. He wobbled when he tried to stand and steadied himself against his desk.

"Mr. Marconi," the teacher said, "maybe you should accompany your good friend."

Same emphasis as the day before. *Good* friend.

Later, Perry shrugged the class off. "He just likes to mess with us. What do you want to bet Lynch drops out?"

"Why would he do that?" Noonan said.

"He's always been a pussy."

"It wasn't very nice," Nan said, "bringing up David Entleman like that."

"And your dad?" Perry said. "That sucked, too. What is it with this guy and our parents?"

"What about David Entleman?" Noonan said.

"He and Lucy were best friends, weren't they?" Nan said.

"I know I'm sticking around until Marconi gets his," Perry said.

"Maybe I won't," Noonan said.

Noonan feared Kozlowski might be right. The next class might well put *him* in the hot seat, the others smirking while he squirmed under the Berg scalpel. Did the man know, for instance, that his mother had been trying all her married life to run away? That on her first attempt his father had caught her, broke open her suitcase and tossed all her intimate apparel into the street? And what about the woman on lower Division? Would he make reference to this when they read a story about adultery? The possibility was real. In the first week of class Nan's, Perry's and Lucy's parents had all been introduced. Did Mr. Berg not understand that there were boundaries, or didn't he know where they were? Despite the man's brilliance, Noonan wasn't sure, and this, more than anything else, was what made the classroom experience both thrilling and scary.

That evening he stopped by Ikey's. The color had returned to Lucy's cheeks, and he said he felt fine, that it must have been something he'd eaten in the cafeteria, but Noonan could tell he was still troubled. "You think he's really crazy?" Lucy said.

"It's possible."

"What happened after I left?"

"He gave me my final exam topic," Noonan told him. "Kozlowski, too."

A few minutes before the bell, Noonan had asked the question that had been on everybody's mind. "Why us?"

Perry had apparently been lying in wait for him, because he immediately chimed in "Which answer would you prefer?" clearly hoping that others would join his laughter and scowling when they didn't.

"Why *not* you?"

"What I mean is," Noonan continued carefully, "this is honors. It's supposed to be for the best students."

"Okay, Mr. Marconi. That will be your personal final exam. An essay on the subject of *why you*. Why the fifteen of you and not the smart Jews you were expecting." Then, when Nan flinched: "You don't mind if I use the word 'Jews,' do you?"

"What I want to know is why *he's* here," Perry said, indicating Three Mock, again sitting right up front, though today he'd not said a word. "He doesn't even go to our school."

Mr. Berg grinned at him. "And that's *your* final."

*

THAT NIGHT, Noonan lay in bed trying to figure out Mr. Berg and wondering why he needed to. The rest of his teachers were simply who they were and transparent in their expectations, which didn't amount to much at all. His history teacher, for instance, had begun class by announcing his intention to keep them busy, then handed out a five-page syllabus amplifying that modest academic goal.

Mr. Berg was more like a dentist with a wire pick, intent on probing each student until he located the nerve he was looking for; to what purpose Noonan couldn't fathom. He obviously wanted them to think, but apparently didn't believe that was possible without first undermining not only their fundamental assumptions but also the very underpinnings of their person-alities, and the man's yellow grin made Noonan doubt he was motivated by sheer goodwill. And while it might be true that he'd settled on him as a favorite, as Lucy believed, Noonan was convinced he had a reason that didn't involve actually liking him. Even when he said, "No fool, our Mr. Marconi," his intonation suggested irony and doubt.

Still, why should any of that matter? So far, the class had been thrilling. He'd unfolded the final petals of "Hope" with delicacy and precision, laying bare both its meaning and the students sitting there. They'd had trouble understanding the poem, he explained, because it had been written by a Negro, Langston Hughes, who lived in Harlem, in black America, which could boast little or no commonality with white America, as represented by Thomaston, New York. Every Negro in Harlem knew what a dream book was, so it was no mistake that Three Mock was the only student—that was the word Mr. Berg had used to describe him, even though he wasn't enrolled in the class—who had any idea what the poem was about. He wasn't smarter, just the only one who had access to a key buried deep in poverty and superstition, racial injustice and despair. Readers in white America were unlikely to discover this key, especially if they had no interest in looking for it, if their parents discouraged the search, if their America was purposely structured to ensure its own prosperity and the continued subjugation of the other America. As Mr. Berg spoke, Noonan was surprised to realize that he himself harbored such subversive thoughts though he lacked the ability to articulate them. This was the class he'd look forward to, the only one that would matter in the end. Given all this, why distrust the man? Even if Mrs. Lynch was right and he was trying to get himself fired, that was no skin off his students' noses. Why not sit back and enjoy the spectacle?

He was about to fall asleep when he heard his father come in, the door off the kitchen banging shut, then the sound of surly muttering in the dark. Since returning to Thomaston, Noonan had slept in the room they'd always referred to as the den, which had no door. The big desk where his father paid the bills—it was locked now—had been moved out to make room for him. The sofa was a pullout; there was a small closet for his clothes. His brothers all doubled up in the second-floor bedrooms. His first night back, in June, Noonan had smelled his father on the thin mattress and known the truth, that he'd driven him back into the master bedroom and also that his mother had understood this would be the inevitable result of her son's return, at least on those nights when her husband wasn't in the West End.

Tonight, he could tell from the clumsy banging in the kitchen that his father had been drinking, but he was surprised when he appeared in the arched doorway and stood there staring as Noonan pretended to sleep. In his inebriation had he forgotten who now occupied the room? Did it take him a moment to realize who was sprawled across the pullout? For the longest time he just stood there, breathing heavily, until finally he said, "You've got it *all* wrong, Buddy Boy. You think you've got all the answers, but you haven't even bothered to ask the questions."

It was a strange sensation, being spoken to in the dark, and stranger still when Noonan thought he heard something of Mr. Berg in his father's voice. Was that possible? Had Sarah's father gotten so far into his head? The two men's voices couldn't have been more different—one deep and gruff, the other thin and brittle—and his father's powerful silhouette bore no resemblance to the emaciated Mr. Berg. Where, then, was the similarity? Something in the message itself, he decided. In honors, the teacher's underlying assumption was that they had the wrong answers because they hadn't asked the right questions. They'd come in thinking they were smart—chosen for honors, after all—but Mr. Berg was there to prove them wrong. Was it possible that Mr. Berg was a bully like his father, just a different kind?

Noonan found himself smiling in the dark, for it occurred to him now that his father might one day become the dying man in the Hughes poem. That after all his sons were grown and departed, he would wake up one day, broke and broken, his health shot, and ask for a fish. Noonan's mother would look that up in her dream book and play the number, maybe even win. She had it coming, God knew. Maybe that was how things would play out: his father dead (no fish) and his mother with the winnings. Except this wasn't a very good reading of the poem. Its title was "Hope," sure, but it offered little for either the dying man or his wife, merely the longest of odds and the ignorance necessary to make the odds look short.

For some reason Noonan's thoughts drifted from the poem to Lucy. At first he'd assumed it was the discussion of parents, the first great mystery in a life full of them, that had sent Lucy into his funk, but maybe not. According to Nan, he'd been best friends with that kid who'd taken his life. Noonan had been surprised to hear about this friendship, and now it occurred to him why. Back in June, that first day he'd gone over to Ikey's, Lucy had rattled on for hours, catching him up on everything that had happened while Noonan was away at the academy, and there hadn't been a single mention of David Entleman. Probably he just hadn't wanted to revisit such a sad subject.

Poor Lucy. Except for Sarah, he'd been mostly unlucky in his friends, including Noonan himself, who always tried his best to conceal his ambivalence. But maybe in his heart of hearts Lucy knew. With a start Noonan thought about that day at the railroad trestle. By then the Marconis had moved out of the West End, though Noonan still missed his friends from the old neighborhood. Sometimes, instead of going straight home after school like he was supposed to, he'd head down to Berman Court in the hopes of running into Jerzy and the others, which was how he happened to find them the afternoon they'd put Lucy in the trunk and pretended to saw it in half. It had been his panicked, muffled screams that drew Noonan to the trestle, and he should've made Jerzy let him out right then. Why hadn't he? Because the danger wasn't real. The boys were just taking turns sawing away at a crossbeam that was five feet above the trunk. They'd tried to scare Noonan with the same trick earlier in the summer. Unlike Lucy, he'd climbed into the trunk on a dare. Then, once he was inside, they told him they were going to saw him in half, but they were his friends and he could tell they weren't sawing on the trunk itself. Eventually, when Lucy got tired of screaming and really listened, he'd realize that, too. That's why Noonan hadn't intervened. They'd free him soon, Jerzy had whispered, after they'd had a little fun, and afterward they'd all be friends. Noonan remembered rationalizing, as he trudged up the bank, that the experience would be good for Lucy, who was scared of his own shadow. When he was finally set free, he'd understand that there'd been nothing to fear.

But this wasn't the truth, the whole truth and nothing but. Not so help him God. In fact he'd been resentful of Lucy for a long time. From the beginning, really. He hated being taken out of Cayoga Elementary and sent to school with the weird Catholic kids, and he particularly hated that his mother insisted he make friends with Lucy Lynch, the weirdest of them all. He resented having to accompany him to and from school, but when he complained about how weird Lucy was and how none of the other kids liked him, his mother had grown even more insistent, reminding him the Lynches were both neighbors and nice

413

people, especially Mrs. Lynch, who'd confided how the other kids made fun of her son with that cruel nickname and were always trying to scare him.

For his mother's sake, Noonan tried his best, though he soon grew weary of being Lucy's only friend. To him, moving away from Berman Court meant a blessed end to that solemn duty. Sure, he was sorry about what happened on the trestle, but he still didn't want to be his friend anymore, and his father, for perhaps the first time, took his side. When the Lynches had followed them to the East End, it was his father who, over his mother's objections, had negotiated the friendship down to just Saturdays, when he and Lucy rode around pretending to surf in Mr. Lynch's milk truck. There, he learned that Lucy's experience in the trunk hadn't left him wiser, only more needy and clinging. So when they moved to the Borough, he'd felt relieved a second time.

He was sleepily pondering all this when he heard his father again, in the bathroom this time, and wondered if he'd return to the den with further observations. But the toilet flushed and the door to his parents' bedroom opened and closed, and his mother asked softly if everything was all right. He thought again about Mr. Berg's confession, if that's what it was, that he never knew what his father did for a living, knew even less than the Mock kid did about his. Noonan's own problem was the reverse. He knew his father all too well.

Realizing that he'd once more balled his hands into fists, he decided it might be more pleasant to fall asleep thinking about Nan Beverly, who really *was* pretty and *did* have a good body and who *would*, against her better judgment, surrender to him one day. They had several classes in common, and today she'd suggested they study together sometime. Later, in the locker room he'd overheard some boys saying he was her new boyfriend. Somewhere, though, on the gray border between wakefulness and sleep, Nan became Sarah, and he was visited by yet another unwelcome, groggy thought: what would happen to

Lucy if he stole her away? That he should have such a thought, even in passing, shamed him, and he rolled over so as not to face the den's arched doorway, lest he imagine Mr. Berg with that yellow grin of recognition. And in that instant he decided what to do about Mr. Berg: he'd learn everything he could from the man while keeping him at arm's length.

He slept, then, and didn't dream. When he awoke the next morning there was nothing to look up, no number to bet.

THE BRIDGE OF SIGHS

THE JUNIOR HIGH has emptied out, its art room locked up by the time I arrive. Fortunately, I know the custodian, Tom Shipley, whom I find in the broom closet screwing a cap back onto a pocket flask. "Mr. Mayor," he says, grinning at me as if he's the one who caught me in the act. "I do something for you?"

I tell him my wife has a new painting in the art studio that I'm here to look at, and that same knowing grin suggests I have some other, secret purpose, but that no matter what it is, he won't tell on me. I follow him up the corridor in my squishy shoes, still soaked from the Cayoga Stream, leaving footprints on his shiny floor. Tom keeps a big nest of keys attached to his belt by a chain, and when he inserts one to unlock the art room door, he has to go up on tiptoe and thrust his pelvis forward, a vaguely obscene gesture.

"I won't be long," I tell him, already spotting my wife's painting across the room. In that moment of recognition my heart contracts like a fist, just as it did when I saw that first drawing of hers, the one of her little brother in the Congregationalist hall when we were kids. I'd been filled with wonder, not just that Sarah had this talent, but that something so compelling could've been so completely hidden, and that she trusted me with the knowledge of her little brother's death and how she'd felt about that horrible loss. She'd invited me into her heart. Me, Lucy Lynch. By the time she drew Ikey's the next day I was already in love, with Sarah, with the intimacy of her gift and with the prospect of being known and understood so fully. I was, in other words, still a child. It hadn't yet occurred to me how difficult it is to be fully known to yourself, much less to another person. "And how well do you know yourself?" her father once asked me in the English honors class he taught.

"Take your time," Tom says. "The door locks automatic."

When he's gone, I pull up a stool and take off my ruined loafers. Next to the easel with Sarah's canvas is a music stand on which she's propped a glossy Italian travel book, so I pick this up and read about the photograph she's using. From across the room it looked like a painting of a railroad overpass, but in fact I see it's a stone bridge in Venice, the Bridge of Sighs, which connects the Doge's Palace in St. Mark's Square to the adjacent prison. Crossing this bridge, the convicts—at least the ones without money or influence—came to understand that all hope was lost. According to legend, their despairing sighs could be heard echoing in the neighboring canals. A melancholy subject, it seems to me. Tonight I will ask Sarah why she chose it.

Perhaps because I saw him earlier, a man without money or influence, or because he's lost just about everything a man can lose, I find myself thinking about Gabriel Mock and the night Whitcombe Hall burned to the ground, finally putting an end to the decades-long debate whether money should be raised for its restoration. It was nearly midnight when the fire trucks arrived, and the Hall, actually little more than a shell, was engulfed in flames. A very drunk Gabriel Mock capered nearby, just inside his fence, whooping and hollering and having a grand old time. Did you do this? the police demanded. Did you set this fire? Johnny K.'s boy the one done it, Gabriel told them. You want to know who's responsible, ask Johnny K. Junior.

Perry Kozlowski, he meant. To the astonishment of everyone who knew Perry as a boy, he'd become a college professor out west. He hadn't stepped foot in Thomaston for nearly twenty years, not since his father died and his mother moved away, but he *was* in town that particular weekend, as Gabriel had good reason to know. In fact, that afternoon he'd delivered the commencement address at Thomaston High. Neither Sarah nor I had attended, though we later heard that Perry had credited her father with saving his life by "turning him on" to books, transforming his blind, objectless rage into what he called "a passion for knowledge." Apparently, that oblique mention of the anger that had once possessed him was his only reference to the beating he'd given Three Mock behind the theater. The younger people in the audience had no memory of that incident, but even their elders were on Perry's side when Gabriel, roaring drunk even then, in the middle of the day, disrupted the ceremony. It must have been a bad moment for Perry, to be confronted on such a public occasion by his accusing and unforgiving past in the person of a tiny black man. People said he turned very pale, and even after Gabriel had been escorted none too gently from the auditorium—to a chorus of "Send him out!"—it took Professor Kozlowski several moments to get back on track, though everyone agreed he gave a good speech, that he seemed a changed man. And maybe he was, but I had to smile when I heard that before returning home the next day he'd accidentally broken the nose of our assistant principal, elbowing him in a pickup basketball game.

Even though I chaired the Committee for the Restoration of Whitcombe Hall, I couldn't really find it in my heart to blame Gabriel, if indeed it was he, not a lightning strike, that caused the fire. I understood. I did. It would've been too much for any one man to bear—his son long dead in Vietnam, and our high school commencement address delivered by the very person who'd once beaten him into a coma. I myself had been willing to let bygones be bygones. If it weren't for Sarah, normally the most forgiving of souls, and my mother, I probably would have attended. I never missed graduations, and I'll admit I was curious to see what kind of man Perry had become. Sarah was willing to concede that he might've changed, but she couldn't forgive what he'd done, and of course my mother was even more outraged by his triumphant return. It was she, when Gabriel was arrested out at Whitcombe Park, who insisted we make his bail.

Poor Gabriel. He'd vomited in his cell during the night and did so again on the steps of the police station when we left. I remember how he sat there in the bright morning sun, staring at but not seeing or smelling the awful mess he'd made, as horrified passersby gave both of us wide berth. "What kind of a town we livin' in, Junior, you tell me that?" he asked. By which he meant *How could any town so honor the boy who'd savagely assaulted his son?* Gabriel's "setbacks" were often tied to such unanswerable questions. "What kind of a country we livin' in," he'd asked me two decades earlier when the news came of his son's death. "Take a boy and send him halfway round the world to get killed. Boy that don't never speak. Don't say nothin' to nobody. Ask him if he want to go over there and kill people, and he don't say nothin', so they send him over." And of course, he frequently asked, as my mother had, what kind of people stood by while a boy got beat half to death.

What kind of town? What kind of country? What kind of people? If my father had been on the courthouse steps that day, he might have been able to summon his deeply held conviction that ours was a good town, a good country, and that we were good people, but I couldn't think what to say, and Gabriel seemed grateful that things made no better sense to me than they did to him.

At some point, half in this shameful, sorrowful past and half in the thrall of my wife's new painting, I feel a terrible confusion come over me, followed by that all-too-familiar vagueness, the sense that time itself has slowed. I finally realize I'm having a spell, that I've been flirting with one all day, maybe for the last several days. I should've paid attention this morning when Owen wondered if that's what was happening, and later when I found myself standing ankle deep in the Cayoga with no memory of having slipped in. As always, knowing I'm "spellbound" isn't nearly as helpful as it should be. It's like knowing you're asleep and dreaming, an awareness that should wake you up but doesn't.

In the throes of an episode I'm often peaceful, serene. I know full well that my life is "elsewhere," that I should return to it, but "elsewhere" is such a long way off and I'm so very tired. Besides, where I am isn't so terrible. That had been true even in the trunk.

Eventually I hear Sarah calling to me. I turn toward her voice reluctantly, not wanting to refuse her anything she might want, even though I just now remember what I hid in my desk drawer and am terribly, terribly ashamed.

"Lou," my wife says. "I'm right here."

"Where?" I try to say, but I know this isn't the sound that comes out. I turn toward the door, expecting her to enter the art room, but what I see framed in its tiny rectangular window is my uncle's face. But this makes no sense. Uncle Dec hasn't lived in Thomaston for years. Then when I blink, I recognize the face as belonging to José Ocariz, our junior high history teacher. He looks nothing like Dec, but his expression is the one my uncle wore the first time I had a spell in his presence: "This is some weird shit, Bub."

"This is some weird shit, Bub," I say, or something like that, or maybe I'm only thinking it. I turn away from José to Sarah's painting, since this must be where she is and I should join her there, so I do. Inside the Bridge of Sighs it's dark and I'm alone, stepping carefully on the smooth stones. I hear Sarah call my name again, but now her voice is farther away. I try to resolve this paradox. If I'm moving toward her, if she's here on the Bridge of Sighs, how can her voice be retreating? I keep moving, though her voice, each time she calls, is fainter and more distant. Should I turn around, return to the art room and await further instruction? No, I think. I love my wife. I do. But I think again of the letter and am too ashamed to face her. The direction I'm traveling in is the right one. I feel sure of this, though I can't say why. I will cross this Bridge of Sighs even though I now realize Sarah won't be there to greet me. On the other side of the bridge is profound darkness, but I'm not afraid. Whatever lies beyond the Bridge of Sighs will be my new life.

I'm in the middle of Sarah's bridge when I see a man leaning over the railing and staring down at the red water below. I recognize him, of course, and yet again I am ashamed. I try to sneak by, but he says, "Is that you, Louie?" so I go over and stand beside my father. After a moment he says, "You promised," and of course I know which promise he's talking about, though I made it long ago. "You promised you'd never do like you're doing," he explains, unnecessarily. Allowing myself to just drift away, is what he means. On that long ago day when he gave me a tour of the Borough in his milk truck, I promised him I'd never do that, and here I am breaking my oath.

"But you're gone," I tell him. "You died." How can I be bound by my promise when my father is dead?

"You always done good till now," he says sadly, as if he can't understand what's come over me.

I'd like to tell him no, he's wrong, that I've not always done as I should, that I've failed as a son, as a father and especially as a husband, but of course he'd never believe any such thing, any more than he'd have believed I gave Karen Cirillo free cigarettes from Ikey's. "It's just that I'd rather stay here with you," I tell him in my small, whiny child's voice, hoping he'll let me have my way, as he so often did when he was alive.

"I miss you, too," he tells me. "It ain't that. It's just . . ."

I wait for him to complete his thought, but instead he reaches down and takes my hand.

"Here, Lou," my wife says, her voice close now. "Open your eyes."

Are my eyes closed? I don't think so, but then I open them and there she is, my Sarah, on her knees next to my chair. It's she, not my father, who's squeezing my hand. She is, literally, "at hand," a phrase that takes on a magical new meaning. And I must be saying something—maybe trying to explain that I've actually been *inside* her painting, perhaps the finest one she's ever done, because I can feel words, like pebbles, in my throat.

ALL AND SUNDRY

SARAH WAS mostly proud of how she'd handled her parents' breakup. She hadn't cried or pouted or gotten angry with them. They were, after all, two strong-willed people who'd made up their minds. She herself was not strong-willed, nor was her mind made up as to whether the separation was a good or bad thing, so she quickly recognized the futility of attempting to alter the course of unalterable events. Enduring what couldn't be cured, she supposed, was what people meant by being adult, though it was ironic that so few of them—including her parents —had mastered the skill themselves. By age twelve she'd already learned to cut her losses and derive what comfort she could from doing so. Generally she was happy or, failing that, reasonably content, though she sometimes wondered if she'd conceded the inevitable too quickly. What if the only thing concessions got you was the habit of conceding?

Still, what remained after the separation was not nothing. Both her parents cared for her, and she mostly succeeded in trying not to think that their happiness apparently counted for more than her own. She divided her time unequally between them—residing in Thomaston with her father during the school year, on Long Island with her mother every summer, which arrangement hadn't been discussed with her but worked as well as any she herself might've proposed had anyone asked her opinion. By the time she entered junior high she was used to it, the rhythm of her comings and goings feeling natural or at least familiar. The only real difficulty was the transition, when the baton was passed between her father and mother in mid-June and then again over the Labor Day weekend.

Her parents' lives couldn't have been more different. Her father was an ascetic by nature and nurture, and her life with him was regimented and predictable. The hours after school were much the same as those in school, where a glance at the wall clock told you where you were and what you were meant to be doing: ten o'clock, chem lab; eleven, study hall; noon, lunch. At home, they alternated cooking duties, though following the same dozen or so recipes, and they ate at six sharp. Fridays they went out for pizza. Saturday mornings they went to the supermarket.

At her mother's you could search in vain for any structural principle. They shopped when they ran out, her mother purchasing whatever struck her fancy. If the produce looked good, she'd fill the cart with fruits and vegetables, most of which would be thrown out later in the week once they'd spoiled. She shopped until she grew bored, whereupon she'd proclaim, "That's enough for today," and promptly join the checkout line, which was why they were forever running out of necessities, like milk or toilet paper, and having to improvise. Her mother's tiny kitchen was full of cookbooks that she'd read around in, as if they contained poems, for an hour or so before deciding to order Chinese takeout. "What?" she said when Sarah hinted that a little organization in their lives might not be amiss. "You want me to be all buttoned up, like your father?" A *little* buttoning up, Sarah thought, might not have hurt. On hot sunny days, her mother often came home early from her studio and took a sweating shaker of martinis up onto the roof of the apartment house to sunbathe in the nude, a habit that altered the flight path of many a small aircraft. Entering her mother's world each summer, after the inflexible routine of her father's, gave Sarah vertigo, and swapping again in September was no easier. She tried not to think about the genetic implication that one day she would have to confront and resolve their contradictions or else lose her mind.

The apartment house was called the Sundry Arms, and it catered, by design or serendipity, to recently divorced men. "All and Sundry. That's who lives here," her mother joked, because the landlord's name was Harold Sundry. Though not much below medium height, Harold, thanks to a very large head, seemed dwarflike. His legs were of unequal length, which gave him a strange, rolling gait, and by watching him you couldn't quite tell where he was heading until he arrived there, though it was probably someplace in the Sundry Arms. Sarah never once saw him outside the complex, and he appeared to spend his every waking moment getting a recently vacated apartment ready for a new tenant. He himself lived in the outsize front unit that doubled as the complex's office. Every June Sarah was amazed that no one, except for her mother, remained from the previous summer. Where did they all go? Anywhere and everywhere, apparently. A few, those willing to grovel, returned to their permanently aggrieved wives and distrustful children. Others found apartments in the city. The luckiest moved in with new women. Still others moved to the Sundry Gardens, which was owned and operated by Harold's ex-wife Elaine, who'd gotten it in the divorce and now lived in the large front unit directly across the street from her ex-husband's. "Kiss my ass, Elaine," he often could be heard calling on warm evenings when the traffic had died down and he imagined his ex-wife's window might be open.

According to Sarah's mother, both complexes owed their existence to the fool's errand institution of marriage, which since she left hers had become her favorite subject, one she could riff on for hours. One of the stranger things about her parents' separation was how it had loosed her mother's tongue. Back when they were still together, she had mostly just stared at her husband in disbelief. Sometimes she'd open her mouth as if to say something, or a big bunch of somethings, but then she'd glance at her daughter and close it again. Now she just talked and talked. It was as if she'd committed to memory every single thing she'd meant to say for all those years and was letting it all loose in a flood. Away from her husband, she just hemorrhaged words and ideas, and whole philosophies on pretty much any topic, though marriage remained her favorite.

Matrimony, she explained, was based on two fallacies, both real doozies. The first was the ridiculous notion that people knew what they wanted. There was no evidence in support of this contention and never had been, but they seemed to enjoy believing it anyway, blinded as they were by love and lust and hope, only the last of which sprang eternal. The second fallacy, built on the shifting sands of the first, was equally seductive and even more idiotic—that what people thought they wanted today was what they'd want tomorrow. Sarah's mother filed this under the general heading of "Failures of Imagination," which was probably the biggest category in the entire history of categories, its origin almost certainly divine. Human beings, she believed, were a failure of God's imagination. "Look around the Sundry Arms," she was fond of saying, "and tell me God *intended* this shit." Divorce, she maintained, made a better sacrament than marriage, if you had to have one. It signaled that at least one person and probably two had come to his or her senses and taken a long hard look at not only their spouse but the institution that had encouraged such irrational behavior. Thinking clearly at last, such people embraced freedom, usually in the guise of adultery, and shortly thereafter you had need of the Sundrys, Arms and Gardens.

Elaine's Sundry Gardens was the better of the two complexes, both newer and larger, with unfurnished two- and three-bedroom apartments. The divorced men who moved in there had been clever enough to see what was bearing down on them in time to make modest preparations and draw up an evacuation plan. They'd hired lawyers (or were lawyers themselves), squirreled money away in accounts their wives knew nothing about, taken careful inventory of what they could and couldn't live without when the inevitable day arrived, making plans to secure what they could and replace what they couldn't. What they managed to salvage usually fit into a small U-Haul truck that took no more than an afternoon, with the help of an old college friend or two, to load and unload. On the other hand, the shell-shocked walking wounded who moved into the furnished one-bedroom units of the Sundry Arms arrived with little more than a suitcase or two, packed under the supervision of a woman whose Hell Hath No Greater Fury was her lone parting gift. Yet something about them appealed to Sarah's mother. "Here comes another one," she'd say when she spotted a bewildered man in the courtyard below, trying hard to follow Harold Sundry's rolling gait, zigging when Harold zagged. "No idea whether to eat shit, chase rabbits or bark at the moon." Most of them didn't look like they possessed enough energy, wit or imagination for adultery, but here they were, so they must have. For weeks they'd be like bugs on their backs, her mother explained, their little legs churning dutifully in the air, seeking traction where there wasn't any and not even realizing what they really needed, which was for someone to come along and flip them over so they could scurry off again.

Why her mother actually liked the Sundry Arms and preferred such men to their craftier, more self-sufficient counterparts across the street was something Sarah didn't like to think about too deeply. One reason, she suspected, had to do with the fact that one of the many things the Sundry Arms men arrived without were the younger women who'd wrecked their marriages, whereas Sundry Gardens men were alone only until their secretaries found someone to sublet their apartments in Chelsea. At any rate, her mother seemed to consider it her duty to cheer up her new neighbors, to help them understand that their stay, though brief, needn't be joyless. Most of them seemed grateful for her efforts on their behalf. When they left—a month, two months, six months later—it was Sarah's mother and not their more immediate neighbors to whom they bequeathed what wouldn't fit into those same suitcases: the half-empty bottle of Drambuie, the like-new Teflon-coated frying pan, the apartment-sized stereo unit. Thanks to their generosity, she was constantly upgrading her possessions, and over the years she'd learned the wisdom of helping these sad, beleaguered men outfit themselves in the first place, knowing that one day soon whatever they purchased would be hers, so why not go top of the line?

Harold liked Sarah's mother, too, and his fondness was also profitable. There was a lot of breakage at the Sundry Arms, whose residents seemed to grasp immediately that they'd found a port in a storm. They also imagined that port to be temporary, that they'd be staying only until their wives came to their senses. When they discovered how wrong they were, furnishings tended to go airborne. Whenever a tenant moved out and Harold had to replace a lamp or chair, he put the new one in Sarah's mother's apartment and rotated her used one into the newly vacant space. "Wow," the new arrivals said, when she showed them her apartment, "yours is nice." They didn't quite know what to make of it; she could tell. The layout was identical to their own, as was much of the furniture, but she had been given a special dispensation from Harold to replace the heavy, dark drapes with fancy blinds and the Motel 6 artwork with her own colorful designs. Harold himself couldn't get over how nice her place looked. "These men are all deeply and easily confused by sleight of hand," her mother explained.

Summers, she insisted that Sarah take the bedroom. "Most of the time I fall asleep in front of the TV anyway," she reasoned, which was true enough, even if it wasn't the whole story. Sometimes Sarah woke to conversation that wasn't on the television and realized that what had awakened her was someone knocking. Once she thought she recognized the male voice in the front room as belonging to Harold, but she couldn't be sure, and other times the voices were definitely not his. These half-overheard conversations were always short, and when Sarah heard the front door open and shut again, she felt certain that she was now alone in the apartment. Sometimes, an hour or two later, she'd hear her mother return. One morning she'd awakened at the usual time and found the sofa empty, only to discover her mother snoring there when she emerged from the shower. Another day, up early for a babysitting job, she'd dressed in the dark and moved quietly around her mother's sleeping form, slipping out the front door, closing it quietly behind her, then kicking over the two martini glasses somebody had thoughtfully returned, leaving them on the step.

"How much does your father know about this place?" it occurred to her mother to ask one day. The answer, in fact, was very little. (They were still separated then, and it would be years before her mother got around to filing for divorce.) "That Sundry place?" he asked each September. "She's still living there?" He was jumping, just as her mother knew he would, to precisely the wrong conclusion. If she still had the same furnished one-bedroom apartment, then she must still be having a tough go of it. Sarah never let on that she spent far more every month on her studio than she did on her apartment. She'd changed studios three times, actually, each time to a larger, better lighted space. And of course her father had no idea about the men—all and Sundry—or the martini glasses, or the large bottle of Beefeater gin she replaced weekly, or that she always bought the largest jar of green olives available at the super-market, or that she was forever running out of toothpicks.

As she was about most things, Sarah was of two minds about such behavior. Sometimes she was embarrassed by her mother's freewheeling promiscuity, but was it any more discomforting than her father's celibacy? Since his wife's departure, he hadn't been out on a single date. Once, when she told him she wouldn't mind if he had a woman friend, he'd just looked at her funny and said he was still married to her mother. That would've been romantic had it not been totally devoid of affection, had Sarah not known that while her father looked forward to the day when economic reality would force her mother to return, he didn't really miss her. "Being married to your father was a lot like being a nun," her mother had observed more than once, and Sarah suspected that even if he'd known about the men at the Sundry Arms, it wouldn't have inspired sexual jealousy. No, he wanted his wife back out of I-told-you-so spite.

Her father didn't date or drink, but there was *something*. Sometimes, when she returned home after spending the evening with Lou at Ikey's, she'd find him asleep in his chair, the phonograph needle bumping the label of one of his jazz records, a strange, sweet smell in the air. Or she'd wake up in the morning and there'd be a stale version of that same cloying aroma lingering in the house. She was about to ask her father about it when she remembered the very first time she'd smelled it in the parking lot one Friday night outside Angelo's Pizza. There a skinny, shabbily dressed Negro was idling near the entrance, and he'd nodded familiarly at her father. "Got what you be needin', brother, whenever you be needin' it," the man said, seemingly to no one in particular. A group of people was coming out of the restaurant as they were going in, and Sarah's first thought was that he'd been addressing one of them, but once inside, the longer she thought about it, the more certain she was that he'd been talking to her father, a conclusion reinforced by the fact that he'd taken no notice whatsoever of the man. Her father always went out of his way with Thomaston's Negroes, starting up conversations whether the occasion warranted it or, to judge from their startled reactions, not. Yet that evening he'd ignored the skinny black man entirely, and they'd passed close enough for her to catch a whiff of the sickening sweet odor that clung to his clothes. Was it possible that such a man had something her father wanted, or needed, as he'd claimed? If so, Sarah wasn't sure she wanted to know what it was. "Promise me," her mother had told her that first summer Sarah stayed at the Sundry Arms, "that if you ever see a syringe lying around the house, you'll tell me." Frightened by the prospect of stepping on a needle, Sarah promised she would, but she never saw a syringe "lying around" and couldn't find one in the medicine cabinet either, though she routinely looked to make sure. But what would she do if she found one? Keeping her mother's secrets meant she was honor bound to keep her father's, too, didn't it? Assuming he had any?

As DIFFERENT as her parents were, Sarah's strategy for living with them was the same: keep busy, fill the days. In Thomaston, she joined as many after-school clubs as would have her and volunteered at the library and the Shady Rest Nursing Home, explaining to her father that such activities looked good on college applications. And now, of course, there was Ikey Lubin's, her second home. On Long Island's South Shore, filling the days was easier. The summer people for whom she'd babysat since she was twelve started arriving around Memorial Day, and the first thing many of them did was call Sarah's mother in the hopes of getting in the front of the queue for her daughter's services. "Really? Not until mid-June?" they said, their voices rich with panic. The idea that they'd have to look after their own children until then, every hour of the livelong day, was really too much to bear. "You're here!" they'd exclaim when she finally arrived. "Can you come Tuesday? No? Wednesday, then? Don't tell me Gwen Spencer got to you before me? What did that woman do, meet your train?"

No joke. Sometimes, desperate mothers did precisely that. Having learned the date of her arrival, they'd pretend to be at the station to meet their husbands. "Sarah!" they exclaimed. "I'm so glad I ran into you. Are you free Saturday night? Can we book you Saturdays for the whole summer?" Sarah could've charged far more than she did—her mother urged her to—but she preferred instead to be selective, working only for people she liked and whose children weren't monsters.

Just once, the summer between her sophomore and junior years, was she tempted by an offer for more work at greater pay.

One of the mothers, aware that Sarah was a budding artist, had offered her the large apartment over their garage, which she could use as a studio when she wasn't looking after the children. It was tempting, because this particular family was her favorite, and the two girls adored her. The husband was young and good-looking, a former college athlete who worked for an ad agency in the city. Monday through Thursday he commuted on the LIRR, which meant that his wife and daughters were alone in the overly large house. She liked how he'd sometimes sneak up behind his wife in the kitchen when he thought Sarah and his daughters were off somewhere, put her in a big bear hug and kiss the back of her neck while she squealed and frantically pedaled her feet in the air as if she were on an invisible bicycle. The round table in the large kitchen had five chairs, which meant that Sarah would fit in quite naturally and wouldn't crowd them at all, even when the husband was there on his three-day weekends.

It presented a stark contrast to her mother's apartment at the Sundry Arms, where the two of them had to eat sitting on barstools at what was euphemistically called the breakfast nook. "*Please*," the little girls begged, tugging on Sarah's fingers. "*Please* come live with us." "Now, girls," their mother chided, "that's something Sarah has to decide with *her* mom." But Sarah could tell she herself was almost as excited as her daughters, and later, when she drove Sarah back to the Sundry Arms, she'd sweetened the pot, assuring her that of course she could have Sundays off. This was the day Sarah and her mother always spent together, and she didn't want to come between them. In fact, maybe Sarah could take every other weekend, Saturday and Sunday both.

Should she mention the offer? Her instinct was no. She didn't want to hurt her mother's feelings. But then, she thought, what harm would it do? She wouldn't have to make it sound like something she was interested in, but rather something wanted *of* her. Then she could gauge her mother's reaction. Who knew? It was possible her mother would see it as mutually beneficial.

431

They *were* squeezed tight at the Sundry Arms, and Sarah knew her presence did cramp her mother's style, manwise. Also, an artist herself, she'd certainly understand how nice it would be for Sarah to have space to work, a room with good light, where she wouldn't constantly be having to put her brushes and paints away so they could have space to eat. So maybe.

Deep down, though, she knew better. Her mother harbored ambivalent feelings about most of the families Sarah sat for, admitting they were pleasant enough and certainly had nice houses but always managing to find something amiss. She wouldn't let Sarah work for people she hadn't met. She interviewed them in their own homes, then voiced her suspicions about them after they returned to the Sundry Arms. The bigger the house, the more lavish its grounds and well mannered its owners, the more convinced she'd be that something had to be wrong. If you looked hard enough, you'd find it, and usually her mother didn't even have to look all that hard. "I don't envy *that* woman," she'd remark after being introduced to a new family. "Did you notice that the husband kept trying to look down my blouse?"

"Maybe you should've worn a bra," Sarah would say, a suggestion her mother was sure to ignore.

"I give that marriage two years, max. I like what they did with the kitchen, though. Someday before I die I want a big kitchen with an island."

At any rate, when Sarah finally did mention the offer, her mother's crestfallen expression caused her to lie and say she'd already told the woman no. "Who does she think she is?" her mother said, and Sarah felt guilty for weeks, mostly because she realized, after turning it down, how much she'd been looking forward to a seat at that table, to being part of that family. She had no way of knowing that by the end of the summer the couple's marriage would be in ruins, their summerhouse for sale. The two little girls had cried and cried when informed they'd be heading back to the city early and wouldn't be seeing Sarah anymore. According to the mother, they'd been even more inconsolable over that than the fact that their father wouldn't be living with them.

"You didn't see that coming?" Sarah's mother said when she heard the news.

What she saw, a week later, was the husband coming out of Sundry Gardens. He looked just the same, which for some reason had surprised her. Could a man betray his wife and children and still look the same? Wouldn't there be visual evidence of his faithlessness? She knew that was silly, but still. And there'd been a woman with him. Pretty, though no prettier than the wife he used to sneak up behind in the kitchen. Sarah wondered if he did the same thing with this new woman, and whether she would ever suspect what was going on behind *her* back. There'd also been a little girl with them, younger than either of the man's daughters. The adults had each taken her by the hand and were swinging her between them as they made their way to the parking lot. When the husband saw Sarah across the street, he smiled and waved, but she pretended not to see and then not to hear when he called her name. She knew what he wanted of her, and she would *not* babysit for him.

Lies, Sarah reluctantly concluded, were simply part of how adults operated. Everybody had secrets, it seemed, and to keep them people lied. That knowledge didn't trouble her terribly except when she ran across someone like that husband, who was particularly good at it. She didn't consider herself gullible, but of course gullible people never did, and what if she was wrong? Probably best to play it safe and avoid deceitful people. One of the things she loved best about her boyfriend was that, like his father, Lou seemed incapable of deceit. But she'd also begun to realize there was more than one way to lie. Some people lied to each other but also, bizarrely, to themselves. Sometimes they had to in order to lie to others. Weren't her own parents like that? The official reason she lived with her mother during the summer was that she could make far more money babysitting on Long Island than she could in Thomaston. Her father reminded her of this each time he put her on the train. He would miss her terribly, he said, but she'd make good money and her college fund would grow, just like it had last summer. And, he went on, a girl needed time with her mother. Even though all of this was true, it was still mostly a lie. Her father wouldn't miss her, at least not as much as she missed him. It wouldn't take him weeks to get used to her absence. He wouldn't spend hours imagining what was going on at the Sundry Arms. When he took her to the station in June, she could tell by how he shifted his weight from one foot to the other and kept eyeing the platform clock how anxious he was to see her off. By the time the train pulled out of the station he'd be speeding back to Thomaston, where a fresh ream of typing paper awaited him. This was the *real* reason she was going—so her father could work on his book, uninterrupted.

At the end of the summer the same thing would happen in reverse. Under the high, vaulted ceiling of Grand Central, she'd listen to the same half-truths she'd heard on the platform of the tiny station in Fulton. "Oh, sweetie," her mother would lament, "summer's too short. You just *got* here. You know why I had to leave your father, don't you? You know I wasn't leaving *you*. You mean more to me than my own life. Tell me you believe that, sweetie, because I couldn't bear it if you didn't. And you know that if things ever get too awful with your dad, you can come live with me, right? You wouldn't even have to call. You're old enough now. You can just get on the train and call me when you get to the city. And you know how to get out to the country. . . ."

Sarah knew her mother believed everything she said when she said it, but she also knew she could make such promises because it was safe to do so. Whatever happened in Thomaston, no matter how terrible her longing for her mother was during the long winter months, Sarah would never abandon her father, never show up on her doorstep expecting to stay. Her mother was what happened during the summer when her father was writing his book. Her father was what happened during the school year when her mother was enjoying her independence. That was what her parents had negotiated. Any revisions would also be negotiated between them, and she'd merely be informed of their decision.

Still, she knew that parting was harder on her mother, who, unlike her father, stayed with her until the last possible moment, sometimes actually boarding the train with her, making sure she was settled in with her luggage safely stowed on the racks above. Once she miscalculated and the door hissed shut in front of her, and she'd had to stay on the train all the way to Fordham. Sarah suspected—no, she knew—that the apartment would feel empty when she returned, that for weeks she'd be dogged by an emotion she didn't want to admit was guilt. Maybe that feeling never entirely went away. But neither was it strong enough for her to consider returning to her marriage, her husband, to life in Thomaston, New York. Gradually her guilt would abate, and she'd convince herself of the wisdom of keeping things as they were, since there was no help for it. She did love the freedom her apartment represented, and it wasn't big enough for two, at least not all year. And what her mother said about Sarah being more important to her than her own life simply wasn't true, or not true enough to change things. That was the terrible secret her mother held deep in her heart, the one she hoped her daughter didn't suspect. And it was different only in degree from the secret her father harbored—that once his fingers started flying over the keys, his life was full and sufficient.

Maybe everyone was like that. Maybe lies were necessary to survival. When she was younger, such possibilities had been painful to contemplate. But by the summer before her senior year, Sarah had grown used to them. She'd long ago forgiven her parents for their secrets, as well as for the half-truths they first told to themselves and then to her. Of course by that summer she had a secret of her own.

435

*

THE REALIZATION that she had one came to Sarah gradually. She suspected it when she left Thomaston in June. By August, she was sure. But did he really qualify as a secret? How could he? She'd only met him once, and briefly, at Ikey Lubin's. He wasn't what you'd call remarkably handsome, nor did he seem exceptionally bright or charismatic. In fact, she was at a loss to explain how he'd managed to impress her, unless it was because of Lou, who'd prepared her for someone truly extraordinary. Maybe she'd heard so many of her boyfriend's stories about Bobby Marconi's exploits that by the time she actually met him it was no longer possible to take him at face value. That was the only explanation she could come up with.

Thinking that he might feel like less of a secret if she spoke his name out loud, she brought him up, ever so casually, shortly after she arrived at her mother's. "It's like he's one person," she said, trying to put her vague sense of the boy into words, "but deep down he's trying to be another."

"Careful," her mother cautioned. "He sounds like your father."

"Five-yard penalty," Sarah told her.

Her mother was an avid pro-football fan and the year before had dated a Sundry Arms tenant named Frank, who'd claimed to play for the New York Giants. Well, not exactly *play*. He said he was on something called the taxi squad, the function of which, he stressed, was *not* to drive players to the game. He described being on the squad as a kind of limbo where you might get the call to suit up on any given Sunday, though probably not. Sarah had wondered if her mother might be getting serious about him, but then he'd disappeared, as Sundry Arms men always did, and her mother explained that no, they'd just had some laughs. Now all that remained of Frank were the football metaphors she and her mother used to establish and enforce boundaries. Her mother threw flags when Sarah was too inquisitive about the

436

exact nature of her relationships with various men, whereas she whistled her mother's disparaging remarks about her father. She let her mother skate when she offered general remarks like "Never trust a man who lives in his head" or "Don't, whatever you do, marry out of pity." More than likely these *were* oblique allusions to her father, but not necessarily. However, direct references—"that pencil dick"—drew flags every time. It was a game, of course, but also a means of dealing with important things without making them Important Things. At one level it was an invitation to disclosure, to greater intimacy, but it also contained built-in checks and balances that could be invoked when necessary. Sarah's mother seemed to want, perhaps even need, to tell her daughter about her Sundry Arms boyfriends, though her partial confessions were often more confusing than illuminating. She wanted her to understand that at long last she was having a little fun, which life owed you, right? And when the time came, she hoped Sarah would have a rich, rewarding sex life. "You're going to like sex *a lot*," she said more than once, though she wouldn't say precisely what she'd like about it. The joys of sex aside, the men actually in her mother's life mostly offered a large and varied list of male character traits to identify early and then avoid. For this reason she hoped that when Sarah was her age, she wouldn't still be "playing the field," though of course she wasn't advocating marriage either, far from it. More like a life partner, the sort of person you'd be *tempted* to marry. But *anything*, and she did mean *anything*, was preferable to being married to an arrogant, egomaniacal snob. A flag on that one— "Fifteen yards! Unnecessary roughness!"

Sarah thought she understood her mother's need to both surrender and withhold information. She felt the same conflicting impulses herself, though their circumstances were different. What her mother needed to share was experience, her long suit. If she could tell her daughter what she'd learned about men, maybe Sarah might be spared some heartache. Sarah's long suit —as she knew better than anyone—was her lack of experience.

She needed to talk about a boy she'd only just met and knew nothing about, beyond what her boyfriend had told her. But that wasn't all. She would also have liked to discuss Lou and what wasn't happening between them, about how his respect for her seemed to preclude much in the way of passion before marriage. In fact she would've liked to talk about boys in general, and what sort her mother imagined her falling in love with. She'd gotten explicit advice from her father, who claimed to know exactly the kind of boy who would make her happy. He'd explained more than once how things would go. She'd meet her future husband at Columbia, probably during her junior year. He'd most likely be a graduate student, probably in English. They'd wait for her to finish her degree, then marry and live for a year in graduate student housing before getting a small apartment in Park Slope, which was safe and nice and more affordable than Manhattan. Sarah's husband would be ambitious, a young man with aspirations that were alien to Thomaston. Sure, it was hard for her to understand all this now, but in the end *she'd be glad she waited.* That was the point her father wanted to stress.

Sarah saw flaws in this blueprint, though she never told him so. First, it shortchanged boys like Lou Lynch and Bobby Marconi, and maybe even places like Thomaston, New York. After all, it wasn't just people in big cities who had big dreams. Wasn't her father himself a perfect example? Though he considered himself an urbanite, he'd grown up, as her mother had delighted in reminding him back when they were still living as husband and wife, on Staten Fucking Island. The other problem was that he seemed to be confusing her life with his own. That is, the boy/man he envisioned her marrying was a better companion for him than for her. She'd made the mistake, last summer, of sharing her father's advice with her mother, who immediately launched into one of her riffs.

As an English major, she predicted, Sarah's future husband would be not only a brilliant scholar, but also that rarer breed, a genuine arbiter of taste, which would manifest itself primarily in an unbounded appreciation of her father's work. He might even make his reputation by writing about her father's novel, which by then would have been published to glowing reviews and perhaps a prize, but which Sarah's future husband thought deserved an even wider audience. Of course a man of such literary discernment would have a half-completed novel in his own desk drawer, and with trepidation he would eventually show this to her father, who would offer the kind of knowing criticism that can only come from a practitioner. Such advice would be difficult to implement because it would go straight to the heart of the matter, but in the fullness of time her husband's book would be completely revised, and Sarah's father would recommend it to his editor. This would lead the younger man to the most difficult decision of his life—whether to dedicate the book to his loving wife, the painter Sarah Berg (who'd of course kept her maiden name), or to his wife's father, without whom, etc., etc. As her mother riffed, Sarah had called penalty flag after penalty, but she was having too much fun to quit, and Sarah secretly had to admit that her father's scenario for her future probably wasn't so very different from her mother's satire of it.

The problem was that her mother had little to offer beyond parody. She was both specific and thorough when advising her daughter about what to avoid in men, but seemingly uninterested in the subject of what she *should* be looking for. Her commandments all took the form of "Thou Shalt Not." Her own vision of her daughter's future was so vague as to appear thoughtless. She wouldn't rule out Thomaston as a source for a future husband, but she conceded it was possible her father might be right—"Even a blind sow finds an acorn now and again." Five-yard penalty—that she'd meet someone in college. Wasn't it possible she'd already met him in Lou Lynch? Her mother had left Thomaston long before Sarah started dating, but she knew the Lynch family and thought they were nice enough. She had considered it odd that people didn't take more note of Mrs. Lynch, who was so smart and funny, but then she laughed at herself for saying something so patently ridiculous. Smart and funny might be fine qualities in unattractive men, but they were the final nails in the coffin of any woman who didn't happen to be drop-dead beautiful as well. And though there was no denying he was a genial fellow, she hadn't been quite so fond of Big Lou. She'd just never taken to big, lumbering men who had to be taught how to work the cheese dip. Out of loyalty, Sarah made an exception to her rule of penalizing only insults to her father, to which her mother replied, "You're right, that wasn't very nice, but he *is* a bit of a doofus, isn't he?" And was promptly awarded another hefty one.

To convince her mother that she was wrong to think poorly of her boyfriend's father, Sarah related the story Lou had told her early on about how, when he was little, some neighborhood toughs had taken him to an abandoned railroad trestle, locked him in a trunk and pretended to saw him in half, a cruel act which had precipitated the first of the terrible spells that had plagued his childhood. Actually, her mother had a vague recollection of the incident. The boy's disappearance had precipitated a panic, everyone in town fearing that he'd been taken by some sick sexual predator. Sarah explained how it had been the middle of the night before Lou came out of his trance. Sluggish and confused, he'd known enough to follow the stream back the way they'd come, and there, waiting on the footbridge to take him home, was Big Lou. It was as if his father'd had some sixth sense and known right where to wait.

Her mother had waited patiently for Sarah to finish, then said, "Sweetie, think about it. That's what a dog would do. With all of that going on, what kind of man goes out and stands in the middle of a footbridge for hours just waiting for something good to happen?"

"But he was right," Sarah insisted, though her mother's reaction did catch her off guard. Having heard the story from Lucy, she'd accepted not just his facts but also his conclusions. "He knew where to wait."

"Sweetie, think," her mother replied. "What was he *doing* on that bridge? You're saying he was there because he *knew* something, had some powerful intuition. But doesn't the opposite make more sense? That he was there because he had no idea what to do? Instead of joining the search and helping his wife and the police, he left her alone to cope."

"That's not what Lou thinks."

"Well, boys love their fathers."

Her mother remembered the Marconis, too. Whispers, mostly. Something wrong with the woman, wasn't there? A little too much left rudder? (That phrase borrowed from another Sundry Arms man who'd served in the navy.) Disappeared for a while and then was magically back home again, put under some sort of house arrest for her own good? Talk about the husband, too, though she couldn't recall what. She *did* remember the dark birthmark on his forehead, though, and the way he had of leaning toward you, too close, and cocking his head, like you'd just said something that made him want to punch you. Or, if you were a woman, maybe do something else. The kind of man who made you wonder what the something else would be like. Anyway, a strange couple, no doubt about that. What sort of kid would be the product of such a union? A pup bred from a rottweiler and a lapdog. At best a deeply conflicted human being, but who knew? Maybe the boy would resolve the conflict and be all right. At worst a volatile, unstable compound, in which case the boy would have to be put down.

"What an awful thing to say!" Sarah blurted, feeling unexpected tears well up.

"I'm just thinking out loud, sweetie," her mother said. "Don't pay any attention."

"But you never even met him," Sarah said.

"If you don't want to know what I think, don't ask."

That was the problem with her. What Sarah wanted was to know what her mother thought *after* she'd given it some thought. Just once, instead of ranting, it would be nice for her to *reflect* on something and maybe respond the next day. That would suggest that the subject Sarah had introduced actually merited serious deliberation. She realized, of course, that this ran contrary to her mother's nature.

"Besides," she reminded Sarah, "you've only met the boy once yourself, so there's no reason for you to get all red faced."

"I'm *not* all red faced," Sarah insisted, though she could feel herself glowing with righteous indignation.

Later that night her mother came into her room and sat on the edge of the bed. "Are you unhappy with Lou?" she asked, and Sarah quickly answered no, though she did sometimes wonder if maybe she was in love with the whole Lynch family, who were a package somehow greater than the sum of its parts, and she thought again of that South Shore family, the fifth chair at their round table that she'd so hoped might be hers. She was aware that her boyfriend, like his father, had a reputation for being a bit of a doofus, but people who believed this didn't know him like Sarah did. Still, she wasn't sure exactly what it meant for one boy to worship another as Lou did Bobby Marconi. Lou was prone to it, of course. He worshipped his father and, she knew, worshipped her, which was nice. Better than nice. If he thought better of people than perhaps they deserved and then proceeded to love them accordingly, didn't she benefit as much as anyone? Even if her mother was right—and Sarah was by no means conceding the point—that Big Lou Lynch wasn't entirely worthy of his son's unquestioning adoration, so what? Didn't that make it like God's grace? Something you might not be worthy of, but would be a fool to reject?

At some point, having failed to explain to her mother (or herself) precisely what was troubling her, it dawned on Sarah that perhaps she could *draw* her way out of this maze of conflicting thoughts and feelings. Why hadn't this solution occurred to her sooner? For years now she'd been drawing her world and in the process discovering her deepest, truest feelings. Until she'd drawn Ikey Lubin's, for instance, she hadn't known that the Lynch corner market represented a yearning—for refuge, a small, safe place in the wider, hostile world. Since then she'd drawn all the Lynches, even Dec, and found in their portraits a deep need for, what? Stability? Belonging? Love? She knew her parents both cared deeply for her, yes, loved her, but they loved her separately, as discrete beings. She'd come to think of their affection for her as Berg Love, something very different from Lynch Love, which was expanded exponentially by the fact that its source was a family. Was it Lynch Love, she wondered, that she most yearned for? In the highly unlikely event that Bobby Marconi might one day fall in love with her, what *sort* of love would it be? From what she knew of his family, it certainly wouldn't be Lynch Love. The boy seemed alone in the world. In her drawing of Ikey's, she'd pictured him outside, about to enter. But what if he never did? Maybe she already knew he wouldn't. Maybe her subconscious had told her right where to put him. Which, if true, might mean he'd never be able to offer what she craved most.

But what if she had it all wrong and there was no such thing as Lynch Love? What if, in the end, Lou brought only himself? What if the context she'd identified was an illusion conjured out of need? What if Ikey Lubin's was just a store, not a family, and the Lynches didn't add up to more than the sum of their parts? Lou himself had admitted they weren't a perfect family, that his mother had been furious when Big Lou bought Ikey's, that in fact Tessa and her husband seldom saw things the same way. But to Sarah the salient fact was that they'd stayed together and worked out their disagreements. Mrs. Lynch might get angry with her husband, but she didn't walk out on him and their son. Was that because she loved the man, or because she wasn't, unlike Sarah's mother, attractive enough to alter the flight path of small aircraft by sunbathing in the nude? It seemed an important question, yet Sarah had to admit she didn't know the answer.

Drawing Bobby might be dangerous. What if she learned

something she preferred not to know? It could happen. It did happen. Every time she drew her father he came out looking like Ichabod Crane. Several times during the course of the summer she'd drawn her mother, a couple times at her suggestion. One sketch had featured her modeling a new two-piece bathing suit, and it buoyed her mother's spirits when Sarah showed it to her. "Not bad for an older broad," she said. "I was right to buy that suit, wasn't I?" But another time Sarah had caught her unawares, early in the morning before she was completely awake. She'd been seated at the breakfast nook in her bathrobe, in front of a steaming cup of coffee, and in her right hand she held a cigarette, the long ash of which had begun to tip. That was the detail Sarah had been most proud of because it suggested how long her mother had sat there, staring off into space. In another second, the viewer couldn't help thinking, the ash would fall. Her mother had taken one look at the drawing, another at Sarah, then gone into the bathroom and shut the door. Sarah expected the shower to come on, but it didn't, and after a few minutes she inquired outside the door if everything was all right. "What you don't understand," came her mother's voice, "is that one day you'll *be* that woman."

In the end, Sarah decided to compromise. She'd draw Bobby Marconi, but not until the end of the summer, by which time maybe it wouldn't be so important. After all, she knew from experience that moving down to the South Shore was never a clean, smooth emotional transition. For weeks Thomaston's insular concerns continued to occupy her waking thoughts, her nightly dreams. Sometimes, even in early July, as she moved from one babysitting job to the next, from a summerhouse to the beach and back again, she was still imagining the Lynches' comings and goings at Ikey's and her father's daily routine without her. But then gradually the world would turn on its fulcrum, and even though she still missed her father and the Lynches, her South Shore life would assume its rightful if temporary primacy and feel less like a seasonal aberration. She was always grateful when that happened, when her other life lost some of its power to haunt. It felt like setting down a big suitcase crammed with all the things you loved. You didn't love them any less, but it was nice not to have to lug them around. And since this was the way of things, why not let nature work in her favor? By August the strong impression Bobby Marconi had made on her might fade. Maybe by then she wouldn't even want to draw him. Maybe, if she let it, the spell would break itself.

LABOR DAY

"Lou's going to be one happy boy when he gets a look at you in September," her mother remarked one morning in early August. Sarah had just stepped out of the shower and was toweling off, unaware that her mother, brushing her teeth at the sink, had been watching her.

"He's not going to see me like this," Sarah assured her.

"He won't have to. Trust me."

When her mother was gone, she studied herself in the mirror with a mix of pleasure and apprehension. Never before that summer had she spent so much time in front of the mirror. It wasn't vanity that drew her so much as wonder. Though well ahead of girls her age in emotional and intellectual maturity, she'd lagged cruelly behind them physically. She got her period late, and her figure remained boyish right through her junior year. Her mother had often reminded her that she, too, had been a late bloomer, but she'd always assumed she was just trying to make her feel better. She still felt certain she'd never have the same generous hips and breasts, though there was no longer any doubt that her mother had been right. The girl who greeted her in the mirror each morning seemed frighteningly new. What if her boyfriend preferred the skinny girl he'd kissed goodbye in June? And there was also the ridiculous notion she couldn't seem to shake, that her belated physical maturity might somehow be related to Bobby Marconi's unexpected appearance. She knew it was beyond crazy. Her father had made a game of the major logical fallacies and drilled her on them back in junior high, so she knew that just because B follows A, it doesn't mean that A

446

caused B. But it *felt* as if her body had been waiting for a reason to do what other girls' bodies had done years before.

Was it because she was so preoccupied with the girl in the mirror that Sarah didn't fully register the striking changes in her mother? She'd noticed on arriving in June that she'd lost weight. "I needed to," she explained, when Sarah remarked on it. But over the summer she lost even more, and her facial features began to look drawn. When she knew she was being watched or photographed, she smiled broadly, sometimes even mugged, but to Sarah it felt wrong, as if her mother were trying to remember what her smile had been like so she could imitate it. When the camera caught her off guard, she looked like the woman Sarah had sketched in her bathrobe, not so much unhappy as anxious, like someone waiting for the doctor to call with test results. Also, she didn't appear to be sleeping well. Previous summers, once her mother stretched out on the sofa with a novel or a movie on TV, she usually zonked out shortly afterward. Sarah would find her the next morning with the book she'd been reading still in her hand, or the television snowy. This year Sarah would often awake at night to the sound of pacing in the front room. And had she really thought about it, there were fewer late-night knocks on the door. Were these things related? This question she would ask herself only later, by which time the answer was obvious.

As ALWAYS, Labor Day weekend ended their summer. To celebrate the renewed intimacy they'd spent these months nurturing, they usually took the train into New York late on Friday afternoon and splurged on a hotel room, a fancy dinner and, if the summer had been especially good, a Broadway show. The city was typically empty, so there were lots of deals to be found. Besides, this made Sarah's departure for upstate on Sunday that much easier. So this year Sarah was surprised by her mother's suggesting they stay on the South Shore. Had she lost a client? She hadn't seemed any more strapped for cash than usual, but maybe something had happened in the last few days or hours that she didn't want Sarah fretting about. Then, for dinner on Saturday, she chose Nick and Charlie's, a nearby waterfront restaurant she didn't even like, claiming it was overpriced and full of tourists who didn't know any better and elderly diners who liked food they didn't have to chew. When Sarah reminded her of this, she just shrugged and said maybe she was getting old herself. That particular comment made Sarah wonder if she was still upset about that sketch of her in her bathrobe.

When Sarah asked if they were going to dress up, as they liked to on their last night together, her mother said hell yes, and the prospect seemed to cheer her up a little, though she didn't show as much skin as she normally did on this occasion. Looking Sarah over she announced that since her daughter looked every bit of eighteen, legal drinking age, they'd put it to the test by ordering her a cocktail. Out in the parking lot, as they backed out, Sarah noticed Harold Sundry leaving his apartment in a jacket and tie. "Did someone die, do you think?" she asked her mother, nodding at him. She'd never seen Harold dressed up before, and unless she was mistaken, he was wearing a special shoe that made his rolling limp less pronounced. At any rate, it seemed he was actually departing the premises, so something had to be up.

At the restaurant Sarah's misgivings grew. There was nothing her mother loved more than a grand entrance—men's heads turning when she passed, their wives noticing, too—but today she seemed uninterested, which was just as well, Sarah thought, because, so far as she could tell, the only heads that turned when they crossed the dining room were appraising her. The two of them were escorted to a table on the deck that had a reserved sign on it, though the hostess deftly whisked it away. "That was lucky," Sarah remarked, imagining that whoever had booked the best table in the restaurant must have canceled at the last moment. Her mother smiled vaguely, as if puzzled by her logic, and when she ordered herself a martini and her daughter a rum and Coke the waitress didn't even give Sarah a second glance. A young couple was seated at an adjacent table, and Sarah's mother, taking a camera from her purse, asked the man if he minded taking a picture of them. This was also a tradition. Her mother kept all their last nights in a scrapbook.

While they waited for their drinks, her mother surveyed the deck rather impatiently, and Sarah once again was visited by the vague sense she'd had off and on all summer, that her mother was waiting for something, a knock on the door, the telephone to ring, something. When the drinks came, she drained half of her martini as if she'd been crawling all day through the desert and just arrived at a watering hole she'd feared was a mirage. It seemed to do the trick, though, because she took a deep breath, regarded Sarah directly and said, "Well, sweetie, I don't know how to do this, so I guess I'll just say it." Unfortunately, Sarah didn't hear what came next because just then she saw Harold Sundry talking to the hostess, who was pointing, she could've sworn, toward their table. "Sarah?" her mother said. "Did you hear me?"

"Yes," Sarah lied, trying to scroll back.

"Well, I wish you'd say something."

And now Harold was rolling toward them, sweating profusely in his dark wool, hopelessly out-of-season sport coat, his shirt collar buttoned so tight that his face was beet red.

"*There* you are," her mother said.

"Sorry," Harold said. "I had to stop for gas."

"Well, sit down. This isn't going well."

"I warned you," Harold said, looking right at Sarah, who, already confused, felt a strong impulse to deny that he'd issued her any warnings whatsoever. They'd barely spoken half a dozen words all summer. *Marry?* Had her mother used that word?

"It's okay, honey," Harold said, speaking to her for real this time. "I'm not such a bad fella once you get to know me."

For the rest of her life Sarah would be thankful she didn't say what was on the tip of her tongue, that she already had a boyfriend, that she was too young to marry, that in any case her father wouldn't stand for anyone except a graduate student in English from Columbia University. She'd actually opened her mouth to say these things when the facts reconfigured themselves in her head. No, her mother wasn't angry with her for growing up and becoming a woman, nor had she arranged for her to marry Harold Sundry as a punishment. How could such a ridiculous notion have taken root even for a second? Was it because the truth was only slightly less bizarre? Sarah turned to her mother, but she refused to come into focus. There was a loud bang—a single shot to a snare drum—that seemed to originate inside her skull. Then nothing.

"WELL, *that's* an evening I won't soon forget," her mother said when they were safely back in the apartment. She touched Sarah's cheek with the back of her fingers. "You're still clammy. You should lie down."

"I'm okay now." She felt suddenly incapable of uttering anything that wasn't completely false. She felt yet another lie already forming on her lips when the phone rang.

"She's okay, Harold," her mother said. "Nothing's happened in the two minutes since we saw you last." Sarah recognized this tone of voice as the same one she'd used on her father. "I will. I will, Harold. Drink a beer and relax. Oh, one won't kill you. All right, go to a movie then. Do whatever. Go across the street and tell Elaine, see if she faints. I know you feel bad. Sarah does, too, and I feel worse than either of you, believe me. You're absolutely right about that, Harold. It *is* a crummy way to begin. No, she likes you fine. Plus you'll grow on her, just like you did on me. I didn't like you at all in the beginning, remember? Well, I didn't, but now I do. We'll talk tomorrow, okay? No, I haven't changed my mind. Don't forget what we talked about, what you said you were going to work on. Being needy, right. Now'd be a good time to start. No, breakfast isn't a great idea. Tomorrow's our last day together. I will, Harold. I promise. Just as soon as I get back from the city."

She hung up, came over and took her daughter gently by the chin. "Oh, sweetie, I hope you aren't going to come out of this with two black eyes."

That snare drum in her head, Sarah now understood, had been her forehead hitting the table. According to her mother, she'd been out only a few seconds, but when she'd awakened she was flat on her back staring up at a ring of faces, her mother's in the foreground, Harold Sundry's among the others, looking like he hoped she'd be able to pick him out of the lineup. Though bathed in perspiration, she otherwise felt fine and in fact was hungry and would've liked to have eaten something. But an ambulance had been called and her mother thought she should get checked out. Harold followed the ambulance in his Buick, and afterward they'd returned to the restaurant for her mother's car. "I'm famished," Sarah told them. "Can we order something?"

"No way I'm walking back in that restaurant," her mother said. "Ever." Back at the Sundry Arms, she ordered a pizza. "Was it really that much of a shock?"

"No," Sarah said. *Liar.* "I mean, sort of. You hate marriage. You're always making fun of people who get married. You say they're delusional."

Her mother made a pained face. "Oh, sweetie, that was just me talking. You know how I love to talk, right? Please tell me you don't believe all the dumb things I say."

There didn't seem to be a polite answer to that question, or even a way to know if it *was* a question. "So, you *want* to be married again?"

"I don't know," her mother admitted. "I had this revelation back in the spring, thinking about how great it was going to be, you coming for the summer, and suddenly I realized I really hadn't been myself since your brother died. I mean, if that hadn't happened, I'd probably still be with your father. It was losing

451

Rudy that made me so desperate, made me want to be a whole different person. Deep down I think I'm really more like the woman you remember, back when we were all together, than the person I am now. Losing your brother made me realize how tired I was of the person I'd become, but now I'm even more tired of this new person. Oh, don't cry, baby. Please don't."

It was the mention of her brother that had done it, of course. How many years had it been since anyone had mentioned his name? *He'd* been the one they couldn't do without, not and still be a family, and she'd tried for a long time to keep him alive, but with a stab of guilt she realized how long it had been since she'd drawn him. She hadn't even brought a picture of him along this summer.

"But *marriage*?" she said, still trying to make sense of it. "Couldn't you . . ."

"Oh, I'd be just as happy to live in sin," her mother admitted, "but Hal's dead set on getting hitched. That damned fool woman across the street's getting remarried, so now he's got to."

Okay, then. Harold Sundry (Hal, now) had entered the conversation. But how to phrase the obvious question: *Of all the men at the Sundry Arms you're marrying* him? "Do you love him?"

Her mother sighed. "I don't know, darlin'. I really don't. I've been trying to make up my mind all summer. He loves me, though. I'm sure of that much. And it's time I quit living like this, don't you think? You've been so sweet not to judge me, all those men dropping by, but I've been judging myself right along. Hal helped me realize that. I need something stable. I need to quit drinking so much, too, and he's promised to help me. Hal's an alcoholic himself, so he knows how to quit."

"What do I tell Daddy?"

"That's not your job, sweetie," she said. "I've been trying to telephone him all week."

"He disconnects the phone," Sarah reminded her. He also canceled the newspaper, refused to answer the door and stacked the unopened mail on the dining room table. No interruptions, none. That was the rule of summer, once the typing began.

"I know, I know," her mother said, rubbing her temples. "But who lives like that? I mean, what if something happened to you, and I had to reach him?"

These were rhetorical questions, Sarah knew, and so felt no obligation to provide answers.

"Maybe Hal and I can drive up in October. He wants to go look at the leaves in Vermont, so maybe we can kill two birds with one stone."

Sarah tried to imagine any part of this scenario actually happening: Harold abandoning the property an entire weekend, the two of them driving to Vermont and staying in some country inn, stopping in Thomaston to share their plans with her father. The last part simply defied imagination. There was no way her mother would ever allow him a good look at Harold Sundry with his big head and his special shoe. "October?" she said. "I can't say anything until then?"

Her mother sighed. "That's not fair, is it? Okay, then I'll just have to tell him over the phone. I'll call tomorrow night after you get back. He'll be expecting me to call then anyway, to make sure you got back safe."

Sarah shook her head. "No, it'll be better if I tell him."

"You really think so?" she said hopefully, and Sarah could tell this was how she wanted it. "Here's another idea! Tell him I died in a car wreck!"

The pizza arrived then, but Sarah found that her mother's failed attempt at humor had routed her appetite. The box looked like it contained the results of a head-on collision, the big lumps of Italian sausage now brain matter, the mushrooms various interior organs, the anchovies strips of flesh and skin. "I didn't realize how hungry I was," her mother said, digging in.

Suddenly energized, she explained how things would be. *Not that different*, she wanted to stress. Better, really. She'd be keeping her studio in town, she assured Sarah, as if this were weighing heavily on her mind. She conceded that Harold didn't fully understand what she did for a living and would've preferred that they partner in the Sundry Arms and share its myriad duties, but in the end he didn't want her to give up something she loved. He was proud that she'd been able to make a go of it all these years, and he could hire help at the Arms as he needed it, just like always. Of course, Sarah would still spend summers with them on the South Shore. There were always vacancies, and Harold promised to set aside the best apartment for the two of them every June, July and August.

And this year's changes, she went on, would be nothing compared with next year's, with Sarah graduating from high school and heading off to college. Okay, right this minute maybe Sarah felt like she was losing her mother to Harold Sundry, but it was more the other way around. If you really thought about it, it was her mother staring loss dead in the face. In no time Sarah would have a husband and family of her own, whereas she'd be alone in the world. It wasn't that she regretted the freedom she'd found here these last few years. She'd needed that after Pencil Dick. No, she'd had *all kinds* of fun and didn't regret *any* of it, but having fun wasn't the same as having a future. You couldn't count on fun to last, that was the thing. Sarah understood that you had to make plans, didn't she? And, if you weren't very good at making plans—and she allowed she wasn't—then you had to rely on someone else to do it for you. Harold saw the future clearly, and he made excellent plans.

Sarah tried hard to focus on what she was saying, but it all came down to words. Her mother was using them, as she so often did, to create a plausible narrative, a story she could live with and embellish, but Sarah had never trusted them. While they'd waited for the pizza to arrive, her mother had shed the nice clothes she'd worn to the restaurant, taken off her makeup and slipped into her robe. In so doing she'd become the very woman in the drawing, and as she talked, the words piling up and running together, her daughter realized she'd been working on this narrative all summer long, all those nights spent pacing in the front room. She'd probably been working on it the morning Sarah had sketched her, catching on paper her sudden loss of confidence, the erosion of her courage, her sheer exhaustion. No wonder she'd felt violated. How cruel that drawing must have seemed. That her mother was at this moment its living embodiment seemed a poor, shabby excuse for what she'd done, and Sarah felt a fissure in herself that she hadn't even known was there, but that was now widening further. She recalled, too, what her mother had told her that night about her one day becoming that woman herself, and she almost hoped this would come true, because she deserved it. How lonely her mother had been. How brave to keep up a strong front for so long. And how little Sarah had intuited of her fear of growing old and ending up alone.

Nor did the irony escape her. Wasn't this searing intimacy exactly what she'd been hoping for this summer? For so many summers? Hadn't she wanted her mother to tell her what she really thought and felt from the bottom of her heart? When she'd asked for advice about her own future, about whether her feelings for Lou were full and sufficient or somehow lacking, wasn't this sort of soul baring what she'd had in mind, her mother's hard-won acknowledgment that one thing was more important than another? Earlier that summer she'd brought up Bobby Marconi without really being able to articulate the question she wanted to ask, yet here her mother was answering it. Passion and independence, she seemed to be saying, were all fine and good, but ultimately not sustainable. In the end it came down to companionship, to friendship, to sacrifice, to compromise. Hadn't Sarah known this all along? Suddenly she understood the question she'd really been trying to ask all summer. Which was more important: to love or be loved?

"Anyway," her mother finally concluded. With very little help from Sarah, she'd reduced the pizza to a stack of thin edges in the middle of the greasy box, "if I'm wrong, I'm no worse off than I was, right? Please say yes, so I can go to sleep."

That night, as sometimes happened when she had too much to think about, Sarah fell immediately into a deep and dreamless sleep, awaking with a guilty start at first light, the events of the previous day both surreal and immediate. Her *mother* was *marrying* Harold *Sundry*? This ending made the whole summer seem implausible, as did the fact that by late afternoon she'd be back in Thomaston living her other life. Her stomach knotted at the thought. Outside her mother's bedroom window it was still gray, almost black. How long before the sun actually came up? They'd set the alarm for seven-thirty, still almost two hours away. She'd packed everything the night before, even her sketch pad. Her suitcases, portfolio and the bag containing gifts for her father and Lou and the other Lynches was sitting in the front room near the door. Sarah closed her eyes, feeling them spill over, and tried to imagine Ikey Lubin's, telling herself she'd be there soon, soothed by both the store and the Lynches, but the image refused to form. *Concentrate*, she told herself. You know it. You know everything about it. Where the register is and the meat counter, too, and the big coolers full of milk and beer along the back wall, though she was arguing with herself in words and could feel the panic rising in her chest until, in the next room, she heard her mother stir. Had she fallen asleep?

Rolling over, she saw a crease of light beneath the bedroom door. Was there a lamp on in the front room? Then a sound like the page of a book turning, except louder. And finally she knew what her mother was doing.

"These are wonderful!" she said when Sarah sat down beside her on the sofa she'd apparently not bothered to unfold that night. All of Sarah's recent drawings and watercolors lay spread out on the coffee table. The sheer volume would have been impressive enough; in just the last few weeks she'd doubled her entire output, and this no doubt contributed to her mother's stunned disbelief. But what she was really responding to, Sarah understood, was the quality. These most recent efforts repre-sented a quantum leap forward, every single one better, far better, than the very best ones from earlier in the summer. "My God, they're *all* wonderful." She was studying Sarah now, with an expression that was almost fearful, as if she suspected that her daughter had made a pact with the devil. "Weren't you going to show them to me?"

She'd meant to, of course, when they returned from dinner last night, or maybe this morning before they headed into the city, when there'd be less time for questions, for explanations. A miscalculation, she now saw. Maybe someone who didn't know any better wouldn't intuit the questions this new work raised, but her mother *did* know better, and she also knew there were reasons for such quantum leaps, even if the artist herself couldn't explain them. While Sarah could pretend not to understand what had happened, at the very least her mother would want to know why she'd been so secretive about work as good as this, when normally she was so open. "I don't understand," she said now, scrutinizing Sarah so closely that her cheeks began to burn with an emotion that seemed equal parts pride and embarrassment.

"I know," she whispered.

"Tell me," her mother said, taking her hand. "How did this happen?"

Her portfolio was leaning up against the coffee table, so Sarah unzipped the inner sleeve and took out the drawing of Bobby she'd finally done back in early August. Feeling guilty in advance, she'd allowed herself just half an hour for his portrait, though she hadn't needed even that long. It was as if the boy already existed on the blank page of her sketchbook and had been patiently waiting there for her pen to locate him. He'd appeared before her so quickly, so effortlessly, that she was almost as startled as she would've been to look up and find him standing there in the flesh. She'd immediately hidden the sketch away in the zippered compartment where she knew her mother wouldn't look, nor would she look at it herself. That was the promise she made and then broke, time and again, slipping it out whenever she had a private moment to study what she'd done, trying to account for what had happened. Had the magic been in her hand or in the subject? There was no telling. What she did know was this: her drawing of Bobby Marconi affected everything she did thereafter. It was as if, having been liberated from the blank page, he now had partial control of her pen.

This part her mother understood at a glance, and she took her daughter in her arms, kissing her feverish forehead with cool lips. "Oh, sweetie," she said. "I'm so, so sorry."

AT GRAND CENTRAL her mother almost succeeded in cheering her up. They'd boarded the train early, loading her suitcases and the bag of gifts overhead, then sat in facing seats, her mother clutching the portfolio and Sarah wishing she'd put it up with the rest of her stuff, out of sight.

"Sweetie, don't you know what this means? It means you have the gift."

"What if I don't want it?"

"You do. You know you do. Don't lie."

But how could she not, since neither statement—I *do* want the gift, I *don't* want it—was completely true. She wanted the gift on her own terms and didn't need her mother to tell her that this wasn't how such gifts were offered. "Will it make me happy?"

"Oh, sweetie . . ."

"Does it make *you* happy?" Because if it did, what need would she have of Harold Sundry?

Her mother looked like she might cry. "You *don't* understand, do you?"

Sarah shook her head, panic again rising.

"I *don't* have it. Oh, I have some talent. Enough to get by. More than most. But it's not the same as yours. What you have comes from some other place."

Sarah's next question was a whisper, so low she wasn't sure she'd spoken. "What about Lou?" Meaning, was her affection for him a lie? Meaning, how could she love him and draw Bobby? Meaning, could she have her gift and Lou, too?

Her mother opened her mouth, then shut it again. "Oh, Lord," she finally said. "I was about to say follow your heart, but I did that and married your father."

Sarah forced a smile. "Five yards."

"Not fifteen?"

She shook her head. She was through giving her mother big penalties.

When the train was at last in motion, it occurred to Sarah that she'd left Thomaston with one secret and was returning with two. Was this how things would go from now on, secrets piling on top of secrets? Was this adult life, or simply the natural consequence of going away in the body of a girl and returning in that of a woman? Would she get used to deceit, like the husband she'd seen coming out of Sundry Gardens with his new girlfriend and her daughter, his face innocent of all misfortune and wrongdoing?

BY ALBANY, Sarah had decided it was time to focus on the task soon to be at hand: putting her father's life back in order. Though she wasn't there to witness them, she knew what his long summer days were like. According to the neighbors, who both awoke and fell asleep to the sound of his typewriter clacking away, she knew he was at his desk at least fourteen hours a day, seven days a week. With Sarah away and no one to please but himself, he did so by dispensing with all social niceties. Rising, he put on a bathrobe to work in, and at night he took it off to go to bed; since he owned two he'd wear one until it was stiff with perspiration before taking it to the cleaners and donning the other. He quit shaving and let his hair grow wild. Last summer, Lou had run into him coming out of Powell's stationery, where he'd gone to replace his typewriter ribbon, and hadn't even recognized him. He looked like Ben Gunn, he told

Sarah; he'd half expected the man to ask him for a piece of cheese.

It was true. When she returned over Labor Day, her father's appearance was always shocking to behold. He looked ten years older, starved and brittle. But his physical condition was only part of it. All summer long words flew off the tips of his fingers and directly onto his typewriter keys, bypassing his larynx entirely, so that by the end of August he was all but incapable of speech. He greeted his daughter with mixed feelings he didn't even try to conceal, though he instructed Sarah not to take his ambivalence personally, and mostly she didn't. In fact, she understood more than he knew.

The book he was writing was an account of his banishment from New York City and his long exile in the wilderness that was upstate in general and Thomaston in particular. Sarah knew all this because one Labor Day, years before, she'd found the manuscript piled neatly on his desk and let her curiosity get the better of her. She recognized her mother in the protagonist's faithless wife, who abandoned him in "Tannersville" and returned to "the city." Fragments of the terrible arguments she'd overheard before her mother finally left were reproduced verbatim. About the only imaginative liberty he seemed to have taken was that the protagonist and his wife were childless, an enormous relief to Sarah, who at thirteen hadn't been anxious to know what her father thought of her. But it did trouble her that Rudy had also been erased. That her father should mimic life's cruelty seemed unforgivable.

Otherwise, however, she understood. The fictional reality of her father's summer, during which he had no daughter either on the page or in the house, was difficult to surrender, and her return—always sudden because he'd managed to lose all track of time—was startling enough to give him the bends. Until he could accustom himself to the reality, she would remain, albeit physically present and undeniable, somehow inconclusive. Over Labor Day she would *become* conclusive, and this painful transition was for her the saddest part of reentry: her father's realization that summer was over, that he had a daughter, that he made his living as a high school teacher in a backwater burg, that he wasn't a writer, not really, and couldn't even pretend to be one again until he completed yet another long season in purgatory. Sarah herself, she came to understand, was her father's discontent personified. These three months in front of his typewriter had convinced him that this was his realest, truest life, and her return each September reminded him—very dramatically—that it was only a vivid illusion. He actually locked the door to his study, refusing to enter the room during the school year lest it remind him of his real work, his real life, that he was cheated out of for nine months of the year. On Tuesday, he always took the stack of pages he'd written to the Thomaston Savings and Loan, placing them with the others in a large safety-deposit box. That nothing in his life was more valuable than the contents of that box couldn't have been more clear.

The good news was that his transformation from writer to teacher, from bachelor to father, though dramatic, was never prolonged. Sarah always returned on Sunday afternoon, and by Tuesday morning he had to appear at the high school prepared to teach another crop of sullen, militantly uneducable Thomaston teens, so for the both of them, Labor Day Monday was full of unremitting labor. Having refused even to think about school during the summer, her father had to generate or modify lesson plans for all his courses. The morning after his daughter's return, he'd rise early, take a long shower, shampoo his mane, shave his beard and actually dress. His trousers would demonstrate that he'd again lost weight and would have to pay another visit to his only friend at the high school, the shop teacher, and ask him to punch an additional hole in his belt. Over breakfast he'd test his vocal cords by quizzing his daughter about her summer, how babysitting had gone, if she'd made any friends, how her mother was faring, and if *she'd* made any friends, and hoping, Sarah could tell, to be told that she was still struggling, still losing accounts to her competitors, still had no man in her life and was therefore closer to admitting she couldn't make it on her own, closer to returning to their lives.

When she was younger, Sarah had worried that the lies she told about her mother's life at the Sundry Arms weren't convincing. After all, when she fudged the truth about her father, her mother's arched eyebrow always let her know she knew better. But her father never seemed suspicious, accepting her bland falsehoods and equivocations as if no daughter of his would *know* how to lie. "He doesn't *want* to know the truth," her mother once explained. "He likes his version of things, and what you tell him allows him to believe what he wants. Think of it as a kindness," she suggested. "Why burst his bubble?" Sarah had never quite gotten the hang of considering lies kindness, but did allow that her mother must be right about why this man with such a questioning mind, a perfect terrier when it came to rooting out the falsehoods of politicians and advertisers and other professional liars, never grilled her or begged details. Normally rational, he craved fantasy where his ex-wife was concerned. Even the fact of their divorce didn't strike him as conclusive. It just meant she was still angry at him. She'd return when she couldn't afford not to.

Sarah's Labor Day was even more laborious, for it fell to her to put their house back in order, throwing open all the windows to air the place out, doing laundry and ironing a week's worth of his dingy, short-sleeved shirts, which no amount of Clorox ever truly whitened, and his black trousers, which *would* whiten if she wasn't careful. She also had to pick up his mess from room to room, then go to the store and replace whatever he'd run out of midsummer and decided to do without. Usually at least half of the lightbulbs in the house had blown, but except for those in the den he hadn't noticed. And once there was light to see by, she'd go through the mail to find out exactly when the electric, phone and water companies were threatening to cut off service, typically right about now.

By suppertime her father was usually a little more like himself, more talkative, more cheerful, more resigned to their life together and the school year that would begin in the morning. Generating his course syllabi tended to raise his spirits, and he'd explain some of his more diabolical plans for testing the critical acuity of Thomaston youth, or for proving how woefully lacking it was. After supper, Sarah would find the scissors and give him a haircut, during which he'd ask if she'd read any good books over the summer, hoping she'd say yes and want to discuss them. But he was far cleverer at talking about ideas, and she didn't want to disappoint him, so she always claimed to have forgotten the authors' names and the book titles, which disappointed him even more, that she should disregard authorship so casually. His worst fear was that she discussed books with her mother, and he was greatly relieved when she assured him that she didn't.

By the time they finished their day of labors and were ready for bed, her father, fully himself at last, would give her a hug and say, "What would I do without you?" and she could tell he meant it, and meant *by* it that he loved her. Still, it was hard not to view the question as rhetorical. What he did without her couldn't have been clearer. Emotionally and physically exhausted, she would fall asleep, pleased and proud to have removed the evidence.

THIS, THEN, was what Sarah had to look forward to in a normal year, with just her mother's secrets to keep. Those empty gin bottles and late-night visits from the men of the Sundry Arms had always been sufficient to tie her stomach in knots. This year, though, with the additional weight of Harold Sundry and the drawing of Bobby Marconi still hidden in her portfolio, she understood how light that burden had been. In half an hour her train would pull into Fulton and her shaggy father, a scarecrow, all skin and bones, would be standing there on the platform to greet her, and then the lies would begin.

If he remembered her. Last year, cramming as many words as he could onto blank pages in those last precious hours, he'd lost track of time and Sarah had waited at the tiny train station for over an hour before finally calling a cab. She'd first tried calling home, of course, but her father hadn't yet reconnected the phone. A thunderous Hudson cab arrived twenty minutes later, its rusted muffler dangling precariously. The driver, a scruffy, pear-shaped man with dark, beady eyes, kept checking her out in the rearview mirror. Did she have a boyfriend, he wanted to know. She said yes, because that seemed like a good idea, but then he'd asked who it was, and when she said Lou Lynch, he blurted, "You mean Lucy?" Most everyone referred to him as Lucy, but Sarah never did and was angry that this strange man should do so. "Last I knew," he said, his beady eyes still fixing her in the mirror, "it was Karen Cirillo pulling him around by his . . ." He let the thought trail off. "You know her?"

Sarah didn't answer. It was beyond strange to hear a middle-aged man speaking with such authority about kids her age, as if he were really sixteen himself and merely disguised as a derelict. "Her ma and me used to be friends," he continued, emphasizing "friends" so as to clarify their relationship. "Karen and me never got along too good. Your Lucy, he used to do cartwheels every time she went into that store. Give her free cigarettes and anything else she wanted." Sarah did remember Karen Cirillo from junior high, beautiful in a cheap sort of way, at thirteen exuding sex from every pore. She supposed it was possible for a girl like Karen to steamroll a boy as shy and awkward around girls as Lucy had been, and still was. But she doubted he'd ever have given her free merchandise from Ikey's.

The driver shrugged, having apparently read her mind. "You don't believe me, ask him." Again he studied her in the mirror. "So now he does cartwheels over you, huh? Gives *you* all that free stuff." Sarah said she paid for everything at Ikey Lubin's, just like she would at any other store, but she could tell he didn't believe her, that he harbored a deep conviction that most everyone else was afforded all manner of advantages expressly denied him. "He never give *me* nothin' free," he said darkly. "Her mom and me spent all kinds of money in that store, and they never give us nothin'."

Suddenly Sarah knew who she was talking to. Lou had told her all about Buddy Nurt, who'd robbed Ikey's years earlier, and now here he was driving her home, his dark little eyes darting back and forth between the road and the rearview mirror. When she shifted her position in the rear seat so she wasn't in his line of sight, he just grinned and adjusted the mirror so she was again.

Sarah was trying to think of how to make him quit looking at her when he sat up straight and said, "Gotcha!" his expression triumphant. "Berg," he said. "That's your daddy. Mr. *Berg*." She couldn't help wincing. Hearing him say her surname was obscene. "What? You think I don't know him?"

Sarah said she had no idea if he did or didn't.

"Know all about Mr. *Berg*," Buddy Nurt assured her. "Know more about him than you do, probably. Drive a cab, you learn all about people. You think I'm lyin'?"

Before Sarah could answer there was a loud bang followed by an ungodly screech of metal, causing Buddy Nurt to use his rearview for its intended purpose. "Son of a bitch," he said. When Sarah turned around, she saw that the cab's muffler was dragging along the macadam and sending off sparks.

Buddy Nurt pulled over onto the shoulder and turned off the engine. "Cocksucker," he said, before getting out. When he popped the trunk, Sarah was able to see what was happening next through the gap. Rudely shoving her suitcases aside, he began rummaging through the clutter of old blankets, greasy rags, cardboard boxes, yellowed, curling newspapers, a tire iron, a case of motor oil, searching for she couldn't imagine what and clearly not finding it. "Motherfucker," he barked before slamming the trunk shut. An idea must have occurred to him, though, because he popped it open again and this time, to Sarah's astonishment, he opened one of her suitcases and rooted around until he found a wire hanger, tossed the dress it was holding aside and went about the task of straightening the hanger. He then disappeared underneath the car, where he must have touched something hot because he yelped and uttered another foul oath. He was directly below her seat, grunting like a pig, his nearness disconcerting even with the undercarriage between them. She was certain those beady little eyes would be looking up her skirt if they could.

Fifteen minutes later they were back on the highway, Buddy Nurt's satisfied expression suggesting that he considered the coat hanger a permanent solution to his muffler problem. "I had to borrow one of your hangers," he told her, as if the maintenance of his cab was their shared responsibility. "You had a bunch of them," he added, so she wouldn't feel ill used. Which, when she thought about it, was probably how he viewed the beer and cigarettes he'd stolen from Ikey's.

His little ferret eyes were back in the rearview now. "So how come you like *him*?" he said, confusing Sarah, in part because the reference to Lou was by then so remote, but also because she happened just then to look out the window and see her father flying by, hunched over the wheel of their Chevy and heading in the opposite direction, toward Fulton, to meet her train.

"There goes your daddy now." Buddy Nurt chuckled. "Guess he don't know I already got you." Nodding at her in the mirror, he was pleased, she could tell, to know something he thought no one else did, no matter what it was. She was hoping with all her heart that this creep would never know anything worth knowing about her when he said, "Sarah, right? Sarah Berg."

WOULD HER FATHER FORGET HER again today? If so, how tempting it would be to just stay on the train. Not because she'd have to call Hudson Cab and risk another ride with Buddy Nurt, but rather because she suddenly felt homeless, adrift. Which made exactly no sense. After all, wasn't she rich in homes—her father's, the Sundry Arms, Ikey Lubin's? Why feel as if she didn't truly belong in any of them when there were people in all three who loved her? Yet how grand it would be to ride on for a few more hours and get off somewhere she'd never heard of and begin a new life there. But her mother was probably right. She was just anticipating the big changes that were going to come in another year. She and Lou would go off to the university, maybe Bobby, too. By then her mother would have remarried. Her father, his book finally finished, would quit his teaching job and return to the city. In a sense, this train was rattling toward a place that was already receding into the distance. Before she knew it Ikey Lubin's, the elder Lynches, her father's house and Thomaston itself would all be reduced to memory. Buddy Nurt, convinced he knew things worth knowing, would continue to drive the eternal Hudson cab, its muffler attached by means of someone else's coat hanger. She would forget and in turn be forgotten. All of this, she told herself, was normal. Certainly nothing to cry about. Sarah closed her eyes, surrendering herself to the rhythm of the rails, and let the stupid, stupid tears fall.

SHE STARTED AWAKE when she felt a hand on her shoulder.

"Your stop, young lady," the conductor said. "That's pretty good. You do it yourself?"

And there in her lap was the drawing of Bobby. She had no memory of removing it from its zippered compartment before falling asleep, but there it was, so she must have.

"I'm guessing you must know that young fella," the man added. She thought he must mean Bobby until she saw he was nodding at the dirty window, where her boyfriend's grinning face was framed. Feeling herself flush, she quickly slid the drawing back into her portfolio. Had Lou seen? Was it *possible* to see inside the coach through such a dirty window? His expression suggested he was seeing his own reflection as much as her.

Outside on the platform he gave her the same big brother's

467

welcome-home hug he did every year, and she would've been disappointed by his lack of passion if he weren't clearly so delighted she was back. "Wow," he said, sounding almost afraid, though admiring, too, as he stepped back to take her in. "You look . . . different." Different. She felt some small disappointment in that word, too.

"I was expecting my father," she said.

"I told you I had a surprise," he said, beaming, and she remembered then that, yes, he'd mentioned something about a surprise when they'd spoken earlier that week. He puffed up with pride now, which made him look very like his own father. "I got my license."

"Wow," she said, trying to sound excited. "That's great."

"I went over to your dad's and he said it was okay if I did the honors," he told her, picking up a suitcase in each hand. "Actually, I think he might've forgotten which train you were on. We had to knock really loud to make him hear, and he answered the door dressed in his bathrobe."

"We?"

"Actually," he said as they emerged from the tiny station into the parking lot, "I've got two surprises."

He was beaming down at her again in that—well, let's face it—goofy way he had. And there, getting out of the Lynch station wagon and grinding a cigarette out underfoot, was the very boy she'd just moments before zipped back into her portfolio, with the same crooked grin she'd given him in the drawing.

"Hey, stranger," she said, surprised at how easy it was to give an old friend's hug to someone who wasn't an old friend. She was also pleased to see how it flustered him.

"You're the one who's been gone, not me," Bobby reminded her.

"But now I'm back, which means you're going to have to shape up. Was that a cigarette I just saw?"

"He's not supposed to be smoking," Lou said, beaming at Bobby now. "He's on the football team. Starting fullback."

BRIDGE OF SIGHS

"You gonna tell on me?" Bobby said.

"I might. You could pay me not to, though."

"How much do you want?"

"A quarter."

He fished in his pocket, found a quarter and handed it to her.

"Okay," she said. "Now your secret's safe."

And so, strangely, were her own. On the train she'd been terrified of them, by her inability to keep them, by their seeming desire to reveal themselves. Now they hardly seemed to matter. Bobby had taken on a dual existence, there before her in the flesh and safely tucked away in the dark. In adult life were realities so compartmentalized? At this possibility she felt her spirits, at low ebb on the train, buoyantly rise up again. If that were the case, she could manage it. She might even be good at it.

"I'll ride in back," Bobby offered.

"Nah," Lou said, going around to the driver's side. "You can ride up front with us. There's room for three."

And he was right. There was.

WINTER BIRDS

TALY IS CANCELED.

I have protested, but feebly, I fear. It's taken all my strength to convince my wife to take me home instead of to the emergency room, and there I've fallen into a fretful sleep on the sofa to the sound of her voice on the phone in the kitchen. By the time I wake up, it's done. Flights, train reservations, hotels, all our plans up in smoke. When I notice the travel books and magazines that for so long threatened to take over the house have also vanished, I study her for signs of anger, because she'd be entitled. But no, she evinces only concern. She is ever Sarah, just as I, alas, am ever Lucy Lynch.

Over a light supper, in the hopes of putting her mind at ease, I remind her about how these things work. My spells, like the valve on a pressure cooker, serve to safely release stress, after which it takes time for the pressure to build again. Years, sometimes. The worse the spell, the greater the relief, the longer between it and the next. What happened today is good news, I tell my wife. It means we won't have to worry for a while. But what, Sarah wonders, if José hadn't found me? What if he hadn't phoned or if she hadn't been able to come immediately to the junior high and summon me back? Grateful though I am to both of them, I remind her that it probably wouldn't have made much difference. It's true the episode could've lasted longer if she hadn't come. I might have returned to myself in the middle of the night, locked in the school, disoriented and confused, but eventually I would've made it home. That was true of my first spell, and of every one since.

470

When we finish eating, I offer to help with the dishes but am shooed away. I'm told I look exhausted, that I should go upstairs and lie down, fall asleep again if I can. Instead I retreat to my study to contemplate this latest humiliation in solitude. While I wish I could make myself believe that I have not betrayed my wife, not only today but in all the days leading up to today, I know better. It's possible that I've been betraying her from the start, when she "drew us together" at Ikey's. That, oddly enough, is where I left off writing my story. I've written far more than I imagined I would, filling two large notebooks, and I now take the second of these and reread the last page. Over supper I've promised her that I won't be writing anymore. I know she fears it's become an obsession that may have contributed to this spell. I suppose it's possible, and anyway I've reached a good place to stop. Sarah has entered my life. She's drawn Ikey's and she's drawn the two of us together, which is what we've been ever since. Bobby is about to enter, which he did, but only briefly.

Our lives have continued, of course, and there's more, much more, to say about them, but I'm content to end on Sarah's drawing, that moment captured and frozen in time. Things would never again be so perfect, so poised between innocence and experience, between past and future. The events of senior year in high school would steal our innocence, after which the losses would commence, Sarah's father to disgrace; her mother to tragedy; Bobby, for us, at least, to Europe and fame; my father . . . my father to malignancy. I meant to write it all because I believed my life to be a hopeful story with a happy ending, the sort my father would've liked, where hard work and faith are rewarded, and the American virtues he most admired are triumphant. After all, Ikey's prospered in the end, vindicating what he'd seen all along. As did our family. Sarah and I bought one of the houses on my father's old milk route in the Borough, just as he said I might one day, if that was what I wanted. She and I married, as he wished, and we've had a son who's a good, gentle man. All of this, every word, is true. It's just not the whole truth, and I suppose that's another reason to leave my story as it stands. Now, today, after the Bridge of Sighs, if I continued to write, it would end up being the story of my betrayal of the woman who has saved my life not once but over and over again. A betrayal that began, I fear, with our marriage.

After high school, Sarah went off to school in the city and I to the state university in Albany, with the unspoken understanding that we'd marry someday, perhaps after we took our degrees. Meanwhile, we'd spend holidays together, maybe even summers. Poor Sarah. Her letters that first autumn in New York were full of anxiety and self-doubt. She said everybody at Cooper Union was more talented than she would ever be, and she wondered out loud if maybe her father had been right. An advocate of traditional liberal arts education, he'd long argued that what undergraduates needed most was to read, and to do so as broadly as possible. Art school, to his way of thinking, was little better than trade school, someplace you'd go if you wanted to learn to fix carburetors or refrigerators. Students required not a narrow set of skills but a broad, sturdy foundation upon which to build a real life of the mind. There'd be plenty of time for studio work later, in graduate study. Back in high school, Sarah'd had little trouble discounting his advice. She'd always known that he undervalued her gift, and also that no matter how sound his abstract argument might be, his underlying purpose was to undermine that gift in the hopes she'd discover another passion that was more to his liking.

But now that he was gone, she began to remember, perhaps for the first time, his advice, and to torment herself with self-doubt. Typically we spoke on the phone on Sunday afternoons, when the rates were low. "What if I'm not that good?" she said one Sunday in late September. I knew she was thinking of her father, of the decade he devoted to his great novel only to have it rejected. "What if I spend years and nothing comes of it?" I told her she was as talented as anyone at CU, and my mother, overhearing, chimed in that otherwise she wouldn't have been admitted. Before we hung up my father got on the line and said her drawing of Ikey's still hung in the place of honor above the cash register and that people commented on it all the time. She was grateful for our reassurance, but her doubts persisted, and when one of her professors was harshly critical of a project she'd devoted many long hours to, she joked that when she flunked out, maybe she'd come join me in Albany, and God help me, I echoed her father's arguments about the value of a broad educational foundation.

And what did I tell Sarah about my own life that first semester at Albany State? The truth, mostly, but not—to borrow one of her father's favorite phrases—"the truth, the whole truth and nothing but, so help me God." I wrote her long letters in which I admitted missing her terribly, which was true. I said I was doing well in my classes (also true), that I attended them regularly and fulfilled all my academic obligations dutifully (true again), but I also gave her to understand that I'd adjusted to university life about as well as could be expected (not even remotely true). That first fall semester I was, in point of fact, a university student in name only. Sarah knew I returned home on weekends to help out at the store. Because I was needed, I told her, which was true enough, but less true than admitting I needed Ikey's on weekends, that once classes were finished I couldn't imagine staying on campus, where I hadn't made a single friend. Worse, I resented Sarah's courage and character: alone in a strange city, battling heroically to conquer her feelings of inadequacy. Whereas I hadn't even tried. I came gradually to understand that this resentment mirrored that which I'd felt toward Bobby when we were boys. Like him, Sarah was dead game, metaphorically willing to surf blind in the rear of any truck, nor would she cry if she got tossed around. But I was still playing it safe, right up front where I could see the dangerous curves well in advance and hold on if I needed to.

Bobby might have been gone that autumn, but he was far from

forgotten. I'd hated to see him go, especially after what happened between him and his father. Now that he wasn't around, however, it had occurred to me that things might be better for me without the constant comparison he offered. While Sarah never mentioned him unless I did first, I knew she hadn't forgotten him either, and why should she when, in the endless nights of my lonely dorm room, even I had to wonder if *they* belonged together. When Sarah wrote that by coming home every weekend I wasn't socializing and making new friends at school, I read into her concern a secret hope that I'd find a new girlfriend so she could be shut of me and available for Bobby, should he ever return. I knew these were crazy ideas, but that didn't make them any easier to banish.

By mid-November, tormented in this fashion by my own unworthiness, I began to sense our future, Sarah's and mine, slipping away. I looked forward starting Monday to our Sunday phone calls, though these often deepened my doubts, because I could tell that every week she was happier, more at home in the city, less fearful of its foreignness, more competent to navigate its treacherous waters. She claimed she was still looking forward to spending the holidays with us, but the same professor who'd been so hard on her earlier in the term had now taken Sarah and another first-year student under his wing and had invited them to come back early, right after the first of the year, to help him install a show. My heart plummeted when she told me she'd agreed, thus lopping off over a week I'd been planning for us to spend together. I both dreaded and longed for Christmas, desperate to see Sarah yet terrified she'd use the occasion to break off our engagement, though we weren't, of course, officially engaged.

Naturally, my fears couldn't have been more unwarranted. From the moment she stepped off the train four days before Christmas, I saw my folly for what it was. She was my Sarah again, or perhaps "our Sarah," as my father called her. She arrived laden with presents and proclaiming it was wonderful to be home, that she'd forgotten what clean air tasted like, and the squealing hug she gave my father had him beaming like Father Christmas the rest of the day. Later, though, when we were alone, she did allow that everything looked smaller than she remembered, which suggested to me it looked shabbier, too. Probably even Ikey's. In our phone calls Sarah had often gone on about how city people dressed, and I was now aware, as never before, of how we Lynches might look to them. My father happened just then to be wearing one of his louder plaid shirts, purchased not at Calloway's, as he'd told my mother, but at our cheaper West End men's store. His cowlick was in full bloom, and the grin he wore at the sight of "our girl" was his very goofiest. I felt my throat constrict with love and embarrassment. But if she felt any embarrassment at all, she gave no sign. She told us, in fact, that on days when she felt low, she imagined all of us going about our daily routines at Ikey's and before long she felt better. "I swear to God, Lou, if you cry I'm going to swat you," my mother warned my father, when she saw his eyes welling up.

But much had changed since graduation. We both felt it. Somehow, Sarah and I weren't quite the same with Bobby gone. We'd always been a threesome, even when he was with Nan Beverly. Sometimes he'd take Sarah's side against me, sometimes my side against her, but he was always there, always trump in whatever game we happened to be playing. When he wasn't actually present, we were busy anticipating his arrival. Everybody else who'd gone off to college and now come home for the holidays wanted news of him, and of course they came to Sarah and me, his closest friends. She didn't appear overly troubled to admit she knew no more than anybody else, but I'd always been proprietary where Bobby was concerned. I did notice, though, that when the bell rang over the door at Ikey's, she always looked up expectantly, and I suspected it was Bobby she imagined would saunter in, because that's exactly who I kept expecting myself. "We'll probably never see him again," I once ventured to say, by which I guess I meant he'd be crazy to come back under the circumstances. Perhaps sensing my feelings were hurt that he hadn't contacted us since fleeing town, Sarah invented a game for us to play. Bobby, we decided, planned to return sometime during the holiday, sneaking back into the country in disguise and just showing up at Ikey's. Anybody who came into the store was Bobby in disguise. "Look, there he is!" Sarah would exclaim when a tiny, elderly woman came in, leaning heavily on a walker. "I recognized him first!"

But, no, he was gone, and he wasn't the only one. Three Mock had been home briefly after boot camp before being sent overseas. Nan Beverly and Perry Kozlowski went off to college in September like the rest of us, but they wouldn't be coming back, their parents having moved away. Jerzy Quinn and Karen Cirillo were still around, though I saw them so seldom that when they did appear they seemed like characters from a novel I'd read long ago and half forgotten. One day I ran into Karen outside the beauty parlor and she had a toddler in tow. "So, Lou," she said, looking at me, or maybe at something behind me, "you still love me, or what?" I told her I was sort of engaged to Sarah Berg. "Never heard of her," Karen said. "She must not be from around here." Rather than explain, I said, "I guess you're married now." Her kid was grinning up at me, fascinated, as kids always used to be with my father. "Married," Karen snorted. "You always were a scream, Lou." I half expected one of the skinny wraiths who'd always attended Karen in junior high to walk up, but none did, causing me to wonder what happened to all of them. When she and her little girl went into the salon, I remember looking around and thinking that half the town, in one fashion or another, had disappeared.

Sarah's Christmas was also made awkward by the fact that, with her father gone, she had nowhere to stay. There wasn't room in our house, which wouldn't have been appropriate anyway, so she'd wangled an invitation from an old girlfriend she'd never been particularly close to and as a result was duty bound to spend time with her and her family, and even then the girl told Sarah she felt used, that next time she wanted to visit the Lynches she'd have to find someplace else to stay. Maybe it was this unpleasantness that cast a shadow over our last few days together, but more likely it was just my sense of unworthiness kicking into high gear as our holiday drew to a close. I was bitterly jealous of how excited Sarah was about the show she was going to help install as soon as she got back to New York. During the two weeks we had together, I'd felt not so much happy as—what?—complete. I'd ask Sarah if she wanted to go out, look up old friends and do things, but she'd said no, she'd rather be at Ikey's most, which caused my mother to shake her head at my father and me, the two of us standing there moist eyed. I didn't know how I'd be able to face her leaving.

On the drive to Fulton I panicked and let all my insecurities come flooding out. I told Sarah how much I loved and missed her, how at times I couldn't help feeling like maybe I was losing her to a better world, the one her father had wanted for her and that would never include me, or Ikey's, or Thomaston. Instead of being repulsed by this display of weakness and mistrust, Sarah just kissed me on the tip of my nose and, looking at me cross-eyed, said I was being silly, although it was a good silly and I was forgiven. She loved me, too, she said, more than ever these last two weeks. She loved not only me but also my mother and father, and dear old Ikey's, and even, when he behaved himself, Uncle Dec. I just had to believe her.

I did. Of course I did. Being Sarah, she wouldn't have said what she didn't mean. She'd given me as unambiguous a declaration of devotion as anyone could hope for, yet when I put her on the train back to the city the thought crossed my mind that even if she *did* mean every word, even if it was the whole truth and nothing but the truth, even if it was so help me God, it wasn't the guarantee I sought. Because I could still lose my Sarah, our Sarah, to some new passion, to someplace she'd never been, to someone she'd never met but would come to love even more than she loved me and us.

Or even someone she'd already said goodbye to, who was gone, but maybe not for good. How could I prevent that? I couldn't. I simply could not.

THAT NEW YEAR was when my father was really diagnosed for the first time. There'd been the earlier scare, his cyst with the "abnormal cells." Afterward he'd gone in for regular exams, but they were expensive and he was feeling good, so gradually he stopped. But that fall he tired easily, and my mother said he'd been sleeping poorly. What I noticed was that he was forever rubbing his right side, just above his ribs, and wincing. "It ain't nothin'," he kept saying. "Just a knot. It'll work out." Except it never did. And then Sarah, who had the advantage of not having seen him every day, immediately remarked that he'd lost weight. "That's it," my mother said, fixing him with the stare that always made him look at his shoes. "Monday morning, *you're* going to the doctor."

It wasn't until after the holidays, though, that he could get an appointment with a specialist, who located the tumor under his arm, right where the cyst had been removed years earlier. My mother was furious, convinced that he'd known for months that something was wrong and refused to do anything about it. The operation to remove the growth was relatively simple, but the chemotherapy that followed exhausted him, making me even more indispensable at home than I'd been the first semester. In mid-January, with the reluctant aid of my academic adviser, I dropped two required courses that met on Monday, Wednesday and Friday, replacing them with Tuesday/Thursday electives that allowed me to catch the late bus and work a four-day weekend at Ikey's, then take the afternoon bus back to campus. Predictably, my mother was livid when she heard what I'd done. "What's the point of college," she demanded, "if you're only there three days a week?"

"It's just this one semester," I countered, the same promise I'd made to my adviser, who'd dutifully warned me that putting off required courses might jeopardize my graduating with the rest of my class. Once my father got his strength back, I told my mother, once he was out of danger, I'd cut back at Ikey's and rededicate myself to becoming a university student in earnest. This argument I knew I could win. After all, I was on scholarship, not wasting the money she'd put aside that now was paying for my father's operation, hospital stay, post-op treatments and convalescence. My mother could argue until she was blue in the face, but they *did* need me and I knew that for a fact.

This victory, however, came at a cost. The conflict that had simmered for so long between my mother and me now came to a rolling boil, and we were at each other constantly. Like so many of the family conflicts I'd witnessed since I was a boy, what we were really arguing about couldn't be acknowledged: in this case, whether my father was going to recover. His surgeon was optimistic. The operation had been a success, he told my mother. They'd caught the malignancy early, before it could spread. Had he waited another couple of months, well, the situation might've been entirely different. Of course he couldn't guarantee there wouldn't be subsequent tumors, but neither was there any cause for undue pessimism. That last was the part my father heard most clearly. "Quit worryin' every minute," he told my mother when she said he was returning to work too soon or trying to do too much. "I ain't gonna die from this little bit I'm doin', and Louie's right here if I need any help." She clenched her teeth and said nothing. My mother prided herself on being what she called realistic and always defended her realism vigorously, but now she couldn't because she knew that optimism, which came to her husband and son naturally, was exactly what a sick man needed to get well. But I knew she was seething inside, and she took out her frustration on all of us. "What the hell do you *want* from me, Tessa?" I heard my uncle ask her one day.

"What do I *want*?" she exploded. "What do I *want*? What I

want is for somebody in this family to—" But she stopped there, glaring homicidally at Uncle Dec, and then at me, before storming out.

"Go easy on her, Bub," he said, somehow aware of how angry I was at her. "If she ever snaps, you can kiss this place goodbye."

"You're full of shit," I told him, the only time in my life I'd ever said such a thing to my uncle, or perhaps to anyone.

For an instant he looked ready to come around the meat counter and teach me some manners, but then thought better of it. "Fine," he said. "Just keep going like you are, ignoring your college work and spending every waking minute in this store. Break her heart, if that's what you want. What the hell do I care?"

THAT MARCH my uncle decided he needed a vacation. He hadn't been back to California since leaving the army and thought he might like to see what was going on out there. There were a couple of good horse tracks he wanted to check out, and you could bet on dogs as well. And if you crossed the border in Tijuana, you could wager on something called jai alai, a lightning-fast sport that men played with big, curved baskets that looked like wicker bananas on their wrists. "Plus," he told my mother, "me being gone will give you and Little Biggy here a chance to see if you've learned anything." This was one of a half-dozen nicknames Uncle Dec alternated between when he wasn't calling me Bub. He'd been training the two of us behind the meat counter for over a year, and we knew everything he did, though the Borough ladies who came into Ikey's still preferred to have him cut their crown roasts. "It's not your fault you aren't sexy like me," he'd kid when they left the store. "Try not to cut your hand off while I'm gone. There's a limited demand for one-armed butchers."

"He's not going to *be* a butcher," my mother said, as if worried I might pursue this new career.

"You be careful your own self," Uncle Dec warned her. "These days you're trying to think about at least five things at once, and when you're holding a meat cleaver you ought to be thinking about just one, the right one."

"Well, with you out of the way, there'll be fewer things going wrong," she assured him.

"What do *you* think, Bub?" he said. "You figure you can survive without me for a month?"

I told him I thought I personally was up to the challenge, at which he snorted and said he imagined I was.

My father, looking pale and thin, happened just then to be sitting on the tall barstool we'd installed so he could work the register more comfortably. "You'll be back in a week if you bet dogs and horses and them mai-tai fellas, too."

"You could be right," said my uncle, who since the operation had been going easy on my father. It was poor sport, he claimed, ridiculing a man in such a weakened condition. "On the other hand, I might win a fortune and buy a house on the beach."

"Send for me if you do," my mother said.

"I can't promise anything," he told her. "I'll probably be surrounded by gold diggers. They say they're all over out there. Just the sort of women a man like me might fall prey to."

"The other thing they say about California is it's due to fall in the ocean," she said, striding out and letting the door swing shut behind her by way of punctuation.

Uncle Dec looked at me and shrugged. "Work on your mother's disposition while I'm gone, will you? It used to be sunnier before she met your father and had you."

WITH MY UNCLE away for the month of March, Sarah would have a place to stay over spring break, which may have been why he chose March over February or April for his vacation. I'd never known him to do anything out of kindness or consideration, but he was very fond of Sarah, so I supposed it was possible. Either that or my mother suggested it. As soon as he was gone, she went upstairs, turned off the heat and flung open the windows to expel what she called the reek of bachelordom, a heady mix of cheap frying oil, too-strong cologne, stale cigarettes, flatulence and old goat. Actually, for a man who'd always lived alone, Uncle Dec was surprisingly clean and tidy. My mother thought the army must have rubbed off on him, because there were no stacks of dirty dishes in the sink, no clothing heaped on the floor at the foot of the bed, and the bathroom, while it would've depressed a woman, at least wasn't gross. No ring around the bathtub, no shaving stubble in the sink, no dried, misadventure urine spattered around the commode.

Given that he'd be gone for the month, my mother decided it would be a good time to paint the whole apartment. The walls were beginning to look dingy, as light-colored walls will when there's a serious smoker in residence. Worse, the scorch mark caused by the electrical fire had again started showing, so there was nothing to do but give it another coat. When I heard her schedule the painter, I asked why she was doing all this. Sarah would only be with us for two weeks, and it wasn't like Dec cared. And he certainly wasn't going to stop smoking.

"Don't you want things to be nice for Sarah?" she said. "In fact, we might as well make a nice guest bedroom out of that storage room." She then proceeded to buy a new queen-size frame, box springs and mattress as well as a nice vanity and chest of drawers. The bathroom got an upgrade, too, as well as a good scrubbing.

All of which made exactly no sense. After all, money was tight. I tried to press my mother on the subject, but she got so angry that I let it slide, because by then we were bickering over everything. Most recently she'd gotten furious when she overheard part of a Sunday phone conversation I had with Sarah about the possibility of her transferring from Cooper Union to Albany for the following year. My father's diagnosis and subsequent operation had frightened her, and she wondered if we might need her closer by to help out.

My mother glared at me when I hung up. "You'd let her do that?"

"Albany has a good art department," I told her weakly. "They'll probably offer her a full ride."

"But it's not Cooper Union, Lou," she said. "Do you have any idea how talented you have to be to get in there? How many kids get turned down?" I reminded her that Sarah was old enough to make up her own mind, but of course she'd have none of it. "If you told her not to, and meant it, she'd stay in New York."

Nor had she been enthusiastic, at least initially, about Sarah spending her spring break with us, an idea I'd floated on New Year's Day, as soon as I returned to Ikey's after putting her on the train. When I entered the store, my impression was that my parents, and even Uncle Dec, had used my absence to argue about Sarah and me, and that I hadn't been gone long enough for them to arrive at a consensus.

"I don't think it's a good idea," my mother said when I mentioned spring break. "It wouldn't be a kindness."

My father objected with his customary shrug. "You saw what a good time she had here."

"I saw what a good time *you* had," she told him, which won her another shrug. My father wasn't about to deny how much he liked having Sarah around Ikey's.

"She had a great time, too," I said. "She told me so."

"We're the only family she's got left," my father pointed out.

"Exactly," Uncle Dec chimed in from behind the meat counter.

My mother sighted him along her index finger. "Don't *you* start in."

"Is this a new rule, Tessa? I don't get to talk?"

"No, it's an old one," she said. "I just haven't been enforcing it. I wish the three of you would quit ganging up on me every time we discuss something."

"It *takes* all three of us to argue with you," my uncle objected, "and we still lose."

"She *had* a good time," I repeated weakly, causing my mother to spin her attention on me.

"You're sure about that?" she said. "You can tell the difference between affection and gratitude?" But even she seemed to realize that this was a low blow.

"You seen how she was—" my father began.

"*Okay,*" my mother interrupted. "Okay. She enjoyed herself over the holidays. My point is that it's no kindness to offer security to somebody who's learning to love independence. Sarah is a *brave girl*. She's just beginning to understand she doesn't *need* a safety net." She turned to me now. "Don't play on her fears. That's not what you do when you love somebody."

Later that night, my parents were still arguing, their voices coming up through the heat register just as they'd done when I was a boy.

"You have to think of her, too, Lou."

"I ain't sayin' that, Tessa. I'm just sayin'—"

"I know what you're saying."

"He ain't had a single one of them spells since—"

"I *know* what you're saying."

"She's been good for him. That's all I'm—"

"I *know* what you're saying. I know, I know, I know."

BUT FOR MY FATHER'S ILLNESS, the conflict over Sarah's spring break would've been even more heated. My mother knew that the last thing he needed was worry. While his chemo dosage was supposedly low, it made him sick to his stomach and weak for days afterward. He'd just start feeling better, and it was time for another round. His appetite disappeared, and he continued to lose weight. For a while it looked like Uncle Dec would have to postpone his trip, but then in late February my father's system seemed to adjust. He began to eat again and regained a little weight and some of his former strength and stamina. A visit from "our girl" in March, he decided, was just what the doctor ordered, even if *his* doctor hadn't ordered it. A few days before Sarah was to arrive, the argument surfaced again when my mother gave my father strict orders not to pressure her about where she'd be going to school next year. "If she doesn't bring the subject up, leave it alone. Let her make up her own mind. She's got her whole future ahead of her, and she doesn't need you telling her what to do."

"Hell, I ain't gonna say nothin'," my father said. "She can do whatever she—"

"Spare me," she snapped. "You know perfectly well what you're going to do, and so do I. When she walks in that door, your face is going to light up like a Christmas tree, and you're going to say, *Welcome home, sweetness,* just like you always do. This is *not* her home, Lou. Her home is a dorm room in New York. Saying otherwise just confuses the poor girl."

"A person can have two homes," he said. "Look at Louie here. He's home with us half the time and down to his school home the other half."

But of course this wasn't true. I spent half my *time* at the university, but *home* was Thomaston. *Home* was Third Street. *Home,* when you came right down to it, was Ikey Lubin's. This, after all, was what my mother and I had been fighting about.

But over spring break Sarah again became part of our family, though instead of working with my father and me in the store, she spent most of her time helping my mother renovate the upstairs flat. On the weekends they went to garage sales and flea markets all over the county looking for good fixtures and other odd items. During the first week they pulled up the ratty carpet, rented a sander to do the hardwood floor underneath, then put down two coats of varnish.

"There ain't no point in talkin' to your mother once her mind's made up," my father told me one afternoon when, thanks to a lull, we had the store to ourselves and the leisure to listen to the droning activity overhead. I could tell he was trying to puzzle it through—why she was spending money sprucing up the flat when it was just Dec living up there. But his March trip, he'd confided to my mother, was a trial run designed to prepare us for his final exit. He'd already stayed longer than he planned, and after all this time anything he hadn't been able to teach us about butchering a pig, we were probably just too stupid to learn.

Of course I knew, or thought I did, what the renovations upstairs were really all about. I just didn't have the heart to explain it to my father, who was still weak, still trying hard to get his strength back. Not wanting to undermine his recovery, I held my tongue and tried to ignore my rising rage every time I thought about what my mother was up to, that she'd do something like this now, when my father was too feeble to offer any opposition, that she refused to come clean about her intentions even to me, that she'd stoop to using Sarah against me.

MY PARENTS HAD PROMISED each other not to pressure Sarah about her decision, and in each other's company they stuck to their pledge of neutrality. But my mother knew it would be impossible for my father not to convey to Sarah his fondest hopes—that she and I would marry, that we'd settle down in Thomaston, that he'd be able to pass Ikey's on to us and to the grandchildren we'd give him. His cancerous brush with mortality had concentrated those hopes, and expecting him not to voice them was like asking him not to breathe. He knew better than to do so when my mother was around, but if she wasn't and I happened to be working out of earshot in the back room, he'd tell Sarah he wished her school wasn't so far away, that Ikey's wasn't the same without her, that I was never so happy as when she was around, that she never had to worry about not having a home and family as long as Ikey's was there, which he figured it would be for a good long time. People would always need things—a half gallon of milk, a four-pack of toilet paper—things they wouldn't make a special trip to the supermarket for. They liked coming into a store like Ikey's, he reiterated, where they knew people, where they could find what they were looking for and there was somebody to ask if they couldn't.

Upstairs, I was certain, a very different conversation was going on, and a very different picture of Ikey's being painted. My mother did Ikey's books every month and knew what a shoe-string operation we ran, how small fluctuations and surprises could throw us for a loop, how hard we had to work for the slender living we made, how we ordered close to the bone so we wouldn't incur losses. Even when we did everything right, we were often flummoxed by unforeseen and unforeseeable circumstances. Yes, we were making a go of it, but each year it was getting harder, not easier, and now there were rumors of a new supermarket coming to town, one that would obsolete the A&P. Ikey's wasn't the kind of star any sensible young person would hitch a wagon to.

Nor was Thomaston. In the years since the tannery closed, no other industry had come in to give hope to those who'd lost their jobs there. FOR SALE signs, more of them every year, bloomed on West End, East End and even Borough properties. The Beverlys, who could afford to, had finally sold their house at a loss. Those who couldn't afford to bail out consulted one demoralized realtor after another, plotting doomed strategies to sell their homes, first at "fair" prices that represented the owners' diminished hopes and expectations, then at "reduced" prices designed to show how "motivated" they were. But only fire-sale pricing attracted serious buyers, of whom there were precious few, and fierce competition for them drove desperate sellers to slash prices further.

So did the now-conventional wisdom that Thomaston had, in fact, been poisoned. Even our local newspaper had finally given up running editorials to counter the Albany whistle-blowers on the pollution of the Cayoga Stream and our tainted ground-water, instead arguing weakly that we weren't that much worse off than our neighboring communities. On weekends, to reassure residents that the Cayoga now ran clean and pure, the paper printed photos of men fly-fishing in the shadow of the abandoned tannery. The problem was that people remembered their poisoning fondly. Back when the Cayoga ran red, they had money in their pockets. Now jobless, once their unemployment was exhausted, they signed up for welfare and drank their government checks in gin mills like Murdick's. Division Street wasn't really even the boundary between the West and East Ends anymore. The poverty and lack of opportunity that had once characterized everything west of Division was now encroaching on formerly respectable East End neighborhoods. Before long, my mother predicted, the banks would own every house and business in town, and then even the banks would leave. Of course Sarah already knew most of this, but I was sure my mother, fearing that her time away might've made her nostalgic, took every opportunity to remind her.

To be honest, what tormented me most when they were alone together was what my mother might be saying to Sarah about me. My mother loved me, I knew that. Why, then, did I suspect her of warning my girlfriend against me? Though we'd never discussed them, Sarah knew when and how my spells had begun and that I'd battled them throughout my adolescence. My father believed they were a thing of the past, that I'd outgrown them like an ugly sweater forgotten in the back of the closet. Would my mother share with Sarah her fear—and, I confess, my own—that I'd never be free of them? Why did I imagine her warning Sarah about what she'd be in for if we married, that she'd spend the rest of her life trapped by not just my condition but also my temperament? "Do you really want to spend the rest of your life in that store?" I could hear her saying. At night, unable to sleep, I cataloged all the things my mother knew about me that I'd rather Sarah didn't: how as a boy I'd been afraid to walk home from school alone after Bobby moved away from Berman Court, how I'd failed to call the turn in the milk truck and gotten

Bobby's wrist broken, how devastated I'd been when the Marconis moved to the Borough, how I'd allowed Karen Cirillo to steal cigarettes from Ikey's.

I knew that these were paranoid fears, evidence merely of self-doubt that at times bordered on self-loathing. These were the very things I should've been telling Sarah myself, if I hadn't been so terrified of losing her. One night I worked myself into such a state that I actually made myself sick and woke my parents by retching violently into the toilet.

The last day of her spring break, my father presented the two of us with a gift certificate to a fancy restaurant located out on the old Albany–Schenectady road that sat on a hill overlooking the canal. Below, in the waning light of evening, dense squadrons of winter birds dove in rigid formation at the water. It was late March, but spring came slowly upstate, its only signs of approach were the snow that had turned brown and water that could be heard tunneling underneath it.

We were given a table by a window through which we could watch the diving birds. How beautiful Sarah looked that night. I can still see her, across the long years, in that lovely, high-necked navy-blue dress, and I remember everyone turning to look at her when we were seated. Our waitress mistook us for newlyweds, which I normally would've taken enormous pleasure in. But I'd been feeling out of sorts all day, as if I might be coming down with something, and conflicted, too, wishing Sarah weren't leaving the next day but glad that my mother wouldn't have further opportunities to poison the well of her affections against me. Also, I was afraid. It had occurred to me that this would be the perfect occasion for Sarah to confess that she was having second thoughts, that maybe we'd been unwise to commit ourselves so young.

When she finally asked why I was so glum, I muttered something about wishing she didn't have to leave tomorrow, and she responded that it wouldn't be that long before we saw each other again, to which I replied spitefully that maybe it would seem a lot longer to me than it did to her. She then reminded me that I could visit her in the city anytime I wanted. In fact, there were people she wanted me to meet, and she'd like to show me her school, as well as all the sights. We could go to the top of the Empire State Building, take a cruise around Manhattan, see Radio City Music Hall. She rattled on like this for a while, her cheer causing my spirits to plummet even further. Of course she could make such offers safely, knowing that I couldn't take her up on them, not with my father still weak from his treatments and Ikey's needing me.

Eventually she ran out of ideas, and when she did I asked what I'd been wanting to all week: what had she and my mother found to talk about up in the flat for the last two weeks? And just that quickly, her eyes were full. "Your poor mother," she said. "She's terrified, you know. She's afraid the doctors aren't telling the whole truth. She doesn't trust Lou-Lou's surgeon because a woman she knows said he lied about her husband, told her there was nothing to worry about, and six months later he was dead."

I'm afraid what I did then was give a harsh, bitter croak that tasted of last night's vomit. "You don't get it, do you? If that's what happens, she gets her way. If they find another tumor, she'll sell the store. She hates Ikey's. She's always hated it. Right from the start she said it would fail, that my father was stupid to buy it. Now she gets to be right. She'll tell him there's no choice. They either have to sell the store or lose the house. She doesn't care what he wants or I want. Why do you think she's spending all that money renovating the flat? Because she thinks that if it's fixed up nice, Ikey's will sell. Then, with the store gone, she'll get her way with me, too. If I don't have Ikey's to come home to, I won't have any choice, will I? I'll have to do what she wants. Stay in school. In Albany. She gets her way about everything."

I might have stopped at any time. I saw the look of horror on Sarah's face deepen with each bitter utterance. Little did she know how much more was right on the tip of my tongue. Like what Nancy Salvatore told me about my mother that day in the store years ago, about my father never knowing what had hit him, and maybe my uncle Dec too. I could still see the woman's obscene sneer, her eagerness to prove she knew my mother longer and better than I did and knew she wasn't who I thought she was. And after that I'd tell Sarah about Uncle Dec, because it now seemed obvious he was the man on the trestle that night I'd woken up in the trunk, and that my mother had been there with him. Once Sarah was convinced of this, she'd understand everything my mother was up to now—renovating the flat over Ikey's, namely preparing to sell the store, so that later, once my father was out of the picture . . .

I might have said all this, but didn't. What stopped me was the look of revulsion on Sarah's face and the fact that I could feel the same obscene knowledge spreading across my features that I'd witnessed that day on Karen's mother's. So I just held my tongue and looked away, out the window, where the ridiculous birds continued diving at the now-black canal, hundreds of them, maybe thousands, flying in precise formation, low over the water, turning the already darkening sky black with their wings. Then they banked all at once and disappeared from sight, as if a living room blind had been yanked open, each blade too thin to register on the eye, until they banked back and the sky was again black with them. Everywhere, nowhere. Everything, nothing. No in between.

I didn't look at Sarah until I heard her say my name with more tenderness than I deserved. "Lou," she said, "are you saying your mother *wants* Lou-Lou to die?"

Hearing her give voice to that thought instantly made me see the lunacy of it. I started to say *No, of course not*, but wasn't that precisely what I'd been saying? And wasn't what I'd almost said even more insane? What evidence did I have that the man on the trestle that night had been my uncle, beyond that they shared a handful of common sayings? That so-and-so was a good egg. That people in hell wanted ice water. But evidence, of course, was not the issue. After all, I was positive that the woman who'd opened the trunk and peered inside at me was *not* my mother. I'd seen her. Why did something I knew to be false continue to haunt me with the terrible power of truth? Did I *want* it to be true? What possible benefit could derive from such a bitter, cruel falsehood?

I must have sat there stunned and mute for a long time, Sarah regarding me with that same tender, confused expression, and I think that if I could've spoken then it would have been to do what I'd suspected my mother of doing: I'd have warned Sarah against me, against the life I was offering her; that her affection for me, and for the rest of us Lynches, was a trap; that this was her chance to escape and tomorrow she should leave Thomaston and never look back. But when I finally spoke, I said, weakly, "It's just . . . ," and then I had to pause again, because suddenly I was aware that the restaurant was blurry around the edges, that it had been since we entered. Sarah herself was out of focus, with a halo encircling her dark curls. A spell, I thought. I'm having a spell. But this realization was less important than my need to explain, so I tried again. "It's just . . . I don't want her to sell Ikey's." I concentrated as hard as I could, wanting to get it right, to be as precise as I could. It wasn't just that I didn't want my mother to sell Ikey's; I didn't want her to be *right* about Ikey's, to be right about *anything*. I wanted desperately for her to be wrong about every single thing she'd ever argued with my father, wrong about our family, our town, our country. I wanted her to be wrong about *me*. But it was more than any of that. "I don't want my father to die," I said.

At which my Sarah, our Sarah, smiled. "Lou-Lou's going to be fine," she said, and she seemed so certain that in my vagueness and confusion I accepted her authority and felt something ponderous lift off of me. "He is?" I said.

Sarah said, "Lou, listen to me. Your mother isn't planning to sell the store. If anything has to be sold, she'll sell the *house*. She knows how much you love Ikey's, that it would kill you to lose it. Maybe she doesn't love Ikey's like you and Lou-Lou, but she loves that *you* love it. It's true she doesn't want to lose your house, but she knows it wouldn't kill her if that's what happens. Do you understand? She's not getting her way. You're getting yours. She wants you to have Ikey's, if that's what you want." She paused then to let all this sink in. "She wants *us* to have Ikey's, if that's what *we* want."

Then she reached across the table and took my hand, and at her touch the spell's aura was gone, the edges of everything sharp and clear again. Utterly vanished as well was the terrible bitterness that had been gnawing at me for days without my being entirely aware, along with the sour taste on the back of my tongue.

"That's what I want," I assured her.

How DISTANT these events seem tonight as I sit alone in my den in the aftermath of a spell powerful enough to blow Italy to smithereens. And as distant as they are in time, they feel even more remote in sentiment. How odd to recall that what I felt that late-March evening so long ago, when Sarah took my hand and banished my spell before it could happen, was *cured*. All my life I'd wanted to believe that my father was right in saying, "There ain't nothin' wrong with our Louie." My mother knew better, knew as I did that there *was* something wrong with me, something that *was* me and that would never go away unless I went with it. No matter how long it is between spells, the next is always lurking, hidden like a malignant cell and awaiting coded instructions to divide, then divide again, until it gains the required mass to steal me away and take me captive. Only then, after it's done what it must, can I be called back. My father was particularly good at this, at making the world feel right and safe for me when I returned.

But not even he had been able to *prevent* a spell. Nobody had ever cast one off once it was under way, as Sarah did when she took my hand in the restaurant. In the depths of despair just moments earlier, I immediately felt giddy with optimism, and so, amazingly, did she, as if she was as stunned by her own power as I was. Even more amazing, having now seen me at my worst, she seemed even more committed to our future than before. We stayed at the restaurant until it closed, mapping out the rest of our lives. Sarah would do one last semester at Cooper Union, then transfer to Albany. There, she'd be a full-time student and stay on campus when I went home on weekends. I'd continue to do whatever I could to help my parents save the store, but Sarah's talent—and suddenly I sounded like my mother—must not be compromised or sacrificed.

Drunk with hope, we determined not only things that were ours to decide but also things that weren't. We concluded that my father's operation had been an unqualified success, just as his doctor proclaimed, and that my mother's apprehensions were born of love, not reason. Before long he'd have his old strength back, and life would return to normal. Then we resolved that Ikey's would prosper, so there'd be no need to sell the house. Further, we figured that the money spent on renovations wasn't being wasted. Now that Sarah had straightened out my thinking, I saw what I'd been blind to before: that as soon as she and I were married, we'd move into the apartment ourselves and stay there until we could manage a down payment on a house of our own. I'd been right that my mother and uncle had been conspiring, but wrong about their intent. They were preparing a place for Sarah and me to live. Later, after she finished her degree, she'd teach art in the local schools and continue to draw and paint. She'd work at Ikey's only when she wanted to. At some point, when it was safe to do so, I'd go back to school and finish my own degree, because that's what my mother had always wanted and sacrificed for. We'd have two children, Sarah and I, a boy and a girl, who would take turns bouncing and giggling on their grandfather's knee. All this we decided, all this and more.

Tonight, our myriad decisions seem as remote as youth itself. Yet I can't bring myself to regard them as folly. As I stare at the

grainy newspaper photo of my hero-father that hangs above my
desk, I'm more disappointed in myself than anything else. Still
shaken by my encounter with him on the Bridge of Sighs, I'm
again visited by a feeling of profound shame, first because I tried
to sneak past my father, then because I begged him to let me stay
there on the bridge instead of returning to Sarah, my life and my
duties. In the final stage of his illness, when he weighed all of a
hundred and twenty pounds and all that was left was pain and
worry, he still loved his life. "I don't want to die," he told me one
afternoon, his lower lip trembling, when my mother was out of
the room. "I ain't afraid. It ain't that. I just want to stay here with
you, is all." Bedeviled by perplexity, he kept saying, "I don't
know what I done to deserve this," as if someone could maybe
explain it to him. But he was clear about what he wanted, at least.
To remain with us, at Ikey's, not to sneak off somewhere like I'd
tried to do this afternoon on the Bridge of Sighs.

I swallow the humiliation of my cowardice as best I can,
reminding myself that tomorrow, after a good night's sleep, I'll
be more myself, but right now the truth is that I'm about as
dispirited as I've been since my father's death, when I realized I'd
have to navigate the long remainder of my life without his star to
guide me. In the weeks and months after he was laid to rest, I
slipped into what I now realize was a deep depression. My
mother and Sarah seemed to understand what was happening
but were powerless to prevent it. No doubt I refused to
acknowledge that I needed help, even if they'd known what to
offer. In my grief and rage I'd become obsessed with the poisoning of our town. I bought a blown-up map of Thomaston and
mounted it on the wall, updating it daily by means of obituaries
in the newspaper, placing a black pin where the newly deceased
had lived. A nurse who worked in the hospital's oncology ward
helped me verify which deaths were due to cancer. In the
beginning I stuck to the relevant facts, recording each subsequent cancer death with another black pin. But before long,
impatient, anxious to indict, I started including people who'd

recently been diagnosed as well as others, like old Ikey Lubin himself, who'd died when I was a teenager. I was mapping, I believed, the tendrils of cancer snaking outward from the polluted stream. In the end, however, my map took on a meta-phorical quality. The black pin behind the Bijou Theater marked where Three Mock had been beaten into a coma, though he actually died years later in Vietnam. I put another on the street where David Entleman hanged himself. I even gave two black pins to the Spinnarkle sisters, who'd fled town rather than face neighbors who now knew their terrible secret.

Gradually, even I came to understand that the purpose of the map had metastasized. Somehow I'd expanded my definition of cancer to include any malignancy, any poison, any wickedness, until what I had was a map of cruelty, of violence, of human frailty, a map so full of personal significance that it was devoid of objective meaning. It was Sarah who helped me realize it had become like the drawing I'd done of Ikey Lubin's as a boy, shading everything so that the longer I worked on it, the darker and murkier it became, and ultimately even the thing I loved most—Ikey's itself—would have disappeared in the prevailing blackness. This was precisely what happened to my enlarged map, the black pins engulfing my entire town. Absent white space, there could be no pattern, no meaning, no significance, except that I'd succeeded in mapping my own despair. I didn't come to this difficult realization all at once but slowly, patiently, over long months as Sarah gently coaxed me back to my life, just as my father had done after my spells.

What occurs to me tonight, though, is this: sure, it's the business of adults to rescue children, but what sort of grown man needs to be repeatedly hauled back into his own life? Wouldn't it be kinder to cut him loose and let him finish his journey? What I told Sarah over supper tonight—that I'd have eventually returned on my own, even if she hadn't been there to help me—may not, this time, be true. Before encountering my father, I'd been deeply content to make that journey across the Bridge of

Sighs, and even now I feel the gentle downward slope of the smooth stones beneath my feet, the gentle and insistent pull of gravity. Keeping my promise to my father not to drift away? That had been uphill, hard. And had he not been there to remind me of my duty . . .

AFTER A TIME, Sarah joins me in the den. I swivel in my chair, and she places another chair right in front of me so we can face each other, knee to knee. Much like an adult would sit with a child, it occurs to me.

"I've been talking to your mother," she says, which doesn't surprise me. "She thinks you should have another scan." Sarah knows I won't like this idea. How many MRIs and CATs have I endured over the years, and to what end? My spells may resemble strokes, but in fact they are not, as the doctors mostly agree, as the scans all show. But this *was* a bad episode. Three full hours I was away, and while it seemed like only a few minutes to me, I now know that from the time my wife joined me in the art room and spoke my name, a good half hour elapsed before my return was complete. So if a scan will put their minds at ease, I'll submit to yet another.

"Is she furious with me?" I ask, because I realize that like everyone else, she'd seen this spell coming.

"Of course not," Sarah tells me. In her opinion I've always sold my mother short, which of course is true, and always has been.

"She must've said something," I venture, though in truth I'm not sure I want to hear her take on today's events, not that her conclusions would be any harsher than my own.

"She thinks there's a part of you that never got out of that trunk," Sarah says, adding, unnecessarily, "the one those boys locked you in." My mother means this observation compassionately, I know. She'd like to absolve me of blame, and not just for Italy, but it's an absolution I cannot accept. What those boys did to me was cruel, yes, though in fact they'd played the same prank on other kids, and I was the only one to suffer lasting consequences. My mother has always considered that a watershed event in my young life, one I never got over, but tell me who hasn't, in one fashion or another, been victimized or found himself imprisoned in this life? Wasn't Jerzy Quinn, the boy most responsible for what happened to me, himself the victim of a childhood far worse than mine? And what about the rest of his gang? In junior high we East Enders believed they were too tough, too cool, to attend our dances at the Y, but the truth was much simpler and more cruel than we understood. How old was I when it finally dawned on me that they simply didn't have the price of admission? They congregated out of sight at the footbridge—*their footbridge!*—within hearing of our pounding music, making a gift of their mocking laughter to those of us who had the necessary fifty cents. They joined us in the gym only after our parents had closed the cashbox and flung the doors wide open. Is it any wonder they came in angry and stomped their way through what little remained of the proceedings? Unlike us, their families lived in close proximity to the toxic stream, ensuring that they would grow exotic tumors later in life, or else they died in Vietnam, while those of us who danced, or nervously looked on, went off to college. I knew every one of those boys in Jerzy's gang, and, except for Perry Kozlowski, they're dead, every one of them. Jerzy himself was the last to go, as always the toughest one, still grinning like a wolf, or so I imagine, when the Jaws of Life pulled him from the wreckage of that fatal head-on. I wept when I read his obituary and wept when I stuffed it into the envelope my wife addressed to Bobby in place of her letter. So tell me, how is it that *I'm* the one who's damaged, who isn't right?

Breaking the silence, Sarah says, "When you were coming out of your spell, you kept trying to tell me something about Lou-Lou."

After a moment I say, "He was there."

"On the bridge?" Clearly she'd prefer to be wrong about an intuition as strange as this one. Over supper I'd explained, trying to make light of it, how I believed I'd actually entered her painting, that I was crossing over the bridge when I heard her calling me, but I'd left out the part about my father being there. I'd wanted her to believe it was she who was responsible for my return. For some reason it seemed important for her not to feel that her power to restore me to myself had been diminished.

"I think he's disappointed in me," I tell her, realizing as I do how crazy this sounds. "I mean, he would be, if he was still here."

"Your father was always proud of you," Sarah replies. "You know that."

Yes. I know this. I do. But I also know his pride was sustained by his refusal, as my mother put it, to know what he knew. And so, taking a deep breath, I do what I should've done weeks ago and open my desk drawer. "Bobby never received your letter," I say, handing it to Sarah, and her expression, as she takes it, is, I think, the saddest I've ever seen on a human face.

Dear Bobby. Though for weeks I've repressed its very existence, I discover I can now recite the letter verbatim. *Remember that drawing I did of Ikey's back before we met, how I put you at the front door about to enter? Well, now the tables are turned and it's we who are on* your *doorstep. Lou and I will be visiting Italy for two weeks in May. Rome first, then Florence. Venice we're saving for last. We've booked a room at Hotel Flora, which we understand is small but nice. We arrive by train on the 17th of next month. Will you invite your old friends across the threshold and into your world? Will you show us your studio and what you're working on? Will you guide us through your city, its Titians and Tintorettos? You remember Lou's mother Tessa, I'm sure. She's on record as believing there's too much water under the bridge for you to be interested in a visit from us. But Venice, I reminded her, is a city of bridges (forgive me,* ponti*). Surely, I told her, you'll be glad to tell us which ones lead to you. Either way, you'll settle a bet. Yours, Sarah.*

Yours, Sarah.

499

I feel my throat constrict at this familiarity. Sarah. No need to add "Lynch." Dear Bobby will know. Forty years? Twice forty? He'd still know.

And the postscript. *When you see me, you're not to comment on the fact that I'm no longer the skinny girl you knew. I will ask you to believe that my hair is really the color you see. Of course you're probably a sad, broken-down specimen yourself. If so, I will pretend not to notice.*

And the postpostscript: *Do you still have the drawing I did of you? The one where you're not completely ugly? Of course not. One of your many wives will have destroyed it. Which, I wonder?*

A love letter. Is there another way to interpret it? That playful, intimate tone is one Sarah hasn't used since we were young, and even then she employed it only with Bobby, which means that in writing to him she became that girl again—sporting, flirtatious, her whole life before her. Who does she miss more, I wonder, the boy she once loved or the girl who loved him?

I don't doubt my wife's faith, innocence or devotion to me, her husband. It's not that. But the human heart, well, it inclines this way and that without permission, ever unruly, ever wayward. It's *this* I've always wished otherwise, the flawed human heart. My mother's, Bobby's, Sarah's and especially my own. Was my father's heart flawed as well? I suppose it must have been, though to me it always beat strong and true.

When Sarah finally looks up, her eyes are full.

"I steamed the envelope open," I confess, feeling my cheeks burn.

"I wondered," she says. "It wasn't like Bobby to ignore us." To ignore *her*, she means. I can see myriad emotions warring within her, but the one that triumphs is relief, and at this my heart sinks even further. At last she says, "Are you going to tell me why?"

"I was afraid," I explain, but I can see she doesn't understand, and I'm visited by an unwanted memory of the day I peered in through the smoky window of the passenger train and saw on Sarah's lap the drawing she'd done of Bobby, the same one she alluded to in her postscript. I knew immediately what it meant, but in a heartbeat I'd hidden both the drawing and its significance away where it would trouble me no further. I think I've remembered it no more than half a dozen times in all the years since.

"Afraid you'd fall in love with him," I manage to tell her. "With Bobby. Again."

CATHEDRAL

Hugh was seated on the grand terrace of his hotel, his bags piled next to the balustrade, when Noonan finally arrived, an hour late. "Dear God, look at you," he said. Noonan had been at work for hours and was covered with paint. There was even some in his hair.

"What time is it?" Lichtner had asked when he shook him awake at dawn.

"Time for you to go home," Noonan told him. "Get up. I need you out of here."

The man sat up on the sofa, blinking at his watch in disbelief. "This is so fucking cruel. I've only been asleep for two hours."

Ignoring his complaints, Noonan busied himself setting up his spare easel. Outside, the newly risen sun was a dull red ball, the same size and shape as the dome of the Salute. A Turner, he thought, if there'd been a Turner handy to see it.

"I could go get us some coffee," Lichtner said wistfully after he'd pulled on his clothes, but Noonan was already going through his supplies and hadn't even responded. If the fool had volunteered to fetch him a big tube of cadmium yellow, he might've taken him up on it, but coffee? A few minutes later Noonan heard the door slam in the courtyard below.

"I'd just about given up on you," Hugh told him now.

"I started something new this morning," Noonan said. "A better painter would've stayed in the studio."

"Tell me."

"It'll be the best painting in the show."

"A whole new canvas? That you can finish in time?"

502

"It'll paint itself."

Hugh grinned. "Excellent. Now can we lose the self-portrait?"

"It's not a self-portrait. It's my father." There, he thought. You said it. And he realized it didn't matter that Hugh knew; it was no longer a secret worth keeping and probably never had been. "Anyway, it doesn't matter. The new one comes first."

He already had a title: *Sarah at the Window*. He'd dreamed the painting whole last night and woke up weeping with gratitude. It had happened before—dreaming a painting—though maybe only ten times in his entire life. The first time he wasn't even a painter yet, had never picked up a brush. It would be the better part of a decade before he'd understand that such dreams were paintings trying to emerge, or, if not an actual painting, the feeling that would be contained within the painting, its source and center on the canvas. Sometimes a single powerful dream would result in half a dozen canvases, a sequence of seemingly unconnected works, though he himself always recognized an emotional linkage, despite being powerless to articulate it. The good news was that he'd never felt much need to explain. When the fit was upon him, as it was now, he had but one need, and that was to paint.

"Your father," Hugh repeated. "Well, I did say it wasn't you, didn't I."

Noonan consulted his watch. "You're going to miss your plane."

"Here's your hat, what's your hurry?" Right on cue, the waiter arrived with Hugh's bill, which he signed with a flick of his wrist. "Walk me to my taxi?"

Noonan supposed that was the least he could do, so he grabbed the larger of his friend's bags, and the two men headed down the terrace to where several water taxis bobbed.

"So," Hugh said, "will you go back to it? After this new one?"

Noonan couldn't help smiling. Yesterday he'd advised him to burn the damn thing; today he was afraid he wouldn't return to it. "It's possible," he said. It was hard to explain how something could be important one minute, irrelevant the next. "Once I know this new one's safe."

Hugh shrugged, accepting what he must, as he'd always done, because what else could he do? "Well, you're behaving like a lunatic this morning. Fortunately, for you that's a good thing. Are you going to be okay?"

Strangely enough, Noonan thought he was. He wouldn't have been given this new painting if he weren't well enough to paint it. Perverse logic, maybe, but there you were. "I'll be fine."

"Is there anything you need? Anything I can do?"

Yes, Noonan thought. Go.

Hugh smirked, as if he'd just read Noonan's thoughts, and stepped into the taxi. When Noonan handed the bag to the driver, Hugh, instead of offering to shake hands, sighed, consulted his watch and said, "You might as well come on board."

What? Was the man insane? Did he expect Noonan to accompany him to the airport? He had a fucking painting to get back to.

"We'll run you over to the Giudecca," Hugh said, then gave instructions to the driver in Italian. "It'll save you ten or fifteen minutes' waiting for the vaporetto."

"Really?" Noonan said, stepping aboard. He could've kissed him. "I'd hate for you to miss your flight." But he didn't say this until they were under way and there was no chance for Hugh to change his mind. This was pure selfishness, he told himself, but in truth he didn't care and never had. Not when there was canvas waiting and paint to put on it.

NOONAN WAS SEVENTEEN when he had the first of what he would come to think of as his "paint dreams." He'd just moved out of his parents' house in the Borough and into a cavernous space above the old Rexall drugstore downtown on Hudson Street. At one time it had been partitioned into small offices, though the interior walls had come down and the whole floor gutted right down to its wood planks. There were tall, soot-blackened windows in both the front, which overlooked the street, and the rear, with a view of the back alley and an abandoned glove shop. The place was unheated and dirty, but the building's owner, a friend of Dec Lynch's, had let Noonan have it for nothing so long as he didn't throw parties or drag in bums off the street. His friends envied him having his own pad until they saw it, after which they couldn't fathom why he preferred sleeping on the cold, hard floor to a nice, soft bed in his parents' home. Only Sarah had immediately seen the beauty of it. After spending the better part of an afternoon scrubbing the rear windows, she'd set up an easel there. Noonan would later come to think of it as his first studio, though it had been someone else who'd painted there. One thing he was sure of: if he hadn't moved out of his parents' house he never would've dreamed the cathedral, and if he hadn't had that first powerful dream, he never would've become a painter.

The cathedral was more vivid than any dream he'd ever had, including the ones that involved sex. Lacking narrative, it had felt more like a vision. He couldn't even be sure how long it had lasted. In dream time it had felt like hours, but he knew that in reality it had probably lasted no more than a minute or two, as the sun streamed in on him through the tall, clean windows, causing his eyelids to flutter and him to swim toward consciousness. He remembered being aware that he was asleep, of both wanting and not wanting to wake up. Awake, he could share his vision, and he didn't want to be the only one to see something so beautiful; but if he woke and called to somebody—maybe Sarah, who'd love it—the wondrous cathedral might disappear. Something told him it would, so he wandered from room to room, breathless, on the verge, simultaneously, of joy and tears.

Cathedral? That was as close as he could come to characterizing the place, which he sensed was not of this world. Its vaulted ceilings were impossibly high, the arched passageways leading between its chambers numberless. It would take years to explore them all, and he wanted nothing more. Not food or drink or love or anything he'd ever tasted in his life so far. In each new chamber he was torn between wanting to stay where he was, to commit every detail to memory, and the even stronger impulse to move on, quickly, from one breathtaking wonder to the next, to discover where each new passageway led, to map the entire cathedral, if something so vast could ever be charted. Though all one building, it was the size of a city, of twenty cities. You could spend a lifetime going from room to room and maybe never again revisit the one you were currently in. Some of the passageways were so narrow he had to turn sideways, others so low he had to crawl on his hands and knees, but each new chamber was bathed in a golden light so soft and radiant that he could feel his heart contract within his chest at its terrifying beauty. *Remember this*, some inner voice kept whispering. *Never, ever forget.*

But that wish, he'd realize later, had been the first sign of wakefulness, and as soon as he opened his eyes the dream began to recede, dull reality assuming its place. He knew that when he fully awoke it would be Saturday, and that afternoon he'd play his final football game of the season. Football! What could be more foolish? Panicking, he tried desperately to fall back asleep. The idea that he might never find the cathedral again—he never would—was in that moment unthinkable. The dream's orgasmic intensity still seized him, even half awake, though he already was thinking of it as a dream, not a real place. He'd glimpsed the miraculous and then, just that quickly, it was gone. He wanted to weep and never quit. In a matter of a few actual minutes, all that remained was the dream's aura, the tingling sense that something marvelous had happened and now was gone forever.

Even at sixty, Noonan could feel his fingertips tingling at the memory, probably because no painting had come from the dream. That first one had come too soon, before he had any idea of what use he would put it to. Each subsequent dream would be a gift, again filling him with wonder and gratitude, though each would also be less intense than the last. That made a kind of sense, he supposed. As he matured as an artist, his power increasingly derived from discipline, from skills honed by habit, and he had less need of inspiration, if that's what the dreams were. The paint gods were frugal. They gave you only what you needed. Last night's had been a pitiful thing, the faintest echo of his cathedral dream, but it was all he'd needed. He'd awakened feeling like he was twenty again and could work forty-eight hours straight if he needed to.

It also occurred to Noonan that last night's just might be his final dream. That possibility he put out of his mind.

THAT FALL Thomaston had suffered through a mediocre season marred by almost pathological inconsistency. The town's gamblers, Dec Lynch foremost among them, found that particularly frustrating. Against his better judgment he'd bet on Thomaston the first game of the season, only to have Mohawk's speedy Puerto Ricans, the very ones Dec had feared, get loose in the home team's porous secondary. Still, the Tanners had made a game of it in the second half, and with time running out had been driving toward a tying touchdown when Noonan, who'd been sure-handed to that point, coughed up the ball and that was that.

"What was I thinking?" Dec Lynch said the next morning when Noonan stopped by Ikey's.

"Sorry, Dec," Noonan said as if he wasn't particularly. "Next week bet on Utica."

But Dec wasn't finished with this week yet. "You know you're allowed to run *around* guys, right? If there's just you and a single defender, there's no law says you gotta go over the top of him. And if you go *around* him you won't drop the ball on impact, because—and here's the real beauty of the thing—there *is* no impact. And the *other* beauty would be that I'd still have money

507

in my wallet, whereas . . ." He took out his billfold then to demonstrate the consequence of trying to go through defenders.

"Bet Utica next week," Noonan repeated. Because Utica was, by all reports, bigger, faster and tougher than Mohawk, and it was an away game to boot.

"Don't worry," Dec told him. "I intend to."

Except that the following Saturday the whole team played well. On the first play from scrimmage, Perry Kozlowski planted Utica's star running back in the turf, and the boy went off the field wobbly, never to return. Noonan ran the ball effectively, though he lacked the speed to be spectacular, and late in the fourth quarter he found himself in the same situation as the previous week, a single safety between him and the goal line, and this time he took Dec's advice. Lowering his head as if he meant to steamroll the Utica defender, he spun at the last second and left the kid with an armful of air and Dec with an empty wallet for the second Saturday in a row.

It had gone that way pretty much all season, the team zigging when Dec zagged. When he tried to change things up, figuring the Tanners were incapable of having either two good or two bad games in a row, they disproved him then, too.

"Normally I like to go on vacation right after football season," he told Noonan the night before their last game.

He and Lucy and Sarah had congregated at Ikey's, to wait for Nan Beverly to pick them up. Nan, who'd failed her driver's exam twice, had passed on the third try, and they were celebrating by going out for pizza in her father's Caddy.

"But not this year," Dec continued. "This year it'll be Easter before I make back all the money I lost on you nitwits this season. The only bright spot is you're all going to graduate and stop tormenting me."

"I may get held back, actually," Noonan said, mock-serious. "Honors English may do me in." In truth it was his best class, and he was still, for some reason, Mr. Berg's favorite.

"Sweet thing," Dec said to Sarah, who was killing time by

playing a game of crazy eights with Lucy. "Tell your father that if he flunks this kid, I may have to shoot myself."

"That might make him even more determined," she answered, always happy to take the opposite side of any argument that involved Dec.

"There she goes being mean to me again," he said, now trying to make an ally of Noonan. "She does look especially sexy tonight, though, doesn't she? What I'll never understand is why she hangs around with mere boys when there are eligible, single men around, men with good looks and experience both."

"Lou-Lou isn't single," Sarah said, causing Big Lou, at his usual post by the register, to beam.

"I'm talking about me," Dec said. "You must've missed the goodlooking part."

"I just heard the part about you being broke, I guess. Last card," she told Lucy, who commenced drawing, hearts suddenly a rarity. Noonan met Sarah's eye, and when she grinned, he guessed the truth, that the card she held was a wild eight, that Lucy could draw all night and it wouldn't matter, his fate already sealed.

"That's what I've been saying," Dec went on. "This football team is all that stands between me and solvency *and* true love."

"What stands between Dec Lynch and a better life is Dec Lynch," Lucy's mother told him. The two of them were busy tearing down the meat case, stretching sheets of plastic wrap over the tubs of ground beef and ferrying the salads into the walk-in. "I'm guessing a plate of macaroni salad wouldn't completely ruin your appetite," Tessa said, handing Noonan one. Since football season had begun, there was never a time when he wasn't ravenous, and he accepted the plate gratefully.

"Instead of feeding this kid we should be starving him," Dec said. "If he was too weak to play I'd know how to bet."

Finally Lucy found a heart and laid it down. "Why'd you let me draw all those cards?" he said when Sarah put her eight on top of the heart, giving him a kiss on the forehead and her best, throaty laugh. Noonan could almost feel that kiss on his own brow and touched the spot where it would've landed.

Finishing the macaroni salad, he looked up and saw that Tessa had been observing him with her most knowing expression. *She* wouldn't have drawn for that heart like her son just did. She'd have seen her defeat coming and known there wasn't a thing she could do about it.

Outside, a horn tooted, and Nan pulled up to the curb.

"This week I'd bet on us, if I were you," Noonan told Dec on the way out.

"Thanks for the tip," he said. "I'd have to be a complete idiot to take it, but I always feel better knowing your opinion."

BY THE TIME Noonan and his teammates trotted onto the field the next day, he'd all but forgotten his cathedral dream. He'd remembered it a couple of times that morning, feeling just a faint tingle of residual wonder. By afternoon he was able to laugh at the memory, especially since the dream had seemed so urgently important. *Tell everyone.* Tell them what? That somewhere there's a church as big as the world, with more chambers than you could count and ceilings as high as the sky? Good God. He'd been dreaming architecture. What next, biology?

Yet something felt different, brighter, as if some of that golden light had leaked into the real world. On Thomaston's first possession, Noonan took the handoff and ran between the tackles, a play designed to pick up, if all went well, a tough four or five yards. But a gaping hole miraculously opened, and in a heartbeat he was through it and rumbling untouched into the end zone.

And it wasn't just on the field. Even the bleachers seemed brighter, clearer, and when he saw Nan and Lucy and Sarah sitting about halfway up, they looked almost close enough to reach out and touch. Nan seldom paid attention at games. She liked the idea that her boyfriend was the team's star running back, but when time ran out she seldom knew whether he'd had a good game or a bad one, whether he'd fumbled or held on to the ball, scored three touchdowns or been held in check, so she stood and cheered when other people did. "Oh, look!" she was telling Lucy now, pointing at the scoreboard. "We're ahead. Didn't the game just start?" Was it possible he was *seeing* all that? Had he read her lips, or was he just guessing what she'd said? But when Sarah replied, Noonan could read her words as well. "Bobby just ran for a touchdown."

Everywhere he looked, his heightened powers of observation offered up privileged glimpses into private behavior. In the crowd that ringed one end zone he saw Sarah's father in furtive conversation with a tall, emaciated black man named Jackson—first name or last, Noonan didn't know—and then his teacher slipped him something that quickly disappeared into his pants pocket. A moment later Jackson pivoted, as if to depart, and with his other hand deposited something into Mr. Berg's outside coat pocket. Noonan knew this man from Murdick's, where he tended bar on Sunday nights, and knew that he dealt marijuana and who knew what else. Mr. Englander, who owned Murdick's, had been blunt about Jackson. "I don't give a damn what he does as long as he does it in the alley with the door closed. You see him transacting business inside, you have my permission to toss his black ass onto the pavement. Just be careful of that blade he carries."

Noonan spotted his mother sitting, for some reason, over on the visitors' side with his raucous feral brothers, all of them a bane to their teachers but loving to her. They surrounded her now, as if they feared that contact with the world outside their Borough home might overstimulate her. Not much danger of that, Noonan felt sure. Her usual smile was even more serene today, which suggested she'd fortified herself with an additional little pill before leaving the house. He doubted that by tomorrow she'd be any too sure exactly what sort of sporting event she'd attended. She might even wake up and think she'd dreamed her day out. Still, every time he glanced up where she sat, her gaze was fixed on him, his teammates apparently beside the point, and each time he got tackled, she clamped her hand to her mouth. After every play, his brothers had to reassure her. "It's okay, Mom. See? He's up. He's not hurt."

And so it had gone all afternoon. Things normally shrouded in the fog of combat were brightly lit, things happening singly instead of all at once, a slow-motion miracle. When the game was over, Coach Halliday addressed his rowdy, ecstatic team in the locker room for the last time. With the possible exception of Dec Lynch, nobody had been more exasperated by the Tanners' inconsistency than their coach, and today he seemed even more dispirited by their lopsided victory than he'd been by many of their losses. "You see what I been telling you?" he said. He had bad knees from his own days in the semipro leagues, and he needed to be helped up onto the bench so he could address his troops. "You see?"

Noonan, for one, did not, and it didn't look like anyone else did either.

"Marconi," Coach said, barely containing his exasperation. "What have I been telling you guys all season?"

Noonan tried to guess what he might be getting at. He'd told them a lot of things, more than they could absorb at any given moment. Now he seemed to want Noonan to distill all of those things, including the ones they'd forgotten, into a single lesson, *after* an exhausting game. He took a stab. "Fundamentals?"

Coach Halliday rubbed his forehead vigorously, then turned to Perry Kozlowski. "Koz," he said. "What have I been saying since August?"

Perry was visited by a sudden inspiration. "How good we could be if we all worked together?"

"Thank you," Coach said, as if he really was grateful and might well have borrowed the track coach's starter pistol and shot himself in the head if Perry, too, had disappointed him. "Four months I've been telling you that. It's good to know I wasn't wasting my breath. Today, you were a *team*. You understand? Life is teamwork, men. That's all it is. When you think about this game, that's what I want you to remember—how good you were today and how good you could've been all season long if you'd paid attention back in September."

It was a good speech, Noonan thought, and he was moved by it, despite not believing a single word of it. He didn't doubt that Halliday truly thought that life was teamwork, and he supposed he was grateful for his high opinion of their abilities. And of course he was sorry they'd disappointed him by underachieving. But he doubted they'd been any more of a team today than previously. Rather, they'd just played better than usual, probably because this was their last game. Kids who normally missed blocks made them, receivers who usually dropped balls managed to hang on. They'd scored first and benefited from a couple of lucky bounces. Their victory, the way Noonan saw it, was a combination of luck and fate and momentum and who knew what else, but he doubted it could be chalked up to teamwork. More to the point, though Noonan wouldn't have said so to Coach Halliday, he was delighted to see the end of the season, which, far from teaching him that life was nothing but teamwork, had convinced him to eschew all team sports in the future. He'd enjoyed the competition and the physicality, and he understood the necessity of discipline, but the camaraderie that seemed so important to Coach and Perry was left out of him.

When Halliday was done talking, it took two linemen and an assistant coach to help him down and lead him out of the locker room. Then Perry, the team captain, clad only in a jockstrap, leapt up onto the same bench and announced that from that moment forward, everyone on this team was his brother. Noonan had to look away because Perry's entire back was a moonscape of angry purple pimples, bigger and angrier looking than those on his ravaged face. "I'd lay down my life for you guys," Perry proclaimed, his eyes brimming with tears. "Even you, Marconi," he added, getting a laugh.

RICHARD RUSSO

Their old animosity had gradually leaked away over the course of the term. Perry attributed this to the fact they were team-mates, Noonan to Mr. Berg's class. Though Perry still embraced the role of class contrarian and general knucklehead, no one had profited more from the readings and discussions of honors English. Ironically, Noonan thought, that class had become more of a team effort than the Tanners, though Mr. Berg would have scoffed at the idea.

"And I know something else," Perry continued, hitching up his jock-strap. "I know you'd do the same for me."

This, thankfully, seemed to be addressed to the whole team, which absolved him of making a similar declaration that would've been insincere in the extreme. But when Perry hopped down from the bench, he clasped Noonan on the back of the neck with one big paw and drew him forward until their foreheads touched. "I meant what I said up there," he told him.

"I know you did," Noonan said.

"Back in September I wanted to kill you, man," he admitted, and unless Noonan was mistaken, the memory was still fresh enough for some of that old desire to flare again, the grip on the back of his neck tightening. Then it relaxed, one emotion trump-ing an equally bogus one. "But now we're brothers. Forever."

"Okay, then," Noonan said, trying to pull away, although it was apparently too soon for that.

"You know what we should all do tomorrow? We should go down and enlist. Keep the team together."

"Sort of like a suicide pact," Noonan said.

"We could kick some ass over there, this team," Perry said.

"Or," Noonan said, "we could just plan to meet right here every year for homecoming."

Perry, considering this less lethal option, seemed to think it needed some punching up. "Sort of like, no matter where we are, no matter what we're doing, no matter how much it costs, we drop everything and somehow get back here. Prove to Coach we're still a team. That we remember this day."

"I like it," Noonan said, and he did. He particularly liked the fact that it would give them all a full year to forget this day, this pledge and the emotion that inspired it.

Out in the parking lot, after he'd showered and dressed, Noonan saw a man leaning against his motorcycle. For safety Noonan had parked it between two school buses. Dec inspected the bike at least once a week for scratches and dents. He seemed happy enough that somebody was getting some use out of it, but that raised the possibility of damage. "You know this fucking thing's a classic, right?" Dec kept reminding him. "They don't even make Indians anymore. The company's gone out of business." So he always parked out of harm's way, and he didn't allow people to lean on the bike either, like this guy was doing. That Noonan didn't immediately recognize him as his father suggested his sensory apparatus had returned to normal. Either that or it didn't work on his father.

"Nice game," his father said, offering him a cigarette, which he declined.

"I didn't see you there."

"I was, though."

"Whereabouts?"

"I've been to all your games."

"Bullshit," Noonan said—not anger, just an opinion his father could take or leave.

Leave, apparently. "You know a place called Nell's?" he said.

"On the Lake Road?"

"Meet me there, I'll buy you a beer."

"I'm not eighteen."

"I know how old you are. And that you're sleeping in that rat-hole above the Rexall and tending bar at Murdick's on Sundays."

"I'm supposed to meet my friends."

"Meet them after."

"Why?"

"Why not, son?"

*

515

NELL'S SAT five miles out of town atop a hill at the end of a
steep, unpaved road. It appeared to have been built in stages, the
early part of brick, then added on to in clapboard. Noonan
remembered the original restaurant as being prosperous, its
parking lot always full of cars back when he was a boy, but since
then it had fallen on hard times and had changed hands again
and again over the last decade. Whoever Nell was, her sign was
tilting precariously when he roared up the gravel road on his
bike. His father's was one of half a dozen cars in the lot, and
Noonan parked off to the side by the dumpster.

His father was seated at the far end of the bar, talking to a
large woman bartender who looked to be in her early forties and
might've been attractive had she not been so overweight, her
expression so glum. She looked like somebody who could easily
be named Nell and who'd invested her last nickel in the place.

When Noonan slid onto the adjacent stool, his father consulted his watch. "I was about to come looking for you," he said.

"I told you I'd be here."

"I thought maybe you changed your mind."

"I don't do that," Noonan told him, and he could tell from his
smile that they were both referencing the day that spring when
he'd warned what would happen if his mother got pregnant
again.

"A person should change his mind occasionally," his father
said.

"Why?"

"Situations change." Then, before Noonan could offer a
response, he said, "This is Max," and nodded vaguely at the
woman behind the bar, who was wiping her soapy hands on a
towel so they could shake.

"Maxine," she clarified.

"Not Nell?" Noonan said.

"Nell was my sister. She died of leukemia. We named the
place for her."

"And this is Willie, Max's boy," his father added when the

kitchen door swung open and a Down's syndrome kid came in with a bucket of ice. He looked to be about Noonan's age, but he was already balding so it was hard to tell. He grinned and emitted a braying sound that might or might not have been a word, then disappeared back into the kitchen.

"So what kept you?" his father said.

"I stopped by Ikey Lubin's."

His father nodded. "That Lynch kid figure out he's a queer yet?"

"Nice language," Maxine said, glaring at him. It made Noonan like her, though he couldn't help wondering why she imagined she had a place in their conversation. She may have sensed this reaction, because after drawing him a draft beer and sliding it in front of him she busied herself at the other end of the bar.

"He's got a steady girlfriend, actually," Noonan said.

"They'll do that sometimes."

"A person should change his mind now and then," Noonan said. One of the best things about honors English was that Mr. Berg had taught him the value of using other people's words against them. In the two months he and the others had been parrying with Sarah's father, they'd all gotten quicker on their rhetorical feet. They used their new skills outside of class and made short work of anybody who hadn't learned to survive a withering Berg assault. "When situations change."

His father seemed to enjoy the counterthrust himself. "Some situations change. Others don't."

"Have it your way," Noonan said. "What am I doing here?"

"Having a beer with your old man. Let's see your fake ID." He held out his hand. Noonan paused before handing it over. In another month he'd be eighteen anyway, and besides, he doubted his old man meant to confiscate it now, having just bought him a beer.

His father looked the card over, nodding in appreciation. "Nice job. How much did it set you back?"

"Seventy-five."

"I could've got you one for less if you'd asked." He added, when Noonan offered no reply. "But Jass was right. It's a good one."

"Jass?"

"Jasper Englander. Your boss. Why do you think he hired you?"

The last thing Noonan wanted to do was grant his father the satisfaction of yet another surprise when he still hadn't figured out what to make of the first. Was it possible he'd really come to all his games and Noonan had just failed to notice him? What would that mean? For that matter, what did it mean that he'd never suspected his influence when, underage, he got a bartending job from a man who'd been looking at fake IDs all his life?

"You hungry?" his father said.

"No," Noonan lied.

"It's prime rib night. They do it good here."

"I'm not hungry," he repeated.

"Suit yourself," his father said, signaling Maxine, who came down the bar and took his order for a prime rib, medium-rare, just as Noonan would've taken his if he wasn't being so stubborn.

"They let people eat at the bar?" Noonan said when Maxine went into the kitchen.

"Normally, no, but they let me."

"You're special?"

"Well," he said, "I do own the place."

"Right." Noonan snorted, then realized his father was serious. The surprises were coming too fast now, practically tripping over one another.

Maxine returned with a setup and a salad with blue-cheese dressing—also Noonan's favorite—in a small wooden bowl.

"*You*," he said. "You own this place."

His father dug in. "Well, it's my name on the lease, put it like that. What?"

"Nothing," he said. "I was just thinking about the budget you keep Mom on."

"Your mother's a child. If I treated her like an adult, we'd all be broke."

"You're the one who keeps her a child," Noonan said. "You never let her do anything."

"She *can't* do anything. It's not a question of letting her or not letting her."

Noonan shook his head in disbelief. "And you were at the game today?"

"I told you. I've been to all of them."

"Would it have killed you to sit with her? Make her happy for once?"

"Trust me, she was far happier with your brothers."

The prime rib came then, beautifully red, swimming in au jus. Noonan's stomach began to growl. "You sure you don't want one of these?" his father said. "It's not too late."

"I'm not hungry," he said, certain that by now his lie was transparent. "It's those pills. She can't function."

"They don't help," his father admitted, chewing thoughtfully. "They aren't the problem, though." He'd separated the leaner meat from the fatty tail. Even the fat made Noonan's mouth water. "Suppose you're right that I should be around more, act nicer to your mother. What about you? These days, you aren't around much more than I am. If you really cared about her, you wouldn't be living downtown. You'd be home helping out, making things better. Except you know there's no way to make things better, right?"

"I live downtown so I don't run into you. If we lived under the same roof, she'd be even worse off."

"But I *don't* live under that roof. I visit. Just like you." His father pushed his plate away, having eaten, Noonan judged, about half. "Look, I don't give a shit if you lie to me. Say you aren't hungry when you are, that's no skin off my ass. But don't lie to yourself."

"How am I doing that?"

Maxine came over and cleared the plate away. Noonan told himself not to watch it go, but he did anyway.

"Here's what I think. When you were a kid, you saw things a certain way," his father continued. "Who knows? Maybe you were right. But you keep wanting to see things the same way now, even though they aren't. You know they aren't, but you're in the habit. You feel better about things if I'm the bad guy."

"You *are* the bad guy."

"See what I mean?" his father said. "You didn't even have to think about it, and you should've." He called down the bar, "Max, am I a bad guy?"

"Nope."

"Call Willie out here a minute," he suggested, and when the boy appeared in the doorway he said, "William, tell the truth now. Am I a good guy or a bad guy?"

"A good guy," Willie said with no more hesitation than Noonan and even more pleased to have gotten the answer right. "The best guy."

"There you go," his father said, as if only the most unreasonable person could dispute such unblemished testimony.

Noonan chuckled. "I guess that settles it."

"Oh," his father said, "he's not smart like you, so he must be wrong?"

"I didn't say that." He'd implied it, though.

"Okay," his father said, conceding the point. "You tell me. What should I be doing different?"

"I wouldn't know where to begin."

"Begin anywhere. Maybe I should be more like you. Go through life pretending I'm not hungry when I am. Should I make like there's nothing wrong with your mother . . . pretend she's the woman of my dreams?"

"Not a bad idea," Noonan said, mostly out of frustration. "You made her the way she is. Bullying her. Scaring her out of her wits."

"What wits?"

Noonan ignored this. "And you call yourself a man?" His father's birthmark darkened a shade, and Noonan thought, Okay, so we'll do this, right here, right now. Come on. Throw that punch, old man. You know you want to.

But the kitchen door flew open just then, and Willie reappeared, his face contorted and body trembling with what looked like fear. But neither one of them had raised his voice. Had the boy been listening at the door?

"It's okay, Will," Noonan's father said. "Everything's all right."

The boy didn't move. He studied Noonan's father, then Noonan himself, still visibly trembling.

"He doesn't like for people to be angry, do you, Will?"

The boy shook his head violently. His mother came down the bar, put a hand on his shoulder and said, "Shhhh."

His father looked at Noonan. "Tell him everything's fine."

"Everything's fine," he said.

"Try meaning it," his father suggested, the boy still staring at Noonan.

"Everything's okay," he said, sincerely this time, and sure enough, the kid stopped trembling, gave them all a big smile and returned to the kitchen.

"Don't ask," his father said once Maxine was again out of earshot. "I have no idea how he knows, but he does. If you made a fist right now, he'd be back out here before it landed."

"Maybe we should go someplace else."

His father shrugged. "The beer's free here, unless you don't think you can control yourself."

"I guess I was thinking more about you."

He ignored this, signaling to Maxine for two more drafts. "So, you know all about being a man now?"

"How would I? All I've ever known is you."

"But you *haven't* known me."

When Maxine came down the bar, Noonan waved away the beer.

"Leave it," his father told her. "He can drink it or not, his choice. He's a man." When she was gone again, his father changed the subject. "So, tell me about this Beverly girl."

"Why?" Noonan said, setting his beer down, realizing as he did so that he'd taken a swig without meaning to. He'd never mentioned Nan to his father—or mother, for that matter—but somehow he knew.

"She's cute. Marry her and you're set for life," his father said.

"Maybe, but that's not the plan."

"What is?"

Sex, Noonan thought, though she hadn't yet surrendered to him, mostly because he hadn't pressed. And why was that? Sarah, probably. Now that they were all hanging out together, she and Nan had become confidantes, and for some reason she seemed to have concluded that Nan was vulnerable and needed protecting. "She really likes you, you know," Sarah kept telling him, as if affection *caused* vulnerability. To Noonan it just meant they'd eventually have sex. That Sarah should consider it the reason they shouldn't seemed beyond perverse.

"College, maybe," Noonan said, a trial balloon more than anything, curious to see what the old man would think.

"Why not?" his father said, a surprise. Noonan had expected him to recommend the army. "I could maybe help, if that's what you decide."

"Thanks."

His father noticed the tone. "Thanks, but no thanks? Is that what you're saying? Thanks, but I'm not hungry? Thanks, but I'm not thirsty?" He nodded at Noonan's glass, which somehow was empty now.

"So what's this about? We're supposed to be friends, all of a sudden?"

His father shrugged. "Any reason we shouldn't be?"

"Only the last seventeen years."

"We could start the next seventeen tonight."

Could he be serious? "I'll think about it."

"But you don't like the idea."

"Well, it's the timing. Now that you don't scare me anymore, you want to be friends."

"That's one way to look at it."

"What's the other way?"

"Maybe it's not all of a sudden. Maybe you haven't been paying attention. Maybe you're not as smart as you think. Maybe you just prefer what you're used to. Maybe you're afraid something new will throw you off kilter."

"You're saying you've changed."

"I'm saying if you decide to go to college, maybe I can help a little. I'm saying the next time I offer to buy you dinner, you should take me up on it. There's one more thing I'm saying, too, but it'll have to wait, because right now I've got to pee. You must have to take a leak yourself."

"No, I'm fine," he lied.

His father just grinned at him. "Hard to do things different, isn't it."

Once he was gone, Maxine came down the bar. "So how's tending bar down in the Gut?"

"Not bad," Noonan said. And was it any of her business, he'd have liked to ask.

"Murdick's can get a little rough."

"It's pretty quiet on Sundays," Noonan said. "I've only had to eighty-six one guy. He called me a name, but then passed out before I could punch him."

"Well, when you get tired serving beers and bumps to rummies, let me know. I could use a night off every now and then. Sunday would work as well as any other damn day, if that's the only one you can work."

"Now that football season's over, I'm a little more flexible."

"I could teach you how to make a cocktail. Give you a skill. Bartenders don't starve in America," she said, "of course they don't get rich either."

"Thanks. I'll think about it," Noonan told her.

"That's the second time you've said that," Maxine remarked.

And when she smiled, Noonan was surprised. For a woman with such a hard face, her smile was soft and warm. "Tell my old man I said thanks for the beer," he said, sliding off his stool. But then he heard the door to the men's room swing open. When he turned and saw his father returning, he could only stare. In the time it had taken him to empty his bladder, he'd aged ten years.

"What?" his father said.

"Nothing," he said, squinting at him. "You look different."

"Different from what?"

Noonan was about to say *From how you always look*, but stopped. Was it possible that his father was right, that somehow he wasn't paying attention? If the old man suddenly looked a decade older, did that mean that it had been a decade since Noonan had really looked at him? Was this how he'd managed not to see him at all those football games, or failed to recognize him that afternoon, when he was leaning against Dec's bike?

"I'll be back in a minute," his father told Maxine. "My son's a little slow putting two and two together, so I need to bring him up to speed."

Outside, they walked over to the motorcycle. Noonan swung a leg over the saddle and waited for whatever his father wanted to say, so he could leave, but for some reason he seemed reluctant. "Look, I should've met my friends by now," he told him. "If you want to tell me something, shoot."

His father nodded thoughtfully, as if searching for the right words. "It's not something I want to tell you, exactly. I just thought you might like to meet Max."

Noonan blinked at this and was on the verge of asking why on earth he'd want to do that when he understood. "That's *her*," Noonan said. *This* was the woman his father had been involved with all these years?

"Careful," his father said, as if he was about to say the one thing that could provoke hostilities between them. "I just thought you might like to know she's not a bad person. She's had a pretty rough time of it, actually."

"As rough as Mom?"

"Plus, she wanted to meet you."

"Why?"

"She thought it'd do you good. We've been kind of having an argument about you. She said the day would come when you'd wake up and wonder who the hell your old man really was."

"You disagreed."

"Well, it wouldn't have been much of an argument otherwise. But so far, I'm winning."

"That's true, you are," Noonan said, turning the key in the ignition.

"She's stubborn, though," his father shouted over the engine roar. "Like somebody else I could name. Have a good time with your friends."

Noonan watched him disappear back into the restaurant, wondering what the hell this feeling was. Guilt? Come on. But he continued to sit, the bike rumbling beneath him, until finally he laughed, as much to hear his own voice as anything, then shifted into gear. Only when he was out on the highway did he notice his left saddlebag flapping in the breeze. Pulling into the parking lot of the old tannery, he discovered that it contained his father's leftover prime rib. Had Maxine put it there? No, he was pretty sure she hadn't left the bar. The boy, Willie? He didn't think so. Which meant his father must've done it when he went to the restroom or just now when they came out of Nell's together. Had he been holding a doggie bag? One thing was for sure, Noonan thought. He was going to have to start being more observant where his father was concerned.

What he should do, of course, was toss the meat into the weeds, thus making the lie he'd told true or at least consistent. But now, with only himself to lie to, the temptation was too great, and he wolfed down every morsel in the doggie bag, wondering if he'd ever tasted anything so delicious. When he was finished, though, he was as hungry as when he started—and angry. At his father? At himself? How could you tell?

BY THE TIME he arrived at Angelo's, his friends had already left. "You just missed them," Jerry said from behind the counter. "They said to tell you they'd—"

"Be at Ikey Lubin's," Noonan told him. Suddenly the predictability of this, something he usually found comforting, dispirited him. Having been treated to a series of unwelcome surprises at Nell's, there was something demoralizing about returning to these old routines, and he found himself wanting to skip the next six months and wake up in the middle of whatever and wherever came next. By this time next year all of Thomaston would fit neatly in the small rectangle of a rearview mirror.

But for now, there was nothing to do but join his friends at Ikey's. They were seated around the small table where the old geezers had their coffee in the mornings, drinking free sodas, Nan and Lucy arguing about what to name their children, a running gag that had originated in honors back in September when Mr. Berg, immediately recognizing how conventional and conservative both were by nature, had jokingly suggested they get married and start breeding. As the semester wore on he'd continued to treat them as a couple, taking every opportunity to suggest how intellectually and emotionally compatible they were, even speculating, after they'd realized they were soul mates and that their destinies were linked, what their children would be like. It was a laughable notion, and as such easy to embrace. There was something in it for each of them. Nan, who'd been unable, even in jest, to conceal her horror at the idea of one day marrying Lucy Lynch and having his children, discovered that by playing along she could appear less superficial without actually becoming so. Or at least that was Noonan's take on it. She'd had lots of boyfriends, but never a boy for a friend, which made this a whole new kind of experience. Lucy wasn't interested in her romantically, now that he had Sarah, and that had been mildly disconcerting to Nan at first, but then she realized this meant she could trust him and be at ease with him. For his part Lucy was proud to be linked in the popular imagination, albeit comically, with the prettiest girl in the school, who not so long ago had struck him mute with terror. And of course Mr. Berg was right. They did have far more in common than either of them knew even now.

Though Noonan played along, the whole what-will-we-name-our-kids riff made him uncomfortable, perhaps because Sarah's father's jokes always trailed an undercurrent of cruelty. He supposed it was good that Lucy had loosened up enough to laugh at himself, at the shy, skittish boy he'd been most of his life, though Noonan was far from certain his friend understood that he and not Nan was the butt of this particular joke. The idea that a girl like Nan would ever give her heart to a boy like Lucy was what made it funny. And their mock arguments over names implied her willingness to have sex with him, something nobody could picture without bursting into laughter. Noonan hated that Lucy mistook this as a sign of his growing popularity. But maybe Noonan was the one who was wrong. Maybe the time was right for his old friend to adopt a new public persona. Kids still called him Lucy, but affectionately now, and many seemed to have forgotten that the original intent had been to hurt his feelings. Possibly Lucy himself had forgotten. Maybe his popularity now, like his father's, was the just result of his genuine good nature. Sarah, after all, had never given any indication that she shared Noonan's misgivings or seemed at all embarrassed on his behalf, and Noonan was sure she'd never knowingly condone any joke whose purpose, stated or suggested, was the humiliation of her boyfriend.

And why did Noonan himself play along? His primary reason, he had to admit, was selfish. When Lucy and Nan pretended to be a couple, it made an actual couple of him and Sarah. Whereas the two of them bickered over babies' names, he and Sarah would find no shortage of real things to talk about. At Angelo's, or even at Ikey's, Noonan and Lucy always sat opposite each other, which meant you couldn't tell, just by looking, which boy was with which girl. Instead of distinct couples, they became a foursome, easy and relaxed. Back in September, when they first started going places together, they'd configured things differently, and it hadn't worked out nearly as well. With Lucy at Noonan's right, Nan at his left, and Sarah across the table, it had been abundantly clear who was with whom, while now the pretense that Nan and Lucy would end up together resulted in a more complex, though unspoken, truth—that the joke couples made as much sense as the real ones. At the end of the evening Nan and Noonan came back together, as did Lucy and Sarah, but only after they'd spent much of the evening enjoying the opposite symmetry. Was Noonan the only one who recognized this? He suspected that Sarah did, too, but of course there was no way of asking.

At any rate, when he stumbled into this at Ikey's, his already grumpy mood darkened further. If Sarah hadn't broken into one of her radiant smiles, he might've turned around and left. What he really wanted to do was march over and ask Lucy's girlfriend if she wanted to go someplace, just the two of them. In fact, the impulse was so strong that he was grateful when Dec Lynch, fresh from the shower and smelling of cheap cologne that confirmed he'd spend Saturday night as usual, prowling the Gut, intercepted him in the entryway.

"Why don't you just take this?" he said, handing Noonan his wallet, still obviously sore about the outcome of the game. "Apparently you won't be satisfied until it's yours, along with everything in it."

"I tried telling you," Noonan said in his own defense.

"Yeah, well, you didn't try hard enough. And do you want to know what really makes me crazy?"

"No."

"What *really* makes me crazy is I know just as sure as God

made little green apples that you're going to wreck my motorcycle." Noonan had parked it right in front of the store, behind the Beverly Caddy, and Dec stood there regarding it sadly. "I can see the twisted pile of metal in my mind's eye just as clear as I see you standing there."

"Cheer up," Noonan said. "Maybe I'll get killed. Blood on the highway."

Hearing this, Nan cried out "Bob*beeee!*" aghast to hear him even joke about such a thing.

"No, he'd just walk away without a scratch," Dec assured her, as if he considered this yet another dimension of the tragedy. "I can see that, too. I'll be the only victim, as usual."

Despite his facetious tone, Dec's mood seemed every bit as foul as his own, for reasons that ran deeper than a lost bet. The way he stood there in the entryway suggested to Noonan that he couldn't decide whether to stay or leave and never come back. Then Tessa Lynch, who'd been in the back, working in the tiny cubicle they'd recently set up for her there under a bare, hanging lightbulb, came in.

Dec regarded her for a long beat before turning to her husband. "Biggy," he said. "I've got a question for you."

Tessa must have sensed unpleasantness in this innocuous statement, because she said, "Don't start."

"No, really," Dec went on, still looking at his brother. "Why don't you close this place up for the night? Take your wife out someplace."

"I can't just close the store when it's supposed to be open," Big Lou told him.

"Why not? You own it."

"Close the store just because I feel like it?"

"But you *don't* feel like it," Dec said. "Don't tell me you do, because we both know better."

Noonan noticed that Lucy and the others had gone quiet. This wasn't the usual, good-natured Lynch bickering. The lone customer at the register also felt the tension in the air, since after pocketing his change he grabbed his six-pack and was out the door before Big Lou could insist on putting the beer in a paper sack.

"When was the last time you took Tessa anyplace?" Dec demanded.

Big Lou shrugged sheepishly. "That ain't what I'm sayin'—"

"Dec," Tessa said, and there was steel in her voice that Noonan would've paid attention to.

Dec did not. "I tell you what," he continued. "I'll stay home tonight and sell your beer for you. I can't afford to go out anyway. You and Tessa go out."

It was a genuine offer, Noonan could tell, but Dec's motive for making it had nothing to do with kindness. Had something happened before he arrived, or was the cause of this dispute more remote? Dec was clearly pissed about something.

"And where would we go, Murdick's?" Tessa scoffed.

"How the hell should I know?" Dec said, still looking at Big Lou. "Go someplace out of town. You know you aren't going to fall off the end of the earth if you cross the county line, right?"

"Dec," Tessa said. "*You're* the one who wants to go out tonight. So go."

Still refusing to look at her, Dec threw up his hands. "Fine," he said. "But you know what, Biggy? When it happens, it's going to serve you right."

Noonan heard a chair scrape and saw that Lucy had gotten to his feet, his face beet red. He'd never seen his friend mad before, and now he looked ready to combust.

"Sit down, Bub," Dec told him, "before you have one of your famous spells and I get blamed for that, too."

When Lucy remained standing, Tessa said, "Could everybody calm down? Nobody's blaming anybody for anything."

"Yeah, right," Dec said, and let the door slap shut behind him.

Noonan realized that he himself had remained rooted to the spot, and that everybody was looking at him. "You coming or going?" Tessa said.

"I'm trying to decide," he replied, the joke falling flat.

"Tell me about it," Tessa snapped, and then, when she saw her son's face, added, "Oh, quit, for heaven's sake."

"I wonder what all that was about," Big Lou said, staring out at the sidewalk, as if his brother was still there.

"It wasn't about anything," Tessa told him. "Forget it."

Lucy finally sat down, but his expression was still furious. Sarah, Noonan noticed, had taken his hand under the table.

"I don't know what I done to him," Big Lou told Tessa when she joined him at the register. "We been doin' real good, him and me."

"Forget it. He'll be fine in the morning."

"You want to go out someplace?" he said.

"Not tonight."

"We could, sometime," he said, tenderly if without great enthusiasm. "Get Louie to watch the store—"

"If you don't stop talking, I'm going to cry. I mean it."

He reached out and took her hand, and then they were quiet.

That left Noonan and Nan the only people in the store *not* holding hands, so as soon as he sat down, she promptly took his, visibly relieved that the silly bickering was over. "Help us decide," she told him happily. "Which is better, Truman or Spencer?"

NOT LONG after Dec Lynch's angry departure, the rest of them decided to call it a night. Lucy said he thought he might be coming down with something, but Noonan thought it more likely his uncle's strange outburst had upset him and that he blamed his mother for it as much as Dec. Tessa had already left, and when she did, Sarah had whispered something to Lucy that Noonan didn't quite catch, but his friend's facial muscles relaxed a little. Nan was the only one who seemed disappointed the evening was ending so soon, and when Noonan told her he was feeling tired and beat-up after the game, she'd shaken her head in annoyance at both him and Lucy. What they needed, she explained to Sarah, were new boyfriends. She offered Sarah a lift home, but since that was the opposite direction from the Borough, Sarah said she'd catch a ride with Noonan.

"It's pretty cold," he warned her before she climbed on behind him. In fact, he'd been thinking on the way over to Ikey's that he'd have to put the bike up soon. After the first snowfall, it would be unsafe. But Sarah said no, it'd be fine.

They rode in silence, Sarah's arms linked around his middle. Normally she chattered in his ear the entire time she was on the Indian, but not tonight, and Noonan guessed that what had transpired back at Ikey's had upset her, too. Maybe, he thought, his spirits rising a bit, she'd want to talk about it. Once, when he'd given her a ride home back in September, she'd invited him in and they'd talked quietly on the enclosed front porch for over an hour. Sarah had confided how afraid she was that her mother was about to remarry for all the wrong reasons, and her father might go off the deep end when she finally became another man's wife, something he'd always insisted would never happen. These revelations had been so forthright, so trusting and intimate, that Noonan had surprised himself by confessing how strained things were between himself and his father, and how the little pill his mother took every day made her vaguely content but more or less out of it. He even told her that the doctor had warned his father not to get her pregnant again, since she couldn't possibly survive another birth. He'd known better, of course, than to tell her of his threat to kill him if he ignored that warning.

He hoped she'd invite him in again tonight, because she was the one person he wanted to tell about what happened earlier at Nell's. But when they turned into her driveway, the downstairs lights were all ablaze, and Miles Davis was leaking from the stereo inside, and her father must've heard the motorcycle, because they saw him leap from his chair in the living room and begin windmilling his arms around like a madman. That would have been funny except that Noonan knew Sarah was worried about the smell of what could only be marijuana that greeted her when she returned home on weekend nights, especially when, as now, she arrived earlier than expected.

He brought the bike to a shuddering rest, but Sarah made no move to get off. "Is it okay if we just sit a minute?" she said.

It was, it was. He enjoyed the trusting, unself-conscious way she nestled against him on the bike. It was far more enjoyable, in fact, than the passionate good-night kiss Nan had given him outside of Ikey's. Nan loved nothing more than to kiss for show, and tonight she'd been particularly anxious for him to understand what he was missing as a result of being such a grump.

"Do you want me to come in with you?"

"No," she said. "Let's just give him a minute."

So they just sat there, facing the shabby little house where Sarah and her father had lived since her mother left. Eventually, it dawned on him that Sarah was quietly crying.

"Do you think we're all going to end up like them?" she said, and he immediately knew she was talking not just about her present father and absent mother but also about all of their parents—Lucy's, his, maybe even Nan's.

"That's up to us, I suppose," he said.

Mr. Berg, no longer windmilling, came over to the window and peered outside, perhaps wondering why his daughter hadn't come in yet. But you could tell he was seeing mostly his own reflection, and after a moment he gave up and returned to his chair.

"He hates Lou," Sarah said.

"Your dad?" Noonan said, genuinely surprised. "Really?" He would've liked to turn around and face her, but her arms were still wrapped tightly around him, as if she imagined the bike might take off of its own accord. Did she not want him to see her crying? Or was she afraid if she didn't keep him facing forward that he'd take her in his arms?

533

"What kind of grown man hates a boy?" she said. Noonan wanted to say that Lucy was almost eighteen, not a boy anymore, but she added, "He says Lou's everything that's wrong with America."

"That's crazy," Noonan said. The words were out before he could call them back.

"He says he's gullible and a craven conformist," she said. "And something even worse."

"Which is?"

"An innocent. He says there's nothing worse than that." She was clutching Noonan even tighter now. "He wants us to break up."

"Will you?" Noonan said, his own heart clenching.

"Of course not."

"Right."

"He thinks I should be dating you."

Did she want his opinion? He couldn't tell. He also couldn't tell whether she viewed the idea as repugnant or simply impossible. "I don't see how it's any of his business," he said.

She didn't say anything else for a minute. Finally, she put her forehead between his shoulder blades and said, "I hate him sometimes, Bobby. My own father."

"You're lucky," he told her. "I hate my father all the time."

After a moment she said, "Let's make a pact, you and I. That after tonight we'll never say such terrible things again." Only after he agreed did she give him one last squeeze around the waist and climb off the bike. When he started to follow suit, she put a hand on his shoulder. "Don't," she said, so he stayed where he was. She wiped the tears away with her sleeve, then surprised him by taking his hand. "What if it isn't up to us?" she whispered, like a scared child. "What if we're going to end up like them and there's nothing we can do about it?"

Since Noonan didn't know how to answer that, he said, "Do you think there's something going on between Dec and Mrs. Lynch?"

534

She let go of his hand abruptly, as if it had just occurred to her that she was holding it. "No," she said. Her certainty surprised him a little, but he could also tell that his question hadn't surprised her. She, too, had considered the possibility. "Tessa loves Lou-Lou."

You love Lou-Lou, he thought. You don't *want* it to be true. "That doesn't mean—"

"I know what it doesn't mean, Bobby."

"I'm sorry," he said, though he was none too sure why he should feel the need to apologize. "I didn't—"

"It's okay. It's just . . . they're all so dear, the Lynches. I don't know what we'd all do if we lost Ikey's."

And then she was gone.

Instead of backing out of the drive he stayed where he was, astraddle the Indian. Inside, Sarah gave her father—the man she'd just admitted to hating—a hug and a kiss good night, then headed upstairs. A moment later a light came on and she appeared in one of the second-floor windows, bathed in yellow light, and his heart was now like a fist in his chest. It must have dawned on her then that she hadn't heard the motorcycle start up and roar away, because she raised her hand, and when she smiled sadly waggling her fingers in his direction, he tooted and turned his key in the ignition, trying *not* to know what he knew for absolute certain: that he was in love with Lucy's girlfriend and, if she'd have him, that friendship wouldn't stand in the way. And his own girlfriend? Poor Nan didn't even factor into it.

EXCEPT FOR HIS FATHER'S CAR, Nell's parking lot was empty by the time he pulled in and parked the motorcycle beneath the solitary pole-mounted lamp and then stood looking up at the yellow halo of light in the vast blackness of the night sky. It reminded him of something, he couldn't remember what, until suddenly he did: his weird dream about the cathedral that morning. Incredible. It felt like a month ago. How strange to think that the day had begun with clarity. Now, not so many hours later, everything was a hopeless muddle—including, for instance, what the hell he was doing back at Nell's.

His father was sitting in the same spot at the end of the bar, but now he was drinking coffee. Glancing at his watch, he said, "Just in time for last call."

"No thanks," Noonan said, taking the same stool as before. The dining room was empty except for a waitress and a busboy doing setups for the next day. Then Maxine came out of a storage room behind the bar and pushed through the door into the kitchen, where she came up behind her son as he drew a tray of steaming dishes from the washer and grabbed him firmly by the elbows. When she planted a kiss on his balding pate, Noonan could hear his bray of delight before the door swung shut again. He looked over at his father then, trying to fathom how long he'd been a part of this domestic scene.

"That boy," Noonan said. He'd meant to complete some sort of sentence, but instead let the two words just float there in the air between them.

"No relation to you, if that's what you're worried about."

"I wasn't worried, only curious. Also curious about why you prefer her to Mom, or this other family to ours. And maybe when you're done explaining that . . ." Once more, words failed him.

"What?" his father said. "Go ahead. You've got a good head of steam up. You might as well finish."

Except he wasn't sure how. Was there one thing he wanted an explanation for, or everything? Without warning, his father had stopped being a simple man. Did Noonan want an explanation for the kindness he'd shown this Maxine and her idiot kid, or for the mean-spirited bullying he'd offered his mother, his brothers and himself? *The best guy*, Willie had called him. In what reality was his father even a decent guy? It was as if the first seventeen years of Noonan's life had taken place under a full moon that suddenly had waned, allowing his wolf of a father to take on the shape of an ordinary man. How had he managed to miss that transformation? What was it Sarah had asked back at her father's house—whether they'd all end up like their parents? Actually *become* their parents, without having any choice in the matter? He now felt some of his long-cherished loathing begin to leak away, crowded out by the fear that she could be right.

"Look," his father said, after the silence had stretched out too long. "What you need to figure out is simple. What do you want from me? If it's something I can give you, fine. Right now, for instance, if you want a cup of coffee or a piece of pie, just say the word. Next year, if you need help with college expenses, I'll try. I'm not rich, but I've got a little saved. I saved it with you in mind, actually, in case *you* ever changed. If you really don't want anything from me, or want what I don't have or can't give you, then what can I say?"

Noonan studied his father and swallowed the impulse to say something nasty. If he could piss him off, make him really angry, then maybe some of that pure old hatred could be coaxed back. What prevented this was the realization that though his father was offering far less than he was owed, and much, much less than what his mother was, it might just be the best deal he'd ever get from him. Trying to drive a harder bargain would be pointless. "How about a little advice?" he heard himself ask.

This elicited a grin. "Hey, what kind of father doesn't have advice?"

Was this irony? Noonan wondered. Mr. Berg had taught them the three different types: dramatic, verbal and situational. This, unless he misremembered, was verbal, where the speaker says or implies something different from, maybe even the opposite of, what he means. Was his father admitting that even he didn't think much of the job he'd done so far?

Noonan took a deep breath, realizing that what he'd told Sarah earlier was no longer precisely true. He didn't hate his father all the time. He meant to. He had once and surely would again. But what he said was "There's a girl. Two of them, actually."

His father nodded, waiting for the rest.

PASSION CURVE

NOONAN SELDOM MADE predictions about paintings, but when he did he was usually right. Sarah, he'd told Hugh, would paint herself. He worked feverishly in the studio for the rest of the day, quitting only when darkness fell. After taking a shower he discovered, much to his surprise, that he was famished, and not just for food. For about two seconds he considered dropping by Evangeline's gallery but decided against it. Too bad Hugh wasn't still in town, he thought next, then thought better of that as well.

Anne Brettany couldn't have looked more surprised to see who was pounding on her studio door.

"Let me take you to dinner," he said. "Anywhere but Harry's."

They went to a small neighborhood place in Cannaregio, where Noonan's appetite was better than it had been in months. Anne ate like a bird and couldn't stop staring at him.

"What?" he finally said.

"You don't *look* insane," she remarked.

Had Hugh told her about the portrait, or was this a more general reference to the gossip circulating about him? "You could do me a large favor," he told her over espresso. "I'm not looking forward to this flight to New York."

Anne also admitted she was a wreck whenever she flew, and they decided to have Hugh book them on the same flight so they could at least hold each other's hand.

By the time Noonan returned to the studio it was late enough that he had to consider his options. He could take advantage of the agitation and excitement that always accompanied a new canvas and work through the night, thereby avoiding the risk of a night terror. On the other hand, he'd drunk a bottle of wine and he knew from experience that the best time to quit work was when he was going good, when he knew exactly what his next brushstroke would be and why. With some trepidation he decided to take a chance and get the sleep he knew he needed. He'd taken an even bigger chance the night before, allowing Lichtner to bunk down among his paintings. That maybe he'd luck out two nights in a row was his last conscious thought before exhaustion claimed him.

He awoke with the sun in his face, wondering how many hours he'd lost to blessed, dreamless sleep. Standing in his bathrobe, he examined the two paintings resting side by side. Yesterday, without giving it a moment's thought, he'd made his most important artistic decision in a long time by setting up that spare easel. He could've removed his father from the first one, turned the miserable prick's face to the wall and just painted Sarah. Instead he'd allowed them to coexist, and he now began to see the wisdom of that impulse. They wouldn't be companion pieces by any stretch, but they were strangely codependent. The light spilling from Sarah's window had no choice but to fall on his father and the Bridge of Sighs behind him. Though one painting was nearly finished, the other just begun, they would parallel each other for a while.

That, it occurred to Noonan, was how life had been during his senior year in that faraway place called Thomaston, New York. At sixty, halfway around the world, he was able to see clearly what had eluded him at the time—that the narrative of his life had split onto two tracks that ran, at least for a while, closely parallel. He and his friends were on one, their parents on the other, and neither group realized until it was too late that the tracks' convergence in the distance was no optical illusion. The Marconis, the Lynches, the Beverlys and the Bergs. Not one of these families would emerge unscathed from the collision. Only one would survive intact.

*

DESPITE SARAH'S CERTAINTY that there was nothing going on between Dec and Tessa Lynch, he continued to be suspicious. Dec offered no further outbursts, at least in Noonan's presence, and before long things returned to normal at Ikey's. He had the impression that Tessa had privately read her brother-in-law the riot act about his behavior, because for some time he seemed chastened. Still, Noonan couldn't figure out what Dec's outburst had been about in the first place. Unless he was mistaken, Sarah either knew or suspected, but she wasn't telling. "Bobby," she said, regarding him sternly when he asked about it again, "Tessa loves Lou-Lou." End of discussion.

If Noonan remained suspicious of Tessa Lynch, she seemed not to have quite made up her mind about him either. She appeared to be genuinely fond of him, happy whenever he showed up at the store and quick to offer him a plate of food, as if she had two sons instead of one. But even as he gratefully wolfed down whatever she gave him, he was aware that she was observing him closely, especially if Sarah was also present, and something about her expression suggested that she was reminding herself not to trust him. Had she intuited his feelings for Sarah, fearing that he'd one day betray Lucy? Did that—as yet—unwarranted suspicion originate in her own personal experience of betrayal? And what about his own suspicions of her? Wasn't their source his own parents' marriage as much as anything he'd witnessed between her and Dec?

His lingering doubts notwithstanding, the Lynches seemed the most stable of the four families, and Ikey Lubin's seemed an extension of that stability, which perhaps explained why Noonan and his friends spent so much time there. He knew from various things Lucy let drop that the store might fail at any moment, that each new month was a struggle to stay profitable, but to Noonan it seemed as solid as any business in Thomaston, probably because the Lynches themselves were solid, if not terribly exciting, people. It might be that they'd never truly prosper, but neither could he imagine them failing, either their store or themselves. Lucy seemed less sanguine. Of course he was a worrier by nature, but after his uncle's outburst he became ever more vigilant about all things Ikey's. Noonan could tell he hated being away from the store, even for school, and he seemed palpably relieved each afternoon when he returned and found things exactly as he'd left them, with the three adult Lynches at their respective posts and no visible realignment.

Oddly enough, if stability was the criterion, Noonan would've ranked his own family second to the Lynches. True, what his parents had couldn't really be called a marriage, but in most other respects life was less stressful now than when he was a kid. Though his brothers remained feral, they were also remarkably self-sufficient. They doted on their dazed mother and shared responsibility for her care. Now that she wasn't likely to become pregnant, she seemed uninterested in flight. They got part-time jobs and managed to stay out of their father's—and each other's—way. Noonan regarded them less as individual boys than parts of a single organism, each devoted by means of discrete tasks to the survival of the whole. They came home from school with black eyes and swollen, busted lips and wrestled with one another like young wolves, even at the dinner table, while their mother looked serenely on. Their father would come by from time to time to restore something like order, but for the most part he seemed to have surrendered the field.

Noonan and his father had finally managed a truce, maybe something even better, though it stopped well short of trust or affection. Whatever it was, it had something to do with Nell's. There, Noonan discovered, he could encounter his father without fear of conflict, thanks in large part to Willie, whose sensitivity to discord actually seemed to prevent it. The boy was slow witted in the extreme, but Noonan quickly grew fond of him. And his father either liked the boy, or at least didn't mind having him around. It was as though, having neither expectations

nor responsibility for him, he could just let him be, a luxury he'd
never afforded Noonan even for a minute. He wasn't sure either
what his father's feelings were for Maxine, whom he treated with
a kind of gentle consideration that Noonan at first found
impossible to credit. It had to be an act, he thought, the purpose
of which was to convince him that his mother had brought on
herself all the ill treatment she'd suffered at his hands—and, by
extension, Noonan too. He kept waiting for the façade to crack,
for the man he knew to reveal himself to both Maxine and her
son, but so far it hadn't and he began to wonder if maybe it
wouldn't. After all, his father had been part of their lives almost as
long as he'd been with his original family.

At home, though, things could still get tense, so without ever
discussing the matter he and his father had arrived at an
unspoken agreement that on those rare occasions when they
both turned up at the house, one or the other would leave. It was
as if their relationship had become site specific, and it was the
Borough house itself that was toxic.

Noonan had continued to tend bar at Murdick's on Sundays
through the end of November, then moved out to Nell's, where
Max—as he'd started calling her immediately—taught him to
make martinis and manhattans and dozens of other cocktails. He
got his own tips from the patrons, plus a small percentage of the
waitresses' tips from the dining room, which added up to a good
deal more than he'd made drawing beers at Murdick's. After a
month of Sundays Max gave him a couple hours on Friday
nights, too. This was by far the busiest night of the week, and
though the cocktail lounge was small he and Max worked what
she called tits back, trying to keep up with cocktail orders. After
their first Friday night together, he asked, "What did you do
before me?"

"Oh, I'd coax your father off his stool. He wasn't half the
worker you are, though," she said, loud enough that he could
hear. "At least on this side of the bar." This, Noonan guessed,
was a reference to the fact that his father was never without a

drink. The old man drank top-shelf scotch but never got drunk, though it occurred to Noonan that he was perhaps never entirely sober either.

By nine on Fridays the rush was over, after which Max usually told him to go join his friends, and sometimes he did, but just as often he climbed onto the stool next to his father and had something to eat. Other times, if Will was behind in the kitchen, he'd help him by scrubbing pots or ferrying clean glasses out to the bar. With Dec's motorcycle put up until spring, he had to depend on his father for a ride back into town, so often it was easier to settle in at Nell's. Many times he'd look up in surprise when Max announced last call, realizing that somehow the evening had slipped away, that he'd gotten tipsy on free beer, that Nan and Lucy and Sarah had probably waited for him in vain at Ikey's or Angelo's.

"You want to come home tonight?" his father suggested one night when they rolled back into town.

"No, just drop me off at my place," Noonan said.

"Why not come home? It's gotta be cold up there with no heat."

"It is," he admitted, though only on nights when the outside temperature fell below freezing was he uncomfortable. Heat leaked upward from the drugstore, and he had a down sleeping bag and a small electric space heater.

"Your mother misses you," his father said.

"I miss her too," he replied, which was both true and false. In her dreamy, medicated state she wasn't the woman he remembered and loved, and in any case she seemed to have everything she needed in his brothers.

"How long since you spent any time with her?"

"I don't know. How long since *you* did?"

"Okay, if that's the way you want it."

"It's not the way I want it. It's the way it is."

"And you think I'm to blame."

"*I'm* sure not."

"And you think the day won't ever come when you're the reason somebody's unhappy?"

"I don't know."

"It will," his father assured him, pulling up in front of the Rexall. "Take it from me."

"Okay," he said, opening the door.

"Why not let go of this, son? Does it make sense to keep fighting?"

"We're not fighting," he said. "If we were, you'd be bleeding."

"We'd both be bleeding."

That was the other new thing. They were now able to say such things without raising their voices. Both seemed to comprehend that, even though these were potent, dangerous words, they needn't trail dire consequences. It was as if, when they were alone in the car, Willie was their constant companion. They could say angry things as long as they didn't actually become angry. Their barbed exchanges took on the tonal quality of jokes, though they both understood they weren't joking, at least not entirely. In fact, talking about making each other bleed had the power to prevent it.

"Anyway," he replied, getting out of the car, "like you said, there's no reason to fight. You don't get her pregnant again, everything'll be fine."

They were learning, Noonan concluded, to get along, which wasn't lost on his brothers, who were both grateful and suspicious. "So," David had said when he let slip that these days he saw his father pretty regularly at Nell's, "you're on his side now?" Noonan assured him it meant no such thing, but since his brother had introduced the subject, he decided to ask him about something that had been on his mind since that first night. "Do you think he's changed? Dad?"

The answer surprised him. "You both have."

Noonan decided his brother must be practicing some weird new diplomacy. "I mean, does he seem different to you? Less pissed off?"

"You both do."

"Anyway," he said, disappointed but unwilling to push the kid any further, "you don't have to worry. I'm still on Mom's side."

He assumed this would be the end of it, but David surprised him again. "Do you think we're all his?"

"What are you talking about?"

"Me and Philip. We don't look like the rest of you. Or each other."

"That's crazy."

David shrugged. "I walked in on her one day."

"Walked in on her *what*?"

"With the man from the phone company. They had their clothes on and everything, but he was kissing her. And she wasn't, you know, making him stop. When she saw me she just smiled. It was weird."

"Did you ask her about it?"

"No." He was blushing.

"How come you didn't tell me?"

"It was before. You weren't living here then." Something told him this was the one thing his brother was lying about. What he was describing had happened recently.

"She was kissing him back?"

"I don't know," David said, clearly wishing he hadn't brought this up. "I shouldn't have told you. Now you'll—"

"No," he said. "It's not her fault."

"I know," he agreed.

It's not her fault, Noonan repeated to himself. And it was true. It wasn't his mother's fault. Ironically, his brother's story made him even more certain about Tessa and Dec Lynch. Of course it might not have been Lucy's mother's fault either.

THE FAMILY in the most trouble, though, had to be the Bergs. Sarah's new stepfather was an alcoholic, and apparently the idea had been that they would keep each other sober, because, Sarah explained, her mother needed to cut back on her own drinking. For a while it had seemed to work, though lately, when Sarah called on the weekend, her mother's speech was often slurred. But it was her father, in Noonan's opinion, who bore watching. While rattled, he hadn't come completely unglued when his ex-wife remarried, as Sarah had feared he might. And he continued to maintain that once his novel was published and he returned to the city in triumph, she'd drop this new husband like a bad habit. Yet his public behavior, always eccentric, had become dangerously erratic. Back in October, for instance, a group of Jewish mothers had formally accused him of anti-Semitism. Their evidence for this surprising charge was, first, that Mr. Berg and his daughter never attended synagogue and, second, that there wasn't a single Jew in this year's honors English. Nonsense, Mr. Berg responded. He himself was a Jew. *You* don't count, they maintained. How could a Jew not count as a Jew, he replied. If you're going around counting Jews, you have to count them all. Not that he advocated counting Jews. In his view, many people who qualified, by strict definition, didn't measure up, at least not to his standards. Thomaston Jews in general, he maintained, were mostly not the real article. About the most you could say for them was that they were Jew*ish*. The year before, he reminded them, his honors English had been made up almost exclusively of Jews; by the end of the year he'd had it. Enough with the Jews, already. Try something different. So, this year, *no more Jews*. Nor, he assured the Jewish mothers, would he permit his daughter to date their sons. There'd be plenty of time for Jews later, he reasoned, real Jews. Once his daughter got to Columbia, there'd be no scarcity. Not small-town or suburban Jews either. Real New York Jews. At this point the argument grew so heated that Principal Watkins had been called in to mediate. When no satisfactory resolution could be found, he suggested that perhaps the time had come for the honors English course to be rotated among the entire staff. In response to this suggestion Mr. Berg had proposed his own solution. Just as soon as his novel was accepted, he said, he'd be tendering his resignation. When the book was published, he wouldn't be teaching anymore. He'd be taught.

Lucy, who apparently had no idea his girlfriend's father held him in such low regard, agreed with Noonan that he was pushing the envelope, behaviorwise. Still, he was genuinely fond of the man and didn't want to believe there was anything seriously wrong. After all, he argued, wasn't Mr. Berg's lunacy born of genius? Even though Lucy loved and defended Thomaston, he had to admit that the man was out of place there. He was despised by most faculty members and secretly made fun of, but even those who loathed him feared his acid wit, his searing intelligence. For all his eccentricity, he was the best teacher either of them had ever had, and honors was worth more than all their other classes combined, not so much in spite of its instructor being dangerously off center as because of it. The weirder things got, the more boundaries that were ignored, the more interesting things became. But what if one of the boundaries they were crossing was the one that separated sanity from madness? Lucy, perhaps out of loyalty to Sarah, didn't want to believe that this was what they were witnessing. Noonan, though, was apprehensive.

As luck would have it, the first book of the winter term was *Moby-Dick*. They were to read the first half of the book over the holidays, but in the first class it immediately became clear that very few had even begun the novel. While Mr. Berg normally wouldn't tolerate a flagging discussion, that first Monday back he seemed more distracted than incensed. The next day, when they arrived at the classroom, there was no sign of him. Usually, he and Three Mock were already there, the record player set up and Monk or Miles or Louis scratching away, Mr. Berg standing with his feet set wide apart and snapping his fingers to the beat, grinning his yellow grin. Only when they were all present and in the proper mood for unconventional learning would he turn the volume down. That day, though, even Three Mock and the record player were missing. In the center of the room a narrow, rickety stage had been erected, and the desks were all pushed back against the wall. They'd just about concluded that the classroom had been commandeered for some other purpose when they heard a clomping sound out in the hallway, some distance off but steadily drawing nearer. When Noonan looked over at Lucy, he was grinning at him as if the most wonderful thing had just occurred to him.

Mr. Berg's only friend on the faculty was Mr. Davis, the industrial-arts teacher who was thought by most to be mildly retarded, which may have been why Mr. Berg so enjoyed publicly proclaiming him the second-smartest instructor at Thomaston High. Though he never identified the smartest one, everybody could guess who he meant, and his high opinion of Mr. Davis, people said, wasn't so much a compliment to the shop teacher as an insult to everyone else.

What Mr. Davis had fashioned for Mr. Berg today was a short length of two-by-four attached with adjustable, sandal-like straps to his scuffed brown shoe and then fastened tight. Noonan and Lucy had realized in the same moment that it wasn't Mr. Berg clomping toward them down the corridor but mad Ahab himself. Knowing Mr. Berg's fondness for theatricality, Noonan was surprised not to see full sea-captain regalia when he flung the classroom door open and entered, with Three Mock in attendance. But except for the block of wood attached to his shoe, he was dressed as usual, in dark slacks dusted liberally with cigarette ash and a short-sleeved white shirt, its neck stained yellow. With difficulty he mounted the stage—Mr. Davis's awkward apparatus apparently meant to suggest Ahab's whale-bone prosthesis. Three Mock, his black Pip, Noonan supposed, lent a hand until, no longer needed, he retreated to the far corner of the stage.

Mr. Berg stood still for a moment, his back to the class. When he finally spoke, his voice sounded as if it were traveling up from a dark, deep cave. "*All . . . visible . . . objects* . . . are but as pasteboard masks," he said, then fell silent.

"Mr. Berg?" Perry Kozlowski said, and was ignored.

"Some unknown but reasoning thing puts forth the molding of its features from behind the unreasoning mask. If man will *strike*—"

And with this the block of wood came down on the feeble stage to thunderous effect. Everyone jolted upright. Noonan glanced over at Nan, who happened to be sitting closest to the door, and she looked ready to bolt.

Now Mr. Berg pivoted painfully, looking very much like a man whose leg had been shorn from his body, his face contorted, positively aglow with madness. "*Strike* through the mask!" he said, shaking his fist at them so violently that he lost his balance and nearly fell. "How can the prisoner reach outside except by *thrusting* through the wall!"

The question was clearly rhetorical, but Perry raised his hand. "Uh, Mr. Berg?"

Good God, Noonan thought. Did Perry really think he was going to forestall his dramatic performance in order to answer some stupid question like *Will this be on the test?*

Focusing on Perry as he would a mutinous seaman, Mr. Berg clomped over to the edge of the stage and glared down on him with such a murderous expression that Perry actually leaned back in his chair. Ahab's voice became low, conspiratorial. "To me," he confided, "the white whale is that wall. Sometimes . . . I think there's naught beyond." Perry didn't look like this possibility troubled him greatly, though everything else about the proceedings did.

"But 'tis enough," Mr. Berg continued, straightening now and clomping back down the stage, stopping before each member of the class and inspecting the student as a captain would his crew, assessing character and courage. "He tasks me; he heaps me; I see in him hideous strength with an insidious malice sinewing it. That inscrutable thing is chiefly what I hate, and be the white whale agent or principal, I will *wreak* that hate upon him."

Perry, exasperated, was now scanning the novel's table of

contents. "Mr. Berg," he pleaded, "can you at least tell us what chapter you're on?" he pleaded.

Mr. Berg practically flew back down the stage. "Talk not to me of blasphemy, man!" he exploded, as if Perry had done precisely this. "I'd strike the sun if it insulted me!" And to emphasize this point, he again crashed the wooden block down on the stage. "Who's over me?" he demanded to know, first of Perry, then the rest of them. "Who's over me?"

Noonan half expected Perry to suggest Principal Watkins, but to everyone's surprise it was Lucy who spoke. "God?" he suggested, precisely as the *Pequod*'s first mate, Starbuck, had done in the book, if Noonan remembered correctly from his reading the night before. His friend, however, seemed to be raising the point on his own, and Noonan could tell he was serious. He didn't know, though, whether it was the game itself that had turned serious or something outside the game. Was this Starbuck finally standing up to Ahab, or Lucy Lynch confronting the man who despised him?

Mr. Berg said nothing for a long moment, and when he finally did, his whisper was barely audible, intended only, so far as Noonan could tell, for the boy he was fixing: "*Truth . . . knows . . . no . . . confines.*" There was something both vicious and contemptuous in his delivery of these words, something Noonan didn't recall from the novel. Hadn't Ahab considered Starbuck his sole friend, the one man on the *Pequod* who might understand his purpose? Lucy did his best to hold his gaze, but finally had to look down at his desktop. Only then did Mr. Berg turn his attention back to Perry. "Chapter thirty-six," he said in his own voice. "Ahab's speech on the quarterdeck. You were supposed to have read it for today."

He was grinning now, and Ahab's madness had gone out of his eyes, and everyone visibly relaxed. Lucy, in particular, seemed relieved that it had been just a role-playing game after all. Noonan alone detected a more personal madness, its volume having been amped up just a notch. Mr. Berg might have been

551

sane compared with Ahab, but by any other measurement Noonan wasn't so sure.

THERE WAS an explanation for his increasingly bizarre behavior, but Noonan thought this made things worse, not better. *Mr. Berg's novel was finished.* At least that's what he let on to Sarah when she returned from her holiday on Long Island. He had never worked on it except during the summer, when he had two uninterrupted months, but this year, when Sarah went off to spend the week between Christmas and New Year's with her mother and her new husband, Mr. Berg went down to the bank, took the fifteen-hundred-page, single-spaced manuscript from its safety-deposit box, read it through from start to finish—which took him most of the week—and pronounced it complete. The night she returned, they celebrated the event by going out for pizza. The book was not only finished, he told her, it was brilliant. It took his breath away. He'd written the most ambitious, comprehensive and accurate portrait of America since the conclusion of the Second World War. There was nothing to do but publish it and return to New York in triumph.

What worried Sarah, she confessed to Noonan, was the timing of all this. His confrontation with the Jewish mothers had occurred the day after he learned his wife was going to remarry. His turn as Ahab seemed to be occasioned by the wedding. Now, more than ever, he needed something that would prove to his ex-wife that she'd backed the wrong horse. So the novel was not only done, it was perfectly done. Their lives, he told his daughter, were about to change, so she'd do well to prepare for fame and fortune. He'd decided to call the book *Tannersville*, and its publication would detonate the real place that had inspired it, along with everyone in it. How Sarah would laugh one day— she'd have to trust him on this—at the idea she'd ever been serious about a boy from such a place.

Since Mr. Berg's turn as Ahab, Lucy had reluctantly come to

share Noonan's sense of foreboding, and he was particularly concerned when told that Mr. Berg's novel was finished. "He's not even revising?" That was one of the things Mr. Berg had been stressing all year. "Writing *is* revision," he reminded them every time he handed back their essays, each awash in red ink, and he always insisted they make every single correction he'd suggested before moving on to the next assignment.

"Apparently it's word perfect," Noonan said. "Dictated by the Holy Ghost." That, Mr. Berg had told them, was the claim Kerouac had made to his editor when he delivered *On the Road*.

According to Sarah, her father submitted the book in early January to a handful of New York publishers—only the best houses of course and their best editors, men already associated with the likes of Hemingway, Fitzgerald, Faulkner and Ellison—and had immediately commenced racing through the mail every day. By February, upon further reflection, he acknowledged that perhaps his expectations had been unrealistic. The size of the manuscript, the density of its prose, the sheer number of its characters and the complexity of their interconnecting conflicts might *hint* at greatness, but the editors he'd chosen, the busiest and most important men in New York, couldn't be expected to judge its brilliance until they'd read the whole thing. He'd initially imagined them tearing it out of the box and diving right in, but it now occurred to him that the book might have been routed through the infamous "slush pile" of manuscripts submitted by unknown, unagented writers. From this pile it might take weeks, even months, to emerge. Though he'd been very explicit in his cover letter that the manuscript was intended only for the eyes of the editor to whom it was addressed, it might possibly be read first by a junior editor, and a less experienced and discerning reader might not realize what he held in his hands. Mistakes happened, which was why, the more he thought about it, he came to regret trumpeting the novel's imminent publication to that dolt of a principal, Watkins. He didn't doubt the end result, but a delay of any duration guaranteed that

Watkins and his colleagues in the English department would constantly inquire, and he'd have to say he was still waiting for a response and then endure their envious, small-minded snickers. Worse, it meant his ex-wife would be permitted to live that much longer in the bliss of her ignorance. He'd hoped she might commence the process of bitter regret in a more timely manner.

The first rejection came on the Ides of March, a form letter stating that the book didn't suit the publisher's needs at this time. Since the letter was unsigned, there was no way to tell whether the book had been read by the editor he'd selected or by someone else, though Mr. Berg felt confident it must be the latter. He'd been right! Mistakes of this sort not only happened, they happened to him. Another rejection came later in the month, also an unsigned form letter. This one caused him to suffer yet another doubt. Since he'd sent the manuscript off, an even better ending had occurred to him, so he sat down and composed a letter for all the remaining editors, outlining the new ending and explaining why he thought it might conceivably be an improvement over the old, though of course he'd understand if they were wedded to the original. Was it Hemingway who always said, "First thought, best thought"?

This letter's only immediate effect was to generate another form rejection. The day after Mr. Berg received it, a note appeared on the honors classroom door, canceling class without explanation and giving everyone a reading day in the library. But at the end of that period Lucy observed him leaving the principal's office, his face ashen. Had he requested the meeting or been summoned? Had they patched up their disagreement over the Jewish mothers, or was their conflict deepening? Noonan saw Watkins later in the day, and he seemed in excellent spirits. All of this had happened on a Friday. By Monday Mr. Berg was his old self again—manic, sarcastic, mock-confidential, insulting, over the top. But according to Sarah he'd spoken hardly a word all weekend. On Saturday he'd sat on the front porch in the bitter cold, gripping the arms of a wicker chair with white knuckles until the mailman came. He'd taken an envelope into the study and closed the door. Sarah didn't see him again for the rest of the day.

NOONAN WAS NOT in love with Nan Beverly and didn't see any reason why he should be, though his was a distinctly minority view. Almost all the other boys in the school were openly envious of his good fortune. After all, Nan had been going out with him for over six months, much longer than she'd dated anyone else. They couldn't understand why either, because he didn't seem to be working that hard to keep her. He didn't even buy her presents. And when she flirted with other boys in the hopes of making him jealous, a tactic that had never failed her, he didn't seem to care, and it was always the would-be rival who ended up slinking off. Lucy wasn't jealous—he had Sarah, after all—but he did subscribe to the consensus view that his friend had no idea how lucky he was.

"You shouldn't lead her on," Sarah told him one day when they were walking home from school and Lucy was home sick with a cold. They'd not been alone much since the night he'd given her a ride on the Indian. It was winter now, too cold for her to paint in his unheated "studio" above the Rexall and too cold for the motorcycle, which meant he couldn't offer her a lift at the end of their foursome evenings. Unless he was mistaken, she was relieved that there were so few opportunities for them to be alone, as if their conversation that night had been too intimate, that they'd come dangerously close to . . . what?

"How am I leading her on?" he said. He hadn't told Nan he loved her, nor even implied it, so far as he remembered. Of course he hadn't come right out and told her he didn't, but was he obliged to make such a declaration? Sarah seemed to think so.

"It's just that she really likes you," she said.

"Well—"

"And you don't like her nearly so much."

555

"You know this?"

"I do."

"So . . . what? You're saying I should break up with her?"

"No, I'm saying she's vulnerable. If you were honest with her, she could move on to somebody else."

"That would leave me without a girlfriend," he couldn't help pointing out. And it would also be the end of their comfortable foursome.

"I'm your friend."

"But you're Lucy's girlfriend."

"So tell Nan you just want to be friends."

Unfortunately, that simply wasn't true. Though he wasn't in love with her, he was still looking forward to the day in the not-too-distant future when she'd give herself to him. She probably would've done so already, if he'd pressed. He was tempted to point this out to Sarah and maybe get a little credit for gentle-manly restraint. Anyway, in his view, if Nan was vulnerable to anything it was her own vanity. And if Sarah was also worried about protecting her innocence, she was mistaken there as well. In the time they'd been going out, Nan had become increasingly obsessed with sex, or at least the idea of it. "Do you think they've done it yet?" she often asked him of this or that couple. To Noonan these constant speculations were as tiresome as the name-the-kids game she was always playing with Lucy.

In the beginning he thought Nan found sex talk exciting, a kind of verbal foreplay, but he gradually came to suspect that she was deeply anxious and even more deeply conflicted. On the one hand, she didn't want to have sex before her friends did, but neither did she want them to precede her into that promised land. She'd been among the last to get her driver's license, which had been embarrassing enough. She refused to visit Noonan's squalid flat above the Rexall, though on nights when her father let her have the Caddy she liked to drive him out to the old Whitcombe Estate and park in the trees near the entrance. Most nights there'd be two or three other cars in the vicinity, cars they'd sometimes recognize as belonging to friends. At first they'd just necked in the front seat, but lately things had gotten more interesting in the back. Nan now let Noonan put his hands up under her sweater and bra, which was nice, and sometimes they left the car running and the heater on, and she'd take the sweater and bra off, which was nicer still. It was a big backseat, yet Nan wouldn't recline all the way, claiming that they might be tempted to go too far. He suspected the real reason was that she liked to keep an eye on the other cars. Whenever they'd done as much as they were going to do in the backseat and crawled back into the front, she'd wipe the foggy windshield clear and wonder out loud exactly what people parked nearby were doing. She hated to think it might be more interesting and exciting than necking and groping, but she was also distressed, he could tell, by the possibility that she was the only girl out here with her shirt off and her breasts exposed. What she really would've liked was to sneak a peek through those other fogged-up windows, not to actually watch anybody making out, but simply to see if they were ahead or behind her on the passion curve. Nan wanted to be somewhere in the safe middle. Her problem was that the middle, when it came to sex, was hard to locate. Worse, it changed week to week.

Of all the couples she was curious about, none occupied her thoughts more frequently than Lucy and Sarah. "How far do you think they've gone?" she asked at least once a week. He told her he had no idea, though in truth he'd wondered the same thing. Lucy, he'd bet, was terrified of sex. Sarah, he imagined, was not. He supposed Lucy's fear was trump, but who knew?

"They haven't yet," Nan told him triumphantly one night in the backseat as she hooked her bra in back and adjusted her breasts in it. Noonan had some painful adjustments of his own to make. "I asked Sarah this afternoon, and she said they hadn't."

"There," he said. "Now you know."

Then she was visited by an unwelcome thought. "She could be lying."

"I doubt it," Noonan said, and it was true; he did. Though wishful thinking might have been part of it.

"Everybody lies sometimes," Nan said, suddenly serious, her eyes glistening.

Which made Noonan wonder if Sarah was right and Nan *was* vulnerable to something other than her own vanity. It was possible, and he didn't want to hurt her. He did want to have sex with her, though, and Sarah's advising him to walk away struck him as monstrously unfair. Okay, it was true. He didn't love Nan. But he needed a more compelling reason than that. That very compelling reason was Sarah's to give, but so far she hadn't, or even hinted at it, and he doubted she ever would. Though when he scrolled back over their recent conversation, one thing did stand out. When she'd said that she was his friend, and Noonan had said, yes, but you're Lucy's girlfriend, she hadn't confirmed that as a fact. She'd just said he should suggest to Nan that they be good friends. Did she expect him to prove himself as good and decent and selfless as her present boyfriend before he could hope to replace him in her affections? He hoped not, because he *wasn't* that good or decent or selfless. That much should've been obvious. After all, he was his father's son.

THERE WAS no shower or bathtub in his flat above the Rexall, just a commode and a small sink from the days when the whole floor had been rented as office space. Back in the fall the lack of plumbing fixtures hadn't mattered much because he showered every day after practice. On Saturday or Sunday he went home with a full bag of dirty laundry and used the washer and dryer. He promised his mother that when football season was over she'd see him more often because he'd need to shower there, though when the time came he joined the Y instead. It didn't cost that much and was only a block away. He also discovered a Laundromat around the corner where one of the dryers, if you knew the trick, worked for free, so he actually went home less, not more. After the first snow he'd put Dec's Indian up for the winter, and the Borough was just too far away to walk there, or so he told himself. But the real reason he seldom went home anymore was that he couldn't bear to be around his mother, whose deepening serenity he found very unsettling. At Nell's, his father reminded him from time to time that she missed him, that it had been a long time since he'd been to see her, and he always promised to visit, his father's wry smile suggesting every time that he knew he wouldn't.

But in late March his brother David found him at Ikey Lubin's and said that his mother wanted to see him, that she couldn't understand why he'd stayed away so long, that she had something she needed to talk to him about. He'd promised to stop by on Saturday afternoon, and because he'd said this in front of the Lynches, he actually did, lugging along a big bag of dirty clothes. It was supposed to snow like hell that night, the last big storm of the winter, so it would be good to get that job over with. He could find out what his mother wanted, assuming she still remembered, while his clothes were tumbling. Once there, though, he decided he couldn't face her yet and went directly into the laundry room and got a giant load going in the washer, then climbed up on the dryer, crossed his legs and read Ralph Ellison, whom they'd be discussing in honors the following week. He'd just transferred his stuff into the dryer when the door opened and there she stood.

"Mom," he said. "Hi. I was just coming to find you."

When they hugged, she felt feverish and smelled strongly of sleep and medicine. "Don't you want to go into the living room?" he said when she pulled up a rickety plastic chair and sat down.

"No, I like it here," she said dreamily, closing her eyes like a cat. "It's peaceful."

"You're kidding, right?" he said, studying her closely. Peaceful? The dryer was old and noisy, and the washer, when the load got unbalanced, bounced off the wall like an epileptic.

559

"Sometimes, when I'm tired of watching TV or reading magazines, I come in here and just sit and think."

If he'd been surprised back in the fall to realize how much his father had aged, he was equally surprised now to discover how young his mother looked. If anything, she looked younger than she had a decade ago. She'd put on weight, for one thing, which had smoothed out the anxiety wrinkles on her face and neck. Her frame had always been slender, almost fragile, and when pregnant she carried her babies right out in front of her. To Noonan, as a boy, her pregnancies always looked fake, like the ones you saw on television sitcoms. And when she delivered, the extra pounds fell off immediately. This new weight was permanent, and it made her look both soft and young. She exuded a baby-powder scent these days as well, which reminded him of his father's unkind assessment: "Your mother's a child." According to David there was something she wanted to talk to him about, but now she seemed completely absorbed in watching his clothes tumble past the window of the dryer, as if he was in there with them and she was waiting patiently for the end of the cycle.

Finally she said, "Remember the day you went out and gathered up all my clothes and brought them home in that broken suitcase? I was out to here and your father was so angry at me. Remember? And he warned you to leave my things in the street, but you, little as you were, you marched right out and got my suitcase out of the stream and put everything back in the best you could and trudged home on your little legs. Most of the clothes were ruined and I had to throw them away later, but there you were, my little man. I can still see you tugging that suitcase up the front steps."

She delivered this memory as if it were a fond one, worthy of nostalgia. Her own terrible unhappiness, her desperate attempt to escape his father's bullying—these features of the story apparently weren't worth mentioning. He understood, of course, that what she was really nostalgic about was his former devotion to her. Back then, he'd been her little man, whereas now, a couple nights a week, he climbed onto a barstool next to the man he'd once tried so valiantly to protect her from. Which could only mean that he was coming to see things as his father did.

She closed her eyes again and was quiet for so long that Noonan fell into a reverie of his own, until he felt her eyes on him and saw that she was studying him with terrible sadness, as well as an alert awareness that her medications usually prevented. "What's she like?" she asked him.

He knew, of course, who she was talking about, but pretended not to. "Who?"

"That woman."

"Max?" he said, and saw how it wounded her, that he'd called her Max rather than Maxine.

"Yes, her."

"She's not pretty like you," he said, because he imagined that would please her, though it didn't seem to. "Kind of tough looking, actually. I don't know what the attraction is, if that's what you're asking."

"The attraction is she's not me," she said. "Do you like her?"

This was the question Noonan dreaded most. "Mom. We don't have to talk about this."

"Do you like her?"

"She's a hard worker," he said. "She doesn't take any shit from Dad."

"Do you *like* her?"

"Well enough, I guess," he admitted lamely, aware that even so weak an endorsement was a betrayal. "I don't *dis*like her."

"You used to like me."

"I love you, Mom."

She looked askance at him now, as if to acknowledge that, yes, sure he loved her, but *love*, as everyone knew, was no answer. "She has a son."

"Willie," Noonan told her. "He's a sweet kid. He's got Down's syndrome." Why was he telling her this? So she wouldn't be jealous of the woman? "They say he probably won't live to be thirty."

The dryer stopped just then, silence filling the room.

After a moment his mother stood to leave. "Good," she said.

BY THE TIME Noonan left his mother's house it had begun to snow. It was late afternoon, and the sky was low and dark. As he crossed from the Borough into the East End, streetlamps began to click on, one by one, lighting his way, as if that were necessary. He thought about heading straight downtown so he could drop off his laundry bag. From there he supposed he might go out to Nell's, if he could find a ride. If the restaurant was busy, he could help Max behind the bar or bus tables or give Willie a hand in back, in return for which he'd be fed. But if it continued to snow as predicted, business was likely to be slow and there'd be nothing to do but talk to his father, who'd want to know if he'd gone out to see his mother, and he wasn't anxious to recount what had happened there. He'd have to lie, say she seemed fine, that they'd had a pleasant conversation about nothing much in particular. He'd never tell him what she'd said about Willie.

On a normal Saturday night, he and Nan and Lucy and Sarah would've gone to a movie and maybe from there to Angelo's for pizza or back to Ikey's, but Mrs. Beverly had flown in from Atlanta that afternoon, and so Nan was spending the evening with her parents. Noonan had always assumed that if there was one family in Thomaston insulated from strife, it was the Beverlys, though apparently this wasn't the case. Last week, Nan had confided to Sarah that the story her family had told everyone—that Mrs. Beverly had gone on ahead to Atlanta to prepare their new home and lives, that she and her father would join her there after her graduation—wasn't true. In fact, her parents had separated. At issue was the rapid decline in the family's fortune, for which Nan's mother blamed her father,

whom she considered a pale imitation of his father and grandfather, real men of business who would never have allowed the
tannery to fail, any more than they would've frittered away on
bad investments the wealth amassed by previous generations of
Beverlys. A real man would have gone on the offensive, unlike
Mr. Beverly, who'd chosen a more timid course, and was con-
testing the myriad lawsuits directed against them on technical
grounds, practically conceding that these outrageous charges—
that the Beverly family had not only polluted the Cayoga Stream
but also knowingly poisoned the entire community—had merit.
What kind of strategy was that? As a result of his cowardice their
fortune was gone, except for what she'd inherited from her own
parents, and she was damned if he was going to get his hands on
that. Nan loved her father and sided with him as, over the long
winter months, this dispute escalated. She hadn't wanted him to
agree to the trial separation, but he was as passive in defending
his marriage as he'd been about defending the business. He
assured his daughter the separation was only temporary, that he
still loved her mother and was hoping that absence might make
her heart grow fonder. This weekend, he said, would tell if there
was any chance of that.

As much as Noonan didn't want to spend Saturday night with
his father at Nell's, the idea of spending it alone in his unheated
flat was even less appealing, so he decided to stop in at Ikey's. If
Lucy and Sarah had something planned, maybe they'd invite
him to tag along. If not, they'd just hang out there all evening, as
they so often did, and Mrs. Lynch could be counted on to feed
him. He would later regard this decision to stop as his initial
mistake in a night full of them, the first seemingly harmless
domino to fall. On the threshold of Ikey Lubin's, in fact, he
paused for a moment, his hand outstretched, in the exact pose
Sarah had drawn four years earlier, though he didn't think about
that at the time. But he would later realize he might've changed
his mind. Mr. and Mrs. Lynch were there, but they hadn't
noticed him yet. Was it their concerned expressions that made

him pause, their attention focused on the table at the rear of the store where Sarah and Lucy appeared to be in urgent conversation with someone who was partially obscured. He saw Sarah reach out and put a hand on this other person's, and for a moment Noonan thought it had to be a child. In the next instant he was inside, his decision suddenly made.

"Bobby!" Nan cried, leaping to her feet when she saw who it was, her chair tipping over backward as she ran to him. Her eyes, he saw, were red and almost swollen shut. "I hate her!" she sobbed, burying her contorted face in his chest. "I hate her, I hate her, I hate her."

His only thought was how ugly she looked.

IT HAD BEEN CLEAR from the moment her mother got off the plane in Albany that absence hadn't made her heart grow fonder, of her father or even her daughter. In fact, she was spoiling for a fight. Once her suitcases were loaded in the trunk and they'd turned toward Thomaston, she'd made one hateful statement after another, her husband, for the most part, suffering this in silence. By the time they got home, she'd turned her anger on Nan, calling her vain and shallow and spoiled. "If you weren't such a selfish brat, we'd all be living together someplace nice." Last spring, she reminded her daughter pointedly, they'd had a decent offer on their Borough house. But no, Little Miss Special had to finish her senior year with her friends. Why? Because she was scared she wouldn't be the prettiest girl, or even the fifth prettiest, in some new school. In Atlanta, her daddy wouldn't be anybody special, and neither would she. "Well, you know what, little girl? That's life. Get ready for it." Disappointments, she continued, were right around the corner, legions of them. The college sorority she'd have her heart set on? Forget about it. That handsome Sigma Nu? He wouldn't know she was alive. The new convertible she was expecting as a graduation gift? Think again. And that's only what they'd lost by not selling the house when they should've. For the far more significant losses she could thank her beloved father, who was more mouse than man. Did Nan have any idea what he'd made them? Poor. That's what they were now, so get used to it, little girl.

This narrative was far from coherent and broken up by sobs and fury, but Noonan was to hear it several times over the course of the evening. As he listened to it at Ikey's, he felt sorry for the Lynches, who were clearly being treated to the same story all over again, Nan having been there for about an hour by now. Determined to punish both her parents, she'd left home without telling them where she was going. "Let them think I froze to death in a snowbank," she said darkly.

"Aw, you don't mean that," Lucy's father said. But in truth he seemed truly shocked by her recital. Noonan couldn't tell which surprised him more—that anyone would say such things about people as important as the Beverlys, even if the speaker *was* a Beverly, or that Thomaston's longtime first family, who lived in the finest house in the whole county, should exhibit the same resentments and marital recriminations as other people. It was almost as if they were no better than anybody else.

"Mind your own business, Lou," his wife said.

"I ain't sayin' it's my business," Big Lou told them all. "I'm just sayin'—"

"Well, don't," Tessa said. "Don't say a thing. Pretend you don't have an opinion."

Dec Lynch came in then, smelling of aftershave, his black hair slicked wetly back. "What the hell's all this?" he said, taking in the situation at a glance.

"Pretend you don't have an opinion either," Tessa told him.

"I don't," Dec said. "I'm pretty sure I'll disagree with Biggy when all the facts are known, but other than that . . ."

Noonan was afraid Nan would deliver the narrative once more for this new listener, but fortunately all the sobbing had given her the hiccups. "I hate my mother," she said. "She's ruining my life."

"Oh, that," Dec said.

"I mean it," she said, and hiccupped loudly.

"Yeah, I know, Cupcake," he said. "But try to keep things in perspective. In a hundred years, we'll all be dead."

"I'm going to go home and take a whole bottle of aspirin," Tessa said when the door closed behind her brother-in-law. "Whatever you kids decide to do, you better do it quick." She pointed outside, where it was now snowing so hard they could barely see the streetlamps.

OBVIOUSLY, the thing to do was to take Nan back home, but she was adamantly opposed to that. "I'd rather freeze to death in a snowbank," she repeated. They'd recently read *Ethan Frome* in honors, and the story must've taken firm root in her mind. Lucy, taking a tip from his mother, decided that he should get Sarah home while the roads were still passable. Noonan went with him to get the car, leaving Sarah to hold Nan's hand until they returned.

"Poor Nan," Lucy said. "I feel sorry for her."

"I guess." Maybe he had high standards when it came to parental discord, but to Noonan this dispute seemed pretty mundane. After all, Mr. Beverly hadn't cocked his fist at Mrs. Beverly, hadn't called her a dumb cunt or broken open her suitcase and strewn her intimate apparel out the car window on the drive home from the airport. As far as he knew, Nan's father didn't have another woman on the side. And while he didn't doubt that her mother's fury was real, at least that anger was evidence that she was in full possession of her faculties. If you sat her down in front of a clothes dryer, she wouldn't lose her train of thought while watching her own bras spin around. Before leaving Ikey's he'd tried to suggest as much by reminding Nan that other people of her acquaintance had it worse. She'd grudgingly allowed that this might be true, but then remarked that this made them lucky, because they were used to it, whereas her parents had thoughtlessly insulated her against every sort of unpleasantness and now, at the eleventh hour, were unfairly piling their misery on her shoulders. Couldn't they at least have waited until she was safely off at college?

Was it possible Lucy actually sympathized with this absurd argument? Did he really feel sorry for her? If so, Sarah's father had a point. Gullibility and innocence, unmitigated by even a smidgen of healthy cynicism, might not represent everything that was wrong with America, but it *was* a grotesque combination.

He tossed his laundry bag in the back of the Lynch station wagon and climbed in front with his friend, who put the key in the ignition and then just sat there. After a moment he broke into his goofiest grin. "Remember how we used to surf my dad's truck?"

God, Noonan thought. Gullibility, innocence *and* nostalgia. "I remember breaking my wrist."

Lucy nodded seriously, embarrassed by this part of the story. "I should have called the turn." Then, after a moment: "Things were simple back then, huh?"

Before girls? Is that what he was getting at? Or something else?

"Don't you ever wish things just stayed the same?" Lucy said. "That we didn't all have to go off to college and—"

"I can't wait, actually," he answered, trying to cut this off.

"What if it means we never come back? What if we forget?"

"Forget *what*?"

"All of it."

"I imagine we'll remember the important stuff."

"What if it's all important?"

"And there's a quiz?"

He meant this as a joke, of course, and Lucy did grin sheepishly, as if at his own foolishness. But Noonan couldn't shake the feeling that his friend was serious and, for reasons he himself couldn't begin to imagine, had concluded that every single detail of their lives so far was of vast importance. That there would, in fact, be a quiz.

WHEN THEY PULLED UP in front of Ikey's, Nan and Sarah got into the backseat, and Lucy drove slowly downtown. The snow was already halfway up the wheels. Nan was calmer now, her hiccups having subsided, and she suggested they all go out for pizza, but Lucy said the station wagon wasn't all that good in snow, and he didn't want to get stuck. Noonan said pizza sounded good to him, which cheered Nan up a little. When they pulled up in front of the Rexall, he trotted upstairs with his laundry while the others waited in the car, though Sarah, looking worried, was waiting on the landing when he came back down.

She took his hand as she had that night he'd given her a lift home on the Indian. "Be nice to her tonight."

"I thought I was supposed to break up with her. Tell her we should just be friends."

"Not tonight."

"When?"

"I don't know, Bobby. Just not tonight."

Was it because her hand was in his that he leaned forward and kissed her? Or because it was dark there on the landing, the single bare bulb meant to light the stairs having burned out months earlier? Or because Lucy had just shared his profound wish that things would never change. *There*, Noonan thought when his lips touched Sarah's, *they just did*. Or was it because he'd been wanting to for so long? He couldn't say, but one thing was certain. The kiss surprised him a lot more than it did Sarah, who now gave him a maddening smile.

"God," he said, stepping back. "I'm sorry."

"Why?"

He had no ready answer for that, since he wasn't, of course, sorry at all.

"Actually," she said, "you've been working up to that for a while."

"I have?"

"Yes."

"Why didn't you stop me?"

"Because I'm a girl. It was nice."

"But—"

"Go take care of Nan. She needs you." She was pushing him down the steps now, toward the street. "And don't look like you did something terrible. It was just a kiss."

BY THE TIME Lucy dropped Nan and Noonan at the Cayoga Diner and then drove on to take Sarah home, the snow was already up to the top of their boots. They'd stopped first at Angelo's, where there was a handwritten sign taped to the door: CLOSED FOR BLIZZERD. Indeed, the only restaurant open was the diner, and to Noonan's astonishment Nan had never been there, though that made sense once he thought about it. This was the domain of rough, disgruntled men her father had laid off, who blamed him for poisoning their water and causing the cancer that ran through their diminished lives. "My mother would be furious if I went there," Nan said, forgetting for a moment that she hated her, but then her face brightened. "Let's go!"

They had the place to themselves, so they slid into the corner booth where they could watch the street fill up with snow. "Yuck," Nan said when she saw the big plate of greasy fries drenched in brown gravy that came with their burgers, though she was soon lapping them up. Living so recklessly seemed to have improved her spirits, but in no time she was back to recounting her tale of woe for—what?—the fourth time? "Oh, I forgot to tell you this part," she'd say to propel it forward, her face pink with recollected outrage, despite the fact that she *had* told him, twice. Confident he could recite the complete narrative himself, Noonan allowed his mind to drift back to the dark landing. That Sarah considered what happened there "just a kiss" was as unnerving as the kiss itself. He'd long ago recognized that Sarah either had no aura or had found a means of cloaking it, but this reaction was taking ambivalence too far. He'd kissed her when he shouldn't have, and in doing so betrayed both his best friend and his own girlfriend, if that's what the girl chattering at him across the booth actually was. At the very least, kissing Sarah should've clarified matters. Instead he was more confused than ever. He couldn't tell if she'd wanted him to kiss her, nor if she wanted him to do it again. On the one hand, she didn't look like she did, particularly. But neither did she look like she didn't. She hadn't slapped him, or pushed him away. She'd even said it was nice, though this was hardly a ringing endorsement.

The most infuriating thing was that he couldn't remember whether she'd kissed him back. He hadn't known he was going to kiss her until he did, and somehow at the critical moment managed not to pay attention. It was a little like reading a passage in a book, then realizing your mind had wandered and that you couldn't remember a single thing about what you'd just read, though your eyes had passed dutifully over every word. If the kiss had been a paragraph, he'd have gone back and read it again to see if anything rang a bell. But it wasn't a paragraph, and nothing did.

The kiss did have one unforeseen and deeply mysterious consequence, however. As he sat in the Cayoga Diner listening to Nan retrace the day's events, he felt a softening toward her. Back at Ikey's, she'd truly seemed ugly in her rage and sorrow, but now her beauty was largely restored and she was once again the prettiest girl in town. It made exactly no sense to Noonan that kissing one girl should make another more attractive, though right then a lot of things made no sense. Maybe it had to do with the fact that the girl he'd kissed and wanted to kiss again, paying closer attention next time, had specifically asked him to be nice to this other girl, and Lucy—the friend he'd betrayed by kissing the girl he wanted to kiss again—had implied as much himself. By granting their wish, that is, he could make amends for his betrayal. Grant them that much, at least. Because, okay, maybe Nan *was* vulnerable. She'd had what was for her a rough year. Sarah and Noonan were veteran observers of marital dysfunction, and Lucy's parents had struggled mightily for a long time to keep Ikey's afloat. But to Nan economic uncertainty and parental discord were brand-new. They'd thrown her for a loop, and why not? Sure, she'd been coddled and protected and encouraged to be self-centered, but she wasn't stupid. Though most of the books Sarah's father had assigned for honors were subversive to everything she'd been raised to take comfort in, she'd read them diligently, with more wide-eyed innocence than outrage, and occasionally had interesting things to say about them. Take away the trappings of her Borough upbringing, and she was more daring than Lucy, which admittedly wasn't saying much. Still, if Lucy and Sarah wanted him to be nice to Nan tonight, he would.

By the time they finished their burgers and had several cups of coffee, the street outside was deserted except for the groaning snowplows. Larry, who worked the grill and liked chatting with his customers when it was slow, came over and, without invitation, slid into their half-moon booth, confident of a warm reception but not offended in the least when Nan scooted all the way around to Noonan's side. He hated to see good food go to waste, so he finished the last of their soggy fries. He was wearing a gravy-stained T-shirt so thin that his nipples and belly button were plainly visible underneath, and Nan regarded him with undisguised wonderment. What he thought he'd probably do tonight, he confided, was close up early and curl up on a pallet in the back room so he could open on time in the morning, assuming it had stopped snowing by then, the streets were plowed, people could dig themselves out of their driveways, downtown had electricity and all sorts of other assumptions that would probably prove contrary to fact. He seemed determined to explain not only his intentions but also the reasons that buttressed them. He apologized again for having to close early, then sat there smiling benevolently until Noonan said they'd better be going.

Outside, the first thing they noticed was how quiet it had become. The snowplow laboring two blocks up the street was making the only sound, and even that was muffled by the thick blanket of snow. Finally, it seemed, Nan was talked out. They walked in the plowed street as far as the Rexall. There she stopped and looked up at the tall dark windows of his flat, her expression a mix of fear and confusion. Finally she said, "How do you do it?"

He assumed she meant how did he live up there in such a horrid place, all by himself. But apparently not.

"How do you not care?" she elaborated. "Your parents. They don't love each other, right?"

Actually, he'd never discussed them with Nan, so he assumed she must've gotten this from Sarah or Lucy.

"How can you stand that?"

"You just decide," he said, surprised by his own answer.

"You mean you pretend you don't care?"

"No, I mean you decide you don't care, and then you stop caring."

She looked doubtful, as if he'd just told her the secret of flight was making sure you had plenty of elevation, that you should climb to the top of the tallest building you could find and then just take the leap. "Do you think I could do that?"

"I don't know. It took me my whole childhood. You'd have to want to."

"I wonder if I could just not care for the rest of tonight," she said, apparently excited by the idea. "Or the rest of the week."

"And then go back to caring? I'm not sure that's how it works."

"But maybe if they saw I didn't care, *they* would."

"I don't think it works that way either."

"Well, I'm going to try. I just decided. I'm not going home tonight. I want you to show me more places like the diner." She took a deep breath. "I want you to show me the whole West End."

Noonan was tired and would rather have called her father and tell him where he could collect his daughter, but then she put her arms around his neck and said *"Please"* in the pouty little-girl voice she seemed to think was all she needed to get whatever she wanted.

"They won't *believe* this when I tell them!" she said when he'd agreed.

"Oh, they will," Noonan predicted, "and they'll blame me."

They followed the snowplow down Division Street. When they passed Berman Court, he pointed out the second-floor apartment where he'd lived as a boy, before his father got on full-time at the post office. For some reason Nan found it hard to comprehend that both the Marconis and the Lynches had lived there, that he and Lucy had originally been West End kids. He couldn't tell whether she believed that people who started out in places like Berman Court always stayed in them, or that some cosmic screwup had landed them there, a mistake belatedly discovered and rectified.

Next she wanted to see the Hill, where the Negroes lived. "There's nothing there," he told her. "It's just a bunch of houses. There won't be anybody out in this."

"I still want to see it," she said.

So they trudged the half-dozen blocks through deepening snow. When they got to Pine Street, they had to stop because the plows hadn't come here and likely wouldn't before morning.

"It's not fair," Nan said. "Why should they be last?"

Noonan agreed it wasn't fair.

"No, I mean it," Nan insisted.

"So do I."

"Somebody should do something."

"Somebody should."

573

"But nobody ever does," she said sadly, her gaze turning inward. "We all stood and watched Perry beat up that Mock boy. Nobody did anything."

"I wasn't there," he reminded her, not trying to absolve himself, just putting this on the record.

"You'd have stopped it," she said. "I know you."

Noonan was grateful for her good opinion but doubted it was justified. True, he wouldn't have wanted to see Three Mock beaten, but if he'd stepped in it would've been for the pleasure of seeing Perry's fat nose gush bright red blood. Not the best of reasons. All in all, he was just as glad he hadn't been there.

Next, having decided she was with someone who could protect her, Nan announced she wanted to go to Murdick's, a place she'd been hearing about all her life.

"I don't think you'd like it," he said. "Especially on a Saturday night."

But she insisted, and it was only a couple of blocks away. The street looked like it had been plowed earlier in the evening, though another foot of new snow, or close to it, had fallen in the meantime. Snow-covered cars were parked crazily everywhere, front and rear ends sticking out into the street as if the drivers had all been drunk when they arrived, which many of them probably were. Inside, music was throbbing, and a woman shrieked with what Noonan hoped was hilarity. "Let's go in," Nan told him.

"You don't want to do that."

"It sounds like they're having fun."

"Your father wouldn't like you being here."

This, of course, was the wrong thing to say.

"If you don't take me, then I'll go by myself."

But at that moment the front door swung open, and Dec Lynch emerged, unzipping as he did. He looked half in the bag and didn't notice them a few feet off. Arcing his stream over the railing, he tilted his head back, nearly losing his balance, so he could catch falling snowflakes on his tongue, his urine hissing in the snow.

When he'd finished and zipped up, Noonan said, "Hi, Dec."

He swiveled, locating Noonan by sound. "Bobby," he said, offering his hand. Noonan, not that fastidious, shook it. "You better not be riding my bike around in this weather."

"I'm not."

"Good. Don't." Then he noticed Nan. "Hey there, Cupcake," he said, having apparently forgotten completely that a moment before he'd been standing there with his dick in his hand. "You stopped crying, I see. You coming in?"

"No," Nan said, tugging urgently on Noonan's sleeve.

BACK DOWNTOWN, Nan had made up her mind. "I want to," she said. "Tonight."

"It's cold as hell up there," Noonan said. They were again in front of the Rexall, and he was hoping she'd forgotten the place wasn't heated. "It's worse than cold. It's ugly. I only have a sleeping bag." *Also, I'm in love with your friend Sarah, my own best friend's girlfriend. I kissed her earlier tonight and can still taste her lips on my tongue.*

"That's okay," she said.

"That's what you say now."

"I want to," she said.

He saw her wrinkle her nose at the stale urine smell in the dark entryway, and halfway up the steep, narrow stairs she hesitated, clearly frightened. Maybe, he told her, this wasn't such a great idea. No, she was sure. She said this grimly, as if she meant to learn about all of life's tawdry ugliness, including sex, in this one night, so she could be done with it.

Over the months Noonan had learned not to pay any attention to his place, but now he couldn't help seeing it through Nan's frightened eyes. It was huge, like an airplane hangar, and everything was exposed—insulation, pipes, crumbling brick walls. The ceiling had tiles missing, where you could see the crawl space above. Dec's motorcycle sat by the far wall, resting

575

on its kickstand. Back in November he'd needed Lucy's and Perry Kozlowski's help to wrestle it up here, and since then it had been leaking oil onto an old bath mat. In the center of the room sat a ratty sofa, bowed in the middle, and an old footlocker serving the dual purpose of coffee table and clothes bin. Beyond this his unrolled sleeping bag lay on its thin strip of foam padding.

But the most embarrassing detail was the commode, in full sight only a few feet away, and next to it a small, permanently stained sink in the process of detaching itself from the wall. When the toilet flushed, the sink jumped and banged as if someone was out in the hallway pulling on it with all his might. At least Nan wouldn't be witnessing that. Noonan couldn't imagine a circumstance extreme enough for either of them to make use of the commode tonight. Truth be told, he himself used it only the last thing at night, with the lights out, before sliding into the sleeping bag.

"Oh, Bobby," was all she could say, and he could tell she was more deeply affected by where he was living than anything else she'd witnessed on their tour of the West End.

"It's okay," he said. "You get used to it. And it won't be so bad when the weather warms up," he added when he saw her shiver, whether from the cold or moral revulsion he couldn't tell. For some reason her revulsion, if that's what it was, made him proud. Deeply embarrassed, sure, but mostly proud.

Then Nan saw the easel set up by the tall rear windows that overlooked the alley below. She knew that Sarah had used part of the cavernous space as a studio back in the fall, but Noonan could see that the whole arrangement seemed more intimate now. She'd imagined interior walls, and there weren't any, nothing separating the part Sarah used from the part he used. You could still smell her turpentine and linseed oil, which he'd discovered he liked, and her brushes all stood at attention in jars.

He later would wonder if it was Sarah's residual presence there that kept Nan from backing out. For the longest time she quietly studied the evidence, of what, she couldn't quite imagine. Finally, she took a deep breath, turned to Noonan, put her arms around his neck and kissed him.

Unlike the earlier kiss, he paid attention to this one, which was nothing like the kisses Nan offered when she knew other people were watching. Those were dramatic, cinema inspired, moist and fully adult, whereas this was dry and frightened and full of the little girl Nan hadn't been in a long while. And what exactly did it mean, he wondered, to prefer a kiss you couldn't remember to one you could?

Nan must have felt his hesitation, because she said, "Bobby? Don't you want to?"

The answer to that was yes and no. He said only yes.

SOMETIME BEFORE DAWN she woke him, struggling frantically in the sleeping bag and crying, "Let me out! Let me out!" He told her to quit thrashing, but she was beside herself, and he finally had to pin her arms at her sides. "Calm down. Let me unzip us."

Though wild eyed and uncomprehending, she finally quit struggling. "Hurry," she whimpered as he worked to unsnag the zipper.

"You're okay," he assured her, knowing she wasn't. When he finally freed the zipper's metal teeth from the cloth, she became frenzied again and elbowed him in the mouth getting out of the bag. She made it to the toilet just in time, and she looked so pitiful heaving into the bowl that Noonan found he couldn't watch, so he busied himself by rummaging through his footlocker for a washcloth. By the time he found one and wet it in the sink, the worst was over.

"I want to go home," she said, her voice sounding hollow in the bowl. He put the moist towel in her hand, and she used it to wipe her mouth. "Don't watch," she told him. "Go back over there."

He did as instructed while she got shakily to her feet and flushed the toilet, the sink jumping and banging against the wall as if possessed. When it finally stopped Nan again said, "I want to go *home*."

The green face of the alarm clock read 5:17. "It'll be light in another hour," he told her.

"I want to go home *now*." She'd grabbed her elbows and was shivering in the cold, a frightened child. This, Noonan thought, was what Sarah had foreseen and tried to prevent. "Please, Bobby . . . I hate it here. I thought I could, but I can't."

He was about to say *You did*, then thought better of it. Sex was only part of what she couldn't do, which also included his squalid flat, Murdick's, the Hill and he himself. She'd vomited all that, along with Larry's gravy-drenched fries. Last night, the West End had served her vengeful purpose as a means of getting back at her family, but in this black hour before dawn her courage had failed her utterly. Instead of teaching her parents a lesson, she'd taught herself one, and now she wanted that old world back, her own pink bedroom in her own Borough house, even her own angry, bitter mother.

"Where are my clothes?" she said, bewildered, even more childlike.

They were in a pile at her feet, but when Noonan stepped toward her to pick them up, she hissed "Stay away!" and put one hand over the pale patch of her pubic hair.

"Okay," he said, taking a quick step back. "Okay."

"You get dressed, too."

He was as naked as she was, of course, and it occurred to him that when they'd made love she hadn't actually seen him. Her expression now was identical to the one she had last evening when Larry, in his threadbare gravy-stained T-shirt, had joined them in their booth. It would've been funny if she weren't so truly frightened.

"Turn around, okay?" she said. She was holding her panties out in front of her, prepared to step in but unable to do so until his back was turned, as if covering herself would somehow make her more naked instead of less. "Don't watch."

Noonan did as he was told, dressed quickly, then waited for her to finish. When he figured she must be done, he turned around and discovered she wasn't. She was standing there in her bra, about to pull her sweater over her head, which she again refused to do until he turned around.

"Okay, okay," he said, crossing the room to the sink and flipping on the light switch.

"Turn it off!" she snapped, though she was fully clothed now.

He did, but not before glimpsing his bottom lip in the cracked mirror. Her elbow had burst it like a grape, and there was blood on his chin and around his mouth. "Look what you did," he told her, hoping she'd see the humor in the situation or, failing that, at least acknowledge that he, not she, was actually the injured party.

"Take me home" was all she said.

WHEN THEY EMERGED into the street below there was light in the east. Noonan couldn't believe how much it had snowed. Two feet had been predicted, but this looked closer to three. The parking meters had completely disappeared under snowbanks the plows had pushed up. A car wearing a tall snow hat was idling across the street in front of the theater, and he didn't recognize it until the horn tooted.

"That's my father," he told Nan, but if she heard him she gave no sign, standing, frozen, in the doorway. Upstairs, all she'd wanted to do was get home, but now, confronted by all this, she looked like she meant to just stand there until the snow melted. "I'll be right back, okay?"

His father rolled down the window and watched knowingly as he scrambled over the enormous snowbank.

"What are you doing here, Dad?" he said, leaning against the car.

His father flicked his cigarette into the snow and peered around him at Nan, who hadn't moved. Only her head was visible above the snow. "Waiting for you to come down. Would you have preferred I come up?"

"No," he conceded.

"I was going to give you about five more minutes. What happened to your lip?"

"An accident."

"What's the matter with her?"

"Nothing. None of your business."

"That what you plan to tell *her* father?"

"She had a fight with her parents last night, so she stayed with me."

"And?"

"And now she wants to go home." Suddenly, an intuition. "Did her father call you?"

"Me and everybody. He wanted to know where you lived, but I thought it might be better if I came here first."

"Thanks," Noonan said, meaning it.

"He gave me an hour to find you. If his daughter isn't back in"—he consulted his watch—"fifteen minutes, he's calling the cops."

By the time Noonan returned to the doorway, Nan was crying again. "Put your arms around my neck," he told her.

"I don't want to," she said. "I don't love you anymore."

"I'm going to carry you over the snowbank, is all. Then I'm taking you home. Your father's getting ready to call the cops."

"Poor Daddy," she said, snuffing her nose. "Everybody's going to know what we did."

"Nan, listen to me. We got trapped by the storm. There was no phone. That's all anybody needs to know." Across the street, his father got out of the car and stood watching them. "We need to go, Nan," he said. "Try to forget last night. Everything's going to be fine."

"We shouldn't have done it."

"But we did."

"What a horrible thing to say."

"Nan."

"You don't even like me."

"That's not true."

"It's Sarah you really like, I can tell."

"We need to go now."

"I don't know why I ever liked you. All my other boyfriends were nicer to me than you. They're all still in love with me, too."

"I'm going to pick you up now, okay?"

"Okay."

When he did, she linked her arms around his neck. "What if I have a baby?"

"You won't."

"What if I already am?"

It was on the tip of his tongue to say *What if you're already a baby?* but he didn't. "You're not pregnant, Nan."

When they got to the car, his father handed him the keys and opened the door for Nan, who just stood there, confused, as if he expected her to drive.

"Slide across," Noonan told her, suddenly very impatient. She hadn't even acknowledged his father's existence.

"Easy," his father said.

Noonan ignored this. "Where will you be?"

"At the diner," his father said. The lights, Noonan noticed, had just come on down the block, and Larry was once again moving around behind the counter. "You hungry?"

Noonan decided to tell the truth for once. "Yeah," he said, looking at him.

He smiled. "If her old man doesn't shoot you, I'll buy breakfast."

SINCE THIRD WAS one of the few East End streets that had been plowed, Noonan took it, even though it meant passing by Ikey

Lubin's. He was not anxious to run into any of the Lynches, who would put two and two together if they saw him with Nan at this hour of the morning. It was about the time Ikey's opened for business, and sure enough, Big Lou Lynch was lumbering across the intersection.

"Just keep going," Nan said, purposely looking off in the other direction.

He considered this. The man was probably half asleep and wouldn't recognize the car anyway. Then again . . . He slowed, rolling down his window. "Hi, Mr. Lynch," he said.

Lucy's father broke into one of his big, goofy smiles. Then he saw who it was, and the smile disappeared, which meant the Lynches had also gotten a middle-of-the-night phone call. Big Lou peered across at Nan, then back at him, clearly wounded that she hadn't said hello.

Noonan could tell he was wondering if this meant she wouldn't be coming to Ikey's anymore. "I'm taking Nan home," he said. "But I'll swing by on the way back and help you dig out."

"We can manage okay, I guess," Mr. Lynch said, still regarding Nan fearfully.

"It'll be an all-day job," Noonan told him. They'd have to shovel not only the sidewalk in front of the store, but paths out through the snowbanks and the parking lot. "Another shovel will make it go a lot quicker."

"What about your own house? Won't your mom—"

"My brothers will take care of that."

"*Bobby*," Nan said. She was crying again.

"Okay, then," Mr. Lynch said, stepping back. "I guess we could use you."

"He knew," Nan said as soon as the window was rolled up.

"Knew what?"

"What we did."

"Nan," he said, "it was just sex. You were the one who wanted to."

"We're supposed to be married first."

"Well, we weren't. I'm sorry."

"My husband's going to know," she said, crying harder now.

Noonan had no idea what to say to that, but it was a relief to know that whatever future she was imagining didn't include him.

THE SKY WAS LIGHT by the time they arrived at Nan's. All of the Borough streets, even the little ones, had been plowed, and there were half a dozen pickups with snow-blade attachments opening up driveways. The Beverlys' elbow-shaped drive was already plowed, so he pulled right up to the house. Mrs. Beverly, wearing an overcoat, was standing like a statue between the inner and outer doors. Seeing her there, Nan opened her door and stepped out before the car had come to a complete stop. It was so slippery that she almost fell, but then she found her balance. "Wait," he said, taking his key out of the ignition, though she was already running to her mother, who pulled her inside and quickly closed the door, as if the air outside were not just cold but poisonous.

That left Noonan sitting by himself in the drive, wondering whether duty dictated that he follow and knock on that emphatically closed door or be grateful for the clean getaway that apparently was his for the taking. Before he could decide, he saw Mr. Beverly in the rearview mirror coming toward him from the general direction of the garage, its door wide open. Noonan got out to meet him, maybe even offer to shake hands, and struggled to get his footing on a mound of packed snow, still holding on to the handle. Instead of waiting for him to come around the vehicle onto a level surface, Mr. Beverly, his face twitching with anger and fatigue, not to mention, Noonan supposed, a nonstop litany of wifely abuse, came up to him on the bank of snow beside the car. Mr. Beverly was several inches taller and had an athletic build, though according to Nan the only sport he managed gracefully was water-skiing. Staring at Noonan's busted lip, he said, "Did you strike my daughter?" as if the visual evidence suggested this was the only valid conclusion to be drawn.

"No sir." Noonan had started to offer his hand, but saw now there was no point.

"Then how did *that* happen?" Mr. Beverly demanded.

Noonan squinted at him, trying hard to follow his logic. Under the circumstances, mentioning the sleeping bag didn't seem the wisest strategy. "It was an accident," he said. "I'm sorry about last night. We should've called, but Nan was pretty upset—"

"Upset?" her father said. "Did you touch her?"

It was the imprecise nature of this question that caused him to hesitate, and in that pause Mr. Beverly intuited the truth, or something like it. Immediately Noonan saw the man's intention to throw a punch and then, in the next instant, the punch itself. Because he was still holding on to the handle, he was able to lean back without slipping. Mr. Beverly's wildly thrown fist, encountering nothing but air, spun him around on the slick incline, then both feet flew out from under him, and he landed flat on his back, his head cracking on the packed snow before he disappeared completely under the car. Alarmed, Noonan peered over the windshield, expecting him to slide out and stand up on the other side, but instead a groan issued from underneath.

He carefully backed up to the front wheel, then got down onto his hands and knees to look underneath. It seemed Mr. Beverly's overcoat had snagged on the undercarriage, and he was looking straight at Noonan, as if for an explanation. "Ohhhhh," he moaned.

"Let me go around the other side," Noonan said. "I'll pull you out."

But when he got there, he saw that Mr. Beverly was perfectly centered beneath the vehicle. By lying on his stomach, he could reach him, though not with enough purchase to yank him free. "Mr. Beverly?" he said. "Can you move at all?"

His head, apparently, since he was staring at Noonan again.

"Shoulder," he groaned. "*Dislocated.* Happened before. Call ambulance."

He had to ring the doorbell three times before Nan's mother answered, her sleeves rolled up, her forearms wet. "She's in the bathtub," she said. "Washing off your filth."

"Right," Noonan said. "Your husband said to call an ambulance."

"Where is he?"

He pointed under the car.

"You ran over him?"

"He slipped."

"You're a monster."

"No," Noonan said. He wasn't feeling good about himself, it was true, but he was pretty sure he hadn't warranted so harsh an assessment.

"Wait here," she said. "Don't you step one foot into our house. Do you understand me?"

He nodded, and Mrs. Beverly went over to stand next to the car. She wasn't the sort of woman who got down on her knees in the snow. "Jack," she said sharply.

"Ambulance" came her husband's voice.

"Did that boy do this to you?"

"No," Noonan called.

She ignored him. "I'm calling the police," she told her husband.

"No. My fault. All my fault."

"Of course it's all your fault," she said. "What do you think I've been telling you for the last twenty-four hours. This *is* all your fault. My God, what kind of man are you?"

"Hurt."

Mrs. Beverly marched back to the house, and Noonan held the door open for her. "He can just stay there for all I care," she said.

"Would you like me to call the ambulance?"

"I'd like you to leave here and never return."

"Okay," he said. "Except—"

"Go. Get out. Now."

"That's my father's car."

"So walk."

"He'll want it back."

Mrs. Beverly considered this for a second, then screamed, louder than he'd ever heard a woman scream, "Get *out* of here! Get out! Right this minute!"

Noonan walked up the drive, past his father's car. When he heard the front door shut behind him, though, he turned around and cautiously returned to the car, getting down on his hands and knees again.

"Did she call? The ambulance?" Mr. Beverly said, staring at him.

"I don't know."

He nodded. "I'm going . . . to pass out, I think," he said, and closed his eyes. "I'm sorry."

"Me, too," Noonan said. Standing up, he glanced back at the Beverly home one last time. In what he guessed must be her bedroom window, Nan was standing in a pink robe. He waved goodbye, in the sense of so long. She too waved goodbye, in the sense of goodbye.

THE BLIZZARD HAD DUMPED just under three feet of snow, the worst storm in several winters, but by seven-thirty that morning, as Noonan made his way through the snowbound streets of the East End on his way to Ikey Lubin's, the sun came out, and the sky was a robust shade of blue that augured spring. People who'd come out bundled up in heavy coats to tunnel through the monstrous snowbanks now shed them in favor of bulky wool sweaters, and even so their foreheads glistened with sweat as they worked. The warming sun was welcome, but it made the snow heavy and slippery, difficult to shovel. Still, everyone seemed to be in a fine mood, convinced that winter had delivered its final blow. Several people called out greetings as Noonan trudged by in the middle of the street, and though he tried to share their good cheer, it wasn't easy. His girlfriend's father had just tried to punch him, injuring himself in the process; her mother had shrieked like a banshee and called him a monster. Worse, as soon as he got to Ikey's, he was going to have to call his father and explain that he'd left his car in Mr. Beverly's driveway with him pinned beneath it. And then there was the serious stuff. Last night, he'd had sex with a girl he not only didn't love but didn't even like very much. If she got pregnant . . . as if to complete this thought, church bells began to ring. It was Sunday. Somehow he'd forgotten that.

Business at Ikey's was brisk. People were too snowed in to drive any distance, certainly not out to the A&P. By the time Noonan arrived, Lucy and his father had cut a tunnel from the store's entryway to the street, and Big Lou, looking pale and tuckered out, was all too happy to surrender his shovel to him. Midmorning, Dec came down, brutally hungover, and surveyed the situation. "Damn," he said. "I was hoping you'd be done with this Eskimo shit by now."

"Well, we're not," Lucy told him.

"I can see that," Dec said. "You don't mind if I just watch, do you?"

Tessa then came out with another shovel from the storeroom and handed it to him without a word.

"Sunday's my day off," Dec reminded her. "Did you forget that?" But he took the shovel and headed over to the parking lot, where they hadn't even begun yet, and stood there for a good solid minute before throwing up violently into the snow and causing Noonan to wonder who'd be sick next.

Tessa nudged him with her elbow. "See?" she said. "You aren't the only damn fool in the world, are you?"

Maybe not, but that's exactly what he felt like. Nan had been right. Except for Dec, the Lynches all seemed to know about last night. Throughout the morning Lucy had been watching him out of the corner of his eye, and Noonan couldn't tell if his friend was disappointed or just plain scared, knowing what the consequences might be. At noon, Tessa insisted they take a break, heaping paper plates high with cold smoked pork chops and both macaroni and potato salad. Noonan scarfed his down and allowed himself to be talked into seconds. Big Lou, still looking pale and weak, ate little before pushing his plate away.

"You all right, Biggy?" his brother said. "I ask because you look like hell."

"I don't seem to have no strength," he told him.

"You never did," Dec replied. "Even back on the farm you always managed to give me the heavy end of everything." Then he turned to Noonan. "Were you at Murdick's last night?"

"No," he said. They hadn't made it inside, so it wasn't much of a lie.

"Damn," Dec said. "I just had this really vivid recollection of you and Cupcake being there."

After lunch they went at it again. It seemed like every time they made a good, wide opening in the snowbank, the plow came by and shut them in again. There was room for only eight cars in Ikey's tiny lot, but three feet of snow in an area that size was a stupendous amount, and by the time they'd finished clearing it Noonan's bad wrist was throbbing. The pain was strangely welcome, though, and the ache helped him locate the rhythm that hard physical labor demanded, his efforts becoming economical and compact, each swing of the shovel having just enough force behind it to propel the wet slippery snow onto the bank. Though Lucy matched him shovel for shovel, he noticed happily that his friend wasn't taking full shovelfuls and that sometimes the snow he flung came sliding back down the bank at him. Midafternoon, Dec, bent over at the waist like a cripple, said, "Girls, I'll leave the rest of this to you," then disappeared upstairs.

When they finally finished the parking lot, Tessa told Noonan to go home, that he'd done his part, but he knew the

Lynches were still snowed in across the street, so he followed Lucy over there, and they began again. At one point Lucy heard the phone ringing inside and went in to answer it, telling Noonan to rest for a while, but he kept working, as if good-faith exhaustion might appease the angry, jealous God who decided whether small-town girls got pregnant or not. The pain in his wrist was worse now, and that, too, was fine.

Across the intersection people continued to traipse in and out of Ikey's, parking in the lot he and Lucy and Dec had cleared by hand, and for some reason, watching this, he felt a welling up of emotion he didn't immediately recognize as pride, perhaps because there was so little justification for it. Was it possible to achieve such intense satisfaction simply by shoveling snow for a corner grocery? Right then, leaning on his shovel, he felt almost weak with gratitude for the long day's labors, proud not only of himself, but also of the Lynches, even Dec, for their daily devotion to Ikey's. Last night he'd given Nan a guided tour of the West End world that had both fascinated and frightened her. He'd taken secret pleasure in showing her the hard realities she'd been sheltered from, but that had been a very different sort of pride from what he felt now, because in truth he no longer belonged to that West End world any more than she did. And this morning, returning Nan to the Borough, it had struck him that he didn't belong there either. When her mother had screamed at him to get out, he remembered thinking she had every right to do so.

But here, right here, was a place he *could* belong, or at least was worth belonging to, where he'd always be welcome, even if he ended up as dubious a character as Dec Lynch. Back in November, Sarah was in tears at the notion that something might happen to Ikey's. At the time her fear had seemed melodramatic, but now he understood. She was taking a stand against her father's values. Noonan didn't know anything about Mr. Berg's novel, but he was certain nothing like Ikey's was in it. No, he was drawn to extremes, both philosophical and dramatic. The poor black man who dreamed of fish and whose wife played the number appealed to his grand sense of racial injustice, because these people never had a chance. That they thought they did deepened the irony, and oh how Mr. Berg loved irony. On the other extreme were the grand dreamers—the Gatsbys and the Ahabs—who were determined either to conquer or to tear down and reshape whole worlds. In class they'd also read *Death of a Salesman*, though it was clear Mr. Berg didn't care about Willy Loman. He was simply pitiful. Small men with small dreams didn't interest him, even when their dreams demanded enormous faith and endless forbearance. Ikey Lubin's was a small thing. A small, good thing. You could count on it much like you could count on the Lynches, not for what they didn't have but for what they did. Was it something like this—some small, good thing— his father had been yearning for when he invested in Nell's?

"That was Nan," Lucy said when he came back outside and picked up his shovel.

"Really?" he said, surprised. If Nan was calling Lucy, then maybe, even if she was done with Noonan, she still wanted to be friends with him and Sarah. That morning, when she'd waved at him from her bedroom window, he'd gotten the distinct impression she was blowing all of them off.

"She said nothing happened last night," Lucy said, grinning and happy now.

"Is that right."

"She said you almost did, but then you decided not to."

He nodded.

"That was smart," Lucy said, and Noonan could tell his friend was every bit as relieved as if he himself had been the one in jeopardy. "She and her mom made up, too," he added.

Noonan doubted this could be true but didn't say anything.

"They're flying to Atlanta tomorrow for a whole week," Lucy went on. "There are some southern colleges her mother wants her to visit. One's in Atlanta, and they're going to drive to the others."

He wondered if that meant Mr. Beverly would remain behind. Maybe they'd just leave him under the car.

"That's the only bad part," Lucy went on. "I was hoping she'd go to school here in New York. That way you guys could keep seeing each other. She really likes you, and you like her, so . . ."

They continued to work, Lucy chattering happily away, reenergized by his belief that sex had been avoided, that all was well. Noonan couldn't help feeling sorry for him. Nan had shrewdly selected him as the best person to lie to, the person most likely to believe her, also knowing that he'd do his best to convince others. Lucy would always be the sort of person you'd lie to. Something in him wanted you to, so you could tell yourself you were doing him a favor. The first person he'd set out to convince would be Sarah, which was all to the good. All day long Noonan had been worrying about what she'd think of him when she learned he'd slept with Nan just hours after that kiss on the landing.

That last night's secret might be safe for a while should have cheered him, but it didn't, and exhaustion, held at bay until now, finally set in. Suddenly he could barely keep his feet, and every time he tossed another shovelful of snow his throbbing wrist felt ready to snap like a dry twig. It was early evening when they finally finished the driveway, and as they were crossing the inter-section, a photographer from the *Thomaston Guardian* took their picture, dragging their shovels behind them like a couple of twelve-year-olds. At Ikey's he went into the tiny, unheated washroom out back and there sank heavily onto the freezing toilet seat, too tired to rise, his mind scrubbed clean, his body numb. At some point he half realized something was going on out front, some flurry of activity in the store. Had he actually dozed off in there?

That must've been what happened, because when he returned everything in the store had changed. Sarah was there, and Lucy had taken her in his arms. Big Lou, at the register, had silent tears tracking down his cheeks. Tessa wasn't scolding her

591

husband for being sentimental either, and it was this, even more than Dec, shaking his head at him from across the room, that proved this was serious, whatever this was. His first guilty thought was that Sarah'd had an attack of conscience. She'd gotten home yesterday and realized that it hadn't been "just a kiss" after all, but a terrible betrayal. Because of *course* she'd kissed Noonan back. He remembered now that her lips had parted, welcoming him. He was smiling, remembering that, when she noticed him standing there, and their eyes met. In that instant he knew he'd been wrong, that this wasn't about him and had nothing to do with the kiss. Nor had Nan called her to report what he'd done. This was something much bigger, far worse.

"It don't make no sense," Big Lou said, causing Noonan's heart to sink, because this was what he always said when something was horrible, or unfair, or unexpected, something that didn't fit into his overall scheme of things or conform to how he thought the world should operate.

It was Tessa who finally took him aside. The night before on the South Shore, in the same blizzard that had buried Thomaston, Sarah's mother's new husband had lost control of their car and hit a tree. He, apparently, had died on impact. Her mother, who wasn't wearing a seat belt, had been hurled through the windshield. Her injuries, on a normal night, wouldn't have been fatal, but the wreck hadn't been discovered until morning, and by then she'd bled to death in the snow. They'd both been drunk. Sarah had been out when the call came, and when she returned home her father was feeding the pages of his novel into the fireplace. And so she'd known even before he told her.

A car pulled up at the curb, and its horn tooted just as Mrs. Lynch finished relating all this. It was his father, and Noonan knew why he was there. It was Sunday, his night to tend bar at Nell's, and he should've been there an hour ago. "You go on," Tessa said when he told her. "I'll explain. We'll take care of her."

He knew they would. All the Lynches, even Dec, not just

Lucy. He again recalled yesterday's kiss and thinking that in the instant his lips had touched Sarah's everything had changed, but saw now that he'd been wrong. It was, as Sarah had said, just a kiss. When she realized he was standing there and looked into his eyes, he'd seen that for Sarah the kiss had never even happened. She'd held his gaze only briefly, then turned away.

"MAX HAS YOU all prepped," his father told him. "Don't forget to thank her."

Noonan said he wouldn't. His father was clearly not happy with him, and who could blame him? He'd waited for him at the diner that morning for over an hour, before giving up and eating breakfast alone. Then, after Noonan had finally called to explain what had happened at the Beverlys', he'd had to have Max drive him to the Borough to retrieve his car. Now he had to come fetch him for his shift. But arriving at Nell's in the middle of an argument wouldn't do. Willie could tell and would be upset, so they rode in silence all the way.

He did his best behind the bar but screwed up one drink after another. "What the hell's the matter with you tonight?" his father finally asked. Noonan said he was just exhausted from shoveling snow all day, grateful it hadn't occurred to his father to ask about the scene he'd interrupted back at Ikey's. At one point, though, Willie, his psychic tuning fork vibrating as usual, came out of the kitchen, tenderly took his hand in his own and rested his broad forehead on Noonan's shoulder and told him not to worry, that everything would be okay. "Hey, William," his father called down the bar. "Come here a sec." Boys didn't hold hands with boys, Noonan heard his father explain.

"He was just trying to be nice," he said later, when Willie was out of earshot.

"I understand that," his father said. "Next time, when he kisses you, he'll be trying to be nice then, too."

Max, who'd gone into town to visit her mother in her nursing home, returned at nine-thirty, took one look at Noonan and told him to go home.

When they pulled up in front of the drugstore, his father turned off the ignition, and as Noonan started to get out, told him to hold on a minute. "So," he said, "I guess this Berg girl is the one you really like, huh?"

He was far too exhausted for this or any other conversation with his father. "I guess," he said. "I don't know."

"But the Beverly girl's the one you slept with."

"It's kind of hard to explain."

His father shook his head. "Not really. You know what I see when I look at you?"

"Nope." But he knew what was coming.

"Me."

Noonan swallowed what he felt like saying, but was pleased to feel some of the delicious old loathing return.

UPSTAIRS, it was cold. Maybe not as cold as it had been the night before, though it felt even colder. As soon as he crawled into the sleeping bag, he smelled Nan, and his stomach lurched. Unzipping, he dragged the bag over to the lamp and used the same washcloth he'd given her that morning to scrub at the spot of her blood that had dried on the fabric, as if by removing that he could undo the act that occasioned it. But all this accomplished was to start his wrist aching again and to turn a small dry spot into a large wet one. The cloying scent of spoiled, petulant little girl remained.

He tried not to think about how Sarah was lost to him. What he couldn't help wondering was when, precisely, she'd decided on Lou Lynch and not Bobby Marconi. Something told him that when they'd kissed yesterday, her decision hadn't yet been made, which meant she hadn't known for sure until today. Had it become clear only when she learned about her mother? Had she known in that instant of brutal loss whose comforting embrace and genuine kindness she wanted and needed? Or was it when she'd come into Ikey's? And if *he'd* been the one out front and Lucy in the back, would that same grief and loss have propelled her into his arms instead? But these were pointless questions. It didn't matter how or why she'd chosen. She'd just chosen.

Only when Noonan tried to crawl inside the bottom, closed end did he realize he'd put the top of the sleeping bag facing the back of the building instead of the street, as usual. Not that it made any difference, he thought, getting inside and zipping up. He'd be asleep in a minute anyway. Except he wasn't. Despite his exhaustion, he lay awake shivering on the wet spot, the pain in his wrist coming in long leisurely waves now. If Sarah had chosen, then the thing to do was not care. Wasn't that what he'd told Nan last night, that caring was something you could just decide not to do? Hadn't he mastered that trick long ago? In the morning he would wake up and simply not give a shit.

He lay there telling himself this and staring at a strange shape—a cloaked man?—at the far end of the room. It took him a while to recognize the triangle at its apex as the point of Sarah's easel, and for some reason this reminded him of his cathedral dream. He'd thought of it off and on in the intervening months, even considered asking Three Mock if he knew of anybody on the Hill who had a dream book. But that would just give him a number, something he could play, and what he wanted was the dream's meaning. Tonight, oddly enough, he thought maybe he knew it. If he'd had to sum up in a single word what the cathedral had felt like, it was "home."

Earlier, shoveling snow with Lucy, he'd felt like Ikey Lubin's might be home, but he now understood that had been merely a yearning. The Lynch store was no more his home than Nell's was his father's. Ikey's was just a place he'd become invested in. A small, good thing, yes, but not *his* small, good thing. He was welcome there, true, but always as a visitor. In her drawing Sarah had been right to locate him outside, about to enter. Realizing this, Noonan felt, for perhaps the first time, the terrible combination of loss—of something he wasn't sure he could afford to lose—and fear that there might be nothing to replace it. After all, what did it mean if your only true home was a place that didn't even exist outside your own head? Wasn't that just an indication that you didn't belong anywhere?

What he wanted, desperately, was to dream the cathedral again, because this time he'd be ready. The first time he'd wanted to share its wonders. Now he'd know better than to lose his focus. If he had the dream again, he'd know it was meant for him alone, that some things couldn't be shared. The magic and beauty of the cathedral, if that's what it was, could only be revealed to one person at a time, with no distractions. The presence of anyone else, even a loved one, maybe especially a loved one, made it vanish. It was what you got, he now understood, in lieu of a loved one.

As he lay awake staring at the dark, indistinct shape of Sarah's easel, Noonan could not know that he was looking at his future, his destiny, or that he'd spend his adult life in front of easels, his brush often guided mysteriously by a series of what he would come to think of as "paint dreams." All of that was too far away. He did, however, sense a more immediate future, dark shapes moving in the middle distance between his sleeping bag and the easel at the other end of the room. He could sense them gathering force, and he found that by squeezing his throbbing wrist he could make them almost visible in the darkness. The months to come—between the blizzard and graduation—would give these dark shapes substance in the physical world, driving events that would surprise everyone but Noonan. Despite what Nan told Lucy, she and her mother would not return to Thomaston from Atlanta. Her parents would arrange for her to finish her course work and take her exams in absentia. Her diploma would be sent to her through the mail. Lucy, predict-ably, would take this hardest. "How come she doesn't even write, is what I'd like to know," he'd say at least once a week, adding, "To you, especially," hoping Noonan might explain. "Mind your own business, Lou," his mother would tell him. "You, too," she'd warn her husband when he opened his mouth to say it didn't make no sense to him either.

Nor, of course, was Noonan surprised when Sarah's father was arrested in May for possession of controlled substances. He'd seen that coming back in the fall. The charges were ultimately dropped, though not until Mr. Berg agreed to resign his position. A similar accusation, it was learned, is why he'd left his teaching job in New York and come to Thomaston in the first place. When no substitute could be found so late in the semester, he was told he could finish out the term, but then the story broke in the newspaper, and he never returned to class after that. Everyone in honors was awarded an A. Poor Sarah, Noonan thought, grateful she had Lucy and his family for comfort. "We'll take care of her," Tessa had promised when her mother died, and they did.

Of course what shocked people most was what happened between Noonan and his father, but to him, those events, even more than the others, had the feel of a too-familiar story whose plot was set in motion long ago and whose resolution, barring some deus ex machina intervention, was inevitable. David had never stepped foot in the flat above the Rexall, but Noonan wasn't all that surprised to find him there when he returned after graduation practice that afternoon in early June. Nor was he terribly surprised by what his brother had come to tell him—that their mother was pregnant again. And though he'd safely negotiated the turn onto the gravel road that led up to Nell's a hundred times before, he wasn't really surprised that same afternoon when he lost control of the Indian and it slammed into the concrete abutment. All winter long Dec Lynch had been saying that it was just a matter of time before something like that would happen. The only part Dec got wrong was his prediction that Noonan would escape uninjured, because as he rolled clear he felt something give in his wrist. Was there not a beautiful symmetry to this? And of course he wasn't surprised when the restaurant door flew open and poor, befuddled, prescient Willie came barreling down the long drive to meet him, his arms waving wildly above his head, his face a contorted mask of terror, screaming "*No!*" over and over.

Did his father feel that same inevitability? The futility of attempting to alter events that had been preordained so long ago? Because when Noonan entered, he didn't even bother to climb down from his barstool. He did rotate to face his son, showing him once more those mocking eyes he'd known so well as a boy, their former rage turned inward now. Back when Noonan's hatred of his father had been black and pure, he'd looked forward to this day. Now he deeply regretted all those evenings they'd sat on adjacent barstools in an uneasy truce, which had left him more conflicted than he cared to admit, even to himself. But he had warned his father about the consequences if he failed to heed that warning, so what choice did he have? Had Sarah chosen him, he would remember thinking, it might have been different, but she hadn't. And now the time had come to show her just how wise she'd been.

The details of fights were as hard to recall as kisses, and except for his first punch landing flush, his father's teeth collapsing against his knuckles, his barstool still spinning after he'd crashed to the floor, all he remembered was a blur of sight and sound. Max calling the police. Willie, shoved roughly aside in the parking lot, beside himself now, kicking and punching him, howling like a wild animal for him to stop, stop, stop. His father's blood bubbling blackly from his nose and mouth, his eyes no longer mocking, just accepting. Noonan punching with his left fist, his right hanging limp and worthless. He would remember wanting to stop, but not stopping, even when his father's eyes rolled back in his head. He was too honest to tell himself he was doing this for his mother, who didn't want it any more than she wanted another pregnancy. He was simply doing it because he said he would, and so his father, who could never quite bring himself to throw that punch he was forever threatening, would understand, once and for all, that his son was a different sort of man entirely.

LOVE

BY THE TIME I finally come upstairs Sarah has turned off the light, which may or may not mean she's been crying and doesn't want me to see. I undress in the dark, get into my pajamas, then slide into bed next to her. She turns over to let me know she's awake.

"I saw Brindy in the West End this afternoon. She told Owen she was going to Albany," I tell her, because it's important and has been lost in all the turmoil over me.

"I'm sorry," Sarah says, letting her voice fall and leaving me to contemplate exactly what she's sorry about. To share my suspicion? For Owen? That I witnessed this, because now I'll worry? That I need to shift the focus from myself onto our son?

"If he finds out . . ." I let the thought trail off.

"He may already know," my wife says, taking me by surprise. "People know things and pretend not to." Am I mistaken, or is she speaking not only of our son and me but also herself? Finally she says, "Lou, I've decided I need to go away for a while."

I've been half expecting these words for a very long time. How odd they should take my breath away now, especially given the events of the day. I want desperately to beg her not to, but of course I've got this coming. "Where?" I say stupidly. Away, obviously. Away from me.

"I don't know. I just . . . need to be alone, to sort things out. Some time to yourself might do you good, too."

"It won't," I assure her. "Without you—"

"I'm not going to lie to you, Lou. I don't know what I'm going to do. I'm not even sure I know how to be alone. Or who I'd be if

600

we weren't together. Maybe I'll find out. But I want you to understand that I'm not angry. I know how hard you've tried. It was wrong of you to do what you did. But you're not the only one who's ever done a shameful thing."

I wait until she continues.

"Part of what you said before was true," she says finally. "I did love him."

Of course. We both did.

"Or maybe just something about him. His . . ."

Courage.

She clears her throat. "He sent me a postcard when I was at Cooper Union. It didn't say much except that he was in Toronto and all right. He joked about how he'd signed up for an art class and joined a workshop, and I'd better watch out because he planned to catch up to me. I wanted to show you the card, but I knew it would hurt your feelings because he'd written to me, not both of us. I didn't write him back at first, not until Lou-Lou got sick, and then again when we got married. I could tell him things I couldn't say to you, partly because he wasn't here, but also because you take everything to heart so."

Oh Lou, why must you be so . . .

"I wrote him again after your father died and you . . . I panicked, I guess, because of how unhappy you were. And I wrote him when I lost the baby, when I was the unhappy one. That was the last letter. After that, I stopped."

"Why?"

"It started to feel like . . . cheating. He wrote me at a post office box, and I told myself they were just letters, but having that kind of secret didn't feel right. And by then Bobby was married himself, and it wasn't really fair to anybody, so I told him I wouldn't be writing anymore. I said I loved you and I loved our lives, which was true, but mostly it just seemed like it was time to stop. And then Owen came along and we got busy and there wasn't any need."

"Then why start again? Why now?"

601

My eyes have adjusted to the dark. There's just enough light in the room for me to make out her smile, the same sweet smile that's been such a blessing all these years. "Because it was finally safe. Can't you see that? Maybe it was all of us getting older. I don't know, but at some point I realized the danger was past and Bobby was just an old friend. And after so many years, that's also how Bobby would think of me. But it had something to do with my cancer, too. After the operation I wanted to talk to someone who only knew me from before, as I used to be. The person I really wanted to talk to was my mother, but she was gone, and then for some reason I thought of Bobby, remembering how we used to talk."

About things she couldn't say to me.

She takes my hand. "It's sweet that you think of me as a woman another man would want, but—"

"Sarah," I say, my voice barely audible even to me.

"Try not to think of what I'm telling you as a love story, Lou. You and I are the love story, not Bobby and me."

"You'll never come back," I say, surprising myself by the force of my conviction.

Perhaps because she knows me so well, and knows that she'll never convince me on this point, at least not tonight, she doesn't try. "There's one other thing I need to tell you. I want you to understand that writing those letters to Bobby all those years ago isn't the only dishonest thing I've ever done. I've been reading your story, Lou. All this week. I shouldn't have done that without asking you, but I was so frightened. I was scared of something even worse than what happened today."

That I would cross the Bridge of Sighs. That I wouldn't turn back. She doesn't have to spell this out. "Not much of it's true, I suppose. I started out trying to stick to the facts, but I kept getting lost."

"The way you felt about Lou-Lou was true. The way you feel about Ikey's. And I liked what you wrote about me. But will you explain one thing? Why did you say it was some other girl, the one you describe on the stairs at the Y? The one who looked so frightened at being left behind? It *was* me, you know."

"No, that was—" I start to tell her who, because there's no doubt in my mind, but I stop. For some reason I'm having trouble picturing that girl as clearly as I did when I wrote about the incident. Nor can I remember her name.

"You were a step below me on the stair. I knew who you were, but you hadn't met me yet. I wasn't the kind of girl boys noticed. I turned and there you were and—"

"No," I say again, not wanting to get confused. "No, I remember—"

"I was with my best friend, Sally Doyle. She and I went to all the dances together. You were with that poor boy who hanged himself. David."

"No," I say again. I'm literally shaking my head in the dark.

"Lou," Sarah says, sensing my upset. "It's okay, Lou."

I SLEEP FITFULLY, waking an hour before dawn with the certain knowledge that of course Sarah's right. It *was* her on that stair so long ago. I now see the hope and longing in that girl's eyes and recognize them as belonging to the woman sleeping beside me, whose life I've intertwined with my own. Out our bedroom window the eastern sky shows a thin band of gray. I remember waking as a boy during these darkest of hours and being comforted by the clinking of milk bottles. Even though my father never handled our route, that sound told me he was out there making us proud, providing people with what they needed, dependable and sure in all weathers. He was, I believed, an important man with an important job. The sort of job you wouldn't trust to just anybody.

Poor David, I think. How many times have I denied him? This last is the worst. Because Sarah was right about that, too. David *had* been there, standing quietly beside me that Friday night. For moral support we always went to those dances together. His family had recently moved to Thomaston, and he was in desperate need of a friend, and so, as usual, was I. Finally I got to be the mentor and protector, much as Bobby Marconi had been for me, and I remember enjoying that new role. Living on opposite sides of the East End, David and I took turns walking each other home. One Friday after the dance, we went to David's house, and there in the dark driveway he shocked me by kissing me full on the lips, then hurrying inside. The next day, at the theater, he seemed as embarrassed by what he'd done as I was, and neither of us referred to the previous night. But after the movie he walked me home and did it again, this time in broad daylight, right in front of my house. I remember thinking my father was across the street watching, and so I shoved David away and told him I didn't want to be friends anymore. I can still see the look on his face.

I might have let him into my story, explaining that kiss and what followed, the day at school when we learned poor David had hanged himself. No official announcement was made, but by midmorning everybody knew he was dead, that his father had found him dangling in the garage that morning. I might have written about how our stricken teachers had whispered in the halls, and how for the rest of the day both they and the other kids watched me closely, David's only friend, as if they suspected something—that I'd known what he intended, maybe, or that now I'd be next. After school I rode my bike out to Whitcombe Park, gripped Gabriel Mock's fence with white-knuckled fists and indulged my grief, sobbing loudly and with purpose, trying to drain the sorrow from my body, so that when I returned home I wouldn't seem any more distraught than the rest of my classmates.

Over dinner that night, I thought I did a pretty good job of pretending to suffer some lesser version of grief and loss than the one I was feeling. But my mother knew better, as she so often did, knew that I was hurting worse than I let on, because after I'd gone to bed she came into my room with tears in her eyes and told me how sorry she was, and I learned then that no matter how hard you try, you can never empty yourself of tears. "It's a mean old world, sweetie," she said. "It never lets up either. I wish I had better news for you, but I don't."

A month after he took his life, his father came into Ikey's. Apparently David had left a note that mentioned me. I happened to be working in the back room, but I heard my father say, "My Louie ain't that way." Later, after Mr. Entleman left, he came out back and found me sitting on a crate and staring at nothing. "You ain't that way, are you, Louie?" he asked, and I assured him I wasn't. "Boys ain't supposed to like boys that way," he explained patiently. I told him I knew that, and that when David had tried to kiss me I'd pushed him away, that we hadn't been friends since, which reassured him.

Except for what happened in the voting booth, my father had no secrets from my mother, so that night at dinner he told her about the terrible things David's father had said. "The poor boy," my mother sighed, looking at me.

"That don't mean you got to be mean to him or nothin'," my father told me, as if he'd forgotten that David was dead. Probably he just meant that if something like that ever happened again, with some other boy, I wasn't obligated to be cruel, but my mother looked at him as if he'd just sunk to a new low, stupiditywise. "Jesus, Lou," she said, shaking her head in disbelief. "Christ on a crutch."

Was I, as my father put it, "that way"? I didn't know. I did not. Was David? I didn't know that either. He was just a boy. I knew only that he was frightened to be in a strange new place and terribly grateful I'd befriended him. He felt about me like I'd once felt about Bobby. "Adoration" is probably not too strong a word to describe that heady mingling of intense affection and dependence. Back when we lived at Berman Court, and even later on Third Street, during that summer when we surfed my father's truck, I'd *wanted* to kiss Bobby. I had. I'd known it wasn't permitted, but what, I thought, was so wrong about it? I remember thinking about little Gabriel Mock kissing my mother so long ago. How powerful his feelings for her must have been to risk the consequences that were sure to follow. And, like David, he'd done it in broad daylight. Could it be that acts committed in the privacy of darkness became wrong only in the public light of day? Wasn't that the very adult wisdom Perry Kozlowski had tried to convey to me in the balcony of the movie theater shortly before he went out into the brilliant afternoon sunlight and beat Three Mock half to death?

I might have written all this, but did not. Why? The answer to that question, I suspect, can be found in that photo of my father hanging on the wall of my study. My story was written under his watchful eye, and if I've told it dishonestly, it's because I didn't want to embarrass him. To write about David would have meant admitting to my deepest thoughts about what my mother described so accurately as the "mean old world" we share, that its meanness resides deep within each of us. It would've revealed what I've always known to be true, though I've denied it to my mother, my father and myself—that I'm as much her son as his. For my father, the world wasn't a complicated place. Its rules mostly made sense and they were for our own good. I've always wanted to be the person he believed me to be, which at times has kept me from being a better one. A terrible realization, this.

I look over at Sarah and wonder how I'll manage without her, absent her ability to see what's there instead of what I prefer to see. I'll have to make sense of things for myself. She'll wake up soon and then be gone, so for a while I'll watch her breathe and dream. So lovely. She's wearing a cotton nightgown, modest and opaque, but of course it reveals what isn't there, the breast she surrendered last year to save her life, and looking at her now, knowing the small secrets she's kept in her good heart, I feel a little better about my own. Perhaps we are all entitled to keep a small place that's our own.

The line of gray along the horizon is brighter now, and with the coming light I feel a certainty: that there is, despite our wild imaginings, only one life. The ghostly others, no matter how real they seem, no matter how badly we need them, are phantoms. The one life we're left with is sufficient to fill and refill our imperfect hearts with joy, and then to shatter them. And it never, ever lets up.

Blame love.

THE BLUE DOOR

TRUE, IT WASN'T MUCH of a plan. When the Albany train deposited her at Penn Station, Sarah intended to take a taxi up to the Waldorf-Astoria. She and her mother stayed there once over the Labor Day weekend, splurging, they'd called it, though it was her mother paying for it. Sarah's babysitting money, a goodly sum by the end of August, got put away for college. She remembered, during those end-of-summer goodbyes, going to museums, window-shopping, sometimes strolling across town to see the kind of Broadway show her mother liked, something visually extravagant. Beyond that, she hadn't given it much thought. "Ma," Owen kept saying at the train station in Albany, "you're sixty. What're you gonna *do*?"

She supposed he didn't mean to be insulting. He was concerned about her recent illness, so she made an honest effort not to take offense. "I know how old I am," she said. And had she ever mentioned how much she disliked "Ma," instead of "Mom"?

"I know Pop screwed up," he conceded. "I'm mad at him, too."

"I'm *not* mad," she corrected him. Disheartened, it was true, maybe even heartbroken, but if she was angry with anyone it was herself. After all, she knew what Lou could and couldn't do. She'd seen this recent meltdown coming and chose to ignore it.

"Ma," Owen said. "You wouldn't be human if you weren't pissed. I just wish you'd let me into your plan. I'm on your side, remember? Why don't you let me help?"

"You want to help?" she said. "Grab that bag."

Because in fact she had no idea where she'd go or what she'd do when she got there, or when she'd tire of it and return to her life. Or if. Not long ago she'd read a magazine article about a woman, a photographer, who left her life and work in Boston and moved to New Mexico, where she purchased some land and a modest house out in the desert. There she'd experienced what she claimed was an artistic and spiritual rebirth. Had she left her husband, or had he recently died? Sarah couldn't remember. But this woman was a decade older than Sarah, which proved something of the sort could be done. Sarah couldn't decide what she liked most about the idea, the magnificent desert solitude or just the absence of men, their neediness and willful incomprehension. Maybe she'd consult the on-site travel agent at the Waldorf. She'd packed her passport. She could go anywhere she wanted.

ON THE TRAIN she opened the new biography of Frida Kahlo she'd bought, read the first page three times without comprehension, then decided the book would be most useful as a prop. Without it, someone might be tempted to engage her in conversation, which she was determined to avoid. Once under way, she found herself recalling those earlier train rides to and from the city all those years ago. These days, her mother was never far from her thoughts. She'd been forty-six when she died. Just beginning menopause, Sarah supposed. At the time, though, Sarah had been too young to understand what that meant to any woman, much less one like her mother. As a girl, Sarah had always believed her parents' separation had been caused by her little brother's death, the result of grief and loss. Her mother had often intimated as much. "After Rudy," she'd begin, but then the thought would trail off in her typically maddening fashion. Other times she'd say, "Well, the truth is your father and I were never compatible." Sarah had supposed she meant that her father was an intellectual, a man who lived not only for ideas but also the words necessary to compose them, whereas her mother was different. She thought in images, and once she got those to her liking on a canvas or in her sketchbook, any words at all were redundant. What she'd done was either good or it wasn't, and no amount of arguing—her husband's greatest skill—could make it otherwise. The differences between her parents, Sarah imagined, were a lot like those between her father and herself.

She'd been wrong, of course. It went much deeper than that. Sarah didn't have many vivid memories of the time before their separation, but there'd been arguments. "It wouldn't kill you to read a book every now and then," he'd snap. "Any more than it would kill you to put yours down," she'd snap right back. At home, in private, her father belittled everything from her mother's logic to her fondness for TV. In public, often at parties, she scorned his poor social skills and his ignorance of anything that didn't come out of a book. She had been very attractive and loved to dress provocatively and have fun. When her husband held forth on some literary or political subject, she'd pretend to listen with rapt attention until he finished, then she'd laugh and say, "He certainly does *talk* a good game, doesn't he?" Sarah was herself a married woman before it dawned on her that the real reason for her parents' separation had probably been sex. It might be true, as her father always let on, that her mother was a disappointing intellectual companion. But her mother had been hinting, too. Sarah had just been too young to catch on, and of course her mother wouldn't have wanted her to anyway.

As a teenager, she'd understood why her mother had lovers at the Sundry Arms, and the questions her father asked every September when she returned from Long Island suggested that he understood all too well that the freedom afforded by their separation was, for her, largely sexual. Sarah now suspected his feelings about that must have been ambivalent. He always maintained that once his novel was finished and he was famous, her mother would come crawling back. But hard as it must've been for him to admit, he also must have known that he'd never be able to keep up with her in the most important respect. *He talks a good game.* That remark surely burrowed down deep and rankled. His retort took him over a decade to compose and ran to fifteen hundred single-spaced pages. Back then Sarah didn't understand how he could spend so much time and effort on his novel, only to give up when a handful of editors didn't like it. Now she did. Those rejections came at him on two levels: first, he wasn't a very good writer—he didn't even *talk* as good a game as he'd hoped—and also his wife had been right about that other thing he wasn't much good at.

What particularly troubled Sarah about the final year of her mother's life was that her courage had failed her so swiftly. The year before, she'd been roiling with her usual defiance, declaiming against men like Sarah's father and against marriage as institutionalized slavery. Then the change. As if one morning she'd looked at herself in the mirror and saw into the future, that before long even the most desperate and befuddled of the Sundry Arms divorcés would stop coming to her for solace. Probably she saw, too, where all the martinis had settled, in the dark bags under her eyes, her sunken cheeks and breasts. Possibly it wasn't even the bathroom mirror so much as the one on men's faces, where she didn't register anymore or, worse, she registered briefly but then didn't pass the test. Sex had been the currency of her life, and soon she'd be broke. If her husband had talked a good game, well, at least *he* was still in business. That was something you could still do, and maybe even get better at, in your advancing years. Whereas she had *fucked* a good game, which game would soon be over, with nothing to replace it. For all Sarah knew, her father may even have warned her about the day when she'd flirt and no one would flirt back, when men no longer would gather around her at parties for the privilege of looking down her blouse, when she'd have to face what little remained and face it alone. Maybe she'd married Harold Sundry to keep that last part of her father's prediction from coming true.

But Sarah's worst fear was that she herself had played a part in her fatal decision to give up her hard-won freedom and remarry. That final summer she'd been too preoccupied with adolescent concerns to really take in what her mother was going through. And that drawing of her in her bathrobe—looking old and exhausted, as lifeless as the ash on the end of her cigarette. Sarah had spent the summer looking at herself in the mirror, studying her own metamorphosis from girl to young woman. Had she been less self-absorbed, she might've eased her mother's desperation and counseled her against doing anything out of fear. "What you don't understand," her mother had told her when she saw the bathrobe drawing, "is that one day you'll *be* that woman." One day she, too, would be lost, alone, in search of a destination.

And was she that now? Certainly her mother's prediction hadn't come true in the sense she'd meant it at the time—that one day Sarah would wake up and discover that youth and beauty fled and she was no longer the object of men's desire, that menopause would erode her self-confidence, leaving her frightened and desperate, grasping at straws. Because Sarah had emphatically *not* become that woman. Time had taken its toll, of course, there was no denying it. Her body had thickened, her hair grayed. Lines had appeared at the corners of her eyes and deepened, and the skin along her neck had grown slack. But menopause hadn't undermined her, nor had she felt either frightened or desperate, in part because she wasn't alone. She had Lou, whose affection and devotion never wavered, and she had Owen, and she had, well, her life. Maybe her sexual currency in her fifties was less than it had been in her thirties and forties, but sex had been her mother's only currency, or so she'd believed, which amounted to the same thing. Which was why she'd felt less like a woman that last summer, a feeling that Sarah had escaped.

Until now, perhaps. Had her mastectomy finally fulfilled her mother's prophecy, or some irony-rich version of it, at the very moment she'd congratulated herself that they didn't share an emotional destiny? All Sarah knew for sure was that she'd come out from under the anesthesia with a profound sense that her mother had been with her through the whole thing. Not there in the operating theater, or out in the waiting room with Lou and Owen, but *with her* in her drug-induced dreams, riffing the entire time, though Sarah couldn't remember a single word she'd said. In recovery, her first conscious thought had been of her mother's mutilated body lying for hours in the blood-soaked snow. Later, when she could examine what had been done to her, she recalled again the warning that she'd eventually become the woman holding that cigarette with the long, lifeless ash. Had she sold her mother short? Sarah wondered. Had she been wiser than Sarah gave her credit for? What if she hadn't been talking about menopause at all, but rather life's ability to demonstrate just how alone you really are?

In the months following the operation, her mother continued to haunt Sarah's dreams. Which made a kind of sense, she supposed. Her mother had been so badly disfigured by the accident that her casket had been closed, and some subconscious part of Sarah had probably clung to the hope that it was another woman inside. Living with her father when the terrible news came, she'd never felt that she could properly grieve. To give herself over to the devastation of that loss would have shown him the truth, that she'd loved her mother more, this at a time when his own troubles were fast closing in and he was teetering dangerously on the brink. Had her own recent scare given her long-delayed permission to imagine this woman's loneliness and, finally, to grieve her loss?

Possibly. Except that somehow it seemed less like grieving than . . . what? Sarah couldn't quite put her finger on it, but it was more like a conversation between them had been left unfinished, as if one or the other had started to say something important and then been interrupted. But what? Several conversations had been left dangling. Was it possible to be in love with two boys at the same time? Should she worry that one of them always played it safe and the other was both reckless and careless? Was it more important to love or be loved? Was Sarah's great gift—as her mother saw it—incompatible with love? Was that why she'd said, "I'm so, so sorry"? Sarah had tried asking these and many other questions but to little or no avail, her mother invariably retreating further into self-doubt. Then there were all the other conversations they'd have had if her mother hadn't died. Would she think she'd betrayed her gift by marrying Lou and be angry because she'd squandered what she herself would have valued most of all? Sarah just needed one more hour in her company, maybe in one of those small, narrow New York restaurants they'd gone to—except for that final summer—for an oh-so-late supper after the show before Sarah returned home.

One hour: her last conscious thought before the rhythm of the rails lulled her to sleep.

When she awoke, it was with the odd, dreamy sense that her wish had been granted, that the train, whose destination was Penn Station, would make an exception and take her to Grand Central, as it had when she was a girl, where her mother would be waiting at the information kiosk beneath the gold clock. Even more bizarre, her mother would still be forty-six. Damned awkward, that part, being older than your own mother. But otherwise it was a sweet fantasy, and Sarah dreamily indulged it. Maybe they'd *both* move to New Mexico and live in the desert together. By the time the train pulled into the city this lovely vision, instead of diminishing, had become even more powerful, so intense, in fact, that Sarah was actually surprised to realize it was Penn Station, not Grand Central.

She caught a cab and gave the turbaned driver the address of her hotel, but when they passed Grand Central, she changed her mind and told him to pull over. Though she hadn't been inside the terminal in four decades, it was just as she remembered it. The kiosk still stood in the center of the great hall beneath the four-sided gold clock, and there a middle-aged woman, her voice rising in anger, was arguing with an older woman who was inside the kiosk giving out information. How many times had Sarah, as a girl, witnessed her mother, clearly in the wrong but still adamant, having just such altercations with functionaries? Why, this woman wanted to know, would the man at the hotel have instructed her to go to Grand Central if it wasn't the right place? Was it Sarah's imagination, or was her voice identical in tone and timbre to her mother's?

"You must've misunderstood him," the clerk ventured to guess. "If you want to go to Long Island, you need the LIRR out of Penn."

"I *didn't* misunderstand," the traveler insisted. "Don't tell me I did. You weren't even there."

No, she wasn't there, the other woman conceded. She was *here*, and she'd *been* here, working in this very information kiosk, for the past ten years and *knew* which trains ran *where*. "You *want* the Long Island Railroad," she said. "That runs out of Penn Station, whether you want it to or not."

Whereupon her adversary turned to Sarah and said, "Do you *believe* this?"

Though they were the same height, she had the distinct impression that the woman was looking down at her, as you would at a child, and while Sarah saw little physical resemblance to her mother, she recognized her manic exasperation and half expected her to grab her hand when she stormed out.

"You *want* the Long Island Railroad," the clerk called after her, then looked at Sarah, assuming she was next in line. When their eyes met, it was as if she'd been talking to her all along. Which was when Sarah suddenly knew where she was going.

LIKE THE SURROUNDING TOWN, the Sundry Arms had fallen on hard times. Now called just the Arms Apartments, its residents were black and Hispanic, its concrete courtyard weedy with neglect. There was also a smell Sarah wasn't sure she'd ever encountered before, which had nothing to do with cooking or living or, for that matter, dying. After a lifetime in Thomaston, she thought she knew the odor of poverty, but this was different. Stagnancy? Hopelessness? Rage? The courtyard pool had been filled in and a makeshift playground set up, though the slide listed to one side and the seat of the rusted swing dangled from a single chain. Filthy, discolored toys were strewn everywhere, and graffiti bloomed on the interior walls. Towels and sheets were draped over the railings.

Sarah had forgotten that each apartment door at the Sundry Arms had been painted a different bright color. Many were now wide open, and some sported round holes where the knobs had been, a sad acknowledgment that there was nothing inside worth stealing. The nearest apartment looked more like a storeroom than someone's dwelling. Inside, the furniture was piled high with stacks of clothing, both children's and adults', organized by type—undergarments, shirts, pants, outerwear and so forth. Up against the far wall was a mound of what had to be hundreds of pairs of shoes. Did someone *live* here, or was this some sort of communal room where stolen or donated items were collected? And for what purpose? This was much, much worse, Sarah couldn't help thinking, than anything you'd find back home on the Hill, and she now understood why the taxi driver had said, "You sure this is the place you want, lady?" when he dropped her off.

It wasn't as if she'd expected everything to be the same. The Sundry Arms had been sold a year after her mother and Harold died, and a lawyer had called her a few times in the interim. By virtue of their recent marriage, Sarah had stood to inherit part of the complex, but Harold had a daughter of his own, and besides, the place had been mortgaged three times, so the bank would be first in line. In the end the property had sold for half what was due on the loans, which meant that everybody had lost. It now looked like there'd been no winners in the forty years since.

The apartment her mother had rented was at the far end on

the second floor, and Sarah smiled when she saw it still had a bright blue door. Except for Harold's, which was really two units, her mother's had always been the best, and looked like it still might be. There was a window box outside, and the flowers blooming there were the only living, growing things visible, unless you counted the grubby, largely unattended children. One tiny kid with coffee-colored skin and a runny nose had forced his head between the upstairs railings and was crying in a language Sarah didn't recognize for someone to extricate him.

Sarah had no idea how long she'd been standing there, taking it all in, before she was startled by a voice at her elbow.

"You from the state?" said a small, round black woman of indeterminate age. "You look loss."

"I *feel* lost," Sarah admitted. She'd been so sure at Grand Central that coming here was the right thing, as if her mother had left a trail of bread crumbs for her to follow.

"Who you here for?"

"No one," Sarah told her. "I used to live in that apartment, actually. Summers, with my mother."

"Musta been a while ago," the woman said, not disbelieving her exactly, just letting Sarah know that her story needed some work. Several curious children of both genders and half a dozen mixed races toddled over. A tall, lanky black girl who was maybe twelve looked on from the doorway of the apartment crammed with all the clothing and shoes. Why wasn't she in school?

"I *was* thinking about renting an apartment, actually," Sarah told the woman, immediately regretting the emphasis and realizing she'd probably offended her. She'd *been* thinking about renting *until* she saw the skin color of the people living there. That's how it must have sounded.

But if the woman took offense, she gave no sign. "Go 'cross the street. Sundry Gardens," she suggested, then consulted her watch. "Fact, you bess get goin'. Doan mean to be unpolite, but the gangstas all be wakin' up soon."

"Gangsters?" Sarah said, not sure she'd heard right.

"Wannabes, most of 'em," the woman acknowledged. "But aroun' here? If that's what you wanna*be*, that's what you end up *be*in'."

"What if you're a girl?" Sarah smiled at the lanky girl in the doorway, who surprised her by smiling back.

"If you smart, you learn quick." She followed Sarah's gaze and turned to regard the girl. "You doan *wanna*be nothin'. You juss be." She said this loud enough for the girl to hear, and Sarah couldn't help thinking this was for the girl's benefit, suggesting maybe she wasn't as smart as she needed to be.

AT THE OFFICE of the Sundry Gardens, a tough-looking woman roughly Sarah's age, talking with a lighted cigarette dangling from the corner of her mouth, seemed shocked that she'd been across the street. "Lucky you made it out alive. It's Banger Central over there."

From where Sarah stood at the desk she could see into the adjacent living quarters, where a teenage boy with a pimply face was stretched out on a sofa. The layout, from what she remembered, was a mirror image of Harold Sundry's office-apartment. "Banger Central?"

"Gangbangers," the woman explained, ash from her cigarette falling onto the registration form. "Wait till sundown. They come out like roaches, hang out down at the corner in front of the old gas station. Conduct their business right out in the open. The cops drive by every hour or two, pretend they give a shit. The real fun begins after midnight. Hope you don't mind foul language. Muthafuckin' this and muthafuckin' that, calling each other nigger. *Shoot* you if you did."

Sarah smiled, remembering how Harold, forty years ago, would open his window late at night and call across the avenue, "Kiss my ass, Elaine."

"Anyhow, I'm putting you in back where it's quiet. Quiet*er*. So, is your husband dying or what?"

618

"I'm sorry?" Sarah said, brought up short. Had Lou had another spell—how would *this* woman know?

"Women like you, the ones renting by the week? Their husbands are usually in the oncology unit. The motels near the hospital are more expensive. That's not you, huh?"

Sarah shook her head.

The woman waited for her to elaborate, and when she didn't, pushed the paperwork forward for her signature. "Read this," she said, pointing to the asterisked paragraph that explained the refund policy. "You may think I don't mean it, but I do."

That she said "I" instead of the customary "we" made Sarah wonder. "Are you the owner?"

"Yeah. I must look unlucky, huh?"

Sarah considered telling her that unlucky was across the street, but just pushed the signed form back, along with her credit card. "Your last name wouldn't be Sundry, would it?"

"Used to be. I inherited the place from my mother when she smoked herself into an early grave." She stubbed out her cigarette so she could run the card through her machine. "She got it in the settlement when she divorced my old man. He owned that shithole across the street, back when it was white. Got himself a snootful one night and drove into a tree when I was still a kid. People are mostly fools. Maybe you noticed."

Sarah said she had and looked right at her when she said it, but Harold's daughter didn't catch on. Indeed, she seemed pleased that they were philosophically compatible. "You decide to stay beyond the week, which you won't, I can probably make you a better deal. I'm putting you on the second floor because my grandson's a Peeping Tom," she said, handing Sarah her key. The boy in the next room had to have heard, but he didn't react. "Draw your curtains anyway, 'cause he can climb like a monkey. It's his one skill." Sarah had gotten as far as the office door when the woman said, "Thomaston." She'd lit another cigarette and through the smoke was studying the personal data on the form. "Where's that?"

"Upstate."

"Why's it ring a bell?"

"The woman who was in the car with your father the night he ran into that tree used to live there," she said. "She was my mother."

The woman's mouth opened but nothing came out. It was still open when Sarah closed the office door.

GIVEN THE PROXIMITY of gangbangers and voyeurs, Sarah slept surprisingly well, a deep dreamless slumber from which she awoke refreshed. She rented a car, drove to the cemetery and found the stone that marked the grave where her mother and Harold Sundry lay side by side. She didn't remember much about the burial, just how bitterly cold it had been. Cold enough to freeze the tears to her cheeks, if she'd cried, but she hadn't. To her astonishment, it was her father who'd completely lost control, breaking down in violent, angry sobs. It had been the first of many breakdowns. He would never again be in charge of anything, not a class, not his daughter, not even himself. He left Thomaston shortly after her graduation and took a job clerking at a used-book store in Albany, where he died three short years later. But in a sense she buried them both that day.

After laying a wreath, Sarah drove toward the shore through some of the old neighborhoods where she'd babysat during those long-ago summers. The houses didn't look nearly as grand as then, when they'd been vacation homes. Many now had a run-down, year-round feel, and the vehicles parked among the weeds were mostly pickup trucks and windowless vans that sported logos of the sort her mother used to design; their wheel wells were rich with salt rust. Money, it seemed, had found another outlet.

After a while she drove back into town, looking for traces of her mother's spirit. The restaurant where Sarah had fainted when her mother told her she was marrying Harold was still open but under a different name, and the old textile mill where she'd rented studio space had been razed. The supermarket where they'd gone for weekly groceries now felt like an extension of the Arms, its produce as brown as its customers, its shelves stocked with items long past their sell-by dates, though apparently good enough for poor people. There Sarah bought cereal, milk and orange juice, bread and cheese, enough to get her through a day or two. By the time she returned to the Sundry Gardens she felt utterly dispirited, wondering what had possessed her to pay for an entire week. The day she'd just spent was more than sufficient to convince her this was a mistake. Yesterday, her anticipation had been palpable. It had felt like the children's game where some object is hidden and one child is given clues by the others how to find it. *You're getting warmer . . . warmer . . . even warmer.* That's how Sarah had felt on the LIRR. Pulling up in front of the Arms, she'd been so certain— *You're scalding hot!*—that she hadn't really seen where she was, what she was looking at. Even inside the complex, with the squalor of that courtyard so conspicuous, how her heart had leapt at the sight of that blue door! Later, crossing the street to Sundry Gardens, she had again heard those voices, mocking now: *You're getting cooler . . . cooler . . . cold.* Today they'd whispered throughout her travels and, when she returned to her apartment and locked the door against the outside world, announced gleefully *You're like ice!*

Shut up, she thought. Who asked you?

More than anything she wanted to call home, to tell her husband and son to expect her return shortly. Maybe she'd spend a night or two in the city, like she'd originally planned. What prevented her from making this call, she supposed, was pride. After explaining to everyone that she needed to be alone, she hated to admit she didn't know how to go about it. Not that Lou would have cared. He'd be relieved and overjoyed to see her, beyond grateful that things were returning to normal. And Owen, very much his father's son, would be glad, too, for many of the same reasons. It was Tessa she'd have trouble facing. They'd always been friends, but over the years, since Big Lou's death, had grown ever closer. Just how close was, of necessity, their secret. Though she'd never understood why, Sarah had long known that Lou distrusted his mother and was suspicious of her intentions. Once, before they were married, he'd accused her of planning to sell Ikey's the minute his father was "out of the way," and Sarah had been hard pressed to persuade him that the opposite was true, that Tessa was merely trying to insulate the store against the terrible eventuality that her husband's cancer might return. When Lou finally understood how wrong he'd been, he was mortified and for some time thereafter racked by guilt for having believed his mother capable of such treachery, but before long other and different suspicions returned. After they were married, when Sarah and Tessa spent time together, he always wanted to know what they'd talked about, as if convinced his mother was warning her against him, though nothing could have been more remote from the truth.

It *was* true, though, that Tessa Lynch's confidences usually coincided with those times when her son was most troubled, a spell bearing down or having just occurred. The most dramatic of these had happened shortly after Big Lou's death. His passing had hit them all hard, but for many months both women had wondered if Lou would ever bounce back, and that was when Tessa decided to tell her about Dec Lynch. Sarah had long feared there'd been something between them, yet it turned out that she'd had it all wrong. Dec had been Tessa's first lover, before she'd even met Big Lou, who at the time was still trapped on his parents' failing farm. Dec had recently returned to Thomaston after being discharged from the army, and according to Tessa everything about him was dangerous and exciting. Her father, having heard all about him, had forbidden her to have *anything* to do with the Lynch boy, but when Dec bought a brand-new Indian motorcycle and offered her a ride, she'd immediately climbed on. And by the end of that first ride she'd decided she wanted *everything* to do with Dec Lynch. Which meant she'd have to lie. To avoid scrutiny they'd usually meet somewhere downtown and roar off on the Indian. Later, Dec would drop her off a few blocks from home so her parents wouldn't connect her return to the rumble of the motorcycle in the quiet night.

She was a natural the way she rode, Dec told her, leaning into the curves instead of away, as you would if you were afraid. And when he saw she wasn't, he couldn't help wondering what *would* frighten her, so he let out the throttle. But though the Indian went like the wind, Tessa never once told him to slow down, and his inability to scare her, she thought, scared *him* a little. She didn't tell Sarah about the sex, of course, but the motorcycle metaphor left no doubt in her mind that they leaned into the curves there, too. In retrospect, Tessa admitted, their affair seemed like a madness, almost viral in its feverish intensity. Had they stayed a couple, she said, they probably would've ended up robbing banks. Whenever they were together, a feeling of complete abandonment came over them, their individual wildness made exponential by proximity.

Then one night that delicious recklessness nearly cost them their lives. They'd gone to a rowdy roadhouse near the Pine Mountain summit, and though they hadn't drunk a lot, maybe two or three beers each, they'd lost track of the time. Roaring back down the mountain well past Tessa's curfew, Dec had tried to pass a whole line of slow-moving vehicles on the narrow, two-lane blacktop. They'd sailed by about half of them when Tessa saw the truck round the curve below, its headlights blinding them. Both of them had known instantly that they weren't going to make it. The truck driver laid on his horn, but Dec kept the Indian right on the yellow centerline and Tessa put her forehead between his shoulder blades and closed her eyes tight, waiting for the impact that didn't come. When she opened her eyes again the road was clear. Dec, she realized, hadn't even slowed down, and they howled with joy and adrenaline all the way back into town.

That night, though, alone in bed, Tessa remembered what hadn't really registered fully at the time, that in the split second they were between the truck and the sedan they were passing, when her eyes were closed, she *felt* how close they'd come, the tug of both vehicles on her knees, and then, finally, she *was* afraid. Shivering in the dark, she tried to calm down by telling herself that in the morning, in the clear light of day, the terror would evaporate, but it didn't, not even a little, and so she came clean with her father, telling him not only that she'd been seeing Dec Lynch but also that things had gotten out of hand and she didn't know how to stop.

Dec was then living on the third floor of a rooming house in the Gut, and her father paid him a visit. It being morning, Dec was still asleep, and he came groggily to the understanding that his girlfriend's father was seated on the edge of his bed holding a gun and telling him before he was fully awake that he was never to see his daughter again. "I got one of those myself," Dec told him, nodding at the gun. Very matter of fact, not at all threatening, just a tidbit of information the other man might find interesting. Tessa's father replied that he didn't care what the boy had or didn't have, just so long as he agreed he'd never have his daughter. According to Tessa, Dec hadn't been particularly frightened by the handgun. Though he had no idea what life held in store for him, he doubted he'd be killed by a pale insurance agent who didn't know enough to flip the safety off when threatening somebody with a gun. But the occasion did give Dec the excuse to step back and assess the wildness that came over himself and Tessa whenever they were together. "Could be we're not that good for each other," he said the next time he saw her, more than a little worried about how she'd take this admission. Maybe she'd conclude that, having had his way with her, he was now tossing her aside. She might just go home and get her father's gun, and if *she* ever pointed it at him he'd by God take *that* seriously. Being shot dead by an angry woman squared better with his overall sense of how life might one day end for him, so he was glad when Tessa, too, confessed to misgivings about the volatility of their relationship. Maybe cooling it wouldn't be a bad thing.

Later that year she met Lou, and her first thought had been: these boys are *brothers*? Dec was quick witted and sharp tongued. He never actually smiled but wore a perpetual smirk, and his talk was layered with sarcasm. By contrast, Big Lou Lynch smiled from ear to ear every time she walked in the door, and his deliberate speech radiated straightforward kindness and goodwill unleavened, at least intentionally, by humor. Where Big Lou always thought things were bound to get better, his brother, whose cynicism ran deep and wide, assumed that in the end things would go badly, though perhaps not so badly for him as for others. If he believed in anything it was his ability to land, catlike, on his feet. "My brother," he warned Tessa when he heard they'd started dating, "will land on his fat ass half the time and on his pointy head the other half."

Tessa's parents had been no more enthusiastic about Lou than they'd been about Dec, but her father realized he couldn't go around pointing a gun at every boy his daughter showed an interest in. Lou, unlike his brother, was by reputation sober and industrious, and he didn't seem the sort of boy who'd pressure his daughter into having sex, as Dec, he suspected, had already succeeded in doing. And Lou was clearly crazy about Tessa, so her father decided his best bet might be to let them go on about their business of being young and stupid, in the hopes that one day she'd wake up, see her new boyfriend for the big doofus he was and wonder what on earth she'd been thinking. He never truly understood, she told Sarah, how deeply she'd been touched by her husband-to-be's simple, good-natured optimism, his reluctance to say an unkind word about anyone. He neither had a devious bone in his body, nor recognized duplicity in others. If some smooth talker conned him out of a quarter, he'd just shrug and say "How come he just didn't come out and ask me for it? I'd have loaned him a quarter." Tellingly, even then Tessa had felt compelled to explain the world to him. "I don't think he wanted to borrow it, Lou. He wanted to own it free and clear. Later, if you felt foolish for giving it to him, that was a bonus." To which Big Lou just shook his head, sadly acknowledging that he guessed there were people like that. In fact, he regarded his own brother as exhibit number one when it came to con artists. "Don't have nothin' to do with him unless you want to lose your shirt," he advised Tessa, unaware she'd already lost that and a lot more. "I'm going to check back with your old man in about twenty years," Dec told her when she and his brother got engaged. "See if he still thinks he pointed that gun at the right Lynch."

Over the years Sarah came to understand that Tessa's confidences served a dual purpose. Most of what she revealed to her daughter-in-law she'd never told another soul, and Sarah sensed what a relief it was to finally disburden herself to another woman. But she also realized that when Tessa talked about her husband and her marriage, she was, by extension, also talking about her son and his marriage to Sarah. Father and son were that much alike. Tessa was offering her not just the wisdom of long, difficult experience but also the comfort that derived from realizing she wasn't alone, that in the end there was nothing to be done about Lou and his father, who weren't likely to change. It had taken a while for that last part to really sink in. When Tessa told her about the brief, nearly tragic fling with Dec, Sarah had not only been relieved to learn that Dec had preceded Big Lou but also imagined her husband might be comforted as well. After all, he couldn't very well blame his mother for something that had happened before she'd even met his father. But when she indicated this, Tessa just smiled and gave her a look that suggested she still had a lot to learn. "Tell him if you want, but it's not the way he thinks. The chronology won't matter. He won't want to think about me and Dec together, period."

Here, too, Sarah understood that her mother-in-law was

talking about sex. Tessa talked only indirectly about her married life, but with Big Lou there'd clearly been no motorcycle involved, no thrilling abandon. He would've been driving one of those slow-moving vehicles she and Dec had flown by coming down the mountain. Her husband, Tessa let on, didn't dislike sex, but was embarrassed by it, by its necessity, by how other people seemed so obsessed with it. Wanting to be a good husband, he recognized that he had duties in this regard, yet the physical act itself seemed to confuse and obscure his feelings for his wife rather than clarify or intensify them. While he'd grown up on a farm and knew there was nothing more natural than sex—and, when his son was born, understood even more fully its benefits and wisdom—he seemed surprised to learn he was expected to continue the practice once they'd achieved their goal.

Sarah was even more circumspect with her mother-in-law about her own married life, partly because it was private but also because there was no need. Tessa understood Lou as well as anyone and how he both was and wasn't like his father. In fact, Sarah grew increasingly certain the only reason Tessa confided as much as she did was to help her understand that if her husband didn't always "lean into the curves" it had nothing to do with her. His devotion would reveal itself in other ways, and his commitment would never waver. Their marriage would be happy, and Sarah, unless she was expecting ecstasy, would suffer few regrets.

"Did *you* have any regrets?" Sarah asked after Tessa'd explained about Dec, and was surprised by her one-word answer.

"Never."

"You were never tempted? Afterward?"

"Oh, sure," she admitted. The flame of their brief passion guttered, then flared up at odd moments, mostly in memory, never entirely extinguished. Even years later, when Dec came to work at Ikey's, she'd feel that old jolt of electricity in a glancing, accidental touch. Whenever this happened, Dec would

invariably grin or even wink at her, as if to say *Yeah, I felt it, too.*
But it was more than either of them wanted, and for perspective
there was also the memory of that truck's headlights and blaring
horn.

Perhaps because they kept these conversations secret from
Lou, Sarah felt guilty, almost as if she were committing an
infidelity, but she was also grateful for every one of them. She
felt like she'd been given not just a friend but a second mother
to replace the one who'd bled to death in the snow. Better yet,
Tessa was able to provide things her own mother hadn't—
sound advice about life and the living of it, the benefit of a wise
woman's experience. Her mother hadn't *been* wise, of course.
That was the point. She'd leaned into the curves right to the
end, long after the road turned into the long, dull straightaway
of Harold Sundry. Neither Tessa nor Sarah would've
characterized their marriages as such. They'd both loved their
husbands more than anyone even suspected, and in return had
been adored. But each of them had walked through an open
door, then heard it slam shut behind them and the mechanism
lock. While neither regretted her decision, knowing the door
was locked was disconcerting just the same, as was the fact that
their husbands, if they'd heard that same slam and click, seemed
untroubled by it. If anything, knowing there was no turning
back was reassuring to them. They never felt trapped, never
wondered about the mountain road not taken, never felt as
though some important part of them was withering as another
flourished, never were greedy for what they didn't have and
would never experience.

Tessa was grateful for the love she'd been given but also
understood how it had trapped her. She'd never had the
opportunity for what Sarah was doing now, escaping that loving
trap, even temporarily. "Go," she'd said when Sarah started,
unnecessarily, to explain her need to get away for a while. "Find
yourself. In fact, keep an eye out for me. I'm out there
somewhere."

Which meant that if she gave up and returned home just because she'd lost the knack of being alone, she'd be betraying Tessa as well. No, she'd give it another day here, at least, and then maybe a few more in the city. If all this was foolish, well, maybe something less foolish would occur to her. She ate a bowl of cereal standing up and then went to bed hoping to feel more optimistic tomorrow.

IN THE MORNING, however, her sense of futility had, if anything, deepened. Fortunately, this wasn't the first time she'd suffered from low spirits, which was why she never went anywhere without her sketch pad. It was as a girl, living across the street at the Sundry Arms, that she learned it was easier to draw than to think her way out of confusion. How low she'd been that last summer until she finally gave in and drew Bobby and how easily, how joyfully he'd leapt from the blank paper. Not that it had relieved her anxiety, of course, or solved the fundamental problem. She'd been in love with two boys, in all probability because each offered her something different, something she needed, or at least she thought they did. Indeed, clarifying the problem should have deepened her crisis. Instead she'd felt intense joy in knowing the truth, even if it was an impossibility: *I love two boys.* Its corollary was even more thrilling: *That's who I am. The kind of girl who can love two boys.* Every other painting and drawing she'd done that summer had been suffused with that confidence. She saw everything more clearly for the simple reason that she knew who was holding the brush or pen. Her mother had recognized her transformation in a glance. "I'm so, so sorry," she'd said. At the time Sarah thought she was sorry about what the drawing of Bobby had revealed, but now she knew better. She'd been worried about the gift itself and the potential for misery that accompanied it.

Locating the sketch pad in the big sleeve on the side of her suitcase, she left the Sundry Gardens and didn't realize she was heading back to the Arms until she was halfway across the street. At this early hour the courtyard was oddly peaceful, with only the sounds of sleepy children and televisions on low leaking out the open doors and windows. A low, cinder-block wall surrounded what had been the swimming pool, so Sarah sat down there and opened her pad to a fresh page. She did a quick sketch of the window box outside her mother's former apartment and felt a little better, if no less foolish, for the effort. She did a couple more sketches on the same page, then got up and moved down the wall to frame the window box within the rusty swing-set. That somehow made both objects more interesting. It might be the basis for a painting later, when she returned home. *If* she returned. ("You *want* the LIRR," the woman had insisted.) She started a new page. She'd only been there for half an hour, but could feel in her blood and busy hand that she was, well, *getting warmer*. Again, the child's game. Was she losing her mind? Wasn't it enough to just sit here and let her pen fly over the rough paper, instead of indulging a fantasy that had already proved futile? On the other hand, what could she lose as long as she acknowledged that it *was* a fantasy?

Sarah was only vaguely conscious of the passage of time, of doors opening and closing, of children emerging into the courtyard, of snatches of adult conversation. "She doin' down there?" "Same woman as the other day?" "She crazy?" There was also the sound of a tricycle with big plastic wheels thumping over cracks in the pavement to the cadence of adult instructions: *don't, don't, don't, don't.* Eventually she became aware of someone watching her, close by, and she turned and saw it was the lanky black girl who'd returned her smile the day before, the one who should've been in school. She was standing awkwardly on one leg, regarding the sketch pad and Sarah herself with a kind of terrible longing.

"Can you teach me?" she said.

Sarah started to say no, felt the word forming on her lips, and saw the girl accept her answer even before it was given and start to leave. Where had she seen that mixture of longing and immediate resignation before?

"Of course I can," she said, though in truth she was none too sure what she meant. That drawing was a skill that could be taught? That she herself had been a teacher most of her adult life? That she could spend the rest of the morning showing the girl a few basics, maybe even go out and get her an inexpensive sketch pad and a starter pen-and-pencil set? Or was she suggesting the girl could actually learn, even in a place like this, if she really wanted to?

"Really?" the girl said, not quite sure she'd heard right, her eyes now big and round.

Really? That's what the Mock boy had said, in exactly that same way. "Really? You would? With me?" In fact, she hadn't even said yes. What she'd said was that she'd ask her father, then warned him not to get his hopes up, because she was never allowed to go out with boys. At the time she thought she was being kind by allowing him to believe the only impediment was her father, that she would've gone with him to the matinee if the choice had been hers, but it wasn't. It had nothing to do with him personally. It wasn't that she didn't like him, or that what he was proposing wasn't permitted because he was a Negro. He'd been expecting one kind of no and she'd given him another, a no that had some yes in it, and didn't include the humiliation he'd expected. But a moment earlier the look of yearning and surrender on his face was the same as the one on this girl's in the split second before Sarah changed her mind. How awful it must be, she thought, to ask for something you knew you'd be denied. How much courage it took to ask anyway, instead of just slinking away and adding this new refusal to the stew of countless others.

"When?" the girl said, thinking perhaps this was where the no would come.

Sarah turned to a fresh page in the sketchbook and motioned for her to sit down on the wall. "How about we start with that window box? The one by the blue door."

631

The girl took the pad and balanced it on her knee like she'd seen Sarah do, then took the pen almost fearfully.

"Like this," Sarah said, showing her how to hold it. "Don't worry about making a mistake. We're going to draw it over and over."

"What comes first?"

"You're the one holding the pen. That means you get to decide."

Sarah couldn't remember seeing anyone more terrified. Finally, the girl drew a tentative horizontal line and immediately looked up at her, as if to ask if the time had come already to give up.

"Good," Sarah told her. "But maybe you'd better tell me your name."

IT WAS KAYLA. And her daddy? "Well, her daddy is anybody's guess, but even if you guessed right, then what?" This was according to Miss Rosa, the small, round black woman who'd spoken to Sarah the afternoon before. "Her mama? Got the HIV. You know where and how. Whole lass year, this girl been bouncin' from one relative to the nex' till they brung her to me. Bringin' me children now, like a cheap toy the wheel come off of. Seventy-three-year-old woman. You tell me," she said with a hint of bitterness that made Sarah like her even more. "You tell me what Jesus thinkin' this time, 'cause I doan know."

If asked to guess Miss Rosa's age, Sarah would've said late fifties, not seventy-three, and she'd been living here for more than thirty years. In fact, she'd been the Sundry Arms' first black resident. Ten years ago, after she'd been "feeling poorly," her doctors had found a tumor the size of a grapefruit in her abdomen, but she'd prayed to Jesus and the tumor shrank and then disappeared altogether. Since then Miss Rosa just left everything to Jesus—money worries, health problems, all of it—

and He provided, and not just for her either. She began to use her apartment as a used-clothing distribution center for young neighborhood mothers, most of them single. Many worked as hotel maids or at other menial jobs on the more prosperous North Shore or in the city while their own mothers, forty-year-old grandmas, looked after their kids. That's why Miss Rosa's apartment was stacked floor to ceiling with all manner of clothing and shoes. She'd traded in her double bed, which she didn't need now that her husband was deceased, to make a little more room. Then people started bringing her other things, too, furniture and food and broken toys, and suddenly she was full to bursting.

Then Jesus provided again. The next-door apartment went vacant, and the very first night there was a fire. The complex's owner had let his insurance lapse and was unwilling to spend what it would cost to clean and repair the damage. Sarah found that fire suspiciously convenient but didn't say so to Miss Rosa, who explained that since the place was just sitting there and she was by then something of a local celebrity, the owner succumbed to public pressure and allowed her to expand her operation, rent-free—in the hopes that this act of generosity might prevent another fire? Sarah wondered. The nearest food pantry was miles away, but Miss Rosa persuaded the staff there to make twice-a-week deliveries of whatever they were thinking about throwing away. Soon the second apartment, too, was crammed from top to bottom.

"My life one gift after another," Miss Rosa said. "Every time I turn aroun', there's Jesus with somethin' new, somethin' I didn't even know I needed till He give it to me. Say to myself, *What my gonna do with this?* But finally I figure out everythin's a gift. That tumor was the first. Takin' it away was the second. You a gift your own self. To me and this child." This was a week or so after Sarah started giving Kayla lessons. "Doan be givin' me that hairy eyeball like you doan believe, 'cause I know better. You too nice a lady to go through life a heathen. Maybe you doan believe now, but you will 'fore you die. You jist got to 'just your thinkin', then you see everythin' clear."

Food, clothing, small appliances, pots and pans. It all turned up in apartments 108 and 110. "Throw it away? Don't. Miss Rosa know what to do with it." She had half a dozen elderly women helping her a couple hours a day each, along with several ancient-looking black men who lugged things and were good at mending toys. The few young men who lived at the Arms were useless at anything other than drug dealing. You seldom saw them before late afternoon, scratching their skinny asses and wondering why there wasn't anything to eat. An odd group, they at once feared Miss Rosa and held her in high esteem, and out of respect, they never conducted their business on the premises. When she gave them a piece of her mind, which she did regularly, they stood and took it, though when she was done they sometimes asked if she'd been born a crazy old woman or grew into it. "Seventy-three-years'-worth-of-smart is what I am," Sarah heard her tell them once. "You all gon be dead 'fore you're thirty, so you tell me who's crazy."

The woman had an amazing memory. Nothing came in that didn't immediately get cataloged in her brain somewhere, somehow, though items often didn't light for long. She'd hold a pair of toddler's sneakers up and say, "I know juss where you-all's goin', doan think I don't. I got me a system," she told Sarah. "Problem is, doan nobody but me know how it works. I juss pray I doan never die or get no Altzeimers, 'cause it'll take ten people smarter'n me to do what I do. That's why Jesus ain't took me yet, I 'spect. Made myself . . . what's the word?"

"Indispensable?" Sarah suggested.

"Thass it."

Do people ever bring you things you wish they'd keep? Sarah asked her one day.

"Not often," Miss Rosa said. "Sometimes."

Kayla was sitting on the wall with the second sketch pad Sarah had bought her that week. Miss Rosa looked at her and nodded.

*

WARMER. That's how Sarah continued to feel each morning when she went across the street. Which was why, at the end of the first week, she again gave the horrible woman in the Sundry Gardens office her credit card. "Another whole week?" she said, clearly suspicious. Her grandson again was stretched out, motionless, on the sofa in the next room. Did he ever get up? "You mind my asking what you do over there every day?" she added while waiting for Sarah's card to be approved.

"Not at all," Sarah told her. "Do you mind my not telling?"

The woman shrugged, but she clearly had something else on her mind. "That girl?"

Kayla had accompanied her into Sundry Gardens the day before. Sarah had made them a simple lunch of sandwiches and canned soup before setting off on their afternoon drive. Two days ago they'd gone all the way out to Montauk, where Kayla had filled half a new sketchbook with drawings of the lighthouse. Afterward they'd eaten an early supper of mussels and clams and fried calamari, none of which the girl had ever tasted before. Her real appetite was for information about Sarah herself, especially her Long Island summers with her mother, so they drove through the old neighborhoods and Sarah told her about the families she used to babysit for. To Kayla, these now-shabby houses looked palatial, much as they had to Sarah at that age. She listened to the stories of who lived where as if she expected to be quizzed on them later, though Sarah quickly learned that *she* was the one who'd be quizzed. Kayla would go anywhere Sarah wanted to take her, but she preferred going back to places and having her repeat the stories she'd told earlier. If Sarah added a new detail, she'd frown and say, "You never said that before." She was equally intolerant of gaps and omissions. "The little sister had golden hair," she'd interrupt peevishly. "That's what you said before."

"I'm going to have to start calling you Sponge, the way you soak everything up," Sarah said.

But Kayla's eyes narrowed in hurt and anger, her body suddenly rigid. "I don't like it when people call me names."

"I'm not calling you a name, Kayla," Sarah replied. "I'm paying you a compliment. You have a good memory."

The girl seemed to accept that but was quiet for the rest of the day, leaving Sarah to puzzle it through. Though she was bright for her age, she was also, Sarah suspected, emotionally stunted, closer to nine or ten than her actual twelve.

She mentioned the incident to Miss Rosa the next morning.

"Been lied to her whole life," she said. "Her mama tell her she's goin' to the store for cigarettes, be back in a hour, then she gone for two days. Child doan believe what you or nobody else tell her. Always checkin' your story out, lookin' for lies. Got to hear it over an' over."

"You're saying she won't ever trust me?"

"I'm sayin' there ain't no bottom to that child's need."

"Kayla," Sarah told her landlady now. "Her name is Kayla."

"She doesn't belong on this side of the street any more than you belong on the other side."

"This is America," Sarah told her.

"Exactly," she said, handing back her American Express card. "That's what I'm saying. Look around. Tell me what you see."

"I see an unpleasant woman," Sarah said, sliding the card back into her billfold. Much to her surprise, the woman's eyes promptly filled with tears. "I'm sorry," she said. "That was uncalled for."

The woman waved off the apology and lit a cigarette, waiting until Sarah was at the door to say, "So what possessed your mother to marry Harold?"

Sarah noted that he was "Harold" rather than "my father." She shrugged. "I don't know. I saw your dad around all the time, but I didn't know they were . . . anyway, he told me I'd like him better once I got to know him. I never got the chance, though."

"Me either," his daughter said. "Not that it was any big loss. He was just a drunk."

"I'm sorry," Sarah said, and again made to leave.

"I've got a lawyer," the woman said. "Just so you know."

"I don't understand. Why—"

"This place belonged to my mother alone, and now it's mine. You think any part of it'll ever be yours, think again."

"I'm sorry," Sarah said again. "But I don't know your name."

"The hell you don't."

"It's true. I don't."

"Pamela," she said, and her hands were shaking so hard she could barely hold on to the cigarette. "Pam. And I hope you don't think I'm a complete goddamn idiot."

"Pamela," Sarah said slowly. "I'm not interested in Sundry Gardens. That's not why I'm here. I don't know how to make you believe me, but it's the truth. It's good you've got a lawyer, but you don't need one for me."

This seemed to calm the other woman a little, though she didn't answer immediately. "It's possible, just possible, that I might believe you, if you'd tell me why you *are* here."

"I wish I could," Sarah said, which was true enough. In fact, she considered telling her a plausible lie that was at least close to the truth. That she'd struck up an improbable friendship with a twelve-year-old black girl who'd managed to get under her skin, probably because she brought to mind a skinny, luckless black boy who'd once taken a terrible beating as a result of sitting next to her in a movie theater. Except she doubted this story would *seem* plausible to Pamela.

The truth? Well, that was simply out of the question. The truth was both beyond ludicrous and too frightening, a half-overheard scrap of conversation between two of Miss Rosa's grandma volunteers, the gist of which was that not everyone living in the Arms was black or Hispanic. The woman living in the apartment with the blue door was a shut-in who'd been here since before Miss Rosa had moved in, and during the past year she'd left the apartment only twice, both times in an ambulance. She was hooked up to an oxygen tank twenty-four hours a day and was a good ninety-five years old.

And this woman was white.

"You bess get home to your man soon," Miss Rosa said one afternoon. They were sitting on the courtyard wall—"resting their bones a spell," as she liked to put it—Kayla was down at the far end and out of earshot, drawing Miss Rosa, her first attempt at a human figure. "I turn out pretty it means you gotta take more lessons, girl. Means you still got a lot to learn." Sarah was writing a postcard to her husband. She'd purchased half a dozen cards at the drugstore the day before, had written him two this morning over breakfast and two more over lunch, when she'd taken Kayla to a sandwich shop in town. In between she'd given Pamela her credit card for another week, reassuring her again that she had no designs on Sundry Gardens. She'd almost told her to charge for the whole next month, but hadn't wanted to freak her out.

Miss Rosa, whose spirits were usually unsinkable, was grumpy today, as if she knew about the transaction across the street and was no happier about it than Pamela. Though she was fond of Sarah, over the last two weeks she'd gone from puzzled by her continued presence to concerned, from mystified to annoyed.

Dear Lou, Sarah wrote. She already knew she wasn't going to send any of the earlier postcards, which had managed to hit all the wrong notes. She'd tried being chatty, totally unlike herself; informative, without providing any actual information, like a White House press release; optimistic, without any apparent grounds; and honest, this being the briefest, since there was so little to say that wasn't a lie. She knew her husband wanted to know only one thing: when was she coming home? And that she couldn't tell him. *I want you to know that I'm well, that I love you, that I'm not angry with you, and that I won't stay away a moment longer than I need to.* A poor offering, she knew, almost not worth the stamp. She'd made the last three statements before she left, and each raised its own obvious question. If she loved him, then what was she doing here? As for angry, as Owen said, who wouldn't be? And how much longer did she need to stay away, having been gone two weeks already? The first few days the urge to call home had been desperate, yet now it had all but disappeared. If this was progress, then toward what? And the first statement was no better: *I'm well.* Was she? Apparently Miss Rosa didn't think so.

Sarah gave up on the postcard and just watched Kayla's pen fly. The girl had filled an entire sketchbook each of the two weeks Sarah had been instructing her. Soon she was going to have to ask the girl to slow down, to think, to exercise more care, but for now, she thought, let her race.

"Some other woman come along and snatch him up," said Miss Rosa, still instructional herself. "Good men is hard to fine. Look round here, you doan believe me."

"You're right," Sarah admitted. For some time she'd been wondering if she might be one of those women who, late in life, came to the reluctant conclusion that men were more trouble than they were worth. Some of them even took female lovers, and while Sarah knew she'd never do that, she could sympathize. Lately, she seemed to have little use for anything male. The lazy, skinny, strutting, no-count boy-men at the Arms were the worst of a bad lot, but in truth she was tired of thinking about men and their needs, including her husband and son. And Bobby. That she wasn't interested in seeing him again suggested just how much things had changed since they called off Italy, since the woman at Grand Central had convinced her that what she wanted was the LIRR. Why not admit it? Italy had been nothing more than an excuse to see Bobby. Lou had been right to be jealous. Her cancer, the resulting operation, had made her desperate. If she could just see Bobby once more, this boy she'd loved and who'd loved her . . . then what? That was the part she

639

hadn't worked out, but she now suspected that if she glimpsed Bobby Marconi in Robert Noonan, then maybe she could convince herself that Sarah Berg still existed in Sarah Lynch. Crazy. Worse than crazy. She could see that now, sitting here on this low concrete wall. Bobby was just another male of the species and, as such, of no particular interest. Unfortunately, she couldn't congratulate herself for discarding this obsession when she'd pretty clearly just replaced it with an even more ridiculous one.

"Serve you right, too," Miss Rosa continued. "End up alone. How you gon feel then?"

"Not having a husband isn't the same as being alone," Sarah pointed out for the sake of argument. "*Your* husband is gone, but I don't know anybody who has a fuller life."

"Tell you one thing, and it ain't two," Miss Rosa said. "My husband shown up alive and said come with me, we leavin', you be sittin' here on this wall all alone and by yourself and nobody to talk to, includin' me."

"I don't believe that," Sarah said.

"Tell you somethin' else. Longer you stay here, the harder it be on that child. Shouldn't be tellin' her all about where you live at neither. That she can visit and such."

This was probably true, and Sarah wished she hadn't. In the beginning the girl had been interested only in her past life, when she was the same age. Any mention of her present life in Thomaston, her husband or grown son made her frown and change the subject. The third time this happened, Sarah asked why she didn't want to hear about where she lived now, and she said that it was a long way away and she'd never see it anyhow, so why talk about it?

"You could visit," Sarah had said. "Especially later, when you're older. It's not the end of the earth. There's a train that runs from here into New York and another that goes close to where I live."

But it was the end of the earth, as far as she was concerned, and Sarah knew it. Montauk had been far enough, and this was off the map.

The very next day, though, she was curious about what sort of town this Thomaston was, so Sarah had told her a few things. "Three stores?" Kayla said, her eyes wide. "You own three?" Not supermarkets, Sarah explained. Little stores, corner groceries. When she said her husband's name was Lou but that most people called him Lucy, Kayla laughed, but then her brow darkened. "He doesn't care if they call him a name?" And so Sarah admitted she didn't think he liked it and especially hadn't liked it when he was a boy. "I always call him Lou," she added, and Kayla said that's what she'd call him, too. Then her expression clouded over again, possibly recalling her stated position that it wasn't anywhere she'd ever visit. "*That's* the apartment you lived in," she declared, pointing to the one with the blue door and window box. "If that was your mama up there, you'd live there now, just you and her, and you wouldn't go back to that other place."

"Thomaston," Sarah said, knowing full well that Kayla hadn't forgotten the name. She just didn't want to say it.

"You'd be here all the time and we'd be neighbors till I grew up and got me a man and moved away."

"But it's not my mother who lives there."

"But it was."

"Yes," Sarah conceded, because she could tell the girl was getting upset. "A long time ago."

The next day she said, "Do you think he'd like me?"

"Who?"

"Lou."

"Yes, I think he would."

"What if I called him Lucy?"

"You said you'd call him Lou."

"But what if?"

"I think he'd like you anyway. He's a nice man. He likes people, and people like him."

641

That seemed to satisfy her. "Ikey Lubin's?" she said when Sarah told her about the store. "That's a funny name."

"I suppose it is," Sarah said, though this had never occurred to her before, and right then it felt a long way away. The end of the earth.

"That girl doan forget nothin'," Miss Rosa told her now. "Repeat every word you say. Got to stop fillin' her mine like you doin'."

"Forgive me, Miss Rosa," Sarah said, "but don't you do the same thing? Telling her how Jesus will make sure things work out all right?"

"That's different," she said. "Jesus doan go into no specifics."

She had a point there. "You think I'm bad for Kayla."

"I think you *bein'* here's bad. An' she's the one gon get hurt when you leave."

"What's going to happen to her, Miss Rosa?"

"Child services. I couldn't before. Had to let her set someplace a while. But now I got to. Gon be thirteen soon. Them boys eyeballin' her already."

Sarah'd noticed that, actually. They looked at Kayla first and then, resentfully, at Sarah. As if the world, which had never given them a fair shake anyway, was really going too far this time, giving this black girl a white woman to look after her, a white woman who was herself looked after by Miss Rosa. How was *that* fair?

"Do you know if she's been—"

"No, jist neglected. Ignored. Told she doan matter. Told to get out the way."

"That's enough."

"Enough is right."

"It's hard to leave her."

Miss Rosa nodded, but something remained on her mind. Finally she said, "Tell the truth and shame the devil."

"What?"

"My mama always say that. Tell the truth and shame the devil. You think I doan see you starin' at that blue door?"

It was true, of course. She had been. Watching it and then turning away, then turning back again.

"You *know* that ole white woman up there ain't your mama, right?"

Sarah didn't answer right away, which made Miss Rosa stare at her even harder. Finally, withering under her scrutiny, she said, yes, she knew. "I visited my mother's grave the first day I was here."

"All right then," Miss Rosa said. "Lease you ain't loss your mind completely."

No, not completely. Sarah *did* realize that that sick old woman was someone else entirely, and if that was true, then it didn't matter if she happened by coincidence to be roughly the same age her mother would've been had she not been killed that night in Harold Sundry's car. Nor did it matter that she never left her apartment or no one ever saw her except the people who delivered her noon meal. She was simply Mrs. R. Feldman, just like it said on her mailbox. How many times had Sarah stared at that name, rearranging the letters a hundred different ways, in search of a clue? And even that wasn't the worst. The worst was that if by some miracle it *had* been some other woman killed in that accident, if Mrs. R. Feldman somehow *was* her mother, living under an alias, it meant she'd have been hiding from Sarah herself for the last forty years, something she never would've done. In other words, if it *was* her mother behind that blue door, then it *wasn't*.

"I know, Miss Rosa," Sarah finally said. "I do." Though she wanted to ask why she, who attributed all good things to Jesus, was allowed an imaginary friend when Sarah wasn't.

"All right then, go on home."

Good advice, and yet. "Did you ever meet her?"

"Meet who? The woman who ain't your mama?" She wasn't even trying to conceal her irritation now. "Sure I met her. Long

RICHARD RUSSO

time ago. Dried-up little ole Jewish lady. Smaller'n me. That what your mama look like?"

"No."

"All right then."

"I know," Sarah said.

And she did, in more ways than one. She'd tried her best to be patient with her husband after Lou-Lou's death, the long hours he spent alone in the study with his blown-up map of Thomaston and its forest of black pins. His inability to see this death as a fact both of life and of their marriage, his inability to look past it and count their remaining blessings, had finally eroded her confidence that things would ever be right and good again between them. For a while she'd even considered leaving him to this painful loss he seemed to cherish more than their own lives. But eventually he'd snapped out of it, thank God, and things did get better. He'd recently confided to her that he never entirely banished the notion that Big Lou's death had been some kind of cosmic mistake, that he still lived on in some parallel existence. That had troubled Sarah deeply, but here she was indulging in exactly the same fantasy.

And Miss Rosa was right. Each day, to sustain that fantasy, she was using a child. Without Kayla she had no reason to return to the Arms every day and to continue her blue-door vigil. She could tell herself that she was acting out of kindness, and maybe her affection for the girl was real, but no matter how many new sketchbooks and lunches she bought, no matter how many hours she spent on tutoring or day trips to Montauk or the North Shore, the truth was she was still using a child. She'd known that much right from the start. When Kayla gave voice to that first plaintive question—"Can you teach me?"— Sarah had been about to say no when it occurred to her that saying yes would allow her to stay, which was what she wanted most. It was the sort of thing her father always did—the right thing for the wrong reason. Like making her go out with the Mock boy because he was a Negro, then later parading him

644

around town to make everybody feel guilty he'd been beaten up. Did he have any idea that Sarah had blamed herself? Did he understand that she'd only said yes because she was sure he'd never allow her to go out with a boy? She knew the Mock boy'd had a crush on her for months, and she didn't dislike him; it wasn't that. Nor did she hold it against him that he was a Negro. But she knew that everyone would stare at them and whisper, that kids who had no idea who she was would now be able to identify her—the Berg girl, who went to movies with Negroes. "I'm proud of you," her father said when the Mock boy climbed the steps and rang the doorbell, by which she understood there was no backing out.

And the Mock boy'd known, too. He wasn't stupid. He could see that she didn't want to go, now that her father had said she could, but he'd already asked her, so what was he supposed to do? "You don't have to sit with me," he said after he'd bought her ticket, letting her off the hook. Everyone—his friends from the Hill, all the West and East End and Borough whites—was already looking at them, talking behind their hands. Her own best friend was worst. She came over when they'd taken their seats—causing several kids nearby to move—and said, "Come sit with me." An order. Not even acknowledging the existence of the boy sitting next to her. "I can't," Sarah told her, and from the tone of her voice it must've been clear how much she wanted to. "Then it's your fault," her friend said, and of course Sarah believed her. If she'd done as her friend wanted, gotten up and left the Mock boy sitting there by himself, he'd have been spared his beating. But how could she have known that a beating was coming? She knew only what her father expected of her and that the Mock boy had a crush on her and still wanted to sit next to her in the dark theater, even though he now knew better than to try to hold her hand or let his arm rest on her shoulder. At one point she heard a sound, looked over and saw he was crying. They didn't speak a single word to each other during the entire movie.

Dear God, Sarah thought. Dear God. She could forgive her poor, scared, thirteen-year-old self, but what did it mean that now, at sixty, she was again using a black child? "Ain't no bottom to that child's need" was the way Miss Rosa had described Kayla. For the last two weeks Sarah had been trying to convince herself that she was addressing at least a few of those needs, but in truth she was giving her only what she could easily afford. *Bottomless need.* What Miss Rosa didn't seem to understand was that this accurately described not only most children but also the scared child that lived, at least part of the time, deep inside most adults. The first time she understood this was that long-ago afternoon in the movie theater after all the other kids had left. Sitting in the manager's office, her nose bloodied in the scuffle, she'd then looked up and seen Lou's face framed in the doorway and seen within him a great kindness and, yes, a terrible need that touched her deeply. He'd worn that same expression when she called him back from her Bridge of Sighs painting, and she remembered thinking that she couldn't bear it anymore, she just couldn't.

"And what if that *was* your mama up there?" Miss Rosa was saying. "What then? Almose a hunnerd years old. Prob'ly doan know who she is half the time and where she is the other half. What you want from her? She gon get her mind back so she can tell you what to do?"

"No," Sarah said. "My mother never was much for giving advice." *Oh, sweetie, I don't know, you've seen what a mess I make of things. Just . . . do the best you can, okay?* Sarah could feel her eyes filling. "But if I could just talk to her one more time." Maybe she didn't know everything she'd say to her mother, but she'd at least let her know she finally understood how life worked, that one day you woke up and found yourself in the throes of what could only be despair, prey to doubts you imagined long banished, your self-confidence shredded. "The last summer we were together, she lost her way and did a very foolish thing. I might have been able to prevent it, but I didn't, and I don't know why. Maybe I was afraid I'd tell her the wrong thing. But now *I'm* the one who's lost and—"

"And you thinkin' about doin' a damn fool thing your own self. Somethin' you want to get talked out of."

Sarah looked her in the eye. "Then you agree, it's foolish?"

"How my s'posed to know if it's smart or dumb if you doan tell me?"

"Can't I just be like Jesus and not go into specifics?"

"No, ma'am."

Sarah took a deep breath. "I think I'd be better for Kayla than child services."

"Keep goin'."

"But I had cancer last year. I'm in remission, but . . . no guarantees."

Miss Rosa nodded.

"I'm thinking about renting an apartment or small house around here. That way we can visit."

"Visit who?"

"You."

"Me an' that door up there, you mean," she said, then, when Sarah offered no comment, "Keep goin'."

"Also, if I'm here, and the cancer comes back—"

"You give the child back."

That sounded horrible, but yes. "I don't think I can go back to my old life. I don't know why, but—"

"Keep goin'."

"That's all."

"No it ain't. Tell the truth and shame the devil."

An even deeper breath. "I want to meet Mrs. Feldman."

Miss Rosa surprised her by taking her hand. "Can't let you take that child nowhere, not even 'cross the street, till I know you ain't crazy. You know I can't, so doan ask me."

Sarah felt Kayla's eyes shift from Miss Rosa onto her, and then her own eyes started leaking. "Why do I feel like she's in there?" she said. "If it's not true, why does it *feel* true?"

647

"I'll pray on it," Miss Rosa said. "You know I will."

TWO DAYS LATER, Miss Rosa abruptly ordered Kayla back into their apartment. It was late afternoon, and the gangsta children had mostly risen and come out, shirtless, to hang over the railings and practice looking lethal. Sarah thought maybe that was why the girl had been sent inside, then realized it wasn't. They'd just returned from a drive to Orient Point, where Kayla had sketched the ferry that ran between there and New London, Connecticut. It had been a mostly uncomfortable outing.

"What's the funny name of that store?" she'd asked.

"You know perfectly well," Sarah said. She'd taken to heart what Miss Rosa had said about filling her head with talk of Thomaston and Lou and Ikey Lubin's. Kayla wasn't making things easy, though.

"*You're* supposed to say."

"That's good," Sarah said. She'd gotten the line of the ferry right—not easy, because it was deceiving. She was beginning to slow down, to really see before cutting loose with the ink.

"You're right," she said. "I do know. It's Mikey's." And when Sarah didn't respond, chanted, "I'm right. It's Mikey's, Mikey's, Mikey's."

Once the girl was safely inside, Miss Rosa said, "Here's the way it's got to be. You gon go 'cross the street and call that man and say you comin' home. I ain't lettin' this child be an orphan twice, you understand me?"

"But—"

"You thinkin' about makin' a new life, then go make it, but if you want this child you gon take her back to your ole life an' that good man that's waitin' on you. You doan make that call, *I* call child services."

"If you could just give me a little more time—"

"Hear me out, then you can have your say. Won't make no difference, but you tell me if it make you feel better."

Sarah tried not to look up at the blue door but did anyway.

"You make that call today an' tomorrow morning you an' me gonna go upstairs, say hello to that ole white woman."

She felt her heart leap with anticipation and, surprisingly, fear. If the woman inside the apartment wasn't her mother, she'd lose the blue door, and the door, she realized, had become almost enough. "She agreed? You spoke to her?"

"Five minutes," Miss Rosa went on. "I told her you juss want to say hello 'cause of your mama. So we gon say hello and you gon see this old Jewish lady ain't your mama and then we're gon *leave*. You understand all that?"

Sarah nodded, not wanting to trust her voice.

Miss Rosa was smiling now. "Then you gon live like a woman with a brain in her head and not no lunatic. Maybe help a child, too."

Sarah had only to look at Miss Rosa to know this was the best deal—the only deal—she was going to cut with her. "This is what Jesus advised?"

"Jesus tole me to use my own bess judgment, an' that's all we're gon say about Jesus, too. I didn't live so long to get talked out of Him, no ma'am, so doan even try."

Sarah then went back to Sundry Gardens to make the promised call. "I'm going to be bringing someone with me," she warned her husband. "You'll love her." If you love her, he said, so will I, and she felt the dam of her emotions break, a relief every bit as intense as when the oncologist told her she was in remission. So profound, in fact, that the next morning she told Miss Rosa that it wasn't even necessary to trouble Mrs. Feldman after all. The madness had passed. She was going to be fine.

Surprisingly, Miss Rosa would have none of it, and they climbed the stairs and knocked on the blue door. A feeble voice inside said the door was unlocked, so Miss Rosa opened it wide. The first thing Sarah saw was her mother, and the second was the carpet coming up to meet her.

*

THE NEXT AFTERNOON Sarah said goodbye to both Miss Rosa and the Arms. With the help of a couple of the grandmas, the old woman had managed to clear mounds of clothing off a love seat, where they sat at an angle, their knees almost touching. Miss Rosa was a small woman, but today, indoors, among the towers of clothing and shoes, she seemed like she might be on the verge of disappearing altogether.

"Hope you doan think you gon be any smarter when you my age," she said, wiping away her tears, " 'cause it doan work that way. Stupid's what you get. Stupid waitin' to be dead. Doan know why but Jesus muss want it, 'cause that's the way it is."

"You're the farthest thing from stupid, Miss Rosa," Sarah told her.

"Then you explain it," she said. "All lass week I'm after you to get home to your good man, and now you goin' and I'm beggin' you to stay. Tell me that ain't stupid. My husband use to say to me *Rosebud, how my s'posed to get what you want when you doan know what it is? Make up you mind, woman, 'fore I lose mine tryin' to please you.* I think sometimes he left when he did 'cause he couldn't take it no more, tryin' to please a woman who doan know her own mind one day to the next. Feel sorry for that man you got, 'cause it look like he's in the same boat. Wass this?"

She was studying the envelope Sarah had just handed her. It contained all the information she'd need if someone came looking for Kayla: their address and the phone number of the Borough house, the phone at Ikey's, plus Owen's name and phone number, just in case. Also a check. "That's to help with your work here, Miss Rosa," she explained when the old woman discovered it. "I talked it over with Lou, and he agrees."

"It's too much," she said, but the check disappeared into her apron pocket before her voice fell. "I know 'zactly what I'm gon do with it, though."

She looked past Sarah now, out the front door to where Kayla sat fidgeting on the wall next to the big suitcase they'd bought her the day before. She'd been sent outside while the two women said their goodbyes. "You gon take that child to church some-times, or juss let her grow up heathen?" The question, neither completely serious nor critical, did suggest to Sarah that she was having eleventh-hour misgivings. Or, more probably, she was just feeling, as Sarah was herself, the magnitude of what they were about to do, which was nothing less than altering a human destiny. Or maybe fulfilling it.

"She looks frightened," Sarah admitted.

"Course she is."

"We'll take good care of her," she said. "Not just me. My husband—"

"I know that. Wouldn't let her go nowhere with you otherways."

They now stood up, and when they did Kayla leapt to her own feet outside, shifting from one foot to the other, then back again, as if trying to determine which provided the firmer foundation.

"I'm going to hold you to your promise to come visit," Sarah said. "We'll send you the money for the train."

"The good Lord willin'," she said. "I juss got to find somebody to be me for a few days when I'm gone."

The two women hugged. "There's no you but you, Miss Rosa."

"Thass true," the other woman said, smiling. "Take two or three of my ladies to be me, and even then they gon need help."

They went outside into the courtyard, and Kayla began to make a strange sound that neither one of them immediately recognized as crying until her face finally came undone.

"Stop that now," Miss Rosa told her. "Be seein' you in no time, and I 'spect to hear good reports 'bout how you gettin' on. Bend down and give this ole lady a kiss. You gon be a good girl?"

"I will," Kayla blubbered, "I promise."

"I 'spect at lease one drawin' a week. Want you to draw me this town you goin' to and I specially want to know what this lady's man look like, so draw me a good one there. Anything else catch your eye, you juss draw it for me. Good drawin's a powerful thing, no mistake. Juss don't make it so good I fall down in a faint and get me two black eyes, like some folks." She let the girl go and turned to Sarah. "That remind me," she said, "you ain't looked up at that blue door even once. I guess you're gon be okay."

"I think so," Sarah said. "I hope Mrs. Feldman will be, too." The old woman's terrified face, partially obscured by her foggy oxygen mask and haloed by a cloud of wild white hair, had been the first thing Sarah saw when she came to on the floor of the apartment. That's what she felt worst about. What if her passing out like that had given the old woman a heart attack? Her nose had bled copiously, and her blouse was a sticky sheet of bright red blood. How horrifying for the poor old woman. Except for the people who brought her noon meal and cleaned her apartment and replaced her oxygen tank, no one was allowed beyond the blue door. At the urging—badgering, most likely—of Miss Rosa, she made an exception for Sarah, and this was the result. A bloodstained carpet.

"Know what I think?" Miss Rosa said. "I think the good Lord forgot about that old woman, livin' all alone like she does and never talkin' to Him. He's gon remember her real soon, though, because I'm gon remind Him."

"You don't like her?"

"What kind of person live like that? Like she in a cave. Never stick her head outside. Doan say hello to nobody."

"Didn't you ever want to be alone, Miss Rosa? Just worry about yourself instead of spending all your time making things right for other people?" That, of course, was what Sarah had intended to do when she left Thomaston, what the fantasy of moving to New Mexico had been about. And here she was, about to return home with yet another person to worry about.

"Too lonesome. Ain't how it 'sposed to be. No ma'am. I gon remind the good Lord 'bout that old woman. I think she done slip His mind."

Sarah couldn't help but smile. She'd noticed more than once

during the last month that although Miss Rosa was the soul of generosity, when she didn't understand something, she responded by not *wanting* to. That Mrs. Feldman chose to live her life locked up in her apartment, refusing to speak even to her neighbors, simply made no sense, and that was the end of it. "Aren't you afraid? What if Jesus has forgotten you?"

"He ain't forgot me," she said, patting the pocket where she'd put Sarah's check. "He send me somethin' new every day to let me know He's cogitatin' on how to use me. I doan forget Him and He doan forget me. That's the deal we got." She studied Sarah critically. "How come you didn't take it? She said you could have it. Belong to your mama. What she want with a picture of two folks she doan even know?"

"She told me her own daughter died at about the age I was in the drawing. I guess I reminded her of the girl. That's why she's kept it all these years."

Miss Rosa shrugged, unconvinced. "Doan matter," she said. "Nothin' gone happen to it. When her time comes, I'll make sure it doan go nowhere. 'Less you doan want it."

"No, I do," Sarah said. The drawing had put the worst of her guilt to rest. She knew now that her mother's last months hadn't been all regret and despair, that she'd not completely lost her sense of herself, which in turn meant Sarah needn't blame herself for it. The drawing belied all that. It was full of pride, and not just of Sarah, by making clear where Sarah's beauty came from. And while her mother hadn't romanticized herself by diminishing the effects of age, it certainly suggested Harold Sundry had just won the lottery and, if he didn't appreciate that, he'd lose it in a heartbeat. And if she'd been jealous of her daughter's youth and beauty, this would have found its way into their portrait, and there wasn't a trace. Moreover, a despairing woman wouldn't have done the drawing at all. A work of art, any work of art, is a hopeful thing, and this had been her way of telling her daughter not to worry. She'd probably hung the drawing in the apartment meaning to surprise her the following summer, but then she'd died. Sarah had never been a fan of ghost stories, though if that's what this was, it was a dandy. Had her mother's ghost haunted her old apartment, she was a loving spirit who, once her job was done, had fled.

"Won't coss you nothin' either," Miss Rosa was saying, eyeing the blue door rather malevolently, Sarah thought. "I got my ways, you know I do."

Together, the three of them walked out to the street, Kayla pulling her new wheeled suitcase behind her. Sarah was packed, but she had to return to Sundry Gardens to collect her own luggage and give her key to Harold's daughter. At the curb Miss Rosa gave Kayla another hug and elicited another promise to be good and say her prayers. When she turned back to Sarah, she seemed to have something on her mind. "I juss wish you'd say how you knowed it was in there," she said.

"I didn't," Sarah told her. "I didn't know the drawing even existed." She'd gone through all this before, that at the end of her last summer with her mother they'd gone to dinner at a nearby restaurant, where her mother brought out her camera and asked a man to take their picture. To judge from the clothes they had on in the drawing, she'd then used this photo as a basis for the drawing that hung in Mrs. Feldman's apartment. She'd also told Miss Rosa that a minute after the photo was taken she'd fainted upon hearing that her mother was going to marry Harold Sundry, and that in the forty years between then and now she hadn't fainted once, not until she walked into Mrs. Feldman's apartment and saw her mother's face framed on the wall.

But Miss Rosa wasn't buying it. "Must've known and you forgot," she'd said when she first heard this story. "Your mama told you about that picture and said she was gon put it up on the wall. You juss forgot. Too spooky otherways. Thass why I believe in Jesus. Ain't nothin' spooky 'bout Him. Know what you gettin' and it ain't no voodoo neither."

Which she repeated now. "Jesus doan spookify things. Got all the trouble we needin' in this neighborhood without ghosts. No haints allowed nowhere I live, an' thass final. Tell you what, though. I get back inside, I'm gon look blue door up in my dream book and play the number. Could be a sign. Could be Jesus got it in His mind for me to be rich and He's just now gettin' round to it. Fine with me."

"And me," Sarah told her.

"Me, too," Kayla said, beaming. "I *like* money."

HOME

NOONAN WAS already on his third draft beer when he saw Hugh grinning at him in the mirror that ran along the back wall. Dressed all in black when he visited Noonan in Venice, he was now in white, this being spring in New York, and from his breast pocket he took a silk handkerchief and swatted it theatrically at the stool before sitting down.

He surveyed the Soho bar with distaste and pushed away the wooden bowl of in-the-shell peanuts. "You might've picked someplace where we could order champagne, at least."

"I don't like champagne."

When the bartender tore himself away from the ball game that was on above the bar, Hugh ordered a designer vodka Noonan had never heard of.

"Okay, I'll bite," he said. "How did you find me?" Weary of the introductions and flesh-pressing, the unctuous praise and New York small talk, he'd sneaked out an hour ago, hoping that in his absence people might pay more attention to Anne. About the only truly enjoyable part of the event—and this was a complete surprise—had been talking with the small group of Columbia grad students who'd arrived in the wake of their professor, Popov, aka Irwin the Contrite, still a supercilious little putz, but mellower now, either that or Noonan was. The students were a motley crew, grotesquely tattooed and horribly stapled, some of them, in all looking like torture survivors who'd managed somehow to retain their innocence. They seemed to think he knew something they didn't, whereas to Noonan, the opposite was likely closer to the truth. They kept referring, with great enthusiasm, to painters and other artists he'd never heard of, but they didn't seem troubled in the least by his ignorance, as if he'd earned it, given his stature. "We'll catch you up in no time," one young woman predicted. That she and her friends, who paid hefty tuition, should be required to educate him, who would be paid a hefty salary, evidently didn't bother her. "And what would I give you in return?" he asked, a question he wrongly thought might stump them. "You'll tell us our work sucks and why," one boy said gloomily, though without visible resentment. "*Does* your work suck?" Noonan had asked the boy. "Yes," said a young woman who was apparently his girlfriend. "Definitely," another young man said. "We all suck. But you'll inspire us and whip us into shape. And on Friday afternoons we all go out drinking and you'll buy the beer."

How could you not like them? Noonan doubted he'd make them worse painters, though doing no harm didn't strike him as a particularly lofty academic goal. Did they know he couldn't give them what they wanted most: a blueprint? Did they understand he couldn't tell them how it was done, only how he'd done it? He could tell them he'd painted and had kept painting. He could look at their work and ask them questions about it. He could maybe correct a few bad habits. And, on Fridays, he could buy the beer.

"I saw you turn right when you left the gallery," Hugh was explaining, "so I did the same and entered the first dive where it looked like a man could get into a knife fight."

This last he said just as the bartender arrived with his vodka. "Pay no attention to this man," Noonan told him. "He's a homosexual."

"So am I," said the bartender, glaring at Noonan pointedly. "What of it?"

When he finally drifted back down the bar, Hugh said, "A New York fag with no sense of irony? Where do these people come from? I do rather like the cut of his jib, though."

"Irony isn't everything," Noonan noted, sliding off his stool so he could retrieve the bowl of peanuts, which he set between them. Extracting a nut from its skin, he tossed the empty shell over his shoulder onto the floor. The two men sat there grinning at each other until Hugh's grin turned into a chuckle, and Noonan couldn't help joining in.

"Fantastic," Hugh said.

"Not bad," Noonan agreed.

"Not bad? Your ass, not bad. Did I or did I not tell you that *Sarah* would sell big?"

The painting was actually titled *Young Woman at a Window*. He'd been calling it *Sarah* from the start but decided at the last minute on *Young Woman* in the unlikely event Sarah should ever see it or, worse yet, Lucy.

Hugh had called from New York the day it arrived. "You weren't kidding, were you? It did paint itself."

"Can you make room?"

"You're joking, right?" Hugh said. "Who is she?"

"Just someone I knew a long time ago."

"A Robert Noonan painting with no worm," Hugh marveled now, just as he had over the phone. "A first. Let me guess. The lovely Sarah escaped imperfection by not submitting to your charms?"

"That might've had something to do with it," he admitted.

"Have you contacted her? Told her she exists on canvas, immortal, her virtue intact? That you've brought her quiveringly to life beneath your stiff but gentle brush?"

"Oh, fuck off," Noonan said. Though in truth he would have liked for her to see it.

"Probably not a great idea, now that I think about it," Hugh conceded. "Is she married?"

"Last I knew."

"Paintings like that have been known to cause divorces. And speaking of divorces, I wouldn't be anxious to show her to the girls either," Hugh said. "One look and they'll know why their marriages to you were doomed before they began. They'll never loan you another dime. Of course, after today you won't need to borrow money for a while."

Noonan had almost dropped the phone when he heard the price tag Hugh had in mind for *Sarah*.

"I just wish I'd known about her a month earlier. I'd have gone back to the printer and raised the price of every other painting in the show."

"Even the *Bridge of Sighs*?" It had brought the second-highest price in the show, only a few thousand less.

"Well, it's not the same painting anymore, is it," Hugh said smugly. No doubt he figured he himself was responsible. He was probably telling people he went to Venice a few months earlier and gave Noonan a good talking-to. What they were viewing was the result. Who knew? Maybe there was some truth to that.

"Still a lot of worm in that one," Noonan said defensively, but Hugh was right, of course. Though not very much had changed, it wasn't the same painting. *Sarah* had changed it. He'd worked on the two canvases side by side, and it was as if the light from Sarah's open window had illuminated the other painting. It fell first on the painting within the painting, of the Bridge of Sighs. Noonan had put it in the painting on impulse, then negated the impulse with shadows so dark that Hugh had seen a gallows there. Once it could be seen for what it was, Noonan had been free to accept it as the controlling metaphor, suggesting the painting had more to do with despair than justice. Up to that point he'd been painting the ogre of his childhood, a man who, though he didn't know it, was about to get what he had coming to him. A portrait of a bully, controller, philanderer and epic hypocrite, whose fist was perpetually cocked in volcanic anger, the reason his mother kept running away, and the reason she needed to swallow those tiny pills with her morning coffee, the reason, long after Noonan had fled, she finally became so vague she'd swallowed one too many.

Once bathed in the light of *Sarah*'s window, he had become

someone who'd already gotten what was coming to him, who'd lost everything, whose crossing of the Bridge of Sighs simply made it official, who knew full well what Bobby Marconi, though old enough to occupy the barstool next to him, had been too young even to suspect—just how mortally tired of himself a man could become, how exhausting and demoralizing being true to one's deepest nature could be, the terrible toll such fidelity exacted. Bobby Marconi had always considered his father's other life with his West End woman evidence of his utter hypocrisy, his need to impose moral order on others, even while granting himself the latitude necessary to maximize his own comfort and pleasure. Now—why not admit it?—Robert Noonan had come to see it differently. His father, at some point, had simply grown weary of his life as a bully, grown weary of himself. When poor, sweet Willie insisted he was not only a good guy but "the best guy," his father must almost have believed him. Had it not been for Bobby, who knew better and gave him to understand in a thousand unsubtle ways that he wasn't fooled by his pretense of having changed, who knew? Maybe he'd have pulled it off. Maybe, with no angry son to contradict him, he actually might have become that "best guy."

This much was certain, Noonan thought, as he revised his portrait. Bobby Marconi had always treated his loathing of his father like a precious commodity, something to be hoarded, something you could run out of, or that could be stolen if you weren't vigilant. Bobby had been a miser. Not really wanting to understand the man he hated, and fearing what sympathy might cost, he'd concentrated on protecting and growing his bitter stash, worrying, just as every miser does that there might not be enough to last, that the day would come when the coffers would be empty. Bobby had never recognized the real danger, that he'd die filthy rich. It was amazing, when you thought about it, how effortlessly hate slipped into the space reserved for love and vice versa, as if these two things, identical in size and shape, had been made compatible by design. How satisfying a substitute each was for the other. All art had its origins in passion, and Noonan knew he wasn't the first artist to be motivated by rage. And it had worked. For a long time it really had, until one day it didn't. Until it became, as Hugh said, "all worm." His night terrors, Noonan now suspected, had been born of the unwelcome intuition that as an artist he'd reached the end, that if he was to continue he'd have to find something new and cross over into unknown territory.

"Okay, enough about paintings," Hugh said, giving in to the bar peanuts. "Let's talk about yesterday."

"We won't know for sure until the tests come back," Noonan said, "but cancer's unlikely, given my symptoms. My former symptoms." If it hadn't been for Hugh, who'd insisted, he'd probably have canceled the tests. After all, the majority of his troubles—shit, was it legions or battalions?—had disappeared as suddenly and mysteriously as they'd arrived. Since the night Lichtner had punched him in the heart and he'd begun the Sarah painting, he'd experienced neither a night terror nor an episode of public grief. Even better, his appetite had returned, and food was again tasting like it was supposed to, or at least the way he remembered it. He was beginning to put back on some of the weight he'd lost, not entirely a good thing. "Curious, though. When I mentioned losing my sense of taste, one of the doctors asked if I was a painter."

"You probably had paint in your beard."

Noonan ignored this. "So cadmium poisoning is one working hypothesis."

"From the oils?"

"Not all of them. Reds and yellows. They seem to think that might explain the night terrors."

"Okay, then. No more reds and yellows."

"Ah, fuck it. We die of what we love."

"Don't we, though," Hugh said, and Noonan couldn't remember if he'd ever heard his friend say anything so seriously.

If cadmium explained the tingling at extremities, the loss of

RICHARD RUSSO

taste and the night terrors, that still left the random bouts of grief. In order to avoid an I-told-you-so, he decided not to tell Hugh about yesterday's other working hypothesis, that over the last nine months he'd been chronically depressed. He still had his doubts about this diagnosis. "Wouldn't I know if I was depressed?" he'd asked. (*Not necessarily.*) "Wouldn't I have to have something to be depressed about?" (*Again, not necessarily.*) Would it just appear, for no reason? (*Not knowing the reason isn't the same as not having one.*) Would it just disappear for no reason? (*Again . . .*) Then, their turn to ask questions. *Did it feel as if a weight had suddenly lifted?* (Yes.) *As if a dark cloud had passed, letting in the sun?* (Yes, that too.) *Was there anything unresolved in his life? Or something he'd recently put to rest? Was he aware that sixty could be a watershed year? That people began to see the figure in the carpet of their lives and that sometimes it threw them?* And then his turn again: Would it all come back? (*Possibly. Possibly not.*) Should he worry? (*Do you enjoy worrying?*) Why did people pay money to go to doctors when priests were free?

"Right now, they're more concerned about my blood pressure than anything else," Noonan continued, trying to sound matter-of-fact.

"How high is it?"

"High," he admitted.

"*How* high?"

"They gave me a prescription," he said. "Told me to avoid stress. You were not named specifically but—"

"Here's what you'll do if you're smart," Hugh said. "Put the money from the show in an account here in the States. The first of each month I'll send you an allowance. Enough to cover your studio and reasonable expenses."

" 'Reasonable' to be defined by you."

"Well, yeah," Hugh replied. "I'm the one who knows what it means. And my guy at Chase has been magic lately. Maybe he could suggest some investments."

"I'll think about it," Noonan said, and maybe he would. He was feeling uncharacteristically flexible these days.

Hugh finished his vodka and pushed the glass away. "I should get back," he said. "Things were winding down at the gallery, and Anne wants to go out to dinner and celebrate. You should come."

"Okay."

Hugh, clearly surprised, regarded him suspiciously. "The lady has a certain glow about her today."

"She sold well, too."

"True," Hugh said, "but unless I'm mistaken, and I seldom am, that's not where this particular glow comes from. And now that I look at you, there's a modest flush about your own usually pale gills."

Noonan declined comment, which elicited a wry smile. Sleeping with Anne hadn't been part of the plan, or wouldn't have been if he'd had one. They'd been lovers once before, albeit briefly, nearly a decade ago, a pleasant enough interlude. Since both were painters, they never had to explain their odd behavior and rituals to each other, a good thing, though oddly disconcerting, too. He supposed he'd grown used to explaining himself, or failing to, so this had felt like skipping a necessary step in the process. Anyway, it hadn't lasted. But last night felt different, their lovemaking unexpectedly moving him. How had Evangeline phrased her question that last time they'd been together? Had their sex spoken to him in any way? He hadn't known how to answer, or perhaps he'd known how but didn't want to hurt her feelings, which were raw and jangly. It occurred to him only later that any woman who asked that particular question was implying strongly that it hadn't "spoken" to her either, at least not above a whisper. Last night with Anne hadn't been a thunderous, buckle-your-knees event, but it had been sweet and tender. They'd both known what they were about, and at their age—though Anne was nearly a decade younger—maybe sweet, gentle was what you got. Or therapeutic. "Okay," Anne had said, mostly to herself, as she'd pulled up the sheet afterward. "Now I can do this tomorrow." By which he understood her to mean the opening. It was an oddly intimate and revealing thing to say, and only a little bit insulting. It suggested trust.

"But for me, you'd have resorted to what? Percodan?"

"Plus a martini."

"Well," Noonan said, feeling sleepy and good, "I'm glad to be of service. Should I go back to my room now?" They were, courtesy of Hugh, staying at the same hotel. "If I fall asleep here, you could be treated to one of my night terrors."

"Not yet. I have a proposal for you," she said, her tone strangely playful now. "I propose we accept Columbia's offer."

Had he mentioned it to her on the flight? He didn't think so. Hugh, then, the blabbermouth. "We?"

"As in 'you and I.' We could share the position."

"Take the whole thing if you want it."

"They don't want me. They want you. But they might accept me if that was the only way they could get you."

He couldn't detect any rancor in this remark, which made him wonder what had become of her usual craving for reassurance, her fragile self-worth.

"How would it work? The teaching."

"I suppose I'd tell them things and you'd correct me."

"Would we be married?"

"I don't think so, no," she said, her turn to be caught off guard.

"Because that's what you make it sound like."

"No, I see us as being the subject of endless gossip, sharing the university apartment and all."

"You'd be taking your life in your hands." Risking a night with him was one thing, a whole semester another entirely. Unless these freak-outs truly were gone for good.

"I don't think you'd hurt me, Noonan. Awake or asleep."

"Why did I think I already had?"

"Oh, that," she said after a pause, suddenly serious. "Well, I guess I don't think you would again."

For some reason he didn't think so either, but after a long history of disappointing women he'd become accustomed to preparing them for the worst at or near the beginning. "What happens when you come home early some afternoon and find me with some pretty grad student?" Not one of Irwin's skinny, sallow-skinned, stapled creatures but some buxom beauty he hadn't met yet.

"What happens if that *doesn't* happen?" Anne said playfully. "When you realize the pretty grad student doesn't want you, or only wants you because you're famous and can make her career? Or, maybe, when it dawns on you that you don't want *her*? That you prefer me instead?"

And the weird, scary part, now, today, in the Soho bar? That she might be right.

Hugh seemed more than a little anxious himself. "Let me think," he said. "Do I approve of this?"

"Did somebody ask you to sign off?"

"Oh, all right, I guess I do. Just promise me it's just a sharing-turpentine sort of arrangement, strictly fluids, that you're not planning to wed the poor woman."

"Mind your own business. Quit worrying about what I do with my stiff but gentle brush."

Hugh was already sliding off his stool. "Should I tell our unironic friend to toss you out by eight-thirty? You're to be at Coco Pazzo by nine."

"Lovely. Italian food. I don't get enough of that."

"Congratulations, Robbie," Hugh said seriously. "You—"

"Go away. I can always tell when you're about to get maudlin."

"Dear God, I *was*, wasn't I." Hugh looked mortified. "Oh, I almost forgot." He reached into his coat pocket. "This was left for you at the gallery."

He handed him an envelope addressed to "Bobby" in a small neat hand. Who called him that anymore?

"The woman who left it said she was an old friend of yours. She didn't quite seem to realize what an unlikely story that was. You may have noticed her, actually. She was with a skinny black girl who had the habit of standing on one foot, like a stork."

Now that Hugh mentioned it, Noonan did have a vague recollection. They'd looked out of place for a gallery opening, and he'd concluded that she was a teacher or social worker trying to expand the cultural horizons of some inner-city kid. He'd particularly noticed the woman because she'd been staring at him, or seemed to be, from behind her dark glasses. Of course that wasn't so surprising, given the occasion. People were always pointing out or staring at the artist at an opening. She'd quickly looked away when their eyes met, the trace of a smile on her face. Later, when he was sneaking out, he'd noticed her again, this time talking to Anne, which had surprised him, since he'd thought it was his own work that had interested her. She'd stood for a very long time directly in front of *Young Woman at a Window*.

The letter was five pages long, but Noonan skipped to the end to verify what he already knew. No wonder she'd stood so long before that painting, as if she were committing its every last detail to memory.

"She was still at the gallery when I came looking for you," Hugh was saying. "No doubt hoping she could talk you into visiting her eighth-grade class in Jamaica Plain. What's so amusing?"

"You have no idea who she was?"

"Should I?"

"Not really. If I didn't recognize her—"

"Dear God," Hugh said, the penny dropping.

DEAR BOBBY, the letter began. He waited until the tavern door closed behind him—"Are you sure you're all right?" Hugh asked. "Because you look a little—" and then moved over to a table near the stained-glass window, where the light was marginally better, if still a bit on the ghostly side. *I hope this letter doesn't come as too much of a shock. I must admit I had a shock myself earlier today when I saw your face (your father's face?) staring up at me from a glossy magazine someone had left on the train. I asked myself, what were the odds of someone leaving that particular magazine right where I'd chosen to sit? Of the magazine being folded open to just the right page and your face staring up at me instead of down at the seat? But this is what happens when we turn sixty. Random stars form constellations full of personal meaning. Anyway, on the train I read the article about your new show, opening this very day—another star in the constellation!—and I knew I had to attend, though I made a pact with myself that I wouldn't approach you, because the gallery would be mobbed (it was) and you'd be surrounded by important people (you were). There was little danger of you recognizing me (you didn't) after forty years. Lou isn't with me, which is just as well, because he'd have been incapable of restraint. He'd have bragged to everyone in the gallery that you were best friends. Indeed, I wonder if you have any idea how many times in an average week he invokes your name.*

That's part of why I'm writing what started out to be a simple invitation. You must pay us a visit, Bobby, and I hope you'll bring your lady friend, Anne. I noticed her at the gallery, the way she kept glancing across the room at you, and she noticed me, too, perhaps for the same reason. Women, unlike men, actually notice things. We talked briefly and it was she who procured the paper this is written on (twice going back for more). I liked her a lot, and her paintings, too. Having her accompany you will make a visit easier on Lou, who believes you and I were in love back when and that we might be again. That's wonderfully sweet, I think. When he looks at me, he sees the girl he married. He's totally blind, in other words.

But destinies turn on individual moments, do they not? Remember how I came over to Ikey's the day I learned my mother had been killed? Lou was there in the store, and so were Tessa and Lou-Lou. They all took one look at me and knew something horrible had happened. Lou took me in his arms, and I think right then I must have had an intimation about the rest of my life, that it would be spent at Ikey's, where it was warm and safe and good. I had no idea you were even there. When you came in from the back room, you were smiling, like maybe you were remembering our one and only kiss the day before, and I remember looking away. Because it came home to me then how wrong I'd been about something I'd believed, or tried to believe, all that year: that I wouldn't have to choose between you. What I never told you, or anyone until now, was that I looked away for shame. You see, before Ikey's I'd gone to your place above the drugstore. When I heard about my mother, it was you I wanted to tell, Bobby. I don't know how long I waited for you there. Long enough to feel like a bad person.

Why am I telling you now? Because, I suppose, it's finally safe. Because I love my husband and my life. I recently doubted that, but I know now that I was wrong to. Things have worked out for the best, and not just for Lou and me. To look at your paintings is to know that you've lived the right life. Your Young Girl *made me think of the night you gave me a ride home on your motorcycle. Remember how I waved to you from my bedroom window? But I particularly admired your* Bridge of Sighs, *which I took to mean you finally made peace with your dad. Such haunted, remorseful eyes you gave him. Your own eyes, if you'll permit me. Does this mean you've forgiven yourself as well?*

Did it? Noonan wondered. How could you know? For some reason he thought about Lucy, how he'd wanted him to explain why some people had to pay at the footbridge while others got to cross for free. That's just the way it is, he'd replied—rather cruelly, it now seemed to him. And not just cruel. Untrue. Because in the end everybody pays.

Not long ago, Sarah continued, *Lou asked me if I thought he'd stolen my rightful destiny by marrying me. I told him the truth, that I loved him and didn't regret anything about our lives together. But do we ever tell "the truth, the whole truth and nothing but, so help me God," as my father used to say, to those we love? Or even to ourselves? Don't even the best and most fortunate of lives hint at other possibilities, at a different kind of sweetness and, yes, bitterness too? Isn't this why we can't help feeling cheated, even when we know we haven't been?*

Love, Sarah.

Everybody pays.

"Hey, dickhead!" came the bartender's voice as Noonan sat staring at the blurred page before him. "No crying in the bar!"

Always a good rule.

It DIDN'T OCCUR to him until he couldn't find Albany among the destinations on the big board at Grand Central Terminal that Sarah's train might be leaving out of Penn Station. Which meant he'd wasted—what, twenty minutes? He'd taken a taxi uptown and now grabbed another, which immediately stalled in crosstown traffic. He used the time to consider how wonderful it was to live in Venice, a city with no cars, and to do the impossible arithmetic of Sarah's head start. How long had it taken her to compose the letter at the gallery while he was drinking beer in that bar? Did she and her companion—who on earth was the black kid, anyway?—have to check out of a hotel first, or had they gone directly from the gallery to the train station? He assumed, though he wasn't sure why, that the kid was traveling with her and not just someone she'd met and would leave in the city. Had their timing been good, or would they have to wait forty-five minutes or longer for the next northbound train? There were far too many variables to calculate.

At Penn Station he didn't see them in the main hall. According to the board, the only train that stopped in Albany was leaving in five minutes, so he noted the track number and dashed off, elbowing his way through the throngs of people. When he found the right track, the train, hissing loudly in anticipation of its departure, looked to have a good dozen cars. "Hurry," a woman in an Amtrak uniform said when he loped toward her, apparently having concluded he meant to board, which he was tempted to, except there was no particular reason to believe they were on this train. They were just as likely to be on the one that left an hour ago, or the one leaving an hour from now. Anne, who'd still been at the gallery when he returned, had told him that all Sarah had said was they had a train to catch. The thing to do, he decided, was head down to the end of the platform and then start back, checking each lighted car. The black girl, bless her, would make Sarah easier to spot and maybe the departure would be delayed. All he really wanted to do was tell her she wasn't alone in feeling cheated, even when, as in his case, life had given more and better than he deserved.

But as he reached the end of the platform the train began moving and he peered anxiously into each car as it creaked past, his heart, unused to such physical exertion, thudding in his chest, his breathing shallow now. He'd just about concluded they weren't aboard when he saw them coming toward him in the next-to-last car. If that was the same black girl from the gallery, and if the dark-haired woman in sunglasses beside her wasn't just a stranger who happened to be occupying the next seat. What was it Sarah had said about unlikely odds? But it *had* to be them for all of this foolish commotion to have any meaning, he thought, for the constellation to *be* a constellation and not just a cluster of random stars.

It was the girl who noticed him waving. Was it a look of recognition she gave him? Did she nudge the woman sitting next to her? Because she looked up from her book at that moment and saw him through the window as the train picked up speed. Did her look of surprise mean she recognized him, or was she simply alarmed that someone was standing so close to the edge of the platform? The Amtrak woman who'd advised him to hurry was now shouting, "Sir! Sir! Step *back*!" Was it Noonan's imagination, or did the passenger break into Sarah's radiant smile in that heartbeat before both the car she was in and the one behind it were gone?

The Amtrak woman had him by the elbow now. "Sir," she said. "You have to step back. The train's gone. There'll be another in an hour. Are you all right?"

Out of breath, Noonan tried to tell her he was fine, but his heart was pounding even harder now, as if it meant to leap out of his chest, and he'd broken into a sweat. In a matter of seconds he was drenched, damned fool that he was, running like this when he hadn't run in years.

"Sir," the woman said, "you need to sit down." She was tugging at him now, but just then he noticed the train across the platform, its doors hissing closed. In the nearest car, a man was looking right at him and grinning nastily. At first Noonan didn't recognize him as Lichtner, who of course was in Venice. They'd run into each other in San Marco the day before he left for New York. Had he followed him here for some reason? Because that's who it was.

"Sir," the woman said firmly. "I'm going to have to ask you to come with me."

"I know that man," he told her, pointing at Lichtner, but then a strange thing happened. At first he thought Lichtner, not wanting to be seen, had pulled a shade down over the compartment window, but then he realized that the shade had come down over his own left eye. He could still see the man out of his right eye, except he wasn't grinning anymore and he wasn't Lichtner either. When that train, too, began to pull away, Noonan became aware of a powerful odor, of something decomposing, pungently, a smell he associated with home and the canals of Venice.

DESTINATION

I SEE HER BIKE first, near the stone pillars that frame the entrance to Whitcombe Park, leaning up against what I still think of as Gabriel Mock's fence. It gives me a bad moment, seeing only the bike, because bad things happen to children, especially when they don't think anything will, and Kayla—God love her—is fearless. Also a child who has become, in record time, more dear to me than I can say.

I pull in at the gate, turn off the ignition and just sit, talking myself out of my unnecessary worry before getting out to look for her. We have forty-five minutes until we need to be at Ikey's for the unveiling of Sarah's new, well, painting, I assume, though it's all very hush-hush. Kayla, having seen whatever it is, has tremendously enjoyed knowing something I don't. We will drink a glass of celebratory Prosecco, which she has informed me is Italian champagne. Actually, the adults will have a glass, and Kayla will be allowed only half, mixed with some juice.

I don't notice old Gabriel Mock sitting in the shade of the pillar until he moves. "Mr. Mock," I say, climbing out. I study him carefully and his eyes are clear, if a little sleepy, and there's no sign of a bottle. "Had me a little nap in the shade," he admits.

I wonder what he's doing out here if he's not "howling," though it's none of my business and he has as much right to be here as anybody. More, actually, considering how many hours he's spent repainting the fence, back when there was a hall for it to surround. "It's a good day for it," I say, and it's true. We've been blessed with a beautiful June afternoon. "You walk all the way out here, Mr. Mock?"

"Partway. Fella give me a lift," he says. "My regular chauffeur's off today. You lookin' for the child belongs to that bike, I bet."

I tell him that's exactly what I'm doing, and that as soon as we've found her I'll give him a lift back into town if he likes.

"Soon as *you* found her," Gabriel corrects me, and he remains seated to further drive home that point. "I'm too old to be chasin' after children, and I never seen legs longer than that girl got. Like a racehorse."

I ask if he has any idea where she might be. Whitcombe Park is huge.

"Out explorin'," he says unhelpfully. "Lookin' for caves. Like somebody else used to do. Tole her what I tole you. Don't go callin' when you fall in a hole. Up to me, she have to live her whole life down in the dark and damp. Get married down there and raise a whole family under the damn ground." He peers around at my new van. "That your *ve*hicle?"

He's seen it before, a couple of times at least, but obviously forgotten. I nod and tell him again it's a minivan, that the rear seats fold down into the floor to make room for Kayla's bike, a feature we'll need once we've located her. In fact she helped me pick it out, lobbying for a deep purple color that wouldn't have been my choice but that's been growing on me, as has the van's other purpose: to allow us to take trips. One of the first things Sarah made clear when she returned was that we'd be showing Kayla more of the world than Thomaston. We've already taken her to see the library in nearby Canajoharie, which boasts a marvelous art collection, as well as to several museums and galleries in Albany, and we're planning a week in Boston this fall. Even Italy is back on, though not until next summer, and of course we won't be driving there. By then we'll know if Kayla is ours and also have the documents required to leave the country.

Those two have made a running joke out of my reluctance to leave home, and naturally I play along. When the time comes for us to go somewhere, Kayla takes me by the hand and drags me to the front door, where I grab hold of the frame, and she grunts until she finally gets me outside and strapped into the van, and away we go to wherever they've planned. When we get there I pretend not to like it, and Kayla patiently explains why I should. Finally I give in and say I'm glad to have come, though I like home, too, and Kayla agrees that where we live is a good place. It's a good game, partly, I suppose, because it's rooted in truth. Anyway, the idea is that I'm gradually being made a traveler; and so far, so good. I'm an old dog with a new trick. I am, I realize, the same man I've always been: Lucy Lynch. But this child, this late gift, has worked a remarkable transformation, taking me out of myself for longer periods than I've ever known.

"Mr. Mock," I say, "your fence has fallen into disrepair." No one has gone near it in at least a decade, and the old, flaking lacquer has been replaced by red rust, a fact that would've given Sarah's father great pleasure. Actually, of late he's been much on my mind. I still remember his vitriolic lectures about our revered ancestor, starting with the delight he took in reminding us that he was a slaveholder who sold arms and liquor to the local Mohawks, whipping them into a bloodthirsty frenzy before loosing them on German and Dutch neighbors as far away as Albany. Tory to the bone, he fled to Canada on the eve of the Revolution, fully intending to return once the insurrection was quelled. Sarah's father believed that on occasion Sir Thomas himself partook of his savages' pagan rites, running naked through the woods with his body painted as garishly as any Mohawk's. His fellow settlers had no idea who it was that buried the tomahawk in their skulls with such force and relish. There was no evidence he played a role in the Cayoga Massacre, but Mr. Berg believed he had, so that when the stream ran red that first time, he became, in a sense, its first polluter. We moderns simply esteemed his wealth, poor pathetic creatures that we are. Gathered at the fence designed to keep us out, we stared with longing at his vast shell of a house, imagining the grand parties to which our own ancestors never would have been invited.

Which always reminds me of the day my father took me here after yet another tour of the Borough. How odd we must've looked, sitting in a milk truck at this very gate, as if intending to make a delivery to a house that hadn't been inhabited in over a century. "I don't know what he done to be so rich," I remember him saying, "but people must've liked him." As he saw it, that's where wealth came from—people liking you more than they did the next fellow. I've always thought the greatest difference between Sarah's father and my own wasn't that one was highly educated, the other not at all. No, their most cherished beliefs were based not in knowledge or its lack, but in temperament. It was my father's habit to give people more credit than they had coming, whereas Sarah's gave them less. I don't think either tendency necessarily makes a man a fool, but both our fathers were anxious that the world conform to their belief. Each was happy when it did, unhappy when it didn't, and neither seemed able to accommodate any contrary evidence, which I know from my own experience can be unhealthy in the extreme. Odd, how I grew up thinking my parents were opposites, my father the optimist, my mother the cynic. In reality, she occupied the middle ground between his willfully blind faith in the basic goodness of his fellow man and Mr. Berg's equally blinkered and needy belief in its corruption.

I'm about to start looking for Kayla when she calls "Lou-Lou!" and I see her coming down the fence at a dead run. Need I say how much it pleases me that she uses the pet name Sarah once gave my father?

A moment later she's hanging off me, her spindly arms locked around the back of my neck. "You're getting heavier every day," I say when she finally lets go.

"And *faster*," she says, as if I've altogether ignored the most important part. "Watch!" And then she dashes off, sprinting a good fifty yards to the nearest large oak, her arms churning, and then back again, out of breath now, resting her forehead on my breastbone. Most days she wants me to see how much faster she's gotten than the day before, as if I had a stopwatch and had measured the various distances in advance.

"Girl makes me tired just watchin'," Gabriel says.

"You and me both, Mr. Mock," I agree, gathering her in. When she finishes hugging me, she goes over and gives Gabriel another, which I can tell makes his day. The first time she told him he stank, but since then he's passed hygienic muster, so I'm not the only one who's been transformed by Kayla's arrival in our midst. For nearly a decade Gabriel's merely been going through the motions, living more meaningfully in memory's twilight than reality's noonday sun.

"I think I might be an Olympic track star," she tells us with a sigh, adding this possibility to the long, long list we've been cataloging. Energy restored, she begins to skip. "I'm really good at a lot of things, huh?"

"Better not let your grandma Tessa hear you bragging," I warn her.

At the mention of my mother, her face clouds over. "How come she doesn't like me?"

"She likes you fine," I assure her, just like I do every day. In this respect Kayla could be a direct descendant of my father. She just can't understand why anybody wouldn't like her, an opinion that could derive only perverse obstinacy. In truth, I don't know why my mother hasn't warmed to her. I doubt it has anything to do with Kayla herself, only in what Sarah and I are attempting: to adopt her and to finish the job of raising her in Thomaston, an experiment doomed, in her view, to failure. "You haven't seen enough heartbreak?" she said when I first explained this. She was referring to Gabriel Mock, of course, and his son, and to every other black kid she'd known growing up, most of whom still live on the Hill. She seems to think our purpose is a social experiment akin to Mr. Berg's, though nothing could be further from the truth.

"If it makes you feel any better," I tell Kayla, "I was never sure she liked me either."

But she misses most of my attempted reassurance because she's gotten hold of my left hand and is straightening out my fingers, which curl up again as soon as she lets go.

"What do you think?" I ask. "Better today?"

"Definitely," she says, though what we have here is another subjective measurement, like her sprint to the oak.

"I think so, too," I say, winking at Gabriel. "What do you think, Mr. Mock?"

"Never mind them fingers," he advises her. "Fix that crooked grin. Makes him look even more like his daddy and he looks enough like him already."

She comes up on tiptoe, puts an index finger to the corner of my mouth and pushes up, so my smile isn't lopsided anymore. The slightly cramped fingers on my left hand and my asymmetrical smile are the only effects remaining from my stroke last month. At the end of the day my left foot will sometimes drag a little, but otherwise I'm back to normal and I feel better than I have in a long while. The cholesterol medication seems to be doing the trick, and Kayla has made it her personal mission to make sure I don't cheat on my new diet. People don't seem to realize that for me, the stroke was a gift, a demonstrable physiological event that actually left some evidence in its wake. For the first time a CAT scan did reveal damage. Not severe or irreparable, of course, and I'm grateful for that, but proof something had happened, something that could be documented. Instead of my not being *right*, something was *wrong* with me, a tiny semantic difference to anyone except me. Ironically, on the basis of this sole event, it's now been decided that I've probably been suffering from ministrokes all along. TIAs, they're called, common enough, if rare among children. The other possible explanation for my spells is even more esoteric, something called organic brain syndrome, which so far as I can tell is a grab bag of symptoms that remain unexplained by any other diagnosis. The most honest of the numerous specialists I've consulted just shrugged and admitted, "There's so much we don't know."

The rear seats of our van fold down into the floor with minimal effort, a job Kayla loves to perform, so I let her do it while I help Gabriel Mock into the middle seat. Then she and I lift her bike into the newly created space and close the door. But once I'm behind the wheel and she's belted into the seat next to me, she remembers something so exciting she almost triggers the air bags. "I found the cave!" she practically shouts.

My heart flutters even more frantically than it did when I pulled up and saw her bike leaning up against the fence and no Kayla. "Did you go in?" I finally ask.

She stares at me wide eyed. *"No way!"* she says, shuddering at the mere thought, which makes me happy, knowing that her brashness has limits.

Also, I take heart in the knowledge that we're not so different, she and I. Because I remember vividly the day I found the cave entrance myself. I'd been searching for it all that summer, and I felt hugely disappointed that it was just a hole in the side of the hill, small enough to be hidden by a bush, nothing like the caves you saw in movies, with openings large enough for a warrior to ride into on a great steed. I also recall standing there in despair, having found what I'd been searching for for so long yet was now afraid to explore. I got down on my hands and knees to squint into the dark opening, trying to see inside, but it was like staring straight down into a pool of black water, and I caught a whiff of something rancid inside. And it occurred to me that whatever made that stink might be just inside, staring back out at me. Next summer, I remember telling myself. Next summer I'd be bigger and braver. I'd bring a flashlight. I'd do it. I would. Of course I never did.

All of which reminds me of my unfinished story. I've done no more work on it since the afternoon I made it halfway across Sarah's Bridge of Sighs painting, but I still think about it, especially when, like now, something from those early years occurs to me that I haven't included. Still, the urge to put it all down, to have my complete record, has mostly dissipated, and this I credit to Kayla, who's made the present more urgent than the past. Indeed the present, most days, is all I can handle, all I have need of.

BEFORE GOING to Ikey's we drop Gabriel off at Berman Court. En route he tells Kayla how slow witted I was as a child, how I'd insisted that if you climbed *up* a ladder to the moon, you'd still be looking *up* at the earth when you got there. Naturally, Kayla took my side, making the same argument I'd made so many years ago that *up* was determined by gravity, not direction, but Gabriel was still having none of it, though he winked at me in the mirror to indicate how much fun he was having with all this.

"This is where you used to live when you were a boy," Kayla says after I've helped Gabriel step out of the van and up the walk to the apartment house, and she's pointing up to where our apartment was, as well as the one where Bobby and his family lived.

"Maybe you'll be our family historian," I joke, putting the van in gear and heading for Ikey's.

Kayla, though, takes this possibility seriously. "Maybe," she says. In case she isn't a painter or an Olympic sprinter or any of the myriad possibilities we've discussed of late. Then, once we pull up in front, "Sarah's here," she says excitedly. "Mama, I mean," she quickly corrects herself.

Referring to Sarah as Mama isn't something we've particularly encouraged, since her real mother's still alive and it's possible, if unlikely, she'll one day enter the picture again. But Kayla has a mind of her own and announced shortly after arriving in Thomaston that Sarah would henceforth be "Mama," and she has been, except when things happen unexpectedly or just too fast for Kayla to handle.

Owen's at the register, chatting with a couple of the guys from the Elite Coffee Club, which still gathers at Ikey's in the morning, the sons and even grandsons of the original gang, most

of them. This morning I mentioned there'd be an unveiling of a
new work of art in the afternoon, and they all promised to be
here, and a couple of them actually remembered. Sarah's new
piece, draped, has been hung just to the right of her old drawing
of Ikey's, a place of honor in the store.

"Kayla," my son says when she skips around the counter to
give him a kiss and a hug. "What's shakin', sugar?"

"I found the cave!" she tells him. "Mr. Mock says I don't know
up from down and neither does Lou-Lou, but he's the one that's
confused, not us." Owen chuckles and shoots me a glance.
Kayla's enthusiasm seldom allows for niceties of transition.
We've been trying to get her to slow down by asking, "What
belongs between those two sentences?" and offering various
suggestions: "because," "nevertheless," "still," "also."

On the other side of the wall I hear the whirring vibration of
my mother's mechanical chair. That she, too, is to be present
for the unveiling testifies to how historic an event this has
become. I have to admit I'm puzzled, because Sarah usually
refuses any hint of fanfare about her work, which means that
this has to be more about us than the object itself. Kayla, who's
already seen what lies under the drape, has been excited about
showing me all day long and apparently feels she's waited long
enough. She hops up onto a stool and is about to do the
unveiling herself until Owen says, "Hold on, sugar," and loops
his arm around her waist and gently lowers her back to the
floor, her long legs churning in the air. "We're supposed to
wait for Mom and Grandma Tessa."

But Kayla doesn't want to wait, and she hops right back up on
the stool, determined to uncover what's hidden from view right
this second. Again Owen prevents her, and this time her eyes
flash with anger that's real and bright as he sets her back down.
We don't see this often, though when Kayla's overexcited or
unexpectedly thwarted she can lose control. "Let me *go*," she
says to Owen, who's now standing between her and the stool,
and she tries again to dart around him.

"Hey," he says, his expression serious now. "Who's bigger, you or me?"

And for a moment it seems as if Kayla will push or strike him, anything it takes to remove this obstacle to her will. Since she's decided what she wants to do before Sarah and my mother appear, nothing will make her happy but doing so, and time is running out. We hear the mechanical chair come to rest, and Kayla turns to me, her face a mask of rage. "*Tell* him!" she says.

"Kayla," I say, and we stand in just this attitude until the bell rings over the front door, and this releases the spell. Kayla's fury vanishes without a trace as my mother and Sarah step inside. I meet Sarah's eye, and she takes in at a glance that we've just experienced what she and I refer to as a Kayla moment.

The girl wasn't with us very long before we realized the dark recesses in her personality contained the glowing embers of some past experience, embers that under the right conditions could ignite into a conflagration, only to disappear again so completely that you're not exactly sure what you just witnessed. At first these flare-ups seemed to happen when she hadn't gotten her way, but that explanation doesn't square with all the other times when her will is thwarted without consequence. Rather, the infrequent episodes seem to occur when for some reason Kayla decides she isn't loved, or that someone else is loved more.

Whatever the cause, they have alarmed us sufficiently to discuss them with a social worker from Albany who specializes in children, and she alarmed us further by asking just how determined we were to proceed with Kayla's legal adoption. "You don't know what this child has suffered," she said. "And you may never know the extent of the damage done." Sarah doubts that Kayla has been sexually or otherwise physically abused, though there's no doubt that the love she craved desperately has been withheld, until now. "People get broken," the social worker concluded. "Sometimes they can be repaired, sometimes not. You might do everything right and this could still end badly."

"How will it end if no one does anything?" Sarah asked. She wasn't trying to be confrontational or to deny anything the woman had said, but I'd heard that determination in her voice before and knew what it meant. The social worker herself seemed to suspect, because she then turned to me. "What do you think, Mr. Lynch? Because I can tell you this much for a certainty. You and your wife had better be on the same page."

What did I think? Right then I was thinking about my father, specifically his habit of treating everyone with courtesy and consideration, of how he used to stop on lower Division Street and converse genially with old black men from the Hill whom he knew from his early days as a route man. His kindness and interest weren't feigned, nor did they derive, I'm convinced, from any perceived sense of duty. His behavior was merely an extension of who he was. But here's the thing about my father that I've come to understand only reluctantly and very recently. If he wasn't the cause of what ailed his fellow man, neither was he the solution. He believed in "Do unto Others." It was a good, indeed golden, rule to live by, and it never occurred to him that perhaps it wasn't enough. "You ain't gotta *love* people," I remember him proclaiming to the Elite Coffee Club guys at Ikey's back in the early days. Confused by mean-spirited behavior, he was forever explaining how little it cost to be polite, to be nice to people. Make them feel good when they're down because maybe tomorrow you'll be down. Such a small thing. Love, he seemed to understand, was a very big thing indeed, its cost enormous and maybe more than you could afford if you were spendthrift. Nobody expected *that* of you, any more than they expected you to hand out hundred-dollar bills on the street corner. And I remember my mother's response when he repeated over dinner what he'd told the men at the store. "Really, Lou? Isn't that exactly what we're supposed to do? Love people? Isn't that what the Bible says?"

So when the social worker asked if Sarah and I were in agreement about Kayla, I surprised myself by siding with my mother and saying we're very much on the same page, that we were determined to love this child, that there'd be no half measures.

Which may be why my mother and I have been doing better of late. At first I thought maybe my stroke had softened her, because for the entire time that Sarah was gone she could barely contain her anger and disappointment at what I'd allowed to happen. Perhaps the stroke raised in her mind the possibility that she might, despite her advanced age, outlive me. But more likely her softening toward me reflects my own softening toward her. I go over and give her a hug now, and she clings a beat longer than she used to, and when we release each other she looks me over almost fearfully, as if wanting to make sure I'm okay. I give her a smile to suggest that I am, realizing too late that my crooked smile isn't necessarily my most reassuring feature, though this time it seems to do the trick.

Kayla's now pleading with Sarah to let her undrape this new work. "Please!" she begs, and Sarah says of course she can, *now that we're all here*, letting her know she'd been wrong before, though Kayla's far too happy to absorb that particular lesson. Again she hops up onto the stool, and with a flourish that would make a game-show hostess blush she announces, "Ta-da!" and off comes the cloth.

At first glance it looks like Sarah has simply copied her old drawing of Ikey's, this time using colored pens. The reds, greens, blues and purples of the new work, compared with the black and white of the old, give the impression of a color photograph placed for contrast next to a version done in black and white. But then I begin to notice the differences. Despite the welcome familiarity, the man by the cash register isn't my father, it's me, and the woman at his side is Sarah, not my mother. Over at the meat counter, where Dec stood in the old drawing, there's Owen. I notice Sarah's left enough space next to him to add Brindy later, if she returns, or someone else, if she doesn't. Seated in a thronelike chair in front of the meat case that contains current, updated salads is my mother, looking more like the woman in the first drawing than she does in real life, a kindness she seems to appreciate. In this drawing, too, there's someone on the threshold, about to enter, but instead of Bobby it's Kayla, who in the next instant will complete our lives. There's little to suggest her race, or how else she might differ from us Lynches. We are each of us drawn with a few deft lines that are more suggestive than descriptive. A stranger wouldn't necessarily recognize me in the man at the register or my mother in that chair. We alone know who we are.

Just so there's no confusion, Kayla, continuing her role as hostess, gives us a tour of the drawing. "Ikey Lubin's," she proclaims with another sweeping gesture, before becoming specific. "Lou-Lou, Mama, Uncle Owen, Grandma Tessa." She pauses here for dramatic effect, then identifies herself with an index finger and says, "Me." She's proud, and also challenging any rival interpretation. It's she and no one else who's about to enter our lives. Anyone who sees this differently need speak up now or forever hold his peace. No one does. A quiet group, we've come together in the present to recall the past and share a vision of the future.

"Dear God," my mother finally says, mock-disgusted, because of course tears are rolling down my cheeks and I'm sniffling audibly.

AN HOUR LATER I have Ikey's to myself. Owen has left to meet Brindy and the couples' therapist they've been seeing once a week for the last few months in the hopes of ironing out their differences before giving in to the impending divorce. Why my son would submit to this particular counseling is beyond me. Brindy has freely admitted to the affair she's been having with the West End man and shown no inclination to give him up. According to Owen, the woman who's counseling them seems more concerned with his reluctance to show anger or even resentment than with Brindy's behavior, as if to suggest that Owen has driven her to whatever she's done. "Do you understand how hurtful your silences can be?" she asked at their last session. "Do you understand that stubborn silence can be a form of aggression? That you dehumanize Brindy by refusing to enter into the discourse, to articulate what you want from her? That your silences are a serious obstacle to true reconciliation? Brindy hasn't given up on your marriage, Owen, but your silences tell her that you have. There's another man in Brindy's life now, Owen. Do you realize you haven't even told her you want her to break it off with him? Do you realize how hurtful such coldness can be? If you *want* Brindy to be faithful to you and your marriage, you have to verbalize your feelings."

I study my son, or rather the man in Sarah's new drawing, and something about it conveys his genetic ambivalence. No doubt this marriage counselor reminds Owen of every well-intentioned teacher who ever tried to draw him out. His strategy was always to wait them out, and I doubt very much that it's changed. Eventually, all those teachers gave up and went away, and I'm sure he thinks this counselor will, too. In their last session it was Brindy, not Owen, who snapped under her relentless questioning. "*Look* at him," she told the therapist. "He's not going to talk. Can't you *see* that?"

I can't help wondering if the space Sarah's left next to our son may one day be occupied by the therapist herself, because after that last brutal meeting, she'd asked Owen to remain behind, and surprised him by taking his hand and apologizing for being so rough on him. She was just doing her job, she said, trying, for his sake as much as Brindy's, to achieve a breakthrough, to get him to at least acknowledge what he wanted. Surely he must want *some*thing, she added, giving his hand a squeeze. "I'd figured her for a lesbian," he told us sadly, later that evening. "But I guess not."

What I suppose I like most about my wife's new drawing is that its purpose, across the decades, is the same as her earlier drawing. She drew us—her and me—together in that one, which was how I'd known we were. Now she's telling me that we're still together, that she's returned for good. I'm no longer on probation and probably never was. She has restated her vows, in a sense. In my darkest hour I imagined myself lost in Sarah's Bridge of Sighs, and now she's given me a work of art I can truly live in. This is no Ghost Ikey's, no parallel world. It *is* our lives.

"Are you okay with it?" Sarah asked before driving Kayla home and starting on our dinner. "I thought about putting your dad in. I mean, I feel his spirit in the store every day. It would've been the whitest of lies."

"No," I told her. "You did exactly right. And putting Kayla where Bobby was . . ." But I promptly stopped, unable to continue.

"That felt right, too," she said, raising her index finger to touch Bobby in the old drawing, a gesture that would've troubled me before but doesn't now, and not, I hope, because he's gone. When the phone rang that morning two months ago, I'd expected it would be Sarah, telling me her train had been delayed, or that she and Kayla had decided to stay in the city another day. Instead it was a reporter from the principal Albany newspaper wanting my reaction to the unexpected death of Robert Noonan, the painter and former Thomaston resident who'd died of an aneurysm in New York. She'd called our local paper, where someone remembered that Bobby and I were friends once upon a time and that I could most reliably be reached at Ikey Lubin's market. Bobby had died, the reporter filled me in, during a dinner celebrating his triumphant new show. He'd simply slumped forward in his chair and was gone.

I, too, reach up to touch his figure on Sarah's old drawing. Asked what he'd been like as a boy, I told the reporter how we'd surfed my father's milk truck, that Bobby had been fearless and liked to shut his eyes going into the curves, that he wanted what was coming down the road to be a surprise, even if it meant he got hurt. That story must have struck a chord, because it was picked up in several other obituaries, including the one in *Time*. "Do you think that's what artists have to do if they want to be great?" the reporter asked me, and I told her I didn't know about that, only that Bobby had been brave, that I'd admired his courage and still did. Then she asked if I knew why he'd left Thomaston. Was it because he'd nearly killed his father in an altercation, as she'd heard, or had he left the country to avoid the draft? Was it true he'd gotten a girl pregnant and maybe ran away to avoid marrying her? I quickly made an excuse, telling her the store had gotten busy and I had to hang up. Was there anyone else in Thomaston she could talk to? Anyone who'd known Mr. Noonan well? No, I told her. No one.

Bobby. Hearing that he'd died brought home to me that I'd spent most of my life saying goodbye to him: first when his family moved from Berman Court, and then again a few years later when the Marconis moved from the East End to the Borough. All of this I recounted in my story, and were I to continue it, I suppose I'd have to describe the day Bobby left Thomaston for good, how his mother, looking pale and frightened, had appeared unexpectedly at Ikey's. My father and I were alone in the store, but it was my mother, her old confidante, that Mrs. Marconi had come to see, and my father agreed, like he always did, that if anybody could help, it would be my mother. "They don't have to sit outside," he told her. All of Bobby's brothers were crammed into the family sedan that was parked outside, the oldest at the wheel. "They can come in and have a soda. I wouldn't charge 'em or nothin'."

So in they all trooped and selected their free sodas from the cooler, while I went across the street to fetch my mother. When we returned, she shooed the boys back outside, then led Mrs. Marconi to the table by the coffeepot, where they sat down. My father looked as if he hoped we might be sent away as well. It had been a rough spring: Sarah's mother dying, her father's disgrace, the persistent rumor that Nan Beverly hadn't returned to graduate with the rest of us because she was pregnant and now what had happened between Bobby and his father. All of it had sorely tested my father's optimism, his deep conviction that things would work out all right in the end. "It's like everything's gone crazy," I heard him say to my mother the night before, his voice once more coming up through the heat register. He didn't want to hear any more bad news now, and you had only to look at Mrs. Marconi to know that was all she had.

"The doctor says I could die," we heard her whisper to my mother, who was holding both of her hands in her own, and I remembered the time I'd come home from school and seen them like this in the Marconi kitchen. "What should I do?"

And my mother said, "I'll go with you."

"He'll be so angry."

Hearing this, I looked at my father, and he at me. Clearly, the reality of Mrs. Marconi's circumstance hadn't fully registered. Her husband was in critical condition in the hospital, being fed through a tube, but out of long, sad habit it was still his wrath she feared most, even when her pregnancy might kill her.

"It'll all be over," my mother assured her. "He'll have to accept it."

Frightened though she was for herself, there was something else that scared Mrs. Marconi even more. "They're blaming Bobby," she said, as if this were the height of unfairness. "What if they arrest him?"

Actually, that morning we'd heard the police were just waiting for a judge to issue the warrant. "We'll take care of Bobby," my mother told her.

"How?"

"Lou will see to it," she said, and Mrs. Marconi looked first at my father and then me as if trying to decide which one of us my mother was referring to, or whether either of us could perform such a miracle. "You go home," my mother told her. "Everything's going to be fine."

My father's line. Their roles had reversed. I glanced over at him and saw him thinking the same thing, and he seemed dubious, even though doubting was her job and not his.

Once Mrs. Marconi and her brood drove away, my mother went over to the till and took out the money we always kept under the drawer and held it out to me, but I had money of my own saved up and didn't want Ikey's. When I hesitated, she said, "I'll do this if you can't."

"No, he's my friend," I told her. I'd only hesitated because I wasn't sure Bobby wanted me or anybody else to help him. When I heard what had happened, I'd gone over to his place and knocked on the door. There'd been no answer, but I had the feeling he was inside and didn't want to talk to me. That door was never locked, so I could've gone right in, but in fact I didn't really want to talk to him either, mostly because I didn't know what to say. "Besides, Sarah can come along."

"No," my mother replied, sternly. "Just you."

THE PLAN WAS for me to take Bobby to Lake George, not Albany. There he could catch a bus to Montreal. Under the circumstances, I imagined it would be a somber journey, and I couldn't guess what we'd talk about. Would he tell me he was glad he'd done it, that his father had it coming? Or would he break down and say it was a terrible, awful thing? Would he do what until now he'd steadfastly refused to and admit how badly he was hurting? But I think I knew better than that, that he'd be the same Bobby of his surfing days, just as I was the same Lucy Lynch, as was demonstrated when I again knocked on his door above the Rexall, my eyes already brimming. Though I hadn't told him I was coming, he seemed to be expecting me. He'd gathered his things into one small quadrant of that cavernous space, and his clothes were crammed into a duffel. When I told him what we'd be doing, he just nodded, and I knew we wouldn't talk at all about what had happened.

The drive to Lake George normally wouldn't have taken much more than an hour, but I took a wrong turn and got lost, then found the right road again before getting lost twice more. By then we were laughing like a couple of fools, Bobby saying I had to be the worst driver of a getaway car in the history of crime. I offered to let him take the wheel, forgetting his right hand was in a cast, and that got us laughing even harder. At the bus station he didn't want to take the money I'd withdrawn from the bank, but we both knew he had to, and finally he did. He told me to tell Dec he was sorry about the Indian, sorry he'd made such a mess of things in general, and I didn't tell him he hadn't because we both knew better.

"Remember the footbridge?" I said, mostly for something to say. "How I never had to pay when I was with you?"

"I never should've let them do that," he said, and I knew he meant the trunk.

His admission made me uncomfortable, as if I was the one who owed him an apology, not vice versa. "Will you write?" I asked, and I think maybe a little of the old, juvenile pleading crept back into my voice, like when his family moved to the Borough and I made him promise to call with his new phone number. "When you get where you're going? Sarah will want to write you back. We both will."

He nodded. "You should address the letter to Robert Noonan."

My incomprehension must've been written all over my face. "Why?"

"Because that's my name now. I filled out the paperwork on my eighteenth birthday, but it became official just a couple days ago."

I could only repeat, "Why?"

He shrugged. "To piss him off. Seems like overkill now, I admit."

I saw that he'd registered the word "overkill" and, if his father didn't recover, its possible literal application.

I suppose I looked as horrified as I felt because he said, "Hey, it's okay." But how could that be true? How could it be okay to do something so horrible, so irrevocable? In its own way this was more shocking than the beating. When Bobby shouldered his duffel, I couldn't help myself. I had to ask, "Aren't you afraid?" And I'm not sure what I meant—afraid of going out into the wide world without a destination, or of going anywhere in his now-fatherless condition. To me, they amounted to much the same thing.

"What of?" he said, sounding genuinely curious, as if I had a better view than he of the road ahead and had glimpsed a dangerous curve coming, one it would be my duty to call. Instead, I just told him to take care of himself, and he told me to take care of Sarah, that I was lucky to have her, and I said I knew I was, and part of me knew right then I'd never see him again.

Sarah believes that if Bobby hadn't died in New York when he did, we'd have seen him shortly thereafter. I would like to believe this. I would. I wish Ikey's little bell could've jingled his reentry into our lives once more. I can see him plain as day in my mind's eye, in his surfer's stance, though we wouldn't need that to recognize who it was. Yes, it would have been grand to see him one more time.

Except that would've necessitated yet another goodbye, and there have already been too many. How many times, after all, does the same person get to break your heart?

WHEN OWEN RETURNS from his session with Brindy and the counselor, I suggest we close the store early so he can join us for dinner, but he says no, thanks anyway, Pop. It'll be slow tonight, and closing up at the regular time will do him good, he says. Though he's glad he's here and not at our West End market, which stays open until the gin mills close and people who can't afford to lose start lining up to buy their Lotto tickets.

Owen is looking around the store, taking it all in, as I often do when I have the place to myself, and he ends up studying his mother's two drawings—Ikey's then and now. "This was a good idea Grandpa had," he says.

"It was your grandmother who figured out how to make it work," I feel compelled to remind him. But otherwise I agree. I do. Sometime in the not-too-distant future I'll again raise the issue of selling the West End store, even though Owen's right. It generates twice the income of Ikey's, because of all those desperate people paying taxes on their ignorance, as my mother puts it. That market was one of the top five Lotto convenience stores in the state again last year, a fact that would have shamed my father and does shame me, though we're doing nothing illegal and enjoy the full backing of the state of New York.

"I wish I'd known him," Owen says, looking at my father in the first drawing.

"You would've liked him," I say. "Just about everybody did."

Owen surprises me then by coming around the counter and giving me a hug.

"Whenever I needed him," I say, "he was right there."

"You've been right there, too," he says. "But now? This minute? You should go home. Even your good side's starting to droop."

"Okay, I will," I tell him. It's been a long day. A long, good day, with another coming tomorrow. "I'll open in the morning, though. Sleep in if you feel like it."

That's how we leave it. I'll open in the morning. It's my favorite time of the day, before I unlock the store and let the world in. In that earliest hour Ikey's is crowded with benevolent ghosts. For the rest of the week and all of the next I'll open Ikey's and enjoy every minute of it. The following week we're taking Kayla to Boston, and I'm sure Sarah has planned some other short trips that I don't know about yet. And in the summer, Italy. This time we'll go. We will leave this small, good world behind us with the comfort of knowing it'll be here when we return. But. We will go.

ACKNOWLEDGMENTS

Thanks to Jeff Colquhoun and Kate Russo for their expertise, to Judith Weber, Alison Samuel and Emily Russo for their close, insightful readings. Special thanks to Barbara, my wife, who is always my first reader and often my last after I can no longer bear to look. Nat Sobel has made every single one of my books better, but he absolutely saved this one. And thanks for table space to the following: the Camden Deli, Fitzpatrick's Café, Zoot and Boynton-McKay. And, finally, thanks to Donald Sweet for a great class, years ago, on Langston Hughes.